Handbook of
Adult and
Continuing Education
2010 Edition

Handbook of
Adult and Continuing Education

2010 Edition

Edited by
Carol E. Kasworm
North Carolina State University

Amy D. Rose
Northern Illinois University

Jovita M. Ross-Gordon
Texas State University–San Marcos

A Publication of the American Association for Adult and Continuing Education

Los Angeles | London | New Delhi
Singapore | Washington DC

For information:

SAGE Publications, Inc.
2455 Teller Road
Thousand Oaks, California 91320
E-mail: order@sagepub.com

SAGE Publications India Pvt. Ltd.
B 1/I 1 Mohan Cooperative Industrial Area
Mathura Road, New Delhi 110 044
India

SAGE Publications Ltd.
1 Oliver's Yard
55 City Road
London EC1Y 1SP
United Kingdom

SAGE Publications Asia-Pacific Pte. Ltd.
33 Pekin Street #02-01
Far East Square
Singapore 048763

Printed in the United States of America

Library of Congress Cataloging-in-Publication Data

Handbook of adult and continuing education / Carol E. Kasworm, Amy D. Rose, Jovita M. Ross-Gordon, editors. — 2010 ed.

    p. cm.

"A publication of the American Association for Adult and Continuing Education."
Includes bibliographical references and index.
ISBN 978-1-4129-6050-2 (cloth)

    1. Adult education—United States—Handbooks, manuals, etc. 2. Continuing education—United States—Handbooks, manuals, etc. I. Kasworm, Carol E. II. Rose, Amy D. III. Ross-Gordon, Jovita M. IV. American Association for Adult and Continuing Education

LC5251.H28 2010
374—dc22   2009050795

This book is printed on acid-free paper.

14 10 9 8 7 6 5 4

Acquisitions Editor:	Diane McDaniel
Associate Editor:	Leah Mori
Editorial Assistant:	Ashley Conlon
Production Editor:	Astrid Virding
Copy Editors:	Jamie Robinson, Jacqueline Tasch
Typesetter:	C&M Digitals (P) Ltd.
Proofreader:	Dennis W. Webb
Indexer:	Molly Hall
Cover Designer:	Arup Giri
Marketing Manager:	Erica DeLuca

Contents

THE AMERICAN ASSOCIATION FOR ADULT AND CONTINUING EDUCATION (AAACE)

The American Association for Adult and Continuing Education (AAACE) is the national professional association for all individuals involved in adult and continuing education. The association has its roots in two pioneer organizations: the Adult Education Association and the National Association for Public Continuing and Adult Education. In 1982, these organizations merged to form AAACE.

AAACE's mission is to unify the profession; to provide advocacy for adult and continuing education to legislators and the public; to promote research; to provide professional development opportunities through conferences, seminars, and workshops on a national and local level; and to disseminate information through newsletters, books, pamphlets, and reports.

AAACE members work in a wide variety of settings in education, government, and business. Members include educators and trainers of adults in business, federal, state and local governments, and in community, voluntary, and religious organizations; adult educators who teach literacy skills; directors of adult and continuing education programs at community colleges and four-year colleges and universities; program planners for businesses and those seeking to upgrade their work skills; administrators of basic adult education programs; and professors, students, and researchers.

AAACE's divisions and program units are organized around specialized programs and professional interests. AAACE is also affiliated with state and regional adult and continuing education associations.

AAACE publishes *Adult Learning* magazine four times annually and the research journal *Adult Education Quarterly* in conjunction with SAGE Publications, and also sponsors the *Journal of Transformation Education* published by SAGE. Other publications, sponsored cooperatively with major publishers and other organizations, are also available through AAACE. AAACE has an awards program that recognizes outstanding research and service to the field.

AAACE conducts a variety of conventions and seminars to meet members' needs, including an annual conference so that members may learn and grow together as adult educators. AAACE welcomes new members at any time during the year. For membership and conference information, please visit www.aaace.org, or write AAACE at 10111 Martin Luther King, Jr. Highway, Suite 200C, Bowie, MD 20720.

This *Handbook of Adult and Continuing Education* is part of a series that is published every 10 years. Its aim is to provide an overview of the kinds of organizations, methods, and research that are important to the field. The tables of contents of all previous *Handbooks* may be found on the AAACE Web site, www.aaace.org.

ABOUT THE EDITORS

Carol E. Kasworm is the W. Dallas Herring Professor of Adult and Community College Education in the Department of Adult and Higher Education at North Carolina State University. She received her BA degree in psychology and sociology from Valparaiso University in 1967, her MA in higher education from Michigan State University in 1970, and her EdD in adult education from University of Georgia in 1977. Dr. Kasworm's career has included faculty and academic administrative roles at University of Texas at Austin, University of Georgia, University of Houston-Clear Lake, University of Tennessee-Knoxville, and North Carolina State University.

Her main research and writing interests have focused upon the adult undergraduate experience, including the nature of learning engagement and participation patterns of adult students, the situated influences of varied higher education contexts on adult learners, and the role of adult higher education in a lifelong learning society. She has received a number of honors, including induction into the International Adult and Continuing Education Hall of Fame; the Distinguished Professional Achievement Alumni Award from the College of Education, University of Georgia; the Imogene Okes Research Award, American Association for Adult and Continuing Education; and the Chancellor's Award for Research and Creative Achievement from the University of Tennessee-Knoxville. Among her publications are *Responding to Adult Students in Higher Education* (2002, with C. Polson and J. Fishback), *Accelerated Learning for Adults: The Promise and Practice of Intensive Educational Formats* (2003, coedited with R. Wlodkowski), and *Revitalizing the Residential Conference Center Environment* (1990, coedited with E. Simpson).

Among Dr. Kasworm's professional service contributions, she has assumed leadership roles in the American Association for Adult and Continuing Education, Commission of the Professors of Adult Education, International Adult and Continuing Education Hall of Fame, and American Education Research Association. She also has served on a number of editorial boards, including those of the *Adult Education Quarterly* and the *Journal of Continuing Higher Education*.

Amy D. Rose is Professor of Adult and Higher Education at Northern Illinois University. She received an AB degree in history from the University of Rochester in 1972, an MA degree in medieval history from Columbia University in 1974, an MA in adult and higher education in 1976 from Teachers College, Columbia University, and an EdD in adult and higher education in 1979, also from Teachers College. Dr. Rose received an MPhil in American history in 1980 from Columbia University as well. Prior to coming to Northern Illinois University, she was an administrator at Empire State College in New York.

Dr. Rose's research interests lie in the areas of history and policy of adult education, and she has also written on various forms of nontraditional adult and higher education and programs for women. Among her publications are *An Evaluation Guide for College Women's Re-entry Programs* (1977, with J. D. Mezirow), *Ends or Means: An Overview of the History of the Adult Education* (1991), and *Issues in Assessment: New Directions in Adult Continuing Education* (1997, coedited with M. Leahy). Her most recent research has focused on the history of the GED in the United States.

Dr. Rose has been active in the field. She is a past president of the American Association for Adult and Continuing Education (AAACE) and has served on the AAACE board in a number of capacities. She also has served as a member of the editorial board of *Adult Learning, Adult Education Quarterly,* and *Adult Basic Education and Literacy Journal.*

Jovita M. Ross-Gordon is Professor of Counseling, Leadership, Adult Education, and School Psychology at Texas State University—San Marcos, where she is also Director of the PhD Program in Education and Coordinator of the Master's Program in Developmental and Adult Education. She received a BS degree in speech and language pathology from Northwestern University in 1974, an MA in learning disabilities from Northwestern University in 1975, and an EdD in adult education from the University of Georgia in 1985. Before coming to Texas State University she served as Director of Adult Learning Services at St. Edwards University in Austin, Texas, and Associate Professor of Adult Education and Program Coordinate at Penn State University.

Dr. Ross-Gordon's research centers on teaching and learning of adults, including foci on adult learners in higher education and on issues of diversity and equity in adult higher education and continuing professional education. She has received the Marlowe Froke Outstanding Publication Award from the Association for Continuing Higher Education and the research award from University Continuing Education Association. She is the author or coauthor of numerous articles and book chapters and coauthor of *SuperVision and Instructional Leadership: A Developmental Approach* (2010), now in its eighth edition. She has edited the sourcebooks *Serving Culturally Diverse Adults* (1990) and *Teaching Adults Effectively* (2002) as part of the New Directions for Adult and Continuing Education Series, a series for which she currently serves as Co-Editor-in-Chief. She also is a consulting editor for *Adult Education Quarterly* and the *Canadian Journal for the Study of Adult Education.*

Dr. Ross-Gordon has held numerous positions of national leadership in adult and continuing education, including serving as a member of the Adult Education Research Conference site and steering committees, serving as a member of the executive committee and as chair of the Commission of Professors of Adult Education, and serving on publications, nominations, and Okes Research Award Committees of the American Association for Adult and Continuing Education.

LIST OF CONTRIBUTORS

Mary V. Alfred is Associate Professor of Adult Education and Human Resource Development and Associate Dean for Faculty Affairs in the College of Education and Human Development at Texas A & M University, College Station, TX.

Walter Archer is Academic Advisor, Adult Learning, in the Faculty of Extension at the University of Alberta, Edmonton, AB, Canada.

Richard Banz is Adjunct Instructor at York College of Pennsylvania, York, PA, and a museum consultant.

Lisa M. Baumgartner is Associate Professor of Adult and Higher Education at Northern Illinois University, DeKalb, IL.

Alexandra A. Bell is Associate Professor of Adult Learning at the University of Connecticut, Storrs, CT.

Alisa Belzer is Associate Professor in the Department of Teaching and Learning at Rutgers University, New Brunswick, NJ.

Elisabeth E. Bennett is Director of Education at Baystate Medical Center and Assistant Professor in Medical Education at Tufts University, Boston, MA.

Laura L. Bierema is Professor of Adult Education and Human Resource and Organization Development at the University of Georgia, Athens, GA.

Marcie Boucouvalas is Professor and Program Director of Adult Learning and Human Resource Development at Virginia Tech Graduate Center, Falls Church, VA.

Tuere A. Bowles is Assistant Professor of Adult and Community College Education at North Carolina State University, Raleigh, NC.

Susan J. Bracken is Assistant Professor of Adult and Community College Education at North Carolina State University, Raleigh, NC.

E. Michael Brady is Professor of Adult Education and Senior Research Fellow in the Osher Lifelong Learning Institute at the University of Southern Maine, Gorham, ME.

Stephen D. Brookfield is Distinguished University Professor at the University of St. Thomas, St. Paul, MN.

Shauna Butterwick is Associate Professor of Educational Studies at the University of British Columbia, Vancouver, BC, Canada.

Brendaly Drayton is a PhD candidate in the Adult Education program at The Pennsylvania State University and a research assistant at the Goodling Institute for Research in Family Literacy, University Park, PA.

John P. Egan is Instructor and Instructional Designer and Project Manager in the Office of Learning Technology at the University of British Columbia, Vancouver, BC, Canada.

Leona M. English is Professor of Adult Education at St. Francis Xavier University, Antigonish, NS, Canada.

Jean E. Fleming is Regional Director and Academic Advisor in the Adult Degree Program at Mary Baldwin College, Staunton, VA.

Doris Flowers is Associate Professor of Adult Education and Equity and Social Justice at San Francisco State University, San Francisco, CA.

Sandra L. Fornes is Executive Director, Hidden Angel Foundation, Inc., Gadsden, AL.

Michael W. Galbraith is Professor of Leadership Studies at Marshall University Graduate College, South Charleston, WV.

D. Randy Garrison is Director of the Teaching & Learning Centre and Professor in the Faculty of Education at the University of Calgary, Calgary, AB, Canada.

Margery B. Ginsberg is Associate Professor of Educational Leadership and Policy Studies at the University of Washington-Seattle and Co-Director of the Center of Action, Inquiry and Motivation, Seattle, WA.

Catherine A. Hansman is Professor of Adult Learning and Development at Cleveland State University, Cleveland, OH.

Lilian H. Hill is Associate Professor of Adult Education at the University of Southern Mississippi, Hattiesburg, MS.

Robert J. Hill is Associate Professor of Adult Education at the University of Georgia, Athens, GA.

E. Paulette Isaac is Chair and Associate Professor in Educational Leadership & Policy Studies, at the University of Missouri-St. Louis, St. Louis, MO.

Laurel H. Jeris is Professor of Adult and Higher Education at Northern Illinois University, DeKalb, IL.

Juanita Johnson-Bailey is Professor of Adult Education and Women's Studies at the University of Georgia, Athens, GA.

Melanie S. Jones is Assistant Professor of Adult and Higher Education at Morehead State University, Morehead, KY.

Kathleen P. King is Professor and Director of Adult Education and Human Resource Development at Fordham University's Graduate School of Education, New York City, NY.

Alan B. Knox is Professor of Educational Leadership and Policy Analysis at the University of Wisconsin-Madison, Madison, WI.

Suzanne Z. Kucharczyk is Director of Staff Development and Training at the Shield Institute, and a doctoral student at Teachers College, Columbia University, New York, NY.

Elizabeth A. Lange is Assistant Professor of Adult Education at St. Francis Xavier University, Antigonish, NS, Canada.

Pooneh Lari is a doctoral student and Teaching Assistant in Adult and Higher Education at North Carolina State University, Raleigh, NC.

Clarena Larrotta is Assistant Professor in the Educational Administration & Psychological Services Department at Texas State University, San Marcos, TX.

Randee Lipson Lawrence is an Associate Professor of Adult and Continuing Education at National-Louis University, Chicago.

Victoria J. Marsick is Professor of Education and Co-Director of the J.M. Huber Institute at Teachers College, Columbia University, New York, NY.

Kay M. McClenney is Director of the Center for Community College Student Engagement and Sid W. Richardson Endowed Fellow in the Community College Leadership Program at The University of Texas at Austin, Austin, TX.

Sharan B. Merriam is Professor Emeritus of Adult Education at the University of Georgia, Athens, GA.

Lisa R. Merriweather is Assistant Professor of Adult Education at University of North Carolina, Charlotte, NC.

Catherine H. Monaghan is Program Coordinator and Assistant Professor of Adult Learning and Development at Cleveland State University, Cleveland, OH.

Vivian W. Mott is Professor and Chair of Higher, Adult, and Counselor Education Department at East Carolina University, Greenville, NC.

Fredrick Muyla Nafukho is Professor of Adult Education and Human Resource Development and Department Head, Educational Administration and Human Resource Development, College of Education and Human Development at Texas A&M University, College Station, TX.

Heather Nash is Assistant Professor of Adult Education at the University of Alaska, Anchorage, AK.

Tom Nesbit is Associate Dean of Continuing Education at Simon Fraser University, Vancouver, BC, Canada.

Terry O'Banion is President Emeritus and Senior League Fellow at the League for Innovation in the Community College, Phoenix, AZ.

Marilyn McKinley Parrish is Assistant Professor, Special Collections Librarian Associate and University Archivist at Millersville University, Millersville, PA.

Shari Peterson is Assistant Professor of Human Resource Development and Adult Education University of Minnesota, Minneapolis, MN.

Nancy Lloyd Pfahl is an education consultant in Washington, D.C. and former Chief Development Officer at the College of DuPage, Glen Ellyn, IL.

Cheryl J. Polson is Director of Kansas State University–Fort Leavenworth and Professor of Adult Education at Kansas State University, Manhattan, KS.

Esther Prins is Assistant Professor of Adult Education at Pennsylvania State University and Co-Director of the Goodling Institute for Research in Family Literacy and the Institute for the Study of Literacy, University Park, PA.

Tonette S. Rocco is Associate Professor and Program Leader of Adult Education and Human Resource Development at Florida, International University, Miami, FL.

Elice E. Rogers is Associate Professor of Adult Learning and Development at Cleveland State University, Cleveland, OH.

Ralf St. Clair is Senior Lecturer of Adult and Continuing Education at the University of Glasgow, Glasgow, Scotland.

Lorilee R. Sandmann is Professor of Adult Education at the University of Georgia, Athens, GA.

Vanessa Sheared is Dean and Professor of Education at Sacramento State University, Sacramento, CA.

M Cecil Smith is Professor of Educational Psychology at Northern Illinois University, DeKalb, IL.

Regina O. Smith is Assistant Professor of Adult and Continuing Education Leadership in the Department of Administrative Leadership at the University of Wisconsin-Milwaukee, Milwaukee, WI.

Thomas J. Sork is Professor of Adult Education and Associate Dean, External Programs and Learning Technologies in the Faculty of Education at the University of British Columbia, Vancouver, BC, Canada.

Bruce Spencer is Professor in Labour Relations in the Centre for Work and Community Studies at Athabasca University, Athabasca, AB, Canada.

Leila González Sullivan is the W. Dallas Herring Extension Professor of Adult and Higher Education at North Carolina State University, Raleigh, NC.

Edward W. Taylor is Associate Professor of Adult Education at Pennsylvania State University-Harrisburg, Harrisburg, PA.

Kathleen Taylor is Professor of Education at Saint Mary's College of California, Moraga, CA.

Elizabeth J. Tisdell is Professor of Adult Education & Coordinator of the Adult Education Doctoral Program at Pennsylvania State University-Harrisburg, Harrisburg, PA.

Karen E. Watkins is Professor of Lifelong Education, Administration & Policy at the University of Georgia, Athens, GA.

Michael R. Welton is Adjunct Professor of Adult Education at the Centre for Policy Studies in Higher Education and Training at the University of British Columbia, British Columbia, Canada, and a tutor at Athabasca University, Alberta, AB, Canada.

Colleen Aalsburg Wiessner is Assistant Professor of Adult Education at North Carolina State University, Raleigh, NC.

Arthur L. Wilson is Professor of Adult Education and Chair of the Department of Education at Cornell University, Ithaca, NY.

Cynthia D. Wilson is Vice President of Learning and Research at the League for Innovation in the Community College for Learning and Research, Phoenix, AZ.

Raymond J. Wlodkowski is Professor Emeritus in the College of Professional Studies at Regis University, Denver, CO.

Mary Alice Wolf is Professor of Human Development/Gerontology and Director of the Institute in Gerontology at Saint Joseph College, West Hartford, CT.

Linda Ziegahn is Community Engagement Coordinator at the Clinical and Translational Science Center and the Center for Reducing Health Disparities at the University of California Davis, Davis, CA.

Adult and Continuing Education as an Intellectual Commons

CAROL E. KASWORM, AMY D. ROSE, AND
JOVITA M. ROSS-GORDON

The 2010 *Handbook of Adult and Continuing Education* is part of a long tradition in adult and continuing education. When the *Handbooks* were initially published, starting in the 1930s, they were little more than recitations of programs (Ely, 1948; Rowden, 1934, 1936). However, since the 1960s, these *Handbooks* have evolved into a more thematic and at times reflective and analytic statement about the status of adult and continuing education (Boone, Shearon, White, & Associates, 1980; Boyd, Apps, & Associates, 1980; Charters & Associates, 1980; Knowles, 1960; Knox & Associates, 1980; Kreitlow & Associates, 1980; Long, Hiemstra, & Associates, 1980; Merriam & Cunningham, 1989; Peters & Associates, 1980; Smith, Aker, & Kidd, 1970; Wilson & Hayes, 2000). The recent *Handbooks* present an update of the landscape of practice and knowledge in adult and continuing education, while also defining the field and expanding its knowledge. Our aim is to continue this tradition while also providing new perspectives and understanding of the changes and innovations currently taking place.

Assembling a handbook such as this is a daunting task. Not only is the field of Adult and Continuing Education large and at times inchoate, but the issues facing it are complex and often difficult to untangle. We are attempting several tasks at the same time. On one level, we aim to provide a basic overview of the field that is accessible to novices. In addition, however, we hope to go beyond an introduction to more nuanced analyses of the issues that are meaningful to professionals in the field. Finally, we hope to identify the state of research within Adult and Continuing Education and to note the primary trends that we anticipate will emerge over the next 10 years.

Currently, research indicates that most adults engage in some form of learning in their daily lives. According to Merriam and Brockett, *adult and continuing education* can be defined as "activities intentionally designed for the purpose of bringing about learning among those whose age, social roles, or self-perception, define them as adults" (2007, p. 8). This understanding is different from the historical definitions of adult education described by Stubblefield and Rachal (1992). In tracing changing notions of adult education, they note that in its earliest usage, the term *adult education* was used interchangeably with *home education* and *popular education*. Yet, by the 20th century the term had come to be associated more exclusively with formal educational activities. This change in definition occurred as the field became more institutionalized and moved into the academy. The movement toward professionalization created a constant tension between the desire to narrow the field to formal educational activities and a continuing concern that such an approach deterred the most important and socially relevant aspects of adult learning. Consider for instance the contrast between Bryson's (1936) definition of adult education as "all the activities with an educational purpose that are carried on by people, engaged in the ordinary business of life" (p. 3) and Verner and Booth's (1964) more directed description of adult education as "a relationship between an education agent and a learner in which the agent selects, arranges, and continuously directs a sequence of progressive tasks that provide systematic experiences to achieve learning for those whose participation . . . is subsidiary and supplemental to a primary productive role in society" (p. 32). Stubblefield and Rachal (1992) note that toward the end of the 20th century there was a call for a return to the broader view reflected in the Merriam and Brockett definition. Even today, while many scholars of adult education think of adult education in the broad sense implied by Merriam and Brockett, it is obvious that this conception is not a perspective that is universally held by the average person, by policy makers (for whom public funding for adult education historically has been associated in the United States with basic education or education for economic self-sufficiency), or by adult education practitioners (who may alternatively view their domain of practices as the *only* form of adult education or may not label their work adult education at all).

These varied definitions are also seen in recent adult education participation statistics and trends. One of the historic concerns for adult and continuing education has been, "What counts as adult and continuing education?" According to the most recent survey of the National Center for Education Statistics (NCES), in 2005 44% of adults reported participation in part-time formal adult educational activities (higher education and work-related activities), and 9% reported participation in full-time formal higher education degree or certificate pursuits (NCES, 2007b). This 2005 participation rate represents a significant increase over the 1991 rate, in which 33% of adults reported participation in part-time learning activities (Kopka, Schantz, & Korb, 1998; NCES, 2007b; O'Donnell, 2006). Beyond these statistics, the NCES also has begun to collect data on learning engagements by adults beyond the formal classroom settings. They reported that in 2005 over 70% of adults reported participating in *informal adult learning,* which is defined as learning pursued without an instructor and for personal interest (NCES, 2007a; NCES, 2007c). This means that over 126 million adults were active adult learners in documented learning endeavors in 2005. In addition, 30 years of research on self-directed learning (Merriam, Caffarella, & Baumgartner, 2007; Peterson & Associates, 1979) indicates that most adults are actively engaged in independent, self-directed learning activities anchored to their daily life roles in the spheres of family, work, and community. Such activities are sometimes not considered learning experiences by the layperson, yet they represent adults' active engagement in learning. Some examples include: learning a new computer program, participating in a book club, researching a vacation spot, and studying parenting skills. The statistics suggest that adult learners are a rapidly growing segment within American education. Further, although the statistics demonstrate significant increases in adult participation in formal instructional classroom settings, they also make evident that in our complex, changing worlds, most adults are also actively pursuing learning through informal and self-directed learning.

THE INTELLECTUAL COMMONS FOR ADULT AND CONTINUING EDUCATION

This *Handbook of Adult and Continuing Education* reflects a forum for diverse perspectives, programs and approaches, and issues in the worlds of communities of practice and related research. Thus, the *Handbook* is constructed around the broad thematic approaches that encapsulate the principal concerns of the field. At the heart of all of these approaches is the notion of adult and continuing education as an *intellectual commons.* This commons is envisioned as a place to build upon past formulations and perspectives of the profession and practices, while also providing contemporary contextual frameworks that suggest new understandings of adult learning, innovative practices, and new challenges.

The idea of the commons is rooted in the English town-planning concept. It denotes a central square or village green that is commonly held by all of the townspeople for shared use. More recently, writers have appropriated the term to signify an ideal of shared community commitments and identity outside of geographical limitations. In keeping with this view, Daloz and his colleagues define the *commons* as "a shared public space of a sort that anchored the vision of an American democracy" (Daloz, Parks, Keen, & Keen, 1996, p. 2). This ideal builds on the notion that modern complex societies entail engagement with a plethora of communities on a daily basis. The commons therefore becomes the central place where differing communities can interact, dialogue, and engage. This *Handbook* is using this notion of an intellectual commons as the basis for a discussion of shared values, identities, and goals. But this idea of a commons is not simply an attempt to arrive at consensus or a unitary view. The aim here is to present the diversity of views and approaches present in contemporary adult and continuing education. For Daloz and others, the commons focuses upon a commitment by individuals to the common good and the qualities in individuals that lived their lives in the commons for the public good. Thus, the commons can become a valuable metaphor for the many diverse organized activities and other endeavors that can be openly shared, exchanged, and debated.

Over the last 10 years, the term *commons* has also become a familiar term in two other arenas. First, in the world of knowledge management, libraries, cyber worlds, and journalism, the terms *intellectual commons* and *information commons* refer to freedom of information issues such as intellectual property laws, open source access, and the open education movement. Thus, in this sense the term *intellectual commons* is a designation for those who work toward open access, open source, nonexclusive, unlimited distribution of knowledge in its varied forms (Iiyoshi & Kumar, 2008, p. 254). Second, within the educational community, the term has come to be a metaphor for the commitment of higher education to the enhancement of teaching. In other words, the commons is the central place where teaching and disciplinary rigor can intersect. Huber and Hutchings (2005) suggest that the academic commons, or the community of higher education, requires a new emphasis on the scholarship of teaching and learning—the teaching commons. They state, "the teaching commons is a conceptual space in which communities of educators committed to inquiry and innovation come together to exchange ideas about teaching and learning and use them to meet the challenges of educating students for personal, professional, and civic life" (Huber & Hutchings, n.d).

Building on the metaphor of a meeting space for our professional community (Huber & Hutchings, 2005), we see the intellectual commons as a place for conceptualizing adult and continuing education. In this volume we are attempting to open a dialogue about the role of adult continuing education in society and the interplay between adult learning, education, and broader societal issues. Hence the task of the *Handbook* is complex. We, as editors, are striving through this metaphor of the intellectual commons to introduce the field and analyze it, and to provide an overview of the differing permutations of adult education while also giving a broad sense of the debates and issues that arise in such a broad field.

We hope that this *Handbook* can serve as an intellectual commons, providing a place for digesting the amalgam of disparate values, goals, knowledge, individuals, and structures that is adult and continuing education. The diversity of the philosophical premises underlying much of the field was delineated by Beder (1989) in the 1990 *Handbook*. These purposes include: the facilitation of change in a dynamic society, the support and maintenance of the social order, the promotion of productivity, and the enhancement of personal growth. While Beder presents these as distinct philosophical orientations, it could also be argued that they represent different but overlapping facets of adult education. Each deals with connections among the profession, the individual, and society. Our aim is to explore the multiple perspectives in adult education within differing institutional or organizational formats. In approaching the complexity of adult education in this manner, we hope to illuminate and analyze these different manifestations of adult and continuing education through the lens of an intellectual commons. Based upon the historic traditions of the field, this commons reflects a broad commitment to:

- *The centrality of the adult learner and adult learning.* Understanding adult learning lies at the core of adult and continuing education.

The learning process in both individuals and groups is foundational to understanding the nature of the interaction that lies at the heart of the field. Thus learning and the learner are essential, but not sufficient for understanding the place of adult education within the modern world.

• *The creation of open exchanges of knowledge, theory, and practice.* These complex exchanges involve the creation and sharing of knowledge on adult education and adult learning; knowledge arising from practice and broad cultural understandings, including indigenous knowledge; and critical reflection on all aspects of theory, practice, and research.

• *Adult and continuing education as a field of practice.* It encompasses the attributes of a professional field, while also embracing a notion of itself as a social movement committed to social change—with the multiplicity of purposes, goals, and functions that such a broad commitment entails.

• *The diversity of adult learning venues and collective endeavors.* This diversity of venues and collective endeavors encourages the potential for change while maintaining flexibility in mission, organization, and population served. This diversity includes the sponsorship, facilitation, and study of adult learning in formal, informal, and nonformal settings.

• *The centrality of social justice.* At the heart of adult education practice and ethics is the belief in equity and equality of educational access, support, and impact upon adults and their communities.

• *The future of adult and continuing education within a global context.* Over the past 10 years, the effort to engage in intercultural dialogue and increase global awareness has become a priority. This engagement in the global context includes the goals of developing new practices, establishing collaborative partnerships, and developing new sensitivities to the impact of globalization.

ORGANIZATION OF THIS *HANDBOOK*

We have organized the *Handbook* around the six themes listed above, which in our view comprise

the intellectual commons of the field. Each of these emphases represents our past, our collective present, and our visioning for the future. The sections below describe our conceptualization of these aspects of the intellectual commons and some of the ways that the *Handbook* addresses them.

The Centrality of the Adult Learner and Adult Learning

A commitment to adult learners lies at the heart of adult education's professional identity. Adult learners represent individuals facing myriad intentional and unintentional changes that foster new learning and practices. The world of adult and continuing education focuses both on individual learning and on the varied organizations that support and enhance the processes of learning. The aim of this learning endeavor is to broadly equip adults to effectively engage in the world through individual and collective actions within the spheres of family, work, and community.

The chapters in this section focus on various aspects of adult learners and learning. The central issues of the section explore the key theories and practices related to adult learning and adult development. Although the specific definition of adult is fluid, contextual, and constantly evolving, this *Handbook* focuses on learning experiences intentionally designed for individuals "whose age, social roles, or self-perception define them as adults" (Merriam & Brockett, 2007, p. 8). The chapters focus primarily on the learner, learning, and development, but they also emphasize that adult and continuing education includes a broad sphere of activities and processes. Thus, the adult learner can be understood simultaneously as an individual, as a member of a learning group, as part of a workplace or other learning format, as a member of a community, and as a member of a wider society. The chapters serve as an introduction to these central aspects of adult and continuing education, while also noting the complexity inherent in a generalized discussion of learners and learning.

The Creation of Open Exchanges of Knowledge, Theory, and Practice

Another key facet of this intellectual commons is the sharing, dissemination, and refutation of knowledge and practices. Past models of these exchanges viewed these connections as primarily one of dissemination and implementation. Current models of exchange suggest a more complex set of interactions and exchanges. These new models take into consideration cultural influences at the organizational, local, regional, and national levels. However, they also involve a notion of individual agency, in which the individual must assess the viability of an approach within the context of his or her own philosophical beliefs. Thus, critical reflection, an examination of beliefs, and cultural limitations have been added to our understanding of the connections between research, theory, and practice. The 2000 *Handbook of Adult and Continuing Education* (Wilson & Hayes, 2000) explored the importance of examining the implicit assumptions that affect all aspects of theory building, research, and professional practice in the field. It is our aim to continue this focus, while placing reflection within a broader paradigm that connects the key purposes of adult and continuing education to the practice of the field.

This section of the *Handbook* has been crafted to provide readers who are novices in the field with a foundational baseline of the historical background and contemporary understandings of the field of practice and study of adult education. The intent of this section is to provide a general overview of the theorizing and research in the field, the societal context affecting adult and continuing education, and some of the differing ways that these foundational areas can be conceptualized, while also emphasizing that adult and continuing education is itself the embodiment of an open exchange of knowledge, theory, and practice. By this we mean that adult and continuing education is conceptually dynamic and fluid. The conceptual frameworks at the core of this section are varying, and these differences add to the organizational richness of the field. They also provide a broad framework for analyzing and understanding the practice of adult and continuing education. In addition, each of these chapters presents a framework for analysis that is complementary. These complementarities are at the heart of the intellectual commons. They provide a vibrant critique of practice and research as well as broad bases for our current understanding of the field today. Thus, it is the goal of this

section to provide an overview of key contemporary understandings of the field and an intellectual organization of the landscape of key strands of scholarship and practice perspectives.

Adult and Continuing Education as a Field of Practice

One of the central premises of this *Handbook* is that adult and continuing education is a distinct field of practice that requires unique skill sets. Given the many definitions of adult education, it should come as no surprise that understanding the field requires a multiplicity of approaches. Adult and Continuing Education is simultaneously a process, a philosophical approach, a view of learning, and a commitment to the learner. In addition, Adult and Continuing Education occurs in a variety of settings, including formal (educational settings), nonformal (organized activities outside educational organizations, such as in businesses and industry, churches, and professional associations), and informal (learning in everyday settings) contexts (Coombs, Prosser, & Ahmed, 1973). Because of this diversity, several questions arise when examining the field of practice. Are there common skills that educators in all of these contexts utilize? If so, what are they? Do adults learn in a similar fashion in all of these contexts? If so, how do we categorize this learning? If not, what are the differences? The chapters in this section examine some of the central premises of this issue. They begin by looking at the commonalities of the field and social structure of the profession. The structure is important because of the diversity of job titles and responsibilities that are part of being an adult educator. Thus educators in adult and continuing education may be full-time or part-time professional educators or volunteer workers. These chapters seek to describe the professional knowledge and skills that are part of being an adult educator, as well as to lay out the extreme permeability of these categories. The chapters in this section of the *Handbook* offer syntheses of the key principles and scholarship that guide current practice and beliefs, as well as an introduction to the central intellectual commons of adult and continuing education, specifically in terms of the varying tasks of adult and continuing educators. These chapters also consider the facilitation and design of learning, program planning, and delivery of adult education experiences; assessment and evaluation within adult and continuing education; and management and leadership of adult and continuing education. In addition to these core areas of knowledge, the chapters in this section examine the issues attached to the notion of adult and continuing education as a field with a particular professional identity.

The Diversity of Adult Learning Venues and Collective Endeavors

Another feature of this intellectual commons is a diversity of adult learning venues and collective group venues and the related multiplicity of roles by adult educators. Because adults do not engage in learning efforts solely within one context, it is essential that adult and continuing educators examine the various contexts and potential for collaboration and partnership. This multiplicity of contexts includes formal educational endeavors in schools, businesses, and community organizations, as well as informal and nonformal contexts.

Adult and continuing education is usually embedded within larger organizations that are primarily designed for another purpose. This marginalization affects the funding, structures, and policies that make up the field. Yet this organizational diversity can also be a strength in that it expands both access to and the definition of adult and continuing education. The very structures of adult education agencies both encourage and discourage participation. They are designed to enhance social and/or economic mobility, yet often fail to provide this mobility. As practitioners and researchers, adult educators continue to be boundary spanners and change agents in negotiating and brokering among these institutional venues. Thus, the examination of these varying contexts adds to the idea of the intellectual commons as a negotiated and constantly changing set of realities.

In this section, the chapter authors examine the totality of practice; that is, the range of educational providers and the concomitant roles and identities of adult educators within these various contexts. Within the framework of the intellectual commons, this organizational diversity can be seen as a key part of the continuing experimentation and innovation that takes place within the field. Because of the complexity and variation of adult and continuing education activities, the chapters in this section focus on key contexts that serve significant numbers of adults or that provide uniquely delineated practices serving large numbers of adults. Recognizing that we all live in a dynamic and evolving world of practice contexts, each chapter provides a contemporary perspective of this community of practice and the key principles, practices, and organizational forms. In order to provide a sense of where the field is currently situated and where it is going, we chose the following contexts for closer examination: 2- and 4-year postsecondary education; the workplace, including both the employee and employer efforts; the military; community-based and faith-based endeavors; health and wellness organizations; cultural institutions; environmental efforts; and Internet-based distance education as a growing entity serving adult learners.

The Centrality of Social Justice

A key aspect of the intellectual commons is a concern for the disenfranchised. In essence, at the core of the work of adult and continuing education is a concern with equity. This concern is examined in this *Handbook* through the lenses of gender, race, ethnicity, class, sexual orientation, and disability. This focus on social justice is often intertwined with how we define the mission of adult and continuing education and ourselves as educators. This stance does not have a clear boundary; there are shifting borders of understanding. Some think of the have-nots as those who have directly or indirectly experienced discrimination based on race, gender, or class. Others see them as those who lack high school diplomas or well-paying jobs, as those without the computer skills required to access information through the Internet, or as individuals who lack conversational English.

The issue of social justice goes beyond programmatic emphasis. In terms of the intellectual commons, we feel that an emphasis on social justice is a core value within adult and continuing education. There is a strong historical tradition within the field that a goal of social change is a principal aspect of the development of adult and continuing education. This long tradition has been demonstrated in the continued interest in the works of Eduard Lindeman and Paolo Freire and in such entities as the Highlander Folk School. This strand of adult education has consistently focused on strengthening the field through study of and action in the community. There have been several different names and approaches within this aspect of the field, including social action, social change, social movements, and social justice. According to Newman (2005), social action "occurs when people act collectively to bring about change" (p. 569). Adult education for social action results in social change. However, social change by itself is not a value. When sociologists talk about social change, they are considering a broader concept of change that can result from social action, but can also result from broader societal shifts such as technological change, population change, or modernization. The notion of social change is descriptive, not prescriptive (Hamilton, 1992).

Social movements on the other hand engage in social action and promote a prescriptive approach to social change. Within adult and continuing education, social movement learning refers to the "(a) learning by persons who are part of any social movement; and (b) learning by persons outside of a social movement as a result of actions taken or simply by the existence of social movements" (Hall & Clover, 2005, p. 384). While much writing in adult and continuing education has used the shorthand of discussing adult education for social change, since the 1990s the more common approach has been to discuss this approach to social change under the rubric of social justice. While social change is not necessarily equitable change, the concept of social justice draws from Rawls's 1999 work *A Theory of Justice*. Within this theory of justice, Rawls insisted that justice is about fairness and that this idea of fairness should replace the previous reliance on the social contract.

Since the publication of the last edition of the *Handbook* (Wilson & Hayes, 2000), this strand of adult education for social justice has become one of the predominant concerns of the field. We have chosen to name this section "The Centrality of Social Justice" because of the broad concerns for equity, fairness, and justice that pervade the section. Thus, social justice is a guiding framework for understanding the role

and mission of adult and continuing education. It is an essential feature of the intellectual commons in that concerns with social justice frame much of the discussion about purpose and structure of adult and continuing education. This concern serves as evidence of adult and continuing education itself as an intellectual commons. This section discusses the contemporary practices and the research embedded in social justice for both adult learning and the creation and facilitation of adult learning environments. Specific chapters examine historic and contemporary understandings of social justice, as well as perspectives on gender and sexual orientation, race and ethnicity, age, disability, class, and place.

The Future of Adult Education Within a Global Context

This *Handbook* has to a large degree taken a focused look at adult and continuing education in North America, particularly the United States. Yet, it is recognized that in the 21st century, adult and continuing education in any one location exists as part of a broader, global endeavor. Thus, throughout many of these chapters there has been an organic and engaged collaboration with international contributors, as well as the growing recognition of international best practices and research. As noted by a number of contributors, our world of professional practice involves the valuing of both local and global perspectives and endeavors. These commingled national and global perspectives represent exciting, innovative accomplishments as well as the continuing exchanges across the adult learning community.

Perhaps one of the more interesting global challenges is to identify key terminology to define policies and practices. One term, *lifelong learning*, has been suggested in many quarters as the rallying cry for extending adult education opportunities, along with its partner terms, *lifelong education* and *learning society*. Yet this term has come to have many meanings and to be associated with many purposes around the world, causing some of adult education's staunchest advocates becoming wary of its use. Historically this term has not been as strongly embraced in the United States as in many other parts of the world, particularly in the policy arena, as represented by the unfunded Lifelong

Learning Act of 1976. The term has been used in scholarly venues within the U.S. to consider the broad landscape of adult and continuing education across the adult lifespan. However, due to the role of education as defined by local and state policy, the term has not been a viable construct for major regional or national initiative. On the other hand, a number of predominantly international collectives and governmental bodies focus upon the lifespan from child to senior citizen for their understanding and engagement in lifelong learning. This latter stance is reflected in the UNESCO's 1972 Report by International Commission on the Development of Education, *Learning to Be: The World of Education Today and Tomorrow* (Faure et al., 1972), and by the most recent efforts of European Commission, which focuses one of its policy areas on lifelong learning "the objectives of which are both to empower citizens to meet the challenges of the knowledge-based society; and to meet the goals and ambitions of the Member States and the candidate countries to be more prosperous, inclusive, tolerant and democratic" (European Commission, n.d.).

Yet many scholars from countries where policies aimed at promoting lifelong have been enacted have come to take a more critical stance as they examine the increasing degree to which the term has become equated with an emphasis on continuing learning as a way to increase status in the marketplace. According to this critique, the emphasis on the market place devalues learning for noneconomic purposes. (Cruikshank, 2002; Griffin, 2006; Grummel, 2007). Other scholars, focusing on Asia and Africa, have examined how well Western concepts of lifelong learning and learning society embrace international worldviews and social contexts, as well as the degree to which ideals of equitable access to adult education for all are being met by current lifelong learning policies as implemented (Atchison, 2004; Preece, 2006; Wang, 2008).

This final section examines adult education within a global context. It examines the global demands that impact the future of practice and scholarship in adult and continuing education. Current understandings and disjunctures between philosophy and practice are also explored. Specific chapters consider the worlds of adult learners and their society through the lenses of globalization, access and participation

in adult education, the commitment to community, informal learning in a virtual era, reflections upon the nature of a professional identity, and related trends linking research and practice.

CONCLUDING THOUGHTS

This *Handbook* is a decennial opportunity to take stock of the field of adult and continuing education. The 2010 *Handbook* is designed to continue in this important tradition. In these six sections of the intellectual commons, we hope that the reader will gain an understanding of key aspects of adult learning and development and related processes, knowledge of frameworks that inform current practice, and an overview of fundamental features of the field of practice and of the varying institutional and collective endeavors within the field. Further, this *Handbook* has taken a special stance to speak to importance of social justice and the enhanced global connections that inform adult and continuing education. We believe that the notion of the intellectual commons conveys the spirit of the field as it grapples with the complex and contradictory phenomena that compose this dynamic world of adult and continuing education.

We also want to emphasize the complexity of this commons. As the authors of these chapters examine the trends, the research, and the current state of practice, they also present analyses of adult and continuing education within these varying contexts and processes. Our aim is to present the multifaceted and complex world of adult and continuing education in North America. We hope that the reader will come to see this field as we do, as an educational endeavor that values all learning while recognizing a collective commitment to fair and equal access to education for all adults. For select institutions, countries, policy makers, and collectives, the field also represents engagements in specific movements and policies to create equitable structures, laws, and processes that embrace varied cultural tenets of a lifelong learning society. Finally, we hope that the notion of the intellectual commons conveys the spirit of the field as it grapples with complex and contradictory phenomena that make up the world of adult and continuing education.

REFERENCES

Atchison, J. (2004). Lifelong learning in South Africa: Dreams and delusions. *International Journal of Lifelong Education, 23*(6), 517–544.

Beder, H. (1989). Purposes and philosophies of adult education. In S. B. Merriam & P. M. Cunningham (Eds.), *Handbook of adult and continuing education* (pp. 37–50). San Francisco: Jossey-Bass.

Boone, E. J., Shearon, R. W., White, E. E., & Associates. (1980). *Serving personal and community needs through adult education. Adult Education Association of the U.S.A. Handbook Series in Adult Education*. San Francisco: Jossey-Bass.

Boyd, R. D., Apps, J. W., & Associates. (1980). *Redefining the discipline of adult education. Adult Education Association of the U.S.A. Handbook Series in Adult Education*. San Francisco: Jossey-Bass.

Bryson, L. L. (1936). *Adult education*. New York. American Book Company.

Charters, A. N., & Associates. (1980). *Comparing adult education worldwide. Adult Education Association of the U. S. A. Handbook Series in Adult Education*. San Francisco: Jossey-Bass.

Coombs, P. H., Prosser, R. C., & Ahmed, M. (1973). *New paths to learning: For rural children and youth*. New York: International Council for Educational Development.

Cruikshank, J. (2002). Lifelong learning or re-training for life: Scapegoating the worker. *Studies in the Education of Adults, 34*(2), 140–155.

Daloz, L., Parks, S., Keen, C., & Keen, J. (1996). *Common fire: Lives of commitment in a complex world. Boston*: Beacon Press.

Ely, M. L. (Ed.). (1948). *Handbook of adult education in the United States*. New York: Institute for Adult Education, Teachers College, Columbia University.

European Commission, (n.d.). *Making a European area of lifelong learning a reality*. Retrieved January 20, 2009, from http://ec.europa.eu/education/policies/111 /life/index_en.html

Faure, E., Herrera, F., Kaddoura, A., Lopes, H., Petrovsky, A., Rahnema, M., & Ward, F. (1972). *Learning to be: The world of education today and tomorrow*. Retrieved November 27, 2009, from http://unesdoc.unesco.org/images/0000/000018/001801e.pdf

Griffin, C. (2006). Research and policy in lifelong learning. *International Journal of Lifelong Education, 25*(6), 561–574.

Grummel, B. (2007). The "second chance" myth: Equality of opportunity in Irish Adult Education Policies. *British Journal of Educational Studies, 55*(2), 183–201.

Hall, B. L., & Clover, D. E. (2005). Social movement learning. In L. M. English (Ed.), *International encyclopedia of adult education* (pp. 584–588). Hampshire, UK: Palgrave Macmillan.

Hamilton, E. (1992). *Adult education for community development*. Westport, CT: Greenwood.

Huber, M., & Hutchings, P. (n.d.). *Building the teaching commons*. Retrieved September 5, 2009, from http://www.carnegiefoundation.org/perspectives/sub.asp?key=245&subkey=800

Huber, M., & Hutchings, P. (2005). *The advancement of learning: Building the teaching commons*. San Francisco: Jossey-Bass.

Iiyoshi, T., & Kumar, M. S. V. (Eds.). (2008). *Opening up education: The collective advancement of education through open technology, open content, and open knowledge*. Cambridge: MIT Press.

Knowles, M. S. (Ed.). (1960). *Handbook of adult education in the United States*. Washington DC: Adult Education Association of the U.S.A.

Knox, A., & Associates. (1980). *Developing, administering and evaluating adult education. Adult Education Association of the U.S.A. Handbook Series in Adult Education*. San Francisco: Jossey-Bass.

Kopka, T., Schantz, N. G., & Korb, R. A. (1998). *Adult education in the 1990s: A report of the 1991 National Household Education Survey*. U.S. Dept. of Ed. NCES. Washington, D. C. National Center for Education Statistics. Retrieved November 11, 2003, from http://nces.ed.gov/pubs98/9803.pdf

Kreitlow, B. W., & Associates. (1980). *Examining controversies in adult education. Adult Education Association of the U.S.A. Handbook Series in Adult Education*. San Francisco: Jossey-Bass.

Long, H. B., Hiemstra, R., & Associates. (1980). *Changing approaches in studying adult education. Adult Education Association of the U.S.A. Handbook Series in Adult Education*. San Francisco: Jossey-Bass.

Merriam S. B., & Brockett, R. (2007). *The profession and practice of adult education: An introduction*. New York: John Wiley.

Merriam, S. B, Caffarella, R., & Baumgartner, L. (2007). *Learning in adulthood: A comprehensive guide* (3rd ed.). San Francisco: Jossey-Bass.

Merriam, S. B., & Cunningham, P. M. (Eds). (1989). *Handbook of adult and continuing education*. San Francisco: Jossey-Bass.

National Center for Education Statistics (NCES). (2007a). *Adult education participation in 2004–2005*. Retrieved June, 2009, from http://nces.ed.gov/pubs2006/adulted/

National Center for Education Statistics (NCES). (2007b). Digest of Educational Statistics, 2007, Table 183. Total fall enrollment in degree-granting institutions, by control and type of institution, age, and attendance status of student: 2005. Retrieved July 28, 2009, http://nces.ed.gov/programs/digest/d07/tables/dt07_183.asp?referrer=list

National Center for Education Statistics (NCES). (2007c). Table 358. Participation of persons, 17 years old and over, in adult education during the previous 12 months, by selected characteristics of participants: Selected years, 1991 through 2005. Retrieved January 30, 2009, from http://nces.ed.gov/programs/digest/d07/tables/dt07_358.asp

Newman, M. (2005). Social action. In L. M. English (Ed.), *International encyclopedia of adult education* (pp. 569–572). Hampshire, UK: Palgrave Macmillan.

O'Donnell, K. (2006). Adult education participation in 2005–05 (NCES 2006–077). U.S. Department of Education. Washington, DC: National Center for Education Statistics.

Peters, J. M., & Associates. (1980). *Building an effective adult education enterprise. Adult Education Association Handbook of the U.S.A. Series in Adult Education.* San Francisco: Jossey-Bass.

Peterson, R., & Associates. (1979). *Lifelong learning in America.* San Francisco: Jossey-Bass.

Preece, J. (2006). Beyond the learning society: The learning world? *International Journal of Lifelong Education, 25*(3), 307–320.

Rawls, J. (1999). *A theory of justice* (Rev. ed.). Cambridge, MA: The Belknap Press of Harvard University Press. (Original work published 1971)

Rowden, D. (Ed.). (1934). *Handbook of adult education in the United States.* New York: American Association for Adult Education.

Rowden, D. (Ed.) (1936). *Handbook of adult education in the United States.* New York: American Association for Adult Education.

Smith, R. M., Aker, G. F., and Kidd, J. R. (Eds.). (1970). *Handbook of adult education.* New York: Macmillan.

Stubblefield, H. W., & Rachal, J. R. (1992). On the origins of the term and meaning of "adult education" in the United States. *Adult Education Quarterly, 42*(2), 106–116.

Verner, C., & Booth, A. (1964). *Adult education.* Washington, DC: The Center for Applied Research in Education.

Wang, C. (2008). Enhancing the interactive relationship between lifelong learning and social changes to carry out a learning society in Taiwan. *International Journal of Lifelong Education, 27*(5), 535–542.

Wilson, A. L., & Hayes, E. R. (Eds.). (2000). *Handbook of adult and continuing education.* San Francisco: Jossey-Bass.

PART I

THE CENTRALITY OF THE ADULT LEARNER AND ADULT LEARNING

1

ADULT LEARNERS

CATHERINE A. HANSMAN AND VIVIAN W. MOTT

The U.S. Department of Education (National Center for Education Statistics [NCES], 2004, 2007) reports that participation levels in adult education activities have, for the most part, steadily increased over the past three decades. These participation increases can be seen in formal adult education programs, such as universities or community colleges, as well as nonformal or informal learning contexts, such as learning in casually formed interest or hobby groups. Because involvement in adult education is so broad and diverse, it is difficult to describe and define a "typical" adult learner. Race, class, gender, sexual orientation, ability, age, and other elements of human difference all influence who adult learners are and the learning activities in which they engage.. Societal factors, such as the aging population, the influx of immigrants, increased numbers of women entering and staying in the workplace, along with shifting technologies, global economic instability, and accelerated knowledge obsolescence, have all contributed to escalated involvement in learning activities (American Society for Training and Development [ASTD], 2008; Bureau of Labor Statistics, 2001; Creighton & Hudson, 2001; Mott, 2009). Usher, Bryant, and Johnston further suggest that these rapid "developments within an increasingly diverse and uncertain world clearly influence the knowledge, skills, attitudes and values a citizen requires to participate in a contemporary democracy" (1997, p. 30). Literature and research concerning adult learners cover a wide range of issues concerning those who are already participating in educational activities, but adults who are not participants remain unknown because they are simply not present in formal educational institutions and often not documented in other learning contexts (Hansman, 2006). In summary, many complex factors must be taken into account when defining and describing who adult learners are, their motivation for learning, the nature of such learning, and the activities in which they engage.

All these issues lead to some intriguing questions, such as: What is the definition of an adult? What developmental and learning theories provide a framework for understanding adult development and learning? Who participates in adult educational activities? Who typically does not participate in educational opportunities, and why? Finally, what challenges do adult educators face to enhance and encourage learning in adulthood, and how can they prepare to better serve adult learners now and in the future?

These questions provide a framework for exploring a wide range of subjects concerning adult learners and learning in adulthood. The purpose of this chapter is to address these issues and promote both deliberation and discourse focusing on adult learners. Understanding the framework concerning adult learners' involvement in formal and informal learning activities, as well as the barriers and incentives to their participation, will further enhance adult educators' knowledge and abilities to work successfully with adult learners.

DEFINING ADULT LEARNERS

What does it mean to be an adult? Should states and governments define when a person is considered an adult? Although the term *adult* may be used to define a "grown up person" (*Collins Webster's Dictionary,* p. 7), Merriam and Brockett (2007) contend that the notion of adulthood as a stage of life is a "relatively new concept" (p. 4). Legal definitions of adulthood generally include some age guidelines that define when a person becomes an adult, such as the ages of 18 to 21 in most of the United States. Bjorklund and Bee describe the adult stage as "emerging adulthood (when adolescence is ending) to the end of life" (2008, p. 4). These authors also categorize adults into four major categories: early adulthood, 20–39; middle adulthood, 40–64; older adulthood, 65–74; and late adulthood, 75 and older. They further distinguish later life in three additional age categories of young-old (ages 65–75), old (ages 65–75), and oldest-old (85 and older), an important distinction given the rapid and consistent rise in the older population. Bjorklund and Bee maintain that as major life tasks, work and personal roles, and educational needs change throughout adulthood, learners of all ages differ in their to motivations, access, and abilities to learn in a variety of venues.

Nevertheless, the definition of adult is for the most part culturally and socially derived. Researchers in other countries and cultures may capture ideas about adults differently than Western cultures, often including other factors besides chronological age in their understandings of adulthood, such as gender, ethnicity, religion, behaviors, and other cultural norms of any particular social milieu. Psychological maturity levels and social roles, as well as life situations, also define adulthood. For instance, persons younger than 18 who are parents or caregivers of others, or "traditional" age university students working full time to support themselves and pay tuition, may be considered adults. So in a real sense, and for the purposes of this discussion, persons may be considered adults when they have taken on the social, psychological, and/or economic roles typically expected of adults in their cultures and collective societies. Bjorklund and Bee (2008) clarify this concept with their caution that "age is just a number" (p. 13), that adulthood has several dimensions that affect learning. While chronological age represents the literal number of years one has lived, biological or functional age (physical condition), psychological (developmental maturity), and social age (perception of roles and expectations at any given point in life) are different measures of age that may significantly impact an adult's desire for and ability to pursue learning.

Life Span and Life Expectancy

The maximum human *life span* is typically considered to be 110 to 120 years (Merriam, Caffarella, & Baumgartner, 2007). In the United States, *life expectancy,* the "average number of years a person can expect to live, based on current age" (Mott, 1999, p. 9), for the total population is 78.1 years (National Center for Health Statistics, 2009), lagging behind the life expectancy of persons in other developed countries. Statistics show that women live longer than men. Although the gap in life expectancy between the Black and White populations has narrowed, it still persists, with life expectancy at birth for Whites 4.9 years longer than that of Blacks (National Center for Health Statistics, 2009).

As a result of longer life expectancy, the population of adults ages 65 and older is increasing at an unparalleled rate. Population projections predict that within the next 10 years, older people will outnumber children for the first time in history. Kinsella and He (2009) reported that "the world's growth rate for the 80-and-over population from 2007 to 2008 was 4.3 percent, while that of the world's older (65 and over) population as whole was 2.1 percent (compared with 1.2 percent for the total [all ages] population" (p. iv). While the world's population is aging, so is the workforce, which has particular educational implications for job training and development.

Older workers (ages 56–65), particularly those in developed countries, continue to participate in job training and job-related adult education, pointing to the continuing need for research concerning learning throughout the life span. Older women, in particular, are much more likely to remain in or return to the workforce—and therefore to need additional training and education—than is any other age group (NCES, 2007). However, since those between the ages of 25 and 44 have higher literacy rates than the older population, illiteracy continues to "hinder older people's social participation and contribution to social development" (Kinsella & He, 2009, p. 94).

Adult Development

Change and development are integral to the human life span, and many development theories attempt to explain this process. Human development is recognized as a lifelong process, but as Jordan (1978) says "In our culture, adulthood as a condition used to be simply assumed; as a process, it now seems to demand an explanation" (quoted in Clark & Caffarella, 1999, p. 3). Clark and Caffarella classify perspectives of human development as biological, psychological, sociocultural, and integrative. The biological perspective acknowledges that the physiological changes in humans are driven by both primary and secondary aging. Biological aging may result in changes in vision and hearing, contribute to the onset of serious illnesses, and cause mobility issues, which may affect the capacity for growth and development as well as interest in learning.

The psychological perspective organizes human development into three categories: sequential models, life events, and transitions. Sequential models of development, such as those proposed by Erikson (1963), Kohlberg (1973), Levinson (1986), and Levinson & Levinson (1996), classify different phases or stages through which all adults travel; each theorist proposed different catalysts, such as age or resolution of key dilemmas in life, that signify when an adult moves to another stage or phase. In the second category, theorists such as Schlossberg (1984) propose that key life events, such as graduations, births, marriages, and job changes may shape personal development. The third category, relational, was first recognized by Gilligan (1982) and Belenky, Clichy, Goldberger, and Tarule (1986). They viewed women's development through the emerging "voice" and understandings of the relational qualities of learning. While their models initially referred to *women's* development, these constructs soon became understood as ways in which development in both men and women could occur.

From a sociocultural perspective, Gardiner and Kosmitzki (2005) maintain that the social and cultural aspects of one's life and environment fuel growth and development throughout the life span. Included in the sociocultural view are considerations of how race, class, ethnicity, social class, gender, sexual identity, and physical ability shape one's growth and development throughout adulthood. Finally, integrative theorists suggest that models of development must be comprehensive and include psychological, sociocultural, and biological changes and interactions throughout the life span (Magnusson, 1995). Sociocultural and integrative perspectives have led to further expansion of theories regarding human development that take into account and honor the intersections and interactions of race, class, gender, ethnicity, ableness, and sexual identity.

As Merriam and her colleagues contend, "the concept of development is most often equated with change" (2007, p. 298), and theories of human development influence the ways in which adult educators may work with adult learners. Understanding these theories may help adult educators examine their role in the lives of their students in order to better facilitate programs and activities for adult learners that foster development.

Adult Learners and Learning Activities

Adult learners are those adults who engage in learning activities that may promote "any sustained change in thinking, values, or behavior" (Cranton, 1992, p. 3). Adult learners participate in many types of formal and informal education activities that they hope will help them "function effectively in the changing world around them" (Taylor, Marienau, & Fiddler, 2000, p. 4), or "for the purpose of achieving some personal sense of fulfillment, for bringing about improvement in their lives, or even for the sake of leisure or recreation" (Mott, 2000, p. 335). Some of the first studies which examined the reasons adult learners participate in educational activities of any kind were conducted by Houle (1961) and Johnstone and Rivera (1965). Houle, in his interviews with 22 adult learners, found that they could be categorized into three groups based on their reasons for participation: (a) *goal-oriented learners,* who seek to achieve specific outcomes; (b) *activity-oriented learners,* who like to be engaged but did not necessarily care what the activity was; and (c) *learning-oriented learners,* who like to learn for learning's sake. In their 1965 survey research,

Johnstone and Rivera discovered that 22% of American adults had participated in learning activities in the year preceding the survey, and that most of these activities involved learning new or practical skills rather than pursuing academic study.

Tough's (1979) research regarding adult participation patterns in learning projects showed that adults engage in a diverse range of learning activities to help them with their day-to-day needs and problems. These needs and problems are wide and varied and can include: training classes in the workplace in order to perform better on the job or achieve promotion, completing necessary coursework for a General Educational Development (GED) credential, learning English as a second language, returning to higher education to complete the classes required to earn an undergraduate or graduate degree, or successfully finishing continuing professional education classes to keep professional licenses or certifications current (e.g., in medicine, law, education). Other adults may engage in less formal and more self-directed activities to enhance their personal or spiritual growth, to take on hobbies, or to learn skills that may improve their daily lives. In short, the learning activities in which adults engage are as diverse as adult learners themselves. There are no "typical" adult learners. Instead, adult learners represent "a diverse set of individuals with distinctive demographics, social locations, aspirations, and levels of preparation" (Pusser et al., 2007, p. 4). As the sociocultural, demographic, technological, and economic shifts continue globally, and as learners continue to be differentiated, their needs and motivations for learning in adulthood will continue to change as well. Research will continue to add new dimensions to this long debated study of just who adult learners are, the motivations that prompt their learning, and the nature of their participation in adult learning venues.

Generational Differences

Another factor facilitating our understanding of adult learners has to do with *generational differences,* an underresearched trend fueled by interest from practitioners in higher education and workplace training programs. Generational differences focus on the birth cohort, sociocultural factors, and historical influences in learners' lives. Lowery (2001) defines a *generation* as

"a series of birth cohorts who share a common location in history and a common peer persona that reflects a collective identity" (p. 72). Generations are frequently described with titles such as *Traditionals* (born prior to 1945), *Baby Boomers* (born 1946 to 1965), *Generation Xers* (born 1965 to the early 1980) and *Millennials* or *Nexters* (born mid-to-late 1980s to 2000) (Lancaster & Stillman, 2002). Because of their experiences and sociocultural influences, persons in different generations or birth cohorts may have wide-ranging values and belief systems, varied life experiences, widely dissimilar learning and work styles, and diverse perspectives on the use and creation of knowledge, technology, and learning. Further, each generation may be motivated by entirely different factors, benefit from support systems distinct from those of other generations, and employ varying strategies to respond to life's demands. Adult educators should consider that—for the first time in history—four distinct generations at once may be present in the workplace and adult education learning environments, potentially posing challenges to effectively serve all adult learners in the same learning context.

Currently, most of the literature on generational differences and its impact on learning and work styles are found primarily in the popular press, and additional empirical research concerning these ideas are needed. Missing thus far from the discourse concerning generations is considerations of how gender, racial, ethnic, class, and sexual identity may also influence individuals within each generation and therefore impact educational access and achievement in adulthood. Further development and empirical research on generational difference should include diverse groups in the research design to develop more accurate understandings of learning differences in and among generations (Hansman & McAtee, 2009).

Concepts of Learning in Adulthood

Learning in adulthood can be "distinguished from childhood in terms of the learner, the context . . . and to some extent, the learning process" (Merriam et al., 2007, p. 423). Individual understandings of learning dominated concepts of learning in adulthood until the late 20th century, when the context of learning and constructivist views of learning prompted new knowledge of learning in adulthood. Malcolm Knowles's assumptions and principles concerning adult learners were widely adopted in the 20th century as helpful in understanding adult learners (Andragogy, defined as "the art and science of helping adults learn" (Knowles, 1980, p. 43), and concepts of self-directed learning contributed to definitions of adult learners. Knowles proposed several assumptions regarding typical adult learners, declaring that adult learners are those who possess independent self-concepts and are capable of directing their own learning from a rich reservoir of their own life experiences; have learning needs prompted by their changing life roles; and are internally motivated toward problem-centered learning that has immediate application to their lives (Knowles, 1980).

Although Knowles's assumptions concerning adult learners are embraced by many adult educators, they are critiqued for not accurately portraying all adult learners and, further, for promoting generic and prescriptive ideas of typical adult learners. For example, contrary to Knowles's notion that adult learners are internally motivated, many adults are externally motivated to learn, striving to improve their employment opportunities, earning potential, and social capital. He also neglected social and learning contexts, which are currently regarded as central to learning (Hansman, 2001, 2008) and have become important in understanding learning in adulthood.

Self-directed learning—"adults assuming control of their learning" (Merriam & Brockett, 2007, p. 137)—is another commonly held assumption about adult learners, but one which varies widely among learners. Merriam (2001) describes the goals of self-directed learning from three perspectives: humanistic, transformational, and emancipatory. The first, from a humanist philosophical stance, posits that adult learners can develop their capacity to be self-directed. That is, depending on their life experiences, existing knowledge, and motivations, learners have varying degrees of self-directedness and can develop it further, motivated by self or others' direction.

A second perspective on self-directed learning is that it may facilitate adults to experience transformational learning through critical self-reflection (Mezirow & Associates, 2000; Taylor, 2008). Transformational learning attempts to explain how adults make meaning from their lived experiences. Mezirow and his associates propose that the process of transformation is set in motion by a disorienting dilemma, such as a job loss, that may stimulate adults to reflect upon and examine their beliefs. This critical reflection may lead to reflective discourse with others, expanding adult learners' historical and cultural understandings of their needs, wants, and interests, which may lead to new self-knowledge and further, opening the door for future learning and development.

A third view of self-directed learning embraces the "promotion of emancipatory learning," where learners are "positioned more for social and political action than individual learning" (Merriam, 2001, p. 9). Brookfield (1993, 2005) has long promoted self-directed learning from this perspective, arguing that "a view of learning that regards people as self-contained, volitional beings scurrying around in individual projects . . . works against collective and cooperative impulses" resulting in "an excessive focus on the self" (p. 84). Given that self-directed learning helps promote the constructivist and contextual nature of knowledge, reflection, creative problem solving, and critical thinking, proponents of self-directed learning advocate the importance of adults' self-directedness as a particularly critical skill for the global marketplace.

Understandings of adult learners have frequently focused on individual learners and psychological approaches to learning and development, but in the past 20 years, expanded understandings of learning have recognized broader contexts and structural factors that may impact learning (Caffarella & Merriam, 2000). These structural factors include the role race, class, gender, ethnicity, ability, power, and oppression play in adult education programs and access to learning opportunities. Thus theorists such as Jarvis (1987) claim that "learning is intimately related to that world and affected by it" (p. 11), and further, that "we live and move and have our being in a social context" (Jarvis, 2006, p. 5). Clearly, the social context of learning has become increasingly important to understanding adult learning. Lave (1988) furthered these ideas, proposing that situated learning theory frames how adults learn. Hansman (2001) explains that context structures learning through the "interactions among learners, the tools they use within these interactions, the activity itself, and the social context in which the activity takes place" (p. 45). Similarly, communities of practice, or CoPs (Wenger, 1998), engage learners in a process of learning constructed around "common interests, ideas, passions, and goals . . . the things that matter to people" (Hansman, 2008, p. 299). In CoPs, adult learners continuously negotiate and renegotiate shared knowledge and understandings; through mutual engagement, participants engage in collective processes and common activities designed to build a joint enterprise of a shared repertoire of knowledge and resources. In other words, learners co-create and share knowledge, framing adult learning as a social endeavor in specific contexts that is shared among learners who may be motivated by different purposes for learning yet joined together for mutual collaboration.

Other considerations of learning in adulthood have expanded to include new understandings of transformational learning (Taylor, 2008), spirituality and adult learning (English, Fenwick, & Parsons, 2003; Tisdell, 2008), somatic/embodied learning experiences as a source of learning and knowledge (Freiler, 2008), critical theory (Brookfield, 2005), and understanding how the brain changes as adults learn (Taylor & Lamoreaux, 2008). These and other ideas and theories will be discussed in more depth in a later chapter concerning adult learning. However, the questions of who adult learners are and how adult educators can best serve them continue to be critical topics of study and discussion among adult educators that are closely connected to an expansion of the notion of adult learning beyond simply cognitive functions. A better understanding of who adult learners are can be seen through analyzing participation patterns in adult educational activities.

PARTICIPATION IN ADULT EDUCATIONAL ACTIVITIES

Adults may engage in learning throughout their lives in a variety of venues and formats, as participation pattern data inform us. Researchers for the Adult Education Survey of the National Household Education Surveys Program (AE-NHES) found that in a combined sample of work-age adults from 2001 to 2005, 54% participated in at least one of the following formal learning activities in the 12 months prior to the survey: English as a second language (ESL) classes; adult basic education/GED classes; apprenticeship programs; work-related or personal interest courses; and college, university, and vocational/technical degree or certificate programs (Kienzl, 2008). Other outcomes of the AE-NHES study showed that 72% of adults with at least a bachelor's degree participated in formal education programs, while only 26% of adults with neither a high school diploma nor a GED credential participated in formal education. Adults with lower education levels also participated less frequently in work-related and personal interest courses, and when they did participate, they took fewer classes, making it less likely for their participation to result in upward mobility or potential personal gain (Creighton & Hudson, 2001; Kienzl, 2008; NCES, 2007). Women, those in rural areas, and those in underrepresented cultural groups remain particularly vulnerable to reduced and less mobility-producing workplace training opportunities (Mott, 1998, 2008). The cost of participation in educational opportunities may be an essential barrier for adults with less education and less than full-time employment, as adults employed full time may have employers who pay for at least some of their educational classes.

The desire for greater self-esteem and feelings of self-worth also factor into adults' participation in formal learning opportunities, particularly in ESL and basic skills/GED preparation classes. O'Donnell (2006) found that "the majority of ESL participants reported having taken ESL classes to either improve the way that they feel about themselves (95 percent) or to make it easier to do things on a day-to-day basis (93 percent)" (p. 2). He also established that 78% of adults taking basic skills/GED preparation classes reported doing so to improve the way they felt about themselves, although 55% viewed the classes as a way to gain employment with a different employer. In addition, 45% viewed basic skills/GED classes as the means to gaining a raise or promotion, 28% found the classes helpful for assisting their children with their schoolwork, and 18% engaged in these classes to qualify for public assistance. These data show that adults recognize education as a path to advance their economic and personal lives as well as help them improve their own feelings of confidence and self-worth, which may encourage them to participate further in other educational opportunities.

More in-depth analysis of the National Center for Education Statistics (NCES) and Bureau of Labor Statistics data reveals some other interesting trends (Bureau of Labor Statistics, 2001; Creighton & Hudson, 2001; NCES, 2004, 2007; O'Donnell, 2006):

- Participation rates in formal education are highest in adults ages 16 to 24 years (53%), followed in order by those in the following groups: ages 25 to 34 (52%), ages 35 to 44 (49%), ages 45–54 (48%), ages 55–64 years (40%), and finally, ages 65 years or older (23%).

- Of respondents who reported participating in formal adult education activities, 46% were White, non-Hispanic; 46% were Black, non-Hispanic; 44% were Asian or Pacific Islanders; and 38% were Hispanic.

- Adult respondents earning more than $75,000 had the highest participation rates, followed by adults earning between $50,001 and 75,000. The group that reported the least amount of participation earned $20,000 or less each year.

- The least participation in any formal adult educational activity was reported by those with less than a high school diploma or equivalent (22%), while those who reported participating the most (66%) already had earned graduate or professional degrees.

- Women participated in educational activities at higher rates than did men. Participation of women learners beyond the age of 35 increased 500% in last three decades.

- Of all adults surveyed, 21% reported participating in personal interest courses, but those with an income of $75,000 or greater and the highest levels of education reported the most participation in this area. Only 16% of adults earning $20,000 or less and 11% of those with less than a high school diploma took personal interest courses.

- Seventy percent of all adults participated in informal learning activities such as learning on computers; using the Internet, books, manuals, videos, or television; participating in clubs or groups; or attending conventions or conferences.

- Nearly half of new job growth in the first decade of the 21st century required college or other postsecondary education.

- Greater numbers of young adult learners (ages 18–24) than in the past share the characteristics of older adult learners in terms of family, work, and financial responsibilities.

FACING FORWARD: CRITICAL ANALYSIS OF THE LANDSCAPE OF ADULT EDUCATION

As we discussed at the beginning of this chapter, the number of adults who participate in all types of adult education activities has continued to grow for the past three decades. However, along with this growth come continual challenges for adult learners, the adult educators who serve them, and the field of adult education as a whole. We conclude this chapter by discussing a few of these.

Changing Workforce

The workforce is transforming in many ways, due to technological, economical, societal, and global alterations. Because of these transformations, jobs in some industries in North America, such as manufacturing, have been altered and downsized, while other jobs have been created and continue to develop in technology and other industries. The industrial economy of the early 20th century that created remunerative work for unskilled labor has given way to an information and service economy that demands higher levels of academic and technical knowledge, as well as other skills such as good communication and problem-solving abilities. Furthermore, major economic changes around the globe have resulted in the downsizing of the workforce, and in many industries, the seemingly permanent loss of some jobs (ASTD, 2008).

The transformation of the world economy over the past several decades has put a premium on an educated workforce. A more fluid and volatile global economy is characterized by more frequent job and career change, which is an important factor in the growing demand for continual learning and skill enhancement. Because of these changes, it is clear that current and future generations of adult workers seeking employment and better quality of life will require more education credentials. Thus 2- and 4-year degrees, certificate programs, and workforce educational and training opportunities are becoming increasingly essential for all workers.

Diversity Challenges

Just as the nature of work is changing, so too is the racial and ethnic composition of the workforce. For instance, "By 2020, the proportion of whites in the workforce between the ages of 25 and 64 is expected to have dropped 19 percentage points to 63 percent, down from its 1980 level of 82 percent. During the same period, the percentage of Hispanic residents aged 25–64 will nearly triple from 6 percent to 17 percent, and the proportion of African Americans in the U.S. population will grow by almost a third" (National Center for Public Policy and Higher Education, 2005, quoted in Kazis et al., 2007, p. 5).

Although the racial composition of the workforce reflects a diverse population, current patterns of participation in education point to less presence in educational settings by minority groups. Groups who have been historically marginalized by race or class continue the struggle to partake in educational opportunities and encounter many impediments, especially financial barriers, to participation. Race, gender, and previous education experiences continue to be accurate predictors of participation in education, even among older learners. Blacks and Whites have higher rates of participation than their Hispanic counterparts or those of other races; women continue to outpace men in both work-related and leisure learning (NCES, 2007). And although the need for education and training is essential in order to obtain a living wage, patterns of participation in education still show that what has been true in the past remains true: "participation reflects a predominantly white, middle-class bias, markedly skewed toward those who are already better educated than most" (Mott, 2006, p. 96). For instance, participation in work-related courses was 8 times higher among adults with a bachelor's degree than for adults without GED/high school diplomas, and participation in work-related courses was higher for employed adults than unemployed adults (Kienzl, 2008).

For adults to remain employable in the current and future labor markets, it is clear that their capacity to learn new skills and adapt to new roles and work situations will be more crucial than ever before. Adult educators need to embrace their roles and responsibilities in facilitating educational opportunities that can help adults develop these aptitudes in various contexts.

Addressing Barriers to Education for Current and Future Adult Learners

Adult educators must address barriers to adults' participation in formal educational opportunities, such as the rising cost of higher education and certificate, vocational, and technical programs, place-bound learning venues, and dependence on technology which may limit many learners. Adult learners may be "institutionally invisible, marginalized, and taken for granted" (Sissel, Hansman, & Kasworm, 2001, p. 18), so research should include nonparticipating adults in an effort to better understand their reasons for their nonparticipation and to try to meet their needs as future learners. The difficulty, of course, is that researchers have little knowledge of or access to nonparticipating adult learners. Not only are researchers hampered by lack of ready access to such adults, but many adults who may have tentatively begun efforts in adult learning are often reluctant to discuss their perceived failures to persevere in the classroom or training context. Adult educators must not only strive to understand nonparticipation and lack of success in adult learning, but also be proactive in local, state, and national policy discussions concerning funding for all levels of adult education (Hansman, 2006).

Program Development for Future Learning

Along with the changing workforce, the accelerated pace of technological change, knowledge obsolescence, social justice issues, and other factors require adult educators to engage in constant program planning and evaluation to meet the ever-changing needs of the content and the context in which adult learning takes place. Important, too, is the challenge of projecting new career fields and addressing the requisite skills and competencies that will present opportunities and challenges for future learners of all ethnicities and races.

With growing competition from private and for-profit educational providers and shrinking resources from local, state, and federal governments, public education programs should consider partnerships and collaborative endeavors, not only to better serve adult learners but to produce programs that are responsive to the ever-changing needs of learners. In addition, service learning and other programs, such as internships and formal mentoring programs for adult learners, which may provide role models and support self-esteem, confidence, and career-related help (Hansman, 2000, 2003; Mott, 2006), should be included in adult education programs to help students gain practical/real-world experiences.

Challenging Perceptions of "Typical" Adult Learners

Adult educators should question "generic" and often stereotypical descriptions of adult learners, realizing that the diverse groups in formal adult education classrooms—different in age, race, class, gender, sexuality, and ability—have divergent learning needs to which adult educators must attend. Educators must find ways to reach adult learners "where they are" and promote critical reflection in learning situations to help further learners' growth and development in increasingly complex societies. Facilitators of adult learning must comprehend and continue to develop understandings of adult learning theories, bridging theory-to-practice barriers in learning contexts.

Expanding the Field of Adult Education

How can adult education expand and gain recognition as a field? Should adult education remain true (or some would argue *return*) to its legacy as a field devoted to education for social justice and democratic action? Or should adult educators pursue the instrumentality and *how-to* nature of a discipline focused on production, pragmatics, and utility? Adult educators must struggle with their own answers to these questions while remaining engaged in policy discussions and developments that will enhance learning opportunities for all adult learners.

The challenges for adult educators and the learners they serve are many. However, there is also much potential for new research and developments in the face of swiftly changing learning contexts and global societies. Adult educators, through authentic practice, critical reflection, collaborative efforts, and continued research, can and must meet the needs of current and future adult learners.

REFERENCES

American Society for Training and Development (ASTD). (2008). *2008 State of the Industry Report*. Alexandria, VA. Retrieved August 6, 2009, from http://www.astd.org/content/research/stateOfIndustry.htm

Belenky, M., Clichy, B., Goldberger, N., & Tarule, J. (1986). *Women's ways of knowing: The development of self, voice, and mind*. New York: Basic Books.

Bjorklund, B. R., & Bee, H. J. (2008). *The journey of adulthood* (6th ed.). Upper Saddle River, NJ: Pearson/Prentice Hall.

Brookfield, S. D. (1993). Self-directed learning, political clarity, and the critical practice of adult education. *Adult Education Quarterly, 43*(4), 227–242.

Brookfield, S. D. (2005). *The power of critical theory: Liberating adult learning and teaching*. San Francisco: Jossey-Bass.

Caffarella, R., & Merriam, S. B. (2000). Linking the individual learner to the context of adult learning. In A. Wilson & E. Hayes (Eds.), *Handbook of adult and continuing education* (pp. 55–70). San Francisco: Jossey-Bass.

Clark M. C., & Caffarella, R. S. (1999). Theorizing adult development. In M. C. Clark & R. S. Caffarella (Eds.), *An update on adult development theory: New ways of thinking about the life course* (pp. 3–7). New Directions for Adult & Continuing Education, No. 84. San Francisco: Jossey-Bass.

Collins Webster's Dictionary. (2007). New York: HarperCollins.

Cranton, P. (1992). *Working with adult learners*. Toronto, Ontario: Wall & Emerson.

Creighton, S., & Hudson, L. (2001). Participation trends and patterns in adult education. *Education Statistics Quarterly, 3*(4), 15–18.

English, L. M., Fenwick, T., & Parsons, J. (2003). *Spirituality in adult education and training*. Malabar, FL: Krieger.

Erikson, E. H. (1963). *Childhood and society* (2nd ed.). New York: Norton.

Freiler, T. J. (2008). Learning through the body. In S. B. Merriam (Ed.), *Third update on adult* learning theory (pp. 37–48). New Directions for Adult and Continuing Education, No. 119. San Francisco: Jossey-Bass.

Gardiner, H. W., & Kosmitzki, C. (2005). Lives across cultures: Cross-cultural human development. Needham Heights, MA: Allyn & Bacon.

Gilligan, C. (1982). In a different voice: Psychological theory and women's development. Cambridge, MA: Harvard University Press.

Hansman, C. A. (2000). Formal mentoring programs. In A. Wilson & E. Hayes (Eds.), Handbook of adult and continuing education (pp. 493–507). San Francisco: Jossey-Bass.

Hansman, C. A. (2001). Context based adult learning. In S. B. Merriam (Ed.), An update on adult learning theory (pp. 43–51). New Directions for Adult and Continuing Education, No. 89. San Francisco: Jossey-Bass.

Hansman, C. A. (2003). Power and learning in mentoring relationships. In R. Cervero, B. Courtenay, & M. Hixson (Eds.), Global perspectives (Vol. 3, pp. 101–121). Athens: University of Georgia.

Hansman, C. A. (2006). Low income adult learners in higher education: Politics, policies, and praxis. In S. M. Merriam, B. C. Courteney, & R. Cervero (Eds.), Global issues and adult education: Perspectives from Latin America, Southern Africa and the United States (pp. 399–411). San Francisco: Jossey-Bass.

Hansman, C. A. (2008). Adult learning in communities of practice: Situating theory in practice. In C. Kimble, P. Hildreth, & I. Bourdon (Eds.), Communities of practice: Creating learning environments for educators (Vol. 1, pp. 293–309). Charlotte, NC: IAP-Information Age.

Hansman, C., & McAtee, K. (2009). The multiple generations in adult and higher education classrooms: What we assume, what we know, what we can learn, and what may be missing. In R. Lawrence (Ed.), Proceedings of the 50th Annual Adult Education Research Conference (pp. 424–425). Chicago: National-Louis University.

Houle, C. (1961). The inquiring mind. Madison: University of Wisconsin Press.

Jarvis, P. (1987). Adult learning in the social context. London: Croom Helm.

Jarvis, P. (2006). Towards a comprehensive theory of human learning: Lifelong learning and the learning society (Vol. 1). London & New York: Routledge.

Johnstone, J. W., & Rivera, R. (1965). Volunteers for learning: A study of the educational pursuits of adults. Hawthorn, NY: Aldine.

Kazis, R., Callahan, A., Davidson, C., McLeod, A., Bosworth, B., Choitz, V., et al.. (2007). Adult learners in higher education (Employment and training administration occasional paper 2007–03). Washington, DC: U.S. Department of Labor, Employment and Training Administration, Office of Policy Development and Research by Jobs for the Future.

Kienzl, G. (2008). Recent participation in formal learning among working-age adults with different levels of education. National Center for Education Statistics, Institute of Education Sciences Issue Brief (NCES 2008–041). Washington, DC: U.S. Department of Education.

Kinsella, K., & He, W. (2009). An aging world: 2008 (U.S. Census Bureau International Population Reports, P95/09–1). Retrieved July 20, 2009, from http://www.census.gov/prod/2009pubs/p95–09–1.pdf

Knowles, M. (1980). The modern practice of adult education. From pedagogy to andragogy (2nd ed). New York: Cambridge Books.

Kohlberg, L. (1973). Continuities in childhood and adult moral development. In P. Baltes & K. Schaie (Eds.), Life-span development psychology: Personality and socialization (pp. 180–204). Orlando, FL: Academic Press.

Lancaster, L. C., & Stillman, D. (2002). When generations collide—who they are, why they clash: How to solve the generational puzzle at work. New York: HarperCollins.

Lave, J. (1988). Cognition in practice: Mind, mathematics, and culture in everyday life. Cambridge, UK: Cambridge University Press.

Levinson, D. J. (1986). A conception of adult development. American Psychologist, 41(1), 3–13.

Levinson, D. J., & Levinson, J. D. (1996). The seasons of a woman's life. New York: Ballantine.

Lowery, J. W. (2001). Millennials come to college: John Wesley Lowery talks with William Strauss. About Campus, 6(3), 6–12.

Magnusson, D. (1995). Individual development: A holistic, integrated model. In P. Moen, G. H. Elder, & K. Lusher (Eds.), Examining lives in context: Perspectives on the ecology of human development (pp. 19–60). Washington, DC: American Psychological Association.

Merriam, S. B. (2001). Andragogy and self-directed learning: Pillars of adult learning theory. In S. B. Merriam (Ed.), An update on adult learning theory (pp. 3–14). New Directions for Adult and Continuing Education, No. 89. San Francisco: Jossey-Bass.

Merriam, S. B., & Brockett, R. G. (2007). The profession and practice of adult education: An introduction. San Francisco: Jossey-Bass.

Merriam, S., Caffarella, R., & Baumgartner, L. (2007). Learning in adulthood: A comprehensive guide (3rd ed.). San Francisco: Jossey-Bass.

Merriam, S. B. (2008). *Third update on adult learning theory.* New Directions for Adult and Continuing Education, No. 119. San Francisco: Jossey-Bass.

Mezirow, J. D., & Associates. (2000). *Learning as transformation: Critical perspectives on a theory in progress.* San Francisco: Jossey-Bass.

Mott, V. W. (1998). Women's career development in midlife and beyond. In L. L. Bierema (Ed.), *Women's career development across the life span: Insights and strategies for women, organization, and adult educators* (pp. 25–33). New Directions for Adult and Continuing Education, No. 80. San Francisco: Jossey-Bass.

Mott, V. W. (1999). Our complex human body: Biological development explored. In M. C. Clark & R. S. Caffarella (Eds.), *An update on adult development theory: New ways of thinking about the life course* (pp. 9–17). New Directions for Adult and Continuing Education, No .8. San Francisco: Jossey-Bass.

Mott, V. W. (2000). Adult and continuing education: A political-economic enterprise. In D. A. Gabbard (Ed.), *Knowledge and power in the global economy: Politics and the rhetoric of school reform* (pp. 335–342). Hillsdale, NJ: Lawrence Erlbaum.

Mott, V. W. (2006). Is adult education an agent for change or instrument of the status quo? In S. B. Merriam, B. C. Courteney, & R. Cervero (Eds.), *Global issues and adult education: Perspectives from Latin America, Southern Africa, and the United States* (pp. 95–105). San Francisco: Jossey-Bass.

Mott, V. W. (2008). Rural education for older adults. In J. A. Ritchey (Ed.), *Adult education in the rural context: People, place, and change* (pp. 47–58). New Directions for Adult and Continuing Education, No. 117. San Francisco: Jossey-Bass.

Mott, V. W. (2009). Evolution of adult education: Is our future in e-learning? In C. V. X. Wang (Ed.), *Handbook of research on e-learning: Applications for career and technical education* (Vol. 2). Hershey, PA: Information Science Reference/IGI Global.

National Center for Education Statistics (NCES). (2004). *Digest of educational statistics.* Washington, DC: U.S. Department of Education.

National Center for Education Statistics. (2007). *The condition of education 2007* (NCES 2007–064). Washington, DC: U.S. Department of Education.

National Center for Health Statistics (NCHS). (2009). *Health, United States, 2008, with chartbook.* Retrieved July 21, 2009, from http://www.cdc.gov/nchs/fastats/lifexpec.htm

O'Donnell, K. (2006). *Adult education participation in 2004–2005* (NCES 2006–077). U.S. Department of Education. Washington, DC: National Center for Education Statistics.

Pusser, B., Breneman, D. W., Gansneder, B. M., Kohl, K. J., Levin, J. H., Turner, M., et al. (2007). *Returning to learning: Adults' success in college is key to America's future.* Indianapolis, IN: Lumina Foundation for Education.

Schlossberg, N. K. (1984). *Counseling adults in transition.* New York: Springer.

Sissel, P. A., Hansman, C. A., & Kasworm, C. (2001). The politics of neglect: Adult learners in higher education. In C. A. Hansman & P. A. Sissel (Eds.), *Understanding and negotiating the political landscape of adult education* (pp. 17–27). New Directions for Adult and Continuing Education, No. 91. San Francisco: Jossey-Bass.

Taylor, E. W. (2008). Transformative learning theory. In S. B. Merriam (Ed.), *Third update on adult learning theory* (pp. 5–15). New Directions for Adult and Continuing Education, No. 119. San Francisco: Jossey-Bass.

Taylor, K., & Lamoreaux, A. (2008). Teaching with the brain in mind. In S. B. Merriam (Ed.), *Third update on adult learning theory* (pp. 49–59). New Directions for Adult and Continuing Education, No. 119. San Francisco: Jossey-Bass.

Taylor, K., Marienau, C., & Fiddler, M. (2000). *Developing adult learners.* San Francisco: Jossey-Bass.

Tisdell, E. J. (2008). Spirituality and adult learning. In S. B. Merriam (Ed.), *Third update on adult learning theory* (pp. 27–36). New Directions for Adult and Continuing Education, No. 119. San Francisco: Jossey-Bass.

Tough, A. M. (1979). *The adults' learning project: A fresh approach to theory and practice in adult learning* (2nd ed). Toronto, ON: OISE Press.

U.S. Department of Labor, Bureau of Labor Statistics. (2001). *Employment outlook 2000–2010: Occupational employment projections to 2010.* Retrieved August 10, 2009, from http://stats.bls.gov/opub/mlr/2001/11/at4ful.pdf

Usher, R., Bryant, I., & Johnston, R. (1997). *Adult education and the post-modern challenge: Learning beyond the limits.* London: Routledge.

Wenger, E. (1998). *Communities of practice.* Cambridge, UK: Cambridge University Press.

2

ACCESS AND PARTICIPATION

MARGERY B. GINSBERG AND RAYMOND J. WLODKOWSKI

Adult participation in formal learning has reached unprecedented levels within the last decade, due to technological advancement, innovative educational programming, the exploitation of adults as a profitable learning market, widespread social acceptance of globalization as a challenge to national economic sustainability, and awareness among middle-income adults that education is the vehicle to career enhancement. Out of context, the sheer numbers are startling: mega transnational universities such as the University of Phoenix with adult student enrollments well beyond 350,000; online students in distance education programs totaling nearly 1.5 million as of 2006 and tripling from 483,113 in 2002 (Romano, 2006); more than 360 colleges and universities offering accelerated learning programs created specifically for working adults (Commission for Accelerated Programs, 2008); and an estimated 90 million adults participating in formal and informal education including adult basic education, English-language learning, workplace learning, and personal development classes (Paulson & Boeke, 2006). If current trends continue, more than 50% of all adults in the U.S. between the ages of 25 and 55 will be involved in some form of adult education by 2010 (Cook & King, 2004).

Yet, when these numbers are examined through the lens of income, race, ethnicity, gender, disability, and credential and degree completion, troubling disparities and challenges emerge. The most underserved group in adult education is the poor (McSwain & Davis, 2007). Among low-income adults aspiring to earn an associate or bachelor's degree, only 8% earned the former and 7% the latter within 6 years (Cook & King, 2004). In workplace learning, similar discrepancies exist in whose learning gets supported, with businesses prioritizing learning programs for top management and knowledge workers rather than low-skilled, low-income learners (Watkins & Marsick, 2009). Since 50% of the people living in poverty in the United States are African American or Hispanic (U.S. Department of Labor, 2003), these groups have the least access. While women now earn more bachelor's degrees in science, technology, engineering, and mathematics than do men, they earn a much smaller percentage of doctorates, especially in the better paying fields of engineering (12%), computer sciences (15%), and physical sciences (21%) (National Science Foundation [NSF], 2004). Although people with disabilities represent one fifth of the U.S. population, their completion rates for attaining a bachelor's degree are minimal (Fabian & Liesener, 2005). The estimated 12 million undocumented workers residing in the United States are among some of the hardest workers with the fewest opportunities for advancement through adult education.

These statistics reflect the legacy of historical injustices and the great difficulty of achieving equity in a discipline committed to it—adult education. They reveal the complexity of knowing what to do to enhance access and participation for all adults. As practioner-scholars, we have worked to make adult education more inclusive through instructional practice that is culturally relevant (Ginsberg & Wlodkowski, 2009). Our successes and challenges have deepened our interest in a better understanding of access and participation, with an emphasis on the pragmatic. Guided by the tradition of critical journalism, we surface questions that can illuminate the knowledge of policy makers, government and educational institutions, and adult educators to more effectively and equitably enhance access and participation. The questions we address are:

1. Who participates in adult education?

2. How can we understand adult participation?

3. What do individuals and institutions such as education, business, and government do to increase or diminish equitable access and participation?

4. What are the innovations, trends, and prospects that could provide greater and more equitable participation?

DEFINITIONS

As we reviewed the literature for this chapter, we found there was a lack of consensus on appropriate definitions for some of the key concepts. Other scholars have noted this problem as well (Fenwick, 2005; Merriam, Caffarella, & Baumgartner, 2007; Paulson & Boeke, 2006). With an understanding of their limitations, we offer the following definitions based upon at least one reference with essentially corresponding meaning:

Adult Basic Education (ABE): The continuum of education that extends from basic literacy and English for speakers of other languages (ESOL) services through adult secondary education (ASE), which includes adult high school diploma and General Educational Development (GED) preparation (Zafft, Kallenbach, & Spohn, 2006, p. 1).

Access: Not only the first time, but any time an adult can enter or make use of a nonformal or formal educational program in an institution such as college or the workplace (Adelman, 2007; Merriam et al., 2007).

Participation: The decision to join or enroll in an adult education program, which can range from ABE to the workplace or college (Comings, 2007).

Persistence: Continuing in an adult education program to the extent that personal educational goals have been met or that some courses or training have been completed and can be applied to acquiring a certificate, license, credential, or degree (Benseman, 2005; Comings, 2007; Merriam et al., 2007). In ABE, persistence can mean adults' engaging in self-directed study or distance education when they must stop attending programs, and their return to such programs when the demands of their lives allow (Comings, 2007, p. 24). In higher education, persistence connotes duration of enrollment, often with accompanying institutional use as a measure of retention and program effectiveness.

Formal learning: Learning sanctioned by an institution such as a college or by a business that leads to credits or some form of certification or diploma (Hrimech, 2005; Merriam et al., 2007). For this learning, there is usually an instructor, a curriculum, and an evaluation process.

Informal learning: Learning that is usually self-directed, independently pursued, and unregulated, often with the purpose of solving problems (Hrimech, 2005; Watkins & Marsick, 2009). With the use of books, technology, and the Internet, this type of learning is very important to adults as a form of knowledge acquisition that provides for learning in the workplace as well as for self-sufficiency and civic contribution.

Nonformal learning: Organized learning such as a workshop or training that takes place at work or in a community organization, but without sanctioning or credit accumulation toward a degree or certificate (Merriam et al., 2007). A community of practice is another example of nonformal learning that occurs as an emergent group to pursue a common interest such as analyzing a particular database or developing a teaching practice.

Workplace learning: Learning where a change in behavior or consciousness, from a new skill to a worker's personal outlook, occurs through and within the organizations, contexts, and activities of work (Fenwick, 2005).

The terms we have defined, while not exhaustive, are foundational to the contents of this chapter.

WHO PARTICIPATES IN ADULT EDUCATION?

The research of Johnstone and Rivera (1965) has informed discussions of participation in adult education for over four decades. The initial portion of their summary, with the exception of its claims about age, has enduring relevance in the United States: "The participant is just as often a woman as a man, is typically under 40, has completed high school or better, enjoys an above-average income, works full time and in a white-collar occupation, is white, Protestant, married and has children, lives in an urbanized area (more likely the suburbs than the city) and is found in all parts of the country . . ." (p. 8).

Researchers have found that in the U.S. within the last decade those workers most likely to participate in nonformal and formal education are 45 to 54 years old, White or Asian American, have a professional or master's degree, earn more than $75,000 per year, and work in professional fields such as education and health care (Hudson, Bhandari, Peter, & Bills, 2005). Participants in postsecondary education among adults 25 and older are predominantly White, women (60%), married with children, and with above average family incomes (Cook & King, 2004; Paulson & Boeke, 2006).

Johnstone and Rivera's (1965) findings for what adults were learning is also similar to that in current literature—practical and skill-oriented subject matter directly useful for work, vocational pursuit, and home life. Formal workplace learning continues to dominate in the 21st century, with 46% of the workforce—nearly 60 million adults in the United States—taking work-related courses, most of which are offered by employers (Hudson, Bhandari, Peter, & Bills, 2005). Whether at work or a postsecondary institution most adults participate in learning for career- or job-related reasons (Aslanian, 2001; Paulson & Boeke, 2006).

Adults found least likely to pursue formal workplace learning have a high school diploma or did not complete high school, are Hispanic, earn less than $30,000 a year, and work in blue collar or service occupations (Paulson & Boeke, 2006). In postsecondary education, low-income adults, in general, are the least likely to enroll, and once enrolled, the least likely to graduate. As Cook and King (2004) document, within 6 years, only 7% of these students earn a bachelor's degree and only 8% an associate's degree. While the proportion of Whites among low-income adult college students is declining, the proportion of African American and Hispanic low-income adult students is increasing. In general, at any age, whether a student acquires a bachelor's degree is largely determined by social class (Selingo & Brainard, 2006). In virtually all societies opportunities to participate in formal education are unequally distributed.

Although the studies are limited, this trend is visible in patterns of adult participation in ABE programs. The adults least likely to participate are those with the least amount of formal education and lowest incomes (Benseman, 2005). For example, within refugee groups nonparticipants tend to be women with little or no formal learning. Findings from a study on persistence in pre-GED classes suggest that among immigrants, those over the age of 30 and parents of teenage or grown children are the most likely to persist (Comings, Parrella, & Soricone, 1999). These older adults face fewer challenges in terms of finances and child care than do younger immigrants. The practical need to learn English contributes to the well-documented finding of greater persistence by immigrants in English for Speakers of Other Languages (ESOL) classes compared to other ABE students (Young, Fleischman, Fitzgerald, & Morgan, 1994).

HOW CAN WE UNDERSTAND ADULT PARTICIPATION?

A score of years ago, one of the most popular models for explaining participation in adult education was Cross's (1981) chain of response model. This reciprocal psychological framework begins with an adult's self-evaluation and attitudes about education, considers his or her life transitions and the importance of goals and expectations for education to meet them, and concludes with the barriers and opportunities to be encountered as well as the information needed to proceed. If the adult's responses all along the chain are positive, the adult will participate.

Using a psychological perspective as well and building on Houle's (1961) classic study on the adult's motivation to participate, Boshier (1991) developed and refined the Education Participation Scale (EPS). This 7-factor scale proposes the following items as influencing and differentiating among diverse adults who participate in educational programs: communication improvement, social contact, educational preparation, professional advancement, family togetherness, social stimulation, and cognitive interest. Although widely applied and researched, such models do not grasp nor sufficiently predict the many complex and changing adult motivations for participating in adult education (Courtney, 1992).

Using a sociological perspective locates participation in an adult's social context rather than the adult's individual motivation and circumstances. These analyses consider such factors as class, race/ethnicity, and gender, as well as how the related patterns of inequality found in adult social, educational, and work lives affect adults' participation. A sociological lens contributes to a historical and broader comprehension of adult participation. As several scholars (Fassinger, 2008; Merriam et al., 2007) have noted, understanding the interaction of sociological and psychological factors offers the fullest and most useful explanation.

In 1981, Cross introduced the concept of barriers emanating from an individual's situation in life, and combining with institutional practices or personal dispositions such as attitudes and self-perceptions, to diminish participation. Although not categorized in the same manner, more recent examination of psychological and sociological factors reveals an interaction that contributes to current inequitable participation. These factors include students' goals and basic skills as they interface with institutional systems such as adult basic education and developmental education.

Two out of every five 18- to 64-year-olds do not have the basic skills in reading and mathematics to succeed in college or today's skilled workforce (Pulley, 2008). Not factoring in English-language learners, there are 57 million adults for whom the lack of basic academic skills poses a barrier to access and participation. Studies (Comings et al., 2000) indicate that ABE students need 150 hours of instruction to have a 75% probability of gaining a one grade or greater equivalent in reading comprehension or English language fluency.

This amount of learning requires most ABE students to have extensive instruction, often for more than a few years, to be able to move on to skilled job training or postsecondary education.

Between 43% and 80% of all entering community college students require one or more remedial courses in math, writing, or reading (Pulley, 2008). Numerous studies provide evidence that adults in this group, as secondary students, often have not been adequately taught (Worthington, Flores, & Navarro, 2005); they have not developed a readiness to learn (Boudard & Rubenson, 2003), have not had sufficient math or science courses (Adelman, 2007), and have lacked educationally supportive role models (Fassinger, 2008). Such disadvantages compound over time and become increasingly difficult for low-income adults to overcome. These adults' capacity to participate is often further diminished when these pre-adult barriers combine with the obstacles in adult education programs.

Adults who participate in adult basic education and higher education exhibit the phenomenon of *stopping out* (i.e., dropping out with the intention of returning), which suggests the need for different institutional perspectives and actions. In a qualitative study, Belzer (1998) found that students who were defined as dropouts in a large urban literacy program did not consider themselves as such. Each student who left planned to return. They were stopping out. These students attributed leaving the program to factors beyond their control such as health problems, financial problems, or family problems that needed to work themselves out. This in-and-out pattern is a form of persistence for many adult basic education students (Comings, 2007). Belzer cautions against framing the issue as dropping out as a result of an obstacle at a single point in time, because it denies the complexity of the issue and the fact that some students see themselves as connected to a program and temporarily unable to attend. Comings (2007) concludes from his research that most ABE students are *intermittent* students who move in and out of program services because they have long-term learning goals, but experience personal and environmental barriers that disrupt their learning and require episodes of departure from their programs. They will likely return as the demands of their lives allow.

In higher education, there are few long-term persistence studies that focus on adult students. The work of Attewell and his colleagues is informative (Attewell, Lavin, Domina, & Levey, 2007). By tracking women who enrolled in the City University of New York system from 1970 to 1972, they found out that within 30 years, 70% had completed a degree, three quarters of these had earned a bachelor's degree, and most had done so in a period longer than 6 years. In their parallel analyses of data from the Longitudinal Survey of Youth, which tracked college students from 1980 until 2000, they found the graduation rate was 61%, and approximately 50% for students entering college with an average of C or below. They also found that 28% of bachelor's degree recipients get their diploma more than 6 years after enrolling in college. This statistic holds more for women, students of color, and low-income students. Due to circumstances such as earning an income and taking care of family needs, they need more time than average to complete college. Similar to the ABE students, many of today's adult learners in college are intermittent students who stop out. Education has to be fitted into the rest of their lives.

Understanding participation in formal and nonformal workplace learning reflects the interaction of societal structures, institutional processes, and individual attitudes and attributes (Rubenson, 1998). With globalization, the chances for acquiring formal and nonformal learning are grim for immigrant workers at the initial stages of English proficiency (Watkins & Marsick, 2009). Today, corporations tend to move work around the globe to find lower operating costs. The U.S. leads the world in this form of offshore or strategic sourcing. Consequently, opportunities for entry-level workers to become skilled workers are lessening. In addition, with estimates that 70% of all workplace learning is informal, formal educational programs are decreasing (Cross, 2007). Corporations want employees to learn continuously of their own accord. For those adults with advanced education and skills, this format may be an exciting possibility. For those adult without such advantages, the potential to participate is constrained.

Analyzing adult participation in adult basic education, higher education, and workplace learning makes it clear that the poor and least formally educated face the most personal and social barriers to participation. Although no individual theory or model provides scientific predictability, evidence for this obvious fact is irrefutable.

What Do Individuals and Institutions Such as Education, Business, and Government Do to Increase or Diminish Equitable Participation?

The most obvious technological change that has allowed informal, nonformal, and formal access to workplace learning and higher education is online learning offered 24 hours a day, 7 days a week, and asymmetrically to accommodate any individual's schedule globally (Conrad, 2005). Adults are the largest age group to use online learning because of its convenience and flexibility. With international competition, the learning demands of all jobs are escalating (Watkins & Marsick, 2009). Workplace learning is now more continuous with online learning as the source for much informal and self-directed learning.

In higher education, many large schools, such as the University of Maryland University College (UMUC), have initiated liberal enrollment policies to allow broad access to adult learners. In March of 2006, Congress passed legislation to delete the requirement that a college had to offer at least half of its courses face-to-face in order to receive federal student aid. This legal change allows more working adults opportunities for federal financial assistance to pursue a postsecondary education. It supports the growing trend of a higher proportion of adults attaining their degrees through online degree programs.

There is widespread global disparity in access to technology. Infoplease (2008) reports that there are 211 million Internet users in the United States, while there are 40 million in India. When we realize the United States has a population of approximately 300 million people and India 1.1 billion people, this proportional difference (70% to 4%) illustrates the profound digital divide at a global level. Everywhere, low-income people lack access to technology and its educational benefits. In addition to the lack of experience and familiarity with personal computers, low-income adults do not receive the institutional cost benefits of online learning (Kelland, 2005). Tuition for online courses is usually the same or higher than for face-to-face courses.

Regardless of the evidence that most formal and informal learning for adults occurs in the workplace (Paulson & Boeke, 2006), there is a global trend in business and industry calling for postsecondary learning among corporate employees (Institute for Higher Education Policy, 2007). Pressures to expand higher education opportunities have increased in almost every region in the world. Rising per-student costs and increasing enrollment rates are an international phenomenon. Under existing circumstances, people with more income and education are most likely to benefit.

As more students enter higher education in the United States, the inequality in financial access for low-income students is increasing (St. John, 2005). Pell grants are the largest federally funded, need-based assistance for low-income adult students. As tuition costs have increased, the purchasing value of Pell grants has declined by nearly two thirds in the last 30 years (Anderson & de Vise, 2009). Most other forms of aid such as tax credits do not offer the same benefit to low-income students that they do to middle-income students, because low-income families frequently lack the tax liability to appreciably benefit from tax credits. Estimates indicate that it would be necessary to double the Pell maximum to recover its losses in purchasing power during this decade.

Further, most student aid policies favor recent high school graduates without dependents (Bosworth, 2007). There is no incentive system in place to encourage employers to invest in the education of their less-prepared adult workers. Nor is there sufficient assistance for low-skilled adults to invest in their own education.

Postsecondary education has been anchored as the threshold qualification for most well-paying and dependable jobs (Carnevale & Desrochers, 2004). In a service/knowledge economy, as more manufacturing jobs are globally distributed, the strong relationship between income and a college education grows, creating a more elitist society where parental education and wealth are passed from one generation to the next. With population growth and underfunding of public higher education increasing, the educational disparity between lower- and higher-income groups is a persistent and predictable economic consequence.

Business and industry primarily rely on postsecondary schools to educate the workforce at the levels necessary to meet their competitive needs. Under 4% of employer training is remedial (Frazis, Herz, & Horrigan, 1995). Rather than investing in basic learning, corporations target their most skilled and educated workers to produce the highest financial returns from their educational investments. Workers must first have postsecondary education to secure jobs that will advance their training (Carnevale & Desrochers, 2004).

Within the last 20 years, community colleges have been the largest gateway for adults to enter postsecondary education. Almost all of the 1,200 community colleges in the United States are open access institutions enrolling a much broader variety of students than baccalaureate-granting colleges. Students of color, low-income students, students with lower academic achievement in high school, and part-time adult students are enrolled in significantly greater proportions in community colleges than in most 4-year colleges (Bailey & Alfonso, 2005).

However, all of public postsecondary education faces daunting fiscal challenges. State budgets for higher education have dropped by at least 13% since 1990 (National Association of State Budget Officers, 2002). Federal budgets have declined as well, with more resources shifting toward national defense as well as business and personal tax cuts. In the U.S., as in many Western countries, reaching out to low-income adults and making access to postsecondary education more available would require considerable investments by federal and local governments and the business community. If funding were available, estimates are that 11 million low-income adults could significantly benefit from postsecondary education and training (Carnevale & Desrochers, 2004). When money from the federal and state government recedes, students pay higher tuition costs. Within this cycle, low-income adult students are the most vulnerable. In 2008, estimates were that the average education debt for graduates who attain a bachelors' degree through loans was $20,000. For the economically distressed, the goal of a college degree and the ability to pay for it is becoming an irresolvable problem (Glavin, 2009). With increasing numbers of less academically prepared students, many of whom are adults, the need for remedial education is surging (Pulley, 2008). Developmental education programs in community colleges attempt to meet this demand; however, these programs tend to be underfunded, generally do not provide college credits, are often not completed, and have low success rates.

WHAT ARE THE INNOVATIONS, TRENDS, AND PROSPECTS THAT COULD PROVIDE GREATER AND MORE EQUITABLE PARTICIPATION?

Nonparticipation in formal learning from the perspective of some adults may be a form of resistance to the status quo, especially for adults from historically marginalized ethnic and racial groups. As Merriam and her colleagues (2007) point out after reviewing 20 years of research on adult participation, "Regardless of the study, the profile of the typical adult learner in formal educational activities remains remarkably consistent: white, middle-class, employed, younger and better educated than the nonparticipant" (p. 78). There are several ways to understand this profile. For example, given the experience of many students of color in secondary schools, it is possible that adult education continues to be a repetitious story: an irrelevant curriculum built upon unexamined cultural norms (Crowther, 2000). Critical race theorists call attention to racism as a central structural entity that permeates every social, economic, and political institution in the United States (Howard, 2008). Today, adult education is a major institution that represents the status quo.

These influences are compounded by the market orientation to recruiting adults for public, private, or for-profit adult education programs. Relying on self-selection to recruit students, the adult education system widens the educational, cultural, and income gaps in society (Rubenson, 1998). Although camouflaged in a liberal progressivism and often housed in universities, the adult education establishment accentuates individual ambitions over communal needs. This orientation promotes the benefits of education with its promise of social mobility, setting the stage for professional growth to trump the expressed need for social change (Wilson, 2009). As members of the adult education community, we believe that recognition of our complicity with the status quo is foundational to suggestions and actions for more equitable adult participation.

Formal education for adults has changed: who conducts it, how it responds to local and global challenges, where it is situated, and how it is financed. Although informal education can develop personal knowledge and advance workplace learning, the trends that legitimize knowledge and secure professional and skilled employment involve formal education. In an increasingly global economy, business and industry expect postsecondary education to provide workforce preparation or, increasingly, they hire employees in other countries.

Currently, 80% of high school graduates attend college within 8 years of graduation and undergraduate enrollment is six times greater than it was 50 years ago (Attewell et al., 2007). With estimates of the number of nontraditional students exceeding 70% of the enrollment in postsecondary education, as well as being the highest population of learners in adult basic education (Zafft et al., 2006), we have to ask: When future rates of more privileged learners participate, can formal education providers offer greater access for underserved adult learners? Given global economic conditions and past educational policies, our response is cautious. There are numerous innovative ideas and practices to expand opportunity in adult education. Although an exhaustive exploration of them exceeds the scope of this chapter, the following examples and policy reports offer a partial representation:

- Prior Learning Assessment (PLA) has become an established global phenomenon, often increasing postsecondary access for underserved adult learners (Spencer, 2005). There are no exact figures available, but there is little doubt that hundreds of thousands of adults have used this process to earn college credit for nonformal, informal, and workplace learning, including various forms of training, volunteer work, and self-directed study. Assessing prior learning includes challenge exams, portfolio assessments, and knowledge demonstrations.

- Accelerated and intensive learning formats reduce the amount of time to earn a degree or credential making a postsecondary education more accessible for working adults. Typically, accelerated courses are between 5 and 8 weeks duration with 20 to 32 contact hours of instruction (Wlodkowski, 2003). Working adults prefer these compressed formats because of their efficiency for completing a certificate or degree (Aslanian, 2001).

• Transition-to-postsecondary-education programs are a promising trend in adult basic education (Zafft et al., 2006). These programs, which are often members of the National College Transition Network (www.collegetransition.org), facilitate access for ABE students to postsecondary education by sustaining their level of academic readiness, promoting more substantial college preparation in ABE courses, and providing advising that supports their resource management to attain further formal learning.

• Although focused on ABE learners, the implications of the findings from the National Center for the Study of Adult Learning and Literacy (NCSALL) multiphase study of factors that support and inhibit persistence are relevant for any long-term formal learning program (Comings, 2007). Confirming the intermittent pathway of most adult learners, the study suggests supportive practices for the three critical stages of their program participation: entrance into services, participation in services, and reengagement in learning.

Within the last decade, advocates of policies to increase access and participation for underserved adult learners have emerged with a number of useful reports (Bosworth, 2007; Gershwin, Coxen, Kelley, & Yakimov, 2008; McSwain & Davis, 2007; Ruppert, 2003). Another valuable resource for ideas, research, and innovations is the Lumina Foundation for Education (www .luminafoundation.org), whose primary mission is to expand access for nontraditional learners. All of these advocates stress the need for stronger community, business, education, and government partnerships. They offer ideas that could significantly increase more equitable adult participation in formal education. Yet, they must be acted upon to have an impact.

Equitable participation is a means to a more just society. At its most basic level, such participation is grounded in every adult being prepared for skilled work and formal education, being able to afford their costs, and having the will and opportunity to learn. Historically, adult educators have been advocates for the common good. Only by example can we reignite the discourse and action for equitable access and participation. Without authentically striving for these fundamental goals, we cannot claim to be agents of social and economic improvement. With such effort, we continue our commitment to provide education for all adults.

REFERENCES

Adelman, C. (2007). Do we really have a college access problem? *Change.* Retrieved November 5, 2007, from http://www.carnegiefoundation.org/change/sub.asp?Key=98&subkey=2385

Anderson, N., & de Vise, D. (2009). Obama to boost funding for Pell grants by $40 billion. *Washington Post.* Retrieved December 3, 2009, from http://nhillman.newsvine.com/_news/2009/10/08/3362590-obama-aims-to-boost-pell-grant-funding-by-40-billion-

Aslanian, C. B. (2001). *Adult students today.* New York: The College Board.

Attewell, P., Lavin, D. E., Domina, T., & Levey, T. (2007). *Passing the torch: Does higher education for the disadvantaged pay off across the generations?* New York: Russell Sage Foundation.

Bailey, T. R., & Alfonso, M. (2005). *Paths to persistence: An analysis of research on program effectiveness at community colleges.* Indianapolis, IN: Lumina Foundation for Education.

Belzer, A. (1998). Stopping out, not dropping out. *Focus on the Basics, 2*(A), 15–17.

Benseman, J. (2005). Participation. In L. M. English (Ed.), *International encyclopedia of adult education* (pp. 455–460). New York: Palgrave Macmillan.

Boshier, R. (1991). Psychometric properties of the alternative form of the education participation scale. *Adult Education Quarterly, 41*(3), 150–167.

Bosworth, B. (2007). *Lifelong learning: New strategies for the education of working adults.* Retrieved August 1, 2008, from http://www .americanprogress.org/issues/2007/12/lifelong_learning.html

Boudard, E., & Rubenson, K. (2003). Revisiting major determinants of participation in adult education with a direct measure of literacy skills. *International Journal of Educational Research, 39*(3), 265–281.

Carnevale, A. P., & Desrochers, D. M. (2004). Benefits and barriers to college for low-income adults. In B. Cook & J. E. King (Eds.), *Low-income adults in profile: Improving lives through higher education* (pp. 31–43). Washington, DC: American Council on Education.

Comings, J. (2007). Persistence: Helping adult education students reach their goals. In J. Comings, B. Garner, & C. Smith (Eds.), *Review of adult learning and literacy* (Vol. 7, pp. 23–46). Cambridge, MA: National Center for the Study of Adult Learning and Literacy.

Comings, J., Parrella, A., & Soricone, L. (1999). *Persistence among adult basic education students in pre-GED classes* (NCSALL Rep. No. 12). Cambridge, MA: National Center for the Study of Adult Learning and Literacy.

Comings, J., Sum, A., & Uvin, J. (2000). *New skills for a new economy: Adult education's key role in sustaining economic growth and expanding opportunity.* Boston: Massachusetts Institute for a New Commonwealth.

Commission for Accelerated Programs. (2008). *Accelerated programs.* Retrieved July 30, 2008, from http://www.capnetwork.org/modules .php?op=modload&name=CAPDatabase&file= index&&letter=All&sortby=institutionname&

Conrad, D. (2005). Online learning. In L. M. English (Ed.), *International encyclopedia of adult education* (pp. 442–446). New York: Palgrave Macmillan.

Cook, B., & King, J. E. (2004). *Low-income adults in profile: Improving lives through higher education.* Washington, DC: American Council on Education.

Courtney, S. (1992). *Why adults learn: Toward a theory of participation in adult education.* New York: Routledge.

Cross, J. (2007). *Informal learning: Rediscovering the natural pathways that inspire innovation and performance.* San Francisco: John Wiley.

Cross, K. P. (1981). *Adults as learners: Increasing participation and facilitating learning.* San Francisco: Jossey-Bass.

Crowther, J. (2000). Participation in adult and community education: A discourse of diminishing returns. *International Journal of Lifelong Education, 19*(6), 479–492.

Fabian, E. S., & Liesener, J. J. (2005). Promoting the career potential of youth with disabilities. In S. D. Brown & R. W. Lent (Eds.), *Career development and counseling: Putting theory and research to work* (pp. 551–572). New York: John Wiley.

Fassinger, R. E. (2008). Workplace diversity and public policy. *American Psychologist, 63*(4), 252–268.

Fenwick, T. J. (2005). Workplace learning. In L. M. English (Ed.), *International encyclopedia of adult education* (pp. 673–677). New York: Palgrave Macmillan.

Frazis, H. J., Herz, D. E., & Horrigan, M. W. (1995). Employer-provided training: Results from a new survey. *Monthly Labor Review, 118*(5), 3–17.

Gershwin, M., Coxen, T., Kelley, B., & Yakimov, G. (2008). *Building tomorrow's workforce: Promoting the education & advancement of Hispanic immigrant workers in America.* Indianapolis, IN: Lumina Foundation for Education.

Ginsberg, M. B., & Wlodkowski, R. J. (2009). *Diversity and motivation: Culturally responsive teaching in college* (2nd ed.). San Francisco: Jossey-Bass.

Glavin, W. F. (2009, November 13). Are too many students going to college? *The Chronicle Review,* p. B7.

Houle, C. O. (1961). *The inquiring mind: A study of the adult who continues to learn.* Madison: University of Wisconsin Press.

Howard, T. C. (2008). Who really cares? The disenfranchisement of African American males in PreK–12 schools: A critical race perspective. *Teachers College Record, 110*(5), 954–985.

Hrimech, M. (2005). Informal learning. In L. M. English (Ed.), *International encyclopedia of adult education* (pp. 310–312). New York: Palgrave Macmillan.

Hudson, L., Bhandari, R., Peter, K., & Bills, D. B. (2005). *Labor force participation in formal work-related education in 2000–01* (NCES 2005–048). Washington, DC: National Center for Education Statistics.

Infoplease. (2008). *Top five countries using the Internet.* Retrieved August 1, 2008, from http://www.infoplease.com/ipa/A0907976.html

Institute for Higher Education Policy. (2007). *The global state of higher education and the rise of private finance.* Washington, DC: Institute for Higher Education Policy.

Johnstone, J. W. C., & Rivera, R. J. (1965). *Volunteers for learning: A study of the educational pursuits of adults.* Hawthorne, NY: Aldine de Gruyter.

Kelland, J. H. (2005). Distance learning: Access and inclusion issues. In R. J. Hill & R. Kiely (Eds.), *Proceedings of the 46th Annual Adult Education Research Conference* (pp. 253 –258). Athens: University of Georgia.

McSwain, C., & Davis, R. (2007). *College access for the working poor: Overcoming burdens to succeed in higher education.* Washington, DC: Institute for Higher Education Policy.

Merriam, S. B., Caffarella, R. S., & Baumgartner, L. M. (2007). *Learning in adulthood: A comprehensive guide* (3rd ed.). San Francisco: Jossey-Bass.

National Association of State Budget Officers. (2002). *State expenditure report, 2001.* Washington, DC: National Association of State Budget Officers.

National Science Foundation. (2004). *Women, minorities, and persons with disabilities in science and engineering: 2004.* Arlington, VA: Department of Resource Statistics.

Paulson, K., & Boeke, M. (2006). *Adult learners in the United States: A national profile.* Washington, DC: American Council on Education.

Pulley, J. L. (2008, April 7). In need of remediation. *Community College Week,* pp. 7–12.

Romano, L. (2006, May 16). Online degree programs take off. *Washington Post,* p. A06.

Rubenson, K. (1998). Adults' readiness to learn: Questioning lifelong learning for all. In *Proceedings of the Adult Education Research Conference, No. 39* (pp. 257–262). San Antonio: University of the Incarnate Word and Texas A & M University.

Ruppert, S. S. (2003). *Closing the college participation gap: A national summary.* Denver, CO: Education Commission of the States Center for Community College Policy.

Selingo, J., & Brainard, J. (2006, April 7). The rich–poor gap widens for colleges and students. *Chronicle of Higher Education,* pp. A1, A13.

St. John, E. P. (2005). *Affordability of postsecondary education: Equity and Adequacy across the 50 states.* Retrieved August 1, 2008, from http:// www.americanprogress.org/issues/2005/ 01/education.html/print.html

Spencer, B. (2005). Prior learning assessment and recognition. In L. M. English (Ed.), *International encyclopedia of adult education* (pp. 508–512). New York: Palgrave Macmillan.

U.S. Department of Labor, Bureau of Labor Statistics. (2003). *A profile of the working poor* (Report No. 968). Washington, DC: U.S. Government Printing Office.

Watkins, K. E., & Marsick, V. J. (2009). Trends in lifelong learning in the U.S. workplace. In P. Jarvis (Ed.), *The Routledge international handbook of lifelong learning* (pp. 129–138). New York: Routledge.

Wilson, A. L. (2009). Lifelong learning in the United States. In P. Jarvis (Ed.), *The Routledge international handbook of lifelong learning* (pp. 129–138). New York: Routledge.

Wlodkowski, R. J. (2003). Accelerated learning in colleges and universities. In R. J. Wlodkowski & C. Kasworm (Eds.), *Accelerated learning for adults: The promise and practice of intensive educational formats* (pp. 5–15). New Directions for Adult and Continuing Education, no. 97. San Francisco: Jossey-Bass.

Worthington, R. L., Flores, L. Y., & Navarro, R. L. (2005). Career development in context: Research with people of color. In S. D. Brown & R. W. Lent (Eds.), *Career development and counseling: Putting theory and research to work* (pp. 225–252). New York: John Wiley.

Young, M., Fleischman, H., Fitzgerald, N., & Morgan, M. (1994). *National evaluation of adult education programs: Patterns and predictors of client attendance.* Arlington, VA: Development Associates.

Zafft, C., Kallenbach, S., & Spohn, J. (2006). *Transitioning adults to college: Adult basic education program models* (NCSALL Occasional Paper). Cambridge, MA: National Center for the Study of Adult Learning and Literacy.

3

Adult Learning

Marcie Boucouvalas and Randee Lipson Lawrence

I n this chapter we situate adult learning in an historical and global as well as holistic framework, inviting readers to think with us about promising advances from various fields that might inform our thinking and practice about learning in adulthood. While adults have been navigating life and learning for millennia, a concerted study of adult learning is of more recent vintage. The 1920s is generally recognized as a watershed period. The philosophical treatise by Lindeman on *The Meaning of Adult Education* in 1926, and the scientific contribution of Thorndike and his colleagues in 1928 that adults indeed had the capacity to learn, lent a strong foundation to the subsequent emergence of literature focused on the adult learner. This *Handbook of Adult Education* series, begun in 1934, is one such example.

The early *Handbooks* repeatedly stressed that any inability of adults to change and adapt was predicated primarily on habituation, or fixed habits. Current literature represents a shift in perspective. Transformative learning, the ability to restructure one's thinking as well as "being," is now understood as based upon a deeper understanding of one's habituation. Harkening to early efforts, where arts-based education figured prominently, we take this posture further in offering art not just as a content area but as an important way of knowing that has potential to fuel transformative learning. All the *Handbooks* have reflected the context of the time, but a thread reappearing in the books of different decades is the importance of learning not just for individual purposes, but equally for societal improvement. Given the globalized, interconnected contemporary context, learning to live together becomes paramount. Accordingly, we fully embrace a concept of adult learning that recognizes the importance not just of individuals but of the contexts in which they navigate, one that equally honors the UNESCO conceptualization of "Education for the 21st Century" as learning to do, know, be, live together, and change (Delors, 1996).[1]

We realize that participation studies, while still researched, are no longer the exclusive focus of researchers. Emphasis has expanded to illuminate the importance of incidental learning, with a growing importance on ways of knowing from various traditions and cultural orientations. Therefore, we broadly conceptualize adult learning to include indigenous knowledge and intuition, attending to cognitive, affective, somatic, and spiritual domains of learning, and their interconnection.

With an understanding of how the current scenario vis-à-vis adult learning intertwines with and augments the past trajectory, we invite you, as you navigate this chapter, to think about the possibilities for the future and your role in creating a deeper and fuller rendition of adult learning and its possibilities. Due to the complexity and voluminous nature of the current principles and scholarship that guide our practice, coupled with space constraints, we can only offer highlights. We begin with a discussion of the holistic viewpoint that frames this chapter and permeates a contemporary understanding of the universe, and then consider multiple theoretical perspectives on adult learning.

Holistic Learning: An Overarching Framework

A holistic understanding of learning views adults as embedded in many systems. Any effort at understanding the adult as learner calls for contextualization. We are products of our multiple identities as well as the larger cultural, societal, and national systems of which we are part. Our increasing global interconnectedness affords an opportunity to better understand how we influence and are influenced by these "greater wholes." Holistic learning is not a learning theory per se. It is a framework for understanding how learning happens. All of the perspectives on learning that will be discussed later in this chapter can be viewed holistically.

While our earliest ways of learning are preverbal and precognitive, traditional schooling has focused on educating the mind, appealing to the intellect. When reaching higher education, many are so conditioned to rational ways of knowing that other ways seem foreign or even exotic. Yet, as indigenous cultures have known for centuries, learning is a holistic process involving the body, heart, and spirit, as well as mind. We learn through many modalities, among them intuition, and by engaging with various creative and imaginative processes.

In a 1994 keynote address at the CAEL International Conference on Experiential Learning, Freire stated: "Teaching and learning are only moments in a greater process which is knowing." It is in this spirit that we embrace the term *holistic*.

We take the position that adult learners, knowingly or unknowingly, navigate many roads in learning, and in life itself. Holistic learning encompasses all of these various roads, including cognitive, somatic, affective, and spiritual domains along with artistic and transpersonal domains. Although these many ways of knowing, and the accompanying learning processes, operate simultaneously and interactively, for the purpose of this discussion we address them individually below.

Cognition: An Expanded Conceptualization

Cognition derives from the Latin root (*cognosco, cognoscere, cognovi, congnitum*) and is defined in the *Oxford English Dictionary* as "the action or faculty of knowing, knowledge, consciousness." Frequently, however, discussions revolving around adult cognition restrict the term to *thinking*, which is actually derived from a different Latin root (*cogito, cogitare, cogitavi, cogitatum*). Thinking, while important, is only one way of knowing (Boucouvalas, 2005), a position that we embrace in this chapter.

The present foundational understanding of cognitive development in adulthood, which is often unfortunately restricted to thinking, was laid by Piaget in his "formal operations" or the ability to think abstractly. Some cognitive developmental scholars have built upon that foundation with the development of postformal cognition, elucidating adult cognitive thought as moving from categorical to relativistic and dialectical thinking, and beyond problem solving to problem finding. Researchers such as Sinnott (1998) and Kegan (1994) have also offered guidance to educators of adults in their writings. Such literature continues to burgeon under the descriptor of postformal thinking. Both Piaget and the postformal researchers acknowledge, however, that knowledge is actively constructed from interaction with one's world, a position that is a central feature of research in situated cognition (cognition is contextually bound) and social cognition, a multifaceted term defined by *Social Cognition*, a journal begun in 1982, as: (a) the processes underlying the perception, memory, and judgment of social stimuli; (b) the effects of social, cultural, and affective factors on the processing of information; and (c) the behavioral and interpersonal consequences of cognitive processes. Perspective taking and reading social cues are integral parts of social cognition, and we continue to learn much from those who have challenges in this area, such as those with learning disabilities and Asperger's syndrome. This expanded view of cognition enables us to offer a broader stance on adult learning.

SOMATIC LEARNING

Somatic or embodied knowing involves accessing knowledge though the body. This most basic form of learning is the least discussed in contemporary adult education literature.

Embodied learning challenges the Cartesian dualistic belief of the mind being separate from the body by calling attention to the body as a source of learning. Imagine making a speech in public for the first time. You feel your face getting warm, you may begin to sweat or your heartbeat may become rapid. You eventually register feelings of fear or embarrassment; however, these visceral sensations are the first indicators. The knowledge is first experienced in the body. As you begin to cognitively process these feelings and bodily sensations you realize that the fear is about forgetting what you are supposed to be talking about, not being able to express yourself in intelligent ways, and possibly making a fool of yourself in public. Once these thoughts come into your awareness you may eventually be able to deal with the feelings, and even find ways to project more self-confidence.

Some forms of adult education (particularly in informal settings) explicitly rely on the body as a source of knowledge. Boal's *Theatre of the Oppressed* (2000) involves ordinary people exploring solutions to individual and community problems by acting them out. For example, a group of tenants experiencing oppression by a landlord who refuses to make necessary repairs to their units might create a scenario where they role-play standing up for their rights. If the individual confronting the "landlord" seems to be stuck, another individual may step in and try a different approach. The informal learning that occurs through embodying the experience can then be applied to the actual situation as well as similar scenarios.

Somatic learning also has global implications. Brockman (2001) suggests that somatic learning is important in that it "provides a basis for talking, transculturally, about knowledge" (p. 332). Murphy (1992) illuminates the latent capacities of the human species in somatic knowing. Unlike spoken language alone,

embodied knowing has the potential to build bridges across difference.

AFFECTIVE LEARNING

The word *emotion* comes from the Latin *e + movere*, which means to stir, to move, or to disturb. Emotions such as anger, sadness, joy, and confusion affect us in deep and personal ways that stir or shake us up in ways we cannot ignore. Emotions take us to places where words alone cannot, thus elevating us to new levels of knowledge acquisition. Emotions often reside outside of our conscious awareness. To learn from these emotions we must bring them into our awareness, which often occurs through imagery, symbol, and through the use of story. We can also surface our emotions through the embodied activities described above.

Critical reflection has become synonymous with adult education as a way to surface our assumptions about ourselves and the world in order to examine them for distortions or faulty reasoning, adopting a more inclusive perspective (Brookfield, 1995; Mezirow, 1991). However, critical reflection is largely a rational mental process, relying heavily on logic.

Emotionality can extend our learning by considering the feelings that underlie the assumptions and imagining alternative realities. For example, a woman with strong negative feelings about people from a different racial group could critically examine her assumptions about people from that group, realize that the assumptions are flawed and inaccurate, and even change her previous beliefs. According to Mezirow, she will have experienced a perspective transformation; however, we assert that for lasting change to occur, the learning needs to take place at a deeper level, an emotional level. Transformative learning has a strong affective component. "Emotionally charged images, evoked through the contexts of adult learning, provide the opportunity for a more profound access to the world by inviting a deeper understanding of ourselves in relationship with it" (Dirkx, 2001, p. 64).

SPIRITUAL KNOWING

The spiritual domain is probably the most misunderstood area of adult learning. Spirituality is often confused with religion. While these concepts may be integrated for some, it is possible to experience a spiritual way of learning outside of any formal religious practice. Although there are many definitions of *spirituality*, we are using the term here as a deep and profound sense of connectedness to something outside of oneself, as well as a connectedness emanating from within, in a transliminal sense. Spirituality is a form of meaning making: a way we construct knowledge by paying attention to the unconscious symbols and rituals that guide us. Spiritual knowing cannot be described in words; however, one knows intuitively when one has had a spiritual experience. Spiritual knowing incorporates all other ways of knowing. For example, Washburn (2003) addresses the interface between the soma and spirituality. According to Native American educator Cajete, "indigenous education at its innermost core, is education about the life and nature of the spirit that moves us" (1994, p. 42). (For more on this topic, see Chapter 26, "Spirituality and Adult Education," in this handbook.)

ARTISTIC WAYS OF KNOWING

Artistic or creative expression is another way to integrate these different learning domains and access knowledge that is hidden from consciousness. Art is indigenous knowledge that cuts across all cultural contexts (Lawrence, 2005); that is, the arts are an inherent instinct native to us all. Working with pastels, writing poetry, dancing, and taking photos are all methods of creative expression that can lead us to profound truths about ourselves and the world at large. Imagery often appears in our creative work as symbol and metaphor, much like our dreams. If we pay attention to these images, we can learn much.

Photographer Freeman Patterson sees art as an expression of the self. "The medium always mirrors my inner self. So accurate is the reflection, that the photographs often reveal the subtle beginnings of emotional transitions that I can recognize consciously only in other ways much later on" (Patterson, 1996, p. 76).

The arts also have a strong role in educating for social justice (Lawrence, 2008). Protest music, slam poetry, guerilla theatre, installation art, and performance ethnography are meant to provoke and disturb, thus creating an emotional response that compels us to take action.

Learning through art not only happens through creative expression, it can also occur through witnessing art such as walking though a gallery or watching a profound drama or ballet. Moreover, artistic knowing can be transpersonal, creating an opening to transcend the small individual self.

TRANSPERSONAL KNOWING

Transpersonal knowing broadens and deepens the epistemological terrain of what is considered "legitimate" knowledge, and how it comes to be known. An understanding of transpersonal knowing derives from the contemporary transpersonal movement that coalesced with the launching of the *Journal of Transpersonal Psychology* during 1969, and spread to other countries and disciplines, including those that focus beyond the individual to groups, organizations, communities, and the cosmos (see Boucouvalas, 1999). Considered an holistic approach to understanding the full human experience in all its levels, states, and structures of consciousness, the transpersonal perspective brings together ancient wisdom with modern science, "Eastern" philosophies with "Western" spiritual understanding, taking into account the whole human phenomenon. Important to understand is that what is knowable in one mode may not be in another.

Study and practice of the transpersonal embraces two dimensions:

1. Transpersonal experiences, which represent temporary shifts in consciousness;

2. Transpersonal development, which represents more lasting shifts, or transformations of consciousness, such that one's worldview and "being" on the planet restructure in a relatively irreversible way based on an increasing identification with and motivation by a larger sense of Self.

These dimensions are described below.

Transpersonal experiences. In expanding one's consciousness beyond one's separate self sense and one's ordinary waking state, transpersonal experiences can occur at any level of health or pathology, a differentiation made by both scholars and clinicians. Glimpses into mystical states, as well as everyday pathways such as music and intimate relations, can usher in such experiences. Transpersonal knowing also includes flashes of insight beyond one's rational mode, which can manifest in a visceral, emotional, cognitive, or spiritual sense. Beauty and awe, direct spiritual experiences, and pain and suffering can trigger transpersonal experiences. Access to transpersonal knowing can occur spontaneously in an unbidden sense, but more often is cultivated through attention training practices. When integrated with everyday life such experiences can lead to transpersonal development. "One of the most common elements of consciousness transformation is an experience of the transpersonal" (Schlitz, Vietan, & Amorok, 2007, p. 161).

Transpersonal development. Cultivating a lived awareness of the limits of ego-centered consciousness and the emergence of a larger sense of Self lies at the heart of transpersonal development, and often leads to a stabilization of wisdom as a way of knowing. Consistent with our expanded conceptualization of cognition, Washburn (2000) speaks of transpersonal cognition. Transpersonal development is not only a shift in worldview but also in the way one navigates the planet.

PERSPECTIVES ON ADULT LEARNING

Given the springboard of holistic learning that captures many modalities, some staples in the literature of adult learning may be addressed afresh. In this section we give a brief overview of adult learning perspectives, including the centrality of experiential learning; self-directed learning; andragogy; and transformative, indigenous, emancipatory, and critical learning perspectives.

Experiential Learning

Experience is a natural part of life. Dewey, whose seminal works have grounded our understanding of experiential learning, stated: "Experience occurs continuously because the interaction of live creature and environing condition is involved in the very process of living" (1934, p. 35). Yet, he emphasizes, it is not enough just to acknowledge that one has had an experience. Learning from the experience is an act of meaning making mediated through communication.

Experience has occupied a central role in the theory and practice relevant to adult learning from Dewey's time to the present, and experiential learning has been conceptualized in many different ways. For example, Kolb's (1984) cyclical model includes concrete experience of and reflective observation on the experience, forming abstract conceptualizations and generalizations, and active experimentation or application of the experience to new situations. Boud, Cohen, and Walker (1993) looked at the individual learner, emphasizing reflection and the context in which the learning occurred. Their model included returning to the experience, attending to feelings around the experience and re evaluating the experience, but they also recognized that there were barriers present at each phase and that one must be flexible and open to the unique challenges and opportunities of each experience. Fenwick (2000) offered five frameworks for viewing experiential learning, including constructivist, psychoanalytic, situative, critical cultural, and enactivist perspectives, along with critiques of each.

Tennant and Pogson (1995) viewed experiential learning from four levels (prior experience, current experience, new experience, and learning from experience). These levels, along with two additional levels—learning from loss and learning from others' experience—are discussed below.

Prior experience. The majority of adult learning happens not in schools but through the ongoing experiences of our daily lives, such as births, deaths, relationships, jobs, and so on. Many colleges and universities, in fact, now award credit for college equivalent learning from such experiences.

One way adults learn is to connect new concepts and theories with something they already know, critically reflecting upon prior experiences in order to make sense of them, thus creating a bridge between the unknown and the known.

Current experience. Most of our formal education began with theories or concepts introduced by teachers and textbooks. Sometime later, we found ourselves putting the theory into practice. Experiential learning assumes that knowledge has been created through practice. Once we learn the theory, we can begin to name what we already know. The theory seems less abstract because we understand how it works in practice.

New experience. As educators, we can create structured shared experiences in our courses via class discussions, simulations, role-play, and other activities. In this way we develop a common knowledge base. As we reflect on and process these experiences as a group, we co-create knowledge.

Learning from experience. Often, learning does not occur until after the experience is over and we take time to process it. In sharing our experiences and reflecting as a group, we find that our individual experiences take on shared meaning. This shared meaning is necessary for collective action to occur. While education is grounded in experience, we do not learn from all of our experiences. As Dewey (1938) cautioned, not all learning experiences are educative; some may even be "miseducative." Adults may enter learning with experiences that have been unpleasant, or worse—painful. Recognizing how this experience manifests in a learning situation is an important part of being an effective adult educator.

Learning from loss. Much can be learned from difficult experiences. Based on the catastrophic natural and human-made disasters during the last decade, the experience of learning from loss may serve as a signature for this period that provides a context for a contemporary discussion of adult learning. In many instances of such megadisasters, a shared community forms. Wall and Louchakova (2002) found that with shared pain a unique meaning of oneness emerges in individuals that assists them in transcending the loss and activates a lasting shift in consciousness and the cultivation of a larger sense of Self. For many, the learning from such an experience is lasting and includes the emergence of a global compassion.

Learning from others' experience. While learning occurs through examining our individual experiences, we also learn from the experiences of others. While one may not have direct personal experience with sexual harassment, racial discrimination, or being an immigrant, listening to the stories of others' experiences often helps us make connections to ideas in new ways, reexamine our

views and assumptions, and see different ways to bridge new and prior learning in potentially powerful ways. We also learn more about our own experiences when we share them with others. We again return to Dewey: "The experience has to be formulated in order to be communicated. To formulate requires getting outside of it, see it as another would see it, considering what points of contact it has with the life of another so it may be got into such a form that he can appreciate its meaning" (1916, pp. 5–6).

Self-Directed Learning

The study of self-directed learning began with the work of Tough and Knowles during the 1960s and has subsequently received concerted study by many. The concept was central to Knowles's andragogical orientation, discussed shortly. Tough's groundbreaking research illuminated the degree to which adults were learning outside of modes in which they "participate" in organized learning. He named the experience the "adults' learning projects" (see, for example, Tough, 1971/1979, 1978, 1982)[2] to indicate that they crafted their own plans to learn—for example, something of necessity (fixing a broken toilet) or value (discovering genealogical roots)—and explored both material and human resources in the process. What was learned about how adults go about learning on their own provided "lessons" for educators of adults, because many successful efforts were antithetical to formal design efforts. Seen globally, though, continued emphasis on self-direction, or the manner in which it has been conceptualized and discussed, may privilege "Western" perspectives, negating collectivist-oriented societies. In introducing the concept of homonomy (coined by Andras Angyal during the 1940s) to the adult education literature to complement autonomy, Boucouvalas suggested that equal attention to the larger homonomous sense of Self (one's identity in being part of a greater whole) would provide a more robust construct for both research and discussions regarding the meaning and practice of self and Self-direction in learning.[3]

Andragogy

In the United States, the name Malcolm Knowles is most closely associated with *andragogy,* a term rooted in 19th-century Europe and referenced by Lindeman during the 1920s. Knowles spent decades crafting what he came to call "the art and science of facilitating adult learning" (see, for example, Knowles, 1950, 1975, 1980, 1991, 1995 and Knowles & Knowles, 1959). A central tenet is the important role of an adult's life experiences (in both quantity and quality) to the learning process. An equally key theme revolves around the concept of self and an adult's self-concept as a mature responsible decision maker except, he observed, when being treated as dependent in a learning situation, a concern which led him to emphasize the importance of developing self-directing learners. He defined that as the growing ability to understand oneself as a learner and develop the capacity to assume one's internal directedness even in other-directed environments, to know how to learn but also when one might need to be taught, and to take responsibility for one's learning or nonlearning—all actions, he suggested, that could help individuals of any age mature as learners.

Andragogy is one of the most widely discussed and critiqued aspects of the adult education literature in America. Most critiques conceptualize andragogy as a method or model, and attempt to discern its effectiveness in general and its exclusivity to adults. An andragogical approach, however, also refers to a way of thinking and being with adult learners and developing adult–adult relationships. While many of Knowles's contemporary critics have expressed concern about his seemingly exclusive emphasis on the individual, his early orientation addressed understanding oneself enough so as to work well in groups and for the benefit of society, and his 1950 book, *Informal Adult Education*, stressed the role of adult education in improving the social order. Perhaps that is why Yugoslavian adult educator Savicevic, when taking a course with Knowles during 1966, informed him that he was practicing andragogy but subsequently critiqued him as Knowles's writings began to emphasize the adult learner per se (albeit retaining the societal vision).

Savicevic, having turned his attention more recently to considering the international nature of andragogy, its similarities and differences of manifestation in different countries, reflected upon Knowles's work, considering "his contributions to dissemination of andragogical ideas throughout the USA . . . [as] huge," concluding that "the history of andragogy will put him on a meritorious place in the development of this scientific discipline" (Savicevic, 2006, p. 20).

Henschke, the foremost biographer of Knowles, has contributed most to understanding the legacy but also the place of Knowles's contributions in the larger global and historical terrain of the various renditions given to the term *andragogy,* from ancient times to the present. Each year an updated paper is presented and published.[4]

Transformative Learning

Transformative learning is similar to experiential learning in that the learning is usually triggered by an experience or series of experiences. Whereas experiential learning results in an expansion of knowledge, transformative learning is both epistemological and ontological, often involving a change in worldview.

Transformative learning was introduced to the field of adult education by Mezirow in 1978. According to Mezirow, transformative learning occurs when one experiences a "disorienting dilemma." Our reality is shaken. Our habitual ways of viewing the world no longer make sense. We experience what Mezirow calls a "perspective transformation" (1991, p. 167) by critically reflecting on our assumptions, recognizing the distortions in them and replacing them with more accurate and inclusive perspectives. This process results in individuals being permanently changed. We can never return to the way we were. While social change is a desirable outcome, according to Mezirow it need not be immediate.

In the last three decades much research in the area of transformative learning has confirmed, enlarged upon, and critiqued Mezirow's theory. O'Sullivan (2002) developed an ecological and planetary model of transformative learning, incorporating power relations, body awareness, and our relationship with the natural world. Dirkx (2006) pointed out that transformative learning can occur by opening ourselves to our unconscious. According to Jung's theory of individuation, knowledge from the unconscious comes to us in the form of symbols and images. Unlike critical reflection, which involves active intellectual engagement, he advocates, similar to Boyd and Myers (1988), contemplation or a quieting of the self to allow imagery, imagination, and self-awareness to occur. In this process our affect or emotions play a pivotal role. Boucouvalas (1997), building on Clark (1993), recognized that the transformative learning perspective of Boyd and Myers, along with Mezirow, Freire (1970), and Daloz (1986, 1999), all involved a change in consciousness illuminating the potential contribution of consciousness studies to broadening and deepening our understanding of transformative learning.

Others have critiqued Mezirow's theories based upon contextuality, rationality, normativity, and individualism. Clark and Wilson (1991) pointed out that transformation cannot be viewed as acontextual. The social and historical milieu in which the learner exists has a significant impact on his or her experience. Tennant (1993) argued that many life changes are the result of normative human development and should not be considered transformative. Feminist theorists such as Belenky and Stanton (2000) have argued that Mezirow's concept of transformative learning, with its emphasis on rationality, often negates women's experience by its failure to take into account relationships and affect. Freire (1970) believed that the primary goal of transformation was social action and that it was not enough to transform individuals.

Transformative learning continues to occupy a prominent space in adult learning theory, including an international conference on transformative learning first established in 1998. A recent publication by Taylor (2008) highlighted the complexities and variations of this perspective.

Indigenous Learning

Although many definitions of *indigenous knowledge* exist, we are using the term to refer to knowledge that is local, organic, rooted in a particular culture, and passed on to future generations through an oral tradition. Indigenous ways of knowing are now being brought into the spotlight and accorded the respect they deserve. During 1992, *Convergence: The International Journal of Adult Education* published an entire issue on indigenous knowledge and learning.

Merriam & Associates (2007) challenged the hegemony of Western ways of knowing that emphasize individualism, autonomy, and independence. These views have been critiqued by many as being Eurocentric. We suggest they are also anthropomorphic or humancentric, in that they assume the dominance and superiority of humans over other beings.

As Abram pointed out in *The Spell of the Sensuous* (1996), human beings in ancient times learned from animals, trees, mountains, rivers, and rocks as well as other humans. This practice is still prevalent in many indigenous cultures today. The Yup'ik's, an Alaskan Native tribe, give thanks to the animals and plants for their gifts through dances and song at the end of the year and request their continued abundance (Frank Andrew, personal communication). They use the term *peoples,* which is inclusive of all beings, human and nonhuman.

While many differences exist among traditions, indigenous cultures have much in common—valuing collectivism, community, interdependence, harmony with nature, balance, and the wisdom of elders. Indigenous learning includes storytelling, myths, dreams and visions, art, ritual, and ceremony.

Learning in Botswana, according to Ntseane (2007) incorporates family, community, and the spirits of one's ancestors. Similarly, Iroquois educator Paula Underwood speaks of the "seventh generation hence" explaining that all major decisions are made with consideration to seven generations in the past and their impact on seven future generations (Breisch, 1998 p. 3).

The *Nguzo Saba,* the seven principles developed by Maulana Karenga in 1965 that have come to be associated with the African American celebration of Kwanzaa, exemplify the values embedded in Afrocentric indigenous perspectives. These include *Umoja* (unity), *Kujichagulia* (self-determination), *Ujima* (collective work and responsibility), *Uamaa* (cooperative economics), *Nia* (purpose), *Kuumba* (creativity), and *Imani* (faith). Educational practices are grounded in these principles (Karenga, 1998).

While indigenous cultures do value formal school-based learning, they place equal or greater emphasis on informal learning. This learning is holistic encompassing mind, body, and spirit as well as harmony with nature. In Native American traditions, learning is experiential. Allen talks about "teaching around the edges," where one learns through the culmination of experience over time "until the student's consciousness opens to grasp ever widening and deepening layers of comprehension and wisdom" (2007, p. 51). Elders also teach through posing questions and transmit knowledge through story (Allen, 2007; Breisch, 1998; Cajete, 1994). Cajete (1994) suggests that indigenous teaching practices are universal archetypes that have implications for people of all cultural traditions. He passionately declares: "These processes have the potential to create deeper understanding of our collective role as caretakers of a world that we have thrown out of balance" (p. 21). Adult educators will encounter learners from many cultural contexts. It is important to be inclusive in considering our teaching practice.

Emancipatory and Critical Perspectives

Critical perspectives approach learning from a power relations framework. Race, class, and gender are central in considering power dynamics and distribution of resources. Critical theoretical analysis views learning in a social context (Welton, 1995), uncovering and exposing unequal power relations that privilege one group's interest over another's, thus preventing emancipatory possibilities.

Since race, class, and gender issues are discussed in other chapters of this book, this section only briefly describes adult learning from these perspectives. We begin with some key ideas from Freire (1970), who advocated for an emancipatory pedagogy based upon his assumptions that adults were capable of critical consciousness: *conscientization*, a process of becoming acutely aware of the oppressive forces that shaped their reality and could therefore be agents in their own learning process, overcoming oppression and transforming their lives. He promoted "problem posing" whereby learners' questions, concerns, and experiences become the context for learning. In problem-posing education, students and teachers are co-investigators in dialogue.

While Freire approached learning primarily from a class analysis, feminist theorists recognized that women learn differently from men and that many of our traditional educational systems emphasize self-direction, autonomy, and competition, which perpetuate hegemony and privilege male domination (Belenky et al., 1986; Hayes & Flannery, 2000; Maher, 1987).

Listening to women's stories, Hayes and Flannery identified themes of affect and intuition in learning; the importance of context; connection between the personal and social, and ethnic and economic influences; learning with others; and learning through play, music, and meditation.

Maher (1987) advocated for a feminist pedagogy because "all human experiences are gendered or centrally shaped by our being either men or women" (p. 187). Feminist pedagogy places value on subjectivity and community, recognizing that multiple realities can coexist and that women's personal stories can inform the educational process.

Since race, gender, and class are interlocking systems of oppression, particularly for people of color, they need to be considered as a collective. Collins (1991, pp. 201–219) talked about an "Afrocentric feminist epistemology" characterized by concrete experience as a criterion of meaning, the use of dialogue in assessing knowledge claims, an ethic of caring, and an ethic of personal accountability.

TOWARD THE FUTURE: INTEGRATING THE NEUROSCIENCES

Many disciplines contribute to our ever-evolving understanding of adult learning. One of the most recent to enter the radar screen of writers in the field, and one that bears watching in the future, is the burgeoning arena of the neurosciences.[5] Neuroscientific awareness, however, is not new to the field of adult education. As early as the 1970s, prominent adult educators such as Kidd and Houle stressed the important potential contribution of the neurosciences to adult learning, with Kidd emphasizing that adult educators stay informed of advances and Houle urging that one draw neuroscientists into the adult education field. During the 1980s one of us (MB) initiated a review of relevant primary literature, complemented by interviews with neuroscientists, which illuminated a neuroscientifc basis to adult learning and the "use it or lose it" phenomenon.[6] Then, as now, we must caution that many neuroscientists voice concern about prematurely generalizing the findings of their research to applied settings. Oversimplification and overgeneralization can result from a lack of appreciation of the complexity of the territory. What we can say with some confidence, however, is that concerted effort is geared to better understanding the adult brain and that promising findings are emerging that affirm a potential neuroscientific basis to adult learning. Barring disease or extreme disuse, life in the adult brain is neither static nor totally decremental in nature. Growing, adapting neuronal structures and networks are evident, and learning itself stimulates such brain changes.

The research upon which these claims are based had begun during the 1960s (Altman, 1962), when findings began to catalyze a paradigm shift from a doctrine of *anatomical fixity* (that neuronal capacity was not amenable to change once adulthood was reached) to one of *neuroplasticity* (the modifiability and regenerative capacities of selected areas of the adult brain; see Gage, 2001), the potential ability of the adult brain to repair itself, and the role that learning plays in that process. Such findings have derived from four sources: (1) controlled experiments with animals; (2) study of living humans who survived brain injuries from accident, illness, or disease and how the brain recovered, or not, from such injuries; (3) autopsies and comparative analyses of injured/diseased and normally functioning brains (thanks to donation of organs to science); and (4) computer imaging technologies.

Influenced by the 1990s "decade of the brain," many interdisciplinary advances have taken root. First to emerge were the cognitive neurosciences (neuronal basis to thought, perception, memory, attention, language, etc.), followed by the more recent social neuroscience (neurological underpinnings of social behavior and interactions) and affective neuroscience (neural basis of emotion). Neuro-education advances are also burgeoning, such as the Neuro Education initiative of Johns Hopkins University's School of Education. Interest in the adult brain has become recognized in the popular press and, during the past decade particularly, practitioner-focused literature has emerged that targets the adult learner. Although a review of that literature is outside the scope and space constraints of this chapter, we can briefly list its common elements, which, to name just a few, include neuronal changes induced by learning throughout life, resulting in individually unique brain patterns; the positive role of enriched and complex environments (including active engaged learning) on growth of neural structures, and conversely, the impact of stressors, especially the inescapable kind, as well as longtime fear associated with learning that may be resistant to extinction; the role of social interaction on neuronal plasticity; and the effect of the environment on gene expression. Also, from a global perspective, the brain seems to reflect how cultural factors affect perception (see Goh et al., 2007). Another major theme is the intertwining of emotion and cognition in the learning process. Goleman (2006), for example, who had popularized Salovey and Mayer's concept of emotional intelligence[7], is now illuminating for lay audiences the link between social and emotional ways of knowing and neuroscientific research. Linkages between the neurosciences and other disciplines, including consciousness studies, are a key to more deeply understanding the reciprocal relationship between learning and brain plasticity: how one affects the other.[8]

We continue to learn much about functioning from what has been lost and what is possible, or not possible, to regain. For example, the incidence of traumatic brain injuries (TBIs) is rising, especially as a result of the wars in Iraq and Afghanistan, and the improvement of medical technology has increased survival rates. Consistent with our discussion on art as a way of knowing, Marianne Talbot formed a dance company a number of years ago comprised of adults with traumatic brain injuries (TBIs) induced by stroke, car accident, drug overdose, and so on, and for over 20 years has observed remarkable improvement in functioning in cases where medical intervention and physical therapy offered a prognosis that no further improvement should be expected (Talbot, 2006). The interactive element of such healing may invoke the social and emotional brain, an area predicted by Heatherton, Phelps, and LeDoux (2004) to occupy a cutting edge of neuroscientifc research on learning over the next decade. Talbot's research on these observations led her to now work as well with returning soldiers with TBIs, to help them transition back into the community (an educational intervention entitled The Hope Project[9]). In general, much work awaits educators of adults with regard to vocational and social reintegration of such individuals, as well as the education of families, caretakers, and other educators of adults.

As universities around the world are establishing research centers and consortia, and hosting conferences that focus on learning and the brain, awareness and interest is increasing, leading to healthy exchanges between neuroscientists and those working with adult learners and educators. Although only the most cursory discussion was possible here, an integrated interdisciplinary approach to understanding the adult brain is clearly emerging.

SUMMARY

In this chapter we have provided a historical, global, and holistic context for understanding adult learning in theory and practice. Our brief historical visit revealed how adult learning has been conceived and addressed in the context of different eras, illuminating simultaneously some golden threads of continuity. We recognized our increasingly globalized, interconnected world, a world that necessitates a balanced cultivation of our individual as well as connected senses of self, as our context for 2010 and beyond. In our discussion of adult learning perspectives we have provided a broad view of the many ways in which learning can be understood. It is important to avoid essentialism and the idea that one size fits all. Critical perspectives are especially useful in helping us challenge our assumptions about learning theories by disrupting systems that privilege some learners while oppressing others. Equally important are the many modes of reflection, including those beyond thinking and conceptual knowing. A deep understanding of adult learning benefits from multidisciplinary contributions.

NOTES

1. The Report to UNESCO of the International Commission of Education for the 21st Century illuminated four pillars that form the foundational purpose of education and learning throughout life in a globalized 21st-century world. Beyond skills development (learning to do), equally important pillars are learning to know and to be, and the pillar that undergirds the rest: learning to live together (see Delors, 1996). More recently, a fifth essential has been added: learning to change.

2. See Tough's The Adult's Learning Projects (1971/1979), 1978, and Tough (1982) as well as his Web site for full texts of his publications (www .allentough.com).

3. Introduction of the concept of homonomy to the field during 1988 was followed by its application to the development of collectives during 1999, and a revisiting of the concept during 2009 in its contribution to the development of a global theory of self-direction in learning.

4. Yearly updates of research progress may be found in the Proceedings of the International Pre Conferences of the American Association for Adult and Continuing Education. Many of these manuscripts have been translated and published in countries such as Romania, Poland, and Serbia. See, for example, Henschke (2009), which was translated into Polish, or see Henschke & Cooper (2007), published in Romania.

5. Neuroscience is a collective term that refers to a variety of branches that include neurochemistry, neurobiology, neuroanatomy, and neuropsychology, as well as the more recent interdisciplinary advances of cognitive neuroscience, social neuroscience, affective neuroscience, and neuroeducation. Use of the term neurobiology alone, as referenced in some sources, is insufficient.

6. Results and discussion appeared during 1988 in the Proceedings of three conferences: the Adult Education Research Conference (Calgary, Canada), Research and Developments in the Neurosciences: Relevance for Adult Education; The Lifelong Learning Research Conference (College Park, MD), Advances in the Neurosciences: Implications and Relevance for Lifelong Learning Professionals; and the National Conference on the Adult Learner (Columbia, SC), Neuroscientific Perspectives on Adult Learning: Contributions and Caveats. The 1980s also witnessed a brain-based movement in K–12 education (not involving adult educators) that, in raising some serious concerns from neuroscientists, has now witnessed more collaborative dialogues between neuroscientists and educators.

7. Based on their research, Salovey and Mayer (1990, 1993) originally proposed the concept of emotional intelligence. Goleman broadened, deepened, and made the concept available to practitioners through his books Emotional Intelligence (1995, Bantam) and Working With Emotional Intelligence (1998, 2001, Bantam).

8. Readers interested in staying abreast of contemporary ongoing developments in the neurosciences are referred to free publications by Dana Foundation that offer excerpts from emerging research: BrainWork: The Neuroscientific Newsletter

and Brain in the News. For a deeper understanding of the research base, see the periodical *Science* (the official publication of the American Association of the Advancement of Science, which has since the 1990s published special issues on cognitive neuroscience), the many specialty journals (e.g., *Journal of*

Neuroscience, Social Neuroscience, etc.), and the *Encyclopedia of Neuroscience* (Squire, 2009).

9. For more information on The Hope Project, see the expert testimony of Talbot to the House Committee on Veterans' Affairs, November 19, 2008 (Talbot, 2008).

REFERENCES

Abram, D. (1996). *The spell of the sensuous.* New York: Random House.

Allen, P. G. (2007). American Indian indigenous pedagogy. In S. B. Merriam & Associates (Eds.), *Non-Western perspectives on learning and knowing* (pp. 41–56). Malabar, FL: Krieger.

Altman, J. (1962). Are new neurons formed in the brains of adult mammals? *Science, 35*(3509), 1127–1128.

Belenky, M. F., Clinchy, B. M., Goldberger, N. R., & Tarule, J. M. (1986). *Women's ways of knowing.* New York: Basic Books.

Belenky, M. F., & Stanton, A. V. (2000). Inequality, development and connected knowing. In J. D. Mezirow & Associates (Eds.), *Learning as transformation* (pp. 71–102). San Francisco: Jossey-Bass.

Boal, A. (2000). *Theatre of the oppressed* (3rd ed.). London: Pluto. (Original work published 1979)

Boucouvalas, M. (1997). An analysis and critique of transformation theory in adult learning: Contributions from consciousness studies. In P. Armstrong, N. Miller, & M. Zukas (Eds.), *Crossing borders, breaking boundaries: Research in the education of adults* (pp. 56–60). London: Birkbeck College, University of London.

Boucouvalas, M. (1999). Following the movement: From transpersonal psychology to a multi disciplinary transpersonal orientation. *Journal of Transpersonal Psychology, 31*(1), 27–39.

Boucouvalas, M. (2005). Cognition. In L. M. English (Ed.), *International encyclopedia of adult education* (pp. 111–113). New York: Palgrave Macmillan.

Boud, D., Cohen, R., & Walker, D. (1993). *Using experience for learning.* Bristol, PA: SHRE and Open University Press.

Boyd, R., & Myers, J. G. (1988). Transformative education. *International Journal of Lifelong Education, 7*(4), 261–284.

Breisch, R. (1998, October–December). A conversation with Paula Underwood. *Entre Nous,* pp. 3–8.

Brockman, J. (2001). A somatic epistemology for education. *The Educational Forum, 65,* 328–334.

Brookfield, S. D. (1995). *Becoming a reflective teacher.* San Francisco: Jossey-Bass.

Cajete, G. (1994). *Look to the mountain: An ecology of indigenous education.* Skyland, NC: Kivaki Press.

Clark, M. C. (1993). Transformational learning. In S. Merriam (Ed.), *An update on adult learning theory* (pp. 47–56). San Francisco: Jossey-Bass.

Clark, M. C., & Wilson, A. L. (1991). Context and rationality in Mezirow's theory of transformational learning. *Adult Education Quarterly, 41*(2), 75–91.

Collins, P. H. (1991). *Black feminist thought.* New York: Routledge.

Daloz, L. A. (1986) *Effective teaching and mentoring.* San Francisco: Jossey-Bass.

Daloz, L. A. (1999) *Mentor: Guiding the journey of adult learners.* San Francisco: Jossey-Bass.

Delors, J. (1996). *Learning: The treasure within.* Paris: UNESCO.

Dewey, J. (1916). *Democracy and education.* New York: Macmillan.

Dewey, J. (1934). *Art as experience.* New York: Capricorn Books.

Dewey, J. (1938). *Experience and education.* New York: Collier.

Dirkx, J. (2001). The power of feelings: Emotion, imagination, and the construction of meaning in adult learning. In S. B. Merriam (Ed.), *The new update on adult learning theory* (pp. 63–82). New Directions for Adult and Continuing Education, No. 89. San Francisco: Jossey-Bass.

Dirkx, J. (2006). Engaging emotions in adult learning. In E. W. Taylor (Ed.), *Teaching for change: Fostering transformative learning in the classroom* (pp. 15–26). New Directions for Adult and Continuing Education, No. 109. San Francisco: Jossey-Bass.

Fenwick, T. J. (2000). Expanding conceptions of experiential learning: A review of the five contemporary perspectives on cognition. *Adult Education Quarterly, 50*(4), 243–272.

Freire, P. (1970). *Pedagogy of the oppressed.* New York: Continuum.

Freire, P. (1994, November). Keynote address at the CAEL International Conference on Experiential Learning, Washington, DC.

Gage, F. (2001). *Neurogenesis and regeneration in the adult nervous system* (The 2001 Florence Mahoney Lecture) [Video]. Bethesda, MD: National Institutes of Health.

Goh, J. O., Chee, M. W., Tan, J. C., Venkatraman, V., Hebrank, A., Leshikar, E., et al. (2007). Age and culture modulate object processing and object scene binding in the ventral visual area. *Cognitive, Affective, and Behavioral Sciences, 7*(1), 44–52.

Goleman, D. (2006). *Social intelligence: The new science of human relationships.* New York: Bantam.

Hayes, E., & Flannery, D. D. (2000). *Women as learners: The significance of gender in adult learning.* San Francisco: Jossey-Bass.

Heatherton, T. F., Phelps, E. A., & LeDoux, J. (2004). Introduction: Emotional and social neuroscience. In M. S. Gazzaniga (Ed.), The *cognitive neurosciences III* (pp. 973–975). Cambridge: MIT Press.

Henschke, J. (2009, November 1–3). A perspective on the history and philosophy of andragogy: An international sketch. In *Proceedings of the International Pre Conference, American Association for Adult and Continuing Education,* Cleveland, OH (translated into Polish for publication).

Henschke, J., & Cooper, M. (2007). Additions toward a thorough understanding of the international foundations of andragogy in HRD and adult education. In *Yearbook of the Romanian Institute for Adult Education* (pp. 7–48). Bucharest, Romania: Editura Academiei.

Karenga, M. (1998). *Kwanzaa: A celebration of family, community and culture.* Los Angeles: University of Sakore Press.

Kegan, R. (1994). *In over our heads: The mental demands of modern life.* Cambridge, MA: Harvard University Press.

Knowles, M., & Knowles, H. F. (1959). *Introduction to group dynamics.* New York: Association Press.

Knowles, M. S. (1950). *Informal adult education.* New York: Association Press.

Knowles, M. S. (1975). *Self-directed learning: A guide for teachers and learners.* New York: Association Press.

Knowles, M. S. (1980). *The modern practice of adult education* (2nd ed.). New York: Association Press.

Knowles, M. S. (1991). *The adult learner: A neglected species* (4th ed.). Houston, TX: Gulf.

Knowles, M. S. (1995). *Designs for adult learning.* Alexandria, VA: American Association for Training and Development.

Kolb, D. (1984). *Experiential learning.* Englewood Cliffs, NJ: Prentice Hall.

Lawrence, R. L. (2005). Knowledge construction as contested terrain: Adult learning through artistic expression. In R. L. Lawrence (Ed.), *Artistic ways of knowing* (pp. 3–12). New Directions for Adult and Continuing Education, No. 107. San Francisco: Jossey-Bass.

Lawrence, R. L. (2008). Powerful feelings: Exploring the affective domain of informal and arts-based learning. In J. Dirkx (Ed.), *Adult learning and the emotional self* (pp. 65–77). New Directions for Adult and Continuing Education, No. 120. San Francisco: Jossey-Bass.

Lindeman, E. C. (1926). *The meaning of adult education.* New York: New Republic.

Maher, F. A. (1987, March). Inquiry teaching and feminist pedagogy. *Social Education, 51*(3), 186–188, 190–192.

Mayer, J. D., & Salovey, P. (1993). The intelligence of emotional intelligence. *Intelligence, 17,* 433–442.

Merriam, S. B., & Associates (2007). *Non-Western perspectives on learning and knowing.* Malabar, FL: Krieger.

Mezirow, J. D. (1991). *Transformative dimensions of adult learning.* San Francisco: Jossey-Bass.

Murphy, M. (1992). *The future of the body: Explorations into the further evolution of human nature.* Los Angeles: Jeremy P. Tarcher.

Ntseane, G. (2007). African indigenous knowledge: The case of Botswana. In S. B. Merriam & Associates (Eds.), *Non-Western perspectives on learning and knowing* (pp. 113–136). Malabar, FL: Krieger.

O'Sullivan, E. (2002). The project and vision of transformative education. In E. O'Sullivan, A. Morrell, & M. A. O'Connor (Eds.), *Expanding the boundaries of transformative learning* (pp. 1–12). New York: Palgrave.

Patterson, F. (1996). *Shadowlight: A photographer's life.* Toronto: HarperCollins.

Salovey, P., & Mayer, J. D. (1990). Emotional intelligence. *Imagination, Cognition, and Personality, 9*(3), 185–211.

Savicevic, D. (2006). Convergence or divergence of ideas on andragogy in different countries. In *Proceedings of the 11th Standing Conference on the History of Adult Education.* Bamberg, Germany.

Schlitz, M. M., Vietan, C., & Amorok, T. (2007). *Living deeply: The art and science of transformation in everyday life.* Oakland, CA: New Harbinger.

Sinnott, J. (1998). *The development of logic in adulthood: Postformal thought and its applications.* New York: Plenum.

Squire, L. R. (2009). *Encyclopedia of neuroscience.* Boston: Elsevier.

Talbot, M. (2006). *The dynamics of a therapeutic dance/movement intervention for individuals with brain injuries: Comparison with physical therapy using Laban Movement Analysis.* Unpublished doctoral dissertation, Virginia Polytechnic Institute and State University/Graduate Center/National Capital Region.

Talbot, M. (2008, November 19). Expert testimony statement to the House Committee on Veterans' Affairs, November 19, 2008 by Marianne Talbot, Ph.D., President, National Rehabilitation and Recovery Foundation: The Hope Project: An independent living program for veterans with TBI. Retrieved January 27, 2009, from http://veterans.house.gov/hearings/Testimony

Taylor, E. W. (2008). Transformative learning theory. In S. B. Merriam (Ed.), *Third update on adult learning theory* (pp. 5–15). New Directions for Adult and Continuing Education, No. 119. San Francisco: Jossey-Bass.

Tennant, M. (1993). Perspective transformation and adult development. *Adult Education Quarterly, 44*(1), 34–42.

Tennant, M., & Pogson, P. (1995). *Learning and change in the adult years.* San Francisco: Jossey-Bass.

Thorndike, E. L., Bregman, E. O., Tilton, J. W., & Woodyard, E. (1928). *Adult learning.* New York: Macmillan.

Tough, A. (1978). Major learning efforts: Recent research and future directions. *Adult Education, 28*(4), 250–263.

Tough, A. (1979). *The adult's learning projects: A fresh approach to theory and practice in adult learning*

(2nd ed.). San Francisco: Pfeiffer. (Original work published 1971)

Tough, A. (1982). *Intentional changes: A fresh approach to helping people change.* Chicago: Follett.

Wall, K., & Louchakova, O. (2002). Evolution of consciousness in response to terrorist attacks: Toward a transpersonal theory of cultural transformation. *The Humanistic Psychologist, 30*(3), 252–273.

Washburn, M. (2000). Transpersonal cognition in developmental perspective. In T. Hart, P. L. Nelson, & K. Puhakka (Eds.), *Transpersonal knowing: Exploring the horizons of consciousness* (pp. 185–212). Albany: State University of New York Press.

Washburn, M. (2003). *Embodied spirituality in a sacred world.* Albany: State University of New York Press.

Welton, M. R. (Ed.). (1995). *In defense of the lifeworld: Critical perspectives on adult learning.* Albany: State University of New York Press.

4

ADULT DEVELOPMENT

M CECIL SMITH AND KATHLEEN TAYLOR

Though the field of adult development as a formal area of study did not yet exist early in the 20th century, the notion that adult learning might transform the lives of adults was presaged by Eduard Lindeman in 1926: "The chief purpose of [adult education] is to discover the meaning of experience; [it is] a quest of the mind which digs down to the roots of the preconceptions which formulate our conduct" (p. x). This was echoed in 1981 when Chickering and Associates, drawing on recently formulated models of adult development, suggested that such outcomes should be a *primary* aim of adult education.

Development is generally associated with individuals' movement in a positive direction. Meaning "to unfold, to grow into latent potential," *development* is more encompassing than *maturation*. Development includes sociocultural expectations and interactions as well as movement toward greater complexity and self-organization (Kegan, 1994; Tennant & Pogsen, 1995). Investigators of life-span development, such as Baltes (1987), view development in complex terms, encompassing both growth (gain) and decline (loss) in capacities and skills with age. As losses in particular functions occur, adults may adapt or compensate for these deficits by, for example, employing memory-enhancing strategies, practicing a skill, or avoiding situations where a declining skill is needed.

In this chapter, we frame development as "a process of qualitative change in attitudes, values, and understandings that adults experience as a result of ongoing transactions with the social environment, occurring over time but not strictly as a result of time" (Taylor, Marienau, & Fiddler, 2000, p. 10). Among the many facets of adulthood affected by development are capacities for lifelong learning, effective responses to an increasingly multicultural environment, self-understanding, and resiliency in the face of loss.

ADULT DEVELOPMENT AND ADULT EDUCATION

The study of adult development is a rapidly growing field of social science. Although research and theory regarding adult development emerged initially from psychological studies of adulthood (Thompson, 2008), many disciplines contribute to and are informed by the study of growth and change in the adult years, including sociology, gerontology, developmental psychology, neuroscience—and adult education.

AUTHORS' NOTE: Authorship order is alphabetical. The authors contributed equally to preparing this chapter.

Research suggests that adult education has the potential to provoke, enhance, support, and sustain development in adulthood. While much adult education literature focuses on learning (i.e., how adults learn, conditions fostering learning, educators' contributions to adults' learning), the last 20 years have seen greater emphasis on the intersection of learning and development (Hoare, 2006). This is not, however, an entirely new thread. Lindeman (1926), an early proponent of adult education, hinted at adult education's developmental aspects, insisting that it "is an agitating instrumentality for changing life" (p. 89).

Rapidly changing societal conditions have led U.S. higher education institutions to establish programs, practices, and initiatives for adult learners (American Council on Education, 2007). Conceptions of adulthood, age, and aging are evolving in contemporary culture. Young adults are putting off marriage and work commitments until their mid-to-late 20s (U.S. Census Bureau, 2006). Definitions and concepts of "family" are in flux, leading to major shifts in gender- and role-expectations (Moen, Kelly, & Maginnis, 2008). The implications of these changes for young adults are dramatic. Jensen-Arnett (2000) has thus proposed a theory of *emerging* adulthood that occurs from the late teens to the late 20s. Jensen-Arnett argues that emerging adulthood is distinct from adolescence and young adulthood in that emerging adults are not constrained by traditional social roles and normative expectations. Emerging adulthood is a period for expansive role exploration beyond adolescence, offering many possibilities. A feature of this life stage is that emerging adults see themselves no longer as adolescents, with the implication of high school or college attendance and financial dependence upon parents. However, emerging adults also see themselves as *not yet adults,* having not acquired the traditional attributes of adulthood: a stable residence, completion of one's education, entry into a career, and marriage and child-rearing.

Developmentalists now recognize the changes that are occurring across the whole of the adult life span. Middle-aged adults are physically active and intellectually engaged for decades longer than in previous eras (Dorner, Mickler, & Staudinger, 2005). Those who once counted on steadily rising through the workplace ranks now expect to change jobs—even careers—several times. More adults want to remain employed long past traditional retirement age (Stein, 2003–2004), citing either economic necessity (Mermin, Johnson, & Murphy, 2007) or that their work is intellectually stimulating as the reason. The workplace is also a setting for maintaining friendships. Increasing diversity, immigration, and social mobility now require more complex understandings of and responses to "difference" among adults. And, as life expectancy increases, attention has focused on the potential for the development of wisdom and positive aging (Ardelt & Jacobs, 2008; Bassett, 2006; Hill, 2006). In response, many higher learning institutions now seek to develop students' capacities and skills for lifelong learning. Adult educators, too, are keen to learn about the processes, characteristics, and trajectories of adults' development, particularly as these intersect with learning.

A number of diverse, sometimes complementary, perspectives can be identified in the theoretical literature. We will focus on three overarching frameworks of adult development. The first centers on development of the individual's ego across the adult life span—and the developmental tasks that provoke ego development, including identity formation. The second focuses on the development of particular "identities"—racial/ethnic and sexual—as key to psychological development and a sense of well-being. The third describes ego/identity/personality development from the perspective of changes in adults' *ways of knowing* themselves and the world around them (i.e., epistemological development). Such changes in individuals' meaning making affect constructions of their identities, self-concepts, relationships, belief systems, and values.

THEORETICAL FRAMEWORKS OF ADULT DEVELOPMENT

Several theoretical perspectives on adult development are oriented to explaining development of the self in response to one's social surroundings. These theories have been termed *phasic* models (Eriksen, 2006) because they focus on the sociocultural expectations and psychological tasks related to growing up and achieving social roles, and to the phases in life when these tasks occur. Phasic theorists include Bühler

(1935), Erikson (1950/1964), Havighurst (1972), Levinson (1986), and Loevinger (1976).

Ego Development in Adulthood

Ego development refers to the development of a sense of self in relation to the surrounding social context of which one is a part in order to become a well-adjusted, effectively functioning individual. As Lerner (2002) notes, reality is shaped by the society in which the individual is developing and the ego must constantly adapt to society's changing demands, which differ across the life span. Erikson's (1950/1964, 1968) model of psychosocial development describes eight age-related stages—from infancy to old age—or phases of development as "crises" that must be resolved. If the ego does not develop the appropriate capabilities to reconcile the extant psychosocial crisis and satisfy changing social demands, it will never be a "*functioning whole*" (italics in original, Erikson, 1959, p. 52).

The threshold of adulthood is the crisis that attends the adolescent's development of a personal *identity* that is distinct from that of others. This is a response to the social demand to individuate—to physically and psychologically separate the self from the family of origin and become one's own person. The young adult must develop healthy *intimacy*, enabling engagement in mutually satisfying relationships, and then become a *generative* middle aged adult who can provide care and nurturing for the succeeding generation. Accomplishing these tasks may lead to a sense of ego *integrality* in the final stage of life.

Ego development occurs alongside cognitive development, and cognitive abilities play a significant role in developing the ego. Erikson, in fact, noted that Piagetian formal operational skills—specifically, the ability to consider multiple perspectives—are essential to identity formation. The adolescent must consider multiple and simultaneous role possibilities (e.g., indifferent student, trusted friend, skilled athlete) and weigh the relative merits of adopting these roles, and must also integrate others' views with their own self-perspective into a new, consistent and coherent sense of self.

By contrast, Levinson (1986) devised the concept of the *life structure,* the "underlying pattern or design of a person's life" (p. 41) as the central motor of the developmental journey. The primary components of the life structure are shaped by the individual's personal relationships, hence the choices that individuals make regarding career, marriage, and family. Levinson argued that the principal focus of Erikson's ego stages is development *within the person* (italics in original; Levinson, Darrow, Klein, Levinson, & McKee, 1978, p. 323), whereas his own focus is on understanding the boundary between the self and the social world, giving equal consideration to both.

Social Role Theory

Sociologists such as Levinson have contributed to a rich understanding of the processes and outcomes of adult development. Reitzes (2003) has investigated adults' social and emotional engagement from a social role perspective, with a view toward understanding the benefits of such engagement (e.g., psychological well-being). Drawing upon symbolic interactionism and identity theory perspectives, Reitzes has examined how adults' "engagement with life" influences their interpersonal relationships and productive activities.

Social and emotional engagement is an investment by the individual into relationships, "as well as an opportunity for social participation" (Reitzes, 2003, p. 427). Such engagement is viewed in terms of role participation and identity construction. Social roles (e.g., neighbor, friend, grandparent) are shared norms among the occupants of social positions, enabling them to anticipate future behaviors and maintain regularity in their social interactions. These specify the knowledge, ability, motivation, and expectations about the proper extent, direction, and duration of feeling states associated with given roles (pp. 427–428). Identities are self-meanings in a role (e.g., regarding oneself as a reliable neighbor or a trusted friend).

Participating in a social role necessitates both "identification of" the role one occupies and "identification with" the role by investing it with intrinsic self-meanings (i.e., infusions of one's self in the role). Individuals add meaning and affect to their roles through at least five processes: role *satisfaction; commitment* to the role; role *salience* (i.e., willingness to participate in or be acknowledged as a role participant); role *centrality* (i.e., importance of the role to the individual); and, *identity meanings* (i.e., how one views one's self in the role).

Role engagement has been shown to have enduring effects on psychological well-being and physical health, according to Reitzes—up to three decades later in some studies. Reitzes identified seven trends drawn from investigations examining the factors that influence role engagement across diverse social roles:

1. Earlier levels of role involvement influence later levels.

2. Gender differences are apparent, reflecting socialization and labor force participation.

3. Work role characteristics (i.e., occupational status) and family factors (i.e., having children) influence role engagement.

4. Patterns of role engagement vary by life-cycle stage.

5. Human capital (e.g., education, income) facilitates role engagement.

6. Engagement in one role encourages engagement in other roles.

7. The greater the identification with a role, the greater the role participation.

This work illustrates the influence of social engagement on adults' development in terms of identity, life satisfaction, and emotional well-being.

The Life Events Perspective

Other sociologically oriented adult development models, which are more a set of perspectives than a specific theory, focus on the influences of life events on adults' development and well-being. Life events are transitional markers of adult development (Hultsch & Plemons, 1979) and most events are normal and predictable (e.g., marriage, child-rearing), although some are not (e.g., economic collapse, wars). A life events perspective emphasizes adult development within a framework of the individual and cultural episodes occurring throughout a person's life (Merriam & Brockett, 2007). Researchers have attended to the timing, sequences, and consequences of life events (George, 1993). Generally, negative outcomes are associated with off-time (e.g., young widowhood) compared to on-time events (which can usually be anticipated, such as the loss of a spouse late in life). Pinhey and Pinhey (2002), for example, examined the emotional consequences of the timing of surgical menopause for women. The investigators hypothesized that younger women who had experienced surgical menopause would report greater emotional distress than older women who had the same surgical procedure, as menopause is perceived as an appropriate event for middle-aged women, but not for younger women. The results of their analyses supported the hypothesis. Women 44 years old and younger were significantly more likely than older women to suffer psychological distress and unhappiness following surgical menopause. Off-schedule life events, such as surgical menopause, can result in considerable emotional trauma because these events are perceived as inappropriate for a particular age or cohort group.

Whether examined primarily through psychological or sociological lenses, awareness of these developmental perspectives is important to adult educators, because education provides a context where adults may consider and enact a variety of *possible selves* (Markus & Nurius, 1987). Indeed, at some level, adults' participation in adult education may be considered identity work (Chickering & Reisser, 1993; D'Amico, 2004), leading to a new sense of self. Specific models have also been proposed that center on students' (and adult educators') race and ethnicity and sexual orientation.

Racial and Ethnic Identity Theories

Adults' racial and ethnic identities are considered essential to their individual development and sense of well-being (Chavez & Guido-DiBrito, 1999). People benefit from developing a conscious identity around race and ethnicity, according to Chavez and Guido-DiBrito. So-called mainstream models of racial identity focus on the universal aspects of group identity—regardless of a specific racial category (Gaines & Reed, 1995). The pioneering work on racial consciousness in young African American children by Clark and Clark (1939) is representative of a mainstream model. Alternative theoretical models (Gaines & Reed, 1995) emerged in the 1970s, represented by Cross (1971), Parham (1989), and Helms (1995). As Chavez and Guido-DiBrito (1999) have noted, most racial identity theorists share a focus on the "intersection between racial perceptions of others (racism) and racial perceptions of self (racial development)" (p. 42).

In general, these perspectives hold that racial minority adults' development must attend to racism and racial stereotypes, as well as question race-based assumptions (which are pervasive and internalized). Most contemporary theories of racial identity development share several characteristics and/or stages.

First, if developed largely within a supportive family or ethnic enclave, the child's identity is likely to move toward a positive self-image based on the parents' worldview (Jackson, 2001). If, however, the social environment is focused primarily on White perspectives, then the child's identity development is more likely to be toward "neutral self-concept and confused ego identity" (Kim, 2001, p. 73).

Second, acceptance of and identification with the dominant culture occurs when the young person from a minority culture internalizes the perspective that "normalcy" is equated with the dominant culture. For most racial groups, this is *Whiteness*, leading to self-denigration, shame, self-alienation, and other hallmarks of negative self-concept that emerge from trying to fit into the majority culture and devaluing one's own (Jackson, 2001).

Third, questioning the dominant assumptions leads to a shift from acceptance to resistance and heightened sociopolitical consciousness—as, for example, the civil rights movement revealed the pervasive nature of racism in American society. Collusion in one's own oppression—using Freire's terminology (1972)—gives way to actively or passively contradicting and "unlearning" established personal and political systems (Jackson, 2001) as well as negative assumptions about oneself and other minorities, and possibly to anger about what is seen as earlier victimization, and for some, active hostility toward the dominant culture.

Such resentment can be redirected by more deeply engaging with and reclaiming one's own culture, history, and heritage and thereby redefining what it means to be "me," rather than be defined (by either oneself or the dominant culture) according to what one is *not*, that is, White—a stance that may not be welcomed by either the dominant culture or those members of one's own group who have been successful at downplaying difference.

Finally, the most complex identity emerges when the person integrates all the experiences and understandings and claims a *both/and* perspective, leading to "blending of individuals'

racial identity with the rest of their social identities" (Kim, 2001, p. 80). This new internalization values what Jackson (2001, p. 26) calls "panethnic cultural perspectives."

There are differences, of course, in how racial and ethnic identities play out among diverse minority groups. Many Asians, whose view of self is deeply affected by the perspectives of the larger social and cultural group, tend to be externally rather than internally focused (Kim, 2001, p. 68). Among Latinos, however, whose ancestors include indigenous people, African slaves, and Spanish conquistadors and whose color palette runs the spectrum, identity emerges primarily via ethnic identification. Ferdman and Gallegos (2001) portray several ethnic "positions," including Latino-integrated, Latino-identified, undifferentiated, White-identified, and so on.

Sexual Orientation

Similar to racial and ethnic identity, the development of identity among sexual minorities has also been characterized in terms of stages of growth (Troiden, 1993). Alderson (2003) discusses several limitations of stage models for gay identity development. Stage models follow a general pattern: the individual's growing awareness of homosexual feelings, followed by testing and exploration, then adoption of a gay identity, and concluding with identity integration (p. 75). Critics of these models point out their irrelevance to minority gay men and well as other sexual minorities (lesbians and bisexuals), and question the assumption of a stable sexual identity across all social–behavioral contexts. Alderson notes the numerous pathways to gay identities that are not adequately captured by stage models. Drawing on both a developmental model and more process-oriented (i.e., self-categorization as gay; social comparison) social identity theory, Alderson proposed an ecological model that accounts for multiple layers of psychological and societal influence on gay identity. He argues that his ecological model provides a holistic perspective on gay identity because it includes both internal and external influences that contribute to gay self-definition. The Alderson model is, however, limited to gay men.

Alderson (2003) defines gay identity as a "status denoting those individuals who have come to identify themselves as having primarily homosexual cognition, affect, and/or behaviour, and who have adopted the construct of 'gay' as having personal significance to them" (p. 78). If the individual encounters more accepting institutions and relationships, then developing a gay identity is less dramatic. Actual sexual behavior is "least important in . . . one's sexual orientation" (p. 81) and can be a misleading indicator of cognitive processes related to sexual identity development, according to Alderson. The theory describes three stages of gay identity development: before coming out, during coming out, and beyond coming out. The impetus for development within and between stages is cognitive dissonance, where there is incompatibility between one's thoughts, feelings, and/or behaviors regarding sexuality. Alderson notes that achieving a positive gay identity is a difficult, lengthy process.

Constructive-Developmental Theory

This approach views development from the perspective that the most fundamental developmental changes are in our *ways of knowing* ourselves and our surround—whether as aging adults in a various environments, members of ethnic-identified groups, or participants in social roles. Thus, rather than focusing on the condition (age, life task, ethnicity, social role), constructive-developmental theories examine how we *construct* those roles—and how that process of construction, itself, evolves.

Piaget's cognitive-structural model is the springboard for these theories. He proposed that cognitive capacities become more complex in response to individuals' interactions with their physical and social environments. Development proceeds in a series of qualitatively different "logics" in which the characteristics of meaning-making in earlier stages are distinct from those of later, more mature stages (Kegan, 1982). Formal operational thought—the capacity for abstract and hypothetico-deductive reasoning—is the highest stage, and is not achieved until late adolescence, if at all.

A number of theorists have claimed that formal operations do not adequately account for the abilities of some adults to consider the relative, nonabsolute nature of knowledge; to accept contradiction as the basis of reality; or to synthesize their contradictory thoughts, feelings, and experiences into a more coherent cognitive organization. Such thinking, which seems to represent a form or level beyond Piaget's final stage, has been labeled postformal operations (Sinnott, 2008). Constructive-developmental models have been in the forefront of describing these more complex ways of knowing.

The basic premise of constructivism is described by Heisenberg (1962): "We have to remember that what we observe is not nature in itself, but nature exposed to our method of questioning" (p. 58). We do not come to know *objective reality* (i.e., something that exists external to ourselves, knowledge of which is there to be "discovered"), but rather, we create (construe, construct) "reality" as we make meaning of whatever happens to, within, and around us. This is not to claim that there is no objective reality, but that what we know of it is necessarily filtered by our lenses of perception (von Glasersfeld, 1996)—and we can no more see these lenses than we can see the eyeglasses we are wearing. We therefore cannot know to what extent these lenses distort or limit our vision.

From the constructivist perspective, development can be likened to lifelong processes of acquiring increasingly effective perceptual lenses; this is another way of describing what Kegan (1982, 1994) called the "subject–object shift." The lens we currently wear—our present way of knowing—is that to which we are *subject*. But when we discard that lens—develop a more complex way of knowing—it becomes *object* to us, and we can therefore see and recognize it as our *former* way of knowing. In this way, we grow beyond that *which held us* to instead *hold it,* in the sense of no longer being confined by it. This is a remarkable consciousness-altering development that education may help many adults to achieve. "Constructive-developmental," then, describes those theories in which development is linked to successively complex and inclusive ways of making meaning.

Constructive-Developmental Models

Three related constructive-developmental models are prominent in adult education: Perry's (1998) model of changes in young adults' (i.e., college students') epistemological beliefs; Belenky and her colleagues' (1986) description of women's "ways of knowing," which parallels Perry's; and Kegan's (1994) "orders of consciousness" model. Kegan's model is presented here as a "meta-model" that incorporates essential elements of the other two. All three models propose that adult development moves toward increasingly complex ways of making meaning, though this does not always occur.

Development, according to Kegan (1994), is a series of qualitative changes in the *form* of knowing, that is, trans-form-ation (2000). This is not, however, limited to cognition: "There is no feeling, no experience, no thought, no perception, independent of a meaning making context in which it *becomes* a feeling, an experience, a thought, a perception, because we *are* the meaning-making context" (Kegan, 1982, p. 11). Of Kegan's five orders of consciousness, three are most relevant to a discussion of adult development: instrumental (second order), socializing (third order), and self-authoring (fourth order).

The transition from each order of consciousness to the next involves a shift from a way of knowing that *has us* to one that *we have*. What we are *subject to* is what we are "identified with, tied to, fused with, or embedded in" (Kegan, 1994, p. 32). However, what we can "reflect on, handle, look at, be responsible for, relate to each other, take control of, internalize, assimilate, or otherwise operate upon" (p. 32) is *object to us*.

Kegan's *instrumental* way of knowing (which appears also to describe Perry's *dualism* or Belenky and her colleagues' *received knowing*) is based on "either/or" thinking and displays cognitive egocentrism oriented to one's own interests, purposes, wants, and needs, although behavior may vary according to external circumstances. The internal, unconscious response to a felt need might be: *I'll do it because I want to,* though the possibility of undesirable consequences may sway the likelihood of acting. For this reason, merely observing behavior is not an effective way to gauge epistemological complexity. People may *act* "properly" without having internalized the underlying propriety.

Instrumental knowers view knowledge as tangible, concrete, and obtainable from those "in the know." Their motivation for acquiring knowledge is utilitarian: to get a better job; to achieve an A in a course. They are relatively unreflective, content to know *what* (facts) and *how* (to do something they want to do), and are unconcerned with understanding *why*. Thus, instrumental knowers may seek more direct guidance from their adult education teachers.

Socializing knowers are oriented to others' expectations and opinions; it is important to gain others' acceptance (Drago-Severson, 2004). They view knowledge in terms of fulfilling social roles and meeting teachers' (and others') expectations. This is the adult learner who asks, "What do you think I should know?" In addition to the potential to "get ahead," they participate in adult education because it may raise them in others' esteem (hence, their own) and gain social approval and affiliation. In Perry's terms, socializing knowers may be early *multiplists* who have yet to make commitments. In Belenky and colleagues' model, they are often *subjective* knowers. Although some may superficially follow the "rules" of *procedural* knowing, they have not internalized the underlying meaning and purposes of those procedures.

Nevertheless, people operating from socialized consciousness have internalized their community's values and other rules for correct living as the most prominent source of the "inner voice" that guides behavior. There is no awareness that the internalized sociocultural framework is in charge—it's just "how I am" or "how things are"—which is why being confronted in classroom or texts with contradictory ideas may be unsettling. Similarly, these individuals find it difficult to accept comments suggesting areas for improvement. Rather than framing such feedback as formative and supportive, it is interpreted as a summative critique depicting the learner as "wrong." Most adults in Western society operate from this way of knowing (Kegan, 1994), and are often a majority in a typical group of learners.

More complex still and less frequently encountered in most adult education classrooms is the *self-authoring* (or self-authorizing) way of knowing, wherein individuals recognize and accept multiple perspectives and their own role in constructing knowledge. Unquestioning reliance on rules and assumptions of one's sociocultural surround gives way to understanding that one is responsible for one's choices and their outcomes. There is tolerance for ambiguity and attention to the "greater good." In Perry's framework, these are adults who can make commitments within relativism. They are well on their way to becoming "constructed knowers," according to Belenky and her colleagues.

Self-authoring knowers thoughtfully construct their own values, which may not accord with those they learned as children. They also have increased capacity to engage in self-directed learning (Taylor, 2006, p. 205) and are self-motivated with regard to their responsibilities in their workplace and community. Though not overly concerned about how others perceive them, they welcome feedback that can help them become more effective. The self-authoring knower participates in adult education *to keep learning and growing as a person.*

According to Kegan (1994), this order of consciousness is the minimum level of competence needed to effectively handle the current pace of cultural, political, and technological change pervasive in Western cultures (and increasingly in other parts of the globe), but less than half of adults in this society have fully achieved self-authoring capacities.

Movement from one form of knowing to another occurs gradually, over several years. These transitions require changes in perspective-taking abilities, as the adult moves from an egocentric to an *other*-oriented point of view and, ultimately, to a broader societal perspective. This kind of growth—from instrumental to socializing to self-authorizing ways of knowing—is highly individualized in terms of when, or if, the next shift occurs. Accordingly, critics view Kegan's model as an excessively individualistic approach to understanding development (Soldz, 1988).

IMPLICATIONS FOR ADULT EDUCATORS

One effective way to foster developmental growth in adults is to more deeply understand developmental processes in general, and to focus, to the extent possible, on each student's process in particular (Taylor, 1996). Adults who find school something of an emotional roller-coaster are comforted to learn that such feelings signal an evolving shift in perspective rather than impending doom. They are usually fascinated to learn more about the processes that unfold before them.

The Holding Environment

From an adult educator's perspective, an intriguing question is: What allows or encourages the kind of development that Kegan describes? There are many strategies and practices adult educators can use to foster learners' development (Taylor et al., 2000). Indeed, there is a wealth of materials on methods such as problem-based learning, case study, scaffolding, and so on. We will focus instead on one overarching strategy that may subsume several others.

According to Kegan (1982), all developing humans need a *holding environment.* In the case of very young children this is literally physical holding: someone whose touch lets us experience comfort when we are sad and joy when we are happy. The metaphorical holding environment of development, however, has three parts: holding on, letting go, and sticking around. Holding on, or *confirmation,* tells learners how well they are doing and lets them know that even if there has been some setback, they are basically okay and can go on. Letting go, or *contradiction,* encourages adults to venture beyond their comfort zone to try the next level of challenge. Sticking around provides *continuity.* It is often difficult for adults, who have years of investment in their current developmental perspective, to shift to a new way of knowing. By continuing to *be there* through sometimes awkward periods of change, a teacher, mentor, or counselor can offer a consistent backdrop for the adult's growth.

From the perspective of the educator, confirmation means acknowledging effort, praising accomplishment, and sharing aspirations. Contradiction means pointing out areas for improvement, providing formative feedback, setting a high but achievable bar. Continuity is being there, *no matter what.* Adult learners in the throes of developmental change can be frustrated and frustrating. The adult educator's most challenging task may be to determine whether the learner needs support, challenge, or something else entirely.

Although "developmental intentions" (Taylor et al., 2000) may be laudable, adult educators must remember that their task is to provide environments within which adults may—or may not—*choose* to develop (Daloz, 1988). However well intentioned, it is not up to adult educators to decide someone else's life course. As Brookfield (1990) has observed, in some traditional societies, development can mean cultural suicide, when people who no longer fit the accepted mold are denied further connection to their communities.

It is also essential that educators periodically reflect on their own process as developing adults. It is understandably tempting to avoid challenges to one's existing perspectives and instead remain in the realm of the familiar and comfortable—perhaps even when it concerns new ideas about learning, teaching, and development.

REFERENCES

Alderson, K. G. (2003). The ecological model of gay male identity. *Canadian Journal of Human Sexuality, 12*(2), 75–85.

American Council on Education. (2007). *Framing new terrain: Older adults and higher education.* New York: MetLife Foundation.

Ardelt, M., & Jacobs, S. (2008). Wisdom, integrity, and life satisfaction in very old age. In M C. Smith (Ed.), *Handbook of research on adult learning and development* (pp. 730–758). New York: Routledge.

Baltes, P. B. (1987). Theoretical propositions of lifespan developmental psychology: On the dynamics between growth and decline. *Developmental Psychology, 23,* 611–626.

Bassett, C. L. (2006). Laughing at gilded butterflies: Integrating wisdom, development, and learning. In C. Hoare (Ed.), *Handbook of adult development and learning* (pp. 196–218). New York: Oxford University Press.

Belenky, M. F., Clinchy, B. M., Goldberger, N. R., & Tarule, J. M. (1986). *Women's ways of knowing: The development of self, voice, and mind.* New York: Basic Books.

Brookfield, S. D. (1990). *The skillful teacher.* San Francisco: Jossey-Bass.

Bühler, C. (1935). *From birth to maturity.* London: Kegan Paul, Trench, & Trubner.

Chavez, A., & Guido-DiBrito, F. (1999). Racial and ethnic identity and development. In C. Clark & R. Caffarella (Eds.), *An update on adult development theory: New ways of thinking about the life course* (pp. 39–47). New Directions for Adult and Continuing Education, 84. San Francisco: Jossey-Bass.

Chickering, A. W., & Associates (1981). *The modern American college.* San Francisco: Jossey-Bass.

Chickering, A. W., & Reisser, L. (1993). *Education and identity* (2nd ed.). San Francisco: Jossey-Bass.

Clark, K. B., & Clark, M. P. (1939). The development of consciousness of self and the emergence of racial identification in Negro preschool children. *Journal of Social Psychology, 10,* 591–599.

Cross, W. E., Jr. (1971). Toward a psychology of Black liberation: The Negro-to-Black convergence experience. *Black World, 20*(9), 13–27.

Daloz, L. A. (1988). The story of Gladys who refused to grow: A morality tale for mentors. *Lifelong Learning: An Omnibus of Practice and Research, 11*(4), 4–7.

D'Amico, D. (2004). Race, class, gender, and sexual orientation in adult literacy: Power, pedagogy, and programs. In J. Comings, B. Garner, & C. Smith (Eds.), *Review of adult learning & literacy: Vol. 4. Connecting research, policy, and practice* (pp. 17–70). Mahwah, NJ: Lawrence Erlbaum.

Dorner, J., Mickler, C., & Staudinger, U. M. (2005). Self-development at midlife: Perspectives on adjustment and growth. In S. L. Willis & M. Martin (Eds.), *Middle adulthood: A lifespan perspective* (pp. 243–276). Thousand Oaks, CA: Sage.

Drago-Severson, E. (2004). *Becoming adult learners: Principles and practices for effective development.* New York: Teachers College Press.

Eriksen, J. (2006). The constructive developmental theory of Robert Kegan. *The Family Journal: Counseling and Therapy for Couples and Families, 14*(3), 290–298.

Erikson, E. H. (1959). *Identity and the life cycle.* New York: International Universities Press.

Erikson, E. H. (1964). *Childhood and society* (2nd ed.). New York: Norton. (Original work published 1950)

Erikson, E. H. (1968). *Identity: Youth and crisis.* New York: Norton.

Ferdman, B. M., & Gallegos, P. I. (2001). Racial identity development and Latinos in the United States. In B. W. Jackson III & C. L. Wijeyesinghe (Eds.), *New perspectives on racial identity development: A theoretical and practical anthology* (pp. 8–31). New York: New York University Press.

Freire, P. (1972). *Pedagogy of the oppressed.* London: Penguin.

Gaines, S. O., & Reed, E. (1995). Prejudice: From Allport to DuBois. *American Psychologist, 50,* 96–103.

George, L. K. (1993). Life events. In R. Kastenbaum (Ed.), *Encyclopedia of adult development* (pp. 277–278). Phoenix, AZ: Oryx Press.

Glasersfeld, E. von. (1996). Introduction: Aspects of constructivism. In C. T. Fosnot (Ed.), *Constructivism: Theory, perspectives, and practice* (pp. 3–7). New York: Teachers College Press.

Havighurst, R. J. (1972). *Developmental tasks and education.* New York: McKay.

Heisenberg, W. (1962). *Physics and philosophy: The revolution in modern science.* New York: Harper & Row.

Helms, J. E. (1995). An update of Helms' White and people of color racial identity models. In J. G. Ponterotto, J. M. Casas, L. A. Suzuki, & C. M. Alexander (Eds.), *Handbook of multicultural counseling.* Thousand Oaks, CA: Sage.

Hill, R. D. (2006). *Positive aging: A guide for mental health professionals and consumers.* New York: Norton.

Hoare, C. (Ed.). (2006). *Handbook of adult development and learning.* New York: Oxford University Press.

Hultsch, D. F., & Plemons, J. K. (1979). Life events and lifespan development. In P. B. Baltes & O. G. Brim, Jr. (Eds.), *Lifespan development and behavior* (Vol. 2, pp. 1–36). New York: Academic Press.

Jackson, B. W., III (2001). Black identity development: Further analysis and elaboration. In B. W. Jackson III & C. L. Wijeyesinghe (Eds.), *New perspectives on racial identity development: A theoretical and practical anthology* (pp. 8–31). New York: New York University Press.

Jensen-Arnett, J. (2000). Emerging adulthood: A theory of development from the late teens through the twenties. *American Psychologist, 55*, 469–480.

Kegan, R. (1982). *The evolving self: Problems and process in human development.* Cambridge, MA: Harvard University Press.

Kegan, R. (1994). *In over our heads? The mental demands of modern life.* Cambridge, MA: Harvard University Press.

Kegan, R. (2000). What form transforms? A constructive-developmental approach to transformative learning. In J. D. Mezirow (Ed.), *Learning as transformation* (pp. 35–70). San Francisco: Jossey-Bass.

Kim, J. (2001). Asian American identity development theory. In B. W. Jackson III & C. L. Wijeyesinghe (Eds.), *New perspectives on racial identity development: A theoretical and practical anthology* (pp. 67–90). New York: New York University Press.

Lerner, R. M. (2002). *Concepts and theories of human development* (3rd ed.). Mahwah, NJ: Lawrence Erlbaum.

Levinson, D. J. (1986). A conception of adult development. *American Psychologist, 41*, 3–13.

Levinson, D. J., Darrow, C. N., Klein, E. B., Levinson, M. H., & McKee, B. (1978). *The seasons of a man's life.* New York: Ballantine.

Lindeman, E. C. (1926). *The meaning of adult education.* New York: New Republic.

Loevinger, J. (1976). *Ego development.* San Francisco: Jossey-Bass.

Markus, H., & Nurius, P. (1987). Possible selves. *American Psychologist, 41*, 954–969.

Mermin, G. B. T., Johnson, R. W., & Murphy, D. P. (2007). Why do boomers plan to work longer? *The Journals of Gerontology Series B: Psychological Sciences and Social Sciences, 62*, S286–S294.

Merriam, S. B., & Brockett, R. G. (2007). *The profession and practice of adult education: An introduction.* San Francisco: Jossey-Bass.

Moen, P., Kelly, E., & Maginnis, R. (2008). Gender strategies: Socialization, allocation, and strategic selection processes shaping the adult life course. In M C. Smith (Ed.), *Handbook of research on adult learning and development* (pp. 376–409). New York: Routledge.

Parham, T. (1989). Cycles of psychological nigrescence. *The Counseling Psychologist, 17*(2), 187–226.

Perry, W. G. (1998). *Forms of intellectual and ethical development in the college years: A scheme.* San Francisco: Jossey-Bass.

Pinhey, T. K., & Pinhey, D. L. (2002). Life event timing and the emotional consequences of surgical menopause for Asian-Pacific women in Guam. *Women & Health, 36*(4), 43–54.

Reitzes, D. C. (2003). Social and emotional engagement in adulthood. In M. H. Bornstein, L. Davidson, C. L. M. Keyes, & K. A. Moore (Eds.), *Well-being: Positive development across the life course* (pp. 424–448). Mahwah, NJ: Lawrence Erlbaum.

Sinnott, J. D. (2008). Cognitive development as the dance of adaptive transformation: Neo-Piagetian perspectives on adult cognitive development. In M C. Smith (Ed.), *Handbook of research on adult learning and development* (pp. 103–134). New York: Routledge.

Soldz, S. (1988). The construction of meaning: Kegan, Piaget, and psychoanalysis. *Journal of Contemporary Psychotherapy, 18*(1), 46–59.

Stein, D. (2003–2004). The new meaning of retirement. *ERIC Digest.* Retrieved August 7, 2008, from http://www.ericdigests.org/2001–1/retirement.html

Taylor, K. (1996). Why psychological models of adult development are important for the practice of adult education: A response to Courtenay. *Adult Education Quarterly, 47*, 54–62.

Taylor, K. (2006). Autonomy and self-directed learning: A developmental journey. In C. Hoare (Ed.), *Handbook of adult development and learning* (pp. 196–218). New York: Oxford University Press.

Taylor, K., Marienau, C., & Fiddler, M. (2000). *Developing adult learners: Strategies for teachers and trainers.* San Francisco: Jossey-Bass.

Tennant, M., & Pogsen, S. (1995). *Learning and change in the adult years.* San Francisco: Jossey-Bass.

Thompson, D. (2008). A brief history of research and theory on adult learning and cognition. In M C. Smith (Ed.), *Handbook of research on adult learning and development* (pp. 463–483). New York: Routledge.

Troiden, R. R. (1993). The formation of homosexual identities. In L. D. Garnets & D.C. Kimmel (Eds.), *Psychological perspectives on lesbian and gay male experiences* (pp. 191–217). New York: Columbia University Press.

U.S. Bureau of the Census. (2006, May 25). *Americans marrying older, living alone more, see households shrinking.* Washington, DC: Author.

5

GROUP AND
ORGANIZATIONAL LEARNING

KAREN E. WATKINS AND VICTORIA J. MARSICK

We all know groups, companies, communities, or other institutions composed of many smart individuals who collectively do not benefit from all their members' knowledge. Sometimes, it's quite the opposite. As Peter Senge (1990, p. 9) inquired, "How can a team of committed managers with individual IQs above 120 have a collective IQ of 63?" This chapter is premised on the assumption that collective entities can and do learn, and it explores different conceptions of learning at the group and organizational levels.

Groups, communities, and organizations are human systems, and as such, they are structured consciously or unconsciously in ways that encourage or discourage people's learning. Argyris and Schön (1978, 1996), early scholars of organizational learning, argue that individuals learn on behalf of the system, and their learning is retained and passed on to others through artifacts, practices, processes, structures, or culture. Learning of systems is, therefore, necessarily affected by system properties that act as barriers or supports to learning and sharing knowledge (e.g., leadership, vision and mission, culture, dynamics, structure, communication, management, work practices and processes).

Some theorists (Nevis, DiBella, & Gould, 1995) have argued that group or organizational learning implies a natural state of adaptation to a changing environment, whether outcomes are positive, negative, or neutral. In other words, *all groups and organizations* organically learn. Early scholars took interest in this phenomenon when the environment was more local and stable. As the environment has become global and technology enabled, and subject to rapid change, leaders and educators have argued that systems can reap more benefits by proactively accelerating learning and knowledge sharing.

KEY THEORIES, PRACTICES, AND RESEARCH

Disciplines differently frame group and organizational learning (Dierkes, Berthoin Antal, Child, & Nonaka, 2001). The following framing concepts are drawn from social and organizational psychology.

Group Learning

For many reasons—size, greater ability to bound a system and research it, long history of group dynamics research—it may be easier to identify common agreement about group learning than organizational learning. Its foundation lies in group dynamics—for example, differentiating between task and interpersonal interaction behaviors (Bales & Strodbeck, 1951; Trist & Bamforth, 1951), looking at functional and dysfunctional group behaviors (Bion, 1961), and understanding how stages of group formation affect performance, as embodied in Tuckman's (1965) classic description of groups that move from forming to storming and norming before performing.

Bales and Strodtbeck's (1951) model of group development first distinguished between task-related and socioemotional behavior, as described in Trist and Bamforth's study of coal mining (1951). Group development theory posits that groups function in both social and work modes (i.e., group and task maintenance). Groups maintain themselves by attending to relationship needs that include encouraging, mediating, gatekeeping, and establishing norms. Group task functions help the group do its work and include initiating, information seeking and giving, clarifying, elaborating, and summarizing. Wilfred Bion (1961) identified work states of groups, as contrasted with nonwork states brought on by dysfunctional interpersonal dynamics: flight, fight, dependency, and pairing (i.e., forming cliques that splinter groups). Good group dynamics are necessary but not sufficient for collective learning.

Groups learn when members gain a shared understanding and/or set of capabilities. Various theories shed light on how groups learn—for example, through social learning or social cognitive learning theory, collective learning, or collaborative learning (Bandura, 1977). Theories focus on the impact of interpersonal interactions on what is learned through modeling by others, reinforcement of one's learning, or other social influences on meaning making.

Rose (1996) traces the historical roots and power of group learning in adult education, citing in particular the contributions of Lindeman (1926) and Follett (1919), who conceived of discussion in groups as central to social progress and democratic action. She noted in particular Lewin's (1951) field theory that prompted adult educators and change agents to engage groups in discussion and action for social change.

Teams are a subset of groups with common goals, practices, tasks, and processes. Kasl, Marsick, and Dechant (1997) developed a model of team learning based on research over time in two different organizations. They identified key learning processes—framing/reframing, experimenting, crossing boundaries, and integrating perspectives—that differentiate the degree of shared team learning. The authors hypothesize that some teams remain a fragmented group of relatively individual contributors, whereas other teams form subgroups of pooled learning or even more cohesive subgroups of synergistic learning. Their studies show how team members, to a greater or lesser degree, cross boundaries (physical, mental, or organizational) to seek or give information and ideas. Teams use new ideas to examine the initial ways that they understood or framed situations. They engage in conversations and experiment in ways that help them to reframe their initial understandings and integrate diverse perspectives such that conflicts are resolved or used to make new meanings. Kasl, Marsick, and Dechant also identified team conditions that are critical for effective group learning, specifically, the use of operating principles (e.g., governing effective task, leadership, and interpersonal behaviors), freedom of individual expression, and a cultural norm appreciating and supporting teamwork.

Edmondson (2002) examined group learning in health care and business organizations. She specifically looked at error detection and correction, and identified practices that people engage in when groups learn, such as experimenting and engaging in conversations and feedback so that people learn from errors. Edmonson underscores the "local, interpersonal, and variegated" nature of such learning, and concludes "that team members' perceptions of power and interpersonal risk affect the quality of team reflection, which has implications for their team's and their organization's ability to change" (p. 128).

Diversity is central to engaging new ideas and thinking, although even diverse groups can be configured in ways that reinforce existing views rather than challenging them. According to fMRI studies in the brain conducted by Westen (2007), when individuals hold strong beliefs, their reason can shut down and powerful emotions prevail, reinforcing a priori mindsets and making it difficult or impossible for them to be open to perspectives entailing painful choices.

While honoring conditions that may make it difficult to benefit from diversity, Paige (2007, p. 13) argues that diversity generally leads to better outcomes and notes that "identity diversity produces better outcomes indirectly. Any claim that identity diversity creates collective benefits requires two links. The first link connects identity diversity to cognitive diversity. The second link connects these diverse talents to relevant problems." These concerns are broader than group learning, and they affect human relationships in all settings.

Watson, BarNir, and Pavur (2005) found that work teams with ethnically diverse membership exhibited fewer team-oriented behaviors and more self-oriented behaviors, and were less effective overall. They suggested that ethnic heterogeneity created difficulty early in the team's life cycle, and yet these same differences resulted in more creativity later on (Watson, Kumar, & Michaelson, 2003). Negative effects of diversity diminish over time, particularly with process feedback to teams. Similarly to Westen (2007), Beesley (2004) noted another form of diversity—differences in prior knowledge—that has an impact on team members' ability to assimilate information that is perceived not to fit existing knowledge structures.

Drawing on literacy research based in constructive-developmental theories, Drago-Severson (2004) argues that developmental diversity affects meaning making in ways that catalyze or interfere with group effectiveness. She found that individuals' "way of knowing" influences their capacity to engage in groups, teams, and cohorts. For example, "self authoring knowers" thrive on conflicting views, but not so "rule-oriented knowers," who need clarity, or "socializing knowers," who need important "others" to sanction choices among diverse views. Adults need different forms of support and challenge to work most effectively in teams and to grow from participation, and they have different expectations of team leaders and authorities. Educators and leaders will want to consider different ways adults can demonstrate competence and thus scrutinize group goals, roles, and processes. Enhanced awareness of developmental diversity can help leaders and educators adjust expectations and interventions to improve the fit between learning challenge and *developmental* capacity.

These studies show there are many kinds of diversity, many of which affect team performance. Kleinman and Palmon (2009) observed a four-stage model of decision making from diversity to controversy, insight, and resolution. Their work suggests that all groups experience a period of "stranger-ness" that requires moving from individual to group-oriented functioning.

Underlying these perspectives is a conception that groups as a collective entity can learn. Fenwick (2008) identified eight distinct views of individual and collective relations in learning: individual knowledge acquisition; sense-making/reflective dialogue; levels of learning; network utility; individual human development; individuals in community; communities-of-practice; and co-participation or co-emergence through which individuals reciprocally influence, and are influenced by, the collective. The workplace context was found to be central, yet two contrasting views of the context—as a web of relations or as a container—framed individual ontological orientations.

Group and team learning focus on a local level; yet, these are often the same enabling structures through which individuals implement organizational learning.

Conceptualizing Organizational Learning

Views of organizational learning were at first primarily behavioral, but over time, they have become cognitive and social. According to Easterby-Smith and Lyles (2003, p. 9), "The idea that an organization could *learn* in ways that were independent of the individuals within it was the key breakthrough, which was first articulated by Cyert and March (1963)," who formulated "a general theory of organizational learning" with emphasis on "rules, procedures, and routines in response to external shocks . . . which are more or less likely to be adopted according to whether or not they lead to positive consequences for the organization."

By contrast, Argyris (1999) and Argyris and Schön (1978, 1996) emphasize a cognitive, and sociocultural view. They define organizational learning as Dewey-based inquiry by individuals on behalf of the organization, with a focus on errors that trigger learning when desired outcomes are not achieved. Argyris and Schön differentiate between changing tactics when error occurs in order to achieve one's desired goals (single-loop learning) and probing underlying assumptions, beliefs, or values that show how one has framed a situation and taken actions in unproductive ways (double-loop learning). Double-loop learning helps to reframe thinking and action to achieve stated objectives.

Easterby-Smith and Lyles (2003, p. 10) point out that a contrasting view of organizational learning emanates from a social constructivist perspective. Rational, cognitive views of organizational learning focus on objective ways that products or information can be stored, manipulated, accessed, and used apart from the people who create ideas, learn, and share knowledge. By contrast, a social constructivist view posits that people actively co-create knowledge in action through social processes. Garavan and McCarthy (2008) locate differing views, such as these, along three axes: individual to collective, behavioral to cognitive, and prescriptive to descriptive.

Organizational Learning Perspectives

We have divided our discussion of organizational learning into two broad categories based on differing views of how learning takes place and knowledge is created and utilized:

- An innovation-and-organizational-knowledge perspective that emphasizes storing, retrieving, and managing knowledge, and finding ways to harvest the tacit knowledge embedded in routines and processes to use that knowledge on behalf of the whole system, and

- A culture perspective that emphasizes a more organic process of social construction of meaning and co-creation of knowledge, and that focuses on the ways that culture informs, catalyzes, or inhibits learning and knowledge sharing.

These perspectives are described in greater detail below.

Innovation-and-organizational-knowledge perspective. For organizational learning to occur, results must be embedded in a system's artifacts. The shorthand for this concept is organizational memory (Walsh & Ungson, 1991). Organizations store knowledge that represents rules, procedures,

routines, and other practices that become core competencies for the firm (Hamel & Prahalad, 1990). Some of this knowledge is, and remains, tacit. Other knowledge is made explicit, codified, and invoked through policies or standardized procedures. Organizational memory is achieved and continuously reinterpreted by people who act on behalf of the organization.

Knowledge management and intellectual capital scholars focus on tangible outcomes of organizational learning: knowledge as a product, its management within the system, and its contribution to results, conceptualized as intellectual capital. Many knowledge assets, then, are intangibles resident in people or embedded in systems and products they create. Stewart (1997) described three components of intellectual capital: human capital (people working in a system), structural capital (what remains behind when people leave—i.e., systems, policies, processes, tools), and customer capital (a system of relationships with clients).

Nonaka and Takeuchi (1995) take a social constructivist view. They have proposed an interactive, spiral, iterative organizational learning cycle that moves from socialized tacit knowledge to externalized explicit knowledge that again becomes socialized. Tacit knowledge grows as people unconsciously share experiences, mental models, and skills when they work. Knowledge can be drawn out explicitly, and ideas built into archetypes and tested through new product development. These ideas are explicitly shared throughout the organization, or cross-leveled, so that workers can experiment with them elsewhere in the company. Finally, the newly evolved ideas are resocialized. Five organizational conditions support this knowledge creation process: intention, fluctuation/chaos, autonomy, redundancy, and requisite variety. Nonaka and Takeuchi advocate using this cycle to foster innovation.

The innovation-and-knowledge perspective has led to several foci, including knowledge management, the balanced scorecard (Kaplan & Norton, 1996), technology transfer, intellectual and social capital. Scholars with this view emphasize what of value the organization learned, and how to retain and diffuse that learning. Theories within this perspective are aligned with earlier work on innovation development and diffusion, and on change and change agents.

Learning culture perspective. Schein (1996) argued that we focus too much on individual and group dynamics and that the idea of organizational learning refocuses us on the culture as the primary means of changing the capacity of the organization. Culture, Schein argued, "is both the consequence of the organization's prior experience and learning and the basis for its continuing capacity to learn" (p. 3). In Schein's view, culture influences what organizations do. "And the long-range adaptability of the organization will depend upon its ability to perpetuate the core elements of its culture through socialization processes, while maintaining enough slack to allow for the evolution of new cultural assumptions to take into account new ideas" (p. 3).

Schein and others who adopt this perspective are concerned with changing the organization's capacity to learn toward greater organizational health. Schein defines such health as consisting of these capacities: (1) a sense of identity, purpose, or mission; (2) a capacity on the part of the system to adapt and maintain itself in the face of internal and external changes; (3) a capacity to perceive and test reality; and (4) some degree of internal integration or alignment of the subsystems that make up the total system.

Argyris and Schön (1996) define organizational learning as error detection and correction; and they focus on how culture shapes, supports, or inhibits learning of individuals, groups, and the organization. Single-loop learning involves a change of strategies or tactics in light of a mismatch between what is intended and what occurs. Double-loop learning allows for a deeper analysis of the assumptions, values, or beliefs that cause one to define a situation as one does in the first place. It may not be enough to change strategies or tactics; one may have to redefine the question or situation in order to allow for breakthrough thinking.

A field-based study illustrating this perspective is Meyer's (1982) study of 19 hospitals in northern California. Meyer had completed field observations in each hospital when the doctors went on strike because a malpractice insurer dropped 4,000 California doctors and offered to reinsure them as individuals at a 384% increase. This unanticipated "environmental jolt" allowed him to collect data on the organizations' responses to the strike.

Meyer developed an organizational learning model to describe what happens when a jolt triggers a learning cycle. Strategy (an organization's overall business approach to its environment) and ideology (the beliefs, mission, and values that drive action) determine what captures an organization's attention, and therefore, how its leaders frame the challenge. The organization's response is influenced by structure and the system of relationships in the organization, and by slack, the available human, financial, and technological resources to use in responding to the shock.

Meyer found that the organization either absorbed the impact of the jolt without changing in any fundamental way, or retained new practices or information gained during the change experience. Strategy and slack help organizations absorb the shock of jolts, but lead to change that occurs only incrementally and within the same framework (first-order change or single-loop learning). Slack gives an organization the cushion needed to absorb impact, but an organization's dominant strategy leads organizations to a consistent way of framing problems. For double-loop learning, changes have to occur at the cultural or vision-and-values level, or through a change in the overall system of relationships (the structure).

Scholars and practitioners who adopt this approach focus on how culture shapes action, and how leaders help organizations effectively respond to turbulent environments. This view is aligned with an organization development perspective.

KEY FORMS, PROCESSES, AND STRUCTURES

Scholars who intentionally catalyze group and organizational learning adopt a proactive "learning organization concept" popularized by Senge (1990), who defined it as an organization with five disciplines that enabled continuous, effective, organizational learning. In such organizations, leaders excel at these five disciplines: personal mastery, team learning, mental models, shared vision, and systems thinking—the latter being the integrator and catalyst of the other disciplines. Senge focused on using system archetypes to diagnose and fix systemic problems and on changing organization culture.

Practically speaking, the facilitator of such learning must be a master both of adult learning and of group/organizational development and change processes. The guidelines we proposed (Marsick & Watkins, 1999) for this purpose build on an organization development and action research framework. We think they apply as much today as they did a decade ago. We recommend diagnosing the situation, creating a vision, building alignment around the vision, engaging people in collaborative experiments, monitoring outcomes, and returning to the beginning steps of diagnosis and visioning, leading to a new round of experiments. Two "tools" we advocate to guide change involve diagnosing the situation through a learning culture survey and engaging key stakeholders in action learning to enact change.

Diagnosing and Strengthening the Learning Culture

Watkins and Marsick (1993, 1996, 2003) developed a diagnostic tool, the Dimensions of the Learning Organization Questionnaire (DLOQ), to assess perceptions of organizational learning and culture based on their learning organization model. The instrument diagnoses elements in an organization's climate, culture, systems, and structures that influence an organization's overall adaptiveness. The instrument has been tested and modified through numerous research studies across multiple languages, contexts, and cultures (Watkins & Marsick, 2003).

Yang, Watkins, and Marsick (2004) measured organizational performance against the DLOQ and established a correlation between the learning organization dimensions and measures of knowledge and financial performance. Subsequent studies by Ellinger, Ellinger, Yang, and Howton (2002) and Davis and Daley (2008) used actual organizational performance data to confirm the relationship between the learning culture dimensions and measures of overall knowledge and financial performance. Research results like these have obtained in profit, not-for-profit, government, and other settings. Although other variables could explain financial outcomes—for example, organizational size, access to raw materials, market niche, or competition—study results suggest an important

relationship between the DLOQ learning dimensions and changes in knowledge and financial performance.

Studies confirm the value of diagnosing the organization's learning culture to identify areas to change in order to leverage learning for optimal performance in the organization (see Gephart & Marsick, forthcoming). Research using the DLOQ (Watkins & Marsick, 2003) indicates that measures of individual- and group-level learning—creating continuous learning opportunities, promoting inquiry and dialogue, encouraging collaboration and team learning, and empowering people toward a collective vision—have indirect but significant effects on organizational outcomes. Individual and group learning variables are highly interrelated. Three organizational-level variables—connecting the organization to its environment, creating systems to capture and share learning, and providing strategic leadership for learning—serve as mediators of the relationship between team and individual learning activities and organizational outcomes.

Action Learning

Lewin (1951) believed that to understand social phenomena, a theory needs to be broad enough to encompass the multifaceted nature of human action, and that the way to test that theory was through *action research*. Action research is an iterative cycle of problem formulation, data collection and analysis, intervention, monitoring, assessment and problem reformulation, and it can be thought of as a series of successive approximations—group experiments that, through trial and error, explore and implement changes to systems. Interventions are made and their effects studied on multiple levels of the system, leading to a new set of interventions, and thus reengaging the same cycle.

Action learning (AL), a form of action research, is an approach to developing people that emphasizes learning from and through experience by working on a meaningful problem. AL is currently used in many organizations, often for leadership development, and has been used successfully in profit, not-for-profit, educational, and community settings.

In AL, participants learn as they work in small groups to examine and take action on a problem. A learning coach often works with the group to help the members learn how to balance task accomplishment and learning. Groups can work together on a single project, or peers can support one another through work on unique individual challenges. The focus on individual versus team projects influences the degree of emphasis on individual versus organizational change. Team projects often focus on organizational goals, while individual projects often focus on personal development. AL programs can last from several days to up to a year. AL looks different because purposes vary and its design changes to fit an organization's culture and goals (O'Neil & Marsick, 2007).

AL challenges are complex and systemic, not easily solvable by expert solutions, and have problems over whose solution reasonable people would disagree. Experimentation, questioning, and reflection on results undergird AL. Revans (1998), a British physicist often considered the father of AL, defined learning as interaction between programmed knowledge and questioning insight, captured in the equation: $L = P + Q$. Thus, learning (L) takes place when the programmed knowledge (P) of books and experts has questioning insight (Q) applied to it, enabling new light to be shed on perplexing problems.

AL can build capabilities in individuals, and, through collaboration and sharing, in groups and sometimes the entire system. Key conditions in the organization affect the extent, nature, and duration of learning and whether/how it affects performance. AL can be an effective approach to promoting multilevel group and organizational learning and change, although research on such effects is limited.

In summary, both DLOQ and AL interventions address all three learning levels—individual, group, and organization—through diagnosis, learning via experimentation and reflection, and informed action. Interventions that support group and organizational learning must, like these two approaches, work at multiple levels that take interactive effects into account.

EMERGING TRENDS

The emerging trends discussed here that influence group and organizational learning include globalization's impact and new conceptualizations of how people work in groups, notably communities of practice.

Global Work, Global Competition

With the rise of global competition, global workforces, and widespread access to information through cyber networks, workers' knowledge has become a primary source of national competitiveness. Moreover, national capabilities—for example, human resource policies, economic and technological development levels—advantage some countries over others. Such disparities create the potential for information-rich and information-poor people, organizations, and societies.

Labor force demographics are also changing. According to the Rand Corporation (2004), the U.S. labor force is shrinking, aging, and becoming more diverse. These change are due to fluctuations in birth rates over the last few decades, immigration (especially Hispanics and Asians), and increased participation of women in the labor force. Organizations are outsourcing many jobs to save money and augment a workforce that is too small or unskilled (Workplace Visions, 2005). Education and skill levels create wage gaps. To cut costs, companies increasingly hire part-time or temporary workers and cut training benefits. Changes such as these greatly influence learning in groups and organizations. Time constraints value output over learning, and less available expertise may deplete knowledge assets.

A Rand (2004) study noted that "The new era of globalization—marked by growing trade in intermediate goods and services, expanding capital flows, more rapid transfer of knowledge and technologies, and mobile populations—partly results from inexpensive, rapid communications and information transmission enabled by the IT revolution" (p. 2). As firms move away from vertically integrated organizations, they outsource noncore functions and become more decentralized. This will likely lead to "a shift away from more permanent, lifetime jobs toward less permanent, even nonstandard employment relationships (e.g., self-employment) and work arrangements (e.g., distance work)" (p. 2).

Globalization has increased work done in virtual groups and cross-cultural groups. Consequently, group behavior—and learning and performance—is increasingly affected by differences in communication media, cultural and organizational histories, transitoriness, and even instability. Milton, Watkins, and Daley (2005) studied group facilitator behaviors across nine virtual groups and 312 facilitator interventions. They compared facilitator interventions in these virtual groups with those identified in group and action learning literature. They found few differences in facilitator interventions beyond those that focused on the technology itself. Although research is accumulating on virtual teams (e.g., Shipley, Johnson, & Hashemi, 2009), the escalating reliance on technology, especially by youth, combined with an unstable global economy make it difficult to project how group learning will evolve.

Communities of Practice

Work in the last decade on communities of practice and networks has reframed fundamental ideas about group learning by incorporating new units of analysis and new forms of organizing that accommodate the globally dispersed, diverse, and temporary structures now common in workplaces. Networks are loose configurations of people linked by temporary needs, whereas communities of practice bring people together around a common interest over time. Both networks and communities of practice change in composition and intensity of involvement based on members' motivation to engage, more or less intensively, with one another.

Group learning in communities of practice is situated and explained by social learning theory (Lave & Wenger, 1991; Wenger, 1998). Communities of practice members share a common identity and learn from and with one another as they pursue interests, opportunities, and challenges:

> The concept of practice connotes doing, but not just doing in and of itself. It is doing in a historical and social context that gives structure and meaning to what we do. In this sense, practice is always social practice.
>
> Such a concept of practice includes both the explicit and the tacit. It includes what is said and what is left unsaid; what is represented and what is assumed. It includes the language, tools, documents, images, symbols, well-defined roles, specified criteria, codified procedures, regulations, and contracts that various practices make explicit for a variety of purposes. But it also includes all the

implicit relations, tacit conventions, subtle cues, untold rules of thumb, recognizable intuitions, specific perceptions, well-tuned sensitivities, embodied understandings, underlying assumptions, and shared world-views. Most of these may never be articulated, yet they are unmistakable signs of membership in communities of practice and are crucial to the success of their enterprises. (Wenger, 1998, p. 47)

Network members, by contrast, contact one another when need arises (Van Wijk, Van den Bosch, & Volderba, 2003). It is argued that the nature of learning and knowledge differs when networks involve close ties that bring people together frequently, allowing for sharing of tacit knowledge based on common experiences, versus when networks involve loose ties that allow members to gather information rapidly, though in a shallower and more explicit fashion, by tapping into contacts with whom they seldom interact. Network learning is an important recent development that, like communities of practice, builds bridges between the learning of smaller, more cohesive groups and that of the entire organization.

CONCLUSION

In sum, we have argued that groups learn and organizations may learn through tapping into and sharing knowledge that is then embedded in cultures, structure, practices, and systems so that it persists over time, even when people move on. Diversity is important for generating new ideas and tapping into valuable perspectives and capabilities that are especially important in light of globalization and demographic shifts. Profound changes in the nature of work, of the workforce, and of organizational processes and structures are encouraging new forms of group and organizational learning. The rate of change in the world of work is, itself, undergoing acceleration driven now by radical economic and sociodemographic transformations that will impact work in ways barely—or perhaps not even at all—imaginable. This chapter summarizes the current state of theory and praxis. Academics, in concert with colleagues in practice, will need to investigate and experiment within the evolving context to bring new understandings so that group and organizational learning will operate optimally to benefit a world increasingly under economic and social duress.

REFERENCES

Argyris, C. (1999). *On organizational learning.* Malden, MA: Blackwell.

Argyris, C., & Schön, D. (1978). *Organizational learning: A theory of action perspective.* San Francisco: Jossey-Bass.

Argyris, C., & Schön, D. (1996). *Organizational learning II: Theory, method, and practice.* Reading, MA: Addison-Wesley.

Bales, R. F., & Strodbeck, F. L. (1951). Phases in group problem solving. *Journal of Abnormal and Social Psychology, 46,* 485–495.

Bandura, A. (1977). *Social learning theory.* Englewood Cliffs, NJ: Prentice Hall.

Beesley, L. (2004). Multi-level complexity in the management of knowledge networks. *Journal of Knowledge Management, 8*(3), 71–88.

Bion, W. (1961). *Experiences in groups.* London: Tavistock.

Cseh, M., Watkins, K. E., & Marsick, V. J. (1999). Re-conceptualizing Marsick and Watkins' model of informal and incidental learning in the workplace. In K. P. Kuchinke (Ed.), *1999 Proceedings of the Academy of HRD* (pp. 349–355). Baton Rouge, LA: Academy of Human Resource Development.

Cyert, R. M., & March, J. G. (1963). *A behavioural theory of the firm.* Englewood Cliffs, NJ: Prentice Hall.

Davis, D., & Daley, B. (2008). The learning organization and its dimensions as key factors in firms' performance. *Human Resources Development International, 11*(1), 51–66.

Dierkes, M., Berthoin Antal, A., Child, J., & Nonaka, I. (Eds.). (2001). *Handbook of organizational learning.* Oxford, UK: Oxford University Press.

Drago-Severson, E. (2004). *Becoming adult learners.* New York: Teachers College Press.

Easterby-Smith, M., & Lyles, M. A. (2003). *The Blackwell handbook of organizational learning and knowledge management.* Malden, MA: Blackwell.

Edmondson, A. (2002). The local and variegated nature of learning in organizations: A group-level perspective. *Organization Science, 13*(2), 128–146.

Ellinger, A. D., Ellinger, A. E., Yang, B., & Howton. S. W. (2002). The relationship between the learning organization concept and firms' financial performance: An empirical assessment. *Human Resource Development Quarterly, 13*(1), 5–21.

Fenwick, T. (2008). Understanding relations of individual-collective learning in work: A review of research. *Management Learning, 39*(3), 227–244.

Follett, M. P. (1919). Community is a process. *Philosophical Review, XXVIII,* 576–588.

Garavan, T., & McCarthy, A. (2008). Collective learning processes and human resource development. *Advances in Developing Human Resources, 10*(4), 451–471.

Gephart, M. A., & Marsick, V. J. (forthcoming). *Strategic organizational learning.* New York: Springer.

Hamel, G., & Prahalad, C. K. (1990, May–June). The core competence of the corporation. *Harvard Business Review,* pp. 79–91.

Kaplan, R. S., & Norton, D. P. (1996). *Balanced scorecard: Translating strategy into action.* Cambridge, MA: Harvard Business School Press.

Kasl, E., Marsick, V. J., & Dechant, K. (1997). Teams as learners: A research-based model of team learning. *The Journal of Applied Behavioral Science, 33*(2), 227–246.

Kleinman, G., & Palmon, D. (2009). Procedural instrumentality and audit group judgment: An exploration of the impact of cognitive fallibility and ability differences. *Group Decision and Negotiation, 18*(2), 147–168.

Lave, J., & Wenger, E. (1991). *Situated learning: Legitimate peripheral participation.* New York: Cambridge University Press.

Lewin, K. (1951). *Field theory in social science: Selected theoretical papers.* New York: HarperCollins.

Lindeman, E. (1926). *The meaning of adult education.* New York: New Republic.

Marsick, V. J., & Watkins, K. E. (1999). *Facilitating the learning organization.* Surrey, UK: Gower.

Meyer, A. (1982). Adapting to environmental jolts. *Administrative Science Quarterly, 27*(4), 515–537.

Milton, J., Watkins, K. E., & Daley, B. J. (2005). Virtual OD: Facilitating groups online. In M. L. Morris & F. M. Nafukho (Eds.), *Proceedings of the Academy of Human Resource Development,* Estes Park, CO, Feb. 24–27 (pp. 1287–1294). St. Paul, MN: Academy of Human Resource Development.

Nevis, E. D., DiBella, A. J., & Gould, J. M. (1995). Understanding organizations as learning systems. *Sloan Management Review, 36*(2), 73–85.

Nonaka, H., & Takeuchi, I. (1995). *The knowledge-creating company: How Japanese companies create the dynamics of innovation.* Oxford, UK: Oxford University Press.

O'Neil, J., & Marsick, V. J. (2007). *Understanding action learning.* New York: AMACOM.

Paige, S. E. (2007). *The difference: How the power of diversity creates better groups, firms, schools, and societies.* Princeton, NJ: Princeton University Press.

Rand Corporation. (2004). The future at work: trends and implications. Retrieved October 15, 2005, from http://www.rand.org/publications/RB/RB5070

Revans, R. W. (1998) *The ABC of action learning.* London: Lemos & Crane.

Rose, A. D. (1996). *Group learning in adult education: Its historical roots, Learning in groups: exploring fundamental principles, new uses, and emerging opportunities.* New Directions in Adult and Continuing Education, Number 71. San Francisco: Jossey-Bass.

Schein, E. (1996, June 28). *On organizational learning: What is new?* Invited address to the Third Biennial International Conference on Advances in Management, Sheraton Tara Hotel, Framingham, MA.

Senge, P. (1990). *The fifth discipline: The art and practice of the learning organization.* New York: Random House.

Shipley, M. F., Johnson, M., & Hashemi, S. (2009). Cognitive learning style and its effects on the perception of learning, satisfaction and social interactions in virtual teams. *American Academy of Business, 14*(2), 17. Retrieved February 12, 2009, from http//:www.uhd.edu/computing/ciday/images/

Stewart, T. A. (1997). *Intellectual capital: The new wealth of organizations.* New York: Currency Doubleday.

Trist, E., & Bamforth, K. (1951). Some social and psychological consequences of the longwall method of coal-getting. *Human Relations, 4,* 3–38.

Tuckman, B. W. (1965). Developmental sequence in small groups. *Psychological Bulletin, 63,* 384–399.

Van Wijk, R., Van den Bosch, F. A. J., & Volderba, H. W. (2003). Knowledge and networks. In M. Easterby-Smith & M. A. Lyles (Eds.), *The Blackwell handbook of organizational learning and knowledge management* (pp. 428–453). Malden, MA: Blackwell.

Walsh, J. P., & Ungson, G. R. (1991). Organizational memory. *Academy of Management Review, 16*(1), 239–270.

Watkins, K. E., & Marsick, V. J. (1993). *Sculpting the learning organization.* San Francisco: Jossey-Bass.

Watkins, K. E., & Marsick, V. J. (Eds.). (1996). *In action: Creating the learning organization.* Alexandria, VA: American Society for Training & Development.

Watkins, K. E., & Marsick, V. J. (Eds.). (2003). *Making learning count! Diagnosing the learning culture in organizations. Advances in developing human resources* (Vol. 5, No. 2). Thousand Oaks, CA: Sage and the Academy of Human Resource Development.

Watson, W., BarNir, A., & Pavur, R. (2005). Cultural diversity and learning teams: The impact on desired academic team processes. *International Journal of Intercultural Relations, 29,* 449–467.

Watson, W., Kumar, K., & Michaelson, L. (2003). Cultural diversity's impact on interaction process and performance: Comparing homogeneous and diverse task groups. *Academy of Management Journal, 36*(3) 590–602.

Wenger, E. (1998). *Communities of practice.* Cambridge, UK: Cambridge University Press.

Westen, D. (2007). *The political brain: The role of emotion in deciding the fate of the nation.* New York: Public Affairs.

Workplace Visions. (2005), Learning to compete in a knowledge economy. *Society for Human Resource Management Workplace Trends Program, 3.* Retrieved October 8, 2005, from http://www.shrm.org/trends/visions/

Yang, B., Watkins, K. E., & Marsick, V. J. (2004). The construct of the learning organization: Dimensions, measurement, and validation. *Human Resource Development Quarterly. 15*(1), 31–56.

PART II

CREATION OF OPEN EXCHANGES OF KNOWLEDGE, THEORY, AND PRACTICE

6

THEORETICAL FRAMEWORKS FOR UNDERSTANDING THE FIELD

STEPHEN D. BROOKFIELD

Theorizing is one of the most practical things adult educators do. To adapt Gramsci's (1971) aphorism that all adults are intellectuals, we can say that all adult educators are theorists. That is, all adult educators make decisions and come to judgments based on assumptions, instincts, hunches, and explicit understandings that are theoretical. Deciding what conditions best foster learning, sequencing instructional activities a certain way, presenting ourselves as teachers at the start of a course—all these practical actions have a theoretical dimension to them because they meet three conditions. First, they arise out of a comparative analysis. We ask colleagues how they deal with certain situations, we consult textbooks that purport to describe best practices for us, and we think about our past experiences. Second, these actions are predictive. We do these things because we believe they will have certain consequences such as making new concepts understandable, keeping energy and attention high, or improving students' ability to see the connections between the new knowledge they are learning and their already developed skill sets. Third, we extend our explanation of one event (such as how we dealt with resistance to learning with one student or a particular group of learners) to cover other situations that seem similar. Our assumption is that a hunch that seemed to be borne out with one student or class is useful enough to be broadened to help us deal with others.

A framework of ideas that guides our practice can be called theoretical when it meets the conditions outlined above: (a) it generalizes beyond the case of individual experience (we compare our experiences of dealing with racism in class with accounts of others), (b) it is predictive (a practitioner decides, "If I do A, then B will happen," as in "If I put the chairs into a circle, it will foster good classroom discussion"), and (c) it covers a whole category of events (as when a theory of motivation attempts to explain the different reasons adults show up for learning). These theoretical frameworks are often implicit rather than explicit, but that does not mean they are any less powerful in shaping action. They are the benchmarks we use to assess whether or not we are doing good work. And they are never developed in isolation. What might appear to be our private, idiosyncratic theories of practice are actually connected to, and to some degree shaped by, bodies of thought developed collectively by, and with, colleagues. The collective generation of frameworks for understanding the field is what is called theory development.

In past *Handbooks* some of the dominant theoretical frameworks that have been identified as influencing the field have included behaviorism, humanistic psychology, self-directed and autonomous learning, experiential learning, and conscienti-zation. For the first half of the 20th century the framework of a Dewey-inspired democratic pragmatism dominated, most famously repre-sented by Lindeman (1926/1961; Lindeman & Smith, 1951), was paramount. Here adult educa-tion was conceived as the experimental pursuit of democracy. In the second half of the 20th century a Rogerian-derived humanistic psychol-ogy was strongly influential, particularly in Knowles's adumbration of andragogy as a form of adult-specific educational practice (Knowles, 1984) and his identification of self-directed learning as the natural form of adult learning (Knowles, 1983). Here the emphasis was on helping learners develop their individual poten-tial, both in a self-directed manner and also in problem-solving groups. Concurrently a differ-ent emphasis emerged in the consciousness-raising work of Freire (1993, 2001), in which the focus was on working to challenge material and ideological domination.

In the predecessor to the current volume, the 2000 *Handbook of Adult and Continuing Education* (Wilson & Hayes, 2000), the editors used critical reflection as the guiding theoretical framework. Adult education conceived as criti-cally reflective practice built on the traditions of democratic pragmatism and Freirean praxis to explore how adults came to recognize and sub-vert power dynamics and how they came to acknowledge and challenge hegemony. Critical reflection was the umbrella concept used in the 2000 *Handbook* to encompass a range of profes-sional concerns that placed adult learning and adult educational practice squarely in the social realm. Learning how to challenge racism, clas-sism, sexism, homophobia, and ableism became an explicit part of the adult education agenda.

In this chapter I begin where the 2000 *Handbook* left off. I review some theoretical frameworks that have either entered the dis-course and practice of the field since that time or been reaffirmed as enduringly relevant. All these theories deal with a central question: What does it mean to be critical in a diverse world distin-guished by ideological manipulation and struc-tured inequity? Using the development of critical reflection as a starting point, adult edu-cators have tried to understand what learning people need to oppose the social and economic forces that attempt to turn us into privatized

individuals connected atomistically via cyber-space. They have become increasingly attentive to identity politics and the ways in which hege-mony reconfigures itself in ever more subtle ways to structure access to resources and the exercise of agency along lines of race, class, and gender. The complexities of working with diver-sity and dealing with constant technological rev-olution have rendered easy generalizations and explanatory models hard to come by. But the attempt to develop guidelines for practice has led to the emergence of several theoretical frameworks that currently shape the discourse of adult education. Prominent among these are Africentrism, queer theory, critical theory, criti-cal race theory, feminist theory, postmodernism, and transformative learning theory. This chapter explores these different approaches to under-standing and practicing critically reflective adult education.

AFRICENTRISM

Merriweather Hunn (2004) defines Africentrism as "the written articulation of indigenous African philosophy (an oral tradition) as embodied by the lived experiences of multiple generations of people of African descent" (p. 68). Africentrism draws on African-centered values and traditions to argue that African American learners and educators—indeed all members of the African diaspora—need to work in ways shaped by those values and traditions rather than follow the Eurocentric norm. As developed most promi-nently by Colin (1988, 2002; Closson, 2006), the Africentric paradigm reconceptualizes adult learning and development as a collective, not individual, process in which *I Am Because We Are* (Hord & Lee, 1995). One's own interests and identity are deemed to be inextricably inter-twined with the well-being of the tribal collec-tive, an approach that in Colin and Guy's (1998) view, "differs significantly from traditional Eurocentric perspectives of individualism, competition, and hierarchical forms of author-ity and decision-making" (p. 50). To Colin and Guy, the Swahili notions of *Ujima* (collective work and responsibility) and *Ujamaa* (cooper-ative economics, most famously evident in Nyrere's African socialism) are grounded in African rather than traditional Eurocentric cultural values, and are at the heart of adult learning. The Africentric paradigm conceives adult education as a process of developing African-based cognitive and socioeconomic structures that stress community, interdependence, and collective action.

The aforementioned values match a particular curricular orientation to adult education, one that focuses on self-ethnic liberation and empowerment. Arguing for a philosophy of self-ethnic reliance, Colin and Guy (1998) argue that African American adult education programs must be "designed to counteract the sociocultural and the socio-psychological effects of racism" (p. 47). Adopting Colin's (1988, 2002) emphasis on self-ethnic reflectors, such a curriculum should be developed by members of the ethnic or racial group that have lived the experience of racism and should reflect and affirm the racial identity and traditions of Africans rather than Europeans. Africentric adult education practices and understandings must be generated outside the dominant Eurocentric ideology. In Colin and Guy's opinion, an Africentric practice of adult education "means that the selection, discussion and critique of African Ameripean/African American content must not occur based on using standards or criteria arising from traditional Eurocentric perspectives. Rather, selection of content about African Ameripean/African American adult education is based on an Africentric perspective" (1998, p. 51).

The Africentric theoretical paradigm has prompted other efforts at racially based scholarship and led to an awareness of the importance of racially based ways of knowing (Brookfield, 2003) among majority scholars. It has inspired a continuing and major preconference at the annual Adult Education Research Conference and has widened the range of scholarship evident in the field. In terms of specific adult educational practices, it has underscored the need for programs in which a racial group is taught by members of that group who are attuned to its cultural rhythms and who provide ethnic reflectors for the learners. It has challenged and widened the range of practices seen in adult educational classrooms. Prime examples of this would be the acceptance of "gumbo ya ya," the Creole description for speech in which several people talk simultaneously and conversation constantly overlaps (see Ampadu, 2004); the use

in teaching of "call and response," one of the polyrhythmic realities of African art, music, and dance (see the analysis by Sheared, 1999); and the incorporation of African dialect into formal scholarship, as represented by student essays and classroom presentations and by journal articles and formal research.

QUEER THEORY

In recent years queer theory has entered the field's discourse, enjoining adult educators to consider how people constantly learn to construct, dismantle, and reconstruct sexual identity, and how they understand and practice desire (Hill, 2006a). Exploring this process, one finds it replete with implications for how one thinks, learns, and teaches, and what one believes should be covered in a fully inclusive adult education curriculum. Like postmodernism but unlike Africentrism, critical theory, or critical race theory, queer theory is less a set of theoretical tenets and more a critical posture that questions traditional notions of sexuality. In particular, queer theory problematizes heteronormativity; that is, the dominant, unquestioned belief that heterosexual relationships are not only the empirical norm, but morally superior to gay male and lesbian same-sex relationships. The privilege associated with being "straight" is, according to Rocco and Gallagher (2006), important to identify and challenge, particularly as it forces gay male and lesbian workers to "pass" as straight for purposes of workplace safety or career development.

In choosing the term *queer theory* to describe a theoretical posture of sexual critique, its adherents are mainstreaming what was previously a term of abuse. As Hill (1995) acknowledges, this is a common response of marginalized groups who proudly wave the term of abuse applied to them as a badge of identity, thus turning the tables on the dominant group. Queer theory argues that for some, pinning down their sexuality in a fixed, static way is always likely to be complex, as it is in transgendered relationships or in straight friendships between transvestites and cross-dressers. Classics in the field, such as *Epistemology of the Closet* (Sedgewick, 2008) *interrogate* (to use a favored term) dominant understandings and practices of sexuality. In other words, they question rigorously and continuously how certain ideas and behaviors become accepted as "normal" and others viewed as "deviant."

The *q* in queer theory can never be defined in any stable way, since the notion itself rejects an essentialist epistemology that defines sexuality in a bifurcated, either/or way as gay or straight, hetero or homo (Grace & Hill, 2004). Instead, *queer* celebrates the idea of constantly shifting identities and broadens conceptions of behavioral possibilities. Grace and Hill (2004) argue that queer theory's radical inclusion connects it to theorizing in transformative learning whereby meaning schemes and perspectives are gradually broadened to become ever more permeable and comprehensive. King and Biro (2006) extend this analysis to apply a transformative learning perspective to the development of sexual identity at the workplace.

An interesting example of queering identity is Tisdell's description of her sexuality as contextual (Bettinger, Timmins, & Tisdell, 2006). In describing living as a heterosexual, and then as a lesbian, and then again as a heterosexual, Tisdell rejects the descriptor of bisexual writing "for me my sexual orientation is contextual, and related more to a person and relationship, than with one gender or another" (p. 64). What to others might appear to be sexual confusion is completely normal for Tisdell, since her sexual orientation is "contextually situated as being in love with and committed to a particular person regardless of his or her gender" (p. 64). As Hill (2006b) notes, any attempt to queer organizations, classrooms, or adult education programs is a complex practice with multiple dimensions that "is fraught with paradox and contradiction" (p. 101). In his analysis of queer praxis in adult education, Hill (2004) outlines briefly how research, teaching, and the Internet are queered in a spirit of wildness and mischief, focusing on the intersection of desire with learners' and teachers' bodies.

CRITICAL THEORY

Critical theory, influenced strongly by Jürgen Habermas's theory of communicative action (Habermas, 1984, 1987), places the way humans learn to communicate, and in particular to come to agreement, at the heart of adult education. Habermas's articulation of the ideal speech situation—a form of dialogue in which all relevant knowledge is considered, all strive to understand the others' views, and all are open to changing their minds—has been enormously influential. Mezirow (1991), for example, extended Habermas's theoretical analysis to mean that adult educators had a responsibility to intervene with social and political action any time the conditions for ideal speech were threatened.

However, others within the critical theory tradition, such as Marcuse, stand in contrast to Habermas. Marcuse's (1965) idea of repressive tolerance critiques adult education's concern with dignifying students' experiences by granting equal legitimacy to every contribution to a discussion ("you're entitled to your view, I'm entitled to mine, and they have equal legitimacy"). He contends that this approach suppresses alternative, critical viewpoints that hold certain conditions to be wrong, unjust, and oppressive. Marcuse also argues that widening curricula to include alternative political and racial traditions (for example, Marxism and Africentrism) always marginalizes them by placing them in conjunction with mainstream ideas. Learners have been so conditioned to accept the mainstream that the new idea is always positioned as the exotic "other."

Critical theory assumes that inequity is a permanent structural reality and is accepted without complaint because dominant ideology has convinced the majority that inequity is normal and predictable. The purpose of critical theory is to change this state of affairs. This theoretical impulse finds expression in Freire's (1993, 2001) work and the efforts to raise critical consciousness while teaching basic literacy (Mayo, 1998). It also underpins analyses of adult education's role in combating global capitalism (Allman, 2000, 2001), in abetting social movements (Holst, 2002), and in teaching defiance (Newman, 2006). In addition, the Gramscian notion of adult educators as organic intellectuals aiding in the establishment of working-class hegemony of the majority (Borg, Buttigieg, & Mayo, 2002; Coben, 1998) is grounded in the Marxist critical tradition. In the United States, Horton's (2003) work at the Highlander Folk School is a prominent example of the development of organic or movement intellectuals. Others would be the educational arm of the Black Panther Party (Paulston & Altenbaugh, 1988) and the work of revolutionary organizations such as the Freedom Road Socialist Organization and the League of Revolutionaries for a New America (Holst, 2004). Critical theory also underpins adult educational critiques of the increasing influence of human capital theory within the field (Fenwick, 2004; Schied, Carter, & Howell, 2000). Additionally, prominent African American intellectuals such as West (1993) and Outlaw (2005) have argued for *Critical Social Theory in the Interests of Black Folks* (Outlaw, 2005).

CRITICAL RACE THEORY

Critical race theory (CRT) assumes, like critical theory, that a state of permanent inequity has become accepted as normal in the U.S. (Delgado & Stefancic, 2001). However, whereas critical theory traditionally focuses on exclusion by class, critical race theory is concerned with racism and the dominant ideology of White supremacy. Critical race theory views racism as *the* enduring, all-pervasive reality of American life, and suggests adult educators acknowledge this and make its analysis and confrontation a central feature of study and practice. CRT assumes that racism is endemic and that as legal measures restrict its overt expression (e.g.,Whites-only clubs and organizations), it reconfigures itself in racial microaggressions (Sue, 2003) and aversive racism (Gaertner & Dovidio, 2005). Racial microaggressions are the subtle, daily expressions of racism embodied in speech, gesture, and actions such as who gets called on to contribute in discussions and how those contributions are interpreted. Aversive racism comprises the racist behaviors that liberal Whites enact even as they profess sincerely to be free of racism. Peterson's (1999) early analysis of critical race theory in adult education describes how these subtle forms of racism endure, and the conversations African American adult educators need to have to confront class, power, and language in the fight for dignity.

CRT places considerable emphasis on the use of narrative, particularly counter-storytelling. Counter-storytelling encourages people of color to recount their experiences of racism in ways that reflect their own culture, a process that challenges not just what Whites consider to be racial reality (that civil rights has made racism a nonissue) but also what constitutes appropriate forms of classroom expression or scholarship. Using hip hop as a means of counter-storytelling (Guy, 2004), for example, stands in contrast to mainstream forms of narrative such as formal autobiographies or memoirs. The process of counter-storytelling is complex, however, as Merriweather Hunn, Guy, & Manglitz's (2006) tale of a White adult educator's involvement with the African diaspora preconference of the Adult Education Research Conference illustrates. Here the attempt by a White adult educator to act as an ally to African American educators was seen as both an unwanted invasion and an act of solidarity by different participants at the conference.

Critical race theory argues for a curriculum that stresses the analysis of how White supremacy is permanently embedded in educational texts, practices, and forms of student assessment. It places racism as the central factor of American life and requires adult educators to explore how they collude in its perpetuation. Although originated by scholars of color in critical legal studies, the CRT perspective enjoins White adult educators to explore their own racism. Whites need to scrutinize publicly their own racial micro-aggressions, such as regularly overlooking the contributions of students of color, dismissing the jargon of some groups while employing that of the dominant White culture, citing examples and authors that are exclusively White, or grading students of color differently because they are held to lower expectations. CRT also explores the notion of discriminative justice, echoing Marcuse's (1965) argument that "discrimination is good when it reveals processes of oppression and privilege in classrooms, funding and policies" (Rocco & Gallagher, 2004, p. 39).

FEMINIST THEORY

Feminist theory places women's concerns and the centrality of gender at the forefront of analysis and undertakes a power analysis of gender-based inequality across personal and social relationships, work, politics, and ideologies of sexuality. Some proponents focus more specifically on what are often conceptualized as "women's issues," such as reproductive rights, rape, and sexual objectification via pornography, whereas others conduct a broader critique and dismantling of patriarchy and its ties to capitalism. As with other theoretical perspectives reviewed in this chapter, it is probably more accurate to talk of feminist *theories* and feminist *pedagogies* (Tisdell, 2000) in the plural. For example, theorists such as Mojab (2005) and Hart (2005) insist that gender oppression be understood as intersecting with other forms of class and race-based oppression, and that to separate them is empirically and theoretically untenable.

One element of feminist theory that has influenced adult education has been the articulation of distinctively feminist epistemologies. This perspective emphasizes gender-based modes of cognition such as connected knowing (Belenky, Clinchy, Goldberger, & Tarule, 1986) and maternal thinking (Ruddick, 1995). There has been a vigorous debate in feminist literature regarding the validity of feminist epistemology, and the extent to which this analysis promotes or impedes women's interests (Alcoff & Potter, 1993; Grant, 1993). Writers such as Fraser (1989, 1997) and Gore (1993) have pointed out the dangers of a kind of essentialism that confines women to an ethic of care (Gilligan, 1982). In their view, this emphasis on traditional feminine qualities of nurturance, by implication, reserves the exercise of rationality for men.

By way of response, those identified as arguing for the recognition of gender-based modes of cognition sometimes argue that their position has been oversimplified as representing a wholly biological determination of cognition. For example, in the follow-up text to the influential *Women's Ways of Knowing* (Belenky et al., 1986), Goldberger insists that the volume's authors wished only to demonstrate that "there are hidden agendas of power in the way societies define and validate and ultimately genderize knowledge" (Goldberger, 1996, p. 7). In a new preface to her 1995 book on *Maternal Thinking*, Ruddick points out that "there is nothing foreordained about maternal response" (p. xi), that "mothering is construed as work rather than as an identity or fixed biological or legal relationship" (p. xi), and that "there have always been

men who mother" (p. xii). Hart (1992) argues that mothering by either sex can be viewed as an inherently critical project, particularly when viewed from the social margins rather than from the center of established White masculinist norms.

In the 1980s and 1990s, and on into this century, a group of writers proposed principles of practice to frame the feminist adult classroom and the practice of feminist pedagogy (see, for example, Lather, 1991; Luke and Gore, 1992; Gore, 1993; Maher and Tetreault, 1994; McWilliam, 1994; Diller and her colleagues, 1996; and Weiler, 2001). Elements of feminist pedagogy that have become prominent in adult education concern ways of encouraging the expression of students' voices in personal narratives that use language that reflects students' dialects (an emphasis similar to Africentrism's emphasis on counter-storytelling). There is a curricular focus on gender oppression and the ways this intersects with class and race oppression, the deliberate attempt to equalize classroom participation, the valuing of appreciation as equal to criticism, and a recognition that learning is holistic involving emotional, spiritual, and kinetic dimensions just as much as cognition. These practices have been very influential in adult education, and for many now constitute a dominant ideology of preferred practice.

POSTMODERNISM

Postmodernism eschews its own theoretical status, and many who subscribe to its tenets refuse to claim the label of being postmodern. Often associated with Lyotard's influential *The Postmodern Condition* (1984), the term *postmodern* is more of an intellectual attitude or project than a fixed theoretical "take" on the world. Those that others label as postmodernists are quick to reject applying such a label to themselves. However, certain recurring elements are visible in the cluster of positions that represent what is regarded as a postmodern stance. Prime among these is the rejection of grand narratives, of the "big" ideas such as democracy, progress, equality, or rationality that many believe define the conditions of modern existence. The postmodern position views such ideas as distorted and inaccurate and is highly skeptical of notions of human progress. Its adherents point to the recurring incidence of genocide as proof that humankind has not evolved into rational compassion. The postmodern impulse also rejects the idea of universally applicable truths, instead regarding truth as local and contextual. Struggles must likewise be understood locally as grounded in specific and nongeneralizable conditions. Postmodernism regards developmental trajectories of transformation as misguided and believes that narratives of personal transformation must be analyzed as fictional works of art, not empirically accurate descriptions.

Postmodernism also holds that meaning is malleable and that there is no core, unequivocal meaning waiting to be discovered at the heart of any speech, written text, or visual image. Similarly, it rejects the idea that adults have a core, fixed identity that can be discovered through investigation and analysis. A postmodern stance views human conduct as infinitely malleable so that any person is theoretically capable of acting in any way and holding any belief, depending on the circumstances. This malleability of meaning and identity is a source of pleasure to postmodernists, who often profess a ludic, playful delight in playing with possibilities and alternative constructions.

Within adult education, postmodernism has been influential in shaping how adult educators think about matters such as diversity and power. Books by Usher and Edwards (1984), Usher, Bryant, and Johnston (1997), Britton (1996), and Bagnall (1999) explore how traditional progressive practices within adult education such as negotiating the curriculum, working in discussion circles, and using learning contracts do not have the unitary, fixed, and predictable consequences expected of them. Heavily influenced by Foucault's (1980) analysis of power, postmodernism argues that what seem to adult educators to be liberatory and emancipatory practices are actually experienced by learners as oppressive reconfigurations of power and surveillance. Foucault's (1980) analysis of the way power flows around a situation was used by Gore (1993) to critique participatory educational practices such as the aforementioned circle. Merely moving the chairs in a room does not alter structural power relations. Boshier and Wilson (1998) extended the critical Foucaultian

analysis of power by analyzing the surveillance of students in Web-based courses.

Postmodernism's emphasis on the potentially infinite range of ways people can define and express themselves has helped fuel an explicit acknowledgment of the diversity of adult classrooms in a multiracial, multi-ethnic, and gendered world. It provides intellectual armament for those who want to broaden the range of programs, practices, and materials encompassed by adult education. It also supports practices of classroom and community research that emphasize how adult education must always be grounded in, and responsive to, local conditions. Finally, postmodernism has opened up new avenues of what is considered scholarly research in the field, including the writing of dissertations that are scholarly personal narratives (Nash, 2004).

TRANSFORMATIVE LEARNING

A theoretical impulse that has arisen from within the field of adult education is transformative learning. Building on the work undertaken over the past four decades by Mezirow (1991; Mezirow & Associates, 2000), numerous researchers have explored the empirical confirmation of his chief contention: that as adults mature their life experience impels them to develop meaning schemes (sets of assumptions related to specific situations) and meaning perspectives (assumptions constituting broad worldviews) that are increasingly comprehensive (including a broader range of events) and discriminating (understanding of the differences between particular events and phenomena). Mezirow's work has occasioned critiques and debates regarding whether or not it privileges rationality, mirrors Western epistemology, and neglects social change at the expense of individual development. Mezirow himself has painstakingly replied to all his critics and used their commentaries to hone and refine transformative learning. As a result of his contribution, a new forum, the *Journal of Transformative Education*, and an annual conference on transformative learning have come into existence.

Although transformative theory has been developed, extended, modified, and refined over the years, its core tenets have remained remarkably stable. Mezirow posits a developmental impetus in adulthood that impels adults to develop ways of understanding the world, and ways of constructing meaning, that take account of an ever-widening number of experiences (Erickson, 2007). Some of these meaning-making processes focus on meaning schemes—sets of assumptions concerning events within a specific range of instances, such as the meaning scheme a trainer might develop to explain and respond to resistance and sabotage displayed by learners in a staff development initiative. Other processes deal with much broader sets of assumptions and explanatory mechanisms, and these are called meaning perspectives. A trainer's view of the social purpose or economic function of learning would be an example of a meaning perspective. Adults regularly encounter what transformative learning theory calls disorienting dilemmas—situations that are disturbing and surprising because they contradict very dramatically what we thought were stable understandings of how the world works. Examples of these would be undergoing divorce or marital breakdown, being fired, being betrayed by a supposed friend, being diagnosed with a serious illness, losing someone close, being conscripted, losing one's retirement funds, and so on. All these are things that should not happen to people who carefully follow the rules for marital harmony, career development, or financial planning. When these occur they impel us to reappraise assumptions that until then we thought explained the world adequately. Transformative learning describes the process by which people learn to develop and then integrate new assumptions into existing schemes and perspectives.

Mezirow believes adult learning occurs in four ways—through elaborating existing frames of reference, learning frames of references, transforming points of view, and transforming habits of mind—and names critical reflection as a component of all of these. We transform frames of reference through critical reflection on assumptions supporting the content and/or process of problem solving. We transform our habits of mind by becoming critically reflective of the premises defining the problem. Mezirow contends that the two central elements of transformative learning—objective and subjective reframing—involve either critical reflection on the assumptions of others (objective reframing)

or on one's own assumptions (subjective reframing). He argues that the overall purpose of adult development is to realize one's agency through increasingly expanding awareness and critical reflection. The function of adult educators becomes to assist this development by helping learners reflect critically on their own, and others,' assumptions. Taylor's (2007) regular reviews of transformative learning document how the scope of transformative learning has itself widened to account for holistic, somatic, and emotional dimensions of this process, and for its application within studies of different cultural contexts (Merriam & Niseane, 2008). O' Sullivan, Morrell, and O'Connor (2002) have explored the connections between transformation and spirituality, and the importance of connecting transformation to ecological balance.

CONCLUSION

In this chapter I have tried to show how theoretical frameworks—collections of ideas that arise out of our comparing different sources of evidence, that are predictive, and that cover a broad category of events or situations—are always present in practice. As adult educators we may protest that we are practitioners not theorists, and we may express exasperation or confusion as we hear theoretical concepts bandied about in what seems like inaccessible jargon. But, like it or not, we are all theoreticians. The ways we pursue things dear to us—treating learners respectfully, creating democratic classrooms, empowering adults to take control of their lives—are all informed by theoretical frameworks, whether or not we choose to recognize that fact.

As we consider how to assist learners to exert agency and realize collective interests in a world in which people live their life increasingly in self-protected cyber silos, and in which economic, social, and political forces are seen as being as far removed from daily influence as the weather, theoretical frameworks are crucial. They can help us penetrate hegemony, detect ideological manipulation, and realize when corporate agendas are displacing individual and social well-being. A theoretical understanding helps us read the world in a way that makes it more open to our influence. It also reduces the danger of self-laceration whereby we blame ourselves for an inability to cope with situations that are politically and culturally created. In their different ways, the seven theoretical frameworks described in this chapter all try to understand how adult educators can work in a more critically reflective key with vigor and resolve.

REFERENCES

Alcoff, L., & Potter, E. (Eds.). (1933). *Feminist epistemologies.* New York: Routledge.

Allman, P. (2000). *Revolutionary social transformation: Democratic hopes, political possibilities and critical education.* Westport, CT: Bergin & Garvey.

Allman, P. (2001). *Critical education against global capitalism: Karl Marx and revolutionary critical education.* Westport, CT: Bergin & Garvey.

Ampadu, L. M. (2004). Gumbo ya ya: Tapping cultural stories to teach composition. *Composition Studies, 32*(1), 73–88.

Bagnall, R. G. (1999). *Discovering radical contingency: Building a postmodern agenda in adult education.* New York: Peter Lang.

Belenky, M. F., Clinchy, B. M., Goldberger, N. R., & Tarule, J. M. (1986). *Women's ways of knowing: The development of self, voice, and mind.* New York: Basic Books.

Bettinger, T. V., Timmins, R., & Tisdell, E. J. (2006). Difficult dilemmas: The meaning and dynamics of being out in the classroom. In R. J. Hill (Ed.), *Challenging homophobia and heterosexism: Lesbian, gay, bisexual, transgender, and queer issues in organizational settings.* San Francisco: Jossey-Bass.

Borg, C., Buttigieg, J., & Mayo, P. (Eds.). (2002). *Gramsci and education.* Lanham, MD: Rowman & Littlefield.

Boshier, R., & Wilson, M. (1998). Panoptic variations: Surveillance and discipline in Web courses. In *Proceedings of the Adult Education Research Conference, No. 39* (pp. 43–48). San Antonio, TX: University of the Incarnate Word.

Britton, D. (1996). *The modern practice of adult education: A postmodern critique.* Albany: State University of New York Press.

Brookfield, S. D. (2003). Racializing criticality in adult education. *Adult Education Quarterly, 53*(3), 154–169.

Closson, R. B. (2006). Righteous commitment: A portrait of Dr Scipio A. J. Colin III. *New Horizons in Adult Education and Human Resource Development,* (2), 50–56.

Coben, D. (1998). *Radical heroes: Gramsci, Freire and the politics of adult education.* New York: Garland.

Colin, S. A. J., III. (1988). The Universal Negro Improvement Association and the education of African American adults. Doctoral dissertation, Department of Adult Education, Northern Illinois University.

Colin, S. A. J., III. (2002). Marcus Garvey: Africentric Adult Education for Selfethnic Reliance. In E. A. Peterson (Ed.). *Freedom road: Adult education of African Americans* (Rev. ed.). Malabar, FL: Krieger.

Colin, S. A. J., III., & Guy, T. A. (1998). An Africentric interpretive model of curriculum orientations for course development in graduate programs in adult education. *PAACE Journal of Lifelong Learning, 7,* 43–55.

Delgado, R., & Stefancic, J. (2001). *Critical race theory: An introduction.* New York: New York University Press.

Diller, A., Houston, B., Morgan, K. P., & Ayim, M. E. (Eds.). (1996). *The gender question in education: Theory, pedagogy, and politics.* Boulder, CO: Westview Press.

Erickson, D. M. (2007). A developmental re-forming of the phases of meaning in transformative learning. *Adult Education Quarterly, 58*(1), 61–80.

Fenwick, T. J. (2004). Toward a critical HRD in theory and practice. *Adult Education Quarterly, 54*(3), 193–209.

Foucault, M. (1980). *Power/knowledge: Selected interviews and other writings, 1972–1977.* New York: Pantheon.

Fraser, N. (1989). *Unruly practices: Power, discourse and gender in contemporary social theory.* Minneapolis: University of Minnesota Press.

Fraser, N. (1997). *Justice interruptus: Critical reflections on the "postsocialist" condition.* New York: Routledge.

Freire, P. (1993). *Pedagogy of the oppressed.* New York: Continuum.

Freire, P. (2001). *Pedagogy of freedom: Ethics, democracy and civic courage.* Boston: Rowman & Littlefield.

Gaertner, S. L., & Dovidio, J. F. (2005). Understanding and addressing contemporary racism: From aversive racism to the common in-group identity model. *Journal of Social Issues, 61*(3), 615–639.

Gilligan, C. (1982). *In a different voice: Psychological theory and women's development.* Cambridge, MA: Harvard University Press.

Goldberger, N. R. (1996). Looking back, looking forward. In N. Goldberger, J. Tarule, B. Clinchy, & M. Belenky (Eds.), *Knowledge, difference and* power: Essays inspired by women's ways of knowing (pp. 1–23). New York: Basic Books.

Gore, J. M. (1993). *The struggle for pedagogies: Critical and feminist discourses as regimes of truth.* New York: Routledge.

Grace, A. P., & Hill, R. J. (2004). Positioning queer in adult education: Intervening in politics and praxis in North America. *Studies in the Education of Adults, 36*(2), 167–189.

Gramsci, A. (1971). *Selections from the prison notebooks* (Q. Hoare & G. N. Smith, Eds.). London: Lawrence & Wishart.

Grant, J. (1993). *Fundamental feminism: Contesting the core concepts of feminist theory.* New York: Routledge.

Guy, T. (2004). Gangsta rap and adult education. In L. G. Martin & E. E. Rogers (Eds.), *Adult education in an urban context: Problems, practices, and programming for inner-city communities* (pp. 43–58). New Directions for Adult and Continuing Education Sourcebook, No. 101. San Francisco: Jossey-Bass, 2004.

Habermas, J. (1984). *The theory of communicative action: Vol. 1. Reason and the rationalization of society.* Boston: Beacon Press.

Habermas, J. (1987). *The theory of communicative action: Vol. 2. Lifeworld and system—a critique of functionalist reason.* Boston: Beacon Press.

Hart, M. (1992). *Working and educating for life: Feminist and international perspectives on adult education.* New York: Routledge.

Hart, M. (2005). Class and gender. In T. Nesbit (Ed.), *Class concerns: Adult education and social class.* San Francisco: Jossey-Bass.

Hill, R. J. (1995). Gay discourse in adult education: A critical review. *Adult Education Quarterly, 45*(3), 142–258.

Hill, R. J. (2004). Activism as practice: Some queer considerations. In R. St. Clair & J. Sandlin (Eds.), *Promoting critical practice in adult education* (pp. 85–94). San Francisco: Jossey-Bass.

Hill, R. J. (2006a). What's it like to be queer here? In R. J. Hill (Ed.), *Challenging homophobia and heterosexism: Lesbian, gay, bisexual, transgender, and queer issues in organizational settings* (pp. 7–16). San Francisco: Jossey-Bass.

Hill, R .J. (2006b). Queer challenges in organizational settings. In R. J. Hill (Ed.), *Challenging homophobia and heterosexism: Lesbian, gay, bisexual, transgender, and queer issues in organizational settings* (pp. 97–102). San Francisco: Jossey-Bass.

Holst, J. D. (2002). *Social movements, civil society, and radical adult education.* Westport, CT: Bergin & Garvey.

Holst, J. D. (2004). Globalization and education within two revolutionary organizations in the United States of America: A Gramscian analysis. *Adult Education Quarterly, 55*(1), 23–40.

Hord, F. L., & Lee, J. S. (Eds.). (1995). *I am because we are: Readings in Black philosophy.* Amherst: University of Massachusetts Press.

Horton, M. (2003). *The Myles Horton reader: Education for social change.* Knoxville: University of Tennessee Press.

King, K. P., & Biro, S. C. (2006). A transformative learning perspective of continuing sexual identity development at the workplace. In R. J. Hill (Ed.), *Challenging homophobia and heterosexism: Lesbian, gay, bisexual, transgender, and queer issues in organizational settings* (pp. 17–27). San Francisco: Jossey-Bass.

Knowles, M. S. (1983). *Self-directed learning: A guide for learners and teachers.* New York: Cambridge University Press.

Knowles, M. S. (1984). *Andragogy in action: Applying modern principles of adult learning.* San Francisco: Jossey-Bass.

Lather, P. (1991). *Getting smart: Feminist research and pedagogy with/in the postmodern.* New York: Routledge.

Lindeman, E. C. (1961). *The meaning of adult education.* Montreal: Harvest House. (Original work published 1926)

Lindeman, E. C., & Smith, T. V. (1951). *The democratic way of life.* New York: New American Library.

Luke, C., & Gore, J. M. (Eds.). (1992). *Feminisms and critical pedagogy.* New York: Routledge.

Lyotard, J. (1984). *The postmodern condition: A report on knowledge.* Minneapolis: University of Minnesota Press.

Maher, F., & Tetreault, M. K. T. (1994). *The feminist classroom: An inside look at how professors and students are transforming higher education for a diverse society.* New York: Basic Books.

Marcuse, H. (1965). Repressive tolerance. In R. P. Wolff, B. Moore, & H. Marcuse, *A critique of pure tolerance.* Boston: Beacon Press.

Mayo, P. (1988). *Gramsci, Freire and adult education: Possibilities for transformative action.* New York: Zed.

McWilliam, E. (1994). *In broken images: Feminist tales for a different teacher education.* New York: Teachers College Press.

Merriam, S. B., & Niseane, G. (2008). Transformative learning in Botswana: How culture shapes the process. *Adult Education Quarterly, 58*(3), 183–197.

Merriweather Hunn, L. R. (2004). Africentric philosophy. In R. St. Clair & J. Sandlin (Eds.), *Promoting critical practice in adult education* (pp. 65–74). San Francisco: Jossey-Bass.

Merriweather Hunn, L. R., Guy, T. C., & Manglitz, E. (2006). Who can speak for whom? Using counter-storytelling to challenge racial hegemony. In *47th Annual Adult Education Research Conference Proceedings* (pp. 244–250). Minneapolis: Department of Work and Human Resource Education, University of Minnesota.

Mezirow, J. D. (1991). *Transformative dimensions of adult learning.* San Francisco: Jossey-Bass.

Mezirow, J. D., & Associates. (2000). *Learning as transformation: Critical perspectives on a theory in progress.* San Francisco: Jossey-Bass.

Mojab, S. (2005). Class and race. In T. Nesbit (Ed.), *Class concerns: Adult education and social class.* San Francisco: Jossey-Bass.

Nash, R. (2004). *Liberating scholarly writing: The power of personal narrative.* New York: Teachers College Press..

Newman, M. (2006). *Teaching defiance: Stories and strategies for activist educators.* San Francisco: Jossey-Bass.

O'Sullivan, E., Morrell, A., & O'Connor, M. A. (Eds.). (2002). *Expanding the boundaries of transformative learning: Essays on theory and practice.* New York: Macmillan.

Outlaw, L. T., Jr. (2005). *Critical social theory in the interests of Black folks.* Lanham, MD: Rowman & Littlefield.

Paulston, R. G., & Altenbaugh, R. J. (1988). Adult education in radical U.S. social and ethnic movements: From case studies to typology to explanation. In T. Lovett (Ed.), *Radical approaches to adult education: A reader* (pp. 114–137). London: Routledge.

Peterson, E. A. (1999). Creating a culturally relevant dialogue for African American adult educators. In T. C. Guy (Ed.), *Providing culturally relevant adult education: A challenge for the twenty-first century* (pp. 79–91). San Francisco: Jossey-Bass.

Rocco, T. S., & Gallagher, S. J. (2004). Discriminative justice: Can discrimination be good? In R. St. Clair & J. Sandlin (Eds.), *Promoting critical practice in adult education* (pp. 29–41). San Francisco: Jossey-Bass.

Rocco, T. S., & Gallagher, S. J. (2006). Straight privilege and moral/izing: Issues in career development. In R. J. Hill (Ed.), *Challenging homophobia and heterosexism: Lesbian, gay, bisexual, transgender, and queer issues in organizational settings* (pp. 29–40). San Francisco: Jossey-Bass.

Ruddick, S. (1995). *Maternal thinking: Toward a politics of peace.* Boston: Beacon Press.

Schied, F. M., Carter, V. K., & Howell, S. L. (2000). Silent power: HRD and the management of learning in the workplace. In R. M. Cervero & A. L. Wilson (Eds.), *Power in practice: Adult education and the struggle for knowledge and power in society* (pp. 42–59). San Francisco: Jossey-Bass.

Sedgewick, E. K. (2008). *Epistemology of the closet* (2nd ed.). Berkeley, CA: University of California Press.

Sheared, V. (1999). Giving voice: Inclusion of African American students' polyrhythmic realities in adult basic education. In T. C. Guy (Ed.), *Providing culturally relevant adult education: A challenge for the twenty-first century* (pp. 33–48). San Francisco: Jossey-Bass.

Sue, D. W. (2003). *Overcoming our racism: The journey to liberation.* San Francisco: Jossey-Bass.

Taylor, E. W. (2007). An update of transformative learning theory: A critical review of the empirical research. *International Journal of Lifelong Education, 26*(2), 173–191.

Tisdell, E. (2000). Feminist pedagogies. In E. Hayes & D. Flannery (Eds.), *Women as learners* (pp. 155–184). San Francisco: Jossey-Bass.

Usher, R., Bryant, I., & Johnston, R. (1997). *Adult education and the postmodern challenge: Learning beyond the limits.* New York: Routledge.

Usher, R., & Edwards, R. (1994). *Postmodernism and education: Different voices, different worlds.* London: Routledge.

Weiler, K. (Ed.). (2001). *Feminist engagements: Reading, resisting, and revisioning male theorists in education and cultural studies.* New York: Routledge.

West, C. (1993). *Keeping faith: Philosophy and race in America.* New York: Routledge.

Wilson, A. L., & Hayes, E. R. (Eds.). (2000). *Handbook of adult and continuing education.* San Francisco: Jossey-Bass.

7

HISTORIES OF ADULT EDUCATION

Constructing the Past

MICHAEL R. WELTON

O ver 20 years ago adult education theorist Stephen Brookfield wrote that the "majority of professors and graduate students of adult education in the U.S. do not regard understanding the historical foundations of the field to be a major priority" (1988, p. 291). But several adult education historians were scouring the landscape for a usable history through the 1980s and 1990s. Some wanted to retrieve a past that contested the professionalization of the field of study and practice, yet spoke to the current debates about how the study of adult learning ought to be constructed. This search in the past for "liberatory moments" characterized Michael Welton's 1987 edited work, *Knowledge for the People* (1987). In addition, David Stewart's *Adult Learning in America: Eduard Lindeman and His Agenda for Lifelong Learning* (1987) argued that Lindeman's life and progressive views held "lessons that enrich the lives of persons living today" (p. xiv).

However, this energy for historical studies (critical and mainstream) dissipated after the publication of H.W. Stubblefield and Patrick Keane's *Adult Education in the American Experience: From the Colonial Period to the Present* (1994), Joseph Kett's *The Pursuit of Knowledge Under Difficulties: From Self-Improvement to Adult Education in America, 1750–1990* (1994), and Roger Fieldhouse and Associates' collection, *A History of Modern British Adult Education* (1996). To be sure, obligatory essays on history have appeared in general collections, including Griff Foley's *Dimensions of Adult Learning: Adult Education and Training in a Global Era* (2004) and Tara Fenwick, Tom Nesbit, and Bruce Spencer's *Contexts of Adult Education: Canadian Perspectives* (2006), as well as, here and there, specialized studies such Elizabeth A. Peterson's 2002 *Freedom Road: Adult Education of African Americans*, Welton's 2001 *Little Mosie From the Margaree: A Biography of Moses Michael Coady*, Tom Steele's 2007 *Knowledge Is Power! The Rise and Fall of European Popular Education Movements, 1848–1939*, and Jeff Taylor's *Union Learning in Canadian Labour Education in the Twentieth Century* (2001).

Historical studies in adult education have not been granted sterling professorial and research authority in North American graduate programs of adult education as we have moved into the troubled first decades of the 21st century. From my personal vantage point, it is dispiriting to realize that

AUTHOR'S NOTE: This chapter draws from two of my previously published articles: "What's New in the History of Adult Education?" (1991), *Historical Studies in Education*, 3(1), 285–297; and "In Search of the Object: Historiography and Adult Education," (1993), *Studies in Continuing Education*, 15(2), 133–148.

even when mainstream historians write about topics of interest to adult educators, such as the emergence of public opinion as the foundation for democratic life (see McNairn, 2000) or the lively presence of literary societies (see Gere, 1997, and Winch, 1994), they do not usually think they are writing about adult education history or draw upon adult education theory to inform their analyses. A subfield of adult education history has not yet succeeded in establishing itself as a bona fide, legitimate field of study in the academy. Historical studies are not perceived by the adult education professoriate in the United States, Canada, or Great Britain as either sources for the generation of critical theorems or essential building blocks for foundational studies in adult education. That said, there are enough comprehensive texts available (as well as specialized works) to spark new directions in reinvigorated graduate programs.

In this chapter, then, our attention will focus on selected thinkers' construction of the field of adult educational history. This is necessary to clear imaginative ground for the work ahead, because most historians of adult education just want to get on with it. But with reference to "adult education," what are we supposed to be getting on with? When we study adult learning in different times and places, what forms and processes do we put under the searchlight? Thus, this chapter will proceed by examining various seminal texts in adult educational history (primarily from the U.K. and the U.S.), which have appeared in the last 30 or so years, in order to understand how we think about history. My approach is selective, and cannot be considered as exhaustive. Our focus is on texts whose intent is comprehensive.

Czechoslovakian historian Ivan Savicky (1987) identified the fundamental meta-historiographic problem for historians of adult education as the "theorization of history." By this he means that works of adult educational history have neither defined precisely the object of historical analysis nor articulated the conceptual categories necessary to construct the relationships amongst the elements within the object's boundary. To illustrate: The classic synthetic works on the history of adult education (Grattan, 1955; Kelly, 1970; Knowles, 1962/1977) presented an "outline narrative" (Kelly's depiction). Malcolm Knowles offered a commonsense, whiggish solution to the problem of the object. His text, *A History of*

the Adult Education Movement in the United States, described by Cyril Houle as the "most comprehensive history of adult education in the U.S." (1992, p. 5), simply assumes that a history of adult education will find intimations of the present in the dimly lit gardens of the past. Both Knowles (1977), and Houle in his prestigious book *The Literature of Adult Education: A Bibliographic Essay* (1992), begin in the present (from the vantage point of a thoroughly professionalized and complacent practice), and look to the past to identify institutional precursors to the modern practice. They select only certain objects for inclusion within the arbitrarily constructed boundary (Mechanics' Institutes, lyceum, etc.) in order to celebrate the "swelling growth of the [contemporary] field" (Houle, 1992, p. 21). Plotting the history of American education as romance, Knowles shows how the institutional provision of education for adults gradually shed its amateur qualities, becoming more systematic, expert-dominated, and technically efficient. Knowles's work is the narrative voice of professionalization triumphant.

For revisionist historians (Rockhill, 1985; Schied, 1991), Knowles's and Houle's construction of the boundary of the field created a "distorted image of itself" (Shied, 1991, p. 1). Both Schied and Rockhill claim that adult education's historic roots on social movements have been repressed from the field's memory. In two subtly and fiercely argued essays in *University Adult Education in England and the USA* (1985), Rockhill argues that adult education had been consciously constructed (during the crucial interwar years) to silence the left progressive agenda of education for critical consciousness, social reconstruction, and collective action. To accomplish this task of delegitimating oppositional learning, the emergent professional field had to vanquish alternative knowledge forms and processes, casting them outside the arbitrarily delineated boundary of the field. Schied speaks specifically of the "omission of workers' education, or more accurately, defining workers' education in such a way as to reduce it to insignificance in the study of adult education" (1991, p. 1). He thinks that the exclusion of workers' education from adult education's boundaries is "only part of a much broader omission of virtually any adult education that deals with social change" (p. 2). These boundary disputes indicated pointedly that the historian participates self-consciously in the process of constituting the field of study. Choices are made as to what counts as legitimate "adult education." Schied and Rockhill believe that mainstream adult education history is a censored version of the past.

British socialist and laborite historians of adult education are not preoccupied with the philosophical problems attached to "mapping the territory" (Rubenson, 1982; Welton, 1987b). Brian Simon, one of the leading advocates of "adult education history as workers' history," writes the history of British adult education as the heroic history of a working-class-that-strives-for-independence—from its origins in the 18th century to the present. He selects "independent educational activities" as historical anchor point, and then constructs a "line of continuity" from the Corresponding Societies of the 1790s through the heroic days of the Marxist Plebs League to the present besieged trade union movement. His construction of the "tradition of independent educational activities" (1992, p. 64) as adult education history is comprehensible within his Marxist interpretive framework, which privileges "workers' struggles" as the motor of social change. Echoing feminist concerns, John Field (1992) argues that Simon's limited theorization of history does not illuminate other important objects within the historical field—for example, women's struggles against the patriarchal reproduction of gender relations. The problem, then, with constructing adult education as workers' education is that it leaves out a large part of "empirically ascertainable" adult education.

In *Towards a History of Adult Education in America* (1988) adult education historian Harold Stubblefield offered a well-crafted variant on the reductionist approach. Stubblefield recognizes that in the U.S. prior to World War I adults learned through a chaotic variety of educational forms—chautauquas, lyceum lectures, correspondence schools, university extension, agricultural programs, women's organizations, service clubs. After World War I, he observes, many persons and institutions turned their attention to adult education, and the term *adult education* covered a multitude of activities and social purposes. During the postwar period many thoughtful individuals began to think deeply and systematically about the specific needs of adult learners and adult education

as its own domain of educational practice. Stubblefield is interested in how these "formative thinkers" shaped their views on the nature of adult education, the social conditions calling for new forms of education, aims to be accomplished, appropriate methods, relation of adult education to society, and what the curriculum should be within an organizing paradigm or unifying principle

Stubblefield brings the buzzing facticity of adult learning under some control. But his severely elegant formulation creates severe difficulties. For one thing, constructing adult education history as intellectual history obviously rules out understanding social movements as learning sites. However, even if we accept Stubblefield's compelling guiding premise (adult education history is best theorized as intellectual history), we immediately face numerous problems. Why has he included these particular thinkers? What is the theoretical justification for his selections? No women are included in his historical narrative. Why wouldn't Jane Addams, Ruth Kotinsky, Dorothy Canfield Fisher, Jessie Charters, Hilda Worthington Smith, and/or Eleanor Coit be considered as formative thinkers? (Karlovic, 1993; Sexton, 1993; Thompson, 1993). Black historians would want to include seminal thinkers like Alain Locke (Fitchue, 1993; Guy, 1993; Gyant, 2002) in the list of formative thinkers. M. Anthony Fitchue asserts that the "principal histories of adult education in the United States . . . have all consistently ignored the unique cultural and ethnic experience of African American adult educators" (1993, p. 1; see also Colin, 1988).

Stubblefield himself could be accused of participating in the creation of the myth of the American adult education "great tradition" (as could Welton in his 1987 edited volume, *Knowledge for the People*). By so doing, historians open the way for various deconstructive moves so familiar on today's stormy intellectual scene. Adult education history in Canada and the U.S. has been (and still is) White, male, and middle class in sensibility. Stubblefield also has to confront the question of just how one situates ideas in historical context. When we extrapolate unifying principles from historical context we are not able to see how particular discursive practices are intimately bound up with class, gender, and ethnic interest.

Twentieth Century Thinkers in Adult Education (1987) editor Peter Jarvis believes that by drawing upon the ideas of formative thinkers (such as Coady, Mansbridge, Tawney, Thorndike, Dewey, Freire, Horton, and others), we will come to a clearer understanding of adult education as a field of study." Adult education," he says, "is a unique combination of elements of knowledge from varying backgrounds and concerns of different thinkers, whose work has contributed to the body of knowledge, that may now be called adult education knowledge" (p. 301). However, Jarvis fails to differentiate adequately the production of theoretical knowledge oriented to delineating the boundaries of the field (or theoretical knowledge localized in a region within the field) and the various forms of self-understanding developed by adroit practitioners like Mansbridge, Freire, and Knowles. Analyzing the thought of select formative thinkers cannot contribute to the resolution of the problem of the object. The intellectual history of the field can only be a subregion within the larger delineated field of study. Thinkers like Lindeman and Freire may help us think about the purposes of adult education. But these men are not learning theorists. They are teachers of moral and ethical prescriptions. It is up to us to make sense of their thought and praxis (that is, figure out how to do intellectual history in social context).

During the 1990s four previously mentioned texts offered wide-ranging attempts to write more comprehensive historical accounts of adult education in Britain and the U.S. The works by Joseph Kett, Stubblefield, and Keane as well as Roger Fieldhouse and Thomas Kelly (a revision of his earlier magnum opus) represent a renewed and spirited effort to write more inclusive and comprehensive histories of adult learning and education. After considering these explicitly focused adult educational history texts, I will explicate Lawrence Cremin's educational history. Ironically, his approach to the writing of educational history may hold the key to solving our metahistoriographic problem.

To begin with, British adult education historian and practitioner Roger Fieldhouse, writing in the "Preface" to *A History of British Adult Education* (Fieldhouse & Associates, 1996), simply declares without rationale that he will "overemphasize formal and institutionalized learning at the expense of the less well-recorded autodidact tradition" (p. viii). It is puzzling that in the mid-1990s Fieldhouse can still pose the question of just what is meant by education. Is it teaching or is it learning, is it didactic or self-directed, face-to-face or at a distance? These questions lack intellectual energy and verve.

In his revised classic text, *A History of Adult Education in Great Britain* (first published in 1970, revised in 1992), Thomas Kelly proceeds without apparent alarm with his vision of adult education as the nonvocational education of adults. He, too, does not believe it necessary to defend this exclusionary position. Kelly simply "gets on" with writing often meticulous accounts of adult literacy in the 15th century or Mechanics' Institutes in the 19th century and many other things. Kelly's selective organizing scheme forces him to work with an unacknowledged metaframe, namely, he extols the voluntary learning of adults in times past and present, and laments the loss of this tradition in recent decades.

For his part, Fieldhouse and his associates pile empirical data upon empirical data to serve his agenda of calculating "how influential adult education has been and what effect (if any) it has had on society" (1996, p. vii). This is socialist empiricism with a vengeance! However, Fieldhouse's unwillingness to theorize adult learning in time and place (specifying the learning dynamics of social evolution), as well as the failure to establish what might count as "influence," derails the project. In the end, the various authors uncover much data, adding to Kelly's detail, but do not advance from Kelly's essentially chronological story of various forms of voluntary adult education. Like Kelly, Fieldhouse laments the lost great tradition of "collective effort and social worth" (Fieldhouse & Associates, 1996, pp. 9, 76). As in Simon's work, a melancholic aura pervades this text. Old style workers' education has gone forever; the middle class always seems to co-opt workers' independent initiatives; we never fulfill our emancipatory dreams. All that a socialist labor adult education historian like John McIlroy (1992) can do is retrieve the vision of an alternative working-class education system from the dead past and hope that it will rise like a phoenix from the ashes.

Joseph Kett, an American educational history and outsider to academic adult education, startled this community of scholars with his work

The Pursuit of Knowledge Under Difficulties: From Self-Improvement to Adult Education in America, 1750–1990 (1994). Like others who have stepped into the treacherous waters of adult education history, Kett acknowledges that "exploring the history of continuing and adult education entails making sense of astounding statistics, frustratingly loose terminology, lofty idealism, and base huckstering" (p. xi). He manages to cut through the confusing lexicon of continuing, adult, further, popular, second-chance, education extension, and lifelong learning to the heart of the matter: individuals' pursuit of knowledge in order to improve themselves. This is his organizing scheme, his metaframe, if you will. Kett is a cultural historian of conservative leanings. Basically, Kett argues that this impulse to acquire knowledge is in constant historical tension with formal providers of education. This promising theme unifies Kett's narrative and enables him to frame American history into distinct epochs. He does not, however, provide any defensible justification for beginning his story in the two decades preceding the American Revolution. In the pre–1776 period, Kett identifies the emergent theme of self-improvement (this theme gains prominence in British narratives as well), embodied both in autodidactic projects, and participation in the "institutions of self-improvement" (literary societies, lyceums, Mechanics' Institutes, the Lake Chautauqua assembly) of the 19th century. In the postrevolutionary period, the public's access to education widens in scope.

From 1800 to 1850, claims Kett, the ideal of popular self-education intertwines with urgent calls to diffuse knowledge amongst established educational institutions. Kett informs us that by the 1920s, disillusioned progressives imagined that adult education could counter the lifelessness of public and university schooling. There is a subtext in Kett's study of the American pursuit of knowledge. He thinks that although American adult educators have been animated by a "democratic idealism," they have usually succumbed to diluting their offerings to maintain a clientele. He also believes that by the end of 1980s adult education was not a marginal activity; professional adult educators, however, had "become increasingly marginal to the education of adults" (1994, p. xviii). Contemporary proponents of the learning society will bristle at this latter assertion.

Kett (1994) constructs adult education as the pursuit and diffusion of knowledge. He executes this with some elegance, but there are just too many absences from this text for it to "fill the bill" of an adequate learning history of American society. There are few entries for women, only one entry for African Americans, no entries for Native Americans, and nothing much on working-class history or slavery. Trapped in his elitist cultural hermeneutic, Kett fails to connect culture in interplay with class, race, and gender structures of oppression. He cannot conceive that there is a "great debate" and "bitter struggle" at the heart of our collective existence. We can speak of a class struggle weaving its way as a red thread through our individual histories. This struggle has been essentially about people's huge efforts to create and sustain pedagogical social and learning space that would enable them to gain some mastery over their life situations. Elites have always sought to maintain tight control over the "circle of learning" in order to maintain their "power over." Those below, those on the outside, have fought hard to widen the societal circle of conversation. Class control of pedagogical space is a primary form of conflict that pervades our individual histories as Americans, Canadians, and Britons, and so on. Historians also maintain that we ought to be attentive to two other threads, pink and multicolored, that also weave through our histories: gender and ethnic relations. Women have had to struggle incessantly to achieve their full potential as human beings with the right to all forms of knowledge and occupational mastery. And those of non-European origins, indigenous peoples and many others, have often found themselves outside the banquet halls of power and high status knowledge acquisition. Kett's history is bloodless and lifeless. Reading Kett, one wishes for a solid dose of class analysis from British socialist educational historians (like Brian Simon or John McIroy): the reinvigorating of materialist analyses of culture to the historian's agenda.

In *Adult Education in the American Experience: From the Colonial Period to the Present* (1994), Stubblefield and Keane go beyond Kett in at least admitting that they ought to address the "broad context of adult learning and its relationship to social, economic, and political movements" (p. xii). They recognize from reading Bernard Bailyn (1960) and Cremin (1976, 1977) that one must attend to the metahistoriographic problem of the boundaries of the educational field of study. The also recognize that adult education occurred as part of the cultural transmission process among Native Americans and the early European settlers (Stubblefield & Keane, 1994, p. xiii). But they are writing "primarily for adult education practitioners and scholars, who need a comprehensive history of adult education in the U.S. that interprets their work in relation to the larger field of adult education and to national history" (p. xii).

This is well and good. But the trouble arises, it seems to me, because both men, while aware of class and other forms of conflict in American history, do not want to dwell too long on the dark side of early American conquest of native peoples, the enslavement of Blacks, the domination of workers, and other troubling aspects of American history. They do not encourage us to dwell with those who have suffered the most in American history. They want this book to sit comfortably with mainstream America; thus, one senses that they move quickly through their sketches of Native Americans, providing little insight into the periods of the "Indian Wars" viewed through the learning lens. In fact, Stubblefield and Keane are most comfortable when they are listing various forms of adult education in, say, early America or the national period. There is much of interest here (they add more objects to the field), but they do not attempt to situate the range of learning sites in colonial America within an organizing frame that would help us make sense of why these particular forms of learning were occurring and to what end. At every juncture in American history, they do not tie their analysis to a class, race, and gender structures of oppression (which includes the constituting of what counts as knowledge). Thus, their claim that: "The earlier class, gender, and race relationships persisted, influencing educational provision" (Stubblefield & Keane, 1994, p. 51) rings hollow. They do not theorize and explore this relationship with rigor and depth. In chapter 17 of their book, "Adult Education's Critical and Conserving Functions," Stubblefield and Keane consider the learning dynamics of both the civil rights and women's movements in the post–World War II period. But these critical moments are added on to a narrative that does not consider the critical and conserving impulses as the primary dialectic at

work in human history. In sum, this text, like that of Kett, lacks a political economic, holistic framework within which to situate the learning dynamics of the society as people struggle to make a living, live their lives, and express themselves. Stubblefield and Keane are whigs at heart. Their survey work seems thin once set beside Cremin's works.

The dean of American educational historians, Lawrence Cremin, would never have self-identified as an adult educational historian. But he actually constructs the boundaries of education in a manner that includes both children and adults (see Cremin, 1970, 1976, 1977, 1980, 1988). From the first time I read him, I was struck by the idea that institutions like museums, households, farm movements, and the workplace itself could be understood as educative, forming and shaping outlook and character. Cremin constructs a framework broad enough to include Schied's Freedman Schools, Rockhill's social reconstructionist workers' education, and Knowles's and Houles's beloved lyceums and chatauquas. The sparkling multiplicity of individuals, forms, and institutions that educate found a place within Cremin's cartography of the field.

Cremin knows that he must conceptualize education to avoid either collapsing education into socialization, enculturative or acculturative process, or defining education so broadly that it becomes identical to society. "Any history," he affirms, "is always of the history of something in particular, and the explanatory categories the historian uses in writing about something in particular are almost invariably drawn from other domains—from politics or philosophy" (1977, p. 162). Cremin casts education as the "deliberate, systematic, and sustained effort to transmit, evoke, or acquire knowledge, skills, values, or sensibilities, as well as any outcomes of that effort" (1976, p. 27). This broad, well-known definition allows him to capture the complex interplay of inter- and intragenerational transmission (from adult to children, children to adult, and adult to adult). His definition projects us beyond schools and colleges to the "multiplicity of individuals and institutions that educate" (1976, p. 29). By itself this conceptual move—adding more objects to the field (parents, peers, siblings, libraries, museums, camps, churches, fairs, settlement houses, factories, radio stations, television, newspapers)—is not revolutionary. Cremin's boldly innovative interpretive move posits that educative institutions in any time period form configurations, clusters, or constellations. He speaks of the "tendency of educative institutions at particular times and places to relate to one another in configurations of education" (1977, p. 142). This viewpoint shatters the professionalized, whiggish perspective on adult educational history.

Now historians of adult learning must ask how adults learned about nature, others, and the self in the colonial period, for instance, where "adult education" was unnamed, or not labeled as such. It is this configuration (we will analyze one period in American history in a moment) that transmits knowledge, values, attitudes, and sensibilities (which often cohere in a "vision of life" to the people in different stations in the society). Cremin recognizes that every society harbors "discordant configurations" (1977, p. 21), which exist in tension with the dominant one. This permits him to examine missionary activity and slavery as pedagogical encounters—the "reality of two coexisting modes of life and the two coexisting configurations of education" (1977, pp. 21–22; see also Welton, 2005, for a Canadian case study using this conflicting configurations heuristic). Cremin also asserts that it is necessary to understand that individuals have their own purposes. They move "through institutions and configurations of education in their own ways" (1977, p. 25). These configurations—the affinity of objects for each other—exist in relationship to the larger society. They also change over time. A component may be dropped, or undergo a transformation in purpose and function (in Canada, for example, Mechanics' Institutes often transformed into libraries). New ones are added.

To illustrate, let us examine the period of American history from 1783 to 1876. During this period, the family, church, school, and college—and, to a lesser extent, the newspaper—were the primary educative institutions. But the configuration of education began to change in a number of ways. In *American Education: The National Experience, 1783–1876*, Cremin (1980) tells the story of how the dominant ideology (he terms it the "popular paideia"), comprised of "evangelical pieties, democratic hopes, and utilitarian striving" (p. 14), originated and was transmitted through a myriad of institutions and activities to most Americans. All institutions

were to contribute to the formation of the new American "man" who would not merely seek his own self-interest, but would participate actively in public life and pursue schooling as a practical instrument for personal advancement and a useful tool for bettering society.

Three significant components were added to the old configuration: (1) the institutions of organized work (mill, factory, mine, shop, and office), (2) institutions for the diffusion of special kinds of knowledge (libraries, lyceums, fairs, and museums), and (3) custodial institutions (houses of refuge, orphan asylums, and penitentiaries). During the first century of national life, the educative influence of the school and newspaper probably grew in relation to that of household and church (they were axial in the colonial period). But the educative influence of the external place of work increasingly mediated the influence of all other education during the years of adult employment. Chapter 14 of *American Education*, "Living and Learning" (Cremin, 1980), is of epochal conceptual significance for those committed to understanding how to constitute adult education as an object of study. Cremin observes that the emergent industrial workplace was the primary school for adults, as well as that the evangelical church continued to have significant influence. Thus, with the development of the factory in the 19th century, the values and attitudes traditionally associated with Poor Richard (inner discipline, hard work, punctuality, frugality, sobriety, orderliness, prudence) were taught with renewed vigor and growing intensity by churches, schools, and voluntary associations as well as by the factory.

Cremin, as mentioned earlier, recognizes the existence of alternative configurations in the national period. In a chapter simply entitled "Outcasts," he introduces the concept of a "discordant education"—an "education in which at least two configurations sought to inculcate in the same individuals quite different attitudes via quite different pedagogies" (1980, p. 243). Drawing on the controversial revisionist histories of Black Americans, Cremin argues that the "whip and the bible" were the primary pedagogical instruments instructing Blacks in the White version of their place in the world. But a secondary pedagogy transmitted an alternative culture through family and clandestine religious assembly, enabling the slaves to survive as a people and maintain a Black identity. The dynamics of a "discordant education," Cremin avers, were also present among Native Indians and among numerous subcommunities such as Irish Catholic and Jewish families in New York City.

In conclusion, this survey analysis of how adult education historians construct their "object of their study" has revealed just how tangled up this project is with the values and sensibility of the individual historian. Those with a deep commitment to workers' emancipation write lamentations when they think that this project has vanished from contemporary life. Those with a deep commitment to the professional efficiency and humanistic competence of an adult education professoriate celebrate the growth of the field with its many learning opportunities. Those with particularistic interests in the formation of public opinion, social movements, or literary societies mine history for their ends.

All of this is illuminating. But Cremin, I think, is not simply writing "educational history." His work argues—essentially and brilliantly—that we cannot understand anything deeply significant about history unless we conceptualize the way each society in different epochs constitutes itself as a learning society. The learning society paradigm is now dominant in adult education theory and the popular consciousness. Adult educators come in many guises; what matters most is the way the civil society learning infrastructure is organized to enable men and women and children to stand tall, speak with courage, and express themselves.

REFERENCES

Bailyn, B. (1960). *Education in the forming of American society.* New York: Random House.

Brookfield, S. (1988). Graduate education as a sociocultural product: A cross-cultural analysis of theory and practice in the United States and Great Britain. In S. Brookfield (Ed.), *Training educators of adults.* London: Routledge.

Colin, S. (1988). *The Universal Negro Improvement Association and the education of African American adults.* Unpublished doctoral dissertation, Northern Illinois University.

Cremin, L. A. (1970). *American education: The colonial experience, 1607–1783.* New York: Harper & Row.

Cremin, L. A. (1976). *Public education.* New York: Basic Books.

Cremin, L. A. (1977). *Traditions of American education.* New York: Basic Books.

Cremin, L. A. (1980). *American education: The national experience, 1783–1876.* New York: Basic Books.

Cremin, L. A. (1988). *American education: The metropolitan experience, 1876–1980.* New York: Harper & Row.

Fenwick, T. J., Nesbit, T., & B. Spencer (Eds.). (2006). *Contexts of adult education: Canadian perspectives.* Toronto, ON: Thompson Educational Publishing.

Field, J. (1992). *Learning through labour: Training, education and the state, 1890–1939.* Leeds, UK: Department of Adult and Continuing Education, University of Leeds.

Fieldhouse, R., & Associates. (1996). *A history of modern British adult education.* Leicester, UK: NIACE.

Fitchue, M. F. (1993, May). *The adult education movement: A dialogue across differences in search of Black education history, 1920–1953.* Paper presented at Syracuse University Adult Education Conference, Syracuse, NY.

Gere, A. (1997). *Intimate practices: Literary and cultural work in U.S. women's clubs.* Urbana: University of Illinois Press.

Grattan, H. C. (1955). *In quest of knowledge: A historical perspective on adult education* [Reprint]. New York: Arno Press and The New York Times.

Guy, T. (1993, May). *Cultural pluralism in the adult education movement: Alain Locke and the Association for Adult Education's "Experiment in Negro Education."* Paper presented at Syracuse University Adult Education History Conference, Syracuse, NY.

Gyant, L. (2002). Alain Locke: More than an adult educator. In E. Peterson (Ed.), *Freedom road: Adult education of African Americans* (pp. 67–87). Malabar, FL: Krieger.

Houle, C. O. (1992). *The literature of adult education: A bibliographic essay.* San Francisco: Jossey-Bass.

Jarvis, P. (Ed.). (1987). *Twentieth century thinkers in adult education.* London: Croom Helm.

Karlovic, N. (1993, May). *Jessie Allen Charters: A voice for our times.* Paper presented at Syracuse Adult Education History Conference, Syracuse, NY.

Kelly, T. (1970). *A history of adult education in Great Britain* (2nd ed., rev.). Liverpool, UK: Liverpool University Press.

Kelly, T. (1992). *A history of adult education in Great Britain* (3rd ed.). Liverpool, UK: Liverpool University Press. (Original work published 1970)

Kett, J. F. (1994). *The pursuit of knowledge under difficulties: From self-improvement to adult education in America, 1750–1990*. Palo Alto, CA: Stanford University Press.

Knowles, M. (1977). *A history of the adult education movement in the U.S.* Malabar, FL: Krieger. (Original work published 1962)

McIlroy, J. (1992). Trade union education for a change. In B. Simon (Ed.), *The search for enlightenment: The working class and adult education in the twentieth century.* Leicester, UK: NIACE.

McNairn, J. L. (2000). *The capacity to judge: Public opinion and deliberative democracy in upper Canada, 1791–1854.* Toronto: University of Toronto Press.

Rockhill, K. (1985). The liberal perspective and the symbolic legitimation of university adult education in the U.S.A. In R. Taylor, K. Rockhill, & R. Fieldhouse, *University adult education in England and the U.S.A.* Beckenham, UK: Croom Helm.

Rubenson, K. (1982). Adult education research: In quest of a map of the territory. *Ault Education, 32*(2), 57–74.

Savicky, I. (1987, May). Toward a typology of European adult education historiography. *CASAE History Bulletin,* pp. 19–23.

Schied, F. (1991). *Towards a reconceptualization of the historical foundations of adult education: The contributions of radical German-Americans to workers' education.* Unpublished doctoral thesis, Northern Illinois University.

Sexton, C. (1993, March). *The influences of the turn-of-the-century Midwest on Dorothy Canfield Fisher's educational philosophy.* Paper presented at Syracuse University History of Adult Education Conference, Syracuse, NY.

Simon, B. (1992). *The search for enlightenment: The working class and adult education in the twentieth century.* Leicester, UK: NIACE.

Steele, T. (2007). *Knowledge is power! The rise and fall of European popular education movements, 1848–1939.* New York: Peter Lang.

Stewart, D. (1987). *Adult learning in America: Eduard Lindeman and his agenda for lifelong learning.* Malabar, FL: Krieger.

Stubblefield, H. (1988). *Towards a history of adult education in America:* Beckenham, UK: Croom Helm.

Stubblefield, H., & Keane, P. (1994). *Adult education in the American experience: From the colonial period to the present.* San Francisco: Jossey-Bass.

Taylor, J. (2001). *Union learning: Canadian labour education in the twentieth century.* Toronto: Thompson Educational.

Thompson, M. (1993, March). *The changing language of leadership in adult education: Implications for the acceptance of women as leaders.* Paper presented at Syracuse University Adult Education History Conference, Syracuse, NY.

Welton, M. R. (Ed.). (1987a). *Knowledge for the people: The struggle for adult learning in English-speaking Canada, 1828–1973.* Toronto: OISE Press.

Welton, M. R. (1987b). "Vivisecting the nightingale": Reflections on adult education as an object of study. *Studies in the Education of Adults, 19*(1), 46–68.

Welton, M. R. (2001). *Little Mosie from the Margaree: A biography of Moses Michael Coady.* Toronto: Thompson Educational.

Welton, M. R. (2005). Cunning pedagogics: The encounter between the Jesuit missionaries and Amerindians in 17th-century New France. *Adult Education Quarterly, 55*(2), 101–115.

Winch, J. (1994). "You have talents—only cultivate them": Philadelphia's Black literary societies and the abolitionist crusade. In J. Yellin & J. Van Horne (Eds.), *The abolitionist sisterhood: Women's political culture in antebellum American* (pp. 101–118). Ithaca, NY: Cornell University Press.

8

INTERNATIONAL AND COMPARATIVE ADULT AND CONTINUING EDUCATION

MARY V. ALFRED AND FREDRICK MUYIA NAFUKHO

During the last century, countries the world over have witnessed major and significant changes both locally and globally. Many developing countries have emerged from positions of massive foreign political domination to independence and self-governance. Other significant changes are the globalization of economic systems, the rapid development of technology, the changing demographic composition of the population, and the emergence of information-based and knowledge-based economies. With such transformations and the demand for global competitiveness came the hope for better, relevant, and well-founded education systems that would respond to the need for lifelong learning and adult education. However, as of the beginning of the 21st century, the hope for "education for all" has not been realized (UNESCO, 2007a).

At the national level, governments view education as an important factor in both individual and societal development. With growing concerns about how they will position themselves globally, countries are facing increasing demands to meet a number of often conflicting goals driven by the needs of individuals, businesses, and society at large. As a result, diverse stakeholders' views on schooling often create tensions over educational content, delivery, structure, and outcomes (Kubow & Fossum, 2007). For adult education today, the tension lies around its purpose in an era of internationalization and globalization. The debates take on such issues as economic concerns for equipping adults with appropriate workplace competencies and skills that would allow nations to compete in the global markets; civic concerns for an education agenda that would prepare adults to participate more fully in public life, thus challenging hegemonic and imperialistic ideals; and individual-level concerns for the development of the whole person through lifelong education.

While these debates on the role and purpose of adult education have gone on for decades, the answers that emerge are often multiple and ambiguous, attesting to the discursive and overlapping nature of these issues. Most importantly, responses to these issues are contextual and vary with perspectives, philosophies, practices, and worldviews. In 2006, Gale McClure, then vice president for programs with the Kellogg Foundation, had no question about the purpose of adult education. In the foreword to the book *Global Issues in Adult Education: Perspectives from Latin America, Southern Africa, and the United States,* she wrote, "the impact of adult education throughout the world comes as no surprise to those individuals who are involved in the profession, because the mission of adult education is to help adults, as individuals and groups, achieve their goals and aspirations. . . . Nowhere is this clearer than in the context of international work" (McClure, 2006, p. xi). Because of the complexities of meeting the needs of individuals and society through adult education, it is no surprise that for over 60 years, world nations have come together to plan for the provisions for adult education and lifelong learning. The purpose of this chapter, therefore, is to take an international and comparative view of adult education across nations, and it is organized as follows: (1) a brief history of the development and philosophical foundations of international and comparative adult education; (2) a comparative analysis of the current practice of adult education in selected regions, particularly to the regions' response to CONFINTEA V (the Fifth International Conference on Adult Education, which took place in Hamburg, Germany, in 1997) and its call for "education for all"; and (3) future trends and directions for adult education.

Historical Overview of International and Comparative Adult Education

According to Boucouvalas (2002), efforts at bringing the international community together to collaborate and dialogue about adult education started in 1919 with the establishment of the World Association of Adult Education (WAAE), based in London. This association remained in place until the beginning of World War II, and its objective was to use adult education as a platform to illuminate and address issues that confront individuals, communities, and societies. That period was viewed as a time when adult education was developing its identity—an identity that Charters and Hilton describe as "a kind of 'world sense' of issues and world problems" (1989, p. 2). The WAAE was instrumental in calling together the first international world conference on adult education, which was held in Cambridge, England, in 1929 and was attended by about 300 members with at least 33 national delegates (Harris, 1980).

Since 1949, under the sponsorship of United Nations Educational, Scientific, and Cultural Organization (UNESCO), international adult educators have assembled to dialogue on issues and concerns involving the continuing education of adults worldwide. Five major conferences are worth noting: those in Elsinore, Denmark, in 1949; Montreal, Canada, in 1960; Tokyo, Japan,

in 1972; Paris, France, in 1985; and finally, Hamburg, Germany, in 1997 (Boucouvalas, 2002; Charters & Hilton, 1989; UNESCO, 1997).

Following the 1960 assembly in Montreal, some North American adult educators and scholars (from the U.S. and Canada) gathered at a meeting at Syracuse University to dialogue on issues closer to home that were related to university adult education. That meeting culminated in the formation of the International Congress of University Adult Education (ICUEA). Six years later (in 1966), ICUEA sponsored the first comparative adult education conference, held in Exeter, New Hampshire (Charters & Hilton, 1989), with the purpose of assembling an international group of university adult educators to discuss programmatic concerns and to plan for future directions. Another significant historic organization, the International Council of Adult Education (ICAE), was organized in 1973, thus further highlighting and promoting the agenda for international adult education.

Under the direction of Roby Kidd, the ICEA divided the globe into seven regions and became the association of non-governmental organizations (NGOs) around the world (Boucouvalas, 2002). One unique feature of the ICAE and later the 1997 Hamburg conference was that it assembled not only government officials, but also members of non-governmental organizations, community activists, and the private sector, among others, recognizing that addressing the needs of the populace through adult education takes the collaboration across all sectors. Members of the ICAE took a grass-roots or social action approach, addressing issues that confronted the lives of everyday individuals. According to Boucouvalas (2002), "major world issues such as the environment, peace, gender equity, indigenous knowledge, literacy and others shape the agenda of the ICAE" (p. 24). The ICAE has held several world assemblies, drawing representatives from government as well as non-government organizations. These include the first assembly in Tanzania, Africa, in 1976, and those in Paris, France, in 1982 and Buenos Aires, Argentina, in 1984. More recently, during the last decade of the 20th century, a series of conferences has raised the world's consciousness on some key international issues. These include the following: The World Conference on Education for All: Meeting Basic Learning Needs, held in Jomitien, Thailand, in 1990; The United Nations Conference on

Human Rights, held in Vienna, Austria, in 1993; the International Conference on Population and Development, held in Cairo, Egypt, in 1994; The World Summit for Social Development, held in Copenhagen, Denmark, in 1995; the United Nations Conference on Human Settlements, held in Istanbul, Turkey, in 1996; the World Food Summit, held in Rome, Italy, in 1996; and the 2001 conference in Ocho Rios, Jamaica (Boucouvalas, 2002; UNESCO, 1997).

At each of these conferences, international scholars, practitioners, and representatives from government agencies and non-governmental organizations, among others, discussed the human concerns relative to their specific context, and together they set the agenda for policy, research, and practice of adult education worldwide. Comparative adult education, therefore, emerged as an offshoot of international adult education. According to Charters and Hilton (1989),

> The study of international adult education grew out of the study of adult education itself, and the international aspects of such study took on new importance as national and international events took on major, and sometimes cataclysmic, importance. Further, comparative adult education at the international level began as a body of systemic study after major program developments were perceived to have taken place in international adult education. (p. 2)

It is important, therefore, to take a current view of adult education practice across selected regions to understand how nations are responding to the agenda for continuing education and lifelong learning for all adults, particularly since CONFINTEA V. It is important to highlight some of the results of that conference, as it frames the remainder of the chapter.

CONFINTEA V AND THE AGENDA FOR ADULT LEARNING

Like the other four international conferences sponsored by UNESCO, CONFINTEA V emphasized the role of adult learning and nonformal education to lifelong learning. This is not surprising, because according to Schuetze (2006), "international organizations were the main proponents of Lifelong Learning when the concept was first developed in the early 1970s" (p. 289). However, the fifth CONFINTEA conference marked a turning point in the global recognition of and commitment to adult learning and nonformal education (UNESCO, 2007b). That conference called attention to family literacy as a bridge to formal and nonformal learning and used adult education as the platform from which to plan for human development within a global context. Participants were representatives of world nations and addressed global challenges of the 21st century as they related to "democracy, peace and human rights, respect for diversity and conflict resolution, economic and ecological sustainability, and workforce development" (UNESCO, 2007b). Two landmark documents emerged from the conference that would guide the direction of adult education globally: The Hamburg Declaration on Adult Learning and the Agenda for the Future (UNESCO, 1997). (The full reports can be found on the UNESCO Web site at www.unesco.org)

The Hamburg Declaration identified 27 commitments or positions necessary to promote democracy, equity, and global citizenship through adult education. While each of the commitments is considered significant, because of space limitations only 13 are listed here.

1. Adult education is the key to active citizenship and full participation in society.

2. Adult education constitutes formal, nonformal, and continuing education and each contributes fully to learning across the life span.

3. The education of adults and that of children and youth are not separate but work together to promote learning across the life span, and, therefore, should receive equal attention.

4. Basic education for all means that whatever their age, individuals should have the opportunity to realize their full potential through educational pursuit.

5. Literacy is a fundamental human right and opportunities for literacy engagement and access should be available to all.

6. Women have a right to equal opportunities, and educational systems should expand educational opportunities to all women.

7. The culture of violence should be eliminated and replaced with the culture of peace, based on justice and tolerance.

8. Adult education should reflect the richness of cultural diversity and respect for traditional and indigenous people's knowledge systems.

9. Health is a basic human right, and adult education can provide relevant and sustainable access to health knowledge.

10. Education for environmental sustainability should be a lifelong learning process and adult environmental education can sensitize communities and decision makers towards sustained environmental action.

11. Indigenous and nomadic people have a right to education at all levels and education for members of these communities should be culturally appropriate.

12. Adult education should work to limit the risk of individuals losing sight of the human dimension as a result of technology.

13. Adult education must pay attention to the ageing population and provide learning opportunities that are appropriate and relevant to that population. (UNESCO, 1997, pp. 1–7)

From the declaration, an action plan, namely the Agenda for the Future, was drawn up to serve as a framework for the planning and development of adult education and lifelong learning across the globe. It focuses on some of the issues and concerns facing members of today's societies and highlights the roles that adult education can play in helping individuals address these challenges. It calls for adult education to partner with governmental agencies and nongovernmental organizations, employers and trade unions, universities and research centers, civil and community-based organizations, adult educators, and learners themselves (UNESCO, 1997) in the planning and delivery of education for lifelong learning. Additionally, the agenda brings attention to the changing nature of work resulting from technology and the globalization of economic systems as well as demographic changes caused by the movement of people across nations. Such demographic diversity results in tensions between social groups based on culture, ethnicity, gender roles, religion, and class. All these trends have implications for adult education and lifelong learning activities. In light of some of these challenges, the agenda put forward was organized around the following 10 broad themes:

1. Adult literacy and democracy: the challenges of the twenty-first century

2. Improving the conditions and quality of adult learning

3. Ensuring the universal right to literacy and basic education

4. Adult learning, gender equality and equity, and the empowerment of women

5. Adult learning and the changing world of work

6. Adult learning in relation to environment, health, and population

7. Adult learning, culture, media, and new information technologies

8. Adult learning for all: the rights and aspirations of different groups

9. The economics of adult learning

10. Enhancing international co-operation and solidarity. (UNESCO, 1997, p. 11)

In this chapter, we examine how various regions, through the practice of adult education, are responding to the global challenges that impede human development. Among the challenges included are poverty, health disparities, gender inequities, and economic inequalities, to name a few. Throughout the regions, poverty remains one of the most pressing issues, and it is viewed as a barrier to learning as well as a consequence of low literacy resulting from insufficient education (UNESCO, 2003a). Therefore, for adults around the world, education is viewed as the impetus for human development, and adult education must be reconceptualized and shifted from a purely instrumentalist perspective to a more global agenda for human development.

A COMPARATIVE VIEW OF ADULT EDUCATION IN SELECTED REGIONS

In this section, we highlight some of the regions' responses to the CONFINTEA V call for "education for all." Basically, we present policies and pedagogies of adult and continuing education in selected partner regions. These partner regions include (a) Sub-Saharan Africa, (b) Arab States, (c) Asia and the Pacific Region, (d) Europe and North America, and (e) Latin America and the Caribbean. Using case examples, we focused on how systems of education are repositioning themselves to respond to the agenda for adult education.

All governments have the responsibility to promote and facilitate adult learning; however, in a number of countries—such as Sudan, Somalia, and Angola—this responsibility has been diminished by the impact of war and civil strife, structural adjustment programs, and poor economic performance. While adult education and lifelong learning are being promoted in various parts of the world, Africa is no exception. Youngman (2001) observed that the international trend of increased policy emphasis on adult education and lifelong learning was also being witnessed in Africa. For example, in 1996, the Africa Regional Consultation for UNESCO's Fifth International Conference on Adult Education pronounced the Dakar Declaration on Adult Education and Lifelong Learning. In this declaration, demand for lifelong learning was reported as being on the increase in Africa. In addition, lifelong learning was considered a fundamental right and a prerequisite for individual development and social change (Nafukho, Amutabi, & Otunga, 2005). In 1998, the Seventh Conference of Ministers of Education of African Member States had as its theme "Lifelong Education in Africa—Prospects for the Twenty First Century."

While several African countries recognize the importance of adult education and lifelong learning in addressing individual, organizational, community, and societal development issues, we use the examples of Kenya and Namibia to illustrate the policy efforts being undertaken by the governments of these two African countries.

Republic of Kenya (2003) observed that since CONFINTEA V, the government of Kenya has consistently recognized the important role played by adult and continuing education (ACE) in ensuring the optimal utilization of the country's human resources for individual, community, and national development. For instance, in 1997, the government of Kenya developed the Master Plan on Education and Training (MPET) covering the period 1997 to 2010. This educational plan includes the development objectives and strategies to guide the education sector in the 21st century. Regarding adult and continuing education, this educational plan recommended improvement in the qualitative and quantitative capacity of such education in evolving a functionally

literate society in Kenya and improving social and productive skills among adults. The other key recommendations included the need to use ACE to provide the youth and adults with workplace competencies, strengthen and expand the Adult Basic Literacy and Post-Literacy Programs, promote nonformal education for adults who missed an opportunity to receive education, and invest in adult education and lifelong learning as a strategy to address poverty issues in Kenyan society. In addition, the government of Kenya initiated accreditation of prior informal and nonformal adult learning (see Republic of Kenya, 2003, pp. 5–6) and developed clear policies and strategies aimed at promoting public investment in adult learning.

Besides Kenya, Namibia is the only other African country with an approved government policy on adult education. As noted by Ngatjizeko, Namene, and Tjiho (2003), "As part of the process of the renewal of adult learning in Namibia, a national policy on adult learning [was] drafted, discussed at a national conference and approved by [the] cabinet in July 2003" (p. 1). To ensure implementation of the national adult education policy, several Namibian educational institutions have been involved. Examples of the institutions involved in the provision of adult learning in Namibia include government, nongovernmental organizations, community-based organizations, churches, the University of Namibia, the Polytechnic of Namibia, and the private sector. While reforming education systems in Africa, it is important that the policy makers draw from what is happening in other parts of the world. Every country and/or continent is faced with unique kinds of problems. For example, in the several East Asian countries usually referred to as "Asian Tigers" (e.g., Hong Kong and Taiwan), the economic crisis of the 1990s prompted the reexamination of the role of education in managing economic and social crises. In the case of Hong Kong, the Hong Kong Education Commission (1999) observed, "Our young people must be outward-looking, imbued with a spirit of exploration, able to make use of IT, able to master different kinds of knowledge, and willing to strive to improve through continuous learning. To enhance competitiveness, Hong Kong has to shift to high value-added and technology-based production and services" (p. 9).

In Taiwan, another successful Asian economy, the Ministry of Education (MOE) published an education report aimed at promoting adult and continuing education and establishing a lifelong learning society. The report clearly articulates various implementation strategies for achieving lifelong learning. The strategies include:

1. Constructing a legal system for lifelong education;

2. Nurturing people's notion of lifelong learning;

3. Integrating the lifelong education system;

4. Increasing lifelong learning opportunities;

5. Establishing a recurrent education system;

6. Improving the curriculum, teaching materials, and methods of adult education;

7. Providing administrative support;

8. Processing researches and assessments on lifelong education;

9. Cultivating the international visions and global knowledge;

10. Securing the individual learning right;

11. Motivating the potential of a learning organisation;

12. Encouraging private industries to provide learning opportunities;

13. Integrating the information network of lifelong learning;

14. Establishing commissions of lifelong learning at different governmental levels;

15. Strengthening the foreign language learning in the community;

16. Establishing an accreditation system;

17. Nurturing teachers' notions of lifelong learning;

18. Reforming the school education. (Mok & Chan, 2002, pp. 18–19)

The Ministry of Education in Taiwan also came up with the white paper that contained 14 programs aimed at promoting lifelong learning (see Mok & Chan, 2002, p. 19). While some of these programs may be too ambitious for some areas, we believe that policy makers from the various regions may draw some useful lessons from them.

In the case of the Western countries, in the 1990s especially, adult and continuing education and lifelong learning gained renewed recognition. This renewed recognition of the need to invest in the learning of adult learners has been explained by Youngman (2001) as a result of "changes in the nature of work and global competition; rapid technological development; demographic shifts; the increase in human knowledge and expanded social demand; cultural and lifestyle changes; and political concerns of opportunity and social inclusion" (p. 1). Nafukho and his colleagues (2005), citing the U.S. government (1999), noted that the G-7 Charter on Lifelong Learning emphasized the importance of lifelong learning as a strategy to address societal and economic challenges. In Europe, the European Union chose the theme of lifelong learning for year 1996. Mok and Chan (2002) noted the importance of adult and continuing education, suggesting that

> A dominant theme in current education policy, especially in Europe and North America, has been the creation of access to lifelong learning through the educational system; while international organizations such as IGOs, transnational corporations (TNCs) and non-governmental organizations (NGOs) have been pushing lifelong learning to the educational agendas of national governments. (p. 4)

In the Latin American and Caribbean region, the same can be said, and efforts aimed at promoting adult education and lifelong learning are ongoing. In much of the English-speaking Caribbean, for example, adult education is formally organized within the Ministry of Education and Human Resource Development, with adult education officers appointed to oversee programs and activities throughout the islands. The islands are supported by The Caribbean Council for Adult Education (CARCAE)—a regional body that was established and endorsed by the Caribbean Community (CARICOM) governments to help promote and facilitate the development and provision of adult education in the region (Ellis, Ramsey, & Small, 2000). Working closely with governmental and non-governmental organizations, CARCARE strives to increase awareness about the importance of adult education and has helped broadened the concept of adult learning from one of literacy acquisition to that of lifelong learning. In a CONFINTEA V mid-term report from the small English-speaking island of St. Lucia, it was noted,

Adult learning is more than education for the illiterate. It is a critical pillar of human development worldwide. In today's education for All and Lifelong Learning frameworks and trans-border trade and services, adult learning provides not only high-level skills necessary for the labour market but also the training essential for educators, researchers, business managers, doctors, taxi-drivers, personnel in industry, agriculture, health and a myriad of [other skills] workers need to function productively. It is the trained and retrained individuals who develop the capacity and analytical skills that drive local economies, support initiatives, lead effective governments, and make effective decisions. (CONFINTEA Mid-Term Review, 2003, p. 1)

Adult learning, then, is defined very broadly to include training and development activities in and out of organizations. To that end, the government of St. Lucia, in its national human resource development manifesto, made adult learning and human development key components of that initiative (Scotland, 2004). With a Caribbean agenda to broaden the scope of adult learning, a number of stakeholders collaborated to set an agenda for adult education on the island. As a result, the adult education program, which formerly focused on literacy and numeracy, was renamed in 2001 and became the National Enrichment and Learning Program (Scotland, 2004). At their meeting in 1997, the Caribbean Community (CARICOM) heads of government agreed on a human resource development plan, at the core of which was the education of adults (Jules, 1999). Lifelong learning was at the center of that strategy, and the strengthening of nonformal learning was made a strategic imperative.

Despite the recognized need for adult education among out-of-school youths and adults, adult education remains a low priority in the educational budgets of most Latin American and Caribbean countries. Arnove and Torres (1995) note that in the past three decades, on an average, only 3% of educational funds or less has been spent on programs aimed at adults. They further note that it is not uncommon for governments to be spending only 1% or 2% of their education budgets on adult education in regions where as much as two thirds of the rural population may be illiterate.

Currently, the percentage of the education budget countries allocate to adult education ranges widely. For example, the small British Caribbean island of St. Lucia dedicates to adult education a generous 15.59% of its education budget, Brazil dedicates 7%, Dominican Republic 2.8%, and Ecuador only 0.4% of its education budget (UNESCO, 2003b). The government of St. Lucia appears to be more generous with the adult education dollars because it is working to strategically position the island to compete with the world economy (Jules, 1999). Also, there is the fear that unless the government contributes to the training and development of its population, it will continue to experience the "brain drain" phenomenon (UNESCO, 2003b).

While much progress has been realized in the promotion of adult education and lifelong learning worldwide, there is much yet to be done to meet the global commitment of "Education for All" by the year 2015. Notable accomplishments throughout many parts of the world include large-scale literacy programs, equivalency or second-chance programs, employment skills development programs, and nonformal education programs that are often linked to community development, to name a few. However, the regions still struggle with issues involving poverty, health, education funding, integrating indigenous knowledges, and globalization, among others. Some of these issues are highlighted below as areas of continued concerns.

FUTURE CHALLENGES AND PROSPECTS FOR INTERNATIONAL AND COMPARATIVE ADULT EDUCATION

The radical and uncertain changes in the social, political, economic, environmental, and educational settings the world over require adult educators to transform themselves and the curricula significantly in order to address these challenges. As already shown in this chapter, adult educators in low-income, middle-income, and high-income countries face both challenges and prospects in implementing the agenda for adult education. In concluding this chapter, we briefly examine some of these challenges and prospects.

Challenge 1: Financing of Adult and Continuing Education

The field of adult and continuing education is facing the major challenge of how to finance adult learning programs. Within the broader education sector itself, the main challenge is how to allocate financial resources to various levels of education including adult, continuing, and nonformal education. Given the economic changes and reforms taking place in education, adult educators need to be entrepreneurial and to seek for diverse ways of financing adult education programs. In the case of Africa, Nafukho and his colleagues (2005) outlined several key funding strategies for adult and continuing education programs. These included education taxes, financial support from the private sector, establishment of entrepreneurial activities in all adult learning organizations, voluntary contributions by alumni and other members of society, tax reforms to encourage individuals to donate to adult learning institutions, encouragement of volunteerism (especially among retired citizens), and the establishment of community-based computer learning centers (Nafukho et al., 2005, pp. 160–161). Incorporating some of these strategies could help address the funding barriers that some institutions and agencies face.

Challenge 2: Health Issues

A challenge that cannot be ignored by adult and continuing education educators is the spread of HIV/AIDS. The HIV/AIDS epidemic in many regions of the world has forced governmental and non-governmental agencies, educators, and education institutions to reconceptualize the role of education in combating world problems of such catastrophic magnitude. With an international and comparative approach to education, nations can draw from one another as they plan for adult education to be a "social vaccine" (World Bank, n.d., p. 1) in the fight against many of the world's health problems. Although education can play a central role, the evidence suggests that responses from the education sector have been slow and inadequate, and in some regions nonexistent. This neglect on the part of the education sector is not primarily the result of a lack of resources but a lack of vision as to how education should be reconceptualized to address these social problems. According to the report *HIV/AIDS and Education,*

> This [neglect on the part of education] does not appear to reflect a simple lack of resources: although the overall resource envelope may be inadequate, those resources that are currently

available (e.g., from the World Bank Multi-Country AIDS Program and from the Global Fund) are underutilized by the education sector. Indeed, few educational systems have begun to address HIV/AIDS systematically and many countries have yet to develop a formal strategy for an education sector response to HIV/AIDS. (World Bank, n.d. p. 1)

While Nafukho and his colleagues (2005) view a lack of funding as a barrier to adult education's response to global issues that affect human development, the report *HIV/AIDS and Education* suggests that the barrier is a result not of a lack of resources but of a lack of vision regarding how adult education can embrace globalization and internationalization as means of raising consciousness to the disparities and inequities that impede human development. Indeed, research on North American adult educators' engagement with globalization and internationalization has resulted in similar findings (see Alfred & Guo, 2007; Butterwick, Fenwick, & Mojab, 2003; and Mulenga, 2001).

Challenge 3: Promotion of Indigenous Ways of Learning and Knowing

Adult educators face the major challenge of how to tap the rich indigenous knowledge that is not mainly Western oriented. Currently, adult education students and educators rely on books and learning resources mainly developed in the Western world. On realizing this serious anomaly, UNESCO launched a series of books on adult learning from African perspectives. We need similar books written on Asian perspectives on adult learning, Arabic perspectives on adult learning, and Brazilian perspectives on adult learning, just to mention a few. For example, many countries in Africa, Asia, and Latin America have wonderful and complex indigenous knowledge systems that go back many thousands of years. Much of this knowledge needs to be tapped as a way of managing the current problems facing our societies. In the case of China, for instance, it is a truism that the country has a long heritage and rich Indigenous Knowledge System (IKS) that the rest of the world has benefited from, borrowed from immensely, or appropriated. The creative and innovative IKSs in various regions of the world have been masked by historical misrepresentations and thus are not being utilized to solve the problems facing society.

Challenge 4: Globalization

It is well documented that "for a small segment of the population, globalization means the concentration of wealth and power; for the rest of the human population, it means the globalization of misery and poverty. The numbers of those who fall into the category of 'suffering' are increasing day by day. . . . We certainly need to examine how and why they inhibit human freedom," wrote Ramdas (1997, p. 36). As a result, Ramdas has called for an international and comparative approach to adult education and suggests that in order to make it happen, "We need to reinterpret—and reclaim—globalization" (p. 36). Adult education, especially that of North America, exists within a large instrumentalist, status quo framework (Cruikshank, 1996, 2001; Hall, 1997; Ramdas, 1997). Alternatively, adult education, with its philosophy of social justice and equity, can take a more aggressive position in researching, teaching, and speaking out against the social conditions that impede human development, thus starting a revolutionary movement to address the fundamental issues of human rights. In a plenary address at the CONFINTEA V conference in Hamburg, Germany, Ramdas (1997) noted,

In my view, adult education—in its broadest sense—is uniquely positioned to make an empowering intervention on behalf of the underprivileged in every society, and at the same time, influence macro policy. We need to take an imaginative leap, to move beyond the dialectics of the current discourse which continues to propagate a compartmentalized view of education and learning. I believe that our challenge is to re-interpret adult education as a powerful instrument, to build, in the words of Nelson Mandela, "a new political culture of human rights." (p. 36)

To build this culture of human rights, adult educators must make more purposeful attempts at the internationalization of research, curricula, and pedagogy to bring attention to global issues and to be a partner in finding solutions to these issues. Those involved in the funding, planning, and delivery of adult education, therefore, should answer to the call put forth in 1997 by Lalita Ramdas, then president of the International Council for Adult Education, to build an adult education that goes beyond instrumentalism. A new agenda for adult education, then, is to re/claim adult learning as a lifelong phenomenon with the power to transform human lives across national boundaries. Engaging in the discourse allows space for the development of a critical pedagogy that would highlight and contest the disparities that result from a marginalized position in the world.

REFERENCES

Alfred, M. V., & Guo, S. (2007). Globalization and the internationalization of adult and higher education: Challenges and opportunities for Canada and the U.S. In L. Servage & T. Fenwick (Eds.), *Proceedings of the 48th Annual Adult Education Conference* (pp. 1–7). Edmonton, Canada: University of Alberta.

Arnove, R. F., & Torres, C. A. (1995). Adult education and state policy in Latin America: The contrasting cases of Mexico and Nicaragua. *Comparative Education, 31*, 311–326.

Boucouvalas, M. (2002). International adult education: Past, present, and into the future. *Adult Learning, 13*(4), 23–26.

Butterwick, S., Fenwick, T., & Mojab, S. (2003). Canadian adult education research in the 1990s: Tracing liberatory trends. *The Canadian Journal for the Study of Adult Education, 17*(2), 1–19.

Charters, A. N., & Hilton, R. J. (1989). *Landmarks in international adult education: A comparative analysis.* New York: Routledge.

CONFINTEA mid-term review. (2003). *Six years after CONFINTEA V: Status and future prospects of adult learning. Selected reports from countries/ regions: St. Lucia.* Retrieved December 15, 2009, from http://www.unesco.org/education/uie/ pdf/country/StLucia.pdf

Cruikshank, J. (1996). Are we aiding the enemy? The role of adult education in the new global economy. *Proceedings of the 15th CASAE Conference* (pp. 60–66). Winnipeg, Canada: University of Manitoba.

Cruikshank, J. (2001). Lifelong learning in the new economy: A great leap backwards. *Proceedings of the 20th CASAE Conference.* Laval, Quebec: University of Laval.

Ellis, P., Ramsey, A., & Small, S. (2000). *Education for all in the Caribbean: Assessment 2000.* Monograph Series 27. Kingston, Jamaica: UNESCO.

Hall, B. L. (1997, October 15–17). *Adult learning, global civil society, and politics.* Paper presented at the Midwest Research-to-Practice Conference, East Lansing, MI.

Hamburg Declaration. (1997). In *Final Report: Fifth International Conference on Adult Education* (p. 12). Retrieved December 8, 2009, from http://www.unesco.org/education/uie/confintea/pdf/finrepeng.pdf

Harris, W. J. A. (1980). *Comparative adult education: Practice, purpose, and theory.* London: Longman.

Hong Kong Education Commission. (1999). *Education blueprint for the 21st century—Review of academic systems: Aims of education.* Hong Kong: Hong Kong Government Printer.

Jules, D. (1999). *Adult and continuing education in St. Lucia: Addressing global transformation and the new millennium.* St. Lucia: Ministry of Education, Human Resource Development, Youth, and Sports.

Kubow, P. K., & Fossum, P. R. (2007). *Comparative education: Exploring issues in international perspective* (2nd ed.). Upper Saddle River, NJ: Merrill/Prentice Hall.

McClure, G. (2006). Foreword. In S. B. Merriam, B. C. Courtenay, & R. M. Cervero (Eds.), *Global issues and adult education: Perspectives from Latin America, southern Africa, and the United States* (pp. xi–xii). San Francisco Jossey-Bass.

Mok, K. H., & Chan, D. (2002, May 1–3). *The quest for quality education and learning society in Hong Kong, Taiwan and Shanghai.* Paper presented at the Pacific Circle Consortium 26th Annual Conference. Seoul, Korea.

Mulenga, D. (2001). The impact of globalization on human rights: The challenge for adult educators. *Proceedings of the 20th CASAE Conference* (pp. 54–59). Laval, Canada: University of Laval.

Nafukho, F. M., Amutabi, M. N., & Otunga, R. N. (2005). *Foundations of adult education in Africa.* Cape Town: Pearson and UNESCO.

Ngatjizeko, B., Namene, J., & Tjiho, J. (2003). *Namibia government report on CONFINTEA V Mid-term review.* Hamburg: UNESCO.

Ramdas, L. (1997). Adult education, lifelong learning, global knowledge: The challenge and potential. *Convergence, 30*(4), 34–37.

Republic of Kenya. (2003). Kenya Government report on CONFINTEA V Mid-term review. Retrieved December 15, 2009, from http://www.unesco.org/education/uie/pdf/country/Kenya.pdf

Schuetze, H. (2006). International concepts and agendas of lifelong learning. *Compare, 36*(3), 289–306.

Scotland, M. (2004). National human resource development in St. Lucia. *Advances in Developing Human Resources, 6*(3), 355–362.

UNESCO. (1997). *CONFINTEA adult education: The Hamburg Declaration and the Agenda for the Future.* Retrieved December 15, 2009, from http://www.unesco.org/education/uie/confintea/pdf/con5eng.pdf

UNESCO. (2003a). *Recommitting to adult education and learning: Synthesis report of the CONFINTEA V Midterm Review Meeting.* Retrieved December 12, 2009, from http://www.unesco.org/education/uie/pdf/recommitting.pdf

UNESCO. (2003b). *Regional Latin American report for the CONFINTEA Mid-Term Review Conference.* Retrieved December 8, 2009, from http://www.unesco.org/education/uie/pdf/country/latin_america.pdf

UNESCO. (2007a). *Education for all global monitoring report* 2007. Retrieved August 5, 2008, from http://unesdoc.unesco.org/images/0014/001477/147794e.pdf

UNESCO. (2007b). *North-south exchange on family literacy—Report.* Retrieved May 6, 2008, from http://unesdoc.unesco.org/images/0017/001777/177753e.pdf

U.S. Government. (1999). *G-8 Summit—G-7 Charter on lifelong learning.* Retrieved August 10, 2009, from http://old.tuac.org/statemen/communiq/EvG80k2000e.htm

World Bank. (n.d.). *HIV/AIDS and education.* Retrieved August 18, 2007, from http://go.worldbank.org/U583AZLIY0

Youngman, F. (2001). The prospects for lifelong education for all in Africa: The case of Botswana. *Inchiesta, 30*(29), 42–50.

9

POLICY AND ADULT LEARNING AND EDUCATION

ROBERT J. HILL

dult learning and education (ALE) intersect the policy process in at least three distinct arenas: (1) government policies that specifically impact adult learning and education; (2) the role that adult learning and education play in problem formation, policy formulation, and policy evaluation—key elements in the policy process; and (3) the place of adult educators in policy dynamics. After beginning with policy definitions, this chapter surveys these three main themes.

Policies are prescribed plans that are "action-oriented and problem-oriented . . . [and should express] the 'general will' of the people" (Titmuss, 1974, p. 24). Policy making is more than simply selecting choices between or among alternatives (Jenkins, 1978). It is a complex, more-than-technical enterprise (Spicker, 2006). Policy making is multifaceted and includes political, administrative, economic, and organizational inputs—each with its own educational components.

Numerous groups, including international intergovernmental organizations, non-governmental organizations (NGOs), civil society organizations (CSOs), and corporations are involved in making policy. Policy experts, including those working in adult learning and education, recognize that "policies change all the time in various ways, however, why policies change . . . is not a well-understood phenomenon" (Bennett & Howlett, 1992, p. 275). Not all parties are predisposed to ethical behavior in the policy process. They may be inclined to achieve a particular end at any cost, to spin or distort the meaning of knowledge, to use information selectively, and/or to misrepresent facts (Sabatier, 2007). Ethics, however, are central to the policy process because policies have a profound impact on society (Gostin & Powers, 2006). Since "adult education is a critical practice with moral and political consequences that reach far beyond the walls of the classroom" (Briton, 1996, p. 33), it contributes to the ethical dimension of policy making.

There are multiple perspectives on how policies come about. They range from viewing policy formation as a rational problem-solving activity, in which issues can be uncoupled from the contexts in which they happen (Walt, 1994), to conceptualizing the process as complex, interactive, potentially of long duration, and influenced by specific beliefs, attitudes, values, knowledge, and people's ways of being in the world (Sabatier & Jenkins-Smith, 1993). Elements in policy formation should include: consideration of the policy players' roles and motivations, consideration of the full scope of a problem, open debate, and interrogation regarding whose interests are best served in the policy process. The latter point has significance for adult educators, as seen in the work of Cervero and Wilson (2006), which clearly shows how "interests" are a crucial part of negotiations.

Perry (2008) lucidly explores policy processes as they apply to adult education in a complex international context. A key model that she employs is the advocacy coalition framework (ACF) propounded by Sabatier (1999). The "ACF . . . shifts focus to the agents or coalitions involved in the policy process. . . . At some point, interest groups organize themselves around their beliefs and values and form groups or coalitions" (p. 31). Key here is the idea that behavioral change is a result of "policy learning" (Sabatier, 1988). Knowledge is a crucial policy-relevant resource that directs learning about the severity of problems, their causes, and costs and benefits of policy alternatives (Sabatier, 2007). Focusing on Sabatier and Jenkins-Smith's (1993) assertion that the ACF "has the potential for contributing to a better world" (pp. 231), Perry (2008) points out that this model is highly relevant to adult education. However, it appears never to have been employed in our field.

Public and Social Policy

Policy can have several origins. It may arise from the private sector, or single-handedly from government; public policy, however, is policy that engages more people in its creation than typically occurs in general policy formation (Birkland, 2005). In the process of public policy formation, multiple stakeholders develop understandings of social situations, their causes, and the means to solve them (Birkland, 2005). Birkland (2005) reminds us that despite the "lack of a consensus definition of public policy" (p. 19), there are points of agreement: Public policy is made by a governing body on behalf of the public, it may be interpreted and implemented in both public and private spheres, and it not only sets out what the government intends to do, but also what it will not do. Public policies are thus those policies that refer to the actions of governments, and include the intentions that determine those actions and the outcomes of the struggles over which stakeholders' visions become implemented (Cochran, Mayer, Carr, & Cayer, 2003). In essence, public policies directly or indirectly influence the everyday life of all people, citizens and noncitizens alike.

Social policy accounts for plans or actions designed to create, change, or maintain living conditions that are supportive of human welfare. DeLeon (1988) points out that the science of policy is "an umbrella term describing a broad-gauge intellectual approach applied to the examination of societally critical problems" (p. 7). Marshall (1965) illustrates multiple social policy models. He argued that social policy should be defined by its objectives (e.g., health care, social security, community services), which led Griffin (1987) to suggest that "adult education clearly falls within social policy" (p. 4). In recent years, the contestation within the terrain of adult education as to whether the field's focus should be social or instrumental has heavily impacted our commitment to social policy processes.

Quigley (2005) shows that the terms public policy and social policy are often confused. Public policy in the United States is a phrase "widely used where [it] subsumes social policy" (p. 596). He suggests that outside of the U.S., "public policy has traditionally held a far wider public mandate than social policy" (p. 597). Public policy is "typically far less concerned with the redistribution of valued resources," while social policy includes "the ways and means that the state can improve societies through the creation and redistribution of valued scarce resources through education, health and social services" (p. 596). Community, adult, and continuing education are key elements, even though they are seldom stressed by those doing social policy work. Social policy discourse includes equal opportunity, social justice, and social inclusion of marginalized, oppressed, and underrepresented groups. Social policy takes account of the advocacy and activism of labor and community organizers who build union and constituency-based groups, economic equality, and democratic participation in civil society. Policies, however, are not always progressive regarding resource distribution (and redistribution), aiding those who need assistance. At times governments redirect resources so that the flow is "*from* [italics added] the poor to the rich . . . from one ethnic group to another ethnic group" (Titmuss, 1974, p. 26).

Adult learning and education should raise questions related to the social policy process. For example, will policies be applicable to all (e.g., prisoners and immigrants), and what roles do ALE play in solving problems resulting from contemporary cultural campaigns over notions such as: Education for All (EFA is a set of United Nations policies with the goal of meeting the learning needs of all people by 2015); the Millennium Development Goals (MDGs are concrete plans and practical steps for action by member nations of the UN—for example, to end poverty and hunger, combat HIV/AIDS, and achieve environmental sustainability); gay, lesbian, bisexual, transgender, and Queer rights; overcoming race, religion, minority language intolerance and the hegemony of English, and many more.

In the end, the goals of social policy must improve the well-being of people and assist them to secure education, a living wage, affordable health care, decent housing, a clean environment, and the identity-based right to be different. It is important to note that social policy is more than what governments do to protect individuals' rights and welfare through state-sanctioned social services. It is also about how people learn to solve their own problems (Gee, Hull, & Lankshear, 1996).

GOVERNMENTAL POLICIES AND ADULT LEARNING AND EDUCATION

In this brief chapter, it is impossible to comprehensively cover policy and legislation in the more than 190 member states of the United Nations, or in the 50 states of the U.S. Efforts to explore some of these, however, have occurred. For instance, in 1997, Haddad edited a thorough study of policy and legislation relating to adult learning in 10 countries: Australia, Brazil, Cote d'Ivoire, Hungary, India, Morocco, the Philippines, Switzerland, the United Kingdom, and the United States. The data for this work were derived from a more comprehensive global survey involving 26 countries. A U.S. legislative and policy history, including amendments and new priorities for ALE, is found in the *History of the Adult Education Act* (1998). The history of the act is complicated and convoluted, and includes phases such as civil society agents as primary providers; rapid institutionalization with an emerging university-trained corps of professionals; and in the 1960s policy makers forced to reconceptualize the role of education as social intervention (Cunningham, 2001), which was consequential for adult education policy—and demonstrated the power of adult learning to effect social change at the time.

Hiemstra's (1995) tabulation of landmark policy legislation related to adult education, primarily in the U.S., has uncovered "that the development of adult education has been largely an 'ad hoc' affair. It is a highly pluralistic movement

in a pluralistic society without any evidence of the operation of a 'grand strategy'" (para. 28). He includes the Adult Education Act (AEA) of 1966 (and 1970) in this evaluation. The act was formally known as Title III of the Elementary and Secondary Education Act of 1965 (ESEA), as amended. At the 40th anniversary of the AEA, Halperin (2006) wrote that the paths to adult education legislation were "extremely malleable, porous, and often quirky" (*Reflections on the fortieth birthday of the Adult Education Act of 1966*, para. 3). He characterizes the passage of the AEA as "a small, but potentially momentous, legislative step to support a federally aided network of adult education providers" (para. 1). Halperin goes on to ask, "Who would have guessed then that this relatively unheralded act would spur a national network providing education and literacy services to over 2.5 million adult learners annually ... ?" (para. 2). To him and others, it was momentous because prior to this, "adult educators were barely a presence in the halls of Congress" (para. 6). It should also be noted that,

> [The U.S.] Congress [had been] long dominated by southern conservatives [to whom] 'adult basic education' became conflated with efforts by liberals and the growing civil rights movement to teach 'Negroes' how to pass the literacy tests that southern states had erected as effective barriers to the exercise of voting rights. (para. 9)

In the 1990s there was a growing demand in the U.S. for adults to learn. Cunningham (1998) attributes this to learning "for their own survival as much as well being, in a modern society ... constructed around market forces" (p. 182). A burgeoning neoliberal agenda, production of a hyper-consumer society, and "modernizing" economies to train people for work were the engines driving much learning. Her assertions about the U.S. were, however, globally applicable. Abdi and Kapoor (2009), referencing Prinsloo (2005), argue that "the 1990s saw the development of a culture of adult education in the form of 'lifelong education' [with policy shifts from basic education] as a key objective of governments concerned with balancing issues of economic development and competitiveness in global markets" (p. 22). Cunningham (2001) problematizes the situation by asking whose social needs will determine what educational programs will be offered and funded, and perhaps most importantly, for what purposes? It is recognized that there was a policy-based, global, seismic shift from the social agenda of the period preceding the 1990s to a market-based scheme of economic development after that (Muzvidziwa & Seotsanyana, 2002).

The *National Report on the Development and State of the Art of Adult Learning and Education* (2008) is an important U.S. policy document related to adult education, because it illustrates the ways that politics and policy are inextricably linked. The *National Report* (2008) was written in preparation for the 6th Conference on Adult Education, CONFINTEA VI, which took place in Belem do Para, Brazil, on December 1–4, 2009.

The study *A Review and Critique of the 2008 United States National Report on the Development and State of the Art of Adult Learning and Education* (ALE) by Robert J. Hill, Elizabeth Anne Daigle, Lesley Graybeal, Wayland Walker, Christian Avalon, Nan Fowler, and Michael W. Massey (2008) has shown that the policy implicit in the *National Report* follows economistic geopolitical trends, is steeped in neoliberalism, and is designed to remediate perceived defective low-wage workers—values of the administration for which it was authored. Human values are displaced in favor of an ideology of workforce education and building a knowledge economy. Cuban (2009), citing the report, states that "literacy becomes a tool for individual social mobility with little concern about who and what is left behind" (p. 8). The gendered implications of the study by Hill and his colleagues are developed by Cuban and Stromquist (2009). *A Review and Critique of The 2008 United States National Report on the Development and State of the Art of Adult Learning and Education* (ALE) had wide Internet circulation prior to CONFINTEA VI, and was a part of the international discussion on educational policy. Reference to it was contained in a book published originally in German in volume 4/2009 of the periodical *Bildung und Erziehung* (Hinzen & Knoll, 2009). Wilson (2009) called Hill and colleagues' report "the most trenchant critique yet of US literacy policies" (p. 117).

With the advent of globalization, government policy actions in less technologically developed countries have resulted in a shift from attention to primary and secondary education to "tertiary education as a means for imparting future workers with the skills necessary for economic development" (Abdi & Kapoor, 2009, p. 23). In the U.S., a more technologically developed country, the process has been different because of power imbalances, but driven by similar economic development

intentions. For example, in 2007 the U.S. government narrowly defined adult education as

> teaching or instruction . . . for individuals who are 16 years of age or older, designed to provide: (i) mastery of basic education skills needed to function effectively in society; (ii) a secondary school diploma or its equivalent; or (iii) the ability to speak, read, or write the English language" found in Presidential Executive Order 13445. (*Executive Order,* 2007, Sec 2[b])

In 2008, the U.S. government document on adult education *Bridges to Opportunities: Federal Adult Education Programs for the 21st Century* (U.S. Department of Education, 2008) continued to sustain this limited approach to ALE.

The movement toward "economism," or the reduction of social particulars to economic parameters, is a worldwide phenomenon. Holford (2008) has shown that it is a movement that actually emerged with policy makers in the early 1970s and continues today. Serra and Stiglitz (2008) have suggested that new policy frameworks, stemming from what has been called the "Washington Consensus," impact global governance. Privatization, or the movement of control from the state to corporate domination and to the private sector, is key to the economistic discourse controlling adult learning and education today. In the end, government policy goals of the U.S. and Western Europe, and countries in Africa, Asia, Latin America, and the Caribbean, have at least one commonality—they are geared for economic outcomes, albeit for different reasons and through different mechanisms resulting from colonizer/colonized dualities.

What Washington Means By Policy Reform

The policy shift from humanism, the guarantee of equal rights, and the provision of social services to neoliberalism centered on individual initiative and private enterprise is detailed in "What Washington Means by Policy Reform" (Williamson, 1990). Beginning in the 1970s, the discourse of liberalism changed to new forms of hegemonic corporate and business behavior, and the establishment of market freedoms. Notions of social democracy were eventually overpowered by policy proposals favoring the market, slashing public expenditures for social services, loosening government regulations, and eliminating the discourse of the "public good." These practices, in part, constitute what is termed the

"Washington Consensus." Comprised of 10 policy guidelines that set the stage for conservative actions of Washington's international economic elite (including the World Bank and the International Monetary Fund), the Washington Consensus positioned profits over people, maximized property rights, and allowed economic processes to supersede sociocultural ones.

Policies based on Washington Consensus neoliberalism have had devastating impacts, domestically and internationally, on adult learning and education, in part through imposition of austerity conditions, ensconced in practices that affect the distribution of resources and financing. Consistently, for example, the U.S. Bush administration in the 2000s delivered to Congress budgets with record deficits that virtually froze or shrank the spending necessary for domestic social provisions, while simultaneously proposing record military outlays. According to Abdi and Kapoor (2009), globally, neoliberal policies "have adversely reshaped, redirected, and redefined educational policies" (p. 21) in Africa (Shizha, 2006) and Latin America (Carnoy & Torres, 1992).

Adult Learning and Education and Public Policy

Quigley's work (2000) on social policy was constructed on three maxims: the forethought of the kind of society that adult education has helped to envision, the historical legacy claiming adult education's role as a socially defining agent, and finding a more meaningful role in heralding a just, equitable, and civil society. Merriam and Brockett (2007) remind us that "the debate over what adult education public policy is, what it could be, and what it should be reflects . . . ideological and historically contextualized tensions" (p. 95). For those who understand the primary focus of the ALE enterprise as decontextualized, individual, and private (Hass, 1992), the aims, purposes, and end products of the policy process are different than for those who understand it as contextual, social, and public. As a result, adult educators hold diverse tenets on ALE and public policy, ranging from the belief that social policies in themselves will never solely arise from "political or corporate 'largesse' to serve everyone's best interest" (Quigley, 2005, p. 597), through the " [naïve belief] that education will mean enlightenment

at the policy level" (Quigley, 2005, p. 597), to Boshier's (2005, p. 377) notion that "lifelong learning is largely infused with false hopes." Bouchard (1998) points out that adult educators are faced with the Gordian knot—after accepting the limitations of education as a mithridate for both economic and social inequity, are we to abandon our activities?

In a critique of the field, some adult educators have asserted that our theory and practice exist with, and perpetuate, a "manic market mentality" (Welton, 1995, p. 11). Boshier (2005) has expressed that the current dominance of the lifelong learning paradigm "is a signifier for adapting to the 'needs' of the global economy" by neoliberalists, and that lifelong learning is now socially without a mooring, and is context-impoverished. A similar argument, from a European perspective, is offered by Holford (2008).

The field provides limited critique of how the market has destroyed lives and how adult education has not interrogated policies that favor overconsumption and turbo-capitalism that are devouring people's daily existence (Finger & Asún, 2000). For some, economics is the best education we can have, and equally, education is the best economic stimulus available—thus, most forms of policy in the age of globalization focus on learning for economic competitiveness (Ecclestone, 1999, p. 332). Zuboff (1988) argued, "learning is not something that requires time out from being engaged in productive activity, learning is the heart of productive activity. To put it simply, learning is the new form of labor" (p. 395). Adult education is fueling discourses that drive policy formation in support of this contention.

Adult Educators and the Policy Process

The policy process includes identifying policy actors and stakeholder groups, and exploring the ways they determine interests and influence strategies for involvement. Significant stakeholders in policy include individuals who remain unaffiliated with any group, as well as civil society organizations, governmental bodies, and foundations. Markets have become key stakeholders, lobbying and educating in multiple arenas. There is little agreement on the influences that adult educators, as stakeholders, have had—or currently have—on legislation and policy making. In fact, the ideological and philosophical orientation of adult educators often motivates or precludes participation in policy processes. Over three decades ago, Fay (1972) suggested that "the times now require of us a different kind of adult educator—men and women who can move easily from academia to government to policy study institutes and back to academic posts" (p. 157). This dream has yet to become a reality.

Quigley (2000) cites Knowles as "personally advocating national policy agendas" (p. 209) in adult education. Quigley goes on to argue that "adult educators should be engaged in the informing—the very envisioning—of a better society at the policy formation level"; however, this engagement has "somehow been dropped from our sense of identity" (p. 210). Cunningham (1995) observes that U.S. "federal laws supporting adult education . . . increased markedly [from] 1964 as a response to popular sector demands [but] with little involvement by the adult education profession" (p. 83). Quigley (1993) agrees, arguing that adult educators, at least in North America, have had little impact on social policy formation. He further points out that "our direct involvement in social policy has declined through past decades. There seems to be a consensus within the field that our influence has been on the wane (Thomas, 1987). Few adult educators were . . . involved in the design and passage of landmark social policy legislation through the 1970s and 1980s" (Quigley, 2005, p. 595). There are others, such as Koloski (1989), who suggest that because of the shear diversity, amorphous nature, and vast disciplinary coverage of our field, it is almost impossible for us to impact policy. Even if we do affect policy outcomes, such as during the 1980s when "a fair amount of policy activity related to adult and continuing education [happened]," Koloski (2000) suggests that only a handful of adult educators are involved in the policy debates. Koloski points out that "despite all of our efforts, professional adult educators do not see themselves as having a role in the public policy processes" (2000, para 8).

Quigley (2000) has concluded that we are called to help build a better future through participatory engagement in the democratic systems our founders helped to create—and policy is one opportunity to do this. His writings in 2005, however, seem to take a more cautionary and interrogative tone, asking, "What role, if any, will we play in the social policies of societies into the future?" (p. 595). In the end, "educators, by necessity, are either supporters or opposers of particular positions. As educators we may have some choice over *what* we impose and *how* we impose it, but to impose, we must" (Baptiste, 2008, p. 19). The notion that advocacy is inescapable is not new. Sabatier and Jenkins-Smith (1993) propose that if researchers and policy analysts aspire to have an impact on policy, they generally must abandon the role of neutral technician and instead adopt that of advocate. Cunningham (1995) shows that on the uncommon occasion that adult educators lobby for adult education policy change, they do so without a critical analysis of legislative intent. Increasingly, adult educators' interests have been "limited to policies promoting the instrumental use of adult education often for narrow goals. This is not consistent with the democratic social agenda of many early U.S. adult educators" (p. 83).

During the policy stream, issues move onto the government agenda. Here adult education organizations are, or should be, positioned to assist. Adult educators should be poised to strike when policy windows—opportunities for action—open. But are we? And, if so, we must know the discourses that frame our interventions since actions are always "relative to the frame of reference which contains them" (Bové, 1990, p. 56). In fact, they are a "functions of these frames . . . [and constitute] the truths they claim to discover and transmit" (p. 56).

Cunningham (2001) has suggested that "professional organizations should be a place for collective action directed toward policies for the public good and a place for debating issues among members"; however, she concludes that we "often fall short on both counts" (p. 63). For example, the American Association for Adult and Continuing Education (AAACE) has been criticized for its failure to engage in issues related to social policy formation despite its mission, "advocating [for] relevant public policy and social change initiatives" (*AAACE: Who We Are*, 2008). In fact, at an adult education conference in 1990, AAACE was "charged, and found guilty, by the program organizers of dereliction of duty in failing to honor its founding commitment to educate adults to participate in democratic social action" (Cunningham, 2001, p. 64). In this regard, Cunningham prods, "Can't we mobilize and educate our membership on policy initiatives? Of course we could, if we thought participation and critically informed membership were key to our politics" (p. 66). By way of contrast, the Canadian Association for the Study of Adult Education—Association Canadienne pour l'Étude de l'Éducation des Adults' 21st Annual Conference (2002) was devoted to "Adult Education and the Contested Terrain of Public Policy." In the call for papers, the association asserted that public policy has been privileging the market, claiming that the state and the market have strengthened their alliances, resulting in a widening gap between the rich and the poor. They called for educators, learners, and practitioners to rethink the relationships among adult education, public policy, and civil society.

OUR MOST SIGNIFICANT CONTRIBUTION TO THE POLICY PROCESS

Interrogation of policy trends, especially the turn to the market, has been noticeably absent in the field. Quigley (2000, p. 209), quoting Welton (1997), reminds us that the university-based study of adult education "has been professionally colonized" around a narrow humanist, functionalist, ideology. "The modern practice of adult education [is] depoliticized, dehistoricized, [and made] technicist" (Briton, 1996, p. 9) in a process that abandons its moral and political center. Newman (1994/2007) takes a challenging approach, accusing adult educators of shirking explicit activism and political responsibility to resist and subvert the marginalization and oppression that largely constitute the present moment.

The connections between social justice, education, and policy are intricately woven in relations with the state. Participating in the policy process is one obvious response to the question posed by Zajda, Majhanovich, and Rust (2006), "How can we contribute to the creation of a more equitable, respectful, and just society for everyone?" (p. 13). Adult educators must take seriously the calls of scholars, such as that of Bourdieu and Passeron (1970/1990) for critical policy analysts to engage in a critical sociology of our own contexts of practice; that of Cunningham (1992) for continuing educators to be social activists; and that of Rubenson (1989), who probes, "To what extent does education make society better by making it more egalitarian, and to what extent does education legitimate, and even enhance, existing social and economic inequalities?" (p. 51).

Today, adult education policies are all too often linked to workplace learning, skills development, training, career education, organizational development, and global competitiveness. Online learning, a cash cow for institutions "explicitly devoted to selling services within a competitive marketplace" (Brookfield, 2005, p. 638), has overtaken adult education like a tsunami in multiple settings, including government, universities, and the corporate world. Brookfield (2005) reminds us, however, that such trends "might seem to suggest that the field has become essentially the engine of capitalist development . . . [but] voices critical of this cooptation have emerged" (p. 638). The arena of popular education and learning in social movements (e.g., peace education; feminist movements; the civil rights movement; the environmental movement; the gay, lesbian, bisexual, transgender, and Queer movements), learning within civil society organizations, and learning through community development initiatives are examples of resistant policy actors. Social movement activities, at times the object of adult education research—and to a lesser degree professional adult education praxis—are key elements in influencing the national mood, and ultimately opening the policy window. New social movements in the global North (NSM; e.g., see Welton, 1997), and Subaltern Social Movements in the global South (SSM, groups outside of hegemonic power centers; see Adbi & Kapoor, 2009) are key contemporary policy players in adult learning and education. Cunningham (1998) puts forward the idea that "if one looks at the adult education . . . occurring on the margins within social movements and in community learning, the activities are much more freely constructed and participatory" (p. 177). These are qualities that she and others value as quintessential to democratic policy processes.

Examining the many ways that people solve their common problems is crucial to understanding public policy since public policy is not restricted to government-initiated solutions. Over 35 years ago, Fay (1972) wrote that "we as a nation [cannot] rely solely upon those experts whose view is formed chiefly by what has come to be called policy-oriented research, much of which aims to provide quantitative, technical solutions to social problems" (p. 154). Fay goes on to lament that the unfortunate consequence of relying on experts is a widening gap of knowledge between the specialists and the public, pointing to the undemocratic practice that this encourages. Apart from devising legal, governmental, and institutional strategies for creating and enforcing solutions to community problems, additional stratagems include the role of adult education and learning for civic participation, advocacy, resistance, and contest.

Social policy embraces the formally legislated processes as well as "the informal policies that are operative in areas such as health, education, and literacy, that directly affect the quality of life of citizens" (Quigley, 2005, p. 594). People begin to solve their own problems when they create and interpret their knowledge, and make meaning from their experiences. This includes the demystification of the knowledge held by canonists, and valuing the knowledge of those on the margins. "Democracy depends on citizens making choices about how to deal with problems in their communities. . . . too often we don't stop to talk through the principles that really matter to us, the thoughts behind why we think [that choices] are good—or bad—public policy decisions" (Belcher, Kingston, Knighton, McKenzie, Thomas, Wilder, & Arnone, 2001, p. 1). Our most significant contribution to the policy process may well be though expanding opportunities for democratic life in the public sphere, heeding Welton's (1997) plea for a "rediscovered and reinvigorated concept of civil society" (p. 68).

REFERENCES

AAACE: Who we are. (2008). Retrieved January 3, 2009, from http://www.aaace.org/mc/page .do?sitePageId=66232&orgId=aaace

Abdi, A. A., & Kapoor, D. (Eds.). (2009). *Global perspectives on adult education.* New York: Palgrave.

Baptiste, I. (2008). Wages of niceness: The folly and futility of educators who strive to *not* impose. *New Horizons in Adult Education and Human Resource Development, 22*(2), 6–28.

Belcher, E., Kingston, R. J., Knighton, B., McKenzie, R., Thomas, M., Wilder, J. C., & Arnone, E. (2001). *Framing issues for public deliberation: A curriculum guide for workshops.* Dayton, OH: Kettering Foundation.

Bennett, C. J., & Howlett, M. (1992). The lessons of learning: Reconciling theories of policy learning and policy change. *Policy Sciences, 25,* 275–294.

Birkland, T. A. (2005). *An introduction to the policy process: Theories, concepts, and models of public policy making* (2nd ed.). Armonk, NY: Sharpe.

Boshier, R. (2005). Lifelong learning. In L. English (Ed.), *Encyclopedia of adult education* (pp. 373–378). London: Palgrave Macmillan.

Bouchard, P. (1998). Training and work: Myths about human capital. In S. M. Scott, B. Spencer, & A. Thomas (Eds.), *Learning for life: Canadian readings in adult education* (pp. 128–139). Toronto: Thompson.

Bourdieu, P., & Passeron, J.-C. (1990/1970). *Reproduction in education, society, and culture* (2nd ed.; R. Nice, Trans.). Thousand Oaks, CA: Sage.

Bové, P. (1990). Discourse. In F. Lentricchia, & T. McLaughlin (Eds.), *Critical terms for literary study* (pp. 50–65). Chicago: University of Chicago Press.

Briton, D. (1996). *The modern practice of adult education: A post-modern critique.* Albany: State University of New York.

Brookfield, S. D. (2005). The United States and adult education. In L. English (Ed.), *Encyclopedia of adult education* (pp. 638–640). London: Palgrave Macmillan.

Canadian Association for the Study of Adult Education/Association Canadienne pour l' Étude de l' Éducation des Adults. (2002). *Call for Papers Adult Education and the Contested Terrain of Public Policy.* 21st Annual Conference, May 30-31 & June 1, 2002, Ontario Institute for Studies in Education, University of Toronto. Retrieved January 28, 2009, from http://www .oise.utoronto.ca/CASAE/cnf2002/call2002k.pdf

Carnoy, M., & Torres, C. A. (1992). *Educational change and structural adjustment: A case study of Costa Rica.* Working documents of the operational policy and sector analysis division. Paris: UNESCO.

Cervero, R. M., & Wilson, A. L. (2006). *Working the planning table: Negotiating democratically for adult, continuing, and workplace education.* San Francisco: Jossey-Bass.

Cochran, C. E., Mayer, L. C., Carr, T. R., & Cayer, N. J. (2003). *American public policy: An introduction* (7th ed.). Belmont, CA: Wadsworth.

Cuban, S. (2009). Outside practices: Learning within the borderlands. *Literacy & Numeracy Studies, 16*(2)/*17*(1), 5–18. Retrieved December 8, 2009, from http://epress.lib.uts.edu.au/ojs/index .php/lnj/article/viewFile/1274/1316

Cuban, S., & Stromquist, N. P. (2009, November). "It is difficult to be a woman with a dream of an education:" Challenging U.S. adult basic education policies to support women immigrants' self-determination. *Journal for Critical Education Policy Studies, 7*(2), 154–186.

Cunningham, P. M. (1992). The university continuing educator: Social activist or entrepreneur? *Canadian Association for University Continuing Education Conference Proceedings* (pp. 1–12). Saskatchewan, Canada: Regina.

Cunningham, P. M. (1995). U.S. educational policy and adult education: Social control, social demand and professional adult education preparation. In *Proceedings of the 26th Annual Adult Education Research Conference, University of Saskatchewan, Canada* (pp. 81–90). Saskstoon, Canada: University of Saskatchewan.

Cunningham, P. M. (1998). United States of America. In S. Haddad (Ed.), *Adult education: The legislative and policy environment* (pp. 167–186). Boston: Kluwer.

Cunningham, P. M. (2001). Political hotbeds: Professional organizations as policymakers. In C. A. Hansman & P. A. Sissel (Eds.), *Understanding and negotiating landscapes of adult education* (pp. 63–72). New Directions for Continuing Education, No. 91. San Francisco: Jossey-Bass.

DeLeon, P. (1988). *Advice and consent: The development of policy the sciences.* New York: Russell Sage Foundation.

Ecclestone, K. (1999). Care or control? Defining learners' needs for lifelong learning. *British Journal of Educational Studies, 47*(4), 332–347.

Executive Order: Strengthening adult education. (2007, September 27). Retrieved November 30, 2008, from http://www.whitehouse.gov/news/releases/2007/09/20070927–11.html

Fay, F. A. (1972). Adult education and public policy. *Adult Education, 22*(2), 150–157.

Finger, M., & Asún, J. M. (2000). *Adult education at the crossroads: Learning our way out.* London: Zed.

Gee, J. P., Hull, G., & Lankshear, C. (1996). *The new work order: Behind the language of fast capitalism.* Boulder, CO: Westview.

Gostin, L. O., & Powers, M. (2006). What does social justice require for public helath? Public health, ethics and policy imperatives. *Health Affairs, 25*(4), 1053–1060.

Griffin, C. (1987). *Adult education as social policy.* New York: Croom Helm.

Haddad, S. (Ed.). (1997). *Adult education: The legislative and policy environment.* Boston: Kluwer.

Halperin, S. (2006). *Reflections on the fortieth birthday of the Adult Education Act of 1966.* Retrieved May 30, 2009, from http://librarian.lishost.org/?p=628

Hass, G. (1992). Entrepreneurial education: A paradigm shift. In *Canadian Association for University Adult Education Conference proceedings: The university continuing educator— social activist or entrepreneur?* (pp. 29–34). Saskatchewan, Canada: University of Regina.

Hiemstra, R. (1995). *An annotated chronology of landmarks in the history and development of adult education with particular reference to the U.S.A.* Retrieved May 30, 2009, from http://www-distance.syr.edu/historychron.htm

Hill, R. J., Daigle, E. A., Graybeal, L., Walker, W., Avalon, C., Fowler, N., & Massey, M. W. (2008, December 1). *A review and critique of the 2008 United States National Report on the Development and State of the Art of Adult Learning and Education (ALE).* Report to the International Council for Adult Education Virtual CONFINTEA VI Seminar. Athens, GA: Author.

Hinzen, H., & Knoll, J. H. (Eds.). (2009). Adult education and continuing education policy: Science in between society and politics. *International Perspectives in Adult Education Vol. 63.* Bonn, Germany: Institute for International Cooperation of the German Adult Education Association (dvv International).

History of the Adult Education Act. (1998). National Adult Education Professional Development Consortium, Inc. Retrieved January 3, 2000, from http://www.naepdc.org/issues/AEAHistort.htm

Holford, J. (2008). Explaining European Union lifelong learning policy: Globalisation and competitiveness or path dependency and citizenship? *Proceedings of the Adult Education Research Conference, University of Missouri at St. Louis.* Retrieved August 14, 2009, from http://www.adulterc.org/Proceedings/2008/Proceedings/Holford.pdf

Jenkins, W. (1978). *Policy analysis: A political and organizational perspective.* London: Martin Robertson.

Koloski, J. A. (1989). Enhancing the field's image through professionalism and practice. In B. A. Quigley (Ed.), *Fulfilling the promise of adult and continuing education* (pp. 71–77). New Directions for Continuing Education, No. 44. San Francisco: Jossey-Bass.

Koloski, J. A. (2000). *Public policy in adult education: Where the rubber meets the road.* CenterPoint. American Council on Education. Retrieved January 3, 2009, from http://acenet.edu/calec/centerpoint/CP_pages/current_issue/innovations/innovations_6.html

Marshall, T. (1965). *Social policy in the twentieth century.* London: Hutchinson.

Merriam, S. B., & Brockett, R., G. (2007). *The profession and practice of adult education: An introduction.* San Francisco: John Wiley.

Muzvidziwa, V. N., & Seotsanyana, M. (2002). Continuity, change and growth: Lesotho's education system. *Radical Pedagogy, 4*(2). Retrieved January 1, 2009, from http://radicalpedagogy.icaap.org/content/issue4_2/01_muzvidziwa.html

National Report on the Development and State of the Art of Adult Learning and Education. (2008). A Report Submitted by the United States Department of Education and the United States Department of State to the UNESCO Institute for Lifelong Learning, 6th International Conference on Adult Education, CONFINTEA VI. Retrieved January 3, 2009, from http://www.unesco.org/uil/en/nesico/confintea/confinteanatrep.html#

Newman, M. (2007). *Defining the enemy: Social action in adult education.* Retrieved January 3, 2009, from http://www.michaelnewman.info/defining_the_enemy.html (Original work published 1994)

Perry, H. (2008). *Integration of adult education and public health policy: A case study in Uganda.* Unpublished doctoral dissertation, University of Georgia, Athens.

Prinsloo, R. C. (2005, April 28–30). *Making education responsive to prior learning: From Bologna to Bergen and beyond.* Keynote address at the 29th EUCEN Conference, University of South Africa. Retrieved from http://www.eucen-conf29.uib.no/Proceedings/Final%20Eucden%20Keynote%20Address.%20Rachel%20Prinsloo.doc

Quigley, B. A. (1993). To shape the future: Towards a framework for adult education social policy research and action. *International Journal for Lifelong Education, 12*(2), 117–127.

Quigley, B. A. (2000). Adult education and democracy: Reclaiming our voice through social policy. In A. L. Wilson & E. R. Hayes (Eds.), *Handbook of adult and continuing education* (pp. 208–223). San Francisco: Jossey-Bass.

Quigley, B. A. (2005). Social policy. In L. English (Ed.), *Encyclopedia of adult education* (pp. 594–599). London: Palgrave Macmillan.

Rubenson, K. (1989). The sociology of education. In S. B. Merriam, & P. M. Cunningham (Eds.), *Handbook of adult and continuing education* (pp. 51–69). San Francisco: Jossey-Bass.

Sabatier, P. A. (1988). An advocacy coalition framework of policy change and the role of policy-oriented learning therein. *Policy Sciences, 21,* 129–168.

Sabatier, P. A. (Ed.). (1999). *Theories of the policy process: Theoretical lenses on public policy.* Boulder, CO: Westview.

Sabatier, P. A. (Ed.). (2007). *Theories of the policy process* (2nd ed.). Boulder, CO: Westview.

Sabatier, P. A., & Jenkins-Smith, H. C. (Eds.). (1993). *Policy change and learning: An advocacy coalition approach.* Boulder, CO: Westview.

Serra, N., & Stiglitz, J. E. (2008). *The Washington Consensus reconsidered: Towards a new global governance.* New York: Oxford University Press.

Shizha, E. (2006). Continuity or discontinuity in educational equity. In A. Abdi, K. Puplampu, & G. J. S. Dei (Eds.), *African education and globalization: Critical perspectives* (pp. 187–210). Lanham, MD: Lexington.

Spicker, P. (2006). *Policy analysis for practice: Applying social policy.* Bristol, UK: The Policy Press.

Thomas, A. (1987). Policy development for adult education: The law. In W. M. Rivera (Ed.), *Planning adult learning: Issues, practices and directions* (pp. 57–64). Wolfeboro, NH: Croom Helm.

Titmuss, R. M. (1974). What is social policy? In B. Abel-Smith & K. Titmuss (Eds.), *Richard M. Titmuss: Social policy* (pp. 23–32). London: Allen & Unwin.

U.S. Department of Education. (2008). *Bridges to opportunities: Federal adult education programs for the 21st century. Report to the President on Executive Order 13445.* Retrieved November 30, 2008, from http://www.ed.gov/about/offices/list/ovae/e013445.pdf

Walt, G. (1994). *Health policy: An introduction to process and power.* London: Zed Books.

Welton, M. (Ed.). (1995). *In defense of the lifeworld.* Albany: State University of New York.

Welton, M. (1997). Repair, defend, invent: Civil societarian adult education faces the twenty-first century. In O. Korsgaard (Ed.), *Adult learning and the challenges of the twenty-first century* (pp. 67–75). Odense, Denmark: Odense University Press.

Williamson, J. (1990). What Washington means by policy reform. In J. Williamson (Ed.), *Latin American adjustment: How much has happened?* Washington, DC: Institute for International Economics.

Wilson, A. L. (2009). Adult education in the United States as a subject of policy and politics. In H. Hinzen, & J. H. Knollm (Eds.), *Adult education and continuing education policy: Science in between society and politics* (pp. 107–123). International Perspectives in Adult Education, Vol. 63. Bonn, Germany: Institute for International Cooperation of the German Adult Education Association (dvv International).

Zajda, J., Majhanovich, S., & Rust, V. (2006). Introduction: Education and social justice. *The International Review of Education, 52,* 9–22.

Zuboff, S. (1988). *In the age of the smart machine: The future of work and power.* New York: Basic Books.

10

Sociology of Adult and Continuing Education

Some Key Understandings for the Field of Practice

Shauna Butterwick and John P. Egan

This chapter outlines several critically oriented sociological concepts that speak to adult education as a field of social relations and social action, focusing on ideas that can help underscore both the oppressive and emancipatory possibilities of adult education. Before outlining these concepts, we briefly note other discussions about the benefits of a sociological framework, which has a longer history in studies of schooling (e.g., Bowles & Gintis, 1976), compared with the relatively recent and somewhat fragmented sociological examinations of adult education (Connelly, 1992; Griffin, 1991; Jarvis, 1985; Levinson, Cookson, & Sadovnik, 2002). The ideas of Eduard Lindeman, who wrote about adult education as social action and key to building democracy, are a notable exception (Brookfield, 1987).

Different sociological paradigms have also been explored. How some approaches emphasize the determining character of social structures, while others focus on individuals' ability to make change has been examined (Jarvis, 1985), as has the role of government and capitalist structures on adult learning (Torres, 1987), and the capacity of sociological theory to spotlight adult education's role in maintaining inequality and potential for creating a more just society (Cunningham, 2000; Rubenson, 1989). There are many other scholars, too numerous to list here, who have employed particular sociological concepts in their explorations of specific adult learning contexts; some examples include power dynamics in classrooms (Johnson-Bailey & Cervero, 1998), experiential learning (Fenwick, 2000), workplace pedagogy (Billett, 2002), the socioeconomic outcomes of adult learning (Balatti & Falk, 2002), the learning experiences of immigrant women (Alfred, 2003), and the issue of social class (Nesbit, 2006).

These scholars demonstrate how sociological theory can help us understand adult education as a social phenomenon, and also outline how sociological approaches can illuminate power relations and structures of inequality.

Such an understanding has been eclipsed in an era where transnational discourses around lifelong learning all too often presume adult education as a primarily individuated and instrumental experience with the aim of creating/enhancing flexible and employable workers. While the focus on individual learners has long been a dominant orientation, 21st-century processes of globalized capitalism have contributed to an even more rabid form; thus, a critical reflection on how adult education is mediated by social entities and power relations is even more important.

A social justice orientation to adult education is strengthened, we argue, by critical social theories that explicate how oppression and domination occur—sometimes through the practices of adult educators. Paulo Freire's analysis of oppression and his liberatory approach through popular education (Freire, 1970, 1997) are well known to the field and have been instrumental in building a social justice orientation. But for the purpose of this chapter we purposefully focus on a few key scholars whose ideas may be less familiar: Each has greatly informed our own standpoints as a feminist activist/academic and queer activist/academic interested in and committed to both understanding *and* disrupting how

- Power operates in social relations that maintain inequality;

- Oppression is reproduced through social structures as much as through the tyranny of individuals; and

- Social capital, the networks and relationships that act as a resource for individuals and groups, is implicated in both injustice and social justice.

We recommend these conceptual offerings for their power to explicate adult education as both a disciplining and liberating field of practice. Given the limitations of the chapter, we can only introduce them here; thus, we encourage further reading. Following our discussion of these theoretical contributions, we comment on how these ideas can critically inform a social justice orientation to adult education.

UNDERSTANDING THE STRUCTURAL AND SOCIAL RELATIONS OF OPPRESSION AND DOMINATION

Feminist scholars Iris Marion Young (1990) and Nancy Fraser (1989, 1997) explore the constraints of social justice models that focus on the equal distribution of wealth, income, and material goods, calling for an expanded and integrated notion of justice that addresses what Young calls the "non-distributive," and what Fraser calls "cultural dimensions." For Young, "social justice concerns the degree to which a society contains and supports the institutional conditions necessary for the realization of [the good life]" (1990, p. 37). Part of the problem, Fraser argues, is how to achieve equality while recognizing differences; redistributive justice, to a certain extent, requires the erasure of difference, while recognitive justice must honor and recognize differences. In Fraser's framework these approaches, which have been viewed as oppositional and quite separate, are to be integrated if social justice is to be achieved.

Both Fraser and Young draw attention to the structural, systemic, and everyday dimensions of oppression which occur not only through tyranny, but also through everyday practices that are buttressed by "unquestioned norms, habits and symbols" and "assumptions underlying institutional rules" (Young, 1990, p. 41). Structural oppression, as Young notes, cannot be eliminated "by getting rid of the rulers or making some new laws, because oppressions are systematically reproduced in major economic, political and cultural institutions" (p. 41). While the purposeful day-to-day actions of many individuals maintain and reproduce oppression "these people are usually simply doing their jobs of living their lives, and do not understand themselves as agents of oppression" (pp. 41–42). The structural and everyday reproduction of domination also concerns antiracist scholar Sherene Razack (1998), who challenges liberal orientations informed by pluralistic and ahistorical approaches to understanding difference wherein encounters between unequal groups are to be *managed* through "cultural, racial, or gender sensitivity" (p. 8). She calls for a more historical and anti-imperialist approach, noting how it is often met with great resistance because it involves "disrupting hegemonic ways of seeing through which subjects make themselves dominant" (p. 10).

These scholars recognize that not only are oppressions intertwined, but they are operating in dynamic and complex ways. For any one individual, privilege as well as oppression (or to use Razack's phrase "penalty") can be at work.

This understanding of how oppression operates on social groups and within *social relations,* as much as it affects individuals, is key. Young (1990) defines a social group (in the sociological sense, i.e., a social entity) as any collective of "persons differentiated from at least one other group by cultural forms, practices, or way of life" (p. 43). Social groups exist in *social relation* to each other; that is, "in the encounter and interaction between social collectivities that experience some differences in their way of life and forms of association, even if they also regard themselves as belonging to the same society" (p. 43). Razack's orientation to difference challenges us even further. Pluralistic approaches to the recognition of difference can reflect a denial by dominant groups of their role in constructing the Other. Razack notes how in the practices of institutions like law and education, discussions of cultural difference are not framed as relations, but rather as attributions of one group. A social relations approach is not unidirectional; for example, when considering the colonization of Aboriginal peoples, it is important to ask not only how it changed Aboriginal people, but how it changed White people (Razack, 1998, p. 19). Razack also argues for the notion of *interlocking* systems of oppression wherein "each system of oppression relie[s] on the other to give it meaning" (p. 12).

This emphasis on social relations is important here: It challenges theories of justice (as well as adult education) that are based on "a normative conception of the self as independent . . . autonomous, unified, free and self-made, standing apart from history and affiliations" (Young, 1990, p. 45). Feminist sociologist Dorothy Smith (1987) also brings attention to social relations in her study of domination as structured through what she calls "ruling relations": "The complex or organized institutional practices of government, law, business and financial management, professional organizations and educational institutions that organize our everyday experiences" (p. 3). For Smith (1987), processes of abstraction and generalization, which are extralocal, are at the heart of domination and oppression, and texts and documents serve a central function in this ruling apparatus:

> We are ruled by forms of organization vested in and mediated by texts and documents . . . the practice of ruling involves the ongoing representation of the local actualities of our worlds in the standardized and general forms of knowledge that enter them into the relations of ruling. It involves the construction of the world as texts, whether on paper or in computer, and the creation of a world in texts as a site of action. (p. 3)

Seeking to avoid additive approaches to understanding oppression and debates about which oppression (e.g. sexism, racism, classism) is worse than another, Young mapped out what she calls "five faces of oppression," which include exploitation, marginalization, powerlessness, cultural imperialism, and violence. This scheme integrates distributive and recognitive justice; exploitation, marginalization, and powerlessness are linked to socioeconomic injustice, while cultural imperialism and violence are seen as common results of cultural injustice. As Razack (1998) has argued, these systems or "faces" interlock such that one group's oppression is closely linked to another group's marginalization.

For Young (1990), *exploitation* is a social relation wherein one group has power to determine the value of another group's labor, which involves "social rules about what work is, who does what for whom, how work is compensated, and the social process by which the results of work are appropriated" (p. 50). *Marginalization,* which Young feels is the most dangerous kind of oppression, involves processes whereby some groups' labor is not considered useful: A "whole category of people are expelled from useful participation in social life and thus potentially subjected to severe material deprivation and even extermination" (p. 53). *Powerlessness,* Young's third face of oppression, operates in situations where certain groups "do not regularly participate in making decisions that affect the conditions of their lives and actions" (p. 56). The role of professionals, including educators, in exercising power over others is noted by Young as well as Razack. Both also point to how the power of professionals is felt in other arenas where they are granted authority and influence and considered "respectable."

Cultural imperialism is Young's fourth face of oppression, and is similar to Fraser's notion of cultural domination. It involves "the universalization of a dominant group's experience and culture, and its establishment as the norm"

(Young, 1990, p. 59), which leads to rendering those outside this norm as Other or invisible. A further process of othering involves the construction of stereotypes, which are often essentialized, taken for granted, and regarded as natural by both the dominant groups and those who are othered. The fifth face of oppression is *systemic violence* wherein "members of some groups live with the knowledge that they must fear random unprovoked attacks on their persons or property, which have no motive but to damage, humiliate, or destroy the person" (Young, 1990, p. 61). They suffer not only from actual attacks but from the fear of such assaults which "deprives the oppressed of freedom and dignity" (p. 62). Young emphasizes the social dimension of violence, in which "everyone knows it happens and will happen again . . . always at the horizon of social imagination" (p. 62).

How difference is *constructed* and imagined is key to maintaining these various faces of oppression. Those in dominant positions often fail to acknowledge their role and how institutional structures contribute to constructing differences. Mainstream approaches, furthermore, tend to be pluralistic; they contribute to stereotyping, and emphasize the need for cultural sensitivity. Razack (1998) challenges this approach and calls for an orientation to *histories* of oppression. Instead of constructing a stereotype, this critical historical analysis sees that what might have been named "cultural practices," are "response[s] to an alienating and racist environment" (Razack, 1998, p. 9). Like Young, Razack points to the interlocking dimensions of cultural oppression and violence in those contexts when, for example, violence against women is constituted as a reflection of some essential trait of a specific culture. While Razack does see value in recognizing cultural differences, "for people in reality are diverse," the problem is a superficial reading of difference "that makes power relations invisible and keeps dominant cultural norms in place" (p. 9). Instead of an empty pluralism and a focus on inclusion, Razack argues for a social justice orientation.

METHODS OF ANALYSIS

In order to unpack how oppression is operating in any given circumstance, particular methods are needed. Razack (1998) calls for "historical and site-specific" analysis to illustrate the "shifting positions of power and privilege" and to show how "various systems interlock to produce specific effects" (p. 12). Razack is very much interested in the role of education in the development of critical consciousness: "If we can name the organizing frames, the conceptual formulas, the rhetorical devices that disguise and sustain elites, we can begin to develop responses that bring us closer to social justice" (p. 16). Razack focuses her analysis on education and the law; in the latter case, she notes how "courts come to convert information into fact . . . [in that] those whose stories are believed have the power to create fact" (p. 37). In contrast, the stories from outsider groups are suppressed by legal rules and conventions that function "on the basis of liberalism where the individual is thought to be an autonomous, rational . . . unconnected to other selves" (p. 38).

Challenges to this view argue for an orientation that sees the individual *within* community. One way to illustrate this approach to understanding individuals as located in specific context, histories, and cultures is through storytelling. Razack (1998) notes how stories are central to disrupting dominant practices that maintain relations of inequality, but they are not inherently liberating. When stories of oppression are "told to individuals who are members of the dominant group who are often unwilling to face their own complicity," further marginalization can occur (p. 40). Razack points to several undertakings required to counter the injustice that can be reproduced in storytelling, even as we encourage the voices of Others to be heard. First, we must recognize that in any given situation (e.g., adult education classroom), social hierarchies are present. Second, given this reality, attention must be given to "the contexts of both the teller and the listener" (p. 50). Third, "the risks taken in the course of critical reflection are never equally shared" (p. 50). Fourth, educators must not assume classrooms are safe places. Her final point is critical; we must attend to epistemological diversity, or how we know what we know. "Our different subject positions, borne out in how we know, tell, and hear stories, are ignored at our peril" (p. 51). Razack points to a key challenge especially for educators—to "give up . . . the quest . . . to definitely know"

(p. 53); instead we should pay as much attention to *how* we know as we do to *what* we know.

Fraser's (1989) analysis of the contested character of "needs talk" central to welfare state policies and practices raises similar concerns about speaking and listening across difference. She notes how "in late capitalist welfare state societies, talk about people's needs is an important species of political discourse," one which "involve[s] disputes about what exactly various groups of people really do need and about who should have the last word in such matters" (p. 161). Her analysis focuses on the declaration of needs by marginalized groups and how they are interpreted through expert and professional discourses that reflect dominant interests. To critically examine these processes, she has proposed "a model of social discourse designed to bring into relief the contested character of needs talk" (p. 162), which is not simply pluralistic, but "differentiated into social groups with unequal status, power, and access to resources, traversed by pervasive aces of inequality along lines of class, gender, race, ethnicity and age" (p. 165).

Smith (1987) also provides a powerful method of analysis for explicating the social and institutional relations that maintain the unequal status and lack of power of certain groups, which she calls "institutional ethnography." By institution, Smith is not suggesting a "determinate form of social organization" (p. 161), but rather, institutions as understood as social apparatus. Her analysis helps to illuminate "[how] characteristically, state agencies are tied in with professional forms of organization, and both are interpenetrated by relations of discourse" (p. 160). Like Razack's attention to cultural imperialism and the struggles that arise when stories of the oppressed are interpreted by dominant classes—and similar to Fraser's concerns for how needs are interpreted—Smith's institutional ethnography illuminates how institutional processes are coordinated and mediated by ideology that reflects dominant interests. "The forms of thought and images we use do not arise directly or spontaneously out of people's everyday lived relationships," but are "the product of specialists occupying influential positions in the ideological apparatus" (Smith, 1987, p. 19). The active construction of differences and inequalities by ruling relations is key to engaging in a critical sociological method of analysis.

Smith's approach begins with the distinctive standpoint of women that seeks to "preserve the presence of subjects as knowers and as actors" (Smith, 1987, p. 105). While Razack draws attention to the problematics of storytelling and Fraser helps us analyze the contested character of needs talk, Smith helps us focus on how the ruling relations are operating when stories of the everyday lived experience of oppressed groups are interpreted through dominant frameworks. Institutional ethnography offers a way of "investigating the problematic of the everyday world" (Smith, 1987, pp. 160–161) arising from a standpoint that seeks to explicate the "social and institutional relations determining everyday worlds and . . . how the ordinary worlds may be explored to uncover their ordinary invisible determinations in relations that generalize and are generalizable" (p. 160). An orientation to discourse as a politicized process is also our concern in relation to the concept of social capital, to which we now turn our attention.

SOCIAL CAPITAL, COMMUNITY EDUCATION, AND LIFELONG LEARNING

Social capital as community panacea is perhaps the most powerful contemporary global discourse in social policy, particularly with respect to lifelong learning and community development. Although *social capital* surfaced as a term as early as the 1910s (Putnam, 2000, p. 19), it garnered little currency until the 1970s, when French sociologists Pierre Bourdieu and Jean-Claude Passeron examined educational, professional, and personal outcomes for French public high school graduates. They subsequently used the notion of social capital (along with cultural capital) to more accurately predict why students of similar intelligence, familial economic resources, and access to education would nonetheless experience differing levels of educational success—particularly at the postsecondary level (Bourdieu & Passeron, 1990). Bourdieu's social capital ties *what* you know to *who* you know, and in whose circle you exercise genuine membership: Those with genuine membership in elite circles are advantaged for educational and vocational success—even over more intelligent persons from lesser circles. Over three subsequent decades Bourdieu's body of work continued to revisit the question of social capital and its impact on opportunity.

Some 15 years after Bourdieu and Passeron's work was published in English, American Robert Putnam adapted Bourdieu's use of the term *social capital* to examine civic participation trends, first in Italy (Putnam, Leonardi, & Nanetti, 1992), and later in the U.S. (Putnam, 2000). It is clear that Putnam's work is derivative of Bourdieu's—at least nominally, with respect to the term *social capital.*

We argue, however, that Putnam's (2000) individualistic, wholly localized understanding of social capital impedes social change and engenders inequity and injustice, whereas Bourdieu's (1971, 1986, 1997) provides a robust framework for adult education researchers and practitioners concerned with social justice. In order to understand why Putnam's notion of social capital has been ascendant—while Bourdieu's remains largely marginal—in the realm of public policy, we will begin with a review of each theorist's work.

In *Bowling Alone* (2000), Putman conducts an exhaustive analysis of U.S. trends in religious observance, volunteerism, political action, and other forms of civic participation, taking a strongly structuralist approach. Putnam defines social capital as the "connections among individuals—social networks—and the norms of reciprocity and trustworthiness that arise from them" (p. 19). His social capital posits the value of "social networks" and that social contacts among network members "affect the productivity of individuals and groups" (pp. 18–19). Rather importantly, Putnam takes the concept of reciprocity—of persons doing things for one another because of perceived mutual benefit—and brings it to the fore. For him, reciprocity is an important indicator of the likely stores of any social entity's social capital, since "a society characterized by generalized reciprocity is more efficient than a distrustful" one (p. 21). Putnam sees an erosion in U.S. civil society as a product of reduced social capital.

Putnam (2000) differentiates between two forms of social capital. *Bonding* social capital exists *within* social entities and is good for "undergirding specific reciprocity and mobilizing solidarity" (p. 22). Conversely, *bridging* social capital is found *between* social entities and is more effective for "linkage to external

assets and for information diffusion" (p. 22). Putnam's differentiation between bridging and bonding social capital is useful when considering the specifics of interaction within versus between social entities: In fact, it offers a compelling tool to understand how socially cohesive communities with a great deal of bonding social capital continue to face injustice due to a dearth of bridging social capital. He cursorily acknowledges that bonding social capital "tends to reinforce exclusive identities and homogenous groups" (p. 22).

In the end Putman equates social capital with *civic engagement.* With respect to civic participation, he draws an oversimplified linearization between one complex social dynamic (social capital) and a more narrow and specific category of human activity possibly related to that dynamic (civic engagement). There may well be correlations between measures of civic engagement—voting, membership in political parties, acting as members of community-based organizations—but such participation is not predictive of social capital possessed by individuals or communities (Putnam, 2000, p. 41). And if social capital were largely a function of civic engagement, what value would there be in social capital as a concept distinct from civic engagement?

His emphasis on organizations as representative of all social entities is also flawed: For many, primary sites of social capital accrual include the family (often extended) and neighborhood—both of which, though arguably informal, nonetheless frequently operate as distinct, powerful, social networks. In fact, Putnam leaves little room for extra-institutional social capital accrual—and expenditure.

Putnam (2000) also has some perplexing, troubling things to say about non-governmental organizations (NGOs) and trade unions. In his view, many new NGOs are "professionally staffed advocacy organizations, not member-centered, locally based associations" (p. 51), which represent an erosion of social capital at the community level. As well, Putnam critiques paid community work as less effective at representing community interests. Having paid community workers, according to Putnam, creates a new class of "professional activists." His argument advantages networks whose members have stores of economic, political, and human capital that create bandwidth for volunteerism. Communities whose members are stigmatized or marginalized—particularly those whose members often struggle to meet their material needs—have little (or no) "free" time to advocate on their own behalf. This "professional class" of NGO workers is usually paid meager wages and works extensive amounts of overtime. In social networks defined by gender, sexual orientation, geography, class, ethnocultural community, age, or ability (among others), these workers are not removed from community: They live and work in it. Much of their work isn't about building bonding social capital: It is about building bridging social capital to get government, industry, public education, and other institutions from the public sphere to understand their lives and support their efforts to live better lives.

With respect to trade unions, Putnam (2000) points out "the number of (US) trade unions . . . grew by four percent between 1980 and 1997, while the fraction of employees belonging to unions plummeted by more than 35 percent" (pp. 52–53). He argues that worker disillusionment with union leadership largely accounts for this decline, rather than the political climate of the U.S. in the 1980s: Under the Reagan régime trade unions were undermined by both executive and legislative action and numerous large-scale manufacturing sectors moved their U.S. facilities offshore, eliminating thousands of unionized jobs. A not entirely rigorous analysis.

Finally, one of Putnam's last suggestions is perhaps most problematic. Noting that "part-time workers are typically more involved in social entity activities than *either* full-time employees or people who are not employed at all," he argues for more part-time work, even while acknowledging that "not everyone wants a part-time job, of course, but many do . . ." (Putnam, 2000, p. 407, emphasis in original). "Wanting" to work part-time and earning a living wage while doing so are different things. He is revealing his bias towards those whose economic and social capital is already relatively high, those having the luxury of "choosing" part-time wage earning. But for regularly working people, at a time when sustainable full-time employment is less and less available in many parts of the world—due to the move by many businesses to only employ part-time

(and therefore underwaged and underbenefited) workers—this recommendation is not so much naïve as offensive.

Putnam isn't unaware of issues of power between social entities. He rightly observes that "a well-connected individual in a poorly connected society is not as productive as a well-connected individual in a well-connected society" (p. 21), but he does not directly address why social entities have more power and influence—bridging social capital, in other words—than others. Putnam even acknowledges that "networks and associated norms of reciprocity are generally good for those inside the network, but the external effects of social capital are by no means always positive" and admits that "power elites often exploit social capital to achieve ends that are antisocial from a wider perspective" (p. 22). But merely acknowledging the potential for social capital to be wielded unequally, even hegemonically, *Bowling Alone* fails to explicate issues of power between social entities.

Despite some commonalities, Pierre Bourdieu's conceptualization of social capital as "made up of social obligations ('connections')" (1997, p. 47) stands in stark contrast to Putnam's. Bourdieu's social capital is "the aggregate of the actual and potential resources which are linked to possession of a durable network of more or less institutionalized relationships of mutual acquaintance and recognition" (p. 51). Bourdieu sees social capital existing between rather than within individuals. He notes that the volume of social capital possessed by individuals "depends on the size of the network of connections [they] can effectively mobilize and on the volume of capital possessed in [their] own right by each of those to whom [they are] connected" (p. 51). Both what an individual brings to the network and the relative contribution (in economic, cultural, and social terms) of other members to the network are prominent in Bourdieu's work.

For Bourdieu the notion of *genuine* (rather than nominal) membership—membership that is entitled and unquestioned—in social entities is key. He notes how in elite circles, genuine membership is often "socially instituted and guaranteed by the application of a common name (the name of a family, a class, or a tribe or of a school, a party, etc.)" (1997, p. 51). Possession of such a name, and being known to those who share it, is a powerful mechanism for vetting genuine membership in an elite network. Putnam cursorily acknowledges that social capital acts both within *and* between groups (in its bonding and bridging forms, to use Putnam's typology): Bourdieu puts these power relations at the center of his analyses of how social capital operates.

An important aspect of genuine membership is one's ability to fully participate in network life, according to Bourdieu. Knowing and being known by other members is merely the starting point; if one cannot muster the economic resources needed for full participation, genuine membership is impossible. Among those who meet its criteria, genuine membership yields both material and social benefits. In fact, according to Bourdieu "the profits which accrue . . . are the basis of the solidarity which makes them possible" (1997, p. 51). This shared mutual beneficence is an important part of elite network cohesion, even if some of this work might not seem transparently purposeful. "From a narrowly economic standpoint, this effort [i.e., socializing among the elite] is bound to be seen as pure wastage, but in terms of the logic of social exchanges, it is a solid investment, the profits of which will appear, in the long run" (p. 54).

Bourdieu also rejects the idea that a true liberal meritocracy exists—or even could exist—in stark contrast to Putnam. In Bourdieu's view, persons are born unequal and therefore with different amounts of social capital. Those born into elite and powerful families are endowed with a great deal of social capital, while those born into families with less economic capital also have less social capital (those without families—orphans—start effectively with zero social capital, if not at a deficit). It then follows that one's social capital, in a general sense, would correspond to the social capital of one's family—whether one's family possesses a great deal of social capital, or virtually none. Bourdieu, compared to Putnam, does not deny that social capital can be acquired or lost. But he rejects the liberal notion that public education can wholly revolutionize the transmission of social capital, creating the mythological level playing field. Public education at times mitigates or assuages, rather than eliminates, the significantly natal system of social capital dissemination. This explains why parental income alone does not predict educational attainment.

Putnam's ascendancy does make sense in a lot of ways—even among adult education researchers and practitioners concerned with social justice. He emphasizes the local character of community: The integration of a theoretical discourse that *appears to celebrate* local knowledge *seems* like a positive development, at first glance. Everyone loves that bonding social capital!

But Putnam presumes that the forces that cause familial and community dissonance are also local and internal, and can be remedied at the local level. Most communities possess bonding social capital: Marginalized and stigmatized ones often cannot locally change the forces that create unemployment, poor quality housing, and a lack of access to health care. So the Putnamian discourse allows government to fund local projects for a relatively short period of time, then blame local community when problems do not disappear overnight. Bourdieu refuses to let the positive aspects of local action obscure his understanding of what limits those actions: Hundreds of locally cohesive milieus do not necessarily add up to a great cohesive whole. In fact, often the opposite is true.

TOWARDS A SOCIOLOGY OF ADULT EDUCATION FOR SOCIAL JUSTICE

The above ideas point to the contributions that a critical sociological orientation can bring to the role of adult education for social justice. A social relations view challenges dominant policy claims and program structures that see adult learners as unaffiliated individuals; similarly, it points to how these structures—and how educators—are implicated in the active construction of difference. Equal access is an important right, but it requires nuanced analysis and recognition of group differences, rather than practices and policies that assume all adult learners need and want the same opportunities. Equality of access and outcomes also means recognizing and challenging assumptions about difference and the dangers of stereotyping, which requires knowledge of the historical reality of oppression of particular groups—and educators' relationship to that colonization.

To avoid a facile pluralistic liberal view that stops at mere development of cultural sensitivity, educators must engage in an ongoing critical examination of their own social location in hierarchies of privilege and penalty and encourage their students to do the same. There is no single story to tell about these social relations; some educators and adult learners occupy privileged spaces in relation to their race, class, and gender, and so on, while others, such as persons of color and those living lives as sexual minorities, are often located in lower positions on dominant–subordinate hierarchies of power. Exploring *how* educators and learners come to their knowledge is as critical as focusing on *what* is known. This points to a kind of accountability and ethical stance based on a recognition of the influence of social locations on interpretations—a challenging process. The structures of power that make certain experiences the norm also make it difficult to acknowledge privilege (Curry-Stevens, 2007).

Seeing oppression as structural and reproduced in the everyday illuminates how programs like those found in the welfare system, prisons, and immigration have been significantly shaped by rules and regulations that embody contradictory forces. Working in these contexts towards the empowerment of participants in respectful ways requires a knowledge of adult learners' histories, cultures, and specific circumstances. Determining needs is not a straightforward matter, however; by the time programs are running, participants' needs have already been significantly predetermined through the lens of powerful, dominant interests. Those who work in these programs often engage with practices (or use required curricula) that can reflect a narrow interpretation of needs that are far more disciplining than they are empowering.

Many adult educational practices, at least those in formal settings, also involve the construction of texts and documents where educators and adult learners' experiences must be sorted into predetermined categories that have been created elsewhere, eclipsing the specificities and histories that must be understood for critical consciousness. The paradox of social structures created ostensibly to mitigate social injustice operating via mechanisms that impede, rather than facilitate, agency is both striking and perverse.

The emphasis on the local and lived everyday experiences made by these theorists (excepting, of course, Putnam) is a good fit with the mantra of adult educators "to begin with where learners are at," recognizing the specificities of their communities, families, cultures, and histories and acknowledging their needs as well as their existing knowledge and skills. These scholars, however, offer methods that do not stop at this local or community level of analysis, but extend to understanding of the extralocal: those institutional relations of ruling that organize the everyday and, through careful analysis of how oppression is reproduced through interlocking mechanisms, illuminate how any individual learner and educator is nested in relations of privilege and penalty.

With the Putnamian conceptualization of social capital significantly informing the social and educational policy in the United States, Canada, Australia, and the European Union, an understanding of both Putnam's and Bourdieu's work is essential to challenge policies that focus on short-term delivery of resources to marginalized or stigmatized communities. When "measurable outcomes" are not quickly identified, resources are often withdrawn because of a community's ostensive lack of social capital. Not only do these communities possess a great deal of (bonding) social capital, it is often a dearth of bridging social capital that perpetuates their exclusion. It's a particularly pernicious neoliberal meritocratic discourse, one that focuses on individual choice and responsibility, all the while ignoring structural forces, that facilitates the perpetuation of stereotypes ("they're lazy, they won't work hard, they're not even trying") and the absolution of government to make sustained, long-term resource commitments to assuage inequity and injustice.

As we engage lifelong learning and community education policies that reflect a narrow notion of social capital, one that emphasizes the local and community, but deny how these spaces are constituted by relations of ruling, we need to bring a critical orientation. Working in these contexts requires that we reconsider claims about the power of adult education to reshape social capital and to recognize when policy and programs are grounded in notions of liberal meritocracy. A critical approach to how adult education could contribute to enhancing the social capital of oppressed groups would require an orientation to both local and global.

REFERENCES

Alfred, M. (2003). Sociocultural contexts and learning: Anglophone Caribbean immigrant women in U.S. postsecondary education. *Adult Education Quarterly, 53*(4), 242–260.

Balatti, J., & Falk, I. (2002). Socioeconomic contributions of adult learning to community: A social capital perspective. *Adult Education Quarterly, 52*(4), 281–298.

Billett, S. (2002). Toward a workplace pedagogy: Guidance, participation, and engagement. *Adult Education Quarterly, 53*(1), 27–43.

Bourdieu, P. (1971). *Outline of a theory of practice.* Cambridge, UK: Cambridge University Press.

Bourdieu, P. (1986). The forms of capital. In J. G. Richardson (Ed.), *Handbook of theory and research for the sociology of education* (pp. 241–258). New York: Greenwood.

Bourdieu, P. (1997). The forms of capital. In A. H. Halsey, H. Lauder, P. Brown & A. Stuart Wells (Eds.), *Education: Culture, economy, society.* New York: Oxford University Press.

Bourdieu, P., & Passeron, J. C. (1990). *Reproduction in education, society and culture.* Thousand Oaks, CA: Sage.

Bowles, S., & Gintis, H. (1976). *Schooling in capitalist America.* New York: Basic Books.

Brookfield, S. D. (1987). *Learning democracy: Eduard Lindeman on adult education and social change.* London: Croom Helm.

Connelly, B. (1992). A critical overview of the sociology of adult education. *International Journal of Lifelong Education, 11*(3), 235–253.

Cunningham, P. (2000). A sociology of adult education. In A. Wilson & E. Hares (Eds.), *Handbook of adult and continuing education* (pp. 573–591). San Francisco, CA: Jossey-Bass.

Curry-Stevens, S. (2007). New forms of transformative education. *Journal of Transformative Education, 5*(1), 33–58.

Fenwick, T. (2000). Expanding conceptions of experiential learning: A review of the five contemporary perspectives on cognition. *Adult Education Quarterly, 50*(4), 243–272.

Fraser, N. (1989). *Unruly practices: Power, discourse and gender in contemporary social theory.* Minneapolis: University of Minnesota Press.

Fraser, N. (1997). *Justice interruptus: Critical reflections on the "postsocialist" condition.* New York: Routledge.

Freire, P. (1970). *Pedagogy of the oppressed.* New York: Continuum.

Freire. P. (1997). *Pedagogy of the heart.* New York: Continuum.

Griffin, C. (1991). A critical perspective on sociology and adult education. In P. Jarvis & Assoc (Eds.), *Adult education: Evolution and achievements in a developing field of study* (pp. 259–281). San Francisco, CA: Jossey-Bass.

Jarvis, P. (1985). *The sociology of adult and continuing education.* London: Routledge.

Johnson-Bailey, J., & Cervero, R. (1998). Power dynamics in teaching and learning practices: An examination of two adult education classrooms. *International Journal of Lifelong Education,* http://www.informaworld.com/smpp/title~content=t713747968~db=all~tab=issueslist~branches=17 - v17 *17*(6), 389–399.

Levinson, D., Cookson, P. W., & Sadovnik, A. R. (Eds.). (2002). *Education and sociology: An encyclopedia.* New York: Routledge Falmer.

Nesbit, T. (2006). What's the matter with social class? *Adult Education Quarterly, 56*(3), 171–187.

Putnam, R. D. (2000). *Bowling alone: The collapse and revival of American social entity.* New York: Simon & Schuster.

Putnam, R. D., Leonardi, R., & Nanetti, R. (1992). *Making democracy work.* Princeton, NJ: Princeton University Press.

Razack, S. (1998). *Looking White people in the eye: Gender, race and culture in courtrooms and classrooms.* Toronto: University of Toronto Press.

Rubenson, K. (1989). The sociology of adult education. In S. Merriam & P. Cunningham (Eds.), *Handbook of adult and continuing education* (pp. 51–69). San Francisco, CA: Jossey-Bass.

Smith, D. (1987). *The everyday world as problematic: A feminist sociology.* Toronto: University of Toronto Press.

Torres, A. (1987). *Toward a political sociology of adult education.* Alberta, Canada: Centre for International Education and Development (CIED), University of Alberta.

Young, I. M. (1990). *Justice and the politics of difference.* Princeton, NJ: Princeton University Press.

PART III

ADULT AND CONTINUING EDUCATION AS A FIELD OF PRACTICE

11

PROFESSIONALIZATION OF THE FIELD OF ADULT AND CONTINUING EDUCATION

ALAN B. KNOX AND JEAN E. FLEMING

Issues related to professionalization for the millions of people working in the broad field of adult and continuing education have long been recognized and discussed by leading adult educators (Merriam & Brockett, 2007). These issues are now even more important as the field is increasingly viewed as central to personal and societal change in all spheres of life (Knox, 2002; Ray & Anderson, 2000). Lifelong learning by everyone is essential for people to gain the understanding and commitment they require for making major adjustments in their adult roles, such as family member, worker, and citizen. Because of this central connection between the field and change at all levels, it is essential to continually examine the preparation and performance of those involved in facilitating such changes.

A major challenge is the diversity and decentralization of the field, which requires that professionalization entail concerted efforts by people from the various parts of the field to define its content and processes. In the period covered by this *Handbook,* an overarching challenge for leaders in the field has been to provide a vision that connects local learning to global issues.

The beginnings of a movement toward professionalization of the field can be traced to the 1930s, with the greatest growth developing at the end of World War II as part of an overall stabilization of U.S. culture. In the second half of the 20th century, a focus developed on defining a specialized knowledge base and areas of expertise for the field, on credentialing, on research and the production of theory, and on creating a recognizable and formalized "discipline." Grace, Rocco, and Associates (2009) explain that leaders in this movement saw professionalization as a means to reduce marginalization of the field, and to bring security, status, and stature both in the university setting as a field of academic study and throughout society at large. During the 1960s and 1970s, however, as the field continued its development toward a more professionalized practice with recognizable form and function, those with a "spirit of amateurism" also closely aligned with the field, and they questioned the growing focus on professionalism. Yet, it "nevertheless became a cultural tour de force in the field" (Grace et al., 2009, p. 123).

John Ohliger was among the most vocal critics of this movement questioning precisely what the emphasis on professionalization sought to achieve (Grace et al., 2009, p. 121). He "considered learner freedom to be essential to adult education as a truly social endeavor. As he perceived it, professionalization was a thorn on the side of people's freedom to learn" (Collins, 2009, p. 210).

Conversations centered on professionalization invoke people's philosophical stances on the purposes and missions of adult education, on the merits of professionalism and amateurism, and on the understanding of adult education as a venture or an adventure (Grace et al., 2009). From one vantage point, professionalization can be seen as an attempt to corral the field into respectability, threatening the "free range" soul of a movement that is uniquely in tune with adults' natural tendencies and abilities to learn freely without formalized constraints. Indeed, Ohliger saw professionalization as a way to "tame" the field, and "challenged adult educators to think long and hard about the impact of professionalization on the field of study and practice and, concomitantly, on learner freedom, choice, and independence" (Grace et al., 2009, p. 313).

This chapter provides a rationale for professionalization and explores its potential benefits, in contrast to the critique provided by Grace and his colleagues (2009). Because of continued decentralization of the field, few of the problems regarding restriction of freedom and amateurism that Ohliger feared have materialized. This chapter identifies roles, stages, and career pathways of those who in various ways help adults learn. Both the formalized and decentralized communities of adult learners have retained their power to address individual, societal, and global problems. The challenge presented here is for deeper engagement and commitment by those in adult and continuing education to use scholarship to enhance the transformative energies of their field.

Professionalization of the Field

Professionalization depends on major features of each occupational field (Houle, 1980), and thus there are some distinctive features of professionalization for adult and continuing educators. In a way, the field's diversity defies the type of "unified specialization" linked with a profession (Cervero, 1992; Merriam & Brockett, 2007; Mott & Daley, 2000). As in many fields, people who are engaged reflect on the work they do. Such reflection includes questions about preparation, standards, ethics, and image. Answers to these and related questions can help shape components of professionalization, including publications, association services, communities of practice, formal study, cooperation, and ultimately educational opportunities for adults generally, which impacts the quality and extent of personal and societal benefits.

In this *Handbook,* each chapter addresses relevant aspects of the field and professional practice related to professionalization. The sections of this chapter explore the following seven questions for scholars and practitioners who help adults learn and coordinate programs—to enable them to provide leadership on behalf of professionalization, and to do so in ways that enhance stakeholder support including creativity and benefits to both participants and society.

1. What is the essence of the *professionalization* process for various occupations as rationale for leadership to strengthen the field and increase benefits to people and society?

2. What is the *distinctive* nature of the adult and continuing education field, compared with occupations that have standardized entrance requirements (such as accounting and architecture), and with occupations characterized by decentralized entry and attention to change (such as social work and journalism)?

3. What are the main but interrelated *roles performed* by people who work in the field that need be considered regarding the process and results of professionalization?

4. What are the *career stages* for people working in the field, in terms of: a desirable and feasible progression of those stages; professional concepts to guide the process; desirable proficiencies; procedures to enhance career progression; and criteria for excellence of performance, benefits to learners, organizations, and society?

5. What are the main *influences* on professionalization, such as personal understanding and commitment, publications, and communities of practice?

6. What actual and potential contributions to ongoing professionalization are made by fieldwide *associations* and formal *study?*

7. What are desirable *future directions* for professionalization of the field, regarding leadership, excellence, and benefits?

Decentralization of the Field

For those who work full-time in the adult and continuing education field, their professional role can pose a dilemma. As indicated in the next section, on features of professionalization, those who work full time are especially likely to recognize most of the issues professionalization involves. Each year, about half of all North American adults participate in at least one educational activity, typically on a part-time or short-term basis. Most of the people who help adults learn also do so on a part-time or short-term basis. Although some may assist in this way for many years, few are likely to characterize such activities as central to their career or sense of self (Knox, 1979, 2002; Merriam & Brockett, 2007).

By contrast, a small proportion of (but more than a million) people regard their roles related to educational opportunities for adults as central in their own lives. Collectively, they are associated with every imaginable type of organizational arrangement, in roles as teachers, counselors, administrators, planners, and scholars. Several hundred of these serve as professors of adult education (Merriam & Brockett, 2007).

The dilemma over the adult educator's professional role arises because the scope of the field and its benefits to individuals and society depends on contributions by multiple stakeholders. In addition to people who work in the field, important stakeholders include adult learners, administrators in the larger organization of which adult and continuing education is a part, funders, and policy makers.

Each category of stakeholder is important to program quality and benefits. This broad base of cooperation by various stakeholders reflects the vision and leadership of the relatively small proportion of people in the field who are working full time and have acquired an understanding of essential concepts, past trends, and promising future directions. They are typically the most engaged members. Their more comprehensive understanding of both theory and practice can be acquired in various ways, including formal study (such as in an adult education graduate program), reading, conference participation, and engagement in a local community of practice comprised of other people associated with one or more provider organizations.

Adult learning and change is a very personal, holistic, local process. Essential elements can and usually are discovered and used experientially. The topics and issues that adult learners address are usually connected to past trends and future directions, and to regional, national, and global counterparts. Professionalization can help the engaged and typically full-time members of the field recognize such connections, and then use their understanding of these relationships to assist all of the other stakeholders.

FEATURES OF PROFESSIONALIZATION

Houle's (1980) distinctive contribution was his emphasis on an evolving career-long process of professionalization that reflects the history of each field. This emphasis contrasts with more static inclusion criteria in occupations that have achieved professional status. Houle identified the following 14 features or goals of professionalization related to entry and continuing learning in the professions: agreement on the defining function and mission of the occupation, mastery of theoretical knowledge, capacity to solve problems, use of practical knowledge, self-enhancement, formal training, credentialing, creation of a subculture or community of practice, legal reinforcement, public acceptance, ethical practice, penalties, relation to other vocations, and relations to users of service.

These goals incorporate most subsequent commentary on professionalization (e.g., Cervero, 1992; Mott & Daley, 2000). Together these goals address multiple internal and external stakeholders, desirable standards, leadership, change orientation, collaboration and benefits to learners and society. Houle analyzed 17 occupations at various stages of professionalization, so his rationale can be applied to additional occupations, including adult and continuing education teaching and administration.

Some occupations differ from adult and continuing education teaching and administration regarding formal education in preparation for credentialing and entry to practice; a shared occupational function that spans specialty segments; procedures for periodic recredentialing to protect the public based on further education, examination, and peer review; and emphasis on instruction during preparatory and continuing professional education provided by universities, associations, and enterprises. Such occupational fields include accounting, dentistry, engineering, law, medicine, nursing, pharmacy, and school administration.

Other occupations seem more similar to adult and continuing education teaching and administration regarding centrality of communication, interaction, and change; varied educational and work experience prior to entry to the field; extent of somewhat separate specialties or segments; professional development concurrent with practice; and emphasis on self-directed learning, inquiry, and performance as modes of learning in professional development activities provided by provider organization, association, and university. Such occupational fields include social work, librarianship, journalism, clergy, and acting.

A typical feature of a profession is that in addition to proficiency and performance, there are ethical standards that members are expected to observe, with the assumption that there will be sanctions if they do not (Gordon & Sork, 2001). Other considerations include: program quality, clientele satisfaction, relation between research and practice, and professional identity (Chalofsky, 1996; Hatcher & Storberg-Walker, 2003; Merriam & Brockett, 2007; Polson, 1998; Rose, 1998; St. Clair, 2004; Tobias, 2003; Wilson, 2001). Cervero (1992) urged that the field of adult and continuing education recognize its current stage and focus on options to guide the future professionalization process.

NATURE OF THE FIELD

The broad field of adult and continuing education shares with several others, such as social work, librarianship, and journalism, some features that affect our effort to increase professionalization. One is the decentralization that reflects independent evolution of many segments of the field. This increases the difficulty in achieving a shared vision of the distinctive function and mission of the total field, unlike professional fields such as medicine and law in which earlier agreement on the basic function has undergirded subspecialties. A second feature of our field is the permeability that allows widespread practice prior to formal preparation (Cervero, 1992; Wise & Glowacki-Dudka, 2004).

A tenuous feature of the broad field of adult and continuing education is its diverse segments, along with generic perspectives that can contribute to collaboration. The diverse segments evolved quite separately during the past century, each with some distinctive practices and terminology, each in the context of every imaginable type of organization and adult life

role in society. The early unifying theme was as a social movement (Knox, 2002; Merriam & Brockett, 2007).

During the past eight decades, fieldwide perspectives, resources, and collaboration have received foundation support for fieldwide associations and projects. A major leadership challenge in the field is to achieve a balance between respect and support for the distinctive contribution in each segment of the field (with its strong connections to related organizations and policy makers), and a fieldwide perspective and collaboration on behalf of all adult learners and society generally (Merriam & Brockett, 2007).

ROLES IN THE FIELD

Professionalization efforts vary across three widespread but distinctive roles in the field. Several stakeholder roles are central to professional expectations and performance. These include practitioners, scholars, and people in other influential roles. The permeability of the field aids mobility, but can adversely affect professionalization.

People use many diverse paths as they enter and transition through various roles related to adult and continuing education. Understanding this complexity can help to strengthen communities of practice that can assist career progression and professional contributions to individual adults and to society. For example, initial contact with the field may be as a learner, instructor, coordinator, or policy maker. People working in the field may do so as a volunteer or for pay, may be full or part time, and may serve on a short- or long-term basis. Role transitions are usual, as in the case of a learner who becomes an instructor and then a coordinator, or a practitioner who becomes a scholar. Such complex relationships contribute to program effectiveness but pose a challenge for people who provide leadership regarding professionalization (Cervero, 1992; Houle, 1980; Merriam & Brockett, 2007; Rose, 1998; Wise & Glowacki-Dudka, 2004).

Practitioners

Practitioners may serve as instructors, counselors, or planning committee members, or in roles related to finance or marketing. Expectations for performance are typically shaped by the larger organization that contains their adult and continuing education agency as a minor and dependent part. Organizational influences occur in relation to terms of employment, volunteer contributions, promotion criteria, and setting of program priorities and conditions. Formal preparation is seldom a prerequisite for initial entry, and performance is more important than credentials for progress. Program quality and benefits to learners and society usually depend on cooperation across these practitioner roles, as well as on learners, whose active participation is essential to high quality process and outcomes. Scholars and people in external roles such as policy and finance can also influence practitioner performance. Such local expectations and conditions are typically more influential on role performance than fieldwide standards, preparation, and credentials.

Scholars

A second role perspective is of scholars engaged in research, evaluation, and provision of graduate study opportunities, mainly for practitioners. A few graduates of such programs have become the main source of new faculty. Strengthening the relation between research and practice is important but difficult to achieve (Chalofsky, 1996; St. Clair, 2004). As reflected in association leadership and publications, professors of adult education and their current and former graduate students are major contributors. Students' experience with such graduate courses, and with peers from various segments of the field, provides them with a fieldwide perspective as scholarly practitioners which contributes to their own leadership. They are also in a position to share that perspective, and an understanding of past and future trends and issues, with the overwhelming proportion of the practitioners in their provider organization and specialized associations who lack that grounding and connection.

External Roles

A third perspective that can contribute to role professionalization is that of people outside the field of practice and scholarship, who are associated with government, foundations, associations, larger parent organizations, media, and society generally, and whose view of the field and people who work in it is a major influence. Foundation examples include Carnegie

assistance with the American Association for Adult Education, Ford assistance with the Adult Education Association of the USA, and Kellogg assistance with Houle scholars. Government examples include federal and state executive and legislative leaders who support legislation and policies on behalf of lifelong learning for adults in many domains such as extension, literacy, and retraining.

Educational institution examples include leaders of schools, community colleges, and universities who help with policies and resources in support of educational opportunities for adults as an institutional priority. Support from leaders in such external roles is likely to be increasingly important in efforts to harness expertise from the field to address major public issues (Houle, 1980; Mott & Daley, 2000).

CAREER STAGES

Career development for many people who continue to work in the field tends to move from one stage to the next. The four stages—*entry, creative, transformation,* and *transcendent*—are described below. Actual career routes through such stages vary, as do influences. Each stage has some distinctive professionalization activities available that are responsive to the readiness of people at that stage, and some ways to encourage them to take initiatives. Leadership regarding professionalization of the field generally should consider all four stages, and help people progress through such stages (Merriam & Brockett, 2007; Mott & Daley, 2000). In most professional fields, the main distinction is the criteria for admitting newcomers to the field.

Entry

Many people who enter the field do so based on their experience and interest, rather than as a result of preparatory education and credentialing. Examples include: an effective docent who is encouraged to apply for a paid position as director of museum education, an associate degree graduate who becomes a teacher aide in an adult basic education course similar to one that she took when completing her high school equivalency diploma, and an enterprise manager who transfers to the human resource development department to teach in and coordinate staff development activities. Many such people refer to their entering the field through the back door. Effective interpersonal relations and an interest in learning contribute to initial effectiveness, and without formal preparation there is heavy reliance on experiential learning and coaching by experienced associates. Effective performance is the main criterion for advancement. Many professional development activities for practitioners at the entry stage are aimed at helping some to move to the creative stage.

Creative

Those who fail to identify with their adult and continuing education role and provider continue to learn but move in other career directions. The broader perspective of those who do embrace their role and make progress results from their initiative and creative self-directed learning. Their progress can be enhanced by a culture and community of practice in their provider agency and larger organization. Their emerging perspective and rationale to guide their efforts can be further enriched by participation in association conferences and use of print and electronic materials, such as journals and newsletters. Practitioners at this creative career stage begin to recognize influences and opportunities, and clarify priorities beyond an initial focus on survival concerns and "how to" technical procedures.

Transformation

Practitioners characterized as at the transformation career stage within any segment of the field have usually combined their personal experience and outlook with a growing familiarity with basic concepts, which enables them to reflect on the assumptions and implications of their decisions. Typical concepts and decisions pertain to adult development and learning, helping adults learn, program development and evaluation, program leadership and coordination, and trends and issues related to the field (Knox, 1979). For practitioners who have taken graduate program courses and degrees in adult education and related fields, such concepts and decisions are what they have studied and begun to apply in practice. Graduate study and substantial work experience contributes to their effectiveness and reflection as scholarly practitioners. Many practitioners without comparable graduate study experience are also very effective, as they gain mastery of basic concepts through a wide variety

of learning activities related to their ongoing professional development.

Transcendent

Increasing the number of practitioners and scholars at the transcendent career stage is crucial for both society and the field of adult and continuing education. The people of the United States are confronting an enormous number and severity of interrelated public issues, such as war/peace/terrorism, global economic recession/unemployment, health/poverty, sustainability/energy/conservation, social justice, education, corrections, transportation infrastructure, immigration. Progress on these issues entails ongoing learning and change by all adults. Enlightened leaders in many fields are recognizing that a broad base of understanding, learning, and support is required for constructive change, as has been demonstrated for quality improvement and management.

Transcendent leaders from each segment of the field can strengthen their alignment with policy makers associated with one or more of these major public issues. Because such issues are interrelated, collaboration among leaders throughout the field with a future-oriented global perspective can enhance public respect for interdependence, compassion, and wisdom for adults from all roles and walks of life. Publications on topics such as cooperation with cultural creatives (Ray & Anderson, 2000) and the natural step approach to sustainability (Robert, 2002) illustrate essential contributions by transcendent leaders. Transcendent practitioners and scholars with a collaborative vision benefit from associations, publications, and graduate programs that inform their perspective and enable them to assist the vast majority of people working in the field who lack this fieldwide perspective.

People throughout the field at this transcendent stage have a special opportunity to serve and benefit. Ingredients for their leadership strategy include: a shared vision of the distinctive function and mission of the broad field, and understanding of the importance of each of Houle's other 13 goals of professionalization. They may also recognize the implications from each of the other chapters in this *Handbook* regarding the content of professionalization efforts, connections throughout the field that can lead to collaboration, and an opportunity to enhance their own wisdom and satisfaction.

This may occur from rising to the challenge and making a major contribution. By helping relate more universal trends and issues to local practice, they demonstrate benefits from the field and thus increase general recognition and support of the field. Current public issues that call for increased attention to lifelong learning provide opportunities for people at this transcendent stage to demonstrate their value-added contributions.

INFLUENCES ON CAREERS

There are a number of influences on professionalization of the field beyond the contributions of graduate study and professional associations, which are also affected by these other influences. For example, expansion of the field and turnover produce many job openings. The talents and efforts of each person working in the adult and continuing education field are central to their career performance and development. However, there are various external influences on professional careers, such as the parent organization, materials, and image issues.

The specific provider agency and its larger parent organization (e.g., the human resource development department of an enterprise, the continuing education division of a university) is especially influential on people in adult and continuing education. In addition to overall organizational vitality, finances, and priority for the adult and continuing education function, organizational culture helps to socialize practitioners in both formal and informal ways, such as career ladders and support for practitioner's career development, including self-directed learning, staff development, and in some segments, certification.

With each passing decade, practitioners have an increasing amount of print and electronic materials available for self-directed learning and as part of courses and workshops for people working in the field. Scholars and practitioners from the field and related fields contribute to this resource, which addresses both theory and practice. The image of the field participants, practitioners, materials, and associations is shaped by all of the foregoing and by the ways in which this image is portrayed in the media. In addition, popular images also affect program support, adult participation, staffing, and professional development. Collaborative leadership can help shape the image of the field, especially in conjunction with its relevance to major issues and future directions in society.

Professionalization of the field is understandably connected with the contents of every chapter in this *Handbook*. Each type of provider agency and its larger parent organization affects goals, clientele, procedures, staffing, and finance, which are powerful influences on staff performance. Effective staff and volunteers understand diverse participant characteristics (age, class, place, abilities, aspirations) so that they can be responsive regarding adults' motivation, persistence, and application. Professional development can be enhanced in various ways, including through self-directed learning, technology, and communities of practice. Such concepts constitute the content to achieve Houle's goals of professionalization, such as theoretical and practical knowledge, problem solving, and formal training. Knox (1979) outlined basic proficiencies for the field, such as helping adults learn, program development and evaluation, and program coordination.

PROFESSIONAL PREPARATION

Attention to the defining function and mission of the broad field of adult and continuing education, and to the other 13 goals of professionalization (Houle, 1980), is most likely to result from leadership related to graduate study and fieldwide associations (Cervero, 1992; Chalofsky, 1996; Fleming, 2000; Polson, 1998; Rose, 1998; Sandmann & Smith,1999/2000). A central part of that contribution is strengthening connections between scholarship and practice. This section focuses first on graduate programs and then on associations.

During the past seven decades, graduate programs and associations in the field of adult and continuing education have been major vehicles for preparation of practitioners and scholars working in the field. Contributions by people from graduate programs and associations have overlapped greatly and have been major sources of research and publications.

The first university graduate programs focused on education of adults were established during the 1930s (Cervero, 1992). In the 1960s Houle (1964) listed such programs at 16 universities, most with one professor of adult education. The number of these graduate programs increased and leveled off throughout the 20th century (Kasworm & Hemmingsen, 2007). By the 1970s there were about a hundred such masters and doctoral programs, some with more than four professors of adult education and hundreds of graduate students (mainly practitioners studying part time). In recent decades, some long-standing graduate programs at major universities have been phased out and new programs have been started at regional universities, so the aggregate number of programs and faculty members has been relatively stable. Most programs have a few full-time faculty members who are housed in departments that also include related programs, such as school administration, higher education, and counseling (Imel, Brockett, & James, 2000; Merriam & Brockett, 2007).

University graduate programs have contributed to many additional efforts on behalf of a fieldwide perspective and collaboration. Within AEA and AAACE, the Commission of Professors of Adult Education (CPAE) has served as a vehicle for exchange and cooperation. In 2008, they updated their program standards. Additional contributions to collaboration and a fieldwide perspective include: a *Handbook* about every decade, several journals (e.g., *Adult Education Quarterly* and *Adult Learning*), many books and increasingly electronic media, the Adult Education Research Conference and regional research to practice conferences, the International Adult and Continuing Education Hall of Fame, the Houle, Okes, Wedemeyer, and Knowles awards for outstanding publications and programs, and joint advocacy on behalf of major policy issues.

Similar themes are reflected in the evolution of associations for people who work in the field. Professional development of members is a central function of professional associations. The one or more specialized associations related to most every segment of the field emphasize connections with policy, funding, and priorities related to the larger parent organization. The few fieldwide associations complement the many specialized associations by emphasizing research to practice, generic concepts, and collaboration (Fleming, 2000; Merriam & Brockett, 2007; Polson, 1998; Sandmann & Smith, 1999/2000).

As an indication of the diverse, specialized segments, there are currently more than 50 national associations of people who work in various parts of the field (Knox, 2002). Almost half are related to continuing professional education

in specific professions. Others pertain to adult basic education and literacy, community development, technology, continuing higher education, and human resource development in enterprises. The distinctive character of each segment reflects the mission of the provider organization, the characteristics of the clientele, and relevant content.

The first associations preceded adult education graduate programs, and scholars from various fields who were interested in educational opportunities for adults provided leadership for them, especially those associations with a fieldwide mission (Houle, 1964). The 1926 founding of the American Association for Adult Education (with assistance from Carnegie Corporation), and the related Institute of Adult Education, contributed greatly to handbooks, journals, and books for the field. About three decades later, the successor Adult Education Association of the U.S.A. (AEA) (with assistance from Ford Foundation, which also supported the Center for the Study of Liberal Education for Adults), increased both publications and leadership roles by professors and alums of graduate programs. About three decades later, AEA was succeeded by the American Association for Adult and Continuing Education (AAACE), and both associations included a Commission of Professors of Adult Education. Graduate program faculty and alums have been centrally engaged in the Adult Education Research Conference and in contributions to fieldwide books and journals (Fleming, 2000; Mott & Daley, 2000; Sandmann & Smith, 1999/2000).

In the growing number of associations of people working in the field, the emphasis and leadership have been mainly oriented toward professional practice, with less attention to scholarship and fieldwide perspectives. Collaboration among associations in the field has been seen as desirable over the years, but difficult to achieve. The specialized associations are thriving and target the specific professional development needs of their members. An emerging challenge pertains to the distinctive mission and vision of fieldwide associations and graduate programs.

Some people are associated with graduate programs and with fieldwide associations. Professors of adult education and their students and alumni are active in the Commission of Professors of Adult Education of AAACE, and in leadership positions in AAACE and in the Adult Education Research Conference and similar research to practice groups. Many of these people are connected with the International Adult Education Hall of Fame and with international associations related to the field. People at the transcendent stage are well represented among them. Together, they constitute a critical mass sufficient to accelerate professionalization in the field at transformative and transcendent levels. However, this depends on a commitment to do so.

FUTURE DIRECTIONS

Strengthening a collaborative strategy among various types of providers of educational opportunities for adults entails attention to communication, power, cooperation, and vision. Adult and continuing education can help people understand the important and complex issues that media reports tend to simplify and polarize, and education can enable them to deal with these issues. Local educational programs and use of technology can enable adults to engage in wise democratic action. Cooperative efforts and enlightened leadership across the field can enhance our collective impact in all parts of society. The hallmark of professionalization in the field is the vision to connect local learning to such global issues (Kasworm & Hemmingen, 2007; Knox, 2002; Rachel,1989; Sandmann & Smith, 1999/2000; Wise & Glowacki-Dudka, 2004).

The major public issues that confront our communities, our country, and our world call for lifelong learning and change. The following list suggests ways in which professionalization of the field can make a crucial contribution to dealing with the challenges of the coming decade.

a. Professionalization efforts by graduate programs and fieldwide associations can clarify a future-oriented vision and distinctive global mission of the adult and continuing education field, as a basis for broad societal commitment and support.

b. Professionalization efforts can help to strengthen connections between scholarship and practice in the field, especially for practitioners in part-time and volunteer roles who are not likely to pursue credit and degree courses.

c. Professionalization efforts can explore ways to improve university commitment, resources, and relations among adult education graduate programs and related disciplines and university priorities.

d. Collaborative professionalization efforts can increase collaborative relations across the field's umbrella organizations and various segments.

e. Professionalization can enhance concerted attention to action regarding major public global issues to compliment media overviews and encourage constructive social change.

Each of these potential future directions depends on a compelling vision of the contributions that educational opportunities for adults could make to learners and society generally. For more than a century, people working in the field have made valuable contributions to the adult learners, organizations, and communities they served. They did so early on with little general recognition of the importance of lifelong learning and change. Today, many people throughout society talk about lifelong learning as a given. Our current challenge regarding professionalization is to rise to a new plateau to enhance the expertise and commitment of people engaged in helping adults learn and in coordinating programs, and to do so at the more advanced stages of transformation and transcendence. Our leadership and attention to shared vision and collaboration can help move to this higher plateau. Commitment is the remaining ingredient.

REFERENCES

Cervero, R. M. (1992). Adult education should strive for professionalization. In M. W. Galbraith & B. Sisco (Eds.), *Confronting controversies in challenging times: A call for action.* New Directions for Adult and Continuing Education, No. 54. San Francisco: Jossey-Bass.

Chalofsky, N. (1996). Professionalization comes from theory and research: The why instead of the how to. In R. Rowden (Ed.), *Workplace learning.* New Directions for Adult and Continuing Education, No. 72. San Francisco: Jossey-Bass.

Collins, M. (2009). Moving beyond radical pessimism: Valuing critical perspectives. In A. P. Grace, T. S. Rocco, & Associates (Eds.), *Challenging the professionalization of adult education* (pp. 207–222). San Francisco: Jossey-Bass.

Fleming, J. A. (2000). Professional associations in adult and continuing education. *PAACE Journal of Lifelong Learning, 9,* 1–11.

Gordon, W., & Sork, T. (2001). Ethical issues and codes of ethics: Views of adult education practitioners in Canada and the United States. *Adult Education Quarterly, 51*(3), 202–218.

Grace, A. P., Rocco, T. S., & Associates. (2009). *Challenging the professionalization of adult education: John Ohliger and contradictions in modern practice.* San Francisco: Jossey-Bass.

Hatcher, T., & Storberg-Walker, J. (2003). Developing ethical adult educators: A re-examination of the need for a code of ethics. *Adult Learning, 14*(2), 21–24.

Houle, C. (1964). The emergence of graduate study in adult education. In G. Jensen, A. Liveright, & W. Hallenbeck (Eds.), *Adult education.* Washington, DC: Adult Education Association of the U.S.A.

Houle, C. (1980). *Continuing learning in the professions.* San Francisco: Jossey-Bass.

Imel, S., Brockett, R. G., & James, W. B. (2000). Defining the profession: A critical appraisal. In A. L. Wilson & E. R. Hayes (Eds.), *Handbook of adult and continuing education* (pp. 628–642). San Francisco: Jossey-Bass.

Kasworm, C., & Hemmingsen, L. (2007). Preparing professionals for lifelong learning: Comparative examination of master's education programs. *Higher Education: The International Journal of Higher Education and Educational Planning, 54*(3), 449–468.

Knox, A. (1979). *Enhancing proficiencies of continuing educators.* New Directions for Continuing Education, No. 1. San Francisco: Jossey-Bass.

Knox, A. (2002). A shared vision for adult and continuing education. *Adult Education Quarterly, 52*(4), 328.

Merriam, S. B., & Brockett, R. G. (2007). *The profession and practice of adult education.* San Francisco: Jossey-Bass.

Mott, V., & Daley, B. (Eds.). (2000). *Charting a course for continuing professional education: Reframing professional practice.* New Directions for Adult Continuing Education, No. 86. San Francisco: Jossey-Bass.

Polson, C. (1998). Fostering graduate socialization into adult education. *Adult Learning, 10*(2), 23.

Rachel, J. R. (1989). The social context of adult and continuing education. In S. B. Merriam & P. M. Cunningham (Eds.), *Handbook of adult and continuing education* (pp. 3–14). San Francisco: Jossey-Bass.

Ray, P., & Anderson, S. (2000). *The cultural creatives.* New York: Three Rivers Press.

Robert, K. (2002). *The natural step story.* Gabriola Island, BC, Canada: New Society.

Rose, A. D. (1998). Challenges in training adult educators. *Adult Learning, 9*(3), 4–5.

Sandmann, L., & Smith, W. (1999/2000). AAACE: Its legacy and future direction. *Adult Learning, 11*(1), 34.

St. Clair, R. (2004). A beautiful friendship? The relationship of research to practice in adult education. *Adult Education Quarterly, 54*(3), 224–241.

Tobias, R. (2003). Continuing professional education and professionalization: Traveling without a map or compass? *International Journal of Lifelong Education, 22*(5), 445–456.

Wilson, A. L. (2001). Professionalization: A politics of identity. In C. A. Hansman & P. A. Sissel (Eds.), *Understanding and negotiating the political landscape of adult education.* New Directions for Adult and Continuing Education, No. 91. San Francisco: Jossey-Bass.

Wise, M., & Glowacki-Dudka, M. (Eds.). (2004). *Embracing and enhancing the margins of adult education.* New Directions for Adult and Continuing Education, No. 104. San Francisco: Jossey-Bass.

12

PROFESSIONAL IDENTITY

LAURA L. BIEREMA

We call ourselves "adult educators," yet that term holds different meanings for each of us. You may mean that you are a literacy teacher, continuing education instructor, continuing professional educator, labor educator, nonprofit staff, instructional designer, human resource developer, K–12 educator, corporate trainer, higher education administrator, extension agent, prison educator, organization development consultant, college professor, career development counselor, community activist, health educator, public official, or something else. The dizzying array of adult education occupations and contexts is what makes our field dynamic and diverse, yet difficult to define. Adult education occurs in a range of contexts where professional boundaries may be blurred or contested. The field's breadth means it is fair to assume that what I mean by referring to myself as an "adult educator" may not necessarily be what you mean. Or, you may not even consider yourself an "adult educator." I have spanned the fields of adult education and human resource development for my entire career. My identity as an "adult educator" might be disputed by those "adult educators" who view human resource development (HRD) as embodying the antithesis of adult education's commitment to social justice. Yet, I don't believe the field can deny certain portions of itself, so I write this chapter with an inclusive spirit and as a challenge to broaden the boundaries of our practice both within and beyond adult education—for the good of our profession. This chapter examines adult education's diverse boundaries, with the goals of understanding how our field creates professional identities, analyzing how marginalization shapes the field and its professional identity, and proposing strategies for strengthening our professional identity as a field.

BOUNDARIES OF ADULT EDUCATION

Adult education has been defined as "activities intentionally designed for the purpose of bringing about learning among those whose age, social roles, or self-perception define them as adults" (Merriam & Brockett, 2007, p. 8). Adult education is highly diverse, with manifold goals and settings. A field's boundaries "are held strongly in place by theoretical premises, philosophical foundations, language, the practice arena, and the codification of knowledge in graduate programs" (Jeris & Daley, 2004, p. 101). Boundary issues arise when the various subfields of adult education explore philosophical roots, seek definitions, and both set and resist boundaries (Jeris & Daley,

2004). Truly examining and crossing these boundaries requires reflection and vigor. Jeris and Daley (2004) suggest that as we learn to boundary span it is important to ask how we develop boundaries, recognize their parameters, and can stretch beyond them.

The boundaries of adult education are many, some complimentary, some contested. The explicit social change agenda of programs such as that of the Highlander Center is a stark contrast to continuing professional education aimed at individual compliance with legislation or policy. Teaching someone to read is a more individualized process than educating to inspire a social movement such as the civil rights or women's liberation movement. Corporate training and development may embrace different goals and values than environmental activism. The various types of adult education listed above are weakly threaded together to form a "profession" of adult education that has become highly fragmented and decentralized. Many boundaries exist in adult education, and an immediate and future challenge is to see if the field can span them to create a stronger, more unified field of adult education.

Roth (2004), in discussing boundaries in adult education, notes that they have evolved "at arm's length from one another. Historically, scholars from both camps have been content to fertilize within fenced-in yards rather than explore and nurture common ground" (p. 9). Heaney (2000) observes that the various social visions pursued by adult educators are complicated and often contradictory and offers some examples of "fenced-in yards," such as literacy workers seeking to help individuals improve their job mobility versus activists striving to create shifts in social class, or corporate trainers implementing organization goals versus labor educators advocating resistance to management, or military educators preparing troops for war versus peace educators advancing a nonviolent agenda. Heaney asks how can adult education create a vision without conflict in purposes? He notes that the field is divided, and that puts us at risk:

> An adult education practice that, despite a multiplicity of visions, does not engender strategies for action across the borders of our now divided terrain is destined to reproduce

uncritically and indiscriminately both the best and the worst of the world's conditions. (p. 570)

Just what are adult education's "fenced-in yards," and why are we so reluctant to hop fences? It is useful to scrutinize the boundaries we have created and consider what they enable and prohibit. It is also helpful to consider how we can negotiate and change seemingly impermeable boundaries, like the one that adult education has created between itself and HRD. Exploring boundaries, particularly contested ones, can open the possibility for joint theory development and improved practice, if the boundaries are permeable. When we understand where boundaries interface, we can get closer to making changes in theory and practice and strengthen the whole field of adult education.

ADULT EDUCATION DELIVERY SYSTEMS

Regardless of the particular adult education program's goals, most adult education falls into three broad delivery systems, including institutional, content area, and personnel (Merriam & Brockett, 2007). These delivery systems serve to fragment and fence off segments of the field. The institutional providers include independent adult education organizations, educational institutions, quasieducational organizations, and noneducational organizations. *Independent adult education organizations* provide adult education as their primary function. These institutions can be community based (learning exchanges and grassroots organizations) or private (Literacy Volunteers of America) or proprietary schools and residential centers such as the Highlander Center for Research and Education. *Educational institutions* include public schools and postsecondary institutions serving youth as their main mission. Many adult learners find themselves attending postsecondary institutions. Cooperative Extension Service also falls into this category. Unfortunately, both adult education and adult learners are marginalized in such organizations, even though their numbers are growing, particularly in higher education. *Quasieducational organizations* can be private or public and view education as an important part of their mission. This category incorporates libraries, museums, mass medial, community organizations, religious organizations, and so forth.

Noneducational organizations are similar to quasi-educational organizations, but do not include education as a primary part of their mission. Much of the education that happens in business and industry would fall into this category, and the workplace continues to be one of the largest providers of adult education, with 2006 training expenditures estimated by ASTD to be nearly $130 billion (Workforce Management, n.d.). Merriam and Brockett (2007) identify content areas of adult education, noting that the various delivery systems overlap. Major content areas of adult education include human resource development, continuing professional education, remedial or basic skills education, recreational or leisure learning, citizenship, and technology. Each of these areas has created its own set of professional boundaries, some crossed more readily than others. The third major delivery system of adult education is personnel: those who deliver and receive adult education. Houle's (1970) pyramid of leadership provides a useful metaphor of the adult education's delivery personnel, with volunteers on the bottom, followed by part-time instructors in the middle, finishing with full-time adult educators such as program administrators, professors, training directors, and cooperative extension staff at the top. Each level of personnel likely identifies differently with the field. The range of institutions, content, and personnel involved in the delivery of adult education makes developing both an individual and collective sense of professional identity challenging.

PROFESSIONAL IDENTITY

I often receive quizzical looks from people when they learn I am an adult educator. Most people outside our field have never heard of "adult education," and those of us within in it do not necessarily agree about what it encompasses or in some cases even view ourselves as "adult educators." What are the dimensions of professional identity in adult education? How have we individually formed a professional identity? What are the various "professional identities" that coexist in adult education? To which do each of us belong? How do we form a professional identity within the field itself? These questions persist, and as Imel, Brockett, and James (2000) concluded in the previous *Handbook of Adult and Continuing Education,* "many who practice adult education do not identify with adult education as a field because they do not see its relevance to their work and the learners they serve" (p. 632).

Our personal and professional identity is socially constructed through discourses and interactions within social and professional contexts (Allan & Lewis, 2006). These various settings instruct us on appropriate ways of adult educator thinking and being as we co-create and reformulate our field through talk and action. For instance, how continuing professional education (CPE) professionals view their identity and work may be very different from how literacy teachers understand theirs. Community activists working for social justice may flinch when human resource developers approach their work with the same commitment and passion. Each context of adult education forms a community that has its own set of values, discourses, practices, and theories. Yet, even though professional contexts of adult education differ, we can probably all agree on certain principles—for instance, honoring the experience of the adult learners and giving them autonomy in the learning encounter. This section examines professionalization, defines professional identity, and raises concerns about the fragmented identity of adult education.

Professionalization

There has been enduring debate since the 1920s about whether adult education should become professionalized (Merriam & Brockett, 2007). Professionalization itself represents opposing goals. On one hand, professionalization helps move the field from a marginal status to one of social influence. On the other hand, the field's absorption into professionalization may create a narrowly conceived field of practice that excludes and marginalizes diverse voices and approaches to adult education (Merriam & Brockett, 2007). Given the range of the field, it is not surprising that a single professional identity does not exist. The main issues surrounding the professionalization debate are whether professionalization truly improves practice or whether it constricts who can practice and how we define "good" practice (Merriam & Brockett, 2007). There are fears that professionalization would create an elite class of adult educators, excluding much of the large and diverse population that currently delivers adult education in some form or another. "Professionalization is simply another mechanism by which social power is distributed in society, and all existing asymmetrical power relationships among different races and between men and women are reproduced (often in complex and subtle ways) through this process" (Johnson-Bailey, Tisdell, & Cervero, 1994, p. 65). Regardless of whether or not we believe the field should professionalize, each of us experiences a process of professional identity development.

Professional Identity Defined

The concept "profession" is traceable to the Latin *profiteri,* meaning a public pronouncement of certain principles and intentions and devotion to a certain way of life (duTont, 1995). Professions have either explicit or implicit codes of conduct and are based on rigorous training and study to learn the field. Professions are sustained through research, literature, and legislation (duTont, 1995). The literature base, graduate study, and professional associations have helped establish adult education as a profession (Imel et al., 2000); however, not all adult educators participate in these activities. Professional socialization involves building specialized knowledge and skills, incorporating a sense of occupational identity, internalizing the norms of the profession, and adapting the values and norms into individual behavior and self-concept. Professional socialization can occur formally through a graduate training program, or informally through contact with peers and informal sanctions, according to duTont (1995), who observes,

> Professional socialization is a developmental process of adult socialization. Not only does it involve the recognition of an assumed identity by the outside world, it also involves individuals' recognition of the identity within themselves and the non-deliberate projection of themselves in its terms—referred to as *internalization*—and it depicts the success of past socialization. (p. 165)

Professional socialization causes a new identity to emerge, much of which is formed through academic training. Yet, not all adult educators have received such training.

> The knowledge base is taught through graduate programs to new members, who then participate in professional activities, which in turn solidifies a sense of belonging to the profession. Those who identify themselves with the profession, or are seen by others as members, generally represent formal, institutionalized, mainstream adult education. . . . (Merriam & Brockett, 2007, p. 239)

Considering that graduate training programs, research activities, and professional associations serve as the major functions of professional socialization, it is fair to assume that a large majority of those delivering adult education are excluded from this process, particularly since only 9.4% of the U.S. population holds a master's degree ("Notes on the PhD Degree," n.d.) and less than 1% of the population attains a PhD (U.S. Census, 2004). The well-established academic field of adult education has a more cohesive identity than the field's practitioners. In fact, those working in an educational capacity with adults may or may not identify themselves as "adult educators." Parts of the field that challenge our assumptions of an "adult educator" or the profession itself "rais[e] issues about the meaning of professionalism itself and its relationship to the world of practice" (Merriam & Brockett, 2007, p. 239).

Professional identity in adult education takes two forms. The first is how you conceive of your own professional identity as an adult educator—the individual identification with an adaptation to the field and culture of adult education. Since there are many types of adult education, you might be more inclined to identify yourself as a literacy teacher, health educator, human rights activist, human resource developer, or instructional designer than as an adult educator. The other form of professional identity is how the field itself creates, maintains, and changes its professional identity. In other words, it has a public face with a relatively agreed upon discourse, research, and practice. This "profession" is easier to trace by identifying the many professional groups and conferences that are concerned with adult education, such as the American Association for Adult and Continuing Education, the Adult Education Research Conference, the Standing Conference on University Teaching and Research in the Education of Adults, the Council on Adult Basic Education, the Council for Adult and Experiential Learning, the Academy of Human Resource Development, the University Continuing Education Association, the National Association of State Judicial Educators, the American Society for Training and Development, and dozens and dozens of others. Many associations and conferences also exist on a state-by-state level. Given this range of professional associations, it is no wonder that forging either an individual or collective professional identity is challenging for adult education, since each of these subsets has its own professional identity.

Fragmented Identity in Parallel Universes

The breadth of the adult education field is daunting, mirroring the diversity of learning in adulthood. Some distinguish between adult educators and educators of adults (Griffith, 1989; Merriam & Brockett, 2007). Griffith defines educators of adults as those concerned with specific and practical educational goals, whereas he defines adult educators as those who hold a vision for the field that includes professionalization, academic programs, and interest in a collaborative field. Brockett (1991) offers another understanding, which is not as hierarchical as Griffith's definition, by differentiating between adult educators and those who conduct adult education. These distinctions may help us understand the difference between identity development at the individual versus field level. Brockett suggests by his definition that people may deliver adult education yet not possess any formalized training or professional affiliation in adult education. Brockett describes these distinct practitioners of adult education as working in parallel rather than hierarchically. This pattern of parallel practice has exacerbated the field's fragmentation.

Daley (2006) also writes about how adult education and health promotion exist in parallel universes, with both missing out on what the other field has to offer in terms of theory and practice—at the expense of creating healthy communities. The problem Daley raises is not unique to health promotion, but rather is common across the various subfields of adult education, such as CPE, literacy, higher education, HRD, and so forth. Daley suggests that health promotion models provide guides for adult educators on working collaboratively with health education professionals to create healthy communities. She advocates more alignment in the areas of program planning, teaching and learning, and research. Daley's example is very useful across the various domains of adult education and range of adult educators. Given that adult education has so much parallel activity, it is important to cultivate more communication and collaboration among these parallel entities so that we can create a stronger sense of professional identity.

ADULT EDUCATION AND SOCIAL JUSTICE

Adult education topics, contexts, and professional identities are as varied as its motives. The field has long claimed social justice as a key value, viewing education as an important variable in correcting social ills such as poverty and inequity through an analysis of power and privilege. Yet, for all of the emphasis adult education discourse puts on social justice, evidence of it in practice is difficult to find, and even in the field's literature, "social justice" is indexed only twice in the 2000 *Handbook of Adult and Continuing Education* (Wilson & Hayes, 2000) and not at all in *Learning in Adulthood* (Merriam, Caffarella, & Baumgartner, 2007) and *The Profession and Practice of Adult Education* (Merriam & Brockett, 2007). That is not to say that as adult educators we do not value addressing inequities through education. Rather, I contend that our concern for social justice is not being articulated as a value that is rallying adult educators in a professional sense.

Why is the ideal of social justice lacking prominence as a source of our professional identity? One explanation is that often adult education contexts are highly individualistic, more focused on helping individuals achieve their goals than on addressing broader social problems. Further, many adult education programs are driven by economics and expend more energy filling seats than addressing pressing social issues in order to remain solvent and operational. Adult education programs also may lack a systems focus or analysis and may not offer interventions or strategies that create fundamental change beyond the individual level. Finally, much of the social justice emphasis comes out of academia and the critical theory tradition, which has been accused of being impractical, being elitist, and lacking a bias for action. Practitioners may find complicated and critical academic arguments inaccessible and thus irrelevant to their work.

Elias and Merriam (1995) regard radical adult education (i.e., social justice and transformation-oriented education) as having little impact on the practice of adult education in the U.S. because it occurs within traditional institutions harboring conservative values and social structures. Radicalism is also less embraced by adult educators who tend to be concerned with individual and personal change instead of structural change in society. In addition, Elias and Merriam note that radical adult education philosophy is critique oriented, and criticism of educational practices may not always be welcome by educators or their institutions. Social justice is an honorable vision and an important value for most adult educators. Yet, how well is this vision incorporated into professional identity or practice?

Marginalization of Adult Education Within and Across Boundaries

The fragmented professional identity of the field is complicated by the issue of marginality. "Marginalization occurs when one person's views are valued and voiced at the sociopolitical and historical expense of others" (Sheared, 1994, p. 27). Sheared (2006) defines the margin by contrasting it with the "center." The center is usually the dominant, inside group (often Euro-American heterosexual males) with power and access to resources such as ideology, information, and assets, as well as influence over the politics affecting them. The study of marginality and commitment to eroding it is a hallmark of adult education theory and practice in much the same way as social justice is upheld as our vision. In fact, harboring social justice as a core value also places adult education on the margins, since the goal is to interrogate dominant systems of power and privilege. Adult education programs are marginalized due to diffuse purposes, the service orientation of the field, lack of funding, and the tenuous tie of learners to the provider organizations (Clark, 1956). Adults, by virtue of being of a "nontraditional age" for education, in many institutions may find themselves in settings where they are invisible and unconsidered. Marginality is affected by power relations and is also experienced by historically disenfranchised groups based on race, socioeconomic status, and gender, and other factors that prevent them from having equal access to education.

To be marginalized is to have the status of an outsider, and exist on the periphery of the group that holds the power and access to resources and knowledge, although you are a member of the group at large (Sheared, 2006). For instance, you may be an adult educator, but not part of the group of faculty who controls the education, or the editors who decide what gets published in the journals, or the leaders of associations that determine policy. Marginalization often silences the voices, discourses, and histories of those affected (Sheared, 2006). Marginality is being cast as "other" and usually viewed as of lesser value by the dominant group. Daloz, Keen, Keen, and Parks (1996) suggest that this otherness is where one lives "at the edge of ones tribe or society appears to contribute to the ability to move between tribes" (p. 72).

Types of Marginalization

Marginalization in adult education often manifests socially and institutionally. Social marginalization is based on not being in the center group due to sociological factors or positionalities such as gender, race, class, and so forth. Institutional marginalization is how the structure of organizations and delivery systems of adult education often function to disadvantage it. Social and institutional marginalization are described below.

Social Marginalization. Merriam and Brockett (2007) argue that mainstream adult education has marginalized women, African Americans, Native Americans, Hispanics, the disabled, gays and lesbians, older adults, working class adults, and others. The field marginalizes due to the hegemonic process whereby the exclusion of the voices of all but heterosexual White males comes to be accepted as the norm of the field by all of its participants, including those most negatively affected. It is also determined by power relations in the field and who functions as a gatekeeper of academic programs, journals, conferences, and the knowledge base.

Merriam and Brockett (2007) suggest that the field has an unacknowledged side that is invisible and ignored. Invisible adult education includes the histories and practices of those "whose race or ethnicity, sex, economic class, sexual orientation, able-bodiedness, or lifestyle have differed from mainstream adult educators and learners, thus causing them to be marginalized or disempowered" (pp. 260–261). The ignored aspect of adult education is also community based. Community-based education that relies on collaborative learning, indigenous knowledge production, empowering pedagogies, and the notion of praxis falls outside the mainstream of adult education, which is dominated by economic models, thus causing this type of adult education to also be marginalized.

Institutional Marginalization. The location of adult education also serves to marginalize it. As observed by Clark (1956):

> The adult program is a separate, periphery activity, and its clientele completely outside the compulsory attendance age groups. When an adult education program is initiated, it must make its way within a family of established programs, contending with the strong, central departments for budget support and favorable treatment. (p. 58)

Most adult education programs are housed in institutions that do not view adult education as their primary mission. This is true, for example, in postsecondary institutions or businesses. This problem is compounded by the reality that adult education programs are often funded based on enrollment (Merriam & Brockett, 2007, p. 110). Adult education's marginality also contributes to problems of identity, since many adult education providers do not view themselves as such. Merriam and Brockett (2007) suggest that the field has emphasized the growth of institutional sponsorship and the development of formal programs, dominated by White middle-class males and a drive toward workplace education. A result of this development has been the field's loss of important segments of practice, such as women's education, civil rights movements, immigrant and labor education, and others. Both social and institutional marginalization impinge on the field's ability to influence education and cultivate a unified professional identity.

The Consequences of Marginalization

Marginalization puts adult education at a social, economic, and cultural disadvantage. This is especially problematic because marginalization may become invisible as it weaves through patterns of social and institutional behavior and comes to be accepted as "normal." Hill Collins (1990) explains this normalization process as one where domination seduces, pressures, and forces members of subordinate groups to replace their "individual and cultural ways of knowing with the dominant group's specialized thought" (p. 229). As adult education is marginalized, it becomes more and more difficult to see its marginalization within our institutions and ourselves, and we may even participate in marginalizing the field without realizing it. For instance, in an institution such as higher education, where adults are of low priority, we may find ourselves accepting the substandard facilities and resources available. Or we may not challenge the discourse that others adult learners by suggesting that they are "needy," "nontraditional," "commuter," or "reentry." Marginalization is powerful and problematic since "each individual derives varying amounts of penalty and privilege from the multiple systems of oppression which frame everyone's lives" (Hill Collins, 1990, p. 229). It is important to see ourselves as both members of multiple dominant groups and members of multiple subordinate groups (Hill Collins, 1990) and claim how our actions may both privilege and restrain adult education and learners. In addition to its hegemonic quality, marginalization erodes the power base of adult education to secure resources, influence policy, and reach all adults who seek an education.

FENCE HOPPING AND FUTURE BUILDING

When confronted with parts of our field that we are unfamiliar with, uneducated about, or uncomfortable with, a natural reaction is to dismiss or critique them. Invoking what Argyris (1999, p. 188) called "defensive routines" allows us to discount information or practices that may expose our lack of knowledge or previous errors. Yet, by constructing fences around our carefully guarded areas of adult education, and not challenging ourselves to engage with new, perhaps threatening ideas, we are isolating ourselves from ideas and opportunities that will allow us to grow as professionals and a profession. Further, we are marginalizing aspects of ourselves. This siloing can be dangerous and limit our ability to provide effective, powerful education, or negotiate in the best interest of adult education within and across contexts. It is my belief that adult education is stronger when the various contexts are communicating and collaborating, and we are extending ourselves beyond adult education or our various subsets to expand knowledge and practice. My own practice in adult education and HRD has been shaped by the best of both fields. Yet, working between them has also allowed me to see their shortcomings, sometimes leading me beyond both fields for solutions. When new professional communities are developed, the opportunity is created for exploring new ways of thinking and being within the newly created social context. Learning these new ways of being may impact both individual and collective identity.

This chapter considers adult education's professional identity and how it is shaped by diversity, boundaries, fragmentation, and marginalization. As we anticipate the next decade and beyond, how can we effectively respond to these issues? We can begin this work by embracing marginality, identifying areas of accord and discord, and strengthening professional linkages.

Embracing Marginality

Marginality is generally regarded as an undesirable state, yet Sheared and Sissel (2001) counter that narrative by advocating that we should revel in adult education's marginal status. This sentiment is echoed by other adult educators:

> Marginality does have its benefits including greater independence to be creative and respond to needs and establishing distance from parent institutions to prevent being co-opted into the organization's mission. When one stands at the margins, astride the boundary between tribes, one stands also at the center of a larger, more adequate whole. (Daloz et al., 1996, p. 77)

Since we find ourselves both socially and institutionally marginalized, there is merit in embracing that status and making it work for us rather than against us. Daloz and his colleagues note several gifts of marginality, including greater self-knowledge, improved awareness of others, ease with life at the edge, the ability to promote empathy, and critical thinking across the margin's borders.

Wise and Glowacki-Dudka (2004) also urge us to embrace marginality, suggesting it is largely "volition" in that as adult educators we *choose* to work on the margins. The margins are where dominant ideology and practice are challenged, making them a place of creativity and collaboration. It is on the margins where we gain understanding from insider–outsider perspectives, span disciplinary or ideological boundaries, and use the position and information available to it for creative problem solving, influencing change at the center.

Sheared (2006) suggests there must be recognition of the marginal status, understanding of the power dynamics, and action to change them if we are to move from margin to center. She advocates forming coalitions of mutual success as a means of addressing marginalization, along with defining and interpreting power and hegemony within context. This requires developing multiple centers and margins to move between as issues are negotiated. Sheared emphasizes that before we can understand another marginalized group, we must understand our own. This impels us to cross adult education boundaries we have been afraid to cross, such as that between critical adult education and HRD. This is a particularly perplexing fissure, as these are the only areas of adult education that make group, organization, and system-level interventions an explicit part of their agenda. To some it may seem that they make odd bedfellows, but both are committed to implementing change within their respective contexts, and I contend that they have much to learn from one another, as do other isolated segments of the field. By stepping across boundaries that have been previously written off, we open ourselves to making new and surprising discoveries. Finally, our voice must be developed as those on the margins learn to "acknowledge and share parts of their own reality. . . . multiple voices shaped by history, culture, family, economics, gender, race, sexual orientation, and religion to name only a few conditions" (Sheared, 2006, p. 189). Through communication and collaboration across our boundaries can we develop a stronger voice and advocacy for adult education in all contexts.

Indeed, being on the margin appears to be the best place for adult education to begin stretching across its various boundaries and understanding how cross fertilization of ideas and collaboration between unlikely partners can help to strengthen both our professional identity and the field. Wise and Glowacki-Dudka remind us that we have the skills to foster dialogue and collaboration from the margins and create new partnerships and strategies for social change. Although we can embrace marginality and use it as a force for change, it is also important to remember that those in the center must be included and educated if we are to create lasting structural change. Sheared (2006) advocates the development of a vision to help address these issues, which includes examining who we are, developing a philosophy, and developing strategies aimed at social change.

Identifying Areas of Accord and Discord in the Field

How do we go about embracing marginalization? One way would be to examine points of agreement and disagreement in the field and engage in reflective dialogue about them. Although adult education is a diverse field, there are many boundaries over which there is much accord, such as the humanistic tradition, value of lifelong learning, social and institutional marginalization, commitment to social justice, promotion of learner autonomy, impact of social context on learning, constructivism, influence of technology, and many others. These widely held beliefs make excellent platforms from which a sense of professional identity can be cultivated across the parallel practices of the field.

The boundaries of discord are just as important for the field to identify and discuss and are the margins along which discoveries are made. For instance, the conceptual frameworks in the field differ, each contributing a valuable perspective. We become quite fond of our own frames and unwilling to entertain or attempt to understand others. Yet, the field and our understanding of it would be stronger with more dialogue about the different values, theories, and frames it entertains. The field also differs on units of analysis, with some approaches very individualized and disconnected from social variables such as CPE, while others are more focused on groups, systems, and social change such as social movements or HRD. What can these different approaches learn from considering another's approach? The same discourse or terminology is not uniform across the field, and this is a rich area for learning and bridging across different adult education practices. Finally, the motives of adult education segments vary. Motives may be social, cultural, economic, critical, transformational, developmental, spiritual, and so forth. Rather than ignoring the segment of adult education with motives that do not fit ours, it is educational to appreciate different motives and learn from them.

Strengthening Professional Linkages and Creating New Ones

One way of embracing marginality is to seek more integration across the field and appreciate its multidisciplinary nature. It is probably too much to hope for a unified identity as a field in one so diverse and fragmented as ours. Yet, we need to break out of our parallel existence and find ways to appreciate and embrace the field's variety. Adult education occurs in networks of communities that have a range of relationships with each other. For instance, during my career in HRD in the automotive industry, I worked with a local university and community adult literacy program to enroll interested employees in literacy and GED programs. The participants in the literacy program would not have benefited if the university professor had been unwilling to cross his boundary into the HRD arena, or if I hadn't stepped out of the traditional HRD role and worked with community partners to address the problems of illiteracy and poverty, and asked my corporation to pay for it. The opportunities for such cross-fertilization of the many facets of adult education abound, if we are willing to try new things and take some chances.

The adult education profession has sustained itself for decades and has many expressions of professional identity, including academic programs, books, journals, publications, associations, and conferences. A sense of professional identity could be strengthened with more communication and collaboration across these existing professional outlets. The Adult Education Research Conference celebrated its 50th year in 2009, and the American Association for Adult and Continuing Education has persevered. To date, the field lacks an association dedicated to research in the field and creating one that has strong ties to practice would be one way of bridging between parallel structures of the field. Technology also holds promise for linking previously siloed parts of the field through online social networking, listservs, e-learning, e-mentoring, and blogs. Creating a stronger sense of professional identity requires us to seek cross-fertilization between academia and practice, as well as the various contexts where adult education is practiced and studied. The most we may be able to hope for is making linkages across the varied contexts of adult education and helping people who are educators of adults identify themselves as adult educators.

This chapter has examined the multiple professional identities within adult education by examining our boundaries, similarities, and differences. Our diversity is both a strength and liability. Multiple boundaries, frameworks, and motives create a robust field that serves adult learners across many different institutions and contexts. Yet, at times the field's diversity serves to fragment and fracture adult education as a whole. Each segment of adult education has valuable frameworks and practices. Unfortunately, these attributes do not always translate across our carefully guarded fences. Adult education can move to a position of greater strength and influence when we stop holding our various contexts at arm's length and begin climbing and tearing down fences so that we may embrace the entire field for all that it has to offer adult education and learners.

REFERENCES

Allan, B., & Lewis, D. (2006). The impact of membership of a virtual learning community on individual learning careers and professional identity. *British Journal of Educational Technology, 37*(6), 841–852.

Argyris, C. (1999). *On organizational learning.* Oxford, UK: Blackwell.

Brockett, R. G. (1991). Professional development, artistry, and style. In R. G. Brockett (Ed.), *Professional development for educators of adults* (pp. 5–13). New Directions for Adult and Continuing Education, No. 51. San Francisco: Jossey-Bass.

Clark, B. R. (1956). *Adult education in transition: A study of institutional insecurity.* Berkeley: University of California Press.

Daley, B. J. (2006). Aligning health promotion and adult education for healthier communities. In S. B. Merriam, B. C. Courtenay, & R. M. Cervero (Eds.), *Global issues and adult education: Perspectives from Latin America, Southern Africa, and the United States* (pp. 231–242). San Francisco: Jossey-Bass.

Daloz, L. A. P., Keen, C. H., Keen , J. P., & Parks, S. D. (1996). *Common fire: Leading lives of commitment in a complex world.* Boston: Beacon Press.

duTont, D. (1995). A sociological analysis of the extent and influence of professional socialization on the development of a nursing identity among nursing students at two universities in Brisbane, Australia. *Journal of Advanced Nursing, 21,* 164–171.

Elias, J. L., & Merriam, S. B. (1995). *Philosophical foundations of adult education* (2nd ed.). Malabar, FL: Krieger.

Griffith, W. S. (1989). Has adult and continuing education fulfilled its early promise? In B. A. Quigley (Ed.), *Fulfilling the promise of adult and continuing education* (pp. 5–13). New Directions for Continuing Education, No. 44. San Francisco: Jossey-Bass.

Heaney, T. W. (2000). Adult education and society. In A. L. Wilson & E. R. Hayes (Eds.), *Handbook of adult and continuing education* (pp. 559–572). San Francisco: Jossey-Bass.

Hill Collins, P. (1990). *Black feminist thought: Knowledge, consciousness, and the politics of empowerment.* London: HarperCollins.

Houle, C. O. (1970). *The educators of adults.* In R. M. Smith, G. F. Aker, & J. R. Kidd (Eds.), *Handbook of adult education* (pp. 109–120). New York: Macmillan.

Imel, S., Brockett, R. G., & James, W. B. (2000). Defining the profession: A critical appraisal. In A. L. Wilson & E. R. Hayes (Eds.), *Handbook of adult and continuing education* (pp. 628–642). San Francisco: Jossey-Bass.

Jeris, L., & Daley, B. (2004). Orienteering for boundary spanning: Reflections on the journey to date and suggestions for moving forward. *Advances in Developing Human Resources, 6*(1), 101–115.

Johnson-Bailey, J., Tisdell, E., & Cervero, R. (1994). Race, gender, and the politics of professionalization. In E. Hayes & S. A. Colin (Eds.), *Confronting racism and sexism* (Vol. 61, pp. 63-76). San Francisco: Jossey-Bass.

Merriam, S. B., & Brockett, R. G. (2007). *The profession and practice of adult education: An introduction.* San Francisco: Jossey-Bass.

Merriam, S. B., Caffarella, R. S., & Baumgartner, L. M. (2007). *Learning in adulthood: A comprehensive guide* (3rd ed.). San Francisco: Jossey-Bass.

Notes on the PhD degree. (n.d.). Retrieved February 18, 2009, from http://www.cs .purdue.edu/homes/dec/essay.phd.html

Roth, G. (2004). CPE and HRD: Research and practice within systems and across boundaries. *Advances in Developing Human Resources, 6*(1), 9–19,

Sheared, V. (1994). Giving voice: An inclusive model of instruction—A womanist perspective. In E. R. Hayes & S. A. J. Colin (Eds.), *Confronting racism and sexism* (pp. 27–37). New Directions for Adult and Continuing Education, No. 61. San Francisco: Jossey-Bass.

Sheared, V. (2006). The intersection of education, hegemony, and marginalization within the academy. In. S. B. Merriam, B. C. Courtenay, & R. M. Cervero (Eds.), *Global issues and adult education: Perspectives from Latin America, Southern Africa, and the United States* (pp. 182–192). San Francisco: Jossey-Bass.

Sheared, V., & Sissel, P. A. (2001). What does research, resistance and inclusion mean for adult education practice? A reflective response. In V. Sheared & P. A. Sissel (Eds.), *Making space: Merging theory and practice in adult education.* New York: Bergin & Garvey.

U.S. Census. (2004). What percentage of the US population has a Ph.D. degree? Retrieved August 25, 2009, from http://www.census .gov/population/socdemo/education/cps2004/ tab02–01.pdf

Wilson, A. L., & Hayes, E. R. (2000). *Handbook of adult and continuing education.* San Francisco: Jossey-Bass.

Wise, M., & Glowacki-Dudka, M. (2004). Embracing and expanding the margins of adult education. *New Directions for Adult and Continuing Education, 104,* 87–90.

Workforce Management. (n.d.). 2008 training providers. *Workforce Management: Training & Development.* Retrieved February 18, 2009, from http://www.workforce.com/section/11/feature/ 25/72/12/index.html

13

FACILITATION AND DESIGN OF LEARNING

REGINA O. SMITH

The adult learner population is increasingly diverse with respect to age, gender, race, sexual orientation, culture, work experiences, educational background, learning styles, and epistemologies (beliefs about learning, knowledge, and teaching). This student diversity includes the growing influx of non-European immigrants from Latin America and Asia (Alfred, 2005) as well as the growing number of Africans, African Americans, Asians, Latin Americans, and Native Americans who are already citizens (Merriam, Caffarella, & Baumgartner, 2007).

To take advantage of theories that are more inclusive for the changing adult learner population, a number of adult educators promote a shift in thinking about the design and facilitation of adult learning. A shift to include more contemporary theories requires a shift from teacher-centered to learner-centered instruction (Barr & Tagg, 1995). Learner-centered instruction is characterized by several attributes that change the focus from teaching to learning, passive participation to active involvement, single representation and perspectives to multiple representations and perspectives, and decontextualized to contextualized learning content (Jonassen, 1997; Merriam et al., 2007).

Many adult educators, therefore, embrace the need to change their learning design and facilitation approaches in at least three ways. First, they promote learning that is culturally (Guy, 1999), professionally, and personally relevant (contextualized), which actively engages the learners in social learning activities such as problem solving (Jonassen, 1997; Merriam et al., 2007), simulations, role playing, etc. Second, educators (Cunningham, 1988; Freire, 1970; hooks, 1994; Lindemann, 1921) promote educational efforts that also serve to empower and liberate learners and society. Accordingly, learning must concern itself with social learning conditions that enable learners to challenge and overthrow current societal structures through dialogue, discussion, reflection, and then action (Freire, 1970). Third, researchers (Smith & Berg, 1987; Tennant, 1997) advocate collaborative learning that promotes individual identity change and development. These changes reflect the ways learners make sense of and negotiate the intrapsychic and interpersonal experiences they encounter in these active and contextualized environments. Tennant (1997) explains that traditional thinking about learning emphasizes an ethic of individualism. On the other hand, learners can both make sense of and reshape their thinking in learner-centered environments that emphasize active participation in learning within social contexts with diverse perspectives.

Nevertheless adult educators find that oftentimes, their efforts to move to learner-centered design and facilitation fail. This chapter discusses two main reasons for this failure: (1) incongruence between espoused theories and theories-in-use (Argyris & Schön, 1974), and (2) the separation of the mind, body, and spirit in learning.

INCONGRUENCE BETWEEN ESPOUSED THEORIES AND THEORIES-IN-USE

For the past 20 years, Argyris and Schön's work (1974) has been concerned with the conscious and unconscious reasoning processes that influence actions. Their work is based on the belief that people are the designers of their own actions. They assert that people hold maps, schemata, or theories in their heads to help them plan, implement, and review their actions. They contend that few people are aware of these maps and that oftentimes there is incongruence between the maps (theories) used to plan and the maps used to form their actions. For Argyris and Schön, the distinction is more than merely a distinction between what people do and what people say, but reflects a difference between the "theories in-action" that undergird their actions and the "espoused theories" that they use to guide their intentions. Although it is easy to see this incongruence within the individual teacher, Argyris and Schön also use the same arguments to demonstrate that this incongruency occurs at the student, institutional, and societal levels.

Adult educators who seek to adopt learner-centered perspectives to design and facilitate learning are often unaware of the need to go beyond new facilitation and design strategies and adopt a different worldview about teaching, learning, and the nature of knowledge. For example, a number of adult educators adopt collaborative learning approaches. Collaborative learning is a process by which small, interdependent learners coconstruct knowledge (Vygotsky, 1978) to achieve consensus and shared classroom authority (Bruffee, 1999). The emphasis is on knowledge construction through active learner discussions, as well as a shift of much of the classroom authority and control from the teacher to the small learner groups. During the collaborative process, the learners confront complex real-life situations through messy ill-structured problems (Jonassen, 1997) in which both the problem and the solution are ambiguous. Newcomb (1962) maintains that the consensus-building process places knowledge construction within the small groups,

among peers, rather than between learners and text or teacher and learner. That is, educators shift their design and facilitation to use the small groups rather than the traditional lecture to help learners take some responsibility for their own learning and to share classroom authority (Bruffee, 1999).

Bruffee warns that collaborative learning reflects epistemological beliefs (Schommer, 1994), not simply a set of pedagogical skills. Epistemology (the theory of knowledge), a branch of philosophy, focuses on knowledge creation and how one comes to know. According to Piaget (1952), humans move through significant differences in their organizing structures (assumptions) regarding knowledge and learning, which they use to make meaning of their learning experiences. Although there are many different approaches to epistemological development, many theorists, such as Perry (1970), Kegan (1982, 1994), and Baxter Magolda (1999), assert that these meaning-making structures evolve through predictable stages that represent changes to individuals' assumptions about knowledge and learning (epistemological beliefs). According to Hofer and Pintrich (1997), individual epistemological developments seem to start with a belief of knowledge as right and wrong, and gradually move towards an understanding that all knowledge is relativistic in nature. As individuals develop, they also gain a stronger sense of knowledge as being constructed by themselves. During early stages, teachers view themselves as the transmitter of knowledge and students as passive recipients of the teacher's knowledge. Later, teachers understand that students are also capable of creating valuable knowledge.

Pratt and Associates (1998) contend that epistemic assumptions "will significantly shape, define, and limit a given perspective on teaching" (p. 72). Adult educators' epistemic beliefs shape the way they design and facilitate learning, and ultimately the student's learning experiences. As Bruffee puts it, a change to learner-centered instruction, therefore, requires a change from foundational educational to nonfoundational models, or a change in teacher epistemological beliefs.

The foundational model reflects transmission beliefs, that is, the instructor as transmitter of knowledge and primary classroom authority. The nonfoundational model represents learner-centered beliefs, that is, shared and active construction of knowledge and classroom authority such as those observed in social constructivist as well as many social justice related theories. Social constructivism (Vygotsky, 1978) emphasizes the critical importance of culture and the importance of the social context for cognitive development and knowledge creation among learners.

In collaborative learning the instructor values and builds upon the knowledge, personal experiences, language, strategies, and cultures that the learners bring to learning. The instructor models the collaborative learning process by allowing the learners' knowledge to both challenge and reshape their own thinking (Baxte Magolda, 1999; Bruffee, 1999). That is, the focus is on student learning rather than instructor knowledge.

When instructors with foundational beliefs use collaborative group approaches, the results will continue to reflect their foundational orientations (Bruffee, 1999; Clarebout & Elsen, 2001). For example, Kitchen and McDougall (1999) conducted research into learners' experiences with online collaborative learning. It appears that the instructor's foundational beliefs influenced the types of problems designed for the curriculum. According to Pratt and Associates (1998), beliefs cannot be observed, but must be inferred by what people intend, do, and say. In this particular course, group members with advanced Web-site design skills did most of the work, while other group members expressed dissatisfaction because they were unable to learn Web-site design. Kitchen and McDougall (1999) concluded that learners felt "collaborative interaction gave way to . . . individual task specialization" (p. 254). Rather than working collaboratively, the group members depended upon one person to do the bulk of the work. Therefore, Kitchen and McDougall (1999) concluded, "students did not have an opportunity to develop new skills and knowledge in areas they were previously lacking" (pp. 254–255). When problem solving relies on the subject expertise of one or a few group members, the other members are not able to learn collaboratively or derive the benefits that the collaborative theory promises.

Flannery (1994) explains that failed collaborative efforts are sometimes due to the use of well-structured problems, which reflect foundational thinking and reinforce standard conceptions of instructor authority. Well-structured problems build upon the principle that classroom knowledge is something that learners acquire rather than create. In this way, the instruction is designed to allow learners to learn predefined and identified pieces of information, rather than reflecting the intended social constructivist and learner-centered model. The effort failed because the teachers' epistemological ideas about teaching and learning, as reflected in the well-structured problems, suggest standard foundational beliefs.

According to Pratt and Associates (1998), consciously or unconsciously, our epistemology remains the lens through which we view teaching and learning. Regardless of our intentions (espoused theory), our fundamental beliefs or philosophical understanding of teaching and learning (theories-in-use) will determine our actions during the design and facilitation of adult learning processes. It is in later stages of epistemological development, or from a foundational belief system, that teachers are able to truly design and facilitate instruction that is learner centered, because their intentions and action reflect the ability to allow students to share classroom authority and they believe that students have the ability to create knowledge.

Moving to learner-centered design and facilitation may be incongruent with the students' epistemological beliefs as well. However, researchers such as Bruffee (1999) explain that learners are socialized into a traditional classroom setting characterized by (a) competition, (b) a narrow focus on individual work, (c) destructive criticism of other learners, (d) a willingness to share ideas only with the authority figure (the teacher), and (e) a general lack of trust toward peers.

In the example of collaborative learning, students must accept responsibility for their own learning. They must replace their reliance solely on the teacher and rely on their group members to help them create knowledge; group members must work interdependently and accept responsibility for one another's learning. The newly formed power relations created by the collaborative arrangement create powerful, emotional, and paradoxical tensions.

According to Saltzberger-Wittenberg, Henry, and Osborne (1983) this conflict resides in the dynamic interplay of conflicting teacher–learner expectations, wishes, and fears, rooted in traditional classroom authority configurations. These authors maintain that both teachers and learners hold fantasies that the teacher, who is the ultimate source of knowledge and wisdom, will comfort, teach, and attend to learners' needs. The teacher's ability to live up to such fantasies is problematic in traditional classrooms (Saltzberger-Wittenberg et al., 1983). The learners react by overly criticizing the teacher, arriving late, acting helpless, and so on, when these fantasies fail to manifest (Ringer, 2002). When in groups, learners may engage in various anxious behaviors, such as blaming, ignoring other group members' contributions, and avoiding conflict, which result in precarious learning for group members based on salient traits such as gender, race, age, and culture (Smith, 2005). These tensions create unbearable emotional stress for instructors, who fear losing control and also react negatively (Saltzberger-Wittenberg et al., 1983), fueling the anxious behaviors among group members. Many adult educators also try to resolve this tension by taking control of the group, which then negates the learner-centered approach they were attempting to design and facilitate.

Finally, instructors who want to design and facilitate learner-centered approaches may encounter incongruence between their epistemological beliefs and the beliefs of their colleagues, the institution, and society. For example, instructors who wish to use learner-centered approaches may encounter resistance among their senior colleagues and difficulties with federal standards regarding curriculum design and facilitation policy. Their efforts thus may be devalued and strongly discouraged.

THE SEPARATION OF THE HUMAN MIND, BODY, AND SPIRIT IN LEARNING

The need to adopt a whole person design and facilitation approach is the second reason adult educators fail in their efforts to adopt a learner-centered perspective. Although there is no universal agreement about the origins of the terms *holism* and *whole person learning*, they do share some common elements that are deeply rooted in cultural and historical aspects of indigenous peoples.

According to Fasokun, Katahoire, and Oduaran (2005), holism is a belief that individuals learn through continuous interaction with the community and the environment. According to Erickson (2007), the term *holism* is derived from the Greek word *holo*, which means whole, but the concept of holism is rooted in an ancient Indian Vedic culture that existed thousand of years ago. In the Sanskirt language used by the Indian Vedic culture, the word *sarvah*, which means whole, intact, or uninjured, was used to describe the nature of humans as an integral part of the universe. More specifically, the word *sarvah* means that when the physical form of the human spirit is instilled with an omnipotent source of energy (or spirit) derived from the universe, it is whole, uninjured, and intact (Erickson, 2007, pp. 130–140).

The inference is that holism is the natural state of the human being. That is, there should be interconnectedness within the human being (mind, body, and spirit), between humans, and between humans and the universe (Erickson, 2007). Erickson claims that the unnatural state for humans is a division of the components, with spirit disconnected from the physical body, humans disconnected from one another, and humans disconnected from the universe. Extrapolating from ancient cultures, Erickson concludes that to be healthy is to have the mind, body, and soul/spirit intact.

There are also Western scholars who view holistic learning as integral to education. Heron (1992) views holistic learning as an approach to learning that seeks to engage fully all aspects of the learner mind, body, and spirit. Miller (2006) views holistic education as a way to develop the whole person. He includes the body, mind, and spirit, but adds the social and the aesthetic. Each of these views of holism sees individual learners as an integrated whole within themselves, among their peers, among the members of the community, and among society.

Literature from nursing and medical educators also include the need to both teach and practice in holistic ways to bring the body back into its natural harmony (Erickson, 2007) and patient healing. Holism is also found in human resource development (HRD; Yang, 2004), workplace/workbased learning (Nafukho, 2006; Stephenson, 2001), and organizational learning (Wheatley, 1999) literature. Holism has also been used in mathematics education (Cohen, 2005) to facilitate the use of math in ethical ways for the learners and the community.

Many of the diverse learners who participate in adult education rely on non-Western perspectives like holism that honor the intellectual, emotional, physical, social, aesthetic, spiritual in ways that is visibly absent from much Western adult learning theories and literature (Fasokun et al., 2005; Merriam & Associates, 2007; Merriam et al., 2007; Miller, 2006). Nevertheless, many adult educators continue to use learning theories that fully or partially embrace the technical rational approach to design and facilitate learning. That is, they treat the body and spirit/emotions as separate from the learning process, which can negatively influence student learning.

The technical rational approach (Schön, 1983) to learning facilitation and design is a typical Western approach to learning. This approach focuses on the intellect almost to the exclusion of other ways of knowing, privileging the individual learner, autonomy, and independent thought and action over collective ways of learning that honor community and interdependence (Merriam & Associates, 2007). This approach views individual learners as independent from other learners, their community, and their society. The epistemology behind this approach to learning views knowledge as a fixed entity that is external to the learner, much like behaviorism. The technical rational approach assumes that there is a "correct" body of knowledge that has been scientifically verified and that can be put into a neat and tidy package and used across multiple adult learning contexts (Schön, 1983). During the facilitation and design process, educators ask students to master knowledge and to acquire specific skills or worldviews. The learners are expected to largely ignore the inconsistencies between their everyday reality and the body of knowledge presented, and to adjust their external world to fit the course content. Although the technical rational approach has helped to build the foundation for many of the learning theories today, and they are proven to work in many contexts and among many student populations, they largely ignore the needs of the growing diverse adult population. The technical rational approach largely ignores the cultural (country and community mores; social), emotional (attitudes, interest, attention, awareness, and values), spiritual (perceived sense of connection, religious beliefs, matters of the spirit), and contextual needs of the learners. The holistic approach is offered as an alternative to the technical rational approach.

Many adult educators who teach for social justice readily admit that teaching and learning are always political, social, psychological, and economical acts and that one has to address each of these aspects to provide a systematic way to facilitate change. Consistent with the social justice perspective, holism views the individual as a complex system (Fasokun et al., 2005) that must be considered when designing and facilitating learning. The intellect is not the primary consideration in learning, but rather, learning involves the whole person, with adequate attention to the body, mind, and spirit (Heron, 1992). A look at each element will help to explain the holistic perspective.

The first element is the mind (the intellect by which a person consciously processes or makes sense of information through reasoning and memory). The mind is the primary focus for learning theories such as cognitive approaches to design and facilitation. The focus is on the internal processes that are under the control of the learner (Merriam et al., 2007). When educators use the cognitive approach to design and facilitate learning, they often ignore the emotional issues that learners bring to the classroom. Even when educators recognize that learners bring emotional issues to the classroom, narrowly focusing on the intellect allows them to treat these issues as peripheral to learning, something that one must get out of the way so that learning can take place (Dirkx, Kielbaso, & Smith, 2004). Dirkx and his colleagues cite the way one of the teachers in their study treated the emotional issues the students brought into the classroom. "We may take a few minutes, and you know, let the student vent a little bit. It's like, okay, do you feel better now? . . . Because sometimes that kind of helps the student focus better. So sometimes it may be taking five to ten minutes away from class to kind of find out, okay, how's everybody doing today" (p. 40). That is, the emotional issues are not a part of the learning, but rather, baggage that must receive attention so that the real learning can occur.

Second, a holistic approach recognizes the body (the physical aspects or anatomy of individuals, by which they consciously and unconsciously make sense of or process information through the senses—touch, feel, smell, sight). Many adult educators understand that the emotions are a part of the learning process; however, they often overlook the role of the body in learning.

Often educators design and facilitate learning to promote social justice. Nevertheless, if educators ignore the role the body plays in processing the fear that students face when confronted with the need to speak up for themselves or to try to address inequities in society, the social justice intent might be lost. Crowdes (2000) explains that although we are able to help learners conduct "eloquent and valuable analyses of power, conflict, and the need for change, these skills" may "come to feel like heavy burdens" (p. 25) when learners try to use them in everyday life situations. She further explains that students complain that "as empowered as they feel by their developing multicultural perspectives and sociological imaginations, the ideas remain abstract and disconnected from their daily relationships" (p. 25). Thus, when students experience these issues in real life, they may experience so much stress and tension in their bodies that they become silenced. They have not learned to use the body to learn (Crowdes, 2000). That is, when we fail to teach in ways that honor, for example, the mind–body connection, our learners are ill-prepared to use the information and skills from the class.

Third, the holistic approach recognizes the role of the spirit (the seat of emotion, feeling, and desire) of individual learners, by which each learner relies on gut reactions, perceptions, and other feelings to makes sense of the information presented. When adult educators design and facilitate learning that largely ignores the full role of emotions/spirit, it can greatly influence learning. Horsman (2001) and her colleagues conducted a study of literacy learners who also experience physical or emotional trauma in their lives. The facilitators of the literacy program designed a literacy training program for these learners to emancipate them by helping them gain leadership roles in the community-based organization and ultimately in their personal lives. The trauma literacy learners began to experience physical and emotional discomfort from flashbacks to previous trauma as well as the anxiety found in all group work. The facilitators stepped in and took over the learning groups. Ultimately, the learners complained that they were unable to learn to resolve their own issues and to speak up in the community-based organization meetings. They continued to feel victimized. Horsman and her colleagues tried to use a social justice approach to the leadership training for the trauma literacy victims by empowering them. However, the effort failed because they failed to consider other ways that students make meaning (the physical and emotional pain). She readily acknowledges that participants' experiences affected the body, mind, emotions, and spirit. She concluded that attention to each of these aspects (the whole person) of the leaner is important to facilitate literacy learning for these learners.

Finally, a holistic approach recognizes the interdependence of learners and focuses on the interaction among learners as well as the interaction of the learner, the community, and the larger society. This interdependence encompasses many adult learning theories.

For example, holism is contextual. Contextualized learning is based on the view that people learn more effectively when they are learning something about which they have prior knowledge, that interests them, and that offers them opportunities to use their prior experience to make sense of the new knowledge. Contextualized learning is inherent in indigenous societies, which view learning as a continuous interaction with the community and the environment. For example, Fasokun and his colleagues (2005) explain that most African people experience the subject matter that is taught in the classroom as also an integral part of their everyday living. In addition, drawing largely on the roots of constructivism, cognition theorists such as Brown (1998) explain that contextualized learning allows individuals to make or construct meaning by interpreting and interacting with their environments. He links learning to both the physical learning environment and the social interactions with the people in that environment (Borko & Putnam, 1998; Putnam & Borko, 2000). Thus the notion of contextualized learning drawn from indigenous societies links not only the physical and social learning environment, but also includes society and the daily lives of the learners.

Holism is experiential (Stein, 2004), focusing on people and their interconnectedness with one another. Stein argues that in experiential learning the learners are engaged in learning about interconnectedness rather than learning about objects. He asserts that the focus is "primarily on elements such as the conscious and unconscious contents of individuals' minds; individuals' relationships with others with whom they have a personal link; individuals' relatedness to others with whom they have a connection but no personal link" (Stein, 2004, p. 22).

Holism is culturally responsive. It not only uses the learner's culture in the learning context, but also invites the learner's community to be an integral part of the project. The learning project is designed to help resolve the problems the community faces (Fasokun et al., 2005). For example, Bélanger (1998) conducted a study of the use of holism in literacy education and found that this approach led to significantly higher success than programs based on more formal methods. In a study by Omolewa, Adeola, Adekanmbi, Avoseh, and Briamoh (1998), holistic principles were used to teach people in the community to read and then train them to go out and teach literacy to others. The community was integrally involved in the selection of aspects of the literacy program so that the community could directly benefit from the graduates of the program. The principle of interconnectedness with one another and with the community was apparent in the design and facilitation of the literacy program, which greatly improved the literacy successes. Other examples of aspects of contemporary uses of holism include Vella's (2002) dialogue education, Dirkx and Prenger's (1997) theme-based approach, and Freire's (1970) critical literacy.

IMPLICATIONS FOR ADULT EDUCATION

There are many implications of educators' ability to move to a learner-centered design and facilitation approach that helps to promote congruency between espoused theories and theories-in-use and adopts a holistic perspective. First, there are valid reasons why an educator might be reluctant to use holistic approaches to learning: (a) It becomes more difficult to use current assessment, evaluation, and grading methods to measure learning from a holistic perspective (Miller, 2006). (b) The focus on the soul/spirit has many religious connotations (Orr, 2005).

Although many view spirituality and religion separately, to do so splits aspects of the whole person. This is especially true when the religious aspects of soul/spirit are deeply rooted in the culture or community (Orr, 2005). However, in the Western world, we take great strides to make this separation, and our institutions are not supportive of the promotion of religion in the classrooms. (c) It is difficult to address the emotional issues that surface when the emotional and physical aspects of learning are included (Horsman, 2001). Horsman (1998) readily admits that many teachers are not prepared to deal with emotional issues, and would rather that these issues were reserved for therapists. Nevertheless, when one teaches the whole person, emotional issues are not only important, but they become an integral part of the learning because they present possibilities for healing of unconscious issues learners bring to the classroom (King & Gates, 2007) and healing the soul (Horsman, 2000).

Second, gaining congruence with one's epistemological beliefs is difficult to achieve. Educators must remember that this is a developmental change rather than simply an adoption of new strategies. This must begin with a needs assessment that examines the instructor's and students' abilities to move to the new design and facilitation approaches. This means that adult educators must become holistic practitioners who can understand how it feels to learn holistically, and then teach to the whole person in their classes (King & Gates, 2007). Once the instructor makes the necessary changes, then he or she can begin to design the course developmentally to provide space so that students can move from their current beliefs system to embrace the changes they introduce in the classroom. The learning strategies are less important than the way the strategies are used. Next, instructors need to better understand and include the students' ability to use the mind, body, and spirit as an integral part of the learning design and facilitation.

REFERENCES

Alfred, M. V. (2005). Overlooked in academe: What do we know about immigrant students in adult and higher education? *New Horizons in Adult and Continuing Education, 19*(1). Retrieved from http://education.fiu.edu/newhorizons/journals/volume19no1Winter2005.pdf

Argyris, C., & Schön, D. (1974). *Theory in practice: Increasing professional effectiveness.* San Francisco: Jossey-Bass.

Barr, R. B., & Tagg, J. (1995). From teaching to learning—a new paradigm for undergraduate education. *Change, 27*(5), 13–25.

Baxter Magolda, M. B. (1999). *Creating contexts for learning and self-authorship:*

Constructive-development pedagogy. Nashville, TN: Vanderbilt University Press.

Bélanger, P. (1998). Foreword. In M. Omolewa, O. A. Adeola, G. Adekanmbi, M. Avoseh, & D. Briamoh (Eds.), *Literacy, tradition, and progress: Enrolment and retention in an African rural literacy programme.* Hamburg, Germany: UNESCO Institute for Education.

Borko, H., & Putnam, R. (1998). Professional development and reform-based teaching: Introduction to theme issue. *Teaching and Teacher Education, 14,* 1–3.

Brown, B. L. (1998). Applying constructivism in vocational and career education. *ERIC Clearinghouse on Adult, Career, and Vocational Education, Information Series No. 378.* Washington, DC: U.S. Department of Education, Office of Educational Research and Improvement.

Bruffee, K. A. (1999). *Collaborative learning: Higher education, interdependence, and the authority of knowledge* (2nd ed.). Baltimore: Johns Hopkins University Press.

Clarebout, G., & Elsen, J. (2001). The ParlEuNet-project: Problems with the validation of socio-constructivist design principles in ecological settings. *Computers in Human Behavior, 17*(5–6), 453–464.

Cohen, R. (2005). Journal writing in mathematics education: Communicating the affective dimensions of mathematics learning. In J. P. Miller, S. Karsten, D. Denton, D. Orr, & I. C. Kates (Eds.), *Educating for wisdom and compassion: Creating conditions for timeless learning* (pp. 145–152). Thousand Oaks, CA: Corwin.

Crowdes, M. S. (2000). Embodying sociological imagination: Pedagogical support for linking bodies and minds. *Teaching Sociology, 28*(1), 24–40.

Cunningham, P. M. (1988). The adult educator and social responsibility. In R. G. Brockett (Ed.), *Ethical issues in adult education.* New York: Teachers College Press.

Dirkx, J. M. (1997). Nurturing soul in adult learning. In P. Cranton (Ed.), *Transformative learning in action: Insights from practice.* San Francisco: Jossey-Bass.

Dirkx, J. M., Kielbaso, G., & Smith, R. O. (2004). Epistemic beliefs of teachers in technology-rich community college technical education programs. *Community College Review, 31*(4), 25–47.

Dirkx, J. M., & Prenger, S. M. (1997). *Planning and implementing instruction for adults: A theme-based approach.* San Francisco: Jossey-Bass.

Erickson, H. L. (2007). Philosophy of holism. *Nursing Clinics of North America, 42*(2), 139–164.

Fasokun, T., Katahoire, A., & Oduaran, A. (2005). *The psychology of adult learning in Africa.* Hamburg, Germany: UNESCO Institute for Education; Cape Town, South Africa: Pearson Education.

Flannnery, J. L. (1994). Teacher as co-conspirator: Knowledge and authority in collaborative learning. In K. Bosworth & S. J. Hamilton (Eds.), *Collaborative learning: Underlying process and effective techniques* (Vol. 59). San Francisco: Jossey-Bass.

Freire, P. (1970). *Pedagogy of the oppressed.* New York: Seabury.

Guy, T. C. (1999). Culture as context for adult education: The need for culturally relevant adult education. In T. C. Guy (Ed.), *Providing culturally relevant adult education: A challenge for the twenty-first century* (pp. 5–18). San Francisco, CA: Jossey-Bass.

Heron, J. (1992). *Feeling and personhood: Psychology in another key.* London: Sage.

Hofer, B. K., & Pintrich, P. R. (1997). The development of epistemological theories: Beliefs about knowledge and knowing and their relation to learning. *Review of Educational Research, 67,* 88–140.

hooks, b. (1994). *Teaching to transgress: Education as the practice of freedom.* New York: Routledge.

Horsman, J. (1998). "But I'm not a therapist": The challenge of creating effective literacy learning for survivors of trauma. In S. Shore (Ed.), *Conference proceedings of the Australian Council for Adult Literacy 21st National Conference: Literacy on the line.* Adelaide: University of South Australia.

Horsman, J. (2000). *Too scared to learn? Women, violence, and education.* Mahwah, NJ: Lawrence Erlbaum.

Horsman, J. (2001). "Why would they listen to me?": Reflections on learner leadership activities. In B. Burnaby & P. Campbell (Eds.), *Participatory approaches in adult education.* Mahwah, NJ: Lawrence Erlbaum.

Jonassen, D. (1997). Instructional design models for well-structured and ill-structured problem solving outcomes. *Educational Technology: Research and Development, 45*(1), 65–95.

Kegan, R. (1982). *The evolving self: Problem and process in human development.* Cambridge, MA: Harvard University Press.

Kegan, R. (1994). *In over our heads: The mental demands of modern life.* Cambridge, MA: Harvard University Press.

King, M. O., & Gates, M. F. (2007). Teaching holistic nursing: The legacy of Nightingale. *Nursing Clinics of North America, 42*(2), 309–334.

Kitchen, D., & McDougall, D. (1999). Collaborative learning on the Internet. *Journal of Educational Technology Systems, 27*(3), 245–258.

Lindemann, E. C. (1921). *The community: An introduction to the study of community leadership and organization.* New York: Associated Press.

Merriam, S. B., & Associates (2007). *Non-Western perspectives on learning and knowing.* Malabar, FL: Kreiger.

Merriam, S. B., Caffarella, R. S., & Baumgartner, L. M. (2007). *Learning in adulthood: A comprehensive guide* (3rd ed.). San Francisco: Jossey-Bass.

Miller, J. P. (2005). Introduction: Holistic learning. In J. P. Miller, S. Karsten, D. Denton, D. Orr, & I. C. Kates (Eds.), *Holistic learning and spirituality in education: Breaking new ground* (pp. 1–8). Thousand Oaks, CA: Corwin.

Miller, J. P. (2006). *Educating for wisdom and compassion: Creating conditions for timeless learning.* Thousand Oaks, CA: Corwin.

Nafukho, F. M. (2006). Ubuntu worldview: A traditional African view of adult learning in the workplace. *Advances in Developing Human Resources, 8*(3), 408–415.

Newcomb, T. (1962). Student peer-group influence. In N. Sanford (Ed.), *The American college: A psychological and social interpretation of the higher learning.* New York: John Wiley.

Omolewa, M., Adeola, O. A., Adekanmbi, G., Avoseh, M., & Briamoh, D. (1998). *Literacy, tradition, and progress: Enrolment and retention in an African rural literacy programme.* Hamburg, Germany: UNESCO Institute for Education.

Orr, D. (2005). Minding the soul in education: Conceptualizing and teaching the whole perso. In J. Miller, S. Karsten, D. Denton, D. Orr, & I. Kates (Eds.), *Holistic learning and spirituality in education: Breaking new ground,* (pp. 87–100). New York: State University of New York Press.

Perry, W. G. (1970). *Forms of intellectual and ethical development in the college years.* Austin, TX: Holt, Rinehart & Winston.

Piaget, J. (1952). *The origins of intelligence in children.* New York: International University Press.

Pratt, D. D., & Associates. (1998). *Five perspectives on teaching in adult and higher education.* Malabar, FL: Kreiger.

Putnam, R. T., & Borko, H. (2000). What do new views of knowledge and thinking have to say about research on teacher learning? *Educational Researcher, 29*(1), 4–15.

Ringer, T. M. (2002). *Group action: The dynamics of groups in therapeutic, educational, and corporate settings.* London: Jessica Kingsley.

Salzberger-Wittenberg, I., Henry, G., & Osborne, E. (1983). *The emotional experience of learning and teaching.* London: Routledge.

Schommer, M. (1994). An emerging conceptualization of epistemological beliefs and their role in learning. In R. Garner & P. A. Alexander (Eds.), *Beliefs about text and instruction with text* (pp. 25–40). Hillsdale, NJ: Lawrence Erlbaum.

Schön, D. A. (1983) *The reflective practitioner: How professionals think in action.* London: Temple Smith.

Smith, K. K., & Berg, D. N. (1987). *Paradoxes of group life: Understanding conflict, paralysis, and movement in group dynamics.* San Francisco: The New Lexington Press.

Smith, R. O. (2005). Working with difference in online collaborative groups. *Adult Education Quarterly, 55*(3), 182–199.

Stein, M. (2004). Theories of experiential learning and the unconscious. In L. J. Gould, L. F. Stapley, & M. Stein (Eds.), *Experiential learning in organizations: Applications of the Tavistock group relations approach* (pp. 19–36). London: Karnac Books.

Stephenson, J. (2001). Ensuring a holistic approach to work-based learning: The capability envelope. In D. Boud & N. Solomon (Eds.), *Work-based learning? A new higher education?* (pp. 86–102). Buckingham, UK: Open University Press.

Tennant, M. (1997). *Psychology and adult learning.* London: Routledge.

Vella, J. (2002). *Learning to listen learning to learn: The power of dialogue in educating adults* (Rev. ed.). San Francisco: Jossey-Bass.

Vygotsky, L. (1978). *Mind and society: The development of higher mental process.* Cambridge, MA: Harvard University Press.

Wheatley, M. J. (1999). *Leadership and the new science* (2nd ed.). San Francisco: Berrett-Koehler.

Yang, B. (2004). Holistic learning theory and implications for human resource development. *Advances for Developing Human Resources, 6*(2), 241–262.

14

PLANNING AND
DELIVERING PROGRAMS

THOMAS J. SORK

I recently visited the Cradle of Humankind in Gauteng, South Africa, an area containing some of the oldest hominid fossils yet discovered. As I wandered through the exhibits and read about human habitation, evolution, and migration, I was struck by how important learning was to early humans as they adapted to a changing environment, explored other lands, cultivated crops, hunted and domesticated animals, developed and passed on spiritual traditions, formed communities, governed themselves, fought battles, and made peace. What seems obvious is that learning was an essential process as humans faced the daily challenges of living. Although today the challenges of living may be somewhat different, the role of adult learning is no less important to human survival and growth in an increasingly complex, interconnected, environmentally degraded, conflict-ridden world.

Although humans have been organizing learning experiences for millennia, it is only within the last 60 years or so that formal study of program planning has produced various models, theories, and frameworks to describe or guide the process (Sork, 2000; Sork & Buskey, 1986; Wilson & Cervero, 1997). The *Handbooks of Adult Education* have contained chapters about program planning for the past 50 years, beginning in 1960 with the chapter by London, but even earlier publications presented highly influential guides to practice that left a lasting legacy (Knowles, 1950; Tyler, 1949). As the study of education changed and new analytical-critical lenses through which to view human behavior and social processes were introduced, our understanding of planning became more sophisticated. During the same period, new forms of program delivery were invented and these sometimes required new ways of planning. One can easily imagine our early ancestors assembled in small groups by a crackling fire exchanging stories or acting out important events as a way of teaching and learning. Today learners might be assembled in a virtual community enabled by digital technologies like blogs, wikis, webcasts and various forms of social software to swap stories, communicate ideas, and learn from one another's insights and experiences. The process of learning may not have changed very much, but the options available to promote learning have expanded dramatically.

In addition to new options for program delivery, there has been growing recognition in adult education generally of the importance of diversity in all its forms, although this concern has not yet been explicitly embedded in planning models and frameworks. Some recent work has begun to highlight the planning implications of various forms of diversity (Gboku & Lekoko, 2007), but the literature on program planning continues to be dominated by White male writers from North America (Sork, 2000; Sork & Newman, 2004).

The purpose of this chapter is to summarize contemporary understandings of program planning, including the range of planning theories, the models and frameworks currently available, their strengths and limitations, and the situations in which each might be most useful to practitioners. All of this exists within a dramatically changing context of program delivery that includes the widespread use of digital technologies; the growth of collaborative, even global partnerships for program planning and delivery; concerns about diversity and inclusion; and increased sensitivity to the role of power and ethics in planning.

CONTEXT OF CONTEMPORARY PROGRAM PLANNING AND DELIVERY

Planning and Delivery Across Borders and Boundaries

The quaint image of a small group of like-minded folks sitting around a table planning an educational activity with clear geographic and temporal boundaries is fading as the dominant paradigm in adult education. Today planners are likely to be part of a diverse group from varied cultural backgrounds, pursuing different educational and economic interests using e-mail, Skype, blogs, and other tools to communicate. Planning across geographic, cultural, and temporal boundaries is a particular challenge, partly because few planning models discuss the implications of these developments. Examples of the kinds of challenges that arise in designing programs across cultures can be found in Larsson and his colleagues (2005) and Boud and his colleagues (2006), who developed an online master's program involving universities in Canada, Sweden, South Africa, and Australia. In addition to the expected complications arising from cultural differences and a general lack of understanding of one another's context, the planners also had to represent the norms and traditions of their home locations and interpret and justify the planning process to their colleagues back home. As the field continues to internationalize, this cross-cultural challenge will be faced by more and more planners.

Diversity and Inclusion

There is growing sensitivity about diversity and inclusion in society in general and education in particular. Expectations are high that when programs are planned, those with a stake in the program will have their views heard. Accessibility is now a major concern, not just physical accessibility, but also intellectual accessibility. Many forms of diversity are now recognized as important considerations, even if it isn't always clear how they can and should be accommodated. Race, gender, language, sexual orientation, ableness, religion, facility with language, and economic circumstances are just a few of the many factors that might affect the design and delivery of programs. And with increased mobility of people globally, embedding considerations of diversity in planning and delivery is essential.

Digital Technologies

There are new generations of adult learners who know little of the predigital world. They listen to iPods, watch videos on YouTube, IM their friends, socialize on Facebook, journal on Blogspot, learn on Moodle, search on Google, consult wikis, get their news via RSS feeds, network on LinkedIn, meet mates on e-Harmony, and buy stuff on e-Bay. They have only known a digital world, and they expect learning experiences that incorporate that world. Although those who work primarily in online learning are trying hard to stay on top of this wave (McGreal & Elliott, 2008), those working in more conventional formats must also adapt to this new reality.

These elements of the changing context of program planning and delivery create new challenges for theorists who must reframe their models so they remain relevant. But before suggesting what further work might be needed, we first must review the origins of this body of work and where things stand in 2010.

EVOLUTION AND GENEALOGY OF PLANNING THEORY

There is a large and rich body of literature on planning in adult and continuing education. A large segment of this literature provides advice about how planning should or could be done. A smaller but significant segment consists of research studies that have attempted to understand how planning actually occurs in the messy day-to-day world of practice. A third segment consists of critiques of conventional wisdom about planning and usually proposes new ways of thinking about the process—what is important to consider, how planning is best understood, what elements of planning deserve greater attention, and so on.

The evolution of planning theory up until 2000 has been analyzed and critiqued by others (Sork, 2000; Wilson & Cervero, 1997), so the primary focus here will be on developments since then. But to provide a more complete characterization of this body of work, I'll begin with several observations drawn from earlier analyses.

First, this body of work has been built largely on a foundation of technical-rationality, and this limits its usefulness for understanding and guiding the complex, indeterminate nature of practice (Schön, 1983; Wilson & Cervero, 1997). Many models assume that good planning involves following a detailed stepwise process that leads to a program design to achieve predetermined outcomes. The desire for control and predictability of the ends and means of education has led to increasingly complex models that bear little relationship to the work actually done by planners. Cervero and Wilson (1994, 2006) highlighted the limitations of regarding planning as a purely technical-rational process and moved the negotiation of power and interests to the foreground. Although it might be reassuring to planners to think there is a "right way" to go about planning that will produce successful programs—and that the "right way" can be found in a book—such a belief is incompatible with current understandings of the complex contexts in which planning occurs, the contested nature of ends and means, and the interplay between power and interests among planning actors. The origin of many contemporary planning models can be traced to the work of Tyler (1949), who proposed that curriculum planning in schools could be organized around "four fundamental questions":

1. What educational purposes should the school seek to attain?

2. What educational experiences can be provided that are likely to attain these purposes?

3. How can these experiences be effectively organized?

4. How can we determine whether these purposes are being attained? (p. 1)

This basic framework has influenced generations of planners and instructional designers.

Second, although there are many "generic" models designed to be useful guides for planning in a diverse range of institutional and community settings, there are also specialized models designed for use only in very specific contexts. For example, there are models for planning workplace training/human resource development programs, health education/health promotion programs, literacy/basic education programs, continuing professional education programs, and agricultural extension programs (Sork & Buskey, 1986). Models designed for specific contexts are based on assumptions about features of the context that might be fairly predictable, and so may seem more relevant to those who work there. But even in a broad category like "workplace training," there can be great variation so it remains risky to accept all of the assumptions embedded in these models. Another danger of uncritically adopting these models is that they tend to reproduce existing social relationships rather than question them. In other words, they don't typically include a critical analysis of the status quo as part of the process and therefore are likely to reproduce it.

Third, there is a continuing lack of cumulative knowledge building across planning contexts. Those who write about planning in a specific context tend to refer only to the work of others concerned with that context. Although this is an understandable response to the large and dispersed literature on planning, the consequence is that new ideas and fresh perspectives developed within one context aren't taken up or challenged in other contexts. This impoverishes theory development and limits the range of approaches offered to practitioners.

CONTEMPORARY THEORIES, MODELS, AND FRAMEWORKS

In the past 10 years there have been some noteworthy developments in planning theory, models, and frameworks. These represent evolutionary rather than revolutionary change in the sense that they provide sharper lenses thorough which to view and interpret the dynamics of planning and new or refined ideas about practice. Some of these are responses to critiques or challenges, while others are elaborations on ideas that were too vague or abstract to be clearly understood or applied.

Conventional Understandings of Planning

"Conventional" is used here to label those ways of thinking about planning that are still largely grounded in the technical rational tradition, but which have been refined or elaborated since the previous edition of the *Handbook* (Sork, 2000). One heartening observation about most of the material published since 2000 is that the authors acknowledge the work of others and either attempt to take it into account or provide a rationale for not doing so.

Boone, Safrit, and Jones (2002) have built upon the earlier work of Boone in cooperative extension, and they provide a thorough review of other planning models before elaborating on and updating Boone's original "conceptual programming model." Also to their credit is a careful articulation of their theoretical approach and assumptions. This model is one of the few that explicitly incorporates "a systems view" as a means of characterizing the complex interests and players in the process.

Green and Kreuter (2004) are well known in the health education sector for their PRECEDE-PROCEED model, which is probably the most-researched educational planning model in the world. Now in its fourth edition, their book explains the eight phases of the model in great detail and provides research evidence to support the process. The phases are social assessment and situational analysis, epidemiological assessment, educational and ecological assessment, administrative and policy assessment and intervention alignment, implementation, process evaluation, impact evaluation, and outcome evaluation. As the context of health has changed, the authors have updated the model—and the terminology used—to keep it current. Because health care professionals live in an "evidence-based" world, the model reflects that reality. The impressive detail in the model is also a weakness in that it is very resource intensive to employ fully and requires a high level of expertise to complete some of the phases.

Goldstein and Ford (2002) provide a good example of a planning model from the workplace training sector. Their book, now in its fourth edition, employs an instructional systems approach with three main phases: assessment, training and

development, and evaluation. For each phase there are detailed guidelines for working through the processes in a typical Tylerian sequence. Not surprisingly, given the context, there is no mention of power and interests in planning although attention is given to developing organizational support. The goals of the organization are a given and training is framed as a means to help the organization achieve its goals.

Day and Petrick (2006) are concerned about planning residential wilderness programs for adults. Their primary goal is to provide practical suggestions to those who plan such programs. While it is likely that any general purpose planning model could be used to design such programs, they rightly point out that "something mysterious, unpredictable, and exciting often results from time spent in settings little touched by the ubiquitous hand of human beings—time spent in wild places" (p. x). So this book focuses on how the unique character of a wilderness learning environment—and the unexpected teachable moments such settings provide—can be used to promote transformative experiences.

A recent and welcome addition to this literature is a book by Gboku and Lekoko (2007) on program planning from an African perspective. The book does not present a new planning model, but instead focuses on the uniqueness of the African context. In the words of the authors:

> Education, learning and training are not recent inventions for the many ethnic groups of Africa but a long-standing and integral part of life. In traditional African societies, education, learning and training had and still have their own specific principles, methods and institutional arrangements. These were different to the type of schooling that was later introduced by missionary societies and the colonial administration. African educationalists and policy makers generally neglected these values of African traditional pedagogy, preferring to borrow theories and models from the modern developed countries of the West. Because these theories and models are not rooted in African culture, they cannot be successfully implemented in the African context. (p. 43)

Rather than propose a uniquely African planning model, they emphasize the importance of the following "ten pillars" of the African perspective, which they suggest must be respected regardless of the planning model used:

1. African knowledge and experience must take centre stage in the programme development process and the process must be steered by Africans.

2. Programme developers must have an appreciation and understanding of African indigenous knowledge and experiences and have capacity to integrate the two into programme development.

3. The goal of programme content must be geared to integrating the individuals into their communities and wider African society.

4. Professionals must have faith in the African continent and her people.

5. Programme development must emphasize the needs, goals and expectations of communities or wider African society.

6. Programme developers must adhere to the principle of indigenous African pedagogy, which stresses learning-by-doing for training the intellect, imparting technical skills and instilling moral values.

7. Programme content must be the outcome of the African society's natural and human environment.

8. Programme developers must use both instructional and non-instructional methods of teaching and learning.

9. There must be stakeholder commitment to ensure African solutions to meeting the needs of adult learners.

10. The programme development process must embrace non-African formal education but this must be domesticated to meet the cultural, social, moral, intellectual, economic and political needs of Africa and Africans. (pp. 45–46)

The organization of the chapters suggests a rather conventional arrangement of planning elements—identifying learning needs; determining goals, objectives, and content; identifying and selecting learning materials; marketing; evaluation—but the pillars suggest these would be carried out with a deep appreciation of African culture and indigenous ways of teaching and learning.

Power, Interests, and Negotiation

Cervero and Wilson (1994, 2006) should be credited with introducing the most recent major conceptual shift in program planning theory by challenging the dominance of technical rationality and foregrounding the negotiation of power and interests as the fundamental social process of planning. Although I have argued that "negotiation" may not capture the full range of social processes encountered in contemporary program planning (Sork, 1996), their insistence that power and interests are central to planning has influenced a great deal of recent work in the field. Even if one does not agree with them about how central negotiation is to planning, their body of work and the work of others who draw on theirs cannot be ignored. In their most recent book (Cervero & Wilson, 2006), they use realistic case studies to work thorough familiar elements of planning—like conducting needs assessments, developing objectives, designing instruction, organizing administrative supports, and formulating an evaluation plan—to illustrate the utility of their theory. Since the original elaboration of this theory in 1994, they and others have conducted dozens of studies foregrounding the dynamics of power and interests as an effective way to understand planning. Examples of the range of settings studied include planning literacy programs in Botswana (Maruatona & Cervero, 2004), adult degree programs in higher education (Watkins & Tisdell, 2006), welfare-to-work programs (Sandlin & Cervero, 2003), workplace learning in corporations (Mabry & Wilson, 2001), and public health education (Umble, Cervero, & Langone, 2001).

Cervero and Wilson (2006) continue to lament the influence that conventional notions of planning grounded in technical rationality have on program planning theory:

> This is the problem: instrumental problem solving as a theory of action becomes dysfunctional in the messy human interactions, framed by power relations and interests, that characterize action in the real world. Technical rationality fails at the practical level because it does not enable people to see, much less provide strategies to negotiate, relationships of power. (p. 249)

But this isn't an argument to reject technical rationality completely as a part of effective practice . . . only as the *exclusive* basis for taking practical action.

A useful supplement to their general theory is the work of Yang (1999) and Yang and Cervero (2001), who identify four common patterns of power and influence styles—bystander, tactician, ingratiator, and shotgun—and seven power and influence tactics—reasoning, consulting, appealing, networking, bargaining, pressuring, and counteracting—found among planners. Being mindful of their preferred style and of alternative styles and tactics that can be employed in different planning situations enhances the ability of planners to successfully pursue the ends and means they value, although it is arguable how easy it might be to shift from one style or tactic to another.

Interactive and Question-Based Approaches

Caffarella's (2002) "interactive model of program planning," now in its third iteration, contains many features of conventional models, but more flexibility than is found in most. This flexibility relates to deciding which of the 12 components will be used when planning a specific program and the sequence in which they will be addressed. According to Caffarella:

> What makes this model interactive is that first it has no real beginnings or endings. Rather, persons responsible for planning programs for adults are encouraged to use the relevant parts of the model in any order and combination based on the planning situation. (p. 21)

The twelve components of her model are discerning the context; building a solid base of support; identifying program ideas; sorting and prioritizing program ideas; developing program objectives; designing instructional plans; devising transfer-of-learning plans; formulating evaluation plans; making recommendations and communicating results; selecting formats, schedules, and staff needs; preparing budgets and marketing plans; and coordinating facilities and on-site events (Caffarella, 2002, p. 21).

One of the features of this model that distinguishes it from others is the attention given to devising transfer-of-learning plans. Most other models are silent on this important aspect of planning or just assume that this will be taken care of when designing instruction. This book is rich in examples, exercises, and worksheets so that even novice planners can see how the ideas apply in practice.

In the 2000 edition of this *Handbook,* I proposed a question-based approach to planning

that emphasized the framing of a series of questions related to six common elements of planning—analyze the context and learner community, justify and focus planning, clarify intentions, prepare instructional plan, prepare administrative plan, develop summative evaluation plan—contained within three domains—the technical, social–political, and ethical (Sork, 2000). This emphasis on first posing questions and then deciding the best ways to answer them from a wide range of alternative processes was an effort to break from the idea that good planning involved completing a predictable sequence of tasks. I acknowledged that there was nothing especially new about a question-based approach to planning, since that is essentially what Tyler proposed in 1949—although Tyler thought he knew what the key questions were and how they could be answered. I was also under no illusions that this approach would be widely adopted because it is much more demanding of planners than conventional models (Sork & Newman, 2004). What has yet to be produced is a detailed elaboration of this framework with illustrations of its application in various contexts. One example of how it can be applied in needs assessment has been published (Sork, 2001), but more examples are needed of its use for other elements of planning that include questions in all three domains.

SELECTING AND USING THEORIES, MODELS, AND FRAMEWORKS

There is debate about what planning models, theories, or frameworks might be most useful in adult education. The literature contains a rich assortment of ideas ranging from practical guides that might be useful in specific contexts to general models that require substantial professional judgment and adaptation. Having taught program planning for more than 30 years to students at all points on the continuum from novice to expert, I've developed what might be regarded as a mildly controversial theory about selecting and using models. As a group (an always dangerous opening phrase), novice planners seem attracted to models that are concrete and specific with clearly articulated tasks and practical guidance on how to carry them out. They understand there are political intrigues and power relations in planning that need to be considered and sensible strategies developed. However, they seem first to want to gain a sense of agency about the basic elements of planning, then are more open to exploring the power dynamics and their less-than-predictable manifestations and consequences.

More experienced students like learning alternative ways of thinking about planning and can readily engage in discussions about power dynamics and how they have influenced their own work. In fact, they are often relieved to learn that studies of planners in action show that they just don't use models in the systematic way the literature often suggests. They appreciate being exposed to the work of Cervero and Wilson, because they know from their experience that power is always evident in planning but they just don't have a way of describing and analyzing it. More experienced students also appreciate the freedom and flexibility of the question-based approach to planning, even when they realize it places a lot of demands on them to read the context and make good decisions about what should be done.

So what I have come to is a more or less developmental theory for selecting program-planning models. Novice planners should begin with general models that provide the level of detail and relationship to context they are seeking. A good example of the kind of model I have in mind is Caffarella's interactive model (Caffarella, 2002). Students find this model easy to understand, flexible, and practical for a wide range of settings. A good alternative would be Boone and his colleagues (2002). For specific contexts like workplace learning or health education, the models described above would be good choices.

For more experienced students, knowledge of the work of Cervero and Wilson (2006) is a must while they explore other models that challenge their initial conceptions of what good planning involves. The question-based approach I have been developing (Sork, 2000; Sork, 2001) complements the work of Cervero and Wilson by recognizing the importance of being politically astute while challenging students to avoid fixed ideas about what steps or tasks need to be carried out. But more work is needed to illustrate the application of this framework and test its utility in various settings.

I don't believe it is wise to hope that there will someday be a model, theory, or framework for planning that is universally applicable. As the circumstances in which we plan change, so must the ideas that guide us. My hope is that the diversity of planning frameworks will increase as more people with different backgrounds and analytical perspectives introduce new ways of thinking about this important process.

EMERGING CONCERNS AND NEEDED RESEARCH

Relational Aspects of Planning

Although there are women who continue to write about program planning (for example, Caffarella, 2002, and Sloane-Seale, 2001), it is important to be suspicious of this male-dominated literature. The absence of explicitly feminist voices is problematic because it means this important dimension of adult education practice has not benefited from a thorough gender critique. I continue to wonder if something fundamental is missing from our theorizing about planning that makes it an inhospitable place for women, and particularly for feminists. One possibility is that the relational aspects of planning are theorized without adequate attention to gender, race, class, sexuality, ableness, or other social locations. The attention given to power and interests by Cervero and Wilson (2006) has gotten close, but even where those who have used their framework to characterize planning in which gender, race, and class seemed to play a central role (see Cervero & Wilson, 1996), there was little analysis of how these affected—or might affect—the negotiation of power and interests. So the body of work on program planning would benefit from a thorough feminist critique. Related to this is the continuing dominance of North American, mostly male authors and the possibility that this literature is limited by unrecognized ethnocentrism. The recent appearance of a volume on planning in the African context (Gboku & Lekoko, 2007) is a hopeful sign that the literature will be enriched by writers who bring different cultural and analytical orientations. I am looking forward, for example, to contributions on program planning and delivery from scholars working from Confucian, Gandhian, Friedanian (as in

Betty Friedan's), and Mandelian (as in Nelson Mandela's) perspectives.

Ethics of Planning and Delivery

There has been much progress in the past 10 years to make ethical considerations in planning and delivery of programs explicit. The work of Boone, Safrit, and Jones (2002), Caffarella (2002), Cervero and Wilson (2006), and Sork (2000), among others, includes explicit reference to ethical issues. Studies of practitioners in the U.S. and Canada (Gordon & Sork, 2001) suggest that they are seeking more guidance in how to respond to the ethical dilemmas they face, so this trend in scholarship seems timely. In addition to these discussions of the ethics of planning, more general works on the ethics of practice continue to challenge us to be sensitive to the moral dimensions of this work and the possible harmful effects of our actions (Brockett & Hiemstra, 2004; Burge, 2007; Hatcher & Storberg-Walker, 2004; Ianinska & Garcia-Zamor, 2006; Lawler, 2000a). Although there is still no widely recognized code of ethics for adult educators, the ones proposed have important implications for program planners because they deal with such matters as competence of instructors, claims made about program benefits, how learners are treated, evaluation and assessment practices, marketing, conflict of interest, privacy, and finance (AHRD, 1999; Lawler, 2000b; Siegel, 2000).

Aesthetics of Planning and Delivery

As authors have incorporated an ever-expanding range of issues and concerns, planning models have become more and more complex. One area that has been sorely neglected by theorists is the aesthetics of planning and of programs. By *aesthetics* I mean beauty and the appreciation of beauty. Although aesthetics is often thought of as the domain of philosophers, artists, and art critics, I believe there is an *aesthetic sensibility* that should be applied to educational design. This is not a new idea. Knowles (1970) talked about "the far out notion of adult education as an art form" (p. 129) and proceeded to discuss the principles of "line," "space," "tone," "color," and "texture" as they relate to the design of programs. But the

aesthetics of planning and of programs seem to have been largely overlooked. In the early, primitive days of the Web, it was easier to judge the comparative aesthetic and substantive qualities of courses than it is today (Boshier, Mohapi, & Boulton, 1997), but just like face-to-face programs, there is an aesthetic to Web-based courses that could be better theorized as a consideration in planning. Although Knowles's visually oriented criteria may speak to some program planners, I would add for consideration the criteria of rhythm, flow, and harmony. As we are attending to the subtle and not-so-subtle interplay of power and interests in planning, I hope we might also tune in to the rhythm, flow, and harmony of the programs that result.

CONCLUDING COMMENTS

The feeling of privilege that comes from participating in this decennial summary of what we know and need to know about the planning and delivery of programs is balanced by the fear that something important has been overlooked. But that is inevitable when one person attempts to characterize in a limited space a large and important body of work.

The learning experiences we create—and the relationships formed there—are at the heart of the adult education enterprise. Like Cervero and Wilson (2006), I am fond of the metaphorical planning table as a way to think about the dynamics of the process. But other metaphors may be more generative. As I finish this chapter, I'm attracted to the metaphor of the theater stage where actors in makeup and costumes represent memorable characters in an interesting story, although I prefer to think of planning stories as much more improvisational than the scripts that guide most theatrical productions. As the story unfolds the characters come and go, the best and worst of human nature is on display, human frailties are revealed, circumstances change, surprises occur, dilemmas arise, decisions are made, and relationships are formed and strained. The theater stage is a site that invites drama, creativity, and artistry, as is the field of adult education. In the coming years, the challenge will be to leave behind ways of thinking about the planning and delivery of programs that limit the possibilities and constrain choice, and embrace those with the potential to engage, amaze, and transform.

REFERENCES

Academy of Human Resource Development (AHRD), Standing Committee on Ethics and Integrity. (1999). *AHRD Standards on Ethics and Integrity*. Retrieved December 8, 2009, from http://www.ahrd.org/mc/page.do?sitePageId=56727&orgId=ahrd

Boone, E. J., Safrit, R. D., & Jones, J. (2002). *Developing programs in adult education: A conceptual programming model*. Prospect Heights, IL: Waveland.

Boshier, R., Mohapi, M., & Boulton, G. (1997). Best and worst dressed Web courses: Strutting into the twenty-first century in comfort and style. *Distance Education, 18*(2), 327–349.

Boud, D., Dahlgren, L.-O., Dahlgren, M. A., Sork, T. J., & Walters, S. (2006). Creating a "world class" programme: Reciprocity and constraint in networked global collaboration. *International Journal of Lifelong Education, 25*(6), 609–622.

Brockett, R. G., & Hiemstra, R. (2004). *Toward ethical practice*. Malabar, FL: Krieger.

Burge, L. (Ed.). (2007). Ethical issues in open and distance education [Special issue]. *Open Learning, 22*(2).

Caffarella, R. S. (2002). *Planning programs for adult learners: A practical guide for educators, trainers, and staff developers* (2nd ed.). San Francisco: Jossey-Bass.

Cervero, R. M., & Wilson, A. L. (1994). *Planning responsibly for adult education: A guide to negotiating power and interests*. San Francisco: Jossey-Bass.

Cervero, R. M., & Wilson, A. L. (Eds.). (1996). *What really matters in adult education program planning: Lessons in negotiating power and interests*. New Directions for Adult and Continuing Education, No. 69. San Francisco: Jossey-Bass.

Cervero, R. M., & Wilson, A. L. (2006). *Working the planning table: Negotiating democratically for adult, continuing, and workplace education*. San Francisco: Jossey-Bass.

Day, M., & Petrick, E. M. (2006). *Designing residential wilderness programs for adults*. Malabar, FL: Krieger.

Gboku, M., & Lekoko, R. N. (2007). *Developing programmes for adult learners in Africa*. Hamburg, Germany: UNESCO Institute for Lifelong Learning.

Goldstein, I. L., & Ford, J. K. (2002). *Training in organizations: Needs assessment, development and evaluation* (4th ed.). Belmont, CA: Wadsworth.

Gordon, W., & Sork, T. J. (2001). Ethical issues and codes of ethics: Views of adult education practitioners in Canada and the United States. *Adult Education Quarterly, 51*, 202–218.

Green, L. W., & Kreuter, M. W. (2004). *Health program planning: An educational and ecological approach* (4th ed.). New York: McGraw-Hill.

Hatcher, T., & Storberg-Walker, J. (2004). Developing ethical adult educators: A re-examination of the need for a code of ethics. *Adult Learning, 14*(2), 21–24.

Ianinska, S., & Garcia-Zamor, J-C. (2006). Morals, ethics, and integrity: How codes of conduct contribute to ethical adult education practice. *Public Organization Review, 6*, 3–20.

Knowles, M. S. (1950). *Informal adult education: A guide for administrators, leaders and teachers*. New York: Association Press.

Knowles, M. S. (1970). *The modern practice of adult education: Pedagogy vs. andragogy*. New York: Association Press.

Larsson, S., Dahlgren, M. A., Walters, S., Boud, D., & Sork, T. J. (2005). Confronting globalization: Learning from intercontinental collaboration. *Innovations in Education and Training International, 42*(1), 61–71.

Lawler, P. A. (2000a). Ethical issues in continuing professional education. In V. W. Mott & B. J. Daley (Eds.), *Charting a course for continuing professional education: Reframing professional practice* (pp. 63–70). New Directions for Adult and Continuing Education, No. 86. San Francisco: Jossey-Bass.

Lawler, P. A. (2000b). The ACHE Code of Ethics: Its role for the profession. *Journal of Continuing Higher Education, 48*(3), 31–34.

London, J. (1960). Program development in adult education. In M. S. Knowles (Ed.), *Handbook of adult education in the United States* (pp. 65–95). Chicago: Adult Education Association of the U.S.A.

Mabry, C. K., & Wilson, A. L. (2001). Managing power: The practical work of negotiating interests. In R. O. Smith, J. M. Dirkx, P. L. Eddy, P. L. Farrell, & M. Polzin (Eds.), *Proceedings of the 42nd Annual Adult Education Research Conference* (pp. 263–268). East Lansing: Michigan State University.

Maruatona, T., & Cervero, R. M. (2004). Adult literacy education in Botswana: Planning between reproduction and resistance. *Studies in the Education of Adults, 36*(2) 235–251.

McGreal, R., & Elliott, M. (2008). Technologies of online learning (e-learning). In T. Anderson (Ed.), *The theory and practice of online learning* (2nd ed.; pp. 143–165). Edmonton, Alberta, Canada: Athabasca University Press.

Sandlin, J., & Cervero, R. M. (2003). Contradictions and compromise: The curriculum-in-use as negotiated ideology in two welfare-to-work classes. *International Journal of Lifelong Education, 22*(3), 249–265.

Schön, D. A. (1983). *The reflective practitioner: How professionals think in action.* New York: Basic Books.

Siegel, I. S. (2000). Toward developing a universal code of ethics for adult educators. Pennsylvania Association for Adult and Continuing Education. *PAACE Journal of Lifelong Learning, 9,* 39–64.

Sloane-Seale, A. (2001). Program planning in adult education. In D. H. Poonwassie & A. Poonwassie (Eds.), *Fundamentals of adult education: Issues and practices for lifelong learning* (pp. 116–132). Toronto: Thompson.

Sork, T. J. (1996). Negotiating power and interests in planning: A critical perspective. In R. M. Cervero & A. L. Wilson (Eds.), *What really matters in adult education program planning practice: Lessons in negotiating power and interests* (pp. 81–90). New Directions for Adult and Continuing Education, No. 69. San Francisco: Jossey-Bass.

Sork, T. J. (2000). Planning educational programs. In A. L. Wilson & E. R. Hayes (Eds.), *Handbook of adult and continuing education* (pp. 171–190). San Francisco: Jossey-Bass.

Sork, T. J. (2001). Needs assessment. In D. H. Poonwassie & A. Poonwassie (Eds.), *Fundamentals of adult education: Issues and practices for lifelong learning* (pp. 100–115). Toronto: Thompson.

Sork, T. J., & Buskey, J. H. (1986). A descriptive and evaluative analysis of program planning literature, 1950–1983. *Adult Education Quarterly, 36,* 86–96.

Sork, T. J., & Newman, M. (2004). Program development in adult education and training. In G. Foley (Ed.), *Dimensions of adult learning: Adult education and training in a global era* (pp. 96–117). Crows Nest, NSW: Allen & Unwin.

Tyler, R. W. (1949). *Basic principles of curriculum and instruction.* Chicago: The University of Chicago Press.

Umble, K. E., Cervero, R. M., & Langone, C. A. (2001). Negotiating about power, frames, and continuing education: A case study in public health. *Adult Education Quarterly, 51*(2), 128–145.

Watkins, B. J., & Tisdell, E. J. (2006). Negotiating the labyrinth from margin to center: Adult degree program administrators as program planners within higher education institutions. *Adult Education Quarterly, 52*(2), 134–159.

Wilson, A. L., & Cervero, R. M. (1997). The song remains the same: The selective tradition of technical rationality in adult education program planning theory. *International Journal of Lifelong Education, 16*(2), 84–108.

Yang, B. (1999). How effectively do you use power and interests? In M. Silberman (Ed.), *The 1999 training and performance sourcebook* (pp. 143–155). New York: McGraw-Hill.

Yang, B., & Cervero, R. (2001). Power and influence styles in programme planning: Relationship with organizational and political contexts. *International Journal of Lifelong Education, 20*(4), 289–296.

15

ASSESSMENT AND EVALUATION

MICHAEL W. GALBRAITH AND MELANIE S. JONES

Educators, administrators, policy makers, funders, and stakeholders in adult and continuing education are continually engaged in some aspect of assessment and evaluation. The terms *assessment* and *evaluation* are used interchangeably, with diverse functions and meanings. This is particularly true in the production of the last half century of *Handbooks of Adult and Continuing Education*. Authors of the *Handbooks'* chapters examined the evaluation process in the context of program development and planning and did not specifically address the concept of assessment, with the exception of Boyle and Jahns (1970), who were actually discussing evaluation (Grotelueschen, 1982; London, 1960; Steele, 1989). The previous *Handbook of Adult and Continuing Education* (Wilson & Hayes, 2000) did not mention assessment or evaluation at all, although Sork (2000) wrote a chapter on program planning. Evaluation has been discussed in the adult and continuing education literature with assessment being incorporated, although the two concepts have often been combined into a singular practice or idea.

In this chapter, assessment and evaluation are examined individually as discrete concepts. Their functions and practices are explored, as are related matters that confront adult and continuing educators. Finally, contemporary issues of assessment and evaluation are presented, along with some concluding thoughts.

ASSESSMENT VERSUS EVALUATION

Various authors within adult and continuing education have used the terms *assessment* and *evaluation* interchangeably (Moran, 2001; Queeney, 1995; Rose & Leahy, 1997); however, it is essential to understand that assessment and evaluation are independent concepts and have to be applied as such in order to achieve their intended purpose. Within the classroom, assessment refers specifically to the collection of information to measure learning gains, which indicate learners' individual levels of achievement (Angelo & Cross, 1993; Moran, 2001). From a programmatic perspective, assessment refers to the more comprehensive measurement of achievement of the program itself (Queeney, 1995). Assessment refers to the collection of information, and it measures levels of achievement without comparisons to a set of standards. Evaluation, however, indicates application of the assessment findings to the continued development of student learning or program achievement.

There have been numerous ways of defining evaluation. One of the most used definitions suggests that it means determining whether objectives have been achieved. Stufflebeam and Shinkfield (2007) note that a major problem is that "this definition steers evaluation in the direction of only looking at outcomes" (p. 8). Evaluations should also examine a program's goals, structure, and process. This involves application of a variety of different evaluation methodologies (Knox, 2002). Evaluation implies a certain judgment that can be made, in part, based on assessment information. For learners, this may be a comparison of their assessment results with those of other learners or with a set of standards. Evaluation can be applied to adult education programs by utilizing certain assessment results as benchmarks of comparison with similar programs, defined standards, or historical assessments. Evaluations involve making value judgments, and thus are not value free.

The Joint Committee on Standards for Educational Evaluation has broadly defined evaluation (1981, 1988, 1994, 2003). They call for "evaluations to be systematic and focused on determining an object's value" (Stufflebeam & Shinkfield, 2007, p. 8). The Joint Committee's definition suggests that "evaluation is the systematic assessment of the worth or merit of an object" (p. 3). Stufflebeam and Shinkfield extend this definition of evaluation to say that "evaluation is the systematic assessment of an object's merit, worth, probity, feasibility, safety, significance, and/or equity" (p. 13). For purposes of this chapter, the extended definition will be utilized.

FUNCTIONS OF ASSESSMENT

Assessment, of learning achievement of adult and continuing education students and of achievement of the corresponding programs, serves many functions. Not all the functions are incorporated at any one time, however, as the functions are phaselike and typically occur in a chronological sequence. Hawkins's (1979) work detailed the function of assessment as serving selection and development of strategies in many different settings, including education. This perspective will be the focus here as the functions of assessment are examined within the adult and continuing education context.

The first, and one of the most widely used functions of assessment, is screening (Askov, Van Horn, & Carman, 1997; Moran, 2001). Many times, potential learners are administered an

assessment to help determine the level at which they will begin their studies. Instructors and administrators make decisions as to whether the student is a good fit for a particular course or program. If determination is made in the initial screening that the learner does not fit within the course or program, then the assessor must determine where to refer the learner for services that will be a better fit. Often, this may be a different course, a different field of study, or a different path that involves more preparatory work.

The most widely used function of assessment is to quantify the level of skill or knowledge of a student (Angelo & Cross, 1993). While screening assessments serve to provide an initial impression of where a student is located on the knowledge base continuum, assessments are often used to continually measure student levels of skill or knowledge. Within this phase, there are two major processes required, according to Hawkins (1979). The first is that of formation of a hypothesis, and the second is the actual measurement, as related to the hypothesis. Instructors in adult and continuing education would first hypothesize exactly what they believed students should have learned, up to a certain point in time. Then they would develop and administer an instrument, such as a written test, that would measure the students' level of skill or knowledge up to that desired point in time.

An additional function of assessment is to establish baselines for evaluating and designing learning interventions, teaching methodology, and/or program standards and policies (Bloxham & Boyd, 2007). Much adult and continuing education is by nature developmental education. Instructors want to establish a baseline for students or for groups of students in order to focus method and standards based on the starting level of the students. Baseline assessment eliminates many cookie-cutter approaches to education, and allows instructors to tailor their practice to the needs and educational level of current learners. Program administrators can use baseline student assessments to build standards and policies regarding program requirements, course structure, and instructional methodology that are most conducive to the overall goals and mission of the program (Stufflebeam & Shinkfield, 2007).

Another important function of assessment is to identify skill or problem areas in which students need greater levels of assistance (Moran, 2001). Rather than assess students exclusively to determine levels of achievement, it is important for instructors to use assessments in order to identify widespread skill or problem areas that need to be addressed or re-addressed within the classroom. This more detailed method of assessment analysis may help instructors to discover areas where they could improve practice, offer alternative assignments, or modify teaching strategy. From a program perspective, detailed comparison of various assessments can be utilized to recognize instructional issues, to make comparisons among various instructors, and to ascertain whether specific problem areas exist within classrooms or within the program itself.

A widely used function of assessment is that of monitoring progress (Hart, 1994). Instructors may want to monitor progress continually throughout a course, which allows early indication of learning problems experienced by individual students or by the group as a whole. This function also serves as an indicator for the instructor that student knowledge is developing at desired levels. Program administrators can examine student assessments in order to monitor teacher effectiveness, note progress toward overall goals, and assist in efforts toward modification of program standards (Bloxham & Boyd, 2007).

Finally, assessment is utilized for follow-up, or longitudinal tracking. Within the classroom, instructors may administer a pretest to first determine the students' starting point. It is just as important to administer a postassessment, in order to measure the level of learning over the timeframe of the entire course (Angelo & Cross, 1993). This type of assessment is very valid for program administrators as well. They want to know that courses are maximally effective, are preferred by the learner, and incorporate the right quantity of material to be covered. These issues can be addressed through application of assessments over the long term. It is possible that courses include too much information, include too little information, or are not a good fit within the overall scope of student learning needs.

The aforementioned functions of assessment focus primarily on learning and instruction, but there is another function of assessment that focuses on the performance of the institution. Here, certification or some form of acknowledgment is made that lets the public know that governing standards or standards of accepted practice have been achieved.

Practice of Assessment

Hodnett (2001) notes that "assessment is most effective when it reflects an understanding of learning as multidimensional, integrated, and revealed in performance over time." Assessment of learners' needs should be indicative of the appropriate levels of learning, as well as serve as an impact factor in their life. Helping learners to make personal meaning of learned material will help ensure their lifelong progressive learning.

Within programs, assessment "works best when the programs it seeks to improve have clear, explicitly stated purposes. To properly assess a program, the goals of educational performance and educational purposes and expectations have to be considered" (Hodnett, 2001). The goals are established based on the institution's goals and mission, as well as those goals that are the function of the individual program. In addition, assessment fosters the potential for more widespread improvement when various representatives or stakeholders are involved. Knowledge needs to have relevance to the real world; representatives from the real world can help to ensure programmatic relevance; programmatic relevance can be ensured through ongoing assessment. Finally, learning experiences should be pertinent to all students and fit within this more comprehensive picture of adult and continuing education practice (Rose & Leahy, 1997).

The functions of assessment can be realized through the incorporation of one or more methods of assessment (Wiersma & Jurs, 2005). The purpose here is to highlight various assessment methodologies, allowing practitioners to select the method(s) that would be most appropriate for realizing their specific assessment need, whether in adult basic education (ABE), adult higher education, workplace learning, continuing professional education (CPE), or community-based activities. Below is a complete list of assessment methods generated by Wiersma and Jurs (2005).

- *Criterion-referenced assessment.* With this method, learners' work is compared against certain criteria that are devised within intended learning outcomes.

- *Norm-referenced assessment.* In this method, learners' work is compared against that of other learners. Grades are typically assigned on a normal statistical curve.

- *Qualitative assessment.* This subjective method allows teachers to determine what criteria best suit each learner's individual performance. Learning is expected to build upon prior knowledge.

- *Quantitative assessment.* This method involves comparisons between learners by use of a scale, most frequently a percentage scale that places all learners somewhere on the same continuum.

- *Performance assessment.* This hands-on approach allows learners to apply knowledge by real-life functional methods rather than talking or writing.

- *Formative assessment.* With this method, feedback is provided about how learning is proceeding, giving learners with informal information and guidance for improvement.

- *Summative assessment.* In this type of assessment, learners are graded at the end of a unit, or accredited at the end of a program.

- *Analytic assessment.* In this method, independent aspects of a task, rather than the task as a whole, are weighted in order to derive the final grade.

- *Holistic assessment.* With this approach, the whole learner performance is addressed, rather than certain aspects. Teachers consider attendance, participation, and performance on assessments in order to derive a final grade.

Assessment, without an understood purpose, is a wasted effort. As a solitary event, assessment cannot lead to improvement or change. It must be part of a larger plan that is purposefully designed to promote change. Through assessment, educators meet responsibilities to learners, to stakeholders, and to the public.

FUNCTIONS OF EVALUATION

The functions of evaluation are grounded in the 30 standards adopted by the Joint Committee on Standards for Educational Evaluation (1994), the American Evaluation Association, and the U.S. Government Accountability Office. Stufflebeam and Shinkfield (2007) suggest that "the thirty standards are grouped according to four essential attributes of a sound evaluation:

utility, feasibility, propriety, and accuracy" (p. 87). Utility suggests that evaluation should be useful and should be targeted to those persons and groups that are engaged in the implementation of the program. Feasibility refers to the appropriateness of the selected evaluation method to the program itself. Propriety denotes the need for clear written agreements between all vested parties in order to provide for a successful evaluation where the rights and dignity of all parties are protected. Accuracy refers to the need to properly describe the program, develop the evaluative method, and report the findings in a valid and reliable manner. Stufflebeam and Shinkfield (2007) state that,

> Standards help ensure that evaluators and their clients communicate effectively and reach a clear, mutual understanding concerning the criteria to be met by an evaluation. Such standards are needed to obviate the possibility that either stakeholders or evaluators might unscrupulously bend evaluation outcomes to suit themselves. Without standards that define acceptable evaluative service, the credibility of evaluation procedures, outcomes, or reporting is left in doubt. (p. 81)

Practice of Evaluation

Knox (2002) suggests that evaluation is underused in adult and continuing education practices. He provides, however, numerous reasons for conducting evaluation:

- It may be a response to stakeholders whose interests are likely to be underrepresented in decision making.

- It may be required by the parent organization as a condition of continued support.

- Planning by the provider agency may encompass evaluation findings which might help set priorities.

- Program improvement is aided when stakeholders who are expected to make changes also engage in the evaluation and hopefully gain commitment to the recommendations.

- Accountability prompts the evaluation to document extent of worth and benefits.

- The evaluations may contribute to a rationale for ongoing cooperation by stakeholders.

• It may inform explanations of program functioning; evaluation can contribute to feedback and reflection to help strengthen any aspect of the program. (pp. 6–7)

While there are various reasons for conducting evaluations, there are as many types of evaluations that can be used to reach a particular purpose (Knox, 2002; Lincoln & Guba, 2004; Patton, 1997; Scriven, 2004; Stake, 1967; Stufflebeam & Shinkfield, 2007):

• *Process evaluation.* In this method, the procedures and tasks involved in implementing and carrying out an adult education program are examined. This method can also be used to investigate administrative and organizational aspects of the program. Process evaluation is ongoing, allowing for continual monitoring of the program to ensure counsel and recommendation during the course of the program.

• *Outcome evaluation.* This method can be used to attain descriptive data on a project or program and to document short-term results. An investigation is carried out to determine whether the program caused demonstrable effects on certain predefined target outcomes. One may focus on results of certain tasks, allowing for detailed description of the output of that task (e.g., the number of inquiries received as a result of a public service announcement regarding literacy). In addition, this evaluation approach can also focus on short-term results or immediate effects of the project or program on the target audience (e.g., the percentage of adult students who passed the GED test).

• *Impact evaluation.* This is the most comprehensive form of evaluation (Knox, 2002). This method is so desirable because the focus is placed on the long-range results, changes, and improvements of the adult education program. The downside to this method is that it tends to be expensive and requires an extended timeframe to complete. It is also difficult to directly relate results to any specific activity or program because of other influences that may occur over time.

• *Formative evaluation.* This method is designed to assess the strengths and weaknesses of the program before its implementation. Formative evaluation enables educators to tailor the program to the needs of the target group or program. This allows necessary revisions to be made before implementation. The basic purpose of this proactive method is to maximize effectiveness and increase program success.

• *Summative evaluation.* This type of evaluation uses a combination of measurements and judgments in order to come to conclusions about the impact, outcome, or benefits of a program or method. A summative evaluation occurs following the completion of a program or end of an instructional cycle. It draws together and supplements previous information and provides an overall judgment of the program, project, organization, or person's value.

Evaluation needs to be viewed as a very comprehensive system composed of four major components: *inputs, processes, outputs,* and *outcomes* (Russ-Eft & Preskill, 2001). In evaluation practice, all data are viewed as being inclusive in one of these four major components. Inputs are those factors that help initiate the adult learning program, and include such things as money, students, teachers, curriculum materials, and other capital. Processes refer to the actual administration or implementation efforts of the program, and look at teaching, administrative activities, and all other activities within the program. Outputs are those visible or measurable characteristics of the program, including the number of students served, program completion data, and student achievement data, among others. Outcomes tend to be more intermediate or long term in scope, encompassing such things as job attainment, employment retention, continued education, stakeholder satisfaction, program fidelity, accreditation, and public support.

Within the evaluation process, it is necessary to collect a multitude of data in order to help reach the overall goal or mission of the evaluation. Initially, a determination must be made about what questions to be answered, or what problems need to be solved. These questions most often will result from stakeholder input. Stakeholders may include administrators, educators, funders, learners, instructors, compliance authorities, governing or board officials, and the general public. Once questions are clarified, the data contained within the four major components (inputs, processes, outputs, outcomes) and the specific data and information collected will provide the inclusive elements for the evaluation. In essence, the question(s) of interest determines what data are needed. The type of data used, along with consideration of the question(s), determines what evaluation method is utilized.

Knox (2002) noted that "evaluation uses many research procedures for data collection and analysis, but in evaluation the emphasis is on encouraging stakeholder use of conclusions in a specific context in contrast to research emphasis on generalizability of findings" (p. 8). After the evaluation is completed, the subsequent feedback can allow one to make a judgment concerning merit, worth, needs, and needs assessment in a very systematic manner. Findings from the evaluation need to be the basis on which change is incorporated within adult and continuing education programs. Approaching change from this data-driven perspective helps to eliminate subjective decision making, and provides the focus on the actual identified needs or issues within the program.

CONTEMPORARY ISSUES IN ASSESSMENT AND EVALUATION

There are numerous contemporary issues confronting assessment and evaluation processes and practices. Some of the primary ones are grounded in process, while others are focused in a more sociopolitical and sociocultural dimension.

One of the fundamental issues is the fact that assessment and evaluation are sparsely evident in the adult and continuing education literature. With the exception of Knox (2002) and Jones (2007), very few authors and professional conference presenters talk about assessment and evaluation as pertaining specifically to adult and continuing education. Since this is the case, it is evident that the processes of assessment and evaluation are not accepted as primary elements within these programs. Therefore, the question is raised as to whether or not practitioners are appropriately engaged in assessment and evaluation activities within their programs. In addition, there are other issues that are directly related to this fundamental deficiency of assessment and evaluation.

One such issue is the belief that assessment and evaluation are interchangeable processes. As noted, these activities are independent, yet share certain commonalities and serve explicitly different purposes. The consequences of not properly using assessment and evaluation causes questions to be raised concerning the validity of data collected, and of the implementation of certain practices.

A second, related issue is that the lack of assessment and evaluation within adult and continuing education causes unnecessary or undesired duplication of programs, services, and activities. If services are duplicated, it will result in consequences for the stakeholders, which can include the public. Some of these consequences include lack of appropriate funding, lack of uniformity among related programs, and limited outreach to pockets of the populations that may benefit from the service or program.

Duplication of programs, services, and activities then lends itself to the issue of collaboration. Effective collaboration among programs can include joint efforts in assessment and evaluation, in order to address the issue of accountability. As a result, the strengths and weaknesses of each program are discovered, which leads to an opportunity to correct all of the programs' limitations. When programs can operate collaboratively, and successfully, then many entities benefit. Participants benefit by knowing that they are engaged in a program with proven success. Stakeholders benefit by receiving information that is accurate in determining the value, merit, and worth of the program. Program managers and directors benefit by having a larger support network. And finally, financial benefits may result as collaboration is enhanced. Each of these items then contributes to increased sustainability of program operations.

It is also essential to respect various aspects of student, cultural, program, and institutional diversity in planning implementation of assessment and evaluation activities (Moran, 2001; Stufflebeam & Shinkfield, 2007). When considering the broad concept of diversity, it is necessary to be mindful of the differences in culture, race, gender, sexual orientation, religion, age, socioeconomic status, learning style, thinking style, disability, health status, social interaction style, language, and other personal characteristics. Too often, adult and continuing education classroom environments and the teachers in them reflect the values of the dominant social culture, leaving some students unable to fully participate and feeling marginalized. Because successful assessments and evaluations need to be individualized, it is imperative to take all of the contextual issues into account when developing assessments and planning evaluations.

Here we will primarily focus on the contextual issues of social justice, democratic practice, inclusion of underrepresented groups, and cultural responsiveness (Madison, 1992). There is an idea, seen as controversial by some, that assessment and evaluation should move from being community and individual based to something that better distributes both the benefits and burdens throughout society as a whole (Sirotnik, 1990). This idea advances the position that assessment and evaluation should promote a greater social justice, one that considers the interests of underrepresented groups and/or those who are marginalized or disenfranchised. Ericson (1990) noted that social justice is "the central moral standard that practitioners of evaluation should readily apply to social programs, practices, and institutions" (p. 6).

Engaging in a democratic process of assessment and evaluation permits us to consider these practices as they are connected with issues of control and influence that suggest a larger social, political, and moral configuration. The advantage of approaching assessment and evaluation in this manner is that it allows those who are ethically/racially diverse, and/or those with less power and less money, to have more influence and greater potential for self-advocacy. In situations where self-advocacy is not possible or probable, it becomes the responsibility of those engaged in assessment and evaluation to become representatives of those groups.

Closely related to social justice are the ideas of cultural responsiveness and inclusion of underrepresented groups. Those engaged in assessment and evaluation must understand the sociopolitical and sociocultural contexts of the particular adult and continuing education programs if they are to assess and evaluate effectively. It is impossible to accurately determine how well a program is working without including input from those who are most affected by the program in the evaluation. It is this input that can allow for underrepresented groups to feel more empowered about processes that they have not been directly involved with in the past.

Assessment and evaluation are bound by culture. Language is one primary element of culture that can have a marked influence on assessment and evaluation processes. This influence may be especially negative for those whose ethnicity is not that of the historically dominant culture. Thus the inclusion of various groups in the assessment and evaluation process, something Thomas (2004) calls co-construction, is an important consideration. This idea "involves a redistribution of power, assuming a kind of equality among different stakeholders" (p. 9), and that redistribution "seeks to democratize the evaluation process by lessening the implicit, and sometimes explicit power dynamics between evaluators and project stakeholders" (p. 9).

All the issues discussed above help explain the discrepancy between the ideals of assessors and evaluators and the recognition of their responsibility to social justice, the democratic process, inclusion of underrepresented groups, and cultural responsiveness. In addition to the humanistic factors associated with assessment and evaluation, there are those concepts related to process and practice that must also be a focus. Sparse literature, a belief in the interchangeability of assessment and evaluation, unnecessary duplication of programs, and lack of collaboration all contribute to the current and future status of assessment and evaluation. Until change occurs, people and programs will continue to be subjects that are assessed and evaluated, rather than people who are vested stakeholders and programs that serve to unify and grow the adult and continuing education community.

Conclusions

Assessment and evaluation are independent processes and practices. However, they seem to be rather implicit and underused in the adult and continuing education field. If this trend continues, program decisions will continue "to reflect the interests of the stakeholders with power and resources" (Knox, 2002, p. 6). Assessments and evaluations should be used for planning, improvement, and accountability, and not for the sole purpose of justifying a selected program's existence. Understanding and implementing useful assessment and evaluation approaches can strengthen a variety of adult education programs that wish to make better informed decisions and conclusions.

It is imperative to understand that assessment and evaluation in adult and continuing education programs are not linear processes. The specific method of assessment or evaluation required depends upon context, environment, and where the assessor or evaluator comes into the process.

Often, it is the consideration of time and place that also helps to dictate which assessment or evaluation method(s) should be utilized.

While not the same, assessment and evaluation are highly interrelated. Adult and continuing education programs hoping for sustainability and success require a very deliberate effort to consistently incorporate assessment and evaluation. While assessment previously may have been considered somewhat mundane, its true purpose is now more widely understood, as is the complexity involved within the assessment process. Similarly, evaluation has evolved from a practice that was intermittent and nonformalized into a profession that is guided by widely accepted standards, a national association, and uniform guiding principals for evaluators.

As we look toward the future of assessment and evaluation in adult and continuing education, there are several considerations that need to be addressed. Mark (2007) discusses many notable matters, some of which apply explicitly to adult and continuing education. First, there is the responsibility to increase the evidence and knowledge base about evaluation. As is clear from the literature, there has been little empirical research or formative evaluation work focused on adult and continuing education that has been professionally disseminated.

There is also a need to update the perception about the use and influence of evaluation. Many ideas and opinions exist in adult and continuing education programs pertaining to the role of assessment and evaluation. We need to move beyond stereotypical attitudes, and move toward a more comprehensive understanding and use of assessment and evaluation in order to help secure the futures of many programs and initiatives.

We must also consider the globalization aspect and growth of evaluation (Mark, 2007). There are many different types of programs throughout the world that fall under the scope of adult and continuing education. They could be a source for discovering better systems that could lead to a better understanding of assessment and evaluation on an international scale.

When these important aspects of our future growth are accomplished, practitioners, theorists, methodologists, researchers, and evaluators will benefit from the enhanced knowledge base of assessment and evaluation. Utilization of this knowledge will help those in adult and continuing education plan strategically in order to fulfill their distinct missions and goals.

REFERENCES

Angelo, T. A., & Cross, K. P. (1993). *Classroom assessment techniques* (2nd ed.). San Francisco: Jossey-Bass.

Askov, E. N., Van Horn, B. L., & Carman, P. S. (1997). Assessment in adult basic education programs. In A. D. Rose & M. Leahy (Eds.), *Assessing adult learning in diverse settings: Current issues and approaches* (pp. 65–74). New Directions for Adult and Continuing Education, No. 75. San Francisco: Jossey-Bass.

Bloxham, S., & Boyd, P. (2007). *Developing effective assessment in higher education: A practical guide.* Berkshire, UK: Open University Press.

Boyle, P. G., & Jahns, I. R. (1970). Program development and evaluation. In R. Smith, G. Aker, & J. Kidd (Eds.), *Handbook of adult education* (pp. 59–74). New York: Macmillian.

Ericson, D. P. (1990). Social justice, evaluation, and the educational system. In K. A. Sirotnik (Ed.), *Evaluation and social justice: Issues in public education* (pp. 5–21). New Directions for Evaluation, No. 45. San Francisco: Jossey-Bass.

Grotelueschen, A. D. (1982). Program evaluation. In A. B. Knox & Associates (Eds.), *Developing,* *administering, and evaluating adult education* (pp. 75–123). San Francisco: Jossey-Bass.

Hart, D. (1994). *Authentic assessment.* New York: Addison-Wesley.

Hawkins, R. P. (1979). The functions of assessment: Implications for selection and development of devices for assessing repertoires in clinical, educational, and other settings. *Journal of Applied Behavior Analysis, 12*(4), 501–516.

Hodnett, F. (2001). *Evaluation versus assessment.* Retrieved January 24, 2008, from http://pt3.nmsu.edu/educ621/frank2001–3.html

Joint Committee on Standards for Educational Evaluation. (1981). *Standards for evaluations of educational programs, projects, and materials.* New York: McGraw-Hill.

Joint Committee on Standards for Educational Evaluation. (1988). *The personnel evaluation standards.* Thousand Oaks, CA: Corwin.

Joint Committee on Standards for Educational Evaluation. (1994). *The program evaluation standards.* Thousand Oaks, CA: Corwin.

Joint Committee on Standards for Educational Evaluation. (2003). *The student evaluation standards.* Thousand Oaks, CA: Corwin.

Jones, M. S. (2007, October). *Theory-driven evaluation in adult education program administration.* Paper presented at the 56th Annual American Association for Adult and Continuing Education (AAACE) National Conference, Norfolk, VA.

Knox, A. B. (2002). *Evaluation for continuing education.* San Francisco: Jossey-Bass.

Lincoln, Y. S., & Guba, E. G. (2004). The roots of fourth generation evaluation. In M. C. Atkins (Ed.), *Evaluation roots* (pp. 225–242). Thousand Oaks, CA: Sage.

London, J. (1960). Program development in adult education. In M. S. Knowles (Ed.), *Handbook of adult education in the United States* (pp. 65–81). Chicago: Adult Education Association of the U.S.A.

Madison, A. M. (Ed.). (1992). *Minority issues in program evaluation.* New Directions for Program Evaluation, No. 53. San Francisco: Jossey-Bass.

Mark, M. M. (2007). AEA and evaluation: 2006 (and beyond). In S. Mathison (Ed.), *Enduring issues in evaluation: The 20th anniversary of the collaboration between NDE and ADA* (pp. 115–119). New Directions for Evaluation, No. 114. San Francisco: Jossey-Bass.

Moran, J. J. (2001). *Assessing adult learning: A guide for practitioners* (Rev. ed.). Malabar, FL: Krieger.

Patton, M. (1997). *Utilization-focused evaluation.* Thousand Oaks, CA: Sage.

Queeney, D. S. (1995). *Assessing needs in continuing education.* San Francisco: Jossey-Bass.

Rose, A. D., & Leahy, M. A. (Eds.). (1997). *Assessing adult learning in diverse settings: Current issues and approaches.* New Directions for Adult and Continuing Education, No. 75. San Francisco: Jossey-Bass.

Russ-Eft, D. F., & Preskill, H. (2001). *Evaluation in organizations: A systematic approach to enhancing learning.* Cambridge, MA: Perseus.

Scriven, M. (2004). Reflections. In M. C. Alkin (Ed.), *Evaluation roots* (pp. 183–195). Thousand Oaks, CA: Sage.

Sirotnik, E. A. (Ed.). (1990). *Evaluation and social justice: Issues in public education.* New Directions for Program Evaluation, No. 45. San Francisco: Jossey-Bass.

Sork, T. J. (2000). Planning educational programs. In E. R. Hayes & A. Wilson (Eds.), *Handbook of adult and continuing education* (pp. 171–190). San Francisco: Jossey-Bass.

Stake, R. E. (1967). The countenance of educational evaluation. *Teachers College Record, 68,* 523–540.

Steele, S. M. (1989). The evaluation of adult and continuing education. In S. B. Merriam & P. M. Cunningham (Eds.), *Handbook of adult and continuing education* (pp. 260–272). San Francisco: Jossey-Bass.

Stufflebeam, D. L., & Shinkfield, A. J. (2007). *Evaluation theory, models, & application.* San Francisco: Jossey-Bass.

Thomas, V. G. (2004). Building a contextually responsive evaluation framework: Lessons from working in urban school interventions. In V. G. Thomas & F. I. Stevens (Eds.), *Co-constructing a contextually responsive evaluation framework* (pp. 3–23). New Directions for Program Evaluation, No. 101. San Francisco: Jossey-Bass.

Wiersma, W., & Jurs, S. (2005). *Research methods in education* (8th ed.). Needham Heights, MA: Allyn & Bacon.

Wilson, A. L., & Hayes, E. R. (Eds.). (2000). *Handbook of adult and continuing education.* San Francisco: Jossey-Bass.

16

MANAGEMENT AND LEADERSHIP

CATHERINE H. MONAGHAN

Prior to my academic career, I spent 20 years working in the corporate sector. For 15 years, I was a manager and leader at various levels. I began as an assistant manager of accounting, later becoming the first female vice president of a midsize bank. Although over time many of my ideas about management and leadership have remained the same, today I am more informed and able to articulate why they are important. In addition, some of my ideas about management have changed as I moved toward a more critical viewpoint. As a result, one of my primary research interests is centered in the area of management and leadership from a critical viewpoint (Monaghan, 2004; Monaghan & Cervero, 2006), reflecting my keen interest as an observer of management and leadership.

The purpose of this chapter is to expand the current standpoints of management and leadership in adult and continuing education (ACE). I begin with a discussion of management and leadership, providing definitions and a synopsis of the current thinking about this topic. I present issues, trends, and viewpoints from more critical adult education perspectives to help leaders and managers reflect and evaluate current organizational models. These critical perspectives include three frameworks to broaden and deepen our understanding of management and leadership.

CURRENT STATE OF MANAGEMENT AND LEADERSHIP

What is management? What is leadership? Are they the same? How do they differ? These questions gain in importance as more individuals within organizations take on managerial roles, irrespective of their job titles. Managers are expected to be leaders within their sphere of influence. Some people argue that managers plan, organize, and control in the short term, while leaders are involved in a longer view of the organizational future (Dansey-Smith, 2004). Managers need to lead and leaders need to manage (Sternberg, 2003); however, some leaders may not perform the formal duties of managers, and some managers may not be perceived as leaders (Sadler-Smith, 2006). In summary, management is concerned with achieving objectives. Leadership involves developing objectives while creating relationships among stakeholders to turn visions into reality.

Context

There are a number of settings where ACE managers and leaders hold positions: adult basic education (ABE), higher education; professional continuing education, training, and development;

community health education, to name a few. How does context shape the settings and the role of these leaders and managers? Context includes the historical, cultural, and political aspects of an organization. Theoretically, ACE management and leadership should be different in different contexts. This is because those in ACE need to consider both the learner and the larger community as important stakeholders (Cervero & Wilson, 2006). However, Courtenay (1990), reviewing the literature through 1989, found that only 25% of the books and less than 50% of the articles used by those writing about the ACE context were adult education sources. He also noted, "The body of data that would confirm, for example, that leadership in ABE is in some ways different from leadership in a manufacturing plant is either not available or not published" (p. 72). This is still true today.

Those in management and leadership positions in ACE are foremost adult educators. Because of this, we experience the tension between serving the needs of learners and ensuring the financial success of programs and organizations. In some contexts, such as the corporate sector, this means proving that a training program is effective and profitable. In other contexts, such as ABE and nonprofit organizations, this means securing funding, often from multiple sources, to keep programs running and expanding. It is important to realize that the critical reflection, or lack of it, by ACE leaders within organizations has a tremendous impact on the learners we serve, our communities, ourselves, and our employees.

Management

One way to view management and leadership is strictly in functionalist terms. This means the focus is on the competencies needed to get things done. It is about using models of success for accomplishing objectives. Smith and Offerman's chapter in the 1989 *Handbook* focused on the functional aspects of managing in an ACE context. The authors presented four basic tasks of managing: programming, financing, staffing, and marketing, relating them to the three primary functions of planning, organizing, and evaluating.

Programming involves the development and delivery of education to adults (Caffarella, 2002). The workplace is a major vehicle for adult education. Each year, almost $3 trillion is spent on this type of adult education across the globe. This creates intense competition for learners (Monaghan & Cervero, 2006). With an increasing heterogeneous population, requiring instructional diversity across learning levels, planning becomes more difficult as resources grow scarcer.

Financing, including budgeting, grant writing, and administration, as well as the ability to calculate return on investment (ROI), has become an important part of management in ACE organizations. Over the last two decades, due to decreased public funding, competition among other funding sources, and a continued perception that adult education is a source of funding for other programs, there has been increased pressure on adult education to be self-sustaining.

Managers need the skills to hire, evaluate, and develop their staff (Sadler-Smith, 2006). As more people complete degrees in adult education, the result is a knowledgeable staff in need of innovative leadership and management (Apps, 1994). While salaries are an important consideration, "other factors such as job satisfaction, adequate challenges, and self-leadership" (Smith & Offerman, 1989, p. 255) are equally important.

Marketing is the fourth important function for managers within ACE organizations. From a functional viewpoint, managers need to be sophisticated about marketing strategies, including target marketing and social networking. This expertise includes the ability to execute an effective marketing plan with limited funding. The Internet is also changing the way we market and provide our services, at least for those adults with access. Marketing is an area where managers and leaders need to increase their competencies (Apps, 1994). Ziegler (2005) proposes the use of the Baldridge Education Criteria for performance excellence in the management of ABE programs. She concludes from her study that "adult education administration and quality management may be compatible" (p. 169).

However, an important debate related to marketing and the way we view learners has been sparked within the field of adult education. This debate concerns the move from a service orientation to a product orientation. For example, within a higher education context, do learners really want to "buy" a degree or do they want to acquire skills to help them be successful in their careers? Our view of this transaction, as adult educators, has multiple consequences both for our interactions with learners and for how managers operate and lead organizations. An important question in this debate that needs consideration is "Do such differences collide with or support accepted philosophies of adult education?" (Courtenay, 1990, p. 72). This debate calls on the leadership skills of adult educators.

Leadership

Leaders need another set of competencies. Apps (1994) proposes that adult educators need these leadership competencies: communication skills, human relation skills, well-developed thinking skills, perceptions skills, and a sense of time, which he defines as "the ability to see the relationship of the past to the present with an eye toward the future" (p. 60). In addition, he suggests leaders require competencies in question-framing skills, reflection skills, abstraction skills, and learning skills.

Two models of leadership that receive a great deal of attention in the ACE literature are transactional leadership and transformational leadership (Eddy & Cox, 2008). Under the transactional model, leaders provide rewards and recognition contingent on followers successfully carrying out their roles and assignments. The leader provides the standards for compliance, specifies what constitutes effective performance, and may punish followers for being out of compliance. Transactional leaders "approach their followers with an eye toward trading one thing for another" (Burns, 1978, p. 40). On the other hand, transformational leaders start by offering a vision. The leader then provides opportunities for employee development by encouraging individuals to focus on creative solutions to bring the vision into reality (DeSimone, Werner, & Harris, 2002). The focus is on processes and relationships not just outcomes.

The search for new and more efficient models to enhance management and leadership is ongoing. Senge, Scharmer, Jaworski, and Flowers (2004) propose the U Theory of leadership and organizational change. In this model, leaders consciously work to transform their perceptions, themselves, and their ways of viewing the world. Leaders use this new way of seeing to move to transforming action. One of the mandates for these leaders is to develop within themselves and their followers deeper levels of thinking and learning, leading to actions that serve all stakeholders in a holistic manner.

REFLECTION ON PRACTICE

The economic turmoil at the end of the first decade of the 21st century have made it clear that the old models of capitalism, management, and leadership are not serving us. As an example, traditional higher education institutions, as well as university continuing education divisions, are facing increasing competition from online and corporate universities. Even basic workplace learning, including GED preparation, has competition from for-profit enterprises that are siphoning governmental funding. Therefore, it is important that ACE managers and leaders commit to participate in two important learning endeavors: (1) critical reflection on their practices and (2) expanding their management and leadership paradigms beyond functionalist paradigms that focus on the development of competencies. "Leadership in adult and continuing education is complex, difficult, and sophisticated social practice, and we need all the reflective tools we can garner to aid us in this practice" (Donaldson & Edelson, 2000, p. 205).

Wexler (2005) proposes, "Leaders embody and make sense of different *worldviews* within the context of continuous change, inconsistencies, and multiple meanings" (p. 3). Just looking at the rapid changes in technology and communication, and their impact on ACE over the past 20 years, makes it difficult to envision what ACE will look like in 2030. How do we prepare and lead our organizations for what we may not be able to envision? The answer lies in reflective practice. A number of adult educators have pointed the way. Donaldson and Edelson (2000) stress individual reflection coupled with shared and community discourse. Others suggest that leaders practice "reflection in action" (Schön, 1995). This involves developing the capacity to act and reflect while designing and redesigning action in the moment.

ACE leaders need a deeper kind of reflection and learning. The world is no longer able to retain the illusion of homogeneity. We cannot continue to make decisions based on the illusion that there are models of success that transcend all situations and cultures. An example of trying to retain the illusion of homogeneity is using diversity training to increase awareness within a framework of making adjustments while maintaining the existing structures (Hite & McDonald, 2006). According to Muñoz and Thomas, (2006), leaders at the highest level need to be committed to diversity initiatives; otherwise, such initiatives fail, especially those involving the inclusion of LGBTQ (lesbian, gay, bisexual, transgender, queer) individuals. Superficial nods to diversity no longer work in our world, where globalization and heterogeneity grow stronger, as evidenced by the election of President Barack Obama in 2008.

In order to deepen our critical reflection as mangers and leaders, we need both Schön's (1995) "reflection in action" and Freire's model of praxis. Freire (1970) defines praxis as reflection where "people develop their power to perceive critically *the way they exist* in the world *with which* and *in which* they find themselves; they come to see the world not as static reality, but as a reality in process, in transformation . . . the form of action they adopt is to a large extent a function of how they perceive themselves in the world" (p. 83). We need to reflect critically on both how we view the world and our construction of that reality and how others view the world and their reality. It is only by moving from an awareness of the diversity of the people who work with us, as well as the learners we serve, to a deep embracing of multiple worldviews that we can become effective leaders in the second decade of the 21st century.

The Cultural, Social, and Political Aspects

This level of reflection requires that we acknowledge the cultural, social, and political aspects of management and leadership. ACE managers and leaders need to move past the notion of critical reflection as problem solving to reflect on the "structure of social relations in economic and political terms" (Griffin, 1988, p. 177). Reynolds (1999) points out that "stripping reflection of any socio-political element weakens its capacity for analysis and redefinition while leaving a superficial impression that a more critical approach has been applied" (p. 178). ACE organizations are bound within cultures. As in all cultures, leaders need to attend to politics and power as important aspects of their positions (Cervero & Wilson, 2006). Most of the literature, both scholarly and popular, focuses on the technical aspects of management and leadership. Cultural, social, and political aspects receive less attention.

Who Holds the Power?

In the realm of ACE (Apple, 2003) and in the corporate arena (Alvesson & Willmott, 2003) there is a recognition of the need for discussions about how the sociocultural environment, politics, and power influence the way managers and leaders operate. For instance, in a higher education context, there is a lack of women and minorities in leadership positions. The American Council on Education (2007) states in their report titled *American College President* that "women and people of color still occupy comparatively few presidencies. Furthermore, female presidents are largely concentrated at community colleges and least likely to head research universities" (as cited in Valdata et al., 2008, p. 16). Nationally, about 33% of the vice presidents and provosts are women and 36% of the deans are women (Phuong, 2008). Although the pool of female candidates for presidencies is a third of the population, schools still contend that they are unable to find qualified candidates.

The picture is even bleaker for minorities. While the percentage of woman presidents in higher education more than doubled between 1986 and 2006 to 23%, the percentage of racial and ethnic minorities only increased from 8 to 14% over the same period. Furthermore, if you exclude institutions serving minorities, the figure drops to 10% (American Council of Education, 2007).

Since the 1971 higher education affirmative action mandates, access to education and employment opportunities for African Americans has increased; however, the research demonstrates that when Blacks are compared to their White counterparts, disparity still exists at all levels in academia (Holmes, 2004). Moreover, while there was a very small gain in the number of African American administrators between 1989 and 1995, there was no progress between 1995 and 1997 (Harvey, 2001). In fact, between 1993 and 1999, the percentage of African American administrators at public institutions actually fell from 7.3% to 5.8% (Jackson, 2004). The most important point, though, is that just because women and minorities "are in the house does not mean that [they] are truly invited to the table" (Cole, 2005, p. 14). One Midwest institution, Southern Illinois University Carbondale, where the leadership from the chancellor to the 10 academic deans is male, provides an example (Phuong, 2008). The same types of statistics and stories exist in all adult education arenas, including the corporate sector.

Expanding Management Paradigms

Corporations collapsing along with outdated structures in the face of unprecedented change prompt us to question the current paradigms. Thinking about the need for other paradigms reminds me about a study participant (Monaghan, 2004) sharing a dilemma that occurred during an economic downturn in his family business. The choice was either to lay off workers and doom them to starvation or continue to employ them and then sell the product when the economy recovered. What struck me most was his feeling that he needed to choose between acting in a professional business manner OR acting in an ethical and humane but foolish manner from a leadership viewpoint. This story illustrates how as managers and leaders we can forget that "mainstream management and leadership" rules are constructed by our society, causing us to dishonor or minimize other ways of constructing management and leadership models. This section presents three additional paradigms important for ACE managers and leaders to consider in our practices and philosophies. My hope is that it will also allow practitioners to speak back to a dominant paradigm that breeds racism, sexism, and intolerance of differences. Management and leadership practices, while generally believed to be equitable, impartial, consistent, bias free, and value neutral, are not (Alvesson & Willmott, 2003).

Critical Management Studies

Society increasingly looks to business to solve its problems in the public realm. This is evident in the move to privatize government functions, including that of education. The business paradigm is profit driven; it assumes that the market is the best judge of quality and the best distributor of resources. If business models are going to be applied to addressing social issues, then it becomes imperative that ACE management and leadership address issues of power, privilege, and social justice to counteract systems that privileges some and disadvantages others (Fournier & Grey, 2000).

One theory that addresses issues of power and privilege is critical management studies (CMS). This theory has three key assumptions: (1) the influence of management is all pervasive, affecting our lives at all levels; (2) "mainstream" management and theory is limiting and oppressive, failing to account for the sociopolitical aspects that are the true foundation of organizations and society; and (3) all people, not only managers, have a legitimate interest in management (Alvesson & Willmott, 2003). The purpose of CMS is to foreground "the processes of power and ideology subsumed within the social fabric of institutional structures, procedures, and practices" (Reynolds, 1999, p. 173).

CMS seeks to challenge the myth of objectivity and technical knowledge that forms the basis for "mainstream" management theory and practice. While realizing that technical functions are a necessary part of the productive activity of an organization, its focus is on the sociopolitical phenomenon, particularly its relatively invisible nature and power that underlie these technical functions. CMS is concerned with such questions as who occupies the positions of authority within these technical functions and their resultant divisions of labor (Alvesson & Willmott, 2003). This worldview addresses the oppressive and limiting practices of mainstream management, asking, "Who derives the greatest advantage, in both material and symbolic terms from these divisions?"

CMS theorists contest the notion that only managers and organizations have a legitimate interest in how organizations function. Korten (2000) identified globalization of corporations as a phenomenon driving a larger wedge between the haves and the have-nots while corporations move further from restraints on their power. The purpose of critical managerial discourse and practice is to carefully scrutinize and expose the gap between those voices who claim to speak on behalf of themselves and others (shareholders) and the reality that there are other legitimate voices not allowed in the discourse (Cervero & Wilson, 2006).

Mainstream management normally focuses on characteristics of power that are explicit, observable, and superficial (Alvesson & Willmott, 2003). CMS strives toward the ideal of creating a more just society based on fairness and democracy (Reynolds, 1999), extending the ideal of democracy from the political to the economic sphere. CMS is committed to uncovering alternatives that have been effaced by management knowledge and practice (Fournier & Grey, 2000).

Thus as ACE managers and leaders reflect and learn, we can look beyond the "models of success" or best practices touted by mainstream theories. We can search out, reflect upon, and practice using other paradigms. For example, mainstream management values team building and consensus decision making without concern for the underlying power dynamics that need to be explored to achieve true equality (Rigg & Trehan, 1999). CMS contests the idea that consensus and team building automatically give the employees and other stakeholders more power in the decision-making process.

Engaging in a CMS perspective presents certain dilemmas. As Fenwick (2004) points out, traditional performance measures sustain power and control. These measures often clash with an approach that seeks a more democratic model incorporating representation of the broadest set of stakeholders. We are unable to solve this dilemma as long as we remain wedded to historic measures of success and performance. One opportunity lies in first acknowledging the broader diversity in the general population of students and administrators at all levels. Then, we can enhance our measurement of success in higher education by establishing measures that require proportionate representation of this entire population. As we do so, the goals and objectives change, and the ways of operating to achieve the goals also change.

Afrocentric

Another way of examining and practicing ACE management and leadership is through an Afrocentric lens. Schiele (1994) and other scholars note that Afrocentricity is "a philosophical model based on traditional African philosophical assumptions" (p. 152). This model "1) views the structure of reality from a perspective of interdependency [with] no separation between the spiritual and the material (Asante, 1980);

2) reality is 'both spiritual and material at once' (James Meyers, 1985, p. 34) [and] assumes that all elements of the universe, including people, are spiritual, created from a similar universal substance 3) places considerable emphasis on an affective way of obtaining knowledge [where] knowing (i.e., understanding events and reality) through emotion or feeling is considered valid and critical from an Afrocentric standpoint . . . affect, as a means of knowing, is viewed as offsetting the use of rationality (Akbar, 1984) and 4) significantly underscores the value of interpersonal relationships. The maintenance and enhancement of harmonious interpersonal relationships is considered the most important cultural value in Afrocentricity . . . in which the value in maintaining and strengthening interpersonal bonds overrides the concern over acquiring material objects and accumulating wealth" (Schiele, pp. 152–153). In addition, it "emphases an infinite process of interactions or continuous activity based on what is good for the collective" (Rogers, 2005, p. 704).

A main difference between Afrocentric and Eurocentric models that is applicable to management and leadership is the view of people and relationships. The Afrocentric model emphasizes collectivity and harmony, whereas the Eurocentric view emphasizes fragmentation, domination, and conflict as well as an orientation toward individualism and materialism (Schiele, 1994). Schiele stresses that in the Eurocentric view "people are conceived primarily as individuals separate from other people and nature . . . aggressively and competitively [seeking] control over nature, material items (i.e. objects, property) and other people. . . . Afrocentricity recognizes individual uniqueness . . . it conceives individual identity as collective identity" (1994, p. 154).

Schiele (1994) suggests that administrators in higher education can influence the dissemination and use of more Afrocentric concepts among all administrators. This suggestion has the potential to create a different ACE management and leadership paradigm, one with a holistic view that encompasses true cultural diversity and opens us up to other worldviews and possibilities about how we manage and lead.

Merriweather Hunn (2004) urges adult educators to "make a commitment to challenging and confronting attitudes and practices that contribute to the dominance of the Eurocentric perspective in the field" (p. 70). One way is to use the Afrocentric model to enhance and change our practices in management and leadership. As part of our reflection and praxis as managers and leaders we need to spend time learning about African American and other cultures, history, and experiences while setting the Eurocentric model on the table as just one among many (Merriweather Hunn, 2004). In addition, ACE leaders, "should afford respect, interest, and support . . . when [others] offer suggestions based in other cultural centrisms" (Merriweather Hunn, 2004, p. 71).

Practically, this means that "Our mission in adult education should be to encourage all whom we serve to bring with them to the site of practice their heritage, culture, and history" (Merriweather Hunn, 2004, p. 73). As we incorporate an Afrocentric approach to management and leadership in ACE contexts, we can reflect on what we are doing to learn more about the African American culture and how it can inform our practice. In addition, we can strive to encourage the staff and learners we serve to share their culture, heritage, and history with us. Finally, we can reflect on how this new knowledge and respect for a perspective that is not Eurocentric can actually inform and change our own practices.

Feminist

Feminist scholars also point to a different reality. In most ACE management and leadership literature, feminist perspectives are subsumed under postmodernism and poststructuralism (Donaldson & Edelson, 2000). While feminist perspectives are similar to both viewpoints, they also need to stand alone.

A feminist viewpoint questions whether adaptability and coping with the current structures of organizations is the only way (Gibson-Graham, 1999). In the past, organizations looked at the issues of affirmative action in the workplace and tried to make everything fit into the preexisting structures. There is little acknowledgement that organizations need to change (Gibson-Graham, 1999). Shore's (2006) study revealed that White women who were adult education mangers had learned the hidden rules of managing. These rules included always being positive and not criticizing or doing something else that would threaten another

person. Participants felt that their managerial knowledge rested in understanding the organizational culture gained through the course of their careers. The women also felt they judged those who did not have the same kind of knowledge, and noted that those who did not possess this knowledge were often from different cultural and racial backgrounds.

By applying a feminist lens, including a Black feminist view, leaders reflecting on organization and change would be provided with an interpretive and critical perspective. Feminism foregrounds gender as the defining lens, postmodernism foregrounds the idea of the local as opposed to the universal notions of gender in organizations, while poststructural feminism foregrounds gender and the positionality of those involved in the organization (St. Pierre, 2000). For African American feminists (Collins, 2000), the intersection of race and gender within the experiences of Women of Color is the primary basis for reflection. At first it appears that a feminist perspective is overly complicated, but at the heart of all varieties of feminism is "the question of patriarchy and how to get rid of it" (Mojab & Gorman, 2001, p. 287). A power struggle where the winner takes all is the ground of patriarchy.

An example of organizational change that gives the illusion of less patriarchy is the concept of flattening the organizational structure by eliminating middle-management positions. Management views this in a positive light, claiming that employees experience ownership of their work through increased decision-making responsibilities (Howell, Carter, & Schied, 2002). This might be interpreted as a less patriarchal way of operating; however, research revealed that in actual practice employees experience an increase in workload, usually without any increase in pay. In addition, employees felt that the additional responsibility did not include a "real voice to speak about what they thought was important" (Howell et al., p. 117).

Our reflections could look at how current mainstream management purports to give employees more choices and decision-making powers, but only creates that illusion while increasing workload and stress. As ACE managers and leaders, we have a responsibility to look at the initiatives touted as the panacea to solve our problems. Are these initiatives taking us in the direction of a more equitable society, where all stakeholders are served, or do they just continue the same oppressive system in a new package? In allowing only some voices at the table or counting some voices more than others, we are upholding a view of organizations that says, "Father knows best."

CONCLUSION

In the end, we are always talking about power. However, power in organizations is often only characterized as competition for scarce resources, competing interests, and struggles for power and advantage (Knights & Willmott, 2007). This view is too limiting. "If the power to define is a key element of agency and leadership, then what new variations do we invent to change the discourse and in so doing innovate by redefining meaning and membership, establish new patterns of social engagement, and regaining authorship for ourselves" (Donaldson & Edelson, 2000, p. 202). I have suggested three new paradigms to help us as ACE managers and leaders to change the discourse that can lead to new ways of fostering leadership and direction within the field.

Some people might say I am idealistic and impractical. They might counter that the need to apply a business model to ACE organizations has never been greater. Competition is too fierce and resources and learners are too scarce to spend time reflecting, let alone applying different paradigms representing real change. However, I reply that our philosophical heritage in adult education outweighs these concerns. ACE is about being learner centered and employee centered in the midst of focusing on revenues to sustain our organizations. It is about relationships and a more critical stance focused on "whose interests are served." As Cunningham (2000) so aptly puts it, "The question that currently divides many adult educators is whether to locate their practice in civil society or the economic sector" (p. 577). Today, it is no longer an either-or proposition. The economic sector drives civil society. We have only to look at the number and influence of lobbyists in Washington, D.C., to see the clear connection. As adult educators and leaders, we need to reflect critically on what will be our driving force—our philosophies of adult education or the business model. Perhaps we can use our adult education philosophies to change the business model to be more inclusive and authentic.

Management and leadership in the field of adult education is complex, revolving around the cultural, social, and political nature of organizations. Adult educators need to be reflective practitioners who continue to learn and engage with the various levels of power and interests that occur whenever more than two people show up. In the midst of this reflective engagement and action, it is possible to bring about change and intertwine the economic interests with the human interests of learners, employees, the community, and society. It is not easy, radical change may not happen on our timelines, but it is always worth the effort.

REFERENCES

Akbar, N. (1984). Africentric social sciences for human liberation. *Journal of Black Studies, 14,* 395–414.

Alvesson, M., & Willmott, H. (Eds.). (2003). *Studying management critically.* London: Sage.

American Council of Education. (2007). *Executive summary of The American College President: 20th anniversary.* Washington, DC : American Council on Education, Center for Policy Analysis.

Apple, M. W. (2003). Freire and the politics of race in education. *International Journal of Leadership in Education, 6*(2), 107–118.

Apps, J. W. (1994). *Leadership for the emerging age: Transforming practice in adult and continuing education.* San Francisco: Jossey-Bass.

Asante, M. K. (1980). International/Intercultural relations. In M. K. Asante & A. S. Vandi (Eds.), *Contemporary Black thought: Alternative analyses in social and behavioral science* (pp. 45–58). Beverly Hills, CA: Sage.

Burns, J. M. (1978). *Leadership.* New York: HarperCollins.

Caffarella, R. S. (2002). *Planning programs for adult learners: A practical guide for educators, trainers, and staff developers* (2nd ed.). San Francisco: Jossey-Bass.

Cervero, R. M., & Wilson, A. L. (2006). *Working the planning table: Negotiating democratically for adult, continuing, and workplace education.* San Francisco: Jossey-Bass.

Cole, J. (2005, Winter). Transcending boundaries to build a new academic leadership. *Presidency,* pp. 14–17.

Collins, P. H. (2000). *Black feminist thought: Knowledge, consciousness, and the politics of empowerment* (2nd ed.). New York: Routledge.

Courtenay, B. C. (1990). An analysis of adult education administration literature, 1936–1989. *Adult Education Quarterly, 40*(2), 63–77.

Cunningham, P. M. (2000). Sociology of adult education. In A. L. Wilson & E. R. Hayes (Eds.), *Handbook of adult and continuing education: New edition* (pp. 573–591). San Francisco: Jossey-Bass.

Dansey-Smith, F. (2004). Why "soft" people skills are the key to leadership development. *Strategic HR Review, 3*(3), 28–31.

DeSimone, R. L., Werner, J. M., & Harris, D. M. (2002). *Human Resource Development* (3rd ed.). Mason, OH: South-Western.

Donaldson, J. F., & Edelson, P. J. (2000). From functionalism to postmodernism in adult education leadership. In A. L. Wilson & E. R. Hayes (Eds.), *Handbook of adult and continuing education* (pp. 191–207). San Francisco: Jossey-Bass.

Eddy, P. L., & Cox, E. M. (2008). Gendered leadership: An organizational perspective. *New Directions for Community Colleges, 142,* 69–79.

Fenwick, T. (2004). Toward a critical HRD in theory and practice. *Adult Education Quarterly, 54*(3), 193–209.

Fournier, V., & Grey, C. (2000). At the critical moment: Conditions and prospects for critical management studies. *Human Relations, 53*(1), 7–32.

Freire, P. (1970). *Pedagogy of the oppressed.* (30th anniversary ed.; M. B. Ramos, Trans.). New York: Continuum.

Gibson-Graham, J. K. (1999). *The end of capitalism (as we knew it): A feminist critique of political economy.* Cambridge, MA: Blackwell.

Griffin, C. (1988). Critical thinking and critical theory in adult education. In *Papers from The Transatlantic Dialogue, University of Leeds* (pp. 176–180). Leeds, UK: University of Leeds, School of Continuing Education.

Harvey, W. B. (2001). *Minorities in higher education 2000–2001: Eighteenth annual status report.* Washington, DC: American Council on Education.

Hite, L. M., & McDonald, K. S. (2006). Diversity training pitfalls and possibilities: An exploration of small and mid-size U.S. organizations. *Human Resource Development International, 9*(3), 365–378.

Holmes, S. L. (2004). An overview of African American college presidents: A game of two steps forward, one step backward, and standing still. *The Journal of Negro Education, 73*(1), 21–39.

Howell, S. L., Carter, V. K., & Schied, F. M. (2002). Gender and women's experience at work: A critical and feminist perspective on human resource development. *Adult Education Quarterly, 52*(2), 112–127.

Hunn, L. M. (2004). Africentric philosophy: A remedy for eurocentric dominance. In J. A. Sandlin & R. St. Clair (Eds.), *Promoting critical practice in adult education* (pp. 65–74). New Directions for Adult and Continuing Education, No. 102. San Francisco: Jossey-Bass.

Jackson, J. F. L. (2004). Engaging, retaining, and advancing African Americans in executive-level positions: A descriptive and trend analysis of academic administrators in higher and postsecondary education. *The Journal of Negro Education, 73*(1), 4–20.

James Meyers, L. (1985). Transpersonal psychology: The role of the Afrocentric paradigm. *Journal of Black Psychology, 12,* 31–42.

Knights, D., & Willmott, H. (2007). *Introducing organizational behavior and management.* London: Thomson Learning.

Korten, D. C. (2000). *When corporations rule the world* (2nd ed.). San Francisco: Kumarian Press and Berrett-Koehler.

Mojab, S., & Gorman, R. (2001). The struggle over lifelong learning: A Marxist-feminist analysis. In *Proceedings of the 42nd Annual Adult Education Research Conference* (pp. 285–290). East Lansing: Michigan State University Press.

Monaghan, C. H. (2004). Development of the adult learners' management philosophy through critical management studies courses (Doctoral dissertation, University of Georgia, 2004). *Dissertation Abstracts International* A&I database (Publication No. AAT 3162083).

Monaghan, C. H., & Cervero, R. M. (2006). Impact of critical management studies courses on learners' attitudes and beliefs. *Human Resource Development International, 9*(3), 379–396.

Muñoz, C. S., & Thomas, K. M. (2006). LGBTQ issues in organizational settings: What HRD professionals need to know and do. In R. J. Hill (Ed.), *Challenging homophobia and heterosexism: Lesbian, gay, bisexual, transgender, and queer issues in organizational settings* (pp. 85–96). New Directions for Adult and Continuing Education, No. 112. San Francisco: Jossey-Bass.

Phuong, L. (2008). A "historical problem." *Diverse: Issues in Higher Education, 25*(4), 2.

Reynolds, M. (1999). Grasping the nettle: Possibilities and pitfalls of a critical management pedagogy. *British Journal of Management, 9,* 171–184.

Rigg, C., & Trehan, K. (1999). Not critical enough? Black women raise challenges for critical management learning. *Gender and Education, 11*(3), 265–280.

Rogers, E. E. (2005). Afritics from margin to center: Theorizing the politics of African American women as political leaders. *Journal of Black Studies, 55*(6), 701–714.

Sadler-Smith, E. (2006). *Learning and development for managers: Perspectives from research and practice.* Malden, MA: Blackwell.

Schiele, J. H. (1994). Afrocentricity: Implications for higher education. *Journal of Black Studies, 25*(2), 150–169.

Schön, D. A. (1995). *The reflective practitioner: How professionals think in action.* Aldershot, UK: Arena.

Senge, P. M., Scharmer, C. O., Jaworski, J., & Flowers, B. S. (2004). *Presence: An exploration of profound change in people, organizations, and society.* New York: Random House.

Shore, S. (2006). (Re)thinking equity: The spatial and racial dynamics of managing learning and learning to manage. *Journal of Vocational Education and Training, 58*(4), 497–513.

Smith, D. H., & Offerman, M. J. (1989). The management of adult and continuing education. In S. B. Merriam & P. M. Cunningham (Eds.), *Handbook of adult and continuing education* (pp. 246–259). San Francisco: Jossey-Bass.

St. Pierre, E. A. (2000). Poststructural feminism in education: An overview. *Qualitative Studies in Education, 13*(3), 477–515.

Sternberg, R. J. (2003). WICS: A model of leadership in organisations. *Academy of Management Learning and Education, 2*(4), 386–401.

Valdata, P., Mendoza, V. P., Lum, L., Hawkins, B. D., Pember, M. A., & Nealy, M. J. (2008). Women redefining leadership. *Diverse: Issues in Higher Education, 25*(3), 16–22.

Wexler, M. N. (2005). *Leadership in context: The four faces of capitalism.* Cheltenham, UK: Edward Elgar.

Ziegler, M. (2005). It opens your eyes: Transforming management of adult education programs using the Baldridge education criteria for performance excellence. *Adult Basic Education, 15*(3), 169–186.

PART IV

DIVERSITY OF ADULT LEARNING VENUES AND COLLECTIVE ENDEAVORS

17

ADULT BASIC EDUCATION

RALF ST. CLAIR AND ALISA BELZER

This discussion of adult basic education (ABE), primarily in the United States, is based on a working definition of ABE as education provided to people over the age of compulsory schooling to support them in attaining a level of literacy and numeracy engagement appropriate for their needs. Education in English for speakers of other languages, which often overlaps with ABE in practice, is not within the scope of this chapter because it has key characteristics and complexities in its own right. This discussion covers the nature of ABE as a field, key policies and theoretical ideas, selected examples of ABE in other countries, and new influences on practice.

Two aspects of ABE provision shape policies and practices in critical ways. The first is the complexity of ABE, which is neither highly standardized nor strongly regulated. It is diverse and fragmentary in nature, delivered by many different agencies in a variety of formats. The second aspect is the responsive nature of the field. ABE is highly contextualized, and is shaped by federal, state, local, and other influences unique to each setting. Complexity and responsiveness are not inherently strengths or weaknesses, but both profoundly affect ABE provision across the United States and beyond.

THE NATURE OF ADULT BASIC EDUCATION

As with adult education generally, ABE both benefits and suffers from broad definitions, non-institutionalization, and a marginalized position in the education arena. Periodic national surveys show large numbers of adults in the United States (both immigrants and native-born residents) (Kutner et al., 2007) who could potentially benefit from participating in basic education, yet the justification for funding and policy has been constantly debated, undercut, and revised.

A myriad of funding sources and goals has led to a system of ABE that serves adults in settings ranging from the most informal community contexts to formal adult high schools and community colleges. Instructors may be volunteers with minimal training or may be highly skilled and experienced long-term employees with an advanced degree in education. Instruction can take place individually for an hour or two per week at the convenience of the learner and the instructor, or it can be similar to a full-time job with formally structured classes organized on a semester system in a traditional school setting. Similarly, the instructional content of ABE is highly variable, ranging from basic literacy, numeracy, and language skills to functional and life skills related to parenting and employment. Formal, content area-based high school credit-bearing classes are yet another format.

ABE serves a population of widely varying ages and experiences (U.S. Department of Education, Division of Adult Education and Literacy, 2006). In general, traditional ABE learners are seen as older adults who have interrupted school to have children, to work, or because of other disruptions, and who attend programs for further education as circumstances permit. Participation is often short term, lacking intensity, and episodic due to the conflicting and diverse demands of adulthood (Comings & Cuban, 2007). The field is also experiencing an increase in numbers of ABE learners who are recent school leavers. There is evidence that many are pushed out of high school because of high-stakes testing (Boulden, 2008; Darling-Hammond, 2004) and the perception that a quicker and easier credential can be obtained in the General Educational Development test (the GED exam is primarily a test of reading comprehension and can be sat in one day) (Andrews, 2002; Gonzales, 2006; Marriott, 1993). This group of learners is often willing and able to attend classes full-time, and because of their recent school experience, they may make more rapid progress than those who have been out of school for many years. The field is currently struggling with how to address the different needs of traditional students and recent school leavers (Boulden, 2008; Hayes, 2000; Perin, Flugman, & Spiegel, 2006).

ABE instructors are highly diverse, and they vary in the amount of preservice training and professional development they receive. States require a range of qualifications, from high school graduation to K–12 certification. Without rigorous or consistent credentialing systems in most locations, practitioners enter the field with a wide range of backgrounds, training, and experience. Their diversity has greatly enriched the field (Lytle, Belzer, & Reumann, 1992; Smith, 1990) but also makes it hard to establish a consistent system of professional development and support.

ABE works with a degree of tension between its remedial connotation and its adult population of learners. ABE practices often teeter between approaches reminiscent of traditional schooling and approaches recognizing the participants as self-directed, focused, and mature learners who can make key decisions about what and how they learn. In other words, ABE embodies contradictory educational approaches that may assume learners have a need to be directed and led, while at the same time acknowledging the importance of adult learning principles (Merriam & Caffarella, 1999).

One recent and important development in ABE is the "social practices" approach to teaching. Researchers in the field of New Literacy Studies (Barton, Hamilton, & Ivanic, 2000; Gee, 2001; Street, 1993) have made it clear that the diverse social contexts in which we live profoundly shape the ways people use literacy and numeracy in their day-to-day lives. The implication is that ABE has to address the literacy and numeracy needs of participants as the students define them. This is not to say that definitions of what "counts" as literacy are not externally driven; they often are. This view of learning represents the pervasive tension between systematic and learner-centered goals once more.

In many ways, this ambiguity, along with the broad goals and definitions that describe ABE, has benefited the field. Without the constraints of extensive federal, state, and local policy, the long-established and relatively standardized provision, and the static physical settings of public education for children, ABE has offered tremendous flexibility to practitioners and learners to invent and reinvent the field in innovative, socially progressive, and responsive ways (Belzer & St. Clair, 2003). Yet, the constant need to justify and fight for its existence, along with underdeveloped funding for research and infrastructure, has led to instability, vulnerability, and a need for ABE to reinvent itself in response to the political and policy climate of the day.

Increased funding for 15 years beginning in the early 1990s (funding has now been flat for several years) has been a mixed blessing. Although the field was able to offer more services to more diverse populations (Belzer & St. Clair, 2007), the additional resources have been tied to increased standardization and accountability. Some view this formalization as an important step toward more effectively and efficiently meeting the needs of learners; others see it as a relatively empty gesture simply reflecting the current culture of measurement (Merrifield, 1998; St. Clair & Belzer, 2007).

LOCATIONS OF ADULT BASIC EDUCATION

One concrete indicator of the variability of ABE is the fact that it is situated in so many different kinds of contexts and is funded through so many different sources. Often, the funding source and setting for the program have direct implications for many aspects of provision, including goals and objectives, instructional approaches, assumptions about the meaning of literacy, and the population served. Learners do not always have the option of selecting the location or type of program they attend. Sometimes they are compelled to attend classes in one type of program or another by an employer or a case manager, or they may simply have limited access to diverse programs.

Although several researchers have developed typologies of programs (Fingeret, 1984; Lytle & Wolfe, 1989; Quigley, 1997), none seem to quite capture the current organization of the field. For the purposes of this overview, we suggest that there are three types of ABE program settings offering distinct opportunities to learn. These are *traditional, compulsory,* and *responsive* educational settings.

Traditional educational programs tend to be located in established educational settings such as public schools and community colleges. They offer GED preparation, high school credits, or remedial preparation for college courses, emphasizing academic skills in formats similar to K–12 education. Instruction is often teacher driven, with learners expected to assume a relatively passive role. The primary objective of these types of programs is to assist participants in attaining a school credential (or in the case of the GED, a proxy for a school credential). Increasing social pressures for adults to have postsecondary education credentials make these programs more important. Traditional programs are generally publicly funded and have an emphasis on literacy and numeracy as a neutral set of technical skills that are a means to further education and improved employment.

Compulsory educational settings include welfare-to-work and workforce development programs mandated for recipients of public assistance and programs working with court-adjudicated individuals ordered to attend classes as part of their sentencing agreements. Often located in employment centers, community colleges, and technical/vocational schools, these programs can be highly regulated with strict attendance requirements, a dress code, and required course work. Although they may have academic goals similar to traditional educational programs, these types of

programs may also emphasize life skills, such as job search, financial literacy, and communication. They may encourage acquisition of school credentials but also have an explicit goal of creating more productive, employable, contributing members of society. They also seem to reflect an implicit assumption that ABE can address social problems associated with poverty (St. Clair, 2002; Warner, 2007). This type of program has proliferated since welfare reform in the mid-1990s placed new requirements, expectations, and limits on recipients. Due to funding structures, these programs are often accountable to several bodies.

Responsive programs tend to be more learner centered and are designed to provide instruction that is more likely to meet personal and individualistic goals for self-improvement and fulfillment as a parent, worker, or community member than externally derived objectives (Fingeret & Jurmo, 1989). Many programs of this type are community based. They often view literacy practices as determined by social context and hold that literacy instruction should focus on individual practices and processes for using reading, writing, and numeracy. Some have a further agenda of empowerment and social justice through individual and collaborative action (Gaber-Katz & Watson, 1991; Rogers & Kramer, 2007). Such programs are often located in community spaces including libraries, churches, and community centers, but they may also be found in K–12 schools and in workplaces. Although responsive programs may help learners attain traditional school credentials or gain job-seeking and employment skills, they do this by addressing learners' interests as their first priority. Of the three types of programs discussed here, the responsive programs may be most at odds with the current demands for standardization and accountability because learners' goals may not be congruent with external expectations for ABE. When this occurs, learners and instructors may struggle to reconcile competing and sometimes contradictory goals and objectives (Belzer, 2003; Belzer & St. Clair, 2007).

KEY THEORETICAL IDEAS

It is important to acknowledge the relatively undertheorized and underresearched nature of the field. Unlike initial reading instruction for children, there has been very little research done on literacy development for adults. This is doubly problematic because there is not enough research to know in what ways the teaching and learning process for adult literacy learners is different from that for children. Some theorists have a passionate commitment to the principle of adults and children learning basic skills differently, whereas pragmatists may argue that there is sufficient overlap for child-based research to inform adult practice to some degree (Kruidenier, 2002).

On a broader scale, it is possible to identify three theoretical perspectives on literacy that bear on ABE. The first of these is a skills-based perspective, which sees interaction with texts as based on a definable and measurable series of skills. What people can do as individuals is strongly emphasized in this model, with far less attention paid to the social or collective aspects of literacy. This approach fits within Street's (1984) autonomous category in which literacy skills are viewed as stand-alone and portable, capable of application in any context wherever they are learned.

The meaning of the term *skill* in the skills-based approach varies, and some care must be taken to understand the use in a given context. In some cases, it refers to the component skills of reading, such as decoding text and comprehension. In other cases, such as the English Skills for Life curriculum and much standardized testing in the United States, skills are described in functional terms such as "understand that instructional texts must be read in sequence" with detailed sets of functional subskills (Department of Innovation, Universities, and Skills, n.d. Reading Comprehension Entry 2.1). Although there have been forceful arguments that the skills-based approach oversimplifies and decontextualizes the process of interacting with text (Barton et al., 2000), it does offer some advantages. It provides a concrete way to talk about assessing literacy levels and measuring progress, which is far more difficult in alternative perspectives.

The second perspective on literacy is strongly influenced by the work of Paulo Freire (1972), a Brazilian educator and researcher. Freire argued that literacy and numeracy education were inherently political and that there was no such thing as neutral education—education either led to domestication of humans or their liberation through consciousness raising. The principle that education is an inherently political act

has become a truism in some places, although it very profoundly challenges views of literacy as a collection of functional skills.

The liberatory approach to literacy education has not been widely adopted within ABE systems. There are examples in the Western world, but probably the best-known application is REFLECT, used by 500 organizations in 70 developing countries (Action Aid, 2006). This process typically begins by identifying power and resource issues through maps and other graphical methods, culminating in each participant writing a book to contribute to a local development plan. This is a very highly contextualized view of literacy learning and falls into what Street (1993) calls the ideological approach—the recognition that literacy skills always have meanings and applications beyond the immediate interaction with text.

The third perspective has been particularly influential in the United Kingdom and increasingly across Western Europe. It is the notion of literacy as a set of social practices (Barton, 1994) derived from the theoretical and empirical work of the New Literacy Studies. In this view, the practices associated with reading, writing, and other forms of literacy activity are assumed to be embedded within a specific context and social interaction. The social practices approach suggests that learners do not need to work through a linear hierarchy of skills as if they know nothing of text but may simply need support with some areas within a web of practice. The social practices approach has some ideas in common with the *Equipped for the Future* (EFF) initiative (Center for Literacy Studies, 2004) in the United States, particularly the idea that different areas of life require different abilities and practices.

This extremely brief review of theories of literacy gives a sense of the profundity of differences in conceptualization and implementation in practice across the field. It is important to emphasize that the proponents of each approach do not deny the importance of all aspects of literacy—most would likely agree that decoding matters, as does enhanced political participation. The disagreements center around what appropriately comes first when supporting adults learning how to interact with text and what the role of the program should be. It seems likely that these questions will remain open for some time to come and that such significant differences of perspective could potentially diminish the strength of the field.

POLICIES AFFECTING ADULT BASIC EDUCATION

Our discussion of policy will focus on the federal level. ABE first received federal funding in the 1960s, and federal legislation has played a substantial role in shaping service provision, despite a range of other funding sources. Major increases in federal support in the early 1990s led some commentators to suggest that ABE now had more permanence and stability, which could significantly strengthen it (Fingeret, 1993). Indeed, the 1990s saw a burgeoning of research, program improvement efforts, professional development, and more specialized services for meeting the needs of a diverse population of learners (Belzer & St. Clair, 2003). This period could be characterized as a time of expansion, innovation, hopefulness, and optimism.

Two major pieces of federal legislation were highly influential during this decade and continue to influence the field strongly (Belzer, 2003). The 1996 reform of welfare, although not specifically directed toward ABE, had a significant effect on many potential participants (Sandlin & Cervero, 2003). It set time limits for receiving benefits and mandated specific times, places, and ways to participate in ABE as part of the goal of gaining financial independence from government assistance. Since that time, the welfare system has provided ABE funds and stipulated many aspects of service provision. Programs that receive significant funding through the welfare system generally fall within the category of compulsory programs and have often had to reinvent or revise their program offerings to align themselves better with the requirements of policy (Belzer, 2003; Imel, 2000).

The Workforce Investment Act, passed in 1998, is the most recent significant federal legislation to have had a direct impact on ABE. The two aspects of the legislation bringing about the most notable changes in the field are the consolidation of the workforce development and ABE systems under one related funding stream and the implementation of the National Reporting System (NRS), a performance standards tracking system. The placement of ABE under the umbrella of workforce development has created many new partnerships, which focus on developing employability skills. The NRS emphasis on the accomplishment and documentation of measurable learner outcomes may tend to focus the field on narrow definitions of achievement (Merrifield, 1998).

Each policy has moved the field toward more standardization, more externally driven accountability, and more emphasis on learning for human capital development rather than for human potential development. Every type of program receiving federal funds has been moved in this direction, regardless of its original philosophical commitments. These changes have provided a far clearer mission and a more concrete way to evaluate learner progress and program quality than had previously existed. However, some critics of the field suggest that they have also detracted from the core theoretical underpinnings and commitments of adult education. Although many practitioners and programs may appreciate the increased structure and clarity of the current policy, they also may struggle to maintain the balance between responsiveness to policy and funding requirements and responsiveness to the day-to-day needs, interests, and challenges of the learners (Belzer & St. Clair, 2007).

The funding of two federal research centers over the past 15 years greatly increased the quantity and quality of research for the field. In particular, the National Center for the Study of Adult Learning and Literacy (NCSALL) funded research in a wide variety of areas related to policy and practice and helped to nurture a culture where research informed practice and practice informed research. However, federal funding specifically dedicated to adult literacy research has been discontinued. The only major research currently under way (and nearing completion) is a group of studies designed to compare outcomes of various reading instruction strategies using experimental designs. Although much is still left undone, federally funded ABE research can be described as in a fallow period.

INTERNATIONAL DIMENSIONS OF ADULT BASIC EDUCATION

While the focus of this discussion is clearly centered on the United States, it is informative to consider the ABE provision of other nations to see what differences there are and what lessons they hold. ABE strongly reflects the context in which it has developed, including the form of language, patterns of schooling and economy, political environment, and the history of literacy in the country examined.

One example of an ABE system operating within a similar context to the United States, but having a different philosophical orientation, is Scotland. Like the United States, Scotland has had compulsory education for well over a century but still finds itself with a significant proportion of the population who do not score well on literacy surveys. The International Adult Literacy Survey of the mid-1990s suggested that about half of Scotland's adult population has low literacy levels. As in many countries, the Scottish government responded with increased investment in adult literacy and numeracy education.

Where the Scottish policy makers differed, however, was their theoretical orientation. They chose to develop a system based primarily on the social practices approach (Merrifield, 2005). This was largely due to the government's commitment to social justice and its desire to recognize people's existing strengths by allowing learners to identify their own areas of interest as a starting point for instruction. The system has no common curriculum; learners develop an individual learning plan on entry to adult literacy and numeracy classes and are assessed for progress against this plan. Learners may or may not choose to certify their learning through a series of levels of testing (designed to be as authentic as possible) that map onto a 12-level qualification scale that includes everything from the most foundational skills to PhDs. ABE generally addresses the lowest three or four levels of this scale, up to the examination level expected of a 15-year-old school student.

Overall, the Scottish system is quite different from the U.S. approach to ABE and offers advantages and disadvantages. The extraordinary learner-focused approach can be seen as a benefit, likely to improve motivation and retention. However, it can also make measurement of progress difficult, and it is challenging to link ABE to wider outcomes (St. Clair & Belzer, 2007).

Turning to countries with a different economic and social base from the United States, China is facing some intriguing issues in the development of adult literacy and numeracy

among its population. The issue has been recognized as important since the founding of the Republic in 1949 (Goudong, 1999) and, according to official statistics, has had a major effect on literacy rates. In 1949, 80% of the population was illiterate; by 1990, 16% were considered illiterate (Goudong, 1999); and by 2006, this rate was 7%, with more than 99% of youth considered literate (UNESCO, 2008). A number of key strategies have contributed to this result, including the creation of universal primary schooling and development of special programs for women and ethnic minorities (Goudong, 1999).

One particularly notable aspect of the Chinese approach is the commitment to "prevent first, eradicate second, and upgrade third" (Goudong, 1999, p.72). This has meant putting universal primary schooling in place to reduce the number of people growing up without literacy instruction, making sure that older people who need it return to education, and creating opportunities for further study throughout the population. There is a well-developed interest in ensuring that ABE is relevant by providing instruction in areas of real-life concern to learners such as hygiene, nutrition, and animal care.

The major issues currently facing China concern the literacy gap between rural and urban populations. The coastal cities are developing economically very rapidly and attracting many workers from rural areas. The rural workers often find that they are undereducated for work in the city, however. This creates a policy quandary—is it better to provide upgrading in rural areas before people move to the city or to provide ABE in the cities for newly arrived workers, even though they are often unemployed and worse off than they would be in their villages of origin?

In the United States, Scotland, and China, adult literacy education is used to ameliorate the problem of people who are not well served by universal primary education. In several countries of sub-Saharan Africa, however, primary schooling is not universal, and even when available, it tends to involve older children. For many people in these countries, ABE is their first educational experience, with implications for the type of teaching and learning that is valued and the significance of literacy and numeracy.

For example, one study of classes in Namibia and South Africa (Papen, 2005) found that learners wanted to have ABE delivered in ways that were as school-like as possible. They were not interested in real-life materials or everyday literacy practices, which they saw as imposed on them and uninteresting. They tended to want a teacher-led pedagogy, often in the language of colonization rather than the indigenous language. It is interesting to note that in a country where literacy is not common, instrumental instruction using a skills-based approach is highly valued.

These three examples, lightly sketched though they are, usefully bring forward some of the judgments and balances inherent to ABE provision. They raise questions of how open the curriculum should be; how ABE can best, and most responsibly, serve national economic needs and individual needs; and how literacy education changes its nature in the face of an altered educational marketplace. In the United States, where the provision of ABE has been stable for some time, there may be a need to re-engage with questions such as these in order to create new opportunities for innovative practices.

New Influences and Challenges

A number of issues are likely to grow in importance to the ABE field over the next few years. One important influence is migration. Despite political caution about immigration, particularly across the southern border of the United States, the country still has more than a million people each year attaining naturalized status (Homeland Security, 2008). About 100,000 of these citizens originate in South America alone, with 360,000 from Asia and 41,000 from Russia. This is important for ABE because of the way English as a Second Language instruction (ESL) is delivered in many states. A typical pattern is for people who speak very little English to be in ESL classes until they have basic competence in English and then to transfer into ABE. Even though these learners may be relatively fluent speakers of English, they often have different literacy needs and challenges than native speakers who have attended years of schooling in the United States. These differences create new challenges for ABE instructors, which they often must try to address with limited training and professional development.

This situation creates key questions about which there is still little knowledge. For example, how does learning literacy in a second language interact with first-language literacy? Many immigrants are highly literate in their first language, with professional and advanced degrees. How does this play out in the ABE classroom, especially when they are in the same classroom as people with very limited first-language literacy? To what extent is ABE for skilled immigrants a public responsibility? These questions, and many related ones, would benefit from attention from policy makers and researchers.

The recent push in education toward evidence-based practice is also likely to bear on ABE. Currently, little research knowledge in the field can be considered solidly evidence based (Belzer & St. Clair, 2005), creating a tendency to import research findings from early-reading research with children. This is a troubling phenomenon, as there is not enough evidence to know how legitimate this strategy is. In addition, the possibility of evidence-led frameworks leading to a single "best practices" model of ABE must be considered critically. A universal model would reduce diversity and responsiveness in the field, as well as potentially limiting teaching practices. Although it is appealing to think that we can have definitive knowledge about ABE learners and concretely know how best to teach them, it is important to keep the variety of learner backgrounds, experiences, desires, and needs in the foreground. This diversity should preclude one best way to support their learning.

A further potential influence is the creation of skills-based programming in ABE. England has gone a long way in this direction, with clearly identified pragmatic competencies mapped onto a qualification framework; Canada is currently adopting a system of essential skills. It would be a challenge for the U.S. ABE instructional workforce to deal with a relatively rigid structure involving high levels of instructional uniformity, but it would be surprising if this international trend were not to have some influence on practice. In many ways, being able to point to a set of skill-based outcomes offers a solution to the questions about the value of ABE, although experience elsewhere suggests that it comes at the cost of administrative workload and reduced instructional autonomy, with little evidence of positive outcomes at the societal or individual levels (St. Clair & Belzer, 2007).

Finally, it is important to acknowledge the influence of the nature of the workforce on the field. The fact that instructors are often part-time contract workers and volunteers makes it extremely difficult to strengthen policy implementation and practice of any kind. Instructors typically have limited access to professional development, and given the turnover of instructional staff, it would be difficult to deliver it systematically and comprehensively. There have been discussions on this issue for many years, although entrenched positions and practices have prevented a great deal of structural development (Shanahan, Meehan, & Mogge, 1994); this makes significant change seem unlikely.

CONCLUSION

ABE is an area of adult and continuing education that remains marked by diversity and responsiveness, albeit in tension with increasingly significant standardizing factors. The current, relatively static nature of ABE provision is not underpinned by systemic stability, as in other areas of education, but by retrenchment of the resources investments of the 1990s combined with the lack of any overarching professional or other organizing body capable of bringing about field-driven change.

The field still faces difficult questions, however, to do with both means and ends. ABE suffers from ambivalent policy support, with funding set at levels that enable continuation but rule out substantial development. When combined with a strong policy agenda, this produces a situation where control of objectives and the preferred strategies to address them can be very distant from practice. ABE as an educational activity is as vital, interesting, and complex as ever, but its survival as a field remains uncertain.

REFERENCES

Action Aid. (2006). *Reflect.* Retrieved July 13, 2008, from http://www.actionaid.org/main.aspx?PageID=128

Andrews, H. (2002). Focus on the GED: Who takes it and why? *Southern Regional Education Board Focus*, pp. 1–4.

Barton, D. (1994). *Literacy: An introduction to the ecology of written language.* Oxford, UK: Blackwell.

Barton, D., Hamilton, M., & Ivanic, R. (2000). *Situated literacies: Reading and writing in context.* New York: Routledge.

Belzer, A. (2003). *Living with it: Federal policy implementation in adult basic education. The cases of the workforce investment act and welfare reform* (NCSALL Report No. 24). Cambridge, MA: National Center for the Study of Adult Learning and Literacy.

Belzer, A., & St. Clair, R. (2003). *Opportunities and limits: An update on Adult Literacy Education.* Columbus, OH: ERIC Clearinghouse on Adult, Career, and Vocational Education.

Belzer, A., & St. Clair, R. (2005). Back to the future: Implications of the neo-positivist research agenda for adult education. *Teachers College Record, 107*(9), 1393–1412.

Belzer, A., & St. Clair, R. (2007). The world touches the classroom: Using "anthropolicy" to understand political, economic, and social effects on adult literacy education. . In B. J. Guzzetti (Ed.), *Literacy for the 21st century: Adult literacy* (pp. 17–35). Westport, CT: : Praeger.

Boulden, W. T. (2008). Evaluation of the Advancing Young Adult Learning Project. *Adult Basic and Literacy Education Journal, 2*(1), 3–12.

Center for Literacy Studies. (2004). *Equipped for the future.* Retrieved July 13, 2008, from *http://eff.cls.utk.edu/*

Comings, J., & Cuban, S. (2007). Supporting the persistence of adult basic education students. In A. Belzer (Ed.), *Toward defining and improving quality in adult basic education.* Mahwah, NJ: Lawrence Erlbaum.

Darling-Hammond. (2004). Standards, accountability, and school reform. *Teachers College Record, 106*(6), 1047–1085.

Department for Innovation, Universities and Skills. (n.d.). *Adult literacy core curriculum: Entry 1. The national standards and level descriptors.* Retrieved July 13, 2008, at http://www.dfes.gov .uk/curriculum_literacy/

Fingeret, A. (1984). *Adult literacy education: Current and future directions* (ED246308, Vol. 284). Columbus: Ohio State University, ERIC Clearinghouse on Adult, Career, and Vocational Education.

Fingeret, A. (1993). *Adult literacy education: Current and future directions. An update* (Vol. 355). Columbus: Ohio State University, Center on Education and Training for Employment.

Fingeret, A., & Jurmo, P. (Eds.). (1989). *Participatory literacy education.* New Directions in Literacy Education, No. 42). San Francisco: Jossey-Bass.

Freire, P. (1972). *Pedagogy of the oppressed.* Harmondsworth, UK: Penguin.

Gaber-Katz, E., & Watson, G. M. (1991). *The land that we dream of . . . : A participatory study of community-based literacy.* Toronto, Ontario: OISE Press.

Gee, J. (2001). Identity as an analytic lens for research in education. In W. Secada (Ed.), *Review of research in education* (Vol. 25). Washington, DC: American Educational Research Association.

Gonzales, N. (2006, August 21). High school students turn to GED after exit test failure. *Oakland Tribune.* Retrieved from http://findarticles.com/p/articles/mi_qn4176/is_20060821/ai_n16674521/.

Goudong, X. (1999). Study on literacy programs in China. *PAACE Journal of Lifelong Learning, 8,* 71–75.

Hayes, E. R. (2000). Youth in adult literacy education programs. *Annual Review of Adult Learning and Literacy, 1,* 74–110.

Homeland Security. (2008). *Yearbook of immigration statistics: 2007.* Washington, DC: Author.

Imel, S. (2000). Welfare to work: Considerations for adult and vocational education programs. *ERIC Digest, 217.*

Kruidenier, J. (2002). *Research-based principles for adult basic education reading instruction.* Portsmouth, NH: RMC Research.

Kutner, M., Greenberg, E., Jin, Y., Boyle, B., Hsu, Y., & Dunleavy, E. (2007). *Literacy in everyday life: Results from the 2003 National Assessment of Adult Literacy.* Retrieved July 29, 2008, from http://nces.ed.gov//Pubs2007/2007480.pdf

Lytle, S., & Wolfe, M. (1989). *Adult literacy education: Program evaluation and learner assessment* (Vol. 338). Columbus: Ohio State University, ERIC Clearinghouse on Adult, Career, and Vocational Education.

Lytle, S. V., Belzer, A., & Reumann, R. (1992). *Invitations to inquiry: Rethinking staff development in adult education* (Technical report TR92–02, ED355388). Philadelphia: University of Pennsylvania, National Center on Adult Literacy.

Marriott, M. (1993, June 15). Valuable diploma or meaningless piece of paper? *New York Times.* Retrieved from http://www.nytimes.com/1993/06/15/nyregion/valuable-diploma-or-meaningless-piece-of-paper.html

Merriam, S., & Caffarella, R. (1999). *Learning in adulthood: A complete guide.* San Francisco: Jossey-Bass.

Merrifield, J. (1998). *Contested ground: Performance accountability in adult basic education* (NCSALL Report No. 1). Cambridge, MA: National Center for the Study of Adult Learning and Literacy.

Merrifield, J. (2005). Why England should look north for inspiration. *Reflect 4.*

Papen, U. (2005). Literacy and development: What works for whom? or, how relevant is the social practices view of literacy for literacy education in developing countries? *International Journal of Educational Development 25,* 5–17.

Perin, D., Flugman, B., & Spiegel, S. (2006). Last chance gulch: Youth participation in urban adult basic education programs. *Adult Basic Education Journal, 16*(3), 171–188.

Quigley, B. A. (1997). *Rethinking literacy education: The critical need for practice-based change.* San Francisco: Jossey-Bass.

Rogers, R., & Kramer, M. A. (2007). *Adult education teachers: Developing critical practice.* Mahwah, NJ: Lawrence Erlbaum.

Sandlin, J. A., & Cervero, R. M. (2003). Contradictions and compromise: The curriculum-in-use as negotiated ideology in two welfare-to-work classes. *International Journal of Lifelong Education, 22*(3), 249–265.

Shanahan, T., Meehan, M., & Mogge, S. (1994). *The professionalization of the adult literacy teacher* (NCAL Brief BP94–01). Philadelphia: National Center on Adult Literacy.

Smith, R. A. (1990). *Learning to learn across the life-span.* San Francisco: Jossey Bass.

St. Clair, R. (2002). Stemming criterion bleed: Evaluating literacy education on its own terms. *Adult Basic Education 12*(2), 67–81.

St. Clair, R., & Belzer, A. (2007). The challenges of consistency: National systems for assessment and accountability in adult literacy ducation. In P. Campbell (Ed.), *Assessment practices in adult basic education* (pp. 159–206). Edmonton, Alberta: Grassroots Press.

Street, B. V. (1984). *Literacy in theory and practice.* Cambridge: University of Cambridge.

Street, B. (1993). *Cross-cultural approaches to literacy.* New York: Cambridge University Press.

UNESCO. (2008). *UIS statistics in brief: Education in China.* Montreal, Quebec: UNESCO Institute for Statistics.

U.S. Department of Education, Division of Adult Education and Literacy. (2006). *Adult education and family literacy act, program year 2003–2004, report to congress.* Washington, DC: Author.

Warner, K. (2007). Against the narrowing of perspectives: How do we see learning, prisons and prisoners? *Journal of Correctional Education, 58*(2), 170–183.

18

ENGLISH LANGUAGE LEARNING
FOR ADULTS

CLARENA LARROTTA

The Economic Opportunity Act of 1964 authorized instruction toward the elimination of adult illiteracy. As a result, services for English learners (ELs) within the federally funded adult education system were established (Burt, Fischer, & Peyton, 2003). Forty years later, and due to the constant change in population in the United States, almost half of the students enrolled in adult basic education (ABE) and general education development (GED) programs are ELs. The Center for Adult English Language Acquisition (2007) reports that during 2004 to 2005, a total of "2,581,281 adults were enrolled in adult education programs. Of these, 44.3% were enrolled in English as a Second Language (ESL) programs. University and college students, as well as the many adults served in programs not receiving federal funding, are not included in this number." This increase in demand for ESL instruction has attracted the attention of policy makers, adult educators, and researchers (Burt, Fischer, et al., 2003; Orem, 2005).

The U.S. Census Bureau (2003) reports that in 2003 the foreign-born population in the United States reached 3 million (or 11% of the total population). Out of this group, 53% were from Latin America, 25% were Asian/Pacific Islanders, 14% were Europeans, and 8.0% were from other world areas. Year after year, the foreign-born population keeps growing, and this change is reflected in the ABE and GED classrooms. This ongoing change in student characteristics and their needs calls for a change in adult instruction practices. ABE and GED classrooms can no longer be considered monolingual classrooms.

The need for ESL instruction in ABE and GED programs keeps increasing. For example, Borden and Talavera (2007) explain that they designed a special ESL course in their ABE program to address this need. These authors describe in detail the implementation of an ESL course designed to prepare their adult students to transition successfully into ABE classes. In addition, Mathews-Aydinli (2006) discusses research-based strategies for the ESL classroom to support ELs transition to postsecondary education. Adult ESL education has become a social issue and a matter that requires immediate attention. "The number of adult immigrants who need to improve their English language and literacy skills, gain citizenship, and move from adult education and adult ESL programs to higher education and increased work opportunities is on the rise" (Crandall, Ingersoll, & Lopez, 2008).

In this chapter, we will review the state of adult ESL teaching and learning in the United States. First, a description of the English learners (ELs) in adult ESL classes will be provided. This description will lead to exploring the different adult ESL programs and settings. After describing the students and the teaching/learning settings, we will discuss the nature of ESL and second-language acquisition (SLA). This will be followed by a review of current research and teaching practices in the field. Next, we will consider the implication of adult ESL as a profession and the challenges we may encounter in the field. Finally, a brief overview of what we might expect for the future aims to encourage ESL educators and other professionals in the field to continue this conversation.

Who Are the English Learners in Adult ESL Classes?

Contrary to the stereotypical view portraying immigrants as poor, undocumented, and uneducated, the population of adult ELs is very diverse in terms of legal status, educational background, length of time in the United States, age, the native language they speak, socioeconomic status, cultural practices, ethnicity, and goals (Burt, Fischer, et al., 2003; Center for Adult English Language Acquisition, 2007). Brickman and Nuzzo (1999) classify this population of adults into foreign-born immigrants and U.S.-born adults whose native language is not English. These researchers explain that "many ESL programs teach two distinct nonnative populations: those students who are residents and those internationals who have temporary student visas" (p. 3). Although Brickman and Nuzzo do not explain their use of the term *resident*, it suggests *immigration status;* in other words, a person living in the United States is either a legal resident or an undocumented immigrant. For the purpose of this chapter, the term *residents* will be used interchangeably with the term *immigrants* to encompass legal immigrants and undocumented immigrants living in the United States who are enrolled in adult ESL classes.

From Brickman and Nuzzo's (1999) point of view, depending on the ESL program (academic, nonacademic) and the institution (community college, university, private language institute, or nonprofit), an ESL instructor may encounter two different populations of students: International students or residents. International ESL students are visitors and have a clear idea of when they want to go back to their countries. They come to the United States to obtain a degree or to study English; they retain their culture and have *instrumental motivation* to learn English. Instrumental motivation implies learning English to achieve a specific goal (e.g., pass a test, enroll at school, deliver a speech, accomplish a task). International ESL students want to learn English for self-improvement or to obtain a degree from a U.S. university because it provides prestige when they return to their countries.

On the other hand, residents or immigrant ESL students, in most cases, have left their countries permanently or do not know exactly when they will return. Their motivation to learn English is *integrative.* In other words, immigrant ESL students want to acculturate and adapt to the new community and society. They want to learn English to become part of the daily economy, culture, and society in the United States. Immigrants want to learn English in an effort to seek opportunities for a better life; they want to obtain a better job, to help their children with homework, and to communicate with the people in their community because these activities are essential to them as residents.

Another group in need of adult ESL services has been recently identified in community colleges and universities as *generation 1.5.* Harklau, Losey, and Siegal (1999) describe this group of students as U.S.-born bilingual adults who have graduated from high school but whose English reading and writing skills are not sufficiently developed to allow them to pass classes that require academic reading and writing at a college level. These students have limited or no reading and writing skills in their family's native language. Harklau (2003) explains that:

> Equipped with social skills in English, generation 1.5 students often appear in conversation to be native English speakers. However, they are usually less skilled in the academic language associated with school achievement, especially in the area of writing. Academic writing requires familiarity with complex linguistic structures and rhetorical styles that are not typically used in everyday social interactions.

Generation 1.5 students' language learning needs are very different from those of international students and foreign-born immigrants.

In summary, the adult ESL student population is made up of a multifaceted group of people with different learning needs and backgrounds. For resident and generation 1.5 students, not being fully proficient in English means failing at accessing good job opportunities, social status, sociopolitical participation, and higher education. Regardless of the program or learning setting providing adult ESL instruction, it is very important that all ESL instructors be aware of the different needs of the adult ESL learners they serve.

ESL PROGRAMS AND SETTINGS

Adult ELs are served through a variety of programs such as English for speakers of other languages (ESOL), ABE, and adult secondary education (ASE). These classes are offered through public and private organizations such as federally funded institutions, private language schools, and academic institutions. Adult ESL programs vary in scope and content:

> Some programs, especially those for recent arrivals including refugees, emphasize survival or life skills in the curriculum and focus on improving listening and speaking abilities (oral proficiency). Others stress vocational or work-related topics, citizenship and civics education, family literacy, or academic or GED preparation. Others focus on developing basic literacy skills. (Center for Adult English Language Acquisition, 2007)

Depending on the focus of the program, a wide range of instructional practices is offered to adult ELs. To maximize learning opportunities while accommodating the realities and constraints of adult learners' lives, adult ESL programs need to offer classes that vary in terms of scheduling, location, duration, and content (Burt, Fischer, et al., 2003).

As mentioned before, adult ELs come to the ESL classroom with different learning goals and needs and from a variety of backgrounds; as a result, adult ESL classes range from one-on-one tutoring to small and large classes, depending on the institution and the source of funding. For example, general ESL classes focus on the English language skills that adults need to function in their community and perform everyday life tasks. Family ESL literacy programs focus on the language learning needs of the family members (parents and children) and often have a parenting instruction component. Civics ESL programs address civil rights, citizenship, and

sociopolitical participation. Vocational ESL programs help students develop the necessary skills for obtaining a job. Workplace ESL programs focus on teaching specialized language that ELs will need to use at their workplace. Community college ESL classes help ELs to gain access into higher education, to improve their job skills, or to develop English as a survival skill. Adult academic English programs focus on study skills, cultural awareness, and acquisition of the language level required at the university/college level. These programs focus on preparing students to be able to read large amounts of academic material in English, understand lectures given in English, and communicate their ideas using academic language orally and in writing.

There are different types of English for academic purpose (EAP) classes/programs. For example, English for specific purposes (ESP) programs have traditionally focused on preparing professionals to be able to understand and use literature written/published in English specific to their professional fields. As reported by Johns and Price-Machado (2001), at the present time, ESP instruction is offered in English-speaking countries through vocational ESL programs for residents, English for occupational purposes (EOP) for new immigrant and refugee populations, or in contexts emphasizing academic or business language. These researchers explain that

> ESP continues to be even more common in English as a *Foreign* Language (EFL) contexts [such as China], where an increasing number of adult students are eager to learn business English or academic English in order to pursue their careers or study in English-medium educational situations. (Johns & Price-Machado, 2001, p. 43)

Traditionally, ESP classes have been offered in universities around the world to undergraduate and graduate students in careers such as engineering, mathematics, computing science, medicine, and technology. However, Belcher (2006) clarifies that ESP's growing body of research and theory suggests that ESP has recently expanded to include a diverse range of purposes,

> from the better known EAP and occupational purposes (EOP), the latter including business, medicine, law, but also such fields as shipbuilding and aviation, to the more specific-mission-oriented ESP . . . English for socio-cultural

purposes, for example, for AIDS education, family literacy, and citizenship, or for those with highly specialized needs, such as learners who are incarcerated or who have a disability. (p. 134)

ESP is no longer exclusive of formal academic settings. A possible explanation for this might be that ESP instruction focuses on problems unique to specific learners in specific contexts with the final goal of providing English instruction tailored to address those problems. Nevertheless, regardless of the setting in which ESP classes are offered, some characteristics are essential to the practice of ESP: needs assessment, content-based teaching methods, and content area-informed instructors (Belcher, 2006; Johns & Price-Machado, 2001). EFL is another popular form of English instruction. EFL is the study or learning of English in an environment where English is not already the predominant language, such as in a non–English-speaking country, by someone whose first language is not English. EFL classes are taught at different formal institutions, such as schools, colleges, private language institutes, and universities around the world.

Going back to the topic of ESP, it should be noted that workplace ESL is another possibility for the teaching and learning of English. Workplace ESL is offered through three venues: workplace-based programs, vocational ESL programs, and adult ESL programs. Each makes an important contribution to the options available to immigrants entering or in the workforce (Burt, 2007). To maximize effectiveness of learning in each of these programs, whether conducted as pre-employment training or on the job, six inter-related activities are suggested by the Center for Adult English Language Acquisition (2007):

1. Conducting a *needs analysis* of the language, cultural knowledge, and specific skills needed to perform successfully in a specific workplace or occupation

2. Developing a *curriculum* based on the objectives, which identifies tasks and skills for verbal interaction and for reading and writing on the job

3. Making *instruction* plans including materials that learners will use in the workplace and classroom activities and opportunities for learners to develop knowledge and skills and to put their skills in practice outside the classroom

4. Determining *instructional strategies* that include a variety of activities that focus on the objectives

5. *Evaluating* the program on both a formative and summative basis

6. *Collaborating* with other programs and instructional staff (e.g., adult ESL program and vocational ESL program staff) to provide all of the services needed so that adult immigrants have access to and the opportunity to be successful in workforce preparation programs that provide them with the skills and credentials needed to obtain work that pays a living wage

ESL and Second-Language Acquisition

ESL refers to the study or learning of English in an environment where English is the predominant language by someone whose first language is not English. The term *adult ESL* is used to describe various types of instructional services for adults who do not speak English (Center for Adult English Language Acquisition, 2007). However, it is important to keep in mind that language acquisition and language learning are two different but closely related terms. A language is acquired through the spontaneous communication product of daily life interactions, using the language in different situations such as interacting with neighbors, going shopping, listening to music, watching movies, or reading for pleasure. A language is learned through the conscious process of studying it and usually as a result of some sort of formal education (Krashen, 2003).

Moss and Ross-Feldman (2003) describe second-language acquisition (SLA) as the study of how second languages are learned and the factors that influence the process. Brown (2000) further explains:

SLA is a subset of general human learning, involves cognitive variations, is closely related to one's personality type, is interwoven with second culture learning, and involves interference, the creation of new linguistic systems, and the learning of discourse and communicative functions of language. (p. 271)

There is no unified theory of SLA; researchers from different disciplines (e.g., psycholinguistics,

linguistics, sociology, anthropology) have proposed different theories explaining how a second language is acquired or learned. In addition, SLA researchers examine how *communicative competence* (the ability to interpret the underlying meaning of a message, understand cultural references, use strategies to keep communication from breaking down, and apply the rules of grammar) develops in a second language (Savignon, 1997).

The area of SLA has traditionally focused on how children acquire language. However, recently, with the increase of ELs and the increasing demand for effective ESL instruction for adults, researchers and adult educators have identified the need to shift our attention into studying how adults acquire language. Yet, research in the area of adult SLA has focused on populations in postsecondary educational settings with little SLA research in nonacademic settings (Johnson, 2001; Moss & Ross-Feldman, 2003).

In describing ESL in adult and community-based programs serving primarily adult ELs with literacy needs, Johnson (2001) states that research in these settings has been primarily observational. According to this author, research has focused on moving adults from proficiency in their first language to the ability to function in the second language as full participants in society and on programmatic issues rather than linguistic processes. However, it is also important to understand that conducting research in adult ESL is a challenge. Moss and Ross-Feldman (2003) further explain:

> Investigating issues of culture, language, and education and tracking learner progress over time are not easy [tasks] when complicated by diverse and mobile learner populations and varied learning contexts (e.g., workplace classes, general ESL classes, family literacy classes).

Explaining and predicting how adults learn a second language remains an important area to be investigated (Ellis, 1997; Johnson, 2001; Moss & Ross-Feldman, 2003).

Several researchers agree that it is imperative for teachers to get involved in the process of identifying issues that need attention in the classroom and conduct classroom-based research (Delamont, 1992; Ellis, 1997; Kincheloe, 2003; Loughran, Mitchell, & Mitchell, 2002). Ellis (1997) argues that ESL teachers need to go beyond experimenting and testing other people's ideas in their classrooms:

"Teachers need to engage in the process of conceptual evaluation in order to identify research problems. A familiarity with SLA, then, can help teachers shape problems [they encounter in the ESL classroom] in a way that makes them researchable" (p. 35). Ellis recommends that teachers use SLA theory as a resource to give shape to their research questions and study questions derived from their teaching experience: "It [SLA] can provide teachers with information about the kinds of instruments and procedures they will need to use in order to collect and analyze data" (p. 35). In other words, the suggestion is that teachers use SLA as a tool to support classroom-based research.

CURRENT RESEARCH AND TEACHING PRACTICES

Research seems to support many practices that are currently employed in adult ESL instruction (Moss & Ross-Feldman, 2003). Current teaching practice favors sociocultural approaches to teaching ESL while promoting community building and relationship building between ESL teachers and students (Larrotta & Brooks, 2009). The recent trend in adult ESL is to humanize the teaching/learning process and to facilitate students learning in context while connecting to their lives outside the classroom. In general, researchers believe that language is best learned through social interaction and when learners use the new language for social communication (Gee, 2007; Lantolf, 2006). For example, Florez and Burt (2001) suggest identifying individual, pair, or group projects to help students learn ESL. Using a variety of group work techniques and providing the students with opportunities to interact among themselves, build relationships, and have a good rapport with their instructor, contribute to fostering a safe learning environment and offer the students different possibilities to learn ESL in a communicative and meaningful way. Fleet (2006) recommends incorporating the teaching of culture in the ESL and the EFL classroom starting on the first day. Fleet provides a complete list of class activities and possibilities for helping adult ESL students learn about the target culture. Ullman (1997) elaborates on the importance of understanding how adult ESL learners develop their social identity as they adapt to the new culture and community. Ullman explains that immigrating to a new country affects a person's social identity and requires a readjustment in many different areas of the person's life.

Celce-Murcia (2001) presents communicative language teaching as a student-centered teaching approach. However, "while involvement in communicative events is seen as central to language development, this involvement necessarily requires attention to form" (Celce-Murcia, 2001, p. 25). In other words, the formal aspect of language learning (e.g., the teaching of grammar, vocabulary, and pronunciation) is not overlooked; it is a central part of ESL teaching and learning. For example, some researchers recommend the use of extensive reading (reading large amounts), free voluntary reading (reading because we want to read and without having to report to anyone), and reading for pleasure as possible activities encouraging both communicative language teaching approach and academic ESL learning (Burt, Peyton, & Adams, 2003; Grabe, 2009; Krashen, 2003).

Research suggests that extensive reading, free voluntary reading, and reading for pleasure favor incidental vocabulary learning, the vocabulary we acquire without intentionally sitting down to study. Gass and Selinker (1999) point out that "incidental vocabulary" learning is an effective way of enhancing learners' vocabulary. In the same vein, Gee (2007) believes that "the only way that poor readers can catch up in vocabulary is by doing lots of reading, especially because teaching vocabulary out of context of reading is not very effective" (p. 149). For Gee, reading is an instructed process that works best when it happens as a cultural process. In other words, reading should be taught as connected to the discourses in which learners wish to join: "Learning to read cannot be a generic process . . . it must be a cultural process—learning to use literacy to become and be a certain type of person with other people" (p. 154). In summary, current ESL research points to the need of finding a balance between theory and practice by adapting language learning theory to the classroom context and the learners' needs. These learners' needs are in relation to their communities, identities, cultures, and work environments and are not just the artificial learning needs created within the limitations of the classroom.

Some researchers recommend the following instructional strategies when working with adult ESL learners (Burt, Fischer, et al.,

2003; Celce-Murcia, 2001; Wrigley, Condelli, & Lundmark, 1999):

1. Get to know your students and their needs; begin with assessment of learners' needs and goals.

2. Incorporate principles of adult learning, adult SLA, and working with multicultural groups; model what you expect the students to do and use a variety of teaching/learning techniques.

3. Use scaffolding techniques to support tasks; acknowledge and draw on learners' prior experiences and knowledge.

4. Bring authentic materials to the classroom; incorporate content that is relevant to the lives of the students in your classroom.

5. Balance variety and routine in your activities; involve learners and their input in planning; include ongoing opportunities for assessment and evaluation.

Adult ESL as a Profession

With the increase of the adult EL population and the need for English instruction in ABE and GED programs, the demand for qualified adult ESL teachers has also increased. Therefore, it is of crucial importance that adult ESL teachers gain knowledge and become familiar with SLA theory and the history of language teaching and learning trends (Brown, 2000; Celce-Murcia, 2001). Research points out that sustained, systematic, high-quality professional development has a larger impact on the professional development of adult ESL teachers than one-day workshops (Center for Adult English Language Acquisition & Center for Applied Linguistics, 2008; Crandall et al., 2008; Florez, 1997).

Crandall et al. (2008) and Peyton (2005) present *professional standards* as an effort to professionalize adult ESL education. They explain that *content standards* provide guidance for educators on what students should know and be able to do as a result of instruction. *Program standards* identify the characteristics of effective programs, providing guidance on areas such as curriculum, staffing, professional development, and facilities. *Teacher standards* identify the knowledge and skills that adult ESL teachers need to develop and acquire. Therefore, Crandall et al. (2008) present certification and credentialing of adult ESL educators as two approaches contributing to the effort of professionalizing adult ESL teaching. These researchers examine the requirements for teaching adult ESL in the different states of the United States and provide a list of teacher certification programs that focus on adult ESL education.

Similarly, a report by the National Center for ESL Literacy Education (2002) summarizes the characteristics of effective professional development efforts to include: (a) building teachers' knowledge in the areas of adult learning principles, SLA processes, effective second-language teaching approaches, and techniques for working with multicultural groups; (b) exploring continued, ongoing professional development formats; (c) using technology-based approaches to offer professional development options that optimize financial resources and reach a variety of programs and teachers; (d) promoting reflective practice and professional community-building opportunities such as mentoring and practitioner research; and (e) developing new models for credentialing and certification. Furthermore, Hawk (2000) presents distance-learning opportunities available via the Internet to ESL teachers. This author examines the details of online professional development opportunities, including discussion lists, chat groups, online newspapers and journals, ESL lesson plans, instructional activities and curricula, staff development materials, Web sites of ESL organizations and institutions, and Web portals.

In summary, professional development for ESL teachers should integrate research and practice in SLA, incorporate technology into ESL teaching and teacher preparation, and include professional standards in terms of content, program, and teaching. It is important that adult ESL teachers are provided with a variety of opportunities to keep up to date in their field. Doing this will in turn elevate the status of adult ESL teaching in ABE, GED, and adult ESL literacy programs.

CHALLENGES IN THE FIELD OF ADULT ESL

This section addresses some of the challenges that educators and researchers face in the field of adult ESL. For example, establishing a direct connection between SLA theory and the practice that takes place in the adult ESL classroom seems to be a big concern of many (Yates & Muchisky, 2003). Too many needs to serve and the diversity of learners, programs, and settings add to the complexity of adult ESL instruction. Therefore, creating curricula that incorporate and address students' needs is also a challenge. It is important to point out that challenges vary according to the ESL context, setting, and program, with different issues facing basic education, higher education, and workplace instruction.

Improving the status of the teaching of ESL in ABE and GED programs to attract more teachers to join the field of ESL is also a challenge.

> Many adult ESL teachers express a feeling that the field itself has a low status. Practitioners often work in cramped conditions with limited resources and materials. Most adult ESL teachers are part-time, hourly employees with minimal or no employment benefits. (National Center for ESL Literacy Education, 2002, p. 3)

Providing continual preparation and professional development to these teachers might be a solution. This implies the creation of more accessible opportunities for adult ESL teachers to be equipped with the tools they need in order to serve ELs from a variety of cultural backgrounds and their different language-learning needs.

Teacher training and professional development is another area that needs attention because many teachers lack adequate preparation in TESOL (teaching English to speakers of other languages) (Yates & Muchisky, 2003). Moreover, "a wide range of instructional contexts and content focuses (e.g., workplace, academic, nonacademic, life skills, and volunteer programs) make uniform professional development challenging" (National Center for ESL Literacy Education, 2002, p. 3). ESL teachers need to know about SLA theory and how it is applied in the adult classroom (Celce-Murcia, 2001). Understanding how first language is acquired and knowing how their students' native language works could help ESL teachers serve their students better (Brown, 2000; Yates & Muchisky, 2003).

Finally, there is a need for more private initiatives offering adult ESL instruction. This is particularly challenging in the area of workplace ESL. As stated by Burt (2003), few employers offer ESL instruction because of scheduling problems, the cost it represents, a mistaken perception that it is not beneficial to the organization, and not feeling responsible for ESL training of their employees. Because funding has always been an issue in ESL instruction provided through ABE and GED programs, it is crucial that the private sector contributes to this endeavor. Other types of private adult ESL instruction initiatives, different from workplace instruction, need to emerge.

THE FUTURE OF ADULT ESL

In 2007, 93,840 adults were on waiting lists nationwide for publicly funded ABE and literacy classes, including ESL (National Adult Education Professional Development Consortium, 2007). The near future will bring a larger demand for adult ESL instruction. Nevertheless, formal English instruction may be only part of the process of learning English for immigrants; economic integration, access to the labor market, and social inclusion are also important factors in English language acquisition (McHugh, Gelatt, & Fix, 2007). Immigrants who can speak English are more often employed and are compensated in a more lucrative manner (Chiswick & Taengnoi, 2007). Clearly, immigrants are aware of the importance of being proficient in English as instrumental in making the American dream come true. They are motivated to learn English, and the demand is larger than the capacity to fulfill their needs for ESL instruction.

We can expect an explosion of certificate programs for adult ESL teachers as an effort to professionalize the field. It is evident that we need more teacher preparation options and continual, systematic teacher development possibilities in order to have more qualified teachers and attract more ESL teachers to join us in the field.

However, we will need to make sure that ESL teacher preparation programs include multicultural preparation of these teachers so that they are able to implement culturally responsive methodologies in the adult ESL classroom. We also need to understand what standardization of ESL means for teachers, adult ELs, programs, content delivered, and assessment. Finally, we will need to study social and technological changes affecting ESL teaching and learning. We will continue facing the need for more research focusing on how adults acquire and learn a second language.

CONCLUSION

The main goal of this chapter was to provide the reader with a broader perspective of what adult ESL entails within the context of the United States. We examined adult ELs, the programs they attend, current research and practice, and the challenges we face in the field. We learned that the demand for adult ESL instruction is large and will continue to increase. As a result, recruiting more ESL instructors is imperative and providing them with constant professional development is crucial. Practitioners need to learn about SLA theory and the theory informing language teaching. They need to become more aware of their role in implementing ESL theory and become good consumers by criticizing it and adapting theory to their students' needs and teaching context. They also need to give serious thought to contributing to the research explaining how adults learn a second language and the best practices to help them become successful language users. There is a lot to be done; policymakers, educators, and researchers will need to take action to make change and progress possible.

REFERENCES

Belcher, D. (2006). English for specific purposes: Teaching to perceived needs and imagined futures in worlds of work, study, and everyday life. *TESOL Quarterly, 40*(1), 133–156.

Borden, D., & Talavera, D. (2007). Creating a successful ESL to ABE transition class. *Texas Adult and Family Literacy Quarterly, 11*(1). Retrieved January 29, 2009, from http://www-tcall.tamu.edu/newsletr/apr07/apr07e.html

Brickman, B., & Nuzzo, R. (1999). *International versus immigrant ESL students: Designing curriculum and programs to meet the needs of both* (ERIC Document Reproduction Services No. ED426610).

Brown, D. H. (2000). *Principles of language learning and teaching* (4th ed.). White Plains, NY: Addison Wesley Longman.

Burt, M. (2003). *Issues in improving immigrant workers' English language skills.* ESL Resources: Digests. Retrieved January 29, 2009, from http://www.cal.org/caela/esl_resources/digests/Workplaceissues.html

Burt, M. (2007). *Workplace instruction and workforce preparation for adult immigrants*. Washington, DC: Center for Adult English Language Acquisition and Center for Applied Linguistics.

Burt, M., Fischer, L., & Peyton, J. K. (2003). *Adult English language instruction in the 21st century*. Washington, DC: The National Center for ESL Literacy and Center for Applied Linguistics.

Burt, M., Peyton, J. K., & Adams, R. (2003). *Reading and adult English language learners: A review of the research*. Washington, DC: Center for Applied Linguistics.

Celce-Murcia, M. (2001). *Teaching English as a second or foreign language* (3rd ed.). Carrboro, NC: Heinle & Heinle.

Center for Adult English Language Acquisition & Center for Applied Linguistics. (2008). *Framework for quality professional development for practitioners working with adult English language learners*. Washington, DC: Authors.

Center for Adult English Language Acquisition. (2007). *Frequently asked questions (FAQ # 20): What are factors to consider when planning for, setting up, and evaluating a workplace program for immigrant workers?* Retrieved January 29, 2009, from http://www.cal.org/caela/esl_resources/faqs.html#twenty#twenty

Chiswick, B. R., & Taengnoi, S. (2007). *Occupational choice of high-skilled immigrants in the United States*. Bonn, Germany: Institute for the Study of Labor.

Crandall, J., Ingersoll, G., & Lopez, J. (2008). *Adult ESL teacher credentialing and certification*. Washington, DC: Center for Applied Linguistics. Retrieved January 29, 2009, from http://www.cal.org/caela/esl_resources/briefs/tchrcred.html#

Delamont, S. (1992). *Fieldwork in educational settings: Methods, pitfalls, and perspectives*. London: Falmer Press.

Ellis, R. (1997). *SLA research and language teaching*. Oxford, UK: Oxford University Press.

Fleet, M. (2006). *The role of culture in second or foreign language teaching: Moving beyond the classroom experience* (ERIC Document Reproduction Services No. ED491716).

Florez, M. C. (1997). *The adult ESL teaching profession*. Washington, DC: National Clearinghouse for ESL Literacy Education. (ERIC Document Reproduction Service No. ED413794)

Florez, M. C., & Burt, M. (2001). *Beginning to work with adult English language learners: Some considerations*. Retrieved July 17, 2008, from ww.cal.org/caela/esl_resources/digests/beginQA.html

Gass, S. M., & Selinker, L. (1999). *Second language acquisition: An introductory course*. Mahwah, NJ: Lawrence Erlbaum.

Gee, J. P. (2007). Learning to read as a cultural process. In A. Belzer (Ed.), *Toward defining and improving quality in adult basic education* (pp. 141–157). Mahwah, NJ: Lawrence Erlbaum.

Grabe, W. (2009). *Reading in a second language: Moving from theory to practice*. New York: Cambridge University Press.

Harklau, L. (2003). *Generation 1.5 students and college writing*. Washington, DC: ERIC Clearinghouse on Languages and Linguistics. (ERIC Document Reproduction Service No. ED482491)

Harklau, L., Losey, K. M., & Siegal, M. (Eds.). (1999). *Generation 1.5 meets college composition: Issues in the teaching of writing to U.S.-educated learners of ESL*. Mahwah, NJ: Lawrence Erlbaum.

Hawk, W. (2000). *Online professional development for adult ESL educators*. Washington, DC: Center for Applied Linguistics. Retrieved January 29, 2009, from http://www.cal.org/ncle/DIGESTS

Johns, A. M., & Price-Machado, D. (2001). English for specific purposes: Tailoring courses to student needs and to the outside world. In M. Celce-Murcia (Ed.), *Teaching English as a Second or Foreign Language* (3rd ed., pp. 43–54). Carrboro, NC: Heinle & Heinle.

Johnson, D. (2001). *An annotated bibliography of second language acquisition in adult English language learners*. Washington, DC: National Center for Adult ESL Literacy Education (NCLE).

Kincheloe, J. L. (2003). *Teachers as researchers: Qualitative inquiry as a path to empowerment* (2nd ed.). London: Routledge Falmer Press.

Krashen, S. D. (2003). *Explorations in language acquisition and use*. Portsmouth, NH: Heinemann.

Lantolf, J. P. (2006). Sociocultural theory and L2: State of the art. *Studies in Second Language Acquisition (SSLA), 28*, 67–109.

Larrotta, C., & Brooks, A. K. (Eds.). (2009). *Bringing community to the adult ESL classroom*. New Directions for Adult and Continuing Education, 121. San Francisco: Jossey-Bass.

Loughran, J., Mitchell, I., & Mitchell, J. (2002). *Learning from teacher research*. New York: Teachers College Press.

Mathews-Aydinli, J. (2006). *Supporting adult English language learners' transitions to postsecondary education*. Washington, DC: Center of Adult English Language Acquisition. Retrieved January 29, 2009, from http://www.cal.org/CAELA/esl_resources/briefs/transition.html

McHugh, M., Gelatt, J., & Fix, M. (2007). *Adult English language instruction in the United States: Determining need and investing wisely.* Retrieved August 30, 2008, from http://www.migrationpolicy.org/pubs/NCIIP_English_Instruction073107.pdf

Moss, D., & Ross-Feldman, L. (2003). *Second language acquisition in adults: From research to practice.* Washington, DC: Center for Applied Linguistics. (ERIC Document Reproduction Service No. ED99-CO-0008)

National Adult Education Professional Development Consortium. (2007). *NAEPDC adult student waiting list survey results for program year 2005–2006.* Washington, DC: Author. Retrieved September 5, 2007, from www.naepdc.org/news_views_clues/Part%20II%202005–2006%20WAITING%20LIST%20PUBLISH.xls

National Center for ESL Literacy Education. (2002). *Professional development and adult English language instruction.* Washington, DC: (ERIC Document Reproduction Service No. ED461307)

Orem, R. A. (2005). *Teaching adult English language learners.* Malabar, FL: Krieger.

Peyton, J. K. (2005). *Using the ESL program standards to evaluate and improve adult ESL programs.* Washington, DC: Center for Applied Linguistics. Retrieved January 7, 2008, from www.cal.org/caela/esl_resources/briefs/eslprogstandards.html

Savignon, S. (1997). *Communicative competence: Theory and classroom practice.* New York: McGraw-Hill.

Ullman, C. (1997). *Social identity and the adult ESL classroom.* Washington, DC: Center for Adult English Language Acquisition. (ERIC Document Reproduction Service No. ED413795)

U.S. Census Bureau. (2003). *The foreign born population in the United States.* Washington, DC: Author.

Wrigley, H. S., Condelli, L., & Lundmark, V. (1999). "What works" study for adult ESL literacy students. *Manual from the Classroom Observation and Coding Guide.* Washington, DC: Literacywork International.

Yates, R., & Muchisky, D. (2003). On reconceptualizing teacher education. *TESOL Quarterly, 37*(1), 135–147.

19

ADULT EDUCATION FOR THE EMPOWERMENT OF INDIVIDUALS AND COMMUNITIES

ESTHER PRINS AND BRENDALY DRAYTON

*E*mpowerment has become a popular term in adult education practice, research, and policy. Teachers commonly assert that students become empowered by developing self-esteem. Researchers have shown how popular education can support collective action, for example, against repressive military regimes (Hammond, 1998). And policy makers claim that adult education empowers learners by helping them become more economically productive. These are substantially different conceptions of empowerment and the role of adult education in fostering it. Because empowerment is rarely specified, it demands careful definition and scrutiny. Grounded in a critical, multidisciplinary theoretical perspective, the purpose of this chapter is to analyze how adult education programs equip adults to exercise power individually and collectively in their daily lives, communities, and society, and to delineate the dilemmas inherent in such endeavors. In our theoretical overview, we argue that empowerment entails the exercise of power and therefore cannot be reduced to self-esteem or tokenistic participation. We then use organizational case studies to outline key forms of adult education for empowerment. Although we focus on organizations, we recognize that informal groups can use adult learning and education to achieve personal and collective ends (e.g., Johnson-Bailey, 2006). The chapter concludes by discussing salient challenges for educators.

THEORETICAL PERSPECTIVES OF EMPOWERMENT

Competing views of empowerment fall into three broad categories: functional, psychological, and critical. Rooted in the human capital tradition, the functional perspective defines empowerment as performing more efficiently in one's roles as a worker, citizen, and family member. In this view, adult education is believed to foster empowerment by equipping people with the skills needed to obtain higher wage employment, to improve their health, to help their children succeed academically, and to perform other functional tasks. This conceptualization, however, reflects a static rather than relational view of power relations (Robinson-Pant, 2004a) and fails to question traditional gender roles and other social hierarchies.

In the psychological approach, empowerment entails giving individuals a "voice" and increasing self-esteem and self-confidence—an emphasis consistent with the liberal humanist tradition of adult education. In professional discourse, this is what many educators mean by empowerment (LeCompte & deMarrais, 1992). Although self-respect and expression are crucial, conflating these capabilities with empowerment is overly narrow and individualistic.

Both these frameworks ignore power and the ways in which social structures constrain and enable our capacity to act. To address these shortcomings, we employ a critical perspective grounded in the radical adult education tradition. In this view, empowerment means understanding the causes of injustice and taking action to create more equitable conditions, not only individually but especially in concert with others. This is consistent with bell hooks's definition of agency as "the power to act on our own behalf to change a situation" (quoted in Daniell, 2003, p. 74).

Literature in adult education, citizen participation, and gender and development illuminates key dimensions of empowerment. According to Inglis (1997), adult education for *empowerment* aims to help "individuals attain greater economic, political, and social power" within the existing system, whereas adult education for *emancipation* seeks to transform social systems, particularly through collective action and social movements (p. 4). Transformative learning and critical reflection illustrate the former, whereas Freire's work and the Highlander Folk School (Horton & Freire, 1990) exemplify the latter. This chapter includes examples of both personal and social transformation through adult education.

The citizen participation literature suggests empowerment occurs through community organizing and development activities whereby citizens begin to exercise more control over decisions that affect them and "engage actively with others in the determination of their own affairs" (Gaventa, 1980, p. 18). In addition, empowerment means that citizens and adult learners are able to shape the organizations intended to serve their interests. These should be organizations *of, by, and for* the people (Baum, 1999) because, as Forester (1989) writes, citizens "are profoundly affected . . . not only by what gets *produced* by public and private organizations, but also by how these organizations *reproduce* social and political relations of knowledge and ignorance, consent and deference, trust and dependency, attention and confusion" (pp. 76–77). This literature also reminds us to distinguish tokenistic or manipulative forms of participation from substantive ones (Arnstein, 1969).

Finally, gender and international development scholarship elucidates how adult education can equip women and men to challenge gender hierarchies. From this perspective, education and development endeavors should aim to change the *structural conditions* perpetuating gender inequity, such as the sexual division of labor (Kabeer, 1999; Rathgeber, 1990). According to Stromquist's (1995) model, empowerment encompasses four domains: *cognitive* (understanding causes of gender oppression and developing new perspectives of gender relations); *psychological* (building self-esteem and self-worth); *economic* (engaging in productive economic activities); and *political* (mobilizing for change). Furthermore, Rowlands's (1997) framework highlights the connections among *personal, relational,* and *collective* forms of empowerment, while cautioning that changes in one area (e.g., self-esteem) do not automatically engender changes in another (e.g., collective action).

We offer several caveats about using *empowerment* too loosely. First, individualistic, depoliticized notions of empowerment (LeCompte & deMarrais, 1992) have allowed business and industry (Inglis, 1997) and nongovernmental organizations (NGOs) (Cooke & Kothari, 2001; Leve, 2001) to co-opt this concept, using it to manipulate, promote conformity, and achieve "buy-in" while leaving asymmetrical power relations intact. For instance, leaders routinely elicit participation to manufacture consent—to legitimize a predetermined decision by making people *feel as if* they had a say. Accordingly, this chapter highlights examples of substantive forms of power. Second, educators cannot bestow power on others, for power is not a possession to be granted or withheld (Gore, 1992; LeCompte & deMarrais, 1992). Educators can, however, work to create conditions that allow adults to exercise more control over their educational pursuits and their daily lives. We turn now to describing community-based organizations engaged in just such work.

COMMUNITY-BASED ORGANIZATIONS AND PROGRAMS AIMED AT EMPOWERMENT

While offering an array of services and focusing on myriad issues, empowerment-oriented organizations all use nonformal education as a tool for supporting marginalized groups' struggle for social justice in their respective communities and society. These groups, programs, and organizations focus on distinct issues—for example, adult basic education, immigrant and workers' rights, community health education, environmental justice—and typically work with a specific constituent group, such as farm workers, women, Latinos, immigrants, or low-income families in a particular community. Their scope may be local, regional, statewide, national, or international. For example, Centro Presente (2008) "struggles for immigrant rights and for economic and social justice" for Latino immigrants in Massachusetts by integrating "community organizing, leadership development and basic services" (paragraph 1) such as Spanish Basic Literacy and citizenship classes. Internationally, NGOs engaged in popular education and feminist popular education exemplify education for empowerment (Walters & Manicom, 1996).

Key educational processes include (a) classes and workshops to support community organizing and civic participation (e.g., leadership development courses); (b) popular education (e.g., participatory workshops to support analysis and action on specific problems); and (c) service provision (e.g., General Education Development [GED] degree, English as a second language [ESL], literacy, citizenship classes). Empowerment-focused organizations, however, do more than provide educational services, for service delivery often positions participants as passive recipients or clients, as suggested by this analysis of Centro Presente's transformation from "service provision to active community organizing" (Freiwirth & Letona, 2006):

> Although staff reflected the constituency it served, it largely internalized a hierarchical relationship to clients: staff often viewed themselves as the experts to whom community members came to resolve their problems. More troubling was the board of directors, which had also been operating on a traditional hierarchal governance model and whose members were not of the community being served. (p. 24)

Empowerment-oriented organizations, then, must attend both to what they do and to how they operate, specifically, how they include participants in decision making and in leadership positions.

Organizing-Education

Empowerment-focused programs and organizations can be grouped into two categories: those using adult and popular education as a community organizing methodology (organizing-education) and those focusing specifically on education, providing adult education classes as a tool for individual and community action (education-organizing). In the first type, organizations focus on what Inglis (1997) terms emancipation, for they explicitly aim to change social structures by supporting collective reflection and action, often using popular education. Educational activities are embedded in and directed toward activism, community organizing, and civic participation. Consequently, these organizations aim not to provide direct services or to help individuals achieve personal goals, but rather to organize groups to advocate for their interests. Although personal transformation and development often occur (e.g., Hammond, 1998), these are by-products of educational and organizing work, not the ultimate goal.

A North American example of the organizing-education approach is the American Friends Service Committee (AFSC), a national Quaker organization. AFSC-Austin (Texas) uses popular education workshops to raise consciousness about the global economy, immigrant rights, and peace building, and it sponsors delegations to the U.S.-Mexico border and other activities, all of which involve nonformal education. In addition, AFSC-Austin supports partner organizations' advocacy work such as an immigrants' rights education and leadership development program that provides community organizing experience. It is important that AFSC-Austin's activities not only equip immigrants to improve their lives and communities but also educate U.S. citizens about issues facing immigrants—and challenge them to take action.

Nationwide community organizing networks such as the Industrial Areas Foundation (IAF, established by Saul Alinsky) and Pacific Institute for Community Organization (PICO) illustrate *organizing*-education. While espousing distinct organizing philosophies, both IAF and PICO work with urban U.S. congregations and faith-based community organizations to equip citizens to solve community problems such as affordable housing, health care, and public safety—efforts that have revitalized communities and engaged ordinary people in the work of democracy (Warren, 2001). IAF (2008), for example, identifies power, defined as "the ability to act," as its primary purpose, based on its "radical belief in the potential of the vast majority of people to grow and develop as leaders, to be full members of the body politic, to speak and act with others on their own behalf" (paragraph 3). Leadership development courses are central to both networks, as they teach community leaders to listen to neighbors' concerns, analyze community issues, identify viable solutions, and work with public officials to implement them. In this way, IAF and PICO extend democratic traditions of educational organizing evident in Cooperative Extension (Peters, 2002) and the civil rights movement, for example.

No discussion of adult education for empowerment would be complete without mentioning the Highlander Research and Education Center, an organization that uses popular education, participatory research, and cultural work to develop community leaders and support their struggles for social justice, including civil, human, and labor rights, immigration policy, environmental and economic justice, and other pressing concerns (Horton & Freire, 1990). Although Highlander supports community organizing efforts through its educational work, Myles Horton, Highlander's founder, distinguished organizing focused on *reaching objectives* from Highlander's focus on *developing people's capacity to take action and solve problems*—an approach grounded in the premise that education makes organizing possible:

> Organizing implies that there's a specific, limited goal that needs to be achieved, and the purpose is to achieve that goal. Now if that's it, then the easiest way to get that done solves the problem. But if education is to be part of the process, then you may not actually get that problem solved, but

you've educated a lot of people. . . . The problem is confused because a lot of people use organizing to do some education and they think it's empowerment because that's what they're *supposed* to be doing. But quite often they *disempower* people in the process by using experts to tell them what to do while having the semblance of empowering people. (Horton & Freire, 1990, pp. 119, 120)

In other words, organizers and educators rob people of power whenever they do something for others that they could have done (or learned to do) for themselves, a principle IAF calls the "iron rule" of organizing.

In North America and internationally, popular education, nonformal education, leadership development, consciousness raising, and informal learning have been central to social movements focusing on civil rights, women's rights, the environment, indigenous rights, globalization (e.g., trade, third world debt), sustainable agriculture, and the like (Holst, 2002). In some cases, adult education organizations align with a social movement because they recognize that education alone cannot achieve social transformation; it must be accompanied by changes in legal, political, and economic structures. For example, the Sustainable Livelihood Forum (SLF), a Nepali NGO "explicitly aimed at promoting Nepali Dalit [untouchable] community organizing and social justice through adult education," works closely with the Dalit social movement (Vasily, 2006, p. 1). In so doing, SLF seeks "to identify and change the public and private discourses that maintain caste-based discrimination and practices of untouchability" (p. 7) in Nepal. Like other *organizing*-education organizations, SLF views its adult education and community development work as a means for equipping people to question "the fixed nature of social reality" (p. 52) and to make their own decisions in organization-sponsored projects.

Education-Organizing

By contrast, organizations based on the *education*-organizing approach typically provide adult education classes as a tool for individual and, less frequently, community action. These classes enable adults to meet academic goals—for example, to learn English, obtain a GED diploma, or become citizens—and to understand

and solve personal and community problems. Although these organizations may engage in some community development and organizing, this is not their primary focus. Rather, adult education is used to help individuals enrich their lives and gain some power within the existing system (see Inglis, 1997) instead of supporting collective action to subvert social structures.

Several North American examples illustrate this organizational type. Focusing exclusively on educational issues, Centro Nía in Washington, D.C., provides children and adults with multi-cultural education grounded in social justice and community empowerment, including family literacy, family support services, adult professional development, a bilingual charter school, and educational services for children. What distinguishes Centro Nía (2008) from mainstream adult education and family literacy is its commitment to "ensure that every child receives a high quality education regardless of socio-economic background" and to "include those we serve in every aspect of program design and organizational strategy" (paragraph 4). The recognition of families' cultural identities also differentiates this and other empowerment-oriented programs from dominant approaches emphasizing cultural assimilation to white, middle-class behaviors and values.

BorderSenses of El Paso, Texas, reveals how arts-based adult education can enhance the power of ordinary people to represent their life experiences. For example, BorderSenses (2008) sponsors community-oriented literary projects to enhance people's power through literacy. One such project, Memorias del Silencio (Memories of Silence) (2008), "offer[s] creative writing workshops to GED courses for migrant farm workers and their families" (paragraph 2), resulting in three collections of published stories. This project illustrates how educational initiatives with a singular focus and an orientation toward individual transformation can nevertheless engender powerful consequences—for example, by enabling invisible groups to tell their own stories rather than having others tell their story on their behalf.

International examples of the *education-organizing* approach are numerous. Strikingly, many NGO-sponsored literacy and adult education projects claim to have empowered participants based on such outcomes as increased self-esteem, self-efficacy, and other individual-level indicators. Yet, in many cases, these projects' curricula do not question or challenge gender, age, class, religious, or other hierarchies. For example, indicators of women's empowerment in the Functional Adult Literacy Program (FALP) in Turkey included positive self-concept, self-efficacy, social participation (e.g., voting), reasons for wanting additional children, participation in household decision making, and family cohesion (Kagitcibasi, Goksen, & Gulgoz, 2005). These indicators and outcomes show how empowerment is entangled with the dominant development discourse emphasizing health and family planning, the importance of marrying late, and related topics (p. 475). FALP reportedly enhanced women's "social integration, positive self-concept, and family cohesion" (p. 472). Whether such outcomes constitute genuine empowerment and can be attributed to literacy is a subject of great debate (Bartlett, 2008).

Despite the limited aims and outcomes of many international adult education programs, people nevertheless use the social space these programs afford—and the capacities they develop there—to enrich their lives, which may involve exercising greater power in their relationships, family, and community. For example, Prins (2008) found that although the Alfalit literacy program in two Salvadoran villages did little to improve gender equity or foster collective action, learners identified important psychosocial benefits of attending classes, including a diminished sense of shame, greater confidence and self-expression, expanded friendships, respectful social interaction (*educación*), and enhanced psychological well-being. Although these forms of personal and interpersonal empowerment do not constitute critical consciousness or collective action, they can enhance adults' human capabilities (Nussbaum, 1999) and nurture future collective action. For instance, Friedmann (1992) contends that "political empowerment would seem to require a *prior* process of social empowerment through which effective participation in politics becomes possible" (p. 34). As such, developing the capacity to express one's opinions, establish relationships of trust, and speak in public settings is a necessary yet insufficient foundation for collective, political action.

Adult Education for Women's Empowerment

Much of the literature on adult education for empowerment focuses on women and gender equity, especially in international development and women's social movements. We begin with several North American examples. The first illustrates women's empowerment within a literacy program, Samaritan House in Manitoba, Canada. Through a participatory action research (PAR) project, learners collectively wrote a book about their experiences of living with and overcoming discrimination. The book's introduction reveals that such projects can embolden people and enable them to recognize capacities they never knew they had:

> Working together on PAR gave us the courage to stand up for our rights, and not let people step all over us, using us as doormats. . . . We accomplished something for ourselves that we were told we never could. (Samaritan House PAR Group, 1995, p. 6)

Similarly, WE LEARN (Women Expanding/Literacy Education Action Resource Network) (2008) "promotes women's literacy as a tool for personal growth and social change through networking, education, action, and resource development," including conferences, discussion circles, writing projects, and adult basic education (ABE) student leadership, among others. Additional examples include The Well, a neighborhood-based health education for black women in which participants make programmatic decisions (Elliott Brown, Jemmott, Mitchell, & Walton, 1998); Candora, a women's collective featuring consensual decision making (Scott & Schmitt-Boshnick, 2001); and Community Voices Heard (2008), which involves low-income women of color (primarily welfare recipients) in improving their lives and communities through "public education, grassroots organizing, leadership development, training low-income people about their rights, political education, civic engagement and direct-action issue campaigns" (paragraph 1).

International examples of adult education for women's empowerment abound (e.g., Robinson-Pant, 2004b; Rowlands, 1997). Such initiatives typically involve popular education (Walters & Manicom, 1996) or state- or NGO-sponsored adult literacy programs for poor women. When linked to social movements, such projects have greater potential to alter gender relations, for instance, by changing unjust laws. The most effective empowerment strategies build women's "power from within" while "improving their ability to control resources, to determine agendas and make decisions" (Kabeer, 1999, p. 229). Some scholars (e.g., Stromquist, 2006) claim adult education can equip women to claim citizenship, while others (e.g., Rogers, 2007) contend the dominant literacy-for-citizenship discourse promotes a circumscribed form of citizenship and national identity and mistakenly assumes literacy is a "precondition" for citizenship and empowerment.

The total literacy campaigns (TLCs), sponsored by the Indian government in cooperation with an NGO, demonstrate how adult education can contribute to gender equity and collective action (Srivastava & Patel, 2006). The TLCs mobilized poor women "to change their material conditions and struggle for gender equality" (p. 154). To garner initial support for literacy and development activities, the TLCs employed creative, culturally relevant methods involving folk and conventional media such as films, literacy fairs, songs, and skits. These activities "motivated women to attend literacy classes," which in turn provided "a social space to congregate daily" and share "their common problems and experiences" (p. 156). Such social spaces are vital to empowerment, for they disrupt women's isolation, allowing them to meet with other women and discover common experiences (Prins, 2006; Stromquist, 1997). By teaching more than literacy skills, the TLCs prompted women in various regions to form village councils to discuss local problems, wage an anti-liquor campaign, form women's credit and stone quarry worker cooperatives, and start a bicycle campaign to increase women's physical autonomy and mobility. That many of these initiatives (as well as others sparked by the NGO's educational projects) were co-opted or discontinued underscores the need to provide long-term support to sustain women's collective action.

CHALLENGES

This section identifies several salient challenges that often arise as educators and other professionals work with adults to improve their lives and communities. Because funders can subtly or directly influence what an organization does and whose interests it serves, the first challenge is avoiding co-optation. Indeed, conflict among the goals of funders, educators, and learners is a recurring theme in empowerment discourse. Nonprofit organizations depend on funding to maintain viability (Laverack, 2001), yet accountability to funders creates "constant pressure to manage [organizational] activities around acceptable and predefined agendas" (Kabeer, 1999, p. 262), while simultaneously striving to limit funders' influence over program philosophy, goals, and implementation. In particular, government policies and accountability measures, especially in North America, emphasize individual, instrumental outcomes (e.g., job placement) that may undermine broader purposes such as community action and civic participation. Consequently, educators are forced to balance meeting the needs of students and maintaining their philosophical integrity with keeping the organization open (Beder, 1996; Horsman, 2001).

The experience of Candora, a Canadian nonprofit women's organization, illustrates how funder policies can threaten organizational goals and principles (Scott & Schmitt-Boshnick, 2001). When the government began requiring less time than needed for program completion, Candora first sought to negotiate with legislators by discussing the needs of participants. When this failed, the program enlisted the intervention of community allies and political representatives. Although Candora replaced most of the government funding they had lost, they recognized that adherence to organizational principles that conflict with funder's priorities may result in job loss and program restructuring or closure. This case illustrates how the growing governmental emphasis on work skills, accountability measures, and accelerated time frames can threaten education for empowerment.

Second, educators must learn to negotiate the tension between service delivery and community organizing or, as Baum (1999) puts it, between being an organization *for* the community and an organization *of, by,* and *for* the community. Centro Presente, a Latino rights organization, reveals the challenge of shifting from a hierarchical service delivery entity into a democratic activist organization. After realizing their organizational structure compromised their mission to empower Latinos, the staff sought to establish an organization based on participatory democracy,

self-determination, genuine partnership, and community-level decision making (Freiwirth & Letona, 2006). This shift required getting staff and participants to think like organizers, elevating participant experience to the level of staff expertise, understanding how shared power operates, and addressing staff opposition and turnover. Effective strategies included the incorporation of organizing activities into job descriptions, continuous dialogue about sharing power, and the provision of opportunities for participant leadership development.

The renegotiation of power is a recognized consequence of empowerment for educators and leaders. Consequently, staff members and participants may have difficulty sharing decision-making power, resulting in conflict and staff resistance and turnover (Campbell, 2001; Everett, Homstead, & Drisko, 2007). The challenges of giving up control (staff) or exercising it (learners) arise from different conceptions of shared power, the extra investment of time participation requires of staff and learners, failure to recognize the valuable contribution of participants, and participants' low self-esteem and lack of leadership training. In addition, the risk of losing jobs or government support may inhibit educators' full enactment of empowerment strategies.

The South East Education Task Force, a community-school partnership of 16 schools that was created to give parents a greater voice in school issues, faced just such issues (Baum, 2002). Teachers and parents had divergent understandings of the degrees of authority they could exercise in different arenas. Teachers' view of parental involvement relegated parents to a support position, so when the parents began to question and make suggestions concerning curriculum and classroom practices, the teachers felt they had encroached on an area in which they did not have expertise. In addition, task force participation required extra time, cutting into teachers' personal lives. For school officials, the potential failure of the task force would not only challenge the wisdom and efficacy of directing resources to the partnership but also threaten their job security. The partnership responded by holding regular meetings to foster understanding of shared power and the role of each stakeholder and by soliciting other partners and political alliances to reduce risk to the school and the likelihood and cost of failure.

In community-based settings, educators' lack of familiarity with learners' daily lives can make it difficult to understand why they may hesitate to take collective action. What appears as dependency or lack of motivation to educators may be a legitimate response to a perceived threat to learners' daily survival (Horsman, 2001; Scott & Schmitt-Boshnick, 2001). In sum, it takes "a great deal of trust, commitment, and support to confront the fear of change" (Sauvé, 2001, p. 22) and to face the potential loss of means necessary for survival.

Student self-perceptions also play an important role in negotiating power imbalances. Adult education programs often seek to overcome learners' low self-esteem—a common obstacle to empowerment—by building their self-confidence and "sense of the possible" (Freiwirth & Letona, 2006). For example, Candora addressed power differentials among program stakeholders and legitimized participants' perspectives through shared decision making, promoting a respectful environment where individual voices were recognized, and fostering skill acquisition for self-sufficiency (Scott & Schmitt-Boshnick, 2001). Recognizing some participants' discomfort speaking in group settings, The Well, a black women's health community organization, used suggestion boxes so that women could identify issues anonymously (Elliot Brown et al., 1998).

Deciding what counts as empowerment is a pervasive challenge, especially in gender-focused projects. Guided by neoliberal economic ideology, development institutions such as the World Bank and U.S. Agency for International Development have replaced emancipatory notions of empowerment with a narrow, instrumental focus on promoting "participation in the development process" (Leve, 2001, p. 108) to boost economic productivity. For instance, many women's literacy programs regard literacy as an engine of modernization and development (Agnaou, 2004). Frequently, such programs address women's practical interests (literacy acquisition) but not their strategic interests (socioeconomic equality) and use texts that legitimize existing gender roles and socioeconomic positions (Agnaou, 2004). As such, they fail to change the structural conditions and cultural processes undergirding gender subordination (Robinson-Pant, 2004a), casting doubts on the assumption that participation in adult education

is intrinsically empowering (Agnaou, 2004; Fiedrich & Jellema, 2003).

Even in social justice-oriented organizations, educators may inadvertently perpetuate the prevailing development discourse of individual empowerment, as a study of the REFLECT (ActionAid UK) literacy and development program in Uganda and Bangladesh found:

> The self-directed process of "participating" is considered to be empowering *in itself,* spontaneously fostering autonomy, self-confidence and independence, so that individual women can change their own lives in the ways they want. This results in a picture of women's agency and consciousness that, to a feminist, would seem both overly heroic and at the same time overly paternalistic. (Fiedrich & Jellema, 2003, p. 48)

Thus, any project aiming to improve people's lives through adult education may have unanticipated, contradictory aims and consequences.

Finally, paternalism is an ever-present risk in educational endeavors. Well-meaning educators may unconsciously act as change agents who determine a priori what empowerment entails and impose this perspective without recognizing learners' viewpoints (Fiedrich & Jellema, 2003; Freiwith & Letona, 2006). In most development agencies, "the ambitions and ideals of NGOs, the donors who fund them and the middle class professionals who staff them, shape what can be regarded as empowering and what can't" (Fiedrich & Jellema, 2003, p. 49). In this way, NGOs may implicitly or explicitly equate empowerment with "capitalist individualism," displacing alternative notions of empowerment and forms of resistance (Fiedrich & Jellema, 2003).

Educators in organizations that eschew modernist, top-down approaches to education and development are no less susceptible to imposing their notions of empowerment (Fiedrich & Jellema, 2003). For instance, Ugandan and Bangladeshi REFLECT educators considered themselves "change agents" whose duty it was "to instill modern practices and values among the poor" (pp. 48–49). These concerns echo the criticism that Freire's philosophy positioned educators as change agents who lead participants toward a pre-determined end (Bartlett, 2009). Freire (1994), in turn, insisted that educators should neither impose nor withhold their perspectives. In sum, educators and participants should clarify who determines what empowerment entails, for as Fiedrich and Jellema (2003) observe,

> We suspect that empowerment discourse flourishes for the same reasons that modernization discourse did in the era of decolonization: because it allows room for manoeuvre within an unresolved ambiguity about who is driving the change process and towards what ends. (p. 60)

Conclusion

In this chapter, we have argued for a critical perspective of empowerment focusing on the exercise of power and the social structures that enable or constrain human agency, in place of more palatable but narrow psychological and functional conceptions. Adult education has a rich history of using education as tool for individual and collective action, especially in struggles for social justice. The examples highlighted here provide a glimpse of the varied and creative ways contemporary organizations in North America and internationally integrate education with community development and organizing activities to enrich people's lives and communities.

In these endeavors, educators and participants are beset by challenges such as minimizing funder co-optation, negotiating the tension between service delivery and community organizing, sharing decision-making power, and avoiding paternalism. In particular, staff, volunteers, and community residents must discern the roles of funders, organizational leaders, educators, volunteers, participants, and other stakeholders in deciding what empowerment entails and how to nurture participants' capacity "to act on their own behalf" (Daniell, 2003, p. 74). Educators cannot empower others. But the aforementioned examples reveal that we can cultivate or thwart conditions that allow people to promote human flourishing in their families, workplace, and community, even against seemingly insurmountable odds.

References

Agnaou, F. (2004). *Gender, literacy, and empowerment in Morocco.* New York: Routledge.

Arnstein, S. R. (1969). A ladder of citizen participation. *Journal of the American Planning Association, 35*(4), 216–224.

Bartlett, L. (2008). Literacy's verb: Exploring what literacy is and what literacy does. *International Journal of Educational Development, 28*(6), 737–753.

Bartlett, L. (2009). *The word and the world: The cultural politics of literacy in Brazil.* Creskill, NJ: Hampton Press.

Baum, H. (1999). Community organizations recruiting community participation: Predicaments in planning. *Journal of Planning Education and Research, 18*(3), 187–199.

Baum, H. (2002). *The community approach to school-community partnerships: Challenges and possibilities.* Paper presented at the Annual Meeting of the American Educational Research Association, New Orleans, LA.

Beder, H. (1996). Popular education: An appropriate educational strategy for community-based organizations. In P. Sissel (Ed.), *A community-based approach to literacy programs: Taking learners' lives into account* (pp. 73–83). New Directions in Adult and Continuing Education, No. 70. San Francisco: Jossey-Bass.

BorderSenses. (2008). Home page. Retrieved April 24, 2008, from http://bordersenses.com/

Campbell, P. (2001). Participatory literacy practices: Exploring pedagogy. In P. Campbell & B. Burnaby (Eds.), *Participatory practices in adult education* (pp. 55–76). Mahwah, NJ: Lawrence Erlbaum.

Centro Nía. (2008). History. Retrieved December 31, 2009, from http://www.centronia.org/html/history.html

Centro Presente. (2008). Mission statement. Retrieved April 22, 2008, from http://www.cpresente.org/missionstatement.html

Community Voices Heard. (2008). Mission. Retrieved May 9, 2008, from http://www.cvhaction.org/

Cooke, B., & Kothari, U. (Eds.). (2001). *Participation: The new tyranny?* London: Zed Books.

Daniell, B. (2003). *A communion of friendship: Literacy, spiritual practice, and women in recovery.* Carbondale: Southern Illinois University.

Elliott Brown, K. A., Jemmott, F. E., Mitchell, H. J., & Walton, M. L. (1998). The Well: A neighborhood-based health promotion model for Black women. *Health and Social Work, 23*(2), 146–152.

Everett, J., Homstead, K., & Drisko, J. (2007). Frontline worker perception of the empowerment process in community-based organizations. *Social Work, 52*(2), 161–171.

Fiedrich, M., & Jellema, A. (2003). *Literacy, gender and social agency: Adventures in empowerment.* London: Department for International Development.

Forester, J. (1989). *Planning in the face of power.* Berkeley: University of California Press.

Freire, P. (1994). *Pedagogy of hope: Reliving pedagogy of the oppressed.* London: Continuum.

Freiwirth, J., & Letona, M. E. (2006). System-wide governance for community empowerment. *The Nonprofit Quarterly, 13*(4), 24–27.

Friedmann, J. (1992). *Empowerment: The politics of alternative development.* Cambridge, MA/Oxford, UK: Blackwell.

Gaventa, J. (1980). *Power and powerlessness: Quiescence and rebellion in an Appalachian valley.* Urbana: University of Illinois Press.

Gore, J. (1992). What we can do for you! What *can* "we" do for you?: Struggling over empowerment in critical and feminist pedagogy. In C. Luke & J. Gore (Eds.), *Feminisms and critical pedagogy* (pp. 54–73). New York: Routledge.

Hammond, J. L. (1998). *Fighting to learn: Popular education and guerrilla war in El Salvador.* New Brunswick, NJ: Rutgers University Press.

Holst, J. D. (2002). *Social movements, civil society, and radical adult education.* Westport, CT: Bergin & Garvey.

Horsman, J. (2001). "Why would they listen to me?" Reflections on learner leadership activities. In P. Campbell & B. Burnaby (Eds.), *Participatory practices in adult education* (pp. 77–102). Mahwah, NJ: Lawrence Erlbaum.

Horton, M., & Freire, P. (1990). *We make the road by walking: Conversations on education and social change.* Philadelphia: Temple University Press.

Industrial Areas Foundation. (2008). Who are we? Retrieved April 22, 2008, from http://www.industrialareasfoundation.org/iafabout/about.htm

Inglis, T. (1997). Empowerment and emancipation. *Adult Education Quarterly, 48*(1), 3–17.

Johnson-Bailey, J. (2006). Transformative learning: A community empowerment conduit for African American women. In S. Merriam, B. Courtenay, & R. Cervero (Eds.), *Global issues and adult education: Perspectives from Latin America, Southern Africa, and the United States.* (pp. 307–318). San Francisco: Jossey-Bass.

Kabeer, N. (1999). *Reversed realities: Gender hierarchies in development thought.* London: Verso.

Kagitcibasi, C., Goksen, F., & Gulgoz, S. (2005). Functional adult literacy and empowerment of women: Impact of a functional literacy program in Turkey. *Journal of Adolescent & Adult Literacy, 48*(6), 472–489.

Laverack, G. (2001). An identification and interpretation of the organizational aspects of community empowerment. *Community Development Journal, 36*(2), 134–145.

LeCompte, M. D., & deMarrais, K. B. (1992). The disempowering of empowerment: Out of the revolution and into the classroom. *Educational Foundations, 6*(3), 5–31.

Leve, L. G. (2001). Between Jesse Helms and Ram Bahadur: Participation and empowerment in women's literacy programming in Nepal. *PoLAR: Political & Legal Anthropology Review, 24*(1), 108–128.

Memorias del Silencio [Memories of Silence]. (2008). Introducción [Introduction]. Retrieved April 24, 2008, from http://www.bordersenses.com/memorias/home.html

Nussbaum, M. C. (1999). Women and equality: The capabilities approach. *International Labour Review, 138*(3), 227–245.

Peters, S. J. (2002). Rousing the people on the land: The roots of the educational organizing tradition in Extension work. *Journal of Extension, 40*(3). Retrieved January 14, 2009, from http://www.joe.org/joe/2002june/a1.html

Prins, E. (2006). Relieving isolation, avoiding vices: The gendered meanings of participation in an adult literacy program in El Salvador. *Adult Education Quarterly, 57*(1), 5–25.

Prins, E. (2008). Adult literacy education, gender equity, and empowerment: Insights from a Freirean-inspired literacy programme. *Studies in the Education of Adults, 40*(1), 24–39.

Rathgeber, E. M. (1990). WID, WAD, GAD: Trends in research and practice. *Journal of Developing Areas, 24*, 489–502.

Robinson-Pant, A. (2004a). "The illiterate woman": Changing approaches to researching women's literacy. In A. Robinson-Pant (Ed.), *Women, literacy and development: Alternative perspectives* (pp. 15–34). Routledge: London.

Robinson-Pant, A. (Ed.). (2004b). *Women, literacy and development: Alternative perspectives.* Routledge: London.

Rogers, A. (2007). Women, literacy and citizenship: A critique. *International Review of Education, 53*(2), 159–181.

Rowlands, J. (1997). *Questioning empowerment: Working with women in Honduras.* London: Oxfam.

Samaritan House PAR Group. (1995). *Where there is life, there is hope: Women literacy students and discrimination.* Brandon, Manitoba: Literacy and Continuing Education Branch, Department of Education and Training, Province of Manitoba.

Sauvé, V. L. (2001). A personal journey into participatory education. In P. Campbell & B. Burnaby (Eds.), *Participatory practices in adult education* (pp. 15–27). Mahwah, NJ: Lawrence Erlbaum.

Scott, S. M., & Schmitt-Boshnick, M. (2001). Power and program planning in a community-based context. In P. Campbell & B. Burnaby (Eds.), *Participatory practices in adult education* (pp. 123–142). Mahwah, NJ: Lawrence Erlbaum.

Srivastava, K., & Patel, I. (2006). Community mobilisation, gender equality and resource mobilisation in adult education. *International Journal of Educational Development, 26*(2), 153–165.

Stromquist, N. (1995). The theoretical and practical bases for empowerment. In C. Medel-Añonuevo (Ed.), *Women, education, and empowerment: Pathways towards autonomy* (pp. 13–22). Hamburg: UNESCO Institute for Education.

Stromquist, N. (1997). *Literacy for citizenship: Gender and grassroots dynamics in Brazil.* Albany: State University of New York Press.

Stromquist, N. (2006). Women's rights to adult education as a means to citizenship. *International Journal of Educational Development, 26*(2), 140–152.

Vasily, L. (2006). *Reading one's life: A case study of an adult educational participatory action research curriculum development project for Nepali Dalit social justice.* Unpublished doctoral dissertation, Cornell University, Ithaca, NY.

Walters, S., & Manicom, L. (Eds.). (1996). *Gender in popular education: Methods for empowerment.* London: Zed Books.

Warren, M. R. (2001). *Dry bones rattling: Community building to revitalize American democracy.* Princeton, NJ: Princeton University Press.

WE LEARN (2008). Mission statement. Retrieved May 9, 2008, from http://www.litwomen .org/welearn.html

20

ADULTS IN FOUR-YEAR COLLEGES AND UNIVERSITIES

Moving From the Margin to Mainstream?

LORILEE R. SANDMANN

"For the first time in our society, adults outnumber youth, there are more older adults, the population is better educated than before, and there is more cultural and ethnic diversity" (Merriam, Caffarella, & Baumgartner, 2007, p. 7).

There is also more turmoil. Within this dynamic social context, U.S. institutions of higher education are pressured more than ever to be engines of high value-added jobs to employment-aged adults; the expectation is ensuring global economic competitiveness while simultaneously enduring decreasing state support due to the confluence of powerful socioeconomic pressures on federal, state, and household budgets (Bok, 2003; Cantor, 2006; Cook & King, 2004; Duderstadt, 2000; Newman, Couturier, & Scurry, 2004; Rhodes, 2001; Rowley, Lujan, & Dolence, 1998; Slaughter & Rhoades, 2004). The Commission on the Future of Higher Education states:

> In an era when intellectual capital is increasingly prized, both for individuals and for the nation, [the value of] postsecondary education has never been more important. Ninety percent of the fastest-growing jobs in the new knowledge-driven economy will require some postsecondary education. Already, the median earnings of a U.S. worker with only a high school diploma are 37 percent less than those of a worker with a bachelor's degree. Colleges and universities must continue to be the major route for new generations of Americans to achieve social mobility. And for the country as a whole, future economic growth will depend on our ability to sustain excellence, innovation, and leadership in higher education. (U.S. Department of Education, 2006)

Given this context, what is the place of adult learners in 4-year colleges and universities? This chapter will situate and analyze adults in the 4-year colleges and universities sector of postsecondary education, using the perspectives of adult learners and of higher education providers and programs. Economic pressures are pushing higher education toward academic capitalism, even as instructional technology is broadening educational access. Through these combined forces, adult students are

AUTHOR'S NOTE: The author wishes to thank University of Georgia graduate students Michael W. Massey and Jeremy Schwehm for their contributions to this chapter.

moving from the margins of higher education to gain prominence as an important market for most 4-year colleges and universities. The case will be made, however, that many institutions are slow in developing adult-friendly policies and practices.

This chapter will explore adults in 4-year colleges and universities as snapshots of three increasingly numerous and diverse entities: the adult learner population itself, the providers serving this population, and the programs for adults in 4-year higher education. Next discussed will be relevant policies and practices of access, affordability, and accountability. The chapter will conclude with challenges that warrant attention for the next 10 years.

THE ADULT LEARNER IN HIGHER EDUCATION

The first snapshot focuses on adult learners and their relationship with 4-year colleges and universities. The lack of consistency in defining "adult learner" is an obstacle to synthesizing available research, but this work uses a paraphrase of the American Council on Education's straightforward definition: "Adult learners are defined as those aged 25 and over, who are participating in some type of formal postsecondary instruction" in a 4-year college or university (Paulson & Boeke, 2006, p. v). Formal instruction is a learning program for which there is a dedicated instructor. Thus, 18 to 24 year olds (i.e., "traditional" or "young adult" higher education students) are omitted here. Similarly, community and technical colleges, while fulfilling important missions of formal adult postsecondary education, are considered elsewhere in this handbook, as are programs for basic adult literacy.

Adult Enrollment and Participation

The U.S. population is growing, aging, and diversifying, and adults are increasing both in number and proportion. In 2007, the U.S. population was estimated at 301.6 million, with a median age of 36.6 years and almost two thirds of the population over 25 years of age. The population of adults age 65 and older is projected to increase rapidly for the next two decades (U.S. Census Bureau, 2008). According to Paulson and Boeke (2006), more than 90 million

adult learners are participating in education beyond high school, and it is widely cited that 40% of adults participate in one or more adult education activities each year.

Within this milieu, what is the proportion of adult learners specifically in 4-year colleges and universities? According to the National Center for Education Statistics (NCES, 2007a), about 4 million (or 36%) of the 2005 fall enrollment of nearly 11 million students were 25 years or older. Graduate programs have always been composed primarily of adult learners, so the trends in undergraduate studies are of particular interest. Although the number of adult enrollees in undergraduate programs has increased over the past 10 years, the proportion of such students in 4-year institutions has remained relatively stable near 30%. Younger adult age cohorts participate in higher education in higher percentages than older age groups. For example, in 2005, 25 to 29 year olds were 10.8% of adult undergraduates, 30 to 34 year olds were 6.3%, while 50 to 64 years olds were only 2.8% (NCES, 2007b).

The adult learners enrolled at 4-year, degree-granting providers were about evenly split between full- and part-timers (NCES, 2007a; Paulson & Boeke, 2006; Planty et al., 2008; Snyder, Dillow, & Hoffman, 2007). Within higher education, the proportion of Whites and males has consistently declined, but their numbers have increased. Females are in a small majority but assume a marked majority in older subgroups. From 1990 to 2007, the percentage of Whites declined; all other racial/ethnic groups increased significantly in proportion and numbers.

Those with more formal education and financial resources or who have family with college education backgrounds engage in and succeed in adult higher education at a higher rate than those lacking these resources. Working adults and first-generation adults have greater difficulty, as do the 40% of adult learners who earn less than $25,000 per year (Cook & King, 2004). The size of this low-income subset has important policy implications. Low-income adults participate in higher education at a lower rate than middle- or high-income adults; they face more barriers to getting and staying enrolled, including financial need, family and child care needs, and employment pressures.

Adults participate in higher education to maintain or increase their knowledge or skills. Likely motives include training to enter the workforce, maintaining or improving job skills, making a career transition, or gaining personal satisfaction from earning a degree. Paulson and Boeke (2006) report that those over 25 studying part-time in college or university programs indicate that they had "increased employability in the labor markets" and "improved ability to advance in [their] careers" (p. 18).

Adult learners may delay participation in postsecondary education because they are financially independent with dependents of their own, they wish to get married, or they wish to start or raise a family (Paulson & Boeke, 2006). These adult students are:

- less likely than younger undergraduates to seek a bachelor's degree and more likely to enroll for career advancement and personal satisfaction

- more likely to be pursuing their undergraduate studies as part-time students and more likely to enroll at for-profit institutions than are younger students

- predominantly women

- more likely to be married and have children—especially if they are age 30 or older; the exception is low-income adult students, who are more likely to be single parents

- less likely to apply for aid than traditional-age students, but 85% of those who apply receive assistance

- much more likely to earn a certificate within 6 years than to earn a bachelor's degree (Paulson & Boeke, 2006)

A number of studies on the experiences of adults pursuing degrees provide insight into practices that contribute to their persistence (or lack thereof) to graduation. In one such study, Buteau (2007) followed a class of single mothers who completed bachelor's degrees. Women in this study expressed frustration with faculty members who scolded them for missing class or arriving late without regard to their circumstances. They also reported that were it not for friends, they would have been unaware of the financial aid available to them.

Adult Higher Education

Interest in adult learners has increased because of this population's size and its unique needs—needs that are changing in the face of economic,

technological, workplace, sociodemographic, and globalizing shifts. One change is the generation-long trend of increasing diversity in U.S. higher education. The data on adults in higher education suggest that the most successful 4-year institutions may be those that recognize change, embrace it, and implement the integration of adult curricula and support and delivery systems.

PROVIDERS OF ADULT FOUR-YEAR HIGHER EDUCATION

The second snapshot encompasses providers of adult higher education. We know from the study of adult learners that context matters. Convenience to home or work and affordability influence adult learners' choice of higher education providers (Pusser et al., 2007). Higher education can no longer be seen as a single entity or monolithic knowledge industry. Four-year higher education, traditionally the province of colleges and universities, has become highly and dynamically segmented and stratified. Over the last half-century, enrollment and campus expansions spiked with the advent of the GI Bill; 4-year institutions lost market share to 2-year schools, then to for-profits; the Internet begat asynchronous distance education; and an explosion of student services transformed amenities, expectations, and recruiting. Marketing and retailing in the larger society jumped into the nation's universities due to sophisticated learner-consumers (Bok, 2003; Cantor, 2006; Duderstadt, 2000; Geiger, 2004; Kirp, 2003; Rhodes, 2001; Rowley et al., 1998; Slaughter & Rhoades, 2004; Washburn, 2005).

Segmenting the Adult Providers

Higher education providers are formally divided into publics and privates, which further segment into not-for-profits and for-profits. Publics are not-for-profit corporations by definition. Privates are either not-for-profit, as most are, or for-profit. Even within type, there are unique contextual models for adult learners. For example, 4-year comprehensive universities have relatively open access admission, with curricula more related to the regional economy as compared with liberal arts and research universities with more limited access, admission, and support with broader curricula.

In the academic year from 2005 to 2006, total 4-year Title IV degree-granting institutions numbered 1,053 public and 1,942 private, with 1,534 not-for-profits and 408 for-profits. In Fall 2005, 62% of adult enrollment was in public institutions, 31% in private not-for-profits, and 7% in private for-profits. While the number of private, for-profit institutions is small relative to other providers, adult learners are their primary market. Paulson and Boeke (2006) note that Fall 2004 data from the NCES Integrated Postsecondary Education Data System show that at private, for-profit 4-year institutions, adults constituted 55% of the student population, outnumbering traditional-age students. This finding is historic.

The ever-growing, highly competitive industry of for-profit higher education providers is spearheaded by the University of Phoenix (UOP), At 300,000 students, its enrollment is the largest in any 4-year institution in the United States and one of the largest among higher education institutions worldwide (UOP, 2007). It has two thirds female learners, versus the national proportion, which approaches 57% (Snyder et al., 2007; UOP, 2007). Many for-profits view the changing demographics as a way to access pent-up demand by female adults for home-based programs, even though for-profits may cost more than 4-year, place-based, traditional public universities.

Within 4-year colleges and universities, adult students can have very different experiences. However, some features found across institutional types are known to facilitate adult participation and learning. In a benchmarking study of adult-learner-centered institutions across institutional types, Mancuso (2001) found that at the best-practices institutions (both public and private), the culture was responsive to the individual needs of adult learners; adult learning needs drove institutional decisions and practices; there was a high level of communication about what was occurring, including the way adult learners figured in the institutional mission; and admission and other services made adjustments for adult students. Furthermore, the Emerging Pathways project (Pusser et al., 2007) found four major actions that 4-year institutions can take to enhance adult learning and success:

- Develop pre-baccalaureate, career-related certificate programs that incorporate academic credit applicable toward a degree
- Provide part-time degree programs
- Create year-round, accelerated, and convenient programming
- Facilitate degree mapping (p. 11)

PROGRAMS FOR ADULTS IN FOUR-YEAR COLLEGES AND UNIVERSITIES

College and university programs marketed specifically to adults may be age-segregated programs for adults or age-integrated models. They may be degree-completion programs, accelerated degree programs, night or weekend or workplace programs, distance education programs, contract programs for employers and employees, special appeals and accommodations within existing programs, or hybrids or combinations of these approaches. Typically, they include workplace-oriented curriculum taught by practitioners as adjunct faculty in some accessible, accelerated format, possibly offering assessment and credit for prior life experiences. Accelerated programs, distance education, and nonformal adult education through continuing education and community engagement are increasingly prevalent, and aspects of these program types as key choices of adult learners will be briefly discussed as a third snapshot.

Accelerated Programs

Accelerated learning programs, those programs made of courses offered with fewer than the conventional number of instructional contact hours and for a shorter duration are primarily designed to serve adult students and are one of the fastest-growing transformations in higher education (Wlodkowski, 2003). In 2001, Aslanian reported that 13% of adult students studying for degrees were enrolled in programs offering degrees in less than the traditional length of time and that within 10 years, 25% or more of all adult students will be enrolled in accelerated programs. This is especially evident in particular academic programs, such as MBA programs. Some critics, however, have raised questions about the quality of the learning experience in compressed, intensive time frames, which could sacrifice breadth, depth, analysis, and reflection (Wlodkowski, 2003).

Distance Education

Here, distance education means asynchronous e-learning, not correspondence. The e-learning, distance, or online format accounts for the greatest growth in higher education in the last 10 years (Planty et al., 2008). A major Sloan study surveying thousands of institutions found that online courses are offered by 63% of institutions with traditional undergraduate face-to-face courses, and 44% of face-to-face master's programs offer online coursework (Allen & Seaman, 2007). Furthermore, online enrollments continued to grow far faster than the total higher education student population, and almost 3.5 million students were taking at least one online course in fall 2006, a 10% increase over the previous year. The Sloan studies do not specifically break out enrollment for adult learners, but it was reported that "the appeal of online instruction to non-traditional students is indicated by the high number of institutions which cite growth in continuing and/or professional education as an objective for their online offerings" (Allen & Seaman, 2007, p. 2). The studies further indicate that current patterns are likely to continue with greatest growth in public institutions, associate's institutions, large institutions, and schools that are already fully engaged in online education with a strategic mission and long-term plan that includes online education.

Challenges remain in equity of high-speed access, student supports, and costs; however, technological infrastructure, curriculum, pedagogy, and delivery of instruction have significantly improved (Allen & Seaman, 2007). Students, faculty, and providers are accepting and even expecting anytime-anywhere learning, comparable faculty response time, and the technology to facilitate these.

Continuing Education

Continuing education programs serve adults through both credit and noncredit offerings. The National Survey of Students in Continuing Education (Pusser et al., 2007) reports that continuing-education enrollment is only slightly more likely to be for credit (53.6%) than not (46.4%). The short-term noncredit continuing-education classes serving millions of adult learners (site-based and online) have been called the "hidden college" (Milam, 2005) because this arena is poorly documented. Although such courses are widespread in 4-year institutions, national data sets fail to capture their significance; few states and only 40% of individual institutions document noncredit continuing education efforts. Curricula preferences of adults for continuing education programs reflect a strong labor market orientation, with leading fields of study in credit-based programs being management and business; arts, humanities, and social sciences; and education. In noncredit programs, the topic fields of study are computer and information technology; business and management; and arts, humanities, and social sciences. However, for adults pursuing education through continuing education, choices are limited. The National Survey found that "just over one third of the majors offered elsewhere in the institutions were also available through continuing education" (Pusser et al., 2007, p. 9).

Although continuing-education programs have long been recognized as providing necessary labor market skills, noncredit continuing-education courses are less understood as pathways to further formal education. Because credit for course completion remains key to baccalaureate achievement, this connection calls for greater attention, as does funding for continuing education. Because federal subsidies are currently linked to credit hours, students taking non-credit-bearing courses are generally not eligible. State and federal aid policies that support credit *and* non-credit-bearing programs would better serve the adult learner.

Adult Education Through Community Engagement and Cooperative Extension

In response to charges that higher education has drifted from being a public good to a means of private gain for individuals and corporations, 4-year colleges and universities are practicing a renewed engagement with the public (e.g., Boyer, 1990; Kellogg Commission on the Future of State and Land-Grant Universities, 1999; National Center for Public Policy in Higher Education, 2008), often through service and outreach. These functions are accomplished primarily by two delivery systems: continuing education at most 4-year colleges and universities (just discussed) and cooperative extension in land-grant universities. The federal Cooperative

Extension System, historically a provider of nonformal adult education, began more than 80 years ago to disseminate agricultural research through land-grant universities (Sanders, 1966). Its reach now extends across the country and even internationally. In its 2007 *Annual Reports of Accomplishments and Results,* Cooperative Extension reported 26,267,141 adult and youth direct contacts (personal correspondence, Bart Hewitt, January 28, 2009).

While Cooperative Extension's partnership approach has stood the test of time, mission interpretation and resource allocations present challenges. Extension is working to become more flexible and agile in serving citizens with diverse backgrounds by expanding programming and recruiting and hiring a more diverse staff (ECOP-NASULGC, 2007). An example of this adaptation is the development of eXtension, a coordinated, Internet-based information system, available 24 hours a day, 7 days a week (http://www.extension.org).

PRACTICES AND POLICIES IN HIGHER EDUCATION: IMPLICATIONS FOR THE EDUCATION OF ADULTS

Despite access to a growing number of diverse 4-year college and university options, adults are still largely nontraditional students in traditional institutions. Key policy variables exist both for adults participating in higher education and for society providing education for adults. Major challenges fall into three broad categories: access and support, affordability and funding, and accountability and quality. Although these categories will be discussed independently, they are highly interdependent.

Adult Access and Support

Although touted as a public policy and an important value in higher education, access has historically been limited by both formal and informal admissions barriers as well as affordability for diverse populations with widely varying economic circumstances. Time constraints of employment and family obligations often further disadvantage adult higher education students, so they must choose from

more limited options than those who can undertake full-time, residential study. Older students may also struggle academically due to lack of preparation.

Alternative instructional formats such as evening and weekend programs or accelerated, intensive programs can provide greater access for adult learners (Wlodkowski & Kasworm, 2003). But as noted earlier, it is the proliferation of online degree programs that has significantly changed the education access landscape for adult learners. A remarkable example is the U.S. Army's eArmyU.com program, which now provides educational access to more than 57,000 soldier-students (Stoskopf & Moorash, 2005). However, institutional or individual lack of access to the latest hardware or software is creating a new form of disadvantaged student. Most notably, accessibility remains a major concern for institutions serving lower income, rural, and older students.

Even when new pathways are available and convenient, shortcomings in adult-friendly academic support services may hamper adult students (Pusser et al., 2007). Institutions rushing to develop programs for adults or online learners have often overlooked development of adequate support services (LaPadula, 2003). That adult students need support—especially advising, counseling, and financial aid—is well documented in national surveys and in studies of subgroups of adult learners like Buteau's (2007) work. There is a significant lack of ready access to information about programs, services, and financial aid. Models exist for such support (e.g., in adult student service offices described by Rice, 2003); however, McGivney (2004) finds that higher education lacks a strategic approach to academic guidance for adults. As transient, part-time students, adult learners often cannot use services such as advising and degree maps, counseling, career services, student life, and tutoring. Training for administrators and student affairs professionals often neglects information about adults as learners. Adding to the dilemma, institutions that do provide access to support services for adult students report underutilization because adult students feel that the services are not genuinely open to them or such students are focused primarily on class attendance, have multiple commitments and cannot take advantage of the services, or may satisfy their support service needs elsewhere (McGivney, 1996).

Affordability and Funding for Adults

In addition to access and convenient availability, affordability is crucial to adult participation and persistence in degree achievement. Adult students leave college more often because they lack both time and money for their studies. This situation will likely persist, as the cost of higher education is projected to continue increasing at a rate that exceeds the Consumer Price Index, the nation's basic metric of inflation (Snyder et al., 2007). As institutional costs rise, subsidies have decreased on a per capita basis. With median family income holding steady, students face a greater burden in paying for higher education (U.S. Department of Education, 2006). As a result, they are discouraged from attending college or may take on worrisome debt.

Some adults take advantage of employer subsidies; about 13% of learning expenditures are employer-paid tuition reimbursements (Council for Adult and Experiential Learning [CAEL], 2008; University Continuing Education Association, 2006). At least 20 federal programs provide financial aid or tax benefits to students, but most adult learners are self-funded. Improvement of higher education funding must include the needs of adult students, particularly subpopulations like low-income adults for whom employer subsidies or self-funding are not possible (Cook & King, 2004).

A notable exception to the decrease in public funding is the 21st Century GI Bill, signed in June 2008, which provides aid for military personnel to attend the most expensive public college in their state. Supporters say it has the potential to significantly expand college access for veterans at traditional 4-year institutions; however, the *Chronicle of Higher Education*'s research indicates that for-profit and community colleges are the most popular among students using the bill's benefits. Whereas 6% of all undergraduate students choose for-profit institutions, 19% of students who use the GI Bill benefits do (Field, 2008, p. A-12). Veterans report that these institutions are more convenient and cater to their needs.

Affordability for adult learners at 4-year colleges and universities will probably remain a contested issue. An analysis of changes in the availability of federal financial aid showed a significant positive effect on the enrollment behavior and persistence of adult students (Seftor & Turner, 2002). The Pell grant program, federal work-study, and various tax incentives (Government Accounting Office, 2007) continue to be available. However, the part-time (often students have time or money for only one class per semester), nonresidential, even noncredit patterns of adults often make them ineligible for grants and loans, and family obligations may constrain credit from other funding sources. Beyond GI funding, debate continues about whether providing substantial public resources to adult learners is a good public investment. This is leading to experimentation by private funders such as Lifelong Learning Accounts (LiLAS), employer-based 401(K)s with employees contributing a tax-exempt portion of each paycheck to an education saving account, with the employer matching the money, up to a cap (CAEL, 2009).

Accountability and Quality for Adult Higher Education

Accountability is in demand by state and federal policy makers in return for their support. Consumers and policy makers seek more transparent, understandable information about U.S. institutions' value added (e.g., student learning outcomes, graduation rates, workforce employability). One measure of accountability and consumer protection for adult students is program and institution accreditation. In addition to offering quality assurance, accreditation enables institutions and students to acquire federal dollars; U.S. Department of Education guidelines require accreditation of an institution before it or its students can become eligible to receive federal dollars in any form of grant or loan (Simpson, 2004). The six U.S. regional accreditation organizations have struggled with the issues surrounding adult-focused institutions and degrees and have developed metrics around what constitutes acceptable quality in such categories as online programs, distance education, or, in some cases, programs designed especially for adults. Other sources, such as the Adult Higher Education Alliance (AHEA) and Council for Adult and Experiential Learning (CAEL), provide resources to adult students seeking degree programs most compatible with their needs. These organizations, as well as the American Council on Education and Commission on Colleges at the Southern Association of Colleges and Schools, have also formulated principles of best practices for adult programs and distance learning. Assessment of these principles can guide designers of adult education degrees and adult students in doing diligence and knowing what to expect from a degree program offered with adults' best interests in mind (Simpson, 2004).

FUTURE CHALLENGES FOR ADULTS IN FOUR-YEAR COLLEGES AND UNIVERSITIES

The American Council on Education's Roundtable report *Collective Foresight: The Leadership Challenges for Higher Education's Future* (White & Eckel, 2008) indicates that economic globalization, technological advances, increasing competition, insufficient public resources, and pressure for accountability and transparency will continue to shape higher education. This chapter has shown that the student demographic in 4-year colleges and universities is becoming older and more diverse; new technologies have spawned distance learning as a near-ubiquitous phenomenon; and the for-profit model, while small, is gaining momentum, particularly for adults. More institutions are capitalizing on the trend and offer forms of adult, continuing, and professional education to a wide range of constituencies. Underlying motives range from mission to financial necessity to entrepreneurial spirit.

While significant, the expansion of providers and programs still does not reach the majority of adults in need of further education. The evidence gathered in the Emerging Pathways project (Pusser et al., 2007) suggests that although institutions are becoming sensitive to the challenges adult learners face, institutional actions and strategies are neither generally systematic nor empirically based, nor do they sufficiently account for the diverse identities, characteristics, and needs of the adult learner population. Of the many challenges ahead, four stand out:

- *Adult students as a market:* Mutual benefits can result when higher education institutions look to adult learners as a promising market. However, this approach also bears the potential for exploitation, with educational products (degrees or certificates) sold in a manner designed to undercut the competition, so students spend less time in instruction and study and receive fewer or poorer quality supports. The challenge is to fully engage *with* the adult market in meeting their needs.

- *Systemic support for adult students:* Adult learners often are place bound, have time constraints due to family and work obligations, and have differing education goals and learning preferences than young students. Four-year institutions are challenged to replace outmoded pedagogy, policies, and practices with systemic supports for adult students. Because those adults receiving financial aid are more likely to persist than their peers, state and federal financial aid needs to be a priority and adult-friendly.

- *Research and data needs:* Practitioners and researchers face challenges in accessing and using data on adult learners in 4-year colleges and universities. Even the latest published enrollment and participation data come from a variety of base years. In addition, few sources allow for analyzing information on adults' enrollment choices, financing patterns, or other key information by both age and the interaction of age with other demographic characteristics such as gender, race/ethnicity, and income. Information is particularly lacking on factors affecting degree completion among adult learners; adult student enrollment in noncredit courses at colleges and universities; and the impact of credit-bearing and non-credit-bearing courses on short-term and long-term educational attainment and lifetime earnings.

- *Social equity:* In the next decade, higher education leaders will be challenged to maintain competitiveness while ensuring that higher education remains a relevant social institution with a social justice agenda. The personal and social benefits of higher education include employment and earnings, economic growth and productivity, civic participation and voting, and intergenerational economic and social mobility. Policymakers and academic leaders must strive to eliminate the effects of social stratification by income, gender, race, age, physical ability, or geographic location as barriers to adult education (Cook & King, 2004). Creating strategic partnerships and alliances within, across, and outside higher education will be key to taking on these challenges.

Near the end of the 1990s, eminent management educator and scholar Peter Drucker predicted, "Thirty years from now the big university campuses will be relics" and within a generation, the university would take on a form virtually unrecognizable as an institution that has existed for the past 1,000 years (quoted in Lenzner & Johnson, 1997). A decade later, it appears that Drucker was right:

Higher education is experiencing a radical transformation unparalleled in recent history. Adults are now firmly positioned within higher education and the global knowledge economy. Yet, educational opportunity for all adult learners, not just those filling a market segment, is only one aspect of social justice that the university of the future must adopt as this population makes its way to the mainstream of higher education.

REFERENCES

Allen, I. E., & Seaman, J. (2007, October). *Online nation: Five years of growth in online learning.* Retrieved February 1, 2009, from http://www.sloan-c.org/publications/survey/pdf/online_nation.pdf

Aslanian, C. B. (2001). *Adult students today.* New York: College Board.

Bok, D. C. (2003). *Universities in the marketplace: The commercialization of higher education.* Princeton, NJ: Princeton University Press.

Boyer, E. L. (1990). *Scholarship reconsidered: Priorities of the professoriate.* New York: Carnegie Foundation for the Advancement of Teaching.

Buteau, R. (2007). Balancing acts: A phenomenological study of single mothers who are successful students in higher education. *Proceedings of the Adult Education Research Conference.* Retrieved February 1, 2009, from http://www.adulterc.org/Proceedings/2007/Proceedings/Buteau.pdf

Cantor, J. A. (2006). *Lifelong learning and the academy: The changing nation of continuing education.* ASHE Higher Education Report, Vol. 32(2). San Francisco: Wiley Periodicals.

Cook, B., & King, J. E. (2004). *Low-income adults in profile: Improving lives through higher education.* Washington, DC: American Council on Education.

Council for Adult and Experiential Learning (CAEL). ((2008). *Adult learning in focus: National and state-by-state data.* Chicago: CAEL with The National Center for Higher Education Management Systems.

Council for Adult and Experiential Learning. (2009). *Lifelong learning accounts.* At http://www.cael.org/lilas.htm

Duderstadt, J. J. (2000). *A university for the 21st century.* Ann Arbor: University of Michigan Press.

ECOP-NASULGC. (2007, October). *Strategic opportunities for Cooperative Extension.* Retrieved February 16, 2010 from http://www.aplu.org/NetCommunity/Document.Doc?id=370

Field, K. (2008, July 25). Cost, convenience drive veterans' college choices. *The Chronicle of Higher Education, 54*(46), A1, 12–14.

Geiger, R. L. (2004). *Knowledge & money: Research universities and the paradox of the marketplace.* Stanford, CA: Stanford University Press.

Governmental Accounting Office. (2007, November). *Higher education* (GAO-08–245). Retrieved February 16, 2010, from http://www.gao.gov

Kellogg Commission on the Future of State and Land-Grant Universities. (1999). *Returning to our roots: A learning society.* Washington, DC: National Association of State Universities and Land-Grant Colleges.

Kirp, D. L. (2003). *Shakespeare, Einstein, and the bottom line: The marketing of higher education.* Cambridge, MA: Harvard University Press.

LaPadula, M. (2003). A comprehensive look at online student support services for distance learners. *The American Journal of Distance Education, 17,* 119–128.

Lenzner, R., & Johnson, S. S. (1997, March 10). Seeing things as they really are. *Forbes, 159*(5), 122–128.

Mancuso, S. (2001). Adult-centered practices: Benchmarking study in higher education. *Innovative Higher Education, 25*(3), 165–181.

McGivney, V. (1996). *Staying or leaving the course: Non-completion and retention of mature students in further and higher education.* Leicester, UK: National Institute of Adult Continuing Education.

McGivney, V. (2004). Understanding persistence in adult learning. *Open Learning, 19,* 33–46.

Merriam, S. B., Caffarella, R. S., & Baumgartner, L. M. (2007). *Learning in adulthood: A comprehensive guide.* Lanham, MD: John Wiley.

Milam, J. (2005). The role of noncredit courses in serving nontraditional learners. In B. Passer (Ed.), *Arenas of entrepreneurship: Where nonprofit and for-profit institutions compete.* (pp. 55–68). New Directions for Higher Education, No. 129. San Francisco: Jossey-Bass/Wiley.

National Center for Education Statistics (NCES). (2007a). *Digest of educational statistics 2007* (Enrollment, staff, and degrees conferred in postsecondary institutions participating in Title IV programs, by level and control of institution, sex of student, and type of degree: Fall 2005 and 2005–06). Retrieved February 1, 2009, from http://nces.ed.gov/programs/digest/d07/tables/dt07_177.asp?referrer=list

National Center for Education Statistics (NCES). (2007b). *Digest of educational statistics 2007* (Total fall enrollment in degree-granting institutions, by level, sex, age, and attendance status of student: 2005). Retrieved February 1, 2009, from http://nces.ed.gov/programs/digest/d07/tables/dt07_182.asp?referrer=list

National Center for Public Policy in Higher Education. (2008, April). *Partnership for public purposes: Engaging higher education in societal challenges of the 21st century* (A Special Report by the National Center for Public Policy and Higher Education). Retrieved February 1, 2009, from http://www.highereducation.org/reports/wegner/index.shtml

Newman, F., Couturier, L., & Scurry, J. (2004). *The future of higher education: Rhetoric, reality, and the risks of the market.* San Francisco: Jossey-Bass.

Paulson, K., & Boeke, M. (2006). *Adult learners in the United States: A national profile.* Washington, DC: American Council on Education.

Planty, M., Hussar, W., Snyder, T., Provasnik, S., Kena, G., Dinkes, R., KewalRamani, A., & Kemp, J. (2008, June). *The condition of education 2008* (NCES 2008–031). Washington, DC: National Center for Education Statistics.

Pusser, B., Breneman, D. W., Gansneder, B. M., Kohl, K. J., Levin, J. S., Milam, J. H., & Turner, S. E. (2007). *Returning to learning: Adults' success in college is key to American's future.* Retrieved February 1, 2009, from http://www.luminafoundation.org/publications/ReturntolearningApril2007.pdf

Rhodes, F. H. T. (2001). *The creation of the future: The role of the American university.* Ithaca, NY: Cornell University Press.

Rice, P. J. (2003). Adult student services office. In D. Kilgore & P. J. Rice (Eds.), *Meeting the special needs of adult students* (pp. 53–57). New Directions for Student Services, No. 102. San Francisco: Jossey-Bass/Wiley.

Rowley, D. J., Lujan, H. D., & Dolence, M. G. (1998). *Strategic choices for the academy: How demand for lifelong learning will re-create higher education.* San Francisco: Jossey-Bass.

Sanders, H. C. (1966). *The cooperative extension service.* Englewood Cliffs, NJ: Prentice Hall.

Seftor, N. S., & Turner, S. E. (2002). Back to school: Federal student aid policy and adult college enrollment. *Journal of Human Resources, 37*(2), 336–352.

Simpson, E. G., Jr. (2004). Accreditation issues related to adult degree programs. In J. Pappas & J. Jerman (Eds.), *Developing and delivering adult degree programs* (pp. 81–89). New Direction for Adult and Continuing Education, No. 103. San Francisco: Jossey-Bass/Wiley.

Slaughter, S., & Rhoades, G. (2004). *Academic capitalism and the new economy: Markets, state, and higher education.* Baltimore: Johns Hopkins University Press.

Snyder, T. D., Dillow, S. A., & Hoffman, C. M. (2007). *Digest of education statistics 2006* (NCES 2007–017). Washington, DC: U.S. Department of Education, National Center for Education Statistics, Institute of Education Sciences.

Stoskopf, L., & Moorash, A. (2005). EARMYU: Expanding education access and excellence to highly mobile online learners. *Journal of Asynchronous Learning Networks, 9,* 53–60.

University Continuing Education Association (UCEA). (2006). *Lifelong learning trends: A profile of continuing higher education* (9th ed.). Washington, DC: Author.

University of Phoenix (UOP). (2007). *Factbook.* Phoenix, AZ: University of Phoenix. Retrieved February 16, 2010 from http://www.phoenix.edu/students/student_demographics.htm

U.S. Census Bureau. (2008). Home page. Retrieved February 1, 2009, from http://www.census.gov/

U.S. Department of Education. (2006, September). *A test of leadership: Charting the future of U.S. higher education* (A report of the commission appointed by Secretary of Education Margaret Spellings). Retrieved February 1, 2009, from http://www.ed.gov/about/bdscomm/list/hiedfuture/reports/final-report.pdf

Washburn, J. (2005). *University Inc.: The corporate corruption of higher education.* New York: Basic Books.

White, B. P., & Eckel, P. D. (2008). *Collective foresight: The leadership challenges for higher education's future.* Washington, DC: American Council on Education.

Wlodkowski, R. J., & Kasworm, C. E. (Eds.). (2003). *Accelerated learning for adults: The promise and practice of intensive educational formats.* New Directions for Adult and Continuing Education, No. 97. San Francisco: Jossey-Bass.

Wlodkowski, R. J. (2003). Accelerated learning in colleges and universities. In R. Wlodkowski & C. Kasworm (Eds.), *Accelerated learning for adults: The promise and practice of intensive educational formats* (pp. 5–16). New Directions for Adult and Continuing Education, No. 97. San Francisco: Jossey-Bass.

21

THE LEARNING LANDSCAPE
OF COMMUNITY COLLEGES

NANCY LLOYD PFAHL, KAY M. MCCLENNEY, TERRY O'BANION,
LEILA GONZÁLEZ SULLIVAN, AND CYNTHIA D. WILSON

The need for trained workers, drive for social equality, and inclination to forge institutions of practical value to society spurred development of U.S. community colleges during the early 20th century. Sometimes called "colleges of the people," this form of higher education strives to fulfill its dual promise: "Opportunity *with* excellence. Access *and* student success" (Community College Survey of Student Engagement [CCSSE], 2008, p. i). Because community colleges have been "designed from the ground up to serve American priorities" (Cross, 1999, p. x), communities reap significant benefits as a result of their meeting emergent adult learning needs, regardless of age and preparation for postsecondary study.

Propelled by economic, political, and social forces; open admissions; comparably affordable cost; and convenient locations, 2-year community colleges have proliferated from one experimental technical college in 1901 to 1,045 community colleges, enrolling in 2006 to 2007 more than 6.2 million adults, 35% of all postsecondary students (Provasnik & Planty, 2008). These dynamic institutions have committed to becoming learning colleges where faculty and administrators intentionally apply adult learning practices to help students succeed. They experiment with learning communities and other collaborative learning approaches; develop cultures of evidence to substantiate learning outcomes, inform decision making, and provide a basis for adult learning research; prepare new generations of community college leaders; build local workforces; and provide workforce training models for developing countries.

This chapter includes three sections characterizing the learning landscape. The first describes how community colleges have evolved to build community and increase postsecondary education access to adult learners: the unemployed or underemployed returning to school, displaced workers, employees with degrees returning for career advancement or retirement careers, people seeking professional and leadership development reflecting changes in their fields, and lifelong learners pursuing personal interests. The second discusses contextual issues related to the colleges' history, comprehensive mission, and policy decisions impacting adult learners; it examines how community colleges promote achievement by putting learning first and focusing on success of all students. The third discusses the future of adult learning at community colleges, where almost half the students are over age 25 (Phillipe & Sullivan, 2005).

This chapter's terminology will be *community college*. The term *2-year postsecondary* is misleading. Few students complete studies in 2 years; some certificates require less study time. The American Association of Community Colleges (AACC) accepts the term community colleges as inclusive of multiple monikers: community, junior, technical, 2-year, and baccalaureate degree-granting community colleges.

EVOLUTIONARY CHANGES: ADVANCING ADULT LEARNING THAT BUILDS COMMUNITY

During the past decade, various forces have quickened the pace of change for community colleges. Grounded in their mission, traditionally they have provided adult learners access to postsecondary education and other learning opportunities. Current trends altering them radically include:

- Increases in the number and proportion of older citizens (U. S. Census Bureau, 2008)

- Increasingly diverse student population of minority, self-supporting, immigrant, and first-generation college students, including in Fall 2005 41% (878,834) of all Black undergraduates, 51% (934,399) of Hispanic undergraduates, 45% (405,858) of Asian/Pacific Islander undergraduates, and 51% (78,249) of Native American undergraduates nationwide (Provasnik & Planty, 2008)

- Increase in number of English as a Second Language programs, the largest, fastest-growing programs at many community colleges, where one in four students has immigrated (McCabe, 2003); a minority increase from 33.3% of the U.S. population currently to 54% in 2050 is projected (U.S. Census Bureau, 2008)

- Digital divide, differences between those who do and do not have effective access to information technology

- Growing numbers of academically underprepared and returning adult learners, requiring more intensive learning assessments and strengthened developmental education (Parsad & Lewis, 2003)

- Need for higher education institutions to seek alternatives to state funding at a time of increasing demand on their resources and escalating government pressure to be more accountable for student success (Center for Community College Policy [CCCP], 2000)

- Globalization affecting the world economy and increasing need for more intensive workforce preparation (Jacobs & Dougherty, 2006) in a world now more urban than rural for the first time in history (Giridharadas, 2007)

Creating a volatile climate, these trends challenge community colleges to design and offer programs and services to ensure all students develop skills and competencies needed for living and working in a global community.

Historic Evolution

Scholars have traced community colleges' history and growth: Cohen and Brawer (2008) detail its comprehensive history and evolution; Vaughan (2006) recounts stories of innovation that advanced a new form of local higher education. Although there is divergence of opinion in the literature, the Deegan-Tillery categorization of community college evolution into generations is useful for framing this chapter historically: (1) extension of the high school, 1900 to 1930; (2) junior college, 1930 to 1950; (3) community college, 1950 to 1970; (4) comprehensive community college, 1970 to 1985; and (5) search for a new focus, 1985 to 1995 (Shearon & Tollefson, 1989). Building communities, recommended by the AACC's Commission on the Future of Community Colleges (CFCC), became that focus.

This handbook chapter describes the sixth-generation community colleges committed to adult learning: learning colleges, 1995 to present. The learning college concept derives from quality and productivity challenges of fifth-generation colleges, the work of the CFCC, the seminal work of O'Banion (1997), and the New Expeditions Initiative (NEI).

The CFCC encouraged learning partnerships, curricula that emphasize universal literacy, common learning core, and essentialness of work, lifelong learning, and classroom communities that empower learners for success within local and global communities. In this context, "community must be defined not only as a region to be served, but also as a climate to be created in the classroom, on the campus, and around the world" (CFCC, 1988, p. 49). O'Banion (1997) and Harvey-Smith (2005) articulated foundational learning college principles. NEI further emphasized strengthening community college connections and urgency to "embrace 'learning' rather than 'teaching' as the focus of their educational enterprise" (AACC, 2000, p. 15).

Mission

The mission of comprehensive community colleges includes five components:

- *Education for transfer* to baccalaureate degree-granting institutions

- *Career education* for jobs requiring associate's degrees, more than a high school diploma, but less than an associate's degree

- *Developmental and remedial education,* basic skills, and college prep, including literacy services

- *Business and industry training* to support economic development

- *Community enrichment,* noncredit, lifelong learning courses; music and theater performances; visual arts exhibitions; and dialogues to catalyze action on local, state, and national issues.

While most community college leaders concur about desirability of maintaining a comprehensive mission to meet current and emergent needs, others criticize community colleges' lack of focus and express concern that these colleges divert students from baccalaureate studies (Brint & Karabel, 1991; Dougherty, 2001).

Although community colleges continue "to lead the way by devising new programs and adapting practices to meet needs of previously unserved populations" (Cross, in O'Banion, 1997, p. x), debate continues over appropriateness of developmental programs that serve adults unprepared for higher education. Proponents argue that high-risk students taking developmental and study skills courses are more engaged than lower risk peers (CCSSE, 2008). Critics counter

that college-level remediation covering high school content and skills is inefficient and costly (Bailey, 2008).

Partnership building is a strategy that strengthens community colleges. External partnerships with employers, local school districts, other colleges and universities, community-based organizations, and state and federal organizations support programs and services to meet adult learners' needs (Amey, 2007). Internal collaboration among community college departments and disciplines contributes to refining institutional processes that support learning.

Values

Applying adult learning principles and practices reinforces respect for all learners and acknowledges roles for education in social justice. "Although more traditional colleges struggle to 'recruit minorities,' community colleges achieve their diversity on many dimensions as a natural part of their mission to serve their communities" (Cross in O'Banion, 1997, p. x). Ideally, two decades of focus on building community and more than a decade on learning would lead community college personnel to value richness of diversity, respect each other's contributions to collective learning, and espouse cultures of trust and receptivity to learning from difference. Not everyone, however, has found that these values support dynamic learning environments that address inequalities of students' pre-college backgrounds and ensure long-term success (Dougherty & Kienzl, 2006).

Adult Learning Challenges

Community colleges face multiple challenges including online learning, just-in-time career education, and remedial education. These activities encourage faculty to become more flexible, collaborative, and responsive. Online learning requires faculty willingness to revise classroom strategies and adopt new learning practices, effective across boundaries of space and time.

It is not enough to get students through the open door (Dougherty & Kienzl, 2006). Because adult learners enroll with various preparation levels, community colleges have become gateways for first-generation, self-supporting, and underprepared college students without time to waste. One fourth are single parents, and 29% come from lowest income-level families (Horn & Nevill, 2006). About 42% of first-time public community college enrollees take developmental courses, a result of underpreparation (Provasnik & Planty, 2008), and 98% of public community colleges offer remedial programs (Parsad & Lewis, 2003). Community colleges offer many students their only hope to improve their lives. Typically, such students know what they want and need to learn what is life-relevant. Their motivation is inseparable from their learning; their learning is commensurate with their motivation (Wlodkowski, 2008).

Research findings about impacts of community college remediation are contradictory: Bailey (2008) contends developmental coursework may help early persistence, but not necessarily long-term progress after the second year toward earning a degree. Others have found integration into a college community relates positively to student persistence (CCSSE, 2008; Karp, O'Gara, & Hughes, 2008). Karp and his colleagues learned that community college student-success courses helped to develop information networks that facilitated academic and social integration and improved persistence. Larger-scale studies in Florida and Texas, still in process, appear to contradict these findings: Martorell and McFarlin (in review) have found little indication that these interventions improve either academic or labor market outcomes.

Despite contradictions, baccalaureate institutions have been reluctant to deal with remediation (Parsad & Lewis, 2003). Recognition of student preparation gaps for postsecondary learning has prompted significant investments by higher education institutions, research organizations, and foundations to fund long-term national initiatives such as Achieving the Dream (www.achievingthedream.org). Strong local projects to improve education transitions and college preparation include Puente Project (www.puente.net).

Governance Issues

As community colleges have matured, changing circumstances require all participants to learn. The university model of governance—responsibility for decision making—has become normative (Cohen & Brawer, 2008), trending toward more participation and shared responsibility (Cloud & Kater, 2008). Elected or appointed boards of trustees, primarily laypersons, hire the president; establish policies; oversee human, financial, and physical resources; award academic degrees; and ensure college planning and accountability (McGuinness, 2001, 2002, 2003). Responsible performance requires learning through professional development, such as provided by the Association of Community College Trustees (www.acct.org).

Boards must rethink how they apply local, state, and other resources in global online instructional service areas. Establishing broader partnerships, encompassing pre-K–16 through graduate school, and developing high school and university articulation agreements encourage new forms of cooperation across this continuum (CCCP, 2006).

Internal groups share governance responsibilities. Under authority of a board of trustees and president, administrators may propose policies and implement procedures. Faculty often organizes into a senate that makes academic and student affairs recommendations. Staff may advise on matters affecting those employees. Student input can occur through student board members or trustees and student government organizations.

State-level college governance has become more centralized. As public demand for accountability has grown and resources have diminished, most states have established statewide coordinating and policy-making boards for distributing resources, avoiding duplication of services, addressing assessment and accountability, and advocating on behalf of colleges with state legislatures.

Accreditation, Quality Assurance, and Accountability

Accreditation ensures that community colleges provide quality education for all learners. Community colleges receive institutional accreditation from regional accrediting agencies recognized by the U.S. Secretary of Education and program accreditation from others responsible for program standards and licensure. Regional accreditors establish requirements to define and assess learning outcomes and other student achievement indicators. Calling for higher standards has helped embed the principles of *learning colleges* (described later in this chapter) into community college cultures.

The Commission on the Future of U. S. Higher Education (CFUSHE, 2006) expressed its drive toward increased higher education accountability for learning and addressed learning standards, access, cost and affordability, financial aid, transparency, accountability, and innovation. With no centralized U.S. authority exercising control over postsecondary education, however, the way that community colleges operate varies dramatically, even within states (Cohen & Brawer, 2008).

Funding Issues

As community college enrollments increase, funding is not keeping pace (Cloud & Kater, 2008). State funding formulas have changed to include performance-based funding initiatives (CCCP, 2000). Although the funding mix varies from state to state, from 1918 to 2000, support shifted from 94% local taxes and bonds and 6% tuition to the combination of 46% state support, 20% local support, 20% tuition and fees, and 16% federal and other sources (Cohen & Brawer, 2008).

Even though governing authorities push for learning accountability, "some measure of enrollment" (Cohen & Brawer, 2008, p. 164) remains the primary driver in most states for postsecondary funding formulas (CCCP, 2000). Top five funding indicators are job placement (17 states), transfer rates (16), graduation rates or certificates and degrees awarded (16), retention time to degree (14), and licensure pass rates (11) (CCCP, 2000). Note: The two top indicators do not relate to degree attainment, a controversial issue for accountability (Bailey, Jenkins, & Leinbach, 2006). Given growing student diversity in community colleges, nine states have adopted service to special populations as performance-based indicators (CCCP, 2000).

U.S. Department of Education provides funds for student financial aid and initiatives to enhance program quality through grants such as offered by the National Science Foundation. Other federal agencies pose competitive funding to improve education quality. Such grants influence campus governance and policy decisions. States also provide financial aid and sometimes offer program grants.

REVOLUTIONARY CHANGE: BREAKING WITH TRADITION AND BECOMING LEARNING COLLEGES

Changing from traditional teaching-centered colleges to more learning-centered colleges is less about *what* comprehensive community colleges do—for they continue to offer credit, noncredit, and continuing education to adults—but more about *how* they do it in ways that break with some traditions and reinforce others. Unlike traditional institutions focused on *teaching,* "the learning college places *learning* first and provides educational experiences for learners anyway, anyplace, anytime" (O'Banion, 1997, p. 70). This premise implies integrating and using technology to support learning, regardless of time and place.

Enacting learning-college concepts while community colleges are serving more diverse students, facing leadership and governance challenges, and competing for funding requires all employees to look differently at their roles, with the goal of having "every employed person thinking about how his or her work facilitates the learning process" (O'Banion, 1997, p. 58). For everyone to connect their jobs to learning and accountability requires a change in thinking: Even faculty and academic support personnel must shift from being teachers to becoming learners with their students.

Learning colleges represent a paradigm shift (Cross in O'Banion, 1997) in how community colleges think about and plan for student success. This change requires intentional processes, grounded in commitments to learning and changing. League for Innovation in the Community College (LICC) has nurtured the first 12 experimental learning colleges as catalytic incubators for learning-college concepts (www.league.org). Inclusive professional development is an essential for strategic planning and budgeting processes (Wilson, 2002, p. 24). Raising the bar to achieve learners' goals requires trusting that risks will lead to learning, surfacing and changing problematic assumptions, examining possibilities, collaborating to learn, and using data for decision making (Pfahl, 2003).

Learning College

Foundational to creating more learning-centered community colleges are six key principles

(O'Banion, 1997, p. 47) that assume "placing learning and the learner first" (p. 19) overrides the convenience of institutions and their staffs. To strengthen learning experiences, Harvey-Smith's (2005) seventh principle advocates collaboration between academic and student affairs. She recommends student affairs "lead from the center [where] transformations are more likely to take hold as a result of diverse leadership and involvement of different constituencies" (p. 93).

At its core, the learning-college concept energizes adult learning. Strategies consistent with adult learning practices that power this transition include clarifying and measuring learning outcomes, examining assessment practices, conducting learning research, applying findings to learning practices, integrating technology into learning, drawing on learning-organization principles (O'Banion, 1997), and integrating student affairs and academic programs (Harvey-Smith, 2005).

- *A learning college creates substantive change in individual learners.* "Learning is the driving force of human change" (Jarvis, 2006, p. 5). Adult educators seek to kindle learning in students: new ways of thinking and sensing that will lead to constructive life changes. Learning is both situated and social; people are both material and mental; how learners set their learning goals reflects their changing life-worlds (Jarvis, 2006).

- *A learning college engages learners as full partners in the learning process, with learners assuming primary responsibility for their own choices.* Adult learners know what they want to learn and why. Adult educators must show learners how a class will help them make more informed decisions to reach their goals. Partners in learning, adult educators must acknowledge and access the richest learning resources from within learners themselves (Knowles in Jarvis, 2006, p. 187).

- *A learning college creates and offers as many options for learning as possible.* Providing multiple learning options enables adult learners, faculty, and staff to make the best choices for achieving goals by "transforming the content of their experience" (Jarvis, 2006, p. 187) and applying it to meet the needs of their life-worlds. High achievement requires high expectations coupled with high support (CCSSE, 2008).

- *A learning college assists learners to form and participate in collaborative learning activities.*

Learning is a socially constructed process within a cultural context (Jarvis, 2006). According to the 2008 Horizon Report, "renewed emphasis on collaborative learning" is prompting adult educators "to develop new forms of interaction" (p. 5). Given adult students with years of experience, community colleges flourish with opportunities for learning from difference. Using collaborative strategies and learning practices reinforces the notion that learners create their own knowledge (Barkley, Cross, & Major, 2005).

- *A learning college defines the roles of learning facilitators by the needs of the learners.* Faculty who value adult learners' experience collaborate with them, acknowledging its value and their orientation toward applying knowledge to change how they live. Eliciting narratives and comparing experiences enable adult learners to reflect more constructively on their own and others' life-worlds, identifying new pathways and possibilities (Pfahl & Wiessner, 2007; Wiessner & Pfahl, 2007).

- *A learning college and learning facilitators succeed only when improved and expanded learning can be documented for learners.* Developing a culture of evidence, consistent with the trend for funding tied to learning and productivity measures, requires innovative application of adult learning practices, clarification of learning outcomes and measures, and conducting learning research. When clear about learning outcomes, adult educators can identify appropriate paths for learning assessment and achievement.

- *A learning college integrates and connects its academic programs with student affairs support services to optimize learning success.* Learning is about making connections (Cross, 1999). Enabling adult learners to accomplish their goals requires building internal college partnerships that support learning achievement. "The emerging role of student affairs in learning is one of integration and connectivity; it includes clearer ties and partnerships between student affairs and academic and instructional divisions" (Harvey-Smith, 2005, p. 90).

Challenges to Learning

Learning-college principles have generated dialogue about how to establish generative learning cultures and environments to foster inquiry, assess learning outcomes, become more accountable, and promote student engagement (O'Banion & Wilson, 2010). Trust is foundational: The degree of trust among participants in a culture and their shared values influence the extent of collaboration (Pfahl, 2003).

Establishing Learning Cultures and Environments

Adult learning that promotes intellectual development, effective citizenship, gainful employment, and societal advancement requires creating dynamic learning cultures and varied learning environments (Baker, 2008). Social learning areas, including virtual worlds, "can coexist with and expand traditional education" (Brown & Adler, 2008, p. 22). Understanding how adults learn and taking advantage of technological advances are powerful tools to enrich learning, for robust adult learning practices contribute to generative learning environments and optimize possibilities for achievement.

In a college with traditional practices, putting learning first for everyone, regardless of position, can be challenging. Learning new ways of thinking and interacting requires intentional, honest self-assessment and action. Various factors influence how generative and stimulating learning environments will become: values and attitudes of adult educators and learners toward learning and its assessment; willingness to explore, collaborate, and employ practices consistent with adult learning principles; and use of physical and virtual space. Organizations such as EDUCAUSE (www.educause.edu) provide technology assistance to diversify learning options.

Ensuring Learning Assessment and Accountability

Cultures of inquiry aim to increase knowledge, resolve doubt, and solve problems. This approach applies sound assessment practices, setting the stage for accountability and learning success. Assessment is a continuous process that informs next steps for achieving learning outcomes. Its purposes are improvement of programs to help learners achieve their full potential—assessment *for* learning; informing learners about how they've performed—assessment *of* learning; and identification of accountability measures to use in process improvement and decision making (Baker, 2008). For effective assessment that influences learning outcomes, adult educators

and learners must clarify learning goals and verify evidence documenting learning outcomes. Lack of clarity and agreement renders accountability problematic. Stating outcomes explicitly, assessing achievement regularly, and analyzing verifiable evidence help diagnose learning problems and meet learner and institutional expectations (Baker, 2008).

Adult educators and learners must overcome barriers to assessment and accountability including cynicism about assessment; persistence of ineffective but comfortable practices; repudiation of the need for assessment; pretense—going through the motions without interpreting the meaning of what has happened; and excuses running counter to learning assessment and learner success—lack of time, lack of relevance, and lack of will (Baker, 2008). Even when economically motivated and comparison driven by local, state, and federal governance, assessment and accountability processes emphasize quality over quantity. Nonetheless, some measure of enrollment remains the centerpiece of most state allocation processes (Cohen & Brawer, 2008).

Promoting Student Engagement

Although adult learners may be less likely to engage with colleges than younger undergraduates, due to competing responsibilities and developmental relevancy of such interaction, the Community College Survey of Student Engagement (www.ccsse.org) has found that what matters most for student success is engagement. Surveying more than 700,000 students at 624 participating colleges since 2001, CCSSE has documented effective educational practices in community colleges and relationships among student engagement, college persistence, and academic attainment (CCSSE, 2008; McClenney & Marti, 2006).

Using CCSSE's Web site, participating colleges can benchmark their performance. Benchmarking effectively compares performance with peer institutions, yielding information about institutional quality and student learning in broader contexts. Emerging lessons about what matters most to produce higher levels of student learning, persistence, and degree attainment include the following:

- *Engagement matters for all students, but it matters more to even the playing field for some than for others.* The more engaged community college students are with one another, faculty, staff, and the content of their studies, the more likely they are to persist and succeed. Analyses of high-risk student groups including first-generation college students, students of color, and students underprepared for college-level work indicate that highly engaged high-risk students are most likely to persist.

- *Early engagement is critical.* Community colleges lose many entering students during their earliest weeks of collegiate experience. Investing to strengthen first-term advising, orientation, college success courses, and academic experiences, including learning communities, supplemental instruction, and first-year seminars, likely will pay dividends in terms of heightened learner success (CCSSE, 2008).

- *Effective student engagement happens by design, not by accident.* Given a college population characterized by class attendance mixed with work and family obligations, institutions must design students' experiences to make engagement inescapable, age-appropriate, and relevant to their lives as adults.

- *Developmental education is a top priority for more than 40% of entering community college students* (Parsad & Lewis, 2003). Without more effective academic policies and teaching and learning strategies at the pre-college level, large numbers of adult learners will not have opportunities to succeed in postsecondary learning.

Challenges in Leadership

Community colleges are recruiting new, more diverse generations of leaders prepared to respond to changing circumstances. Leaders viewing learning colleges through lenses of adult education principles and practices commit to supporting all learners, strategic priority-setting, continuous assessment of institutional strengths and weaknesses, evidence-based learning, data-driven decision making, and community engagement. Although presidents set the tone, leaders for learning can emerge throughout community colleges to influence activities at every level. This distribution of leadership empowers participants to achieve learning success.

A number of related organizations prepare community college leaders. AACC and its councils provide various leadership development programs (www.AACC.nche.edu); for example, the National Community College Hispanic Council prepares Latinos/as for community college executive positions, including the presidency (Sullivan, 2007). As a result of such programs, AACC staff has confirmed an increase in the number of women and minority presidents.

Research Challenges

Serious, sustained focus on community college adult learners requires development of cultures of evidence regarding effectiveness of learning strategies. Historically, faculty and administrators have been consumed primarily by *doing things*—implementing projects, programs, and practices—and far less by evaluating impacts on learners. As campuses and state and federal legislators place more emphasis on evidence in their decision making, both classroom and institutional data emerge as powerful prompts for discussion, action, and improvement.

Cultures of evidence offer researchers opportunities to study wide-ranging adult education issues including best practices for creating generative learning environments, classroom strategies to promote success and persistence of adult learners, impacts of remediation on goal achievement, and refinement and integration of institutional processes that support learning success. Centers that specialize in community college research include:

- Center for Community College Research, partner of the National Center for Postsecondary Research, conducts studies on major issues, practices, and policies that affect community colleges and their students (www.cccr.tc.columbia.edu).

- California Community College Collaborative, University of California-Riverside, conducts policy research and designs professional development programs for community college personnel (www.C4.ucr.edu).

- Council for the Study of Community Colleges, University of California-Los Angeles, affiliate of the AACC, conducts and disseminates community college research and provides forums for dialogue (www.cscconline.org).

Local and Global Workforce Challenges

At many institutions, distinctions between vocational and collegiate education have blurred (Cohen & Brawer, 2008) because just as many students transfer to universities from community college career programs as from transfer programs. Traditionally, community college workforce education programs have led directly to employment rather than further study. However, with development of a global economy, two different groups of proponents have emerged: those who advocate vocationalism to prepare individuals for high-tech jobs needing baccalaureates and those who want to increase skills of low-income, displaced, and unemployed workers to become upwardly mobile job-seekers (Jacobs & Dougherty, 2006). In any case, "both strategies require reorientation and . . . commitment of resources" (p. 58).

Given lack of clarity about future occupational labor markets and increased difficulty raising revenues from tuition and state appropriations, the future of workforce education at community colleges seems uncertain; however, "there can be no reversing the perception that one of the colleges' prime functions is to train workers, and ample funds are available to support this function" (Cohen & Brawer, 2008, p. 60). One pragmatic recommendation is "for colleges to create a vertically and horizontally integrated system of workforce training that stretches from noncredit adult education through the baccalaureate" (Jacobs & Dougherty, 2006, p. 60), thereby meeting a broader range of learner interests and economic needs.

Nonetheless, locally directed U. S. community colleges have generated international attention for their workforce training programs and success in placing local workers. For more than 20 years, Community Colleges for International Development (CCID) has collaborated with U.S. community colleges and other countries, forging international partnerships and providing technical development assistance, curriculum development, training, and educational consultation (www.ccid.org).

The quickening pace of international adoption of the community college workforce training

model has enabled indigenous people worldwide to gain economic self-sufficiency and retain higher level positions. The community college movement in India, for example, has grown since 1995–1996 with the opening of Pondicherry University Community College and the first community college sponsored by a nongovernment organization, Madras Community College, and its partners. A decade later, what became a national movement has proliferated to 153 community colleges across 17 states (Alphonse, 2006).

PLANNING FOR THE FUTURE

Community colleges are incubators for adult learning. Learners' diversity of experience, interests, and needs enriches campus learning cultures, challenge adult educators to value and learn from difference, and call for responsive curricula and services. As institutions strive to contribute to every learner's success, and ultimately to the common good, they continue to learn from experience.

Adult educators and learners need to acknowledge when goals they set and realities they enact do not match. In response, educators and learners must reassess their practices, recognizing that simple solutions will not address learning complexity. Becoming more intentional in understanding learners' needs, conducting more consistent and objective assessments, and following rigorous standards for interpreting research data and applying findings will build capacity of community colleges and their faculty to ensure learners' achievement.

At a time when growing numbers of adults enter the open doors of community colleges, expecting to change and better their lives, the resulting challenges require leaders who support continuous experimentation, improvement, and learning on the part of everyone engaged in promoting success of adult learners of all ages.

REFERENCES

Alphonse, X. (2006, January–February). Learning for livelihood. *Frontline, 23*(2). Retrieved January 21, 2008 from www.frontline.in/f12302/f1230200.htm

American Association of Community Colleges. (2000). *The knowledge net: Connecting communities, learners, and colleges.* Washington, DC: Community College Press.

Amey, M. J. (Ed.). (2007). *Collaboration across education sectors.* San Francisco: Jossey-Bass.

Bailey, T. (2008). *Challenge and opportunity: Rethinking the role and function of developmental education in community college.* New York: Columbia University Teachers

College, Community College Research Center (CCRC).

Bailey, T., Jenkins, D., & Leinbach, T. (2006). *Is student success labeled institutional failure? Student goals and graduation rates in the accountability debate at community colleges.* New York: Columbia University Teachers College, CCRC.

Baker, R. (2008, June 11). *Assessment of student learning and institutional effectiveness.* Paper presented at the League Learning College Summit, Johnson County Community College, Kansas City, KS.

Barkley, E. F., Cross, K. P., & Major, C. H. (2005). *Collaborative learning techniques: A handbook for college faculty.* San Francisco: Jossey-Bass.

Brint, S., & Karabel, J. (1991). *The diverted dream: Community colleges and the promise of educational opportunity in America, 1900–1985.* New York: Oxford University Press.

Brown, J. S., & Adler, R. P. (2008, January/February). Minds on fire: Open education, the long tail, and learning 2.0. *EDUCAUSE, 43*(1), 16–32. Retrieved March 1, 2008, from http://www.educause.edu/EDUCAUSE+Review/EDUCAUSEReviewMagazineVolume43/MindsonFireOpenEducationtheLon/162420)

Center for Community College Policy (CCCP). (2000). *State funding for community colleges: A 50-state survey.* Denver: Education Commission of the States. Retrieved July 15, 2008, from www.ecs.org

Center for Community College Policy (CCCP). (2006). *Governance.* Denver, CO: Education Commission of the States. Retrieved August 4, 2008, from www.ecs.org

Cloud, R. C., & Kater, S. T. (Eds.). (2008). *Governance in the community college.* New Directions for Community Colleges, No. 141. San Francisco: Jossey-Bass.

Cohen, A. M., & Brawer, F. B. (2008). *The American community college* (5th ed.). San Francisco: Jossey-Bass.

Commission on the Future of Community Colleges (CFCC). (1988). *Building communities: A vision for a new century.* Washington, DC: American Association of Community Colleges.

Commission on the Future of U.S. Higher Education (CFUSHE). (2006). *A test of leadership: Charting the future of U.S. education.* Washington, DC: U.S. Department of Education.

Community College Survey of Student Engagement (CCSSE). (2008). *High expectations and high support.* Austin: University of Texas, Community College Leadership Program.

Cross, K. P. (1999). *Learning is about making connections.* Mission Viejo, CA: League for Innovation in the Community College.

Dougherty, K. J. (2001). *The contradictory college: The conflicting origins, impacts and futures of the community college.* Albany: State University of New York Press.

Dougherty, K. J., & Kienzl, G. S. (2006). It's not enough to get through the open door: Inequalities by social background in transfer from community colleges to four-year colleges. *Teachers College Record, 108*(3), 452–487.

Giridharadas, A. (2007, November 14). Riding the train of dreams across India. *International Herald Tribune,* p. 2.

Harvey-Smith, A. B. (2005). *The seventh learning college principle: A framework for transformational change.* Washington, DC: National Association of Student Personnel Administrators.

Horizon Report. (2008). Collaboration between the New Media Consortium and the EDUCAUSE Learning Initiative: An EDUCAUSE Program. Retrieved July 10, 2008 from http://www.nmc.org/pdf/2008-Horizon-Report.pdf

Horn, L., & Nevill, S. (2006*). Profile of undergraduates in U.S. postsecondary education institutions: 2003–2004 with a special analysis of community college students* (NCES2006 184). Washington, DC: U.S. Department of Education, Institute of Educational Statistics, National Center for Education Statistics.

Jacobs, J., & Dougherty, K. J. (2006). The uncertain future of the community college workforce development mission. In B. K. Townsend & K. J. Dougherty (Eds.), *Community college missions in the 21st century* (pp. 53–62). San Francisco: Jossey-Bass.

Jarvis, P. (2006). *Towards a comprehensive theory of human learning.* London: Routledge.

Karp, M. M., O'Gara, L., & Hughes, K. L. (2008). *Do support services at community colleges encourage success or reproduce disadvantage? An exploratory study.* New York: Columbia University Teachers College, CCRC.

Martorell, P., & McFarlin, I. (in review). *Help or hindrance? The effects of college remediation on academic and labor market outcomes.* April 2008 version provided by the authors paco@rand.org and isaacmcfarlin@gmail.com

McCabe, R. H. (2003). *Yes we can! A community college guide for developing America's underprepared.* Phoenix, AZ: League for Innovation in the Community College and American Association of Community Colleges.

McClenney, K. M., & Marti, C. N. (2006). *Exploring relationships between student engagement and student outcomes in community colleges.* Austin: University of Texas. Retrieved August 1, 2008, from http://www.inpathways.net/ExploringOutcomesEngagementCommunityCollege/pdf

McGuinness, A. C. (2001). *Governance and coordination: Definitions and distinctions.* Denver, CO: Education Commission of the States (ECS).

McGuinness, A. C. (2002). *Reflections on post-secondary governance changes.* Denver, CO: ECS.

McGuinness, A. C. (2003). *Models of post-secondary education coordination and governance in the states.* Denver, CO: ECS.

O'Banion, T. (1997). *A learning college for the 21st century.* Phoenix, AZ: American Council on Education/Oryx Press.

O'Banion, T., & Wilson, C. D. (2010). *Focus on learning: A learning college reader.* Phoenix, AZ: The League for Innovation in the Community College.

Parsad, B., & Lewis, L. (2003). *Remedial education at degree-granting postsecondary institutions in fall 2000* (NCES 2004–010). Washington: U.S. Department of Education, Institute of Educational Sciences, NCES.

Pfahl, N. L. (2003). *Raising the bar for higher education: Using narrative processes to advance learning and change.* Unpublished dissertation, Columbia University Teachers College, New York.

Pfahl, N. L., & Wiessner, C. A. (Summer & Fall 2007). Creating new directions: Drawing on life experiences in community adult education contexts. *Adult Learning, 18*(3&4), 9-13.

Phillipe, K., & Sullivan, L. G. (2005). *National profile of community colleges: Trends and statistics* (4th ed.). Washington, DC: Community College Press.

Provasnik, S., & Planty, M. (2008). *Community colleges: Special supplement to the condition of education.* Washington, DC: U.S. Department of Education, NCES.

Shearon, R. W., & Tollefson, T. A. (1989). Community colleges. In S. B. Merriam & P. M. Cunningham (Eds.), *Handbook of adult and continuing education* (pp. 316–331). San Francisco: Jossey-Bass.

Sullivan, L. G. (2007). Preparing Latinos/as for a flat world: The community college role. *Journal of Hispanics in Higher Education, 6*(4), 397–422.

U. S. Census Bureau. National news, released August 14, 2008. Retrieved March 2, 2009, from www.census.gov/populations/www/projections/

Vaughan, G. B. (2006). *The community college story: A tale of innovation* (3rd ed.). Washington, DC: Community College Press.

Wiessner, C. A., & Pfahl, N. L. (2007). Choosing different lenses: Using storytelling as a narrative technique to promote knowledge construction and learning in adults. *Journal of Continuing Higher Education, 55*(1), 27–37.

Wilson, C. D. (2002). The community college as a learning-centered organization. In N. Thomas (Ed.), *Perspectives on the community college: A journey of discovery* (pp. 23–26). Phoenix, AZ: League for Innovation in the Community College.

Wlodkowski, R. (2008). *Enhancing adult motivation to learn.* San Francisco: Jossey-Bass.

22

EMPLOYER-SPONSORED LEARNING IN THE WORKPLACE

SHARI PETERSON

The prominent issue for adult educators regarding workplace training and other developmental opportunities sponsored by employers used to be that performance improvement was strictly for the sake of the organization *without regard* for whether or not any personal development accrued to the individual. As a more humanistic focus on learning continued to surface, the perspective began shifting toward an understanding that professional development for performance and personal development for individual gain need not be mutually exclusive objectives (Bierema, 1996; Dirkx, 1996; Peterson & Provo, 2000). In this chapter, employer-sponsored opportunities for *learning* in the workplace are identified as benefitting both the individual and the organization. In the contemporary context of this more humanistic understanding, employer-sponsored learning in the workplace can be defined as the formal and informal provision of learning opportunities through which individuals at every level in the organization have the opportunity to gain knowledge and expertise leading to professional development for accomplishing job tasks and career goals, along with personal development to benefit themselves, their families, and communities.

The purpose of this chapter is to identify key contemporary practices intended to facilitate learning in the context of the workplace and discuss some key related issues. After all, the humanistic perspective presented here is not naïve; indeed, issues of power and justice continue to exist, and the potential for abuse, exclusion, and discrimination is ever present. The content (what adults learn) and how and why adults learn (learning theories) are addressed elsewhere in this handbook. First, the theoretical framework that undergirds the contemporary definition and perspective regarding employer-sponsored learning in the workplace is proposed. Next, contemporary practices are identified, followed by key issues, particularly those regarding diversity and inclusion. The chapter concludes with implications for practice and concomitant questions.

THEORETICAL FRAMEWORK

The two foundational theories that undergird the practice of employer-sponsored learning in the workplace are general systems theory and human capital theory. Other related theories and concepts that may influence adult learning are addressed by other authors throughout this handbook.

According to general systems theory, a system is a collection of parts that interact so as to function as a whole (Kauffman, 1980). A basic systems model is an inclusive framework comprising inputs that lead to processes that lead to outputs, all integrally connected through a feedback mechanism. Thus, general systems theory hypothesizes that when a set of interdependent parts together make up a whole in which each contributes something and receives something, the whole is greater than the sum of its parts. Organizations are systems in which organizational learning takes place (Senge, 1990). According to systems theory, learning can be construed holistically as an input, as well as a process and also as an outcome. For example, learned individuals perform workplace tasks (input); the organization provides a developmental opportunity such as training to those individuals (process); when learning has been enhanced, the organization is now represented by a higher level of individual, thus collective learning (output); the feedback mechanism of systems theory provides for these individuals to transfer their learning to the job (professional development) and to their lives (personal development). Knowles (1984) acknowledged this systemic approach in suggesting that learning does not occur in and of itself; rather, he noted, it is a function of having opportunities to learn and resources to learn—that is, learning is facilitated when there is a learning system in place. Culture, among other things, clarifies the extent to which the organization has a task *versus* learning orientation (Sambrook, 2005). Organizational cultures are complex, representing the thinking, espoused values, and shared norms that define the organization and the way employees function. Thus, a culture of learning is evoked when organizations provide *systemic,* sustained, and continuous opportunities for personal and professional growth and development (Peterson, 2008).

Human capital theory originated as an economic theory in the 1960s and continues to undergird employer-sponsored learning practices. Understandably, portraying human beings as *capital* sparks a discordant tone for many adult educators. Semantics notwithstanding, the theory helps explain the complementary nature of the relationship between improvement for the sake of the organization *and* personal development for the sake of the individual. According to Dobbs, Sun, and Roberts (2008), the essence of human capital theory is that "people invest in themselves according to their own self-interest, for the sake of future gains in life-time earnings" (p. 790), and organizations invest in training according to *their* own self-interest—improved productivity. For both the individual and the organization, the cost of doing so is purportedly offset by the increase in earnings. Billet's (2004) perspective was similar: "workplaces impose certain expectations and norms in the interest of their own continuity and survival, and in the interest of certain participants; but learners also choose to act in certain ways dependent on their own preferences and goals" (p. 320).

The economic objective posited by human capital theory is relevant and realistic because organizations and individuals alike are entitled to anticipate some form of economic gain from the provision of and participation in learning initiatives. Organizations used to engage almost exclusively in organization-specific knowledge and skill development; some still do. Contemporary organizations, however, invest to a great extent in developing a broader knowledge, skill, and attitude base, even with the understanding that they may be developing their employees to be more marketable elsewhere. When organizations recognize the benefit of developing the whole person such that individuals benefit personally and professionally, the organization also reaps more holistic economic rewards. Thus, systems theory and human capital theory are related, providing an even more solid foundation for employer-sponsored learning practices.

EMPLOYER-SPONSORED LEARNING PRACTICES

The practices presented here overlap in a holistic manner. For example, apprenticeships are a form of on-the-job training, as are job rotation, job enlargement, and quality circle initiatives. Similarly, career development may be considered an aspect of leadership development while others might suggest the other way around. In some organizations, mentoring and coaching are managed as aspects of career development, in other organizations as part of leadership development, and in still others as a dimension of both. Thus is the systemic nature of employer-sponsored learning initiatives. Consistent with human capital theory, the practices discussed are collectively advantageous in having the potential to provide economic gain both to the organization and those whom it employs.

Apprenticeships

The purpose of apprenticeships dates back to the Middle Ages—to pass knowledge from experts working in skilled crafts and trades to novices. Contemporary apprenticeships require a blend of classroom and on-the-job training (OJT). The classroom component often is provided by technical or community colleges, enabling apprentices to combine certification in a trade with an associate's degree. In the United States, formal apprenticeship programs are regulated by the Department of Labor's Bureau of Apprenticeship and Training (BAT), which sets the minimum number of hours required in the classroom and on the job (Desimone, Werner, & Harris, 2002). According to BAT, advantages to an organization include (a) a trained and more versatile labor pool with improved problem-solving ability and (b) increased productivity from reduced absenteeism and turnover, both of which lead to a better public image. In addition, organizations may be eligible for wage subsidies and tax credits. Advantages to novices include acquisition of knowledge that skills training alone cannot impart and greater opportunities to secure employment after certification, especially when combined with a degree.

Typically, apprenticeships represent unionized skilled trade and labor industries. The following example is outside the traditional context and format. The Future Leaders Apprenticeship Program (FLAP) was initiated by the auditing firm Deloitte & Touche to specifically recruit African American, American Indian, Asian, and Hispanic accounting majors (Chew, 2007). FLAP scholars were awarded $5,000 educational scholarships to complete degrees if they agreed to join the company and participate in a 2-year leadership program of seminars, meetings with top executives, and mentoring. This exemplary program represents a focus on learning and development that benefits the individual through networking, modeling, and coaching and the organization through recruiting, developing, promoting, and retaining diverse populations, establishing a pipeline of highly qualified and engaged workers.

The advantages of traditional and nontraditional apprenticeships represent a whole that is greater than the sum of its parts, and clearly, there are economic gains for the providers and the participants. The concern, however, is one of inclusion. The benefits accrue only to those who have the potential to succeed in the academic component, leaving behind those with technical potential but little academic acumen.

On-the-Job Training

OJT is one-on-one instruction between employees and supervisors or between coworkers. Formal OJT is structured and refers to planned activities that may range from one-on-one training on a machine at a workstation to mentoring and coaching, as represented by the exemplar apprenticeship program noted above. It can also include assigning employees to shadow other more experienced employees; shadowing generally is considered informal OJT (Desimone et al., 2002). Formal OJT allows for rapid transfer of learning as the employee performs the job tasks in the actual work environment. However, there may be a greater risk of negative unintended consequences with informal OJT. For example, if the experienced employee performs unethically or contrary to job specifications, the learner could acquire inappropriate skills or questionable ethics. The most effective OJT blends classroom instruction with on-the-job application because, consistent with adult learning, it allows for reflection; but unlike apprenticeships, this blend is not required (Daft & Marcic, 2008).

Given that the academic component is the most beneficial form of OJT, as in apprenticeships, then the same concern exists regarding inclusion. In addition, there may be injustices related to power when experienced employees clash with those whom they are assigned to mentor.

Inclusion may also be a concern associated with opportunities to participate in job enlargement and job rotation, motivational practices used in OJT to develop a greater breadth of skills and, in some cases, to relieve boredom associated with repetitive tasks. Through job enlargement, employees expand their current skill set from performing a single task to learning a variety of tasks associated with the same process. Similarly, job rotation provides employees a series of experiences in various positions or departments to learn new skills, enhance understanding of the organization as a whole, and build networks. Both practices facilitate acquisition of more holistic (systemic) views of various jobs, a greater sense of accomplishment and pride (Daft & Marcic, 2008; Desimone et al., 2002), and the potential for economic gain both for the organization and employees.

Quality Circles

Quality Circles (QCs) are another variation of OJT. Used worldwide and derived from Total Quality Management and Continuous Quality Improvement initiatives, QCs consist of 8 to 10 individuals, generally employed as factory workers. The groups meet regularly to identify causes of organizational problems and discuss ideas to improve quality in manufacturing processes, occupational safety and health processes, and product design (Daft & Marcic, 2008). In some organizations, work groups are expected to emerge naturally and informally; in other organizations, they are formally assembled and initiated by managers, union representatives, or by Six-Sigma coaches who are quality improvement specialists specifically trained to lead quality initiatives in organizations designated as *quality-certified.* QCs tend to have considerable autonomy and direct access to senior management, and thus, the process encompasses multiple opportunities for networking. Prior to participating in QCs, members commonly engage in employer-sponsored group facilitation and in problem-diagnosis and problem-solving initiatives (Choo, Linderman, & Schroeder, 2007).

According to Dahlgaard and Dahlgaard-Park (2006), success of QC learning opportunities, both for individuals and the organization, likely depends on an organizational culture in which (a) management accepts that employees closest to the processes may have better ideas on how to improve them, (b) workers are rewarded (e.g., profit sharing, bonuses, recognition) when their ideas prove beneficial to the organization (e.g., cost savings, fewer defects, waste reduction, patentable designs), and (c) specifications are in place that lead to the above. The researchers found that trust, competence, reward, and empowerment were realistic individual developmental outcomes. Organizations that did not focus on coaching to achieve individual developmental factors were less likely to succeed. This research illustrates the holistic influence of systems theory and human capital theory and potential applications not only for QCs, but for other practices discussed here. Still, there may be concerns regarding inclusion and equity for non-union members, members with low seniority but higher skill than those with greater seniority, and cultures with informal norms that do not reward superior productivity.

Career Development

Employees have come to expect opportunities for career development, particularly as they recognize their role in contributing to the competitive advantage of the organization (Gilbreath, 2008; Holbeche, 2001; Pfeffer, 1994). As a general practice, career development refers to employer-sponsored formal or informal opportunities for employees to engage in information gathering and decision making regarding their careers (Peterson, 2007).

According to Holbeche (2001), at one time, career development was part of the psychological contract that automatically came with employment. This contract was based on the assumption that if employees performed their jobs competently, they could expect to be promoted; upward promotion *was* the career path (Holbeche, 2001). In the mid-nineties, major reorganizations resulted in massive terminations and temporary or permanent layoffs, euphemized as *downsizing* or *rightsizing.* The contract had been broken (Pfeffer, 1998). Individuals who no longer felt secure in their jobs and careers, particularly among younger generations, began to demand boundaryless career development—whereby skills and knowledge acquired are not limited to a single job or organization (Hite & McDonald, 2008). This approach has been referred to as protean career development and characterized as changing, self-invented, self-directed, and autonomous. Pfeffer (1998) suggested a similar perspective: Because the *new employment contract* meant organizations would provide challenging jobs and interesting assignments to help employees build skills, but without promise of a lifetime career, employees needed to take individual responsibility for their careers, even if that meant going elsewhere. Other suggestions were that employers replace old career *ladders* with career *tracks* (Holbeche, 2001) or career *paths* (Peterson, 2007), and Gilbreath (2008) referred to *career-conducive organizations*—work settings in which employees and their careers could thrive.

Whatever the term, employees hold employers responsible for identifying skills needed for jobs deemed necessary in the future; for helping them to identify their current skill level, interests, and competencies; and for providing continuous development so they can achieve ever-increasing levels of competency (Gilley & Gilley, 2003). Continuous development includes such practices as team, leadership, and high-potential development, mentoring, and coaching. More specifically, career development might include such formal and informal initiatives as (a) providing opportunities to gain skills leading to advancement, (b) organizing opportunities to discuss career goals with others (e.g., immediate supervisors, other managers, peers in other organizational units), (c) offering help in creating career paths that lead to achievement of career goals, and (d) communicating about *organizational* decisions that impact *individual's* career development (Peterson, 2007). Other practices include self-awareness workshops, labor-market information exchanges, individual and group career counseling, and job-matching programs (Desimone et al., 2002). Holbeche (2001) also offered a host of specific practices associated with career-conducive organizations (e.g., allowing flexible scheduling, job sharing, and personal time; scheduling training and events with awareness of family and community responsibilities; offering alternative rewards for performance; finding alternative assignments within the company when jobs are discontinued).

Advantages to individuals of the many practices noted above include enhanced career decision-making self-efficacy (confidence in gathering information and making decisions about one's career), self-esteem, marketability, promotability, and self-directedness. Advantages to the organization include greater job satisfaction and commitment leading to employee retention because having opportunities to achieve career goals generally precludes the desire to seek them elsewhere (Peterson, 2007). Consistent with human capital theory, these opportunities represent an ongoing economic commitment to the personal and professional growth of employees, while concomitantly providing economic benefit to the organization. As well, these opportunities lead to an organizational whole that is greater than the individual growth of those privileged to have been invited to participate. Thus the conundrum—who is privileged enough to participate?

Leadership Development

Leadership development has become a major initiative as employers increasingly require individuals at every level of the organization to assume leadership roles, including managers and nonexempt employees working in support positions and line functions. Burud and Tumolo (2004) claimed that leaders must be skilled at "facilitating collaboration, handling ambiguity, listening, feeling ambiguity, and appreciating differences" (p. 160) and that people learn those leadership skills "when the organization rotates leadership roles within self-directed work teams, encourages individuals to take leadership roles . . . and employs similar measures that recognize the capacity of all employees to be self-motivated and responsible" (p. 161).

The purpose of team development, the most frequently offered workplace initiative, is for employees to learn to work together in new teams and to adapt in existing teams. The value is systemically enhanced as teams learn collectively. Yet, "individuals do not sacrifice their personal interest to the larger team vision; rather, the shared vision becomes an extension of their personal visions" (Senge, 1990, pp. 217–218). "Individual learning constitutes collective learning . . . [Consequently], lessening interest in individual learning constitutes decreased learning opportunities for the collective" (Lee & Roth, 2007, p. 99).

Employer-sponsored learning initiatives around leadership development include the development of high-potential employees. Referred to as *fast-trackers, hi-pos,* or *high-flyers* in the United Kingdom, they may be present in any level of the organization but are most visible within managerial ranks. What high-potential employees most want from employer-sponsored initiatives are opportunities to develop creative thinking, decision making, problem solving, negotiation, strategic thinking, and communication skills. Because fast-trackers thrive on gaining visibility through understanding business processes, they have identified the single most valuable learning activity as *hardship*—the kind that comes from challenging assignments (Holbeche, 2001). One particularly challenging assignment, although not exclusive to high-potential employees, is the international assignment, or expatriate assignment. When accompanied by cross-cultural training, these are powerful stretch assignments and motivators for learning, according to Littrell and Salas (2005), who cited cross-cultural training as a formal intercultural educative process to acquire behavioral, cognitive, and affective competencies for more effective interaction across diverse cultures. International assignments are moving to the forefront of organizational dynamics as a key element in developing global competencies.

Leadership development, team development, and career development are holistically linked. Individually, each practice is powerful, but when combined, these employer-sponsored practices create a workforce that is greater than the sum of the capacity of the individual employees who participate. In addition, when organizations engage in these practices throughout the organization, not just at the upper levels of management, an even greater synergy is realized. Economic benefits accrue systemwide for individuals and the organization. To that end, progressive organizations engage in mentoring and coaching practices, often holistically within their leadership, team, and career development initiatives.

Mentoring and Coaching Practices

In organizationally sponsored mentoring programs, a senior employee (mentor) encourages, supports, and helps to advance the work of a junior employee (protégé). Formal mentoring programs, purposefully designed and administered, are described by Hegstad and Wentling (2004) as ranging from one-on-one pairings of senior employees with less experienced employees to group or peer mentoring in which two or more employees at any level mentor each other to achieve job or career objectives.

Benefits accruing to mentees include higher compensation, faster or more significant promotions, higher levels of job and career satisfaction, and career maturity (Hezlett & Gibson, 2005; McDowell-Long, 2004). Some studies have shown a relationship between the presence of a formal mentoring program and improved recruitment and retention (e.g., Allen & O'Brien, 2006). However, potential shortfalls include mismatches between mentors and protégés, lack of mentor expertise, manipulation by the mentor, and mentoring that reinforces cultural dysfunction (Higgins & Kram, 2001; McDonald & Hite, 2005). Gibson (2005) identified another critical disconnect that can occur: Although mentors may follow formal guidelines (e.g., meeting frequently and for the appropriate amount of time, offering advice, providing emotional support), they may fall short of sponsoring and supporting the protégé for promotion or key assignments—particularly when the protégé is a woman. Hezlett and Gibson (2005) reported that although women and minorities were as likely as men and Caucasians to have mentors, the process may fail due to lack of role models as mentors.

Similar to mentoring, coaching is a process designed to improve skills, competence, and performance and to enhance personal effectiveness, development, or growth (Hamlin, Ellinger, & Beattie, 2008). Coaching can be arranged concomitantly with or separate from mentoring and has become a major responsibility for managers as an important workplace learning initiative (Dahlgaard & Dahlgaard-Park, 2006; Ellinger, Ellinger, & Keller, 2003). The initiative can originate formally from human resource professionals or can be informally arranged among employees themselves. If employer-initiated, coaches are expected to tailor a program of individual improvement and skill building within the context of organizational goals; most include at least monthly coaching sessions to chart progress toward goal achievement and to address problems. But there is considerable variation in activities depending on desired outcomes, how the coaching was arranged, and the expertise of those involved. Whether formal or informal, for coaching to be successful, both the organization and individual must be committed to the desired outcomes.

Organizations that sponsor career, leadership, and team development with or without opportunities for mentoring and coaching, tend to reflect cultures of learning. When organizations and employees accept this collaborative and systemic approach, recognizing that organizational learning and team learning are inextricably related, that all employees have potential to become leaders, and that a certain level of self-directedness is essential, economic benefits accrue to both. When organizations reject this understanding, the potential for exclusion may be exacerbated based on how individuals are selected to participate, who is selected, and why.

ISSUES

From a contemporary perspective, the employer-sponsored learning initiatives discussed represent opportunities that benefit the organization *and* the individual. Nevertheless, no matter how well-intentioned, within each practice, still resides the potential for discrimination and exclusion.

Workplace literacy programs continue to provide a prime example of these concerns. According to Hull (1993), the focus was on individual *deficits* due to low literacy and other skills—"what people are unable to do, what they lack, how they fail, and the causal relationship assumed between those deficits and people's performance at work" (p. 23). Hull predicted that women, people of color, and immigrants would dominate future work opportunities, and because these groups were identified as having the poorest skills, workplace illiteracy would worsen, thereby threatening productivity and competitiveness. The implication was that fault for organizational nonperformance lay with those less skilled. Hull then argued that workplace literacy programs placed too much faith in the power of literacy and too little credence in people's abilities, particularly those of blue collar and non traditional workers. Because "the popular discourse . . . tends to underestimate and devalue human potential" (p. 28), she raised the question: Under what circumstances will workplace literacy programs be empowering?

Fast-forward to the new millennium. According to D'Amico (2004), presenting an unambiguous or unrealistic picture of the rewards of workplace literacy programs ignores the class-based dissonance between words and worker's lives; after all, most workplace literacy programs exclude custodians and cleaning or part-time employees from participation. Belfiore and Folinsbee (2004) provided another example of this dissonance. Their study of one workplace literacy program identified the instructor's sense of superiority, ironically contradicting the

organization's stated commitment to empowerment; consequently, workers became not only *not* empowered, but disengaged, leading to further dissonance. These barriers, gaps, and misunderstandings continue to persist. Unfortunately, in some organizations, Hull's predictions have materialized.

Fenwick (2008) may know why: Most training structures in organizations maintain patriarchal values, male-oriented communication patterns, and un-family friendly schedules. For example, leadership and management, in which women and minorities are underrepresented, predominate in training, while fewer learning opportunities exist in call centers and food service, where immigrants and women of color are overrepresented.

Opportunities for leadership development and coaching tend to be mostly available to executive-level employees, excluding populations that are underrepresented in those ranks; the latter also have few role models to serve as formal or informal mentors. In addition, for the nearly 20% of U.S. adults with a disability, 35% of whom are employed, leadership and career development are elusive. Fornes, Rocco, and Rosenberg (2008) noted that career development is frequently equated with upward mobility, thus often unrealistic for individuals with disabilities. Job rotation and enlargement, apprenticeships, and other forms of OJT for more specific skills are more readily available, but overwhelmingly are represented by union trade and labor occupations. Exclusion and discriminatory practices also prevail based on sexual preference. According to Rocco, Delgado, and Landorf (2008), in a workplace environment of hostility, opposition to diversity efforts is reinforced, job insecurity and intimidation prevail, and career development is replaced by termination upon discovery or disclosure.

In organizations and occupations where lack of role models, favoritism, and the privileged power structure prevail, individuals with disabilities, aspiring women, immigrants who lack English skills, and other minorities can easily and understandably become discouraged and disengaged. According to Fenwick (2008), this oppressive workplace culture reinforces a *traditional dualism* in which workers may accept and even support the exploitative hierarchy that subjugates them and reproduces the existing power structure. There is much work to be done.

IMPLICATIONS FOR PRACTICE AND CONCLUSIONS

This chapter has focused on employer-sponsored learning practices and the positive outcomes that can accrue based on systems theory and human capital theory. Ideally, individual growth leads to organizational effectiveness, and individual learning leads to collective organizational learning. From this same systems perspective, the overall benefit to the organization is greater than the sum of the individual learning that accrues from apprenticeships, quality circles, and other on-the-job learning opportunities, as well as from career, leadership, and team development, mentoring, and coaching. From a human capital perspective, individuals as well as the organization derive economic gain from engaging in learning opportunities that expand the capacity of each—the individual through acquisition of marketable skills and the organization from enjoying the competitive advantage that is acquired through people (Pfeffer, 1994). When organizations are committed to an empowering culture in which all employees at all levels are valued, when opportunities for learning and growth are offered to all, and not just some, the beneficial outcomes extend beyond the organization as a whole to families and society in general. Unfortunately, systems theory also works under negative conditions. For example, a discriminatory culture breeds discriminatory practices leading to discriminatory outcomes. Thus questions remain. One overarching question is where to go from here?

Given current economic exigencies and the need for organizations to remain profitable to avoid further damage to communities and society from layoffs and closures, all in the face of the ever-present potential for discrimination, three mandates for practice come to mind: respect, responsibility, and research. The first implication for organizational practice is that in planning, designing, and implementing learning opportunities in the workplace, leaders must model and require respect for individual and collective differences, treating all employees with dignity, regardless, as Holbeche (2001) noted, of position, rank, race, gender, or personal choices. All individuals deserve to feel they work in an environment in which they are learning and where there is justice (Rao, 2006). The workplace practices discussed in this chapter have

great potential for positive outcomes—or negative consequences. This is why a key imperative for adult educators is to remain vigilant and continue to disavow employer-sponsored practices that perpetuate disrespect and inequity.

Second, workplaces have a responsibility to provide programs that address the whole person (not only as an employee). For example, an implication for those who design workplace literacy initiatives is to consider extending programs beyond basic skills training (e.g., reading, writing, arithmetic just adequate to perform job tasks) to include opportunities for learning and personal development with a broader potential to impact family and society. For those less *abled*, movement away from a focus on *dis*abilities and toward abilities also has the potential to facilitate systemic and exponential growth that includes families and the broader community.

Third, empirical research is necessary to document the mutual benefit of empowerment derived from the symbiotic relationship between personal growth and organizational improvement, individual and collective learning. One implication for practice is for educators and organizations to collaborate. Researchers might present evidence of the power of positive cultures and expose the destructive outcomes of disempowerment, disrespect, and discrimination. As Fenwick (2008) noted, rigorous in-depth research regarding identity and literacy and power and politics is needed to "illuminate the learning that unfolds in everyday work" (p. 25).

The following conclusions are followed by a sampling of questions that organizational leaders might ask themselves:

- Organizational culture is foundational to learning, and cultures of learning define organizations in which continuous learning is the norm. What must be done to ensure that the norm is one of providing opportunities for learning?

- Organizational cultures also reflect the cultural diversity of employees. Which of our employees representing populations disadvantaged by race/ethnicity, gender, or sexual preference are in positions of leadership to serve as role models, mentors, and coaches?

- According to human capital theory, individual and collective learning are complementary and interdependent. To what extent do our less advantaged populations and those in lower ranks benefit economically from our learning initiatives? To what extent do they go unnoticed and unrewarded?

• Career development is essential, and there is an abundance of literature to support the return on investment of formal and informal career development initiatives. What opportunities do we facilitate? To what extent have we replaced career development opportunities with on-demand and just-in-time training? What career development opportunities exist for support staff (e.g., custodians, cafeteria workers, maintenance)? Who gets to participate? What does it take for our employees to be designated *high potential?* To what extent do our diverse populations land those plum challenging assignments?

• Given the synergistic power of systems theory and the positive economic impact for organizations and employees accruing from human capital theory, what message do our organizational leaders convey?

In some respects, one might question how far opportunities for learning in the workplace have come since the decades-old issue arose of performance improvement for the sake of the organization *versus* for the sake of the individual. On the other hand, there are positive signs that progress is in the right direction. Organizational leaders have the choice as to how to use their power to sponsor equitable learning opportunities serving the best interests of the organization as well as individuals, extending to families and communities. Realistically, not all organizations have the desire or capacity to progress to the humanistic position presented in this chapter. Nevertheless, the definition proffered at the beginning of this chapter can still be useful to organizational leaders who strive toward the collective organizational knowledge, expertise, and competitive advantage that can accrue. These mutual benefits come from employer-sponsored learning opportunities that have as their aim the professional development of employees in order that they might accomplish job tasks and career goals, as well as personal development for themselves, their families, and communities.

REFERENCES

Allen, T. D., & O'Brien, K. E. (2006). Formal mentoring programs and organizational attraction. *Human Resource Development Quarterly, 17*(1), 43–58.

Belfiore, M., & Folinsbee. (2004). Workplace learning and literacies in practice. In *Reading work: Literacies in the new workplace* (pp. 195–220). Mahwah, NJ: Lawrence Erlbaum.

Bierema, L. (1996). Development of the individual leads to more productive workplaces. In R. W. Rowden (Ed.), *Workplace learning: Debating five critical questions of theory and practice* (pp. 21–28). New Directions for Adult & Continuing Education, No. 72. San Francisco: Jossey-Bass.

Billett, S. (2004). Workplace participatory practices: Conceptualising workplaces as learning environments. *Journal of Workplace Learning, 16*(6), 312–324.

Burud, S., & Tumolo, M. (2004). *Leveraging the new human capital.* Palo Alto, CA: Davies-Black.

Chew, C. M. (2007, October). Counting on a more diverse workforce. *Diverse Issues in Higher Education, 24,* 36–37.

Choo, A., Linderman, K., & Schroeder, R. (2007). Method and context perspectives on learning and knowledge creation in quality management. *Journal of Operations Management, 25,* 918–938.

Daft, R., & Marcic, D. (2008). *Understanding management* (6th ed.). Cincinnati, OH: South-Western.

Dahlgaard, J., & Dahlgaard-Park, S. (2006). Lean production, Six Sigma, TQM, and company culture. *The TQM Magazine, 18*(3), 263–281.

D'Amico, D. (2004). Race, class, gender, and sexual orientation in adult literacy: Power, pedagogy, and programs. In J. Comings, B. Garner, & C. Smith (Eds.), *Review of adult learning and literacy* (pp. 17–70). Mahwah, NJ: Lawrence Erlbaum.

Desimone, R., Werner, J., & Harris, D. (2002). *Human resource development* (3rd ed.). Fort Worth, TX: Harcourt.

Dirkx, J. (1996). Human resource development as adult education: Fostering the educative workplace. In R. W. Rowden (Ed.), *Workplace learning: Debating five critical questions of theory and practice* (pp. 41–47). New Directions for Adult & Continuing Education, No. 72. San Francisco: Jossey-Bass.

Dobbs, R., Sun, J., & Roberts, P. (2008). Human capital and screening theories: Implications for human resource development. *Advances in Developing Human Resources, 10*(6), 788–802.

Ellinger, A., Ellinger, A., & Keller, S. (2003). Supervisory coaching behavior, employee satisfaction, and warehouse employee performance: A dyadic perspective in the distribution industry. *Human Resource Development Quarterly, 14*(4), 435–458.

Fenwick, T. (2008). Workplace learning: Emerging trends and new perspectives. In S. Merriam, *Third update on adult learning theory* (pp. 17–27). New Directions for Adult & Continuing Education, No. 119. San Francisco: Jossey-Bass.

Fornes, S., Rocco, T., & Rosenberg, H. (2008). Improving outcomes for workers with mental retardation. *Human Resource Development Quarterly, 19*(4), 281–298.

Gibson, S. (2005). Whose best interests are served? The distinction between mentoring and support. *Advances in Developing Human Resources, 7*(4), 470–488.

Gilbreath, B. (2008). Creating career-conducive organizations: A primary intervention approach. *Advances in Developing Human Resources, 10*(1), 8–31.

Gilley, J., & Gilley, A. (2003). *Strategically integrated HRD* (2nd ed.). Cambridge, UK: Perseus.

Hamlin, R., Ellinger, A., & Beattie, R. (2008). The emergent coaching industry: A wake-up call for HRD professionals. *Human Resource Development International, 11*(3), 287–306.

Hegstad, C. D., & Wentling, R. (2004). The development and maintenance of exemplary formal mentoring programs in Fortune 500 companies. *Human Resource Development Quarterly, 15*(4), 421–448.

Hezlett, S., & Gibson, S. (2005). Mentoring and human resource development: Where we are and where we need to go. *Advances in Developing Human Resources, 7*(4), 446–469.

Higgins, M., & Kram, K. (2001). Reconceptualizing mentoring at work: A developmental network perspective. *Academy of Management Review, 26*, 264–288.

Hite, L., & McDonald, K. (2008). A new era for career development and HRD. *Advances in Developing Human Resources, 10*(1), 3–7.

Holbeche, L. (2001). *Aligning human resources and business strategy.* Oxford, UK: Butterworth Heinemann.

Hull, G. (1993). Hearing other voices: A critical assessment of popular views on literacy and work. *Harvard Educational Review, 63*(1), 20–49.

Kauffman, D. (1980). *Systems one: An introduction to systems thinking.* Minneapolis, MN: Future Systems.

Knowles, M. (1984). *The adult learner: A neglected species* (3rd ed.). Houston, TX: Gulf.

Lee, Y., & Roth, W. (2007). The individual\collective dialect in the learning organization. *The Learning Organization, 14*(2), 92–107.

Littrell, L., & Salas, E. (2005). A review of cross-cultural training: Best practices, guidelines, and research needs. *Human Resource Development Review, 4*(3), 305–344.

McDonald, K., & Hite, L. (2005). Ethical issues in mentoring: The role of HRD. *Advances in Human Resource Development, 7*(4), 569–583.

McDowell-Long, K. (2004). Mentoring relationships: Implications for practitioners and suggestions for future research. *Human Resource Development International, 7*(4), 519–534.

Peterson, S. (2007). Managerial turnover in retail organizations. *Journal of Management Development, 26*(8), 770–789.

Peterson, S. (2008). Creating and sustaining a strategic partnership: A model for human resource development. *Journal of Leadership Studies, 2*(2), 82–94.

Peterson, S., & Provo, J. (2000). A case study of academic program integration in the U.S.: Andragogical, philosophical, theoretical, and practical perspectives. *International Journal of Lifelong Education, 19*(2), 103–114.

Pfeffer, J. (1994). *Competitive advantage through people: Unleashing the power of the workforce.* Boston: Harvard Business School Press.

Pfeffer, J. (1998). *The human equation: Building profits by putting people first.* Boston: Harvard Business School Press.

Rao, S. (2006). Tomorrow's leader. In F. Hesselbein & M. Goldsmith (Eds.), *The leader of the future* (pp. 173–182). San Francisco: Jossey-Bass.

Rocco, T., Delgado, A., & Landorf, H. (2008). Framing the issue/framing the question: How are sexual minorities included in diversity initiatives? *Proceedings of the AHRD International Research Conference* (pp. 201–208). St. Paul, MN: AHRD.

Sambrook, S. (2005). Factors influencing the context and process of work-related learning: Synthesizing findings from two research projects. *Human Resource Development International, 8*(1), 101–121.

Senge, P. (1990). *The fifth discipline: The art and practice of the learning organization.* New York: Currency Doubleday.

23

WORKERS' EDUCATION FOR THE 21ST CENTURY

BRUCE SPENCER

In part, adult education in North America, Europe, and Australia/New Zealand grew out of workers' education. The provision of public lectures, extension classes, and later independent colleges and institutes focused on provision of citizenship education in North America and more generally education for the newly enfranchised working classes drove much of this provision both before World War I and in the interwar period. Adult education developed from early forms of workers' education such as the *Mechanics Institutes,* and *Workers' Educational Association (WEA)* (in Britain and Commonwealth countries), and *Bryn Mawr* and *Brookwood Labor Colleges* (in the United States) (See London et al., 1990 for the USA; Taylor, 2001, for Canada: and Simon, 1990, for the UK).

Workers' education in different forms predates modern labor unions, but a substantial offering of independent working-class education can be dated back only to the turn of the 20th century (Simon, 1990). Labor education (education with the central purpose of supporting the union organizationally) is no more than 100 years old, and it could probably be argued that the main characteristic of labor or union education—representative training—began no earlier than the 1920s with the International Ladies' Garment Workers' Union being one of the first in the United States. Labor education draws from earlier forms of workers' education and could simply be treated as part of a continuum rather than a separate entity.

This chapter will attempt to look at what kinds of workers' education/learning are available at the beginning of 21st century. It will explore the context of employee-organized learning, given the shift of emphasis onto workplace learning; it begins with a discussion of corporate organizational culture before moving on to examine the claimed shift from Taylorism to teams (from factory to knowledge work). It then shifts to examining workers' learning and union education provision and concludes with a discussion of whether or not these examples of union-provided and -sponsored learning offer an alternative education for workers in the tradition of earlier workers' education.

First, it must be remembered that learning at work is not a new phenomenon. While at work, workers learn about the job and how to do the work, as well as how to relate to fellow workers, supervisors and bosses (the social relations of work); they also gain understandings about the nature of work itself and how work impacts on society. Some of what they learn is useful to the employers, to themselves, and to their union organization. Some of this learning has little to do with work itself. It cannot, therefore, be assumed that all learning at work is translatable into organizational learning and is "win-win" for workers and employers alike. Nor can it be argued this learning always results in empowerment for workers; in some circumstances, it may result in greater job control, but in others, it may result in the reverse. The literature, particularly in management studies, tends to slip from discussing workplace learning to empowerment and on to industrial democracy as if they are all one and the same process. For example, it assumes that a statement that a company is "empowering" its workforce means that it is actually happening (Boud & Garrick, 1999; Senge, 1990).

Second, workplace learning literature is generally focused on the informal—including incidental—learning associated with work activities; it is less concerned with nonformal employer and industry vocational training, courses, and programs. Many of these training initiatives are useful to employees and result in workers learning new skills and knowledge. However, some can also be criticized for being narrowly employer-focused, perhaps more concerned with tying employees to a particular employer than with giving workers generic and portable skills. This chapter shares the general focus of the literature and largely ignores specific occupational training courses.

ORGANIZATIONAL CULTURE AND WORKPLACE LEARNING

Workers are encouraged to learn about what is useful for the employer. It is clear that some of their learning may contribute to a "culture of silence" (Freire, 1970), to an acceptance of the way things are. Workers may learn to accept the dominant ideology that supports management rights; for example, the idea that we are all part of a global economy and must strive to outcompete others to survive.

To ignore power and authority at work is to ignore the realities of what it is to be an employee. Organizational culture is that which is determined by management, and learning about that culture is learning to accept it. This perspective is evident in Senge's (1990) early claim that the purpose of management policies is to create a "sense of shared ownership" and control of the enterprise (p. 13) or, more recently, in Eric Newell's (former chairman and CEO of Syncrude Canada Ltd. and chancellor of the University of Alberta) comment, "really, what we are trying to do is engage people to get them

thinking like owners of the business" (quoted in Schwind, Das, & Wagar, 2007, p. 471). All this may appear innocent, but the "sense of ownership" is not the same thing as workers actually owning and controlling: It is also indoctrination.

John Storey (2007), a leading business school professor in the United Kingdom, has commented that the "management of culture" has become a distinguishing feature of human resource management (HRM), and he dates the "remarkable trend" away from "personnel procedures and rules" to the management of culture to the early to mid 1990s (p. 8–10). He comments that "managing cultural change and moving towards HRM can often appear to coincide and become one and the same project," and corporate cultural management is "perceived to offer the key to unlocking of consensus, flexibility and commitment" (p.11).

The idea behind this shift in managerial strategies is clear: Consensus would displace conflict (and collective bargaining), flexibility (a "substitute term for greater management control," Storey, 2007, p. 11) would increase productivity, and commitment would lift labor performance higher—committed employees would "go the extra mile" in pursuit of customer service and organizational goals. To achieve all of this means changing a whole set of workers' behaviors, attitudes, and values, displacing a pluralist (with different interests that sometimes coincide and sometimes conflict) and quasi-democratic culture (with unions challenging management decisions in collective bargaining and through other representative channels) with a unitarist (with everyone in the organization assumed to be sharing exactly the same goals) and a pretend-democratic culture (with claims of empowerment and teams). Workplace learning, therefore, needs to be understood as a new HRM control strategy, not a value-free activity. Keith Forrester (1999) observes that increased competitive pressures on management to improve the quality and quantity of the labor input can result in "the danger that the equally brave new world of pedagogics in relation to 'work and learning' will become part of the new forms of oppression and control in the workplace" (p. 88) rather than empowerment or increased worker control (Spencer, 2002a).

The central contradictions of private enterprise remain: Large corporations create hierarchies of control and power and are driven by the profit motive; these control, power, and profit relations create the social relations within work and society—those of employer and employee, boss and worker. Society's social classes result from these dominant work relations: In fact, it can be argued that, with the shrinkage of well-paid manual and office jobs—described as the "middle class" in North America—even in developed economies, society is polarizing into a large working class and relatively small elite. A veil may be drawn over these contradictions at times with the rhetoric of managers as "leaders" and "coaches" and workers as "associates" or "partners," but unless ownership and control changes and becomes genuinely more equitably distributed, nothing fundamentally has changed.

We live in societies (some would argue in one global society) in which the gap between the richest and the poorest, between those who live fuller lives in the economically developed countries and those who live "half lives at best" in the less developed countries, is growing (Honderich, 2002, p. 6). Many workers in the developed countries have experienced a decline in the value of real wages, and they must struggle to stay abreast of inflation even at low inflation rates, while the incomes of the rich continue to climb. This trend continues with the average of the top 100 CEOs receiving 200 times the average worker's salary in Canada (Beltrame, 2008). How important is this inequality? Sam Pizzigati (2004) in *Greed and Good* argues it is "the root of what ails us as a nation (referring to the United States), a social cancer that coarsens our culture, endangers our economy, distorts our democracy, even limits our lifespans" (p. vii). He comments that CEOs

> have never (in practice) really accepted the notion that empowering employees makes enterprises effective. Empowering workers, after all, requires that power be shared, and the powerful, in business as elsewhere, seldom enjoy sharing their power. The powerful enjoy sharing rewards even less. Corporate leaders have never accepted, either in theory or practice, the notion that enterprise effectiveness demands some sort of meaningful reward sharing. (p. 167)

Even before the financial crisis of 2008, being a worker in a "learning organization" was not a guarantee of job security: It may be true that the company's competitive position depends on a more effective and intelligent use of its human resources, but this does not mean that a corporate decision about location or product development will benefit a particular work group or that the rewards from the collective effort will be equitably distributed among the workforce. Even in those cases where employees are given a small stake in the company, they can lose. In the Enron case, employee shareholdings were locked in and became worthless, while some of the senior executives bailed, taking their inflated funds with them. The decision to close a work site, for example, may have absolutely nothing to do with how that particular workforce has performed or how committed they were to the learning organization.

From Factory to Knowledge Work

The shift from a *Taylorist* workplace to a *knowledge/teams* workplace has been argued repeatedly, the contention being that work on the mind-numbing conveyor belt with Taylor's division of labor (resulting in workers repeating one small task) has been replaced by creative teams striving for ever greater customer satisfaction, according to these accounts. This change is often exaggerated however; factory conditions still exist (if not so much in developed countries, then certainly in the outsourced plants located in less economically developed ones), and new fast food and retail jobs are low-paid, part-time, and insecure. Knowledge jobs are few and can also be insecure; hiding within "knowledge companies" are many boring, routine jobs. There may be a steady demand for very well qualified individuals but that is not the majority of jobs: Setting aside recent growth in construction trades, the greatest growth in the last two decades is in low-paid, casual, and part-time labor. It may be the case that a greater attempt has been made to involve many workers in low-level company decisions, in problem solving, and in customer service, but whether or not these efforts deserve the label *empowering* is at best a moot point—they could equally be described as *limiting* if not as *co-opting*.

A 2003 report by Statistics Canada (Beckstead & Gellatly, 2003) charting the changes in the Canadian economy acknowledges that not all employees in "information and communications technology industries" (ICT) and science industries are "knowledge workers," although as many as half might be classified that way. The report also points out that the number of knowledge workers in other sectors (90% of the Canadian economy) has declined to about 12% (down from 17% in 1981). Only 10% of the Canadian workforce is in ICT and science sectors, and although these sectors can be presented as dynamic (with impressive employment growth in ICT), it would be safe to assume that, by Statistics Canada definitions, less than 20% of the total workforce are employed in knowledge occupations; furthermore, many of these workers are in old knowledge occupations (medicine, dentistry, engineering, law, etc.) rather than new ones (Beckstead & Gellatly, 2003, pp. 35–36). Only one in eight new service jobs, outside of the ICT and science areas, can be described as knowledge jobs (Beckstead & Gellatly, 2003, p. 37). It is important to acknowledge that all workers have knowledge and apply it at work, but it is also important to recognize that Statistics Canada is noting something that workers have been reporting on for some time—the opportunities to apply knowledge at work is in decline, "deskilling" rather than "re-skilling" is the norm, and workers' knowledge is underemployed. Although there may be specific skill shortages, Canada has in general a knowledgeable workforce, with the highest levels of postsecondary participation but not the jobs to match it (Livingstone, 1999). The statistics for other developed economies will vary, but a scan of economic issues in the United States, Australasia, and Europe would suggest the situation is much the same.

More astute researchers have argued that Taylorist measurement and control at work remains or has been expanded (for example, Hennessy & Sawchuk, 2003, discuss the deskilling and "industrializing" of frontline social service workers following the introduction of new technology into their jobs). Taylorism may have changed in form but its essential purpose has not. As Australian Tony Brown (1999) comments,

> Most descriptions contrast team production to the "scientific management" principles of Taylor. In fact the tendency is in the other direction—to specify every move that a worker makes in much greater detail than before. Management chooses the processes, basic production layout and technologies to be used. Speeding up the pace of work is an intended consequence of standardising production, services or software. (p. 15)

All of this is made possible by applying new technology into the "new workplace." Many jobs can be described as white collar and as linked to new technology; some are being dispersed into the home (teleworkers) and are not required to be completed at a particular time or in a specifically designated, employer-owned space—described as postmodern and postindustrial employment. The appearance of worker control over when and how much work is undertaken is illusionary, as the new computer-based work comes with constant monitoring and feedback to the employer—far exceeding what Taylor was able to do with his stopwatch and clipboard. Perhaps what we have today is a more "differentiated" or postmodern Taylorism.

Nor is a shift to a more inclusive team/knowledge workplace (a learning organization) a given in developed economies. As Bratton, Helms-Mills, Pyrch, and Sawchuk (2004) have commented, some organizations may well believe that the company's competitive advantage depends on a happy, committed workforce and may work toward that end (full-time employees, higher skills, job flexibility, workplace learning). Others may equally believe that tight control of labor costs combined with close supervision over employees is the road to success (low-paid, part-time employees, routine jobs). According to Bratton et al., both approaches can work equally well from an employers' perspective (p. 71). It is worth adding that survey material reveals that empowering workers does not generally affect the bottom line, although more say and participation at work can influence employee loyalty (Freeman, Boxall, & Haynes, 2007).

A further aspect is highlighted in a new study of four U.S. workplaces. Focused more on intellectually challenging work, the study revealed that workers felt pressured by management cost-cutting; they were prevented from doing their best work and had little say over process. The result was they *love the work, hate the job* (Kusnet, 2008).

Another problem in the literature is the tendency to treat all organizations the same; this partly reflects the imposition of business rhetoric on nonbusiness organizations such as public services, universities, hospitals, and nonprofit and nongovernmental organizations. All are seen as dealing with "clients" or "customers" within the context of a "business plan" and having to apply business principles to the "bottom line." Scant regard is paid to the notion of the "public good" or the quasi-democratic structures that govern these organizations and distinguish them from corporate capital. Given nurturing circumstances and organizational structures, these organizations may well be capable of more democratic and less hierarchical control involving citizens, workers, their unions, and managers. The workplace "democracy" claimed for corporate learning organizations is never compared to the nonprofit sector, including worker-owned cooperatives with workers participating in major decisions and appointing the CEO (Salamon, 2003).

Workers' Learning

Identifying examples of employee-organized learning is problematic; many situations describing workers undertaking their own workplace learning are more accurately described as responses to manager and supervisor prompting. A few studies undertaken with a workers' perspective throw light on employee knowledge but are often looking at knowledge across the course-training/informal-learning divide, which makes it difficult to sort out which examples of learning are genuinely worker-organized. For example, Livingstone and Sawchuk (2004) provide a number of case studies examining learning in different sectors and report on workers' knowledge generation within company training courses, union education, and informal workplace and out-of-work situations. Examples of employee-organized learning run through the case studies; opportunities may be greater for the auto and small-parts workers than the largely immigrant female garment workers, but all engage in some forms of employee-initiated learning that is both work and non-work related. Issues of control over on-the-job training, pay for knowledge, gender and ethnic divisions, inequitable access to learning, and the struggles of marginalized workers to secure permanent employment are all documented.

Perhaps we should not be surprised to find that union-organized learning at work is concerned with broader issues of worker influence over management policies; workplace insecurity goes hand-in-hand with globalization. Workers are asked to embrace the idea that there are no permanent jobs any more; they must be flexible, move from job to job, and build a "learning profile" more than a career. An interesting international survey of employee voice in six Anglo American countries reports that while workers do engage in learning and knowledge creation activities at work, many would like to have more union representation and more participation in management decision-making processes (Freeman et al., 2007). This lack of representation and access causes workers to be more guarded and less trustful of employers; those with most access are most loyal.

Another new development is the establishment of union learning representatives (ULR) and a union learning fund in the United Kingdom (Shelley & Calveley, 2007). The intention is that ULRs will help connect workers to learning opportunities, essentially occupational related, and help organize employee learning opportunities. Studies to date suggest that in a number of situations, these representatives can make a difference, particularly in terms of training opportunities, although it is too early in the process to be definitive. A major question remains to be answered: Is union involvement in new neoliberal global economic agendas merely incorporation, or can unions and ULRs moderate the impact of these policies and turn these resources to meet broader social goals? Are ULRs worker representatives, or are they primarily agents of government and corporate policy? Also, do they threaten or do they enhance the tradition of independent union education? What is known is that after 4 years of ULRs, only about 10% of workplace representatives *bargained* about learning provision (Kersley et al., 2006, p. 20, 153). These developments are taking place at the same time as freely negotiated recognition agreements are being displaced by partnership agreements that emphasize employer rights including in some cases denying the rights of work groups to democratically determine their own union representative (Wray, 2001).

This discussion of unions accepts the contradictory nature of unionism (as both a force for opposition and accommodation), the tendency toward union incorporation into managerial goals (at both local and national levels of the union), the move toward bureaucratization and oligarchic structures, and so on; it also argues, however, that independent active unionism may provide the best chance to democratize the corporate workplace (to paraphrase Hugh Clegg (1978), collective bargaining *is* a form of industrial democracy). With the decline of union influence in many developed economies, other forms of representation, participation, and worker-initiated learning have emerged—bolstered in Europe by European Union (EU) legislation favoring worker participation. However, the results are mixed; "in most cases, employee representatives [in the participatory structures] are merely informed of upcoming changes by management with no input into decision making" (Freeman et al., 2007, p. 177). While participation/learning organization strategies may be successful in helping employers fight off unions (particularly in the United States and the United Kingdom), the evidence supports the view that much higher levels of participation are found in organizations that *recognize* unions, supporting a view that unionization and employee involvement may be complementary (Freeman et al., 2007, p. 196). It is also noteworthy that union membership in the United States would triple immediately if workers were free to choose union membership (Freeman et al., 2007).

LABOR EDUCATION IN THE GLOBAL ECONOMY

Given this situation, it is important for adult educators to have a better grasp of what learning opportunities workers are developing for themselves within their own organizations. Labor education refers to education and training offered by labor unions (trade unions) to their members and representatives. The extent to which this education is provided directly by unions or by another agency or educational institution for unions varies from country to country and union to union. A main purpose of labor/union education is to prepare and train union lay members to play an active role in the union. Another purpose is to educate activists and members about union policy and about changes in the union environment such as new management techniques or changes in labor law. Labor education is also used to develop union consciousness, to build common goals, and to share organizing and campaigning experience. Unions have a small full-time staff and therefore rely on what is essentially voluntary activity of

their members to be effective at work and in society; the labor education program is thus a major contributor to building an effective volunteer force.

Labor education attracts more participants than any other form of nonvocational adult education in developed countries and is one of the most important forms of nonformal adult education available to working people. However, it is most often underreported and ignored in discussions about adult learning (this in spite of the argument in the first paragraph on the close relationship between adult and workers' education). The 2003 report on the state of labor education in the United States demonstrated that labor education provision had grown since 1968 (the time of the last survey) but that current development was uneven (Byrd & Nissen, 2003). One of the reasons for the lack of knowledge among adult educators in the United States is the division between labor educators and adult educators; another is that most North American labor education is provided in-house by unions—outside the experience of adult educators in the United States and Canada.

Most union members learn about the union while on the job (what is often referred to as informal or incidental learning). They probably will learn more and become most active during negotiations, grievances, and disputes; but they also learn from union publications and communications; from attending meetings, conferences, and conventions; and from the union's educational programs. Although labor education programs cater to only a small number of representatives in any one year, they are designed to benefit a larger number of members because the course participants are expected to share the learning gained with other union members.

Core Labor Education

Most of the labor education courses provided by unions are *tool* courses (for example, shop steward training, grievance handling, and health and safety representative courses). The next largest category is *issues* courses (for example, sexual harassment or racism or new human resource management strategies), which often seek to link workplace and societal issues. A third group of courses can be labeled *labor studies*, which seek to examine the union context (for example, labor history, economics, and politics).

Tool and *issue* courses directly prepare members for active roles in the union and to become representatives of the union; tool courses are targeted at existing or potential union activists. These courses are provided directly by the unions, by labor federations, or by union centrals (such as the Canadian Labour Congress [CLC], the UK Trade Union Congress [TUC], or the Swedish Confederation of Trade Unions [LO]). Tool courses are also provided for unions by educational institutions (for example, by many of the labor studies centers across the United States) or by educational institutions collaboratively with the central bodies or individual unions (for example, with colleges, universities, and the Workers' Educational Association collaborating with the TUC in Britain). They may also be provided by specialized institutions such as the now-defunct Australian Trade Union Training Authority (TUTA) or South Africa's Development Institute for the Training, Support, and Education of Labour (Ditsela).

The intention of the dedicated labor studies courses is to supplement trade union tools and issues courses with a broader educational program and, in some cases, to provide a research basis for union activity—some universities are linking directly with unions to offer research collaborations (for example, Leeds in the United Kingdom and UCLA in the United States) or study and research circles (for example, in Sweden). Although unions are usually represented on the "boards of studies" of the university- and college-offered labor studies programs, they are rarely union controlled, in contrast to the union-run courses. (The variations in terms of the nature, course structures, and delivery of provision of labor education courses are manifest, and this discussion provides but a few examples, drawn mainly from Spencer, 2002b.)

While tools, issues, and labor studies might describe the majority of labor education, the definitions do not encompass all labor education offerings. Unions are increasingly directly involved in a number of membership education programs, some of which have a basic educational skills or vocational purpose. In some cases, union-run literacy and second language courses are tutored by fellow unionists and act as a bridge linking immigrant or illiterate workers to union concerns and publications. Similarly, unions are responsible for a number of worker training programs, which allow the unions to educate workers about union concerns alongside of vocational training. In some countries, skilled and professional unions have a long history of union-sponsored vocational training and education courses. Unions, including noncraft unions, are becoming much more proactive in responding to company restructuring and deskilling and are arguing for reskilling, skills recognition, and skills profiling, as well as challenging employers to live up to their rhetoric on "pay for knowledge." This is a growing area of union educational work and a number of unions in different countries are increasingly becoming more involved in general membership education of all kinds (in some cases running courses in basic literacy skills and vocational training jointly with management, for example in United Auto Workers and United Steel Workers plants and schools).

New Developments in Labor Education

The majority provision of continuing core labor education is targeted at local union representatives. This important work is ever changing, with differing examples evident in all countries where unions are active. There may be more emphasis on peer tutoring in one country and significant content changes in another. There are particular examples of new specific forms of representative training, such as that for European Works Council representatives in Europe; and examples of union representative training in difficult circumstances, such as those in South Africa, where unions are coming to terms with recognition and bargaining after years of opposition under apartheid. We also have reports on more sophisticated educational provision for full-time officers, an underreported area of representative training.

Training recruiters is another new development. The educational components of the U.S. Organizing Institute, the Australia Organising Works, and the UK Organising Academy are important labor education responses to the decline of union influence and to shifting employment patterns. The work undertaken in organizing immigrant workers in Los Angeles is a particular example; it has been successful in linking union activity to community groups and community-based organizing, with labor education playing a key role. The Justice for Janitors campaigns have been most impressive and have relied on educational support to bolster activity, recruitment, and contract negotiation. The region around Los Angeles has bucked the trend in the United States, providing a leading example of union growth. Some of this educational and organizing work involves existing union representatives, and some of it is targeted at new members and would-be representatives.

In Brazil, *Programa Integrar* has come to offer relevant vocational training and educational opportunities for the unemployed and the employed. The program illustrates that even in a hostile climate, union education can succeed; it provides an example to other countries of how to build community links and to argue for alternative worker cooperative employment for union members in opposition to global corporate power. This example links with others in South America, where union members are taking back closed factories and building local economic networks.

Although the use of research circles (workers conducting their own research into workplace or sector problems) has been around for some time, its clear from Swedish experience that this approach has a bright future in terms of strengthening union activity within the union as well as externally. It represents an important alternative for union members wishing to conduct independent workplace learning projects.

Most of the examples above are in the tradition of independent workers' education, whereas the development of ULRs in the United Kingdom and the tradition of joint programs (for example, the UAW-Chrysler National Training Center and UAW-Ford University plus others of collaborative union-company schemes) point to another direction in workers' education. Many of the joint programs are concerned with employee development in relation to employment, and most are specifically aimed at improving vocational skills. In some cases, these programs have been boosted by the desire to develop workers' skills to help them remain employed (up-skilling); in others, they are designed to provide employment opportunities for workers who have been made redundant—there is, of course, no guarantee that reskilling and broader educational upgrading will lead to new jobs. An example of a regional joint union-employer-state program is the Wisconsin Regional Training Partnership, which claims success in both creating new employment opportunities and improving existing employment (Bernhardt, Dresser, & Rogers, 2001). Another development in the same vein is organized labor's Working for America Institute, labor's nonprofit workforce development initiative, by which the AFL-CIO hopes via employer and other partnerships to boost high skills, knowledge work, and good jobs—the so-called "high road" to future employment opportunities.

Conclusions

Many of the labor education initiatives have elements of both accommodation and resistance to current corporate globalization trends. Some courses and programs can be seen as proactive, others as adaptive, while much of labor education remains reactive (see Spencer, 2002b, and the ILO, 2007, for examples). Overall, unions remain an important and positive social organization for working people: It is the absence of strong independent unions that remains a problem for workers in the majority of the globe. Some of the skills-training programs offered through unions may appear to be little different from employer-provided schemes. The thrust of mainstream labor education, however, is toward social purpose and social action; it is aimed at equipping workers with the analytical and organizational knowledge needed to participate democratically in the workplace and society.

There has been an explosion of "work and learning" scholarship in the last decade, with some valuable work identifying issues, marginalized groups, and theoretical models (Fenwick, 2006). Although some writers acknowledge that different interests exist, they still reduce workplace learning to a list of knowledge issues to be resolved and in the process treat it as a reified value-free activity independent of the profit motive. Perhaps the problems with this approach have become clearer with the 2008 financial crisis; libertarian economic policies that value unregulated capital can have major economic effects for labor. While partnership may be an honorable objective and possibly applicable to the nonprofit and voluntary economic sectors, it is difficult to see where exactly the interests of workers, citizens, or the third world figure in the corporate conception of the purposes of workplace learning. "Golden parachutes" are reserved for senior executive use only, and massive state bailouts apply to big corporations and their investors, not to workers.

Discussions of worker-organized workplace learning and more generally union-organized education need to acknowledge the real issues of power, authority, control, and ownership. They need to promote independent workers' learning opportunities for a more real empowerment and a more genuine workplace democracy. Workers' education has moved on from some of the concerns and structures evident in the 20th century, but the democratic imperative remains, and the basic need for an independent workers' education in such an inequitable world is as keen as ever. Adult educators should acknowledge that employer-organized workplace learning is essentially aimed at incorporating workers into management culture. Employee-organized labor education may allow workers to challenge it.

REFERENCES

Beckstead, D., & Gellatly, G. (2003). *The Canadian economy in transition: The growth and development of new economy industries* (11–622-MIE n0.002). Ottawa: Minister of Industry.

Beltrame, J. (2008, January 2). Average Canadians work for shillings while CEOs make a killing. Toronto *Globe and Mail.*

Bernhardt, A., Dresser, L., & Rogers, J. (2001). Taking the high road in Milwaukee: The Wisconsin Regional Training Partnership, *WorkingUSA,* Winter, 109–130.

Boud, D., & Garrick, J. (Eds.). (1999). *Understanding learning at work.* London: Routledge.

Bratton, J., Helms-Mills, J., Pyrch, T., & Sawchuk, P. (2004). *Workplace learning: A critical introduction.* Aurora, Ontario: Garamond Press.

Brown, T. (1999). *Restructuring the workplace: Case studies of informal economic learning.* Sydney: University of Technology, Centre for Popular Education.

Byrd, B., & Nissen, B. (2003). *Report on the state of labor education in the United States.* Berkeley, CA: Center for Labor Research and Education.

Clegg, H. (1978). *Trade unions under collective bargaining.* Oxford, UK: Basil Blackwell.

Fenwick, T. (2006). Work, learning, and adult education in Canada. In T. Fenwick, T. Nesbit, & B. Spencer (Eds.), *Contexts of adult education: Canadian perspectives* (pp. 187–197). Toronto, Ontario: Thompson Educational.

Forrester, K. (1999). Work-related learning and the struggle for subjectivity. In *Researching work and learning: A first international conference* (pp. 188–197). Leeds, UK: Leeds University, School of Continuing Education.

Freeman, R., Boxall, P., & Haynes, P. (Eds) (2007). *What workers say: Employee voice in the Anglo-American workplace.* New York: Cornell University.

Freire, P. (1970). *Pedagogy of the oppressed.* New York: Continuum.

Hennessy, T., & Sawchuk, P. (2003). Technological change in the Canadian public sector: Worker learning responses and openings for labour-centric technological development. In *The Third International Conference of Researching Work and Learning* (pp. 111–119). Tampere, Finland: University of Tampere.

Honderich, T. (2002). *After the terror.* Edinburgh, UK: Edinburgh University Press.

International Labour Organization. (2007). Strengthening the trade unions: The key role of labour education. In *Labour Education, 1–2* (No 146–147). Geneva: Author.

Kersley, B., Alpin, C., Forth, J., Bryson, A., Bewley, H., Dix, G., & Oxenbridge, S. (2006). *Inside the workplace: Findings from the 2004 Workplace Employment Relations Survey.* London: Routledge.

Kusnet, D. (2008). *Love the work, hate the job: Why America's best workers are unhappier than ever.* San Francisco: John Wiley.

Livingstone, D. (1999). *The education-jobs gap.* Toronto, Ontario: Garamond.

Livingstone, D., & Sawchuk, P. (2004). *Hidden knowledge: Organized labour in the information age.* Toronto, Ontario: Garamond.

London, S., Tarr, E., & Wilson, J. (Eds.). (1990). *The re-education of the American working class.* New York: Greenwood.

Pizzigati, S. (2004). *Greed and good: Understanding and overcoming the inequality that limits our lives.* New York: Apex Press.

Salamon, L. (2003). *The resilient sector: The state of nonprofit America.* Washington, DC: Brookings Institution.

Schwind, H., Das, H., & Wagar, T. (2007). *Canadian human resource management: A strategic approach.* Whitby, Ontario: McGraw-Hill Ryerson.

Senge, P. (1990). The leader's new work: Building learning organizations, *Sloan Management Review, 41*(Fall), 7–23.

Shelley, S., & Calveley, M. (Eds.). (2007). *Learning with trade unions: A contemporary agenda in employment relations.* Aldershot, UK: Ashgate.

Simon, B. (Ed.). (1990). *The search for enlightenment: The working class and adult education in the twentieth century.* London: Lawrence & Wishart.

Spencer, B. (2002a). Research and the pedagogics of work and learning, *Journal of Workplace Learning, 14*(7), 298–305.

Spencer, B. (Ed.). (2002b). *Unions and learning in a global economy: International and comparative perspectives,* Toronto, Ontario: Thompson Educational.

Storey, J. (2007). *Human resource management: A critical text* (3rd ed.). London: Thomson Learning.

Taylor, J. (2001). *Union learning: Canadian labour education in the twentieth century.* Toronto, Ontario: Thompson Educational.

Wray, D. (2001, September 11–13). *What price partnership?* Paper presented at *Work Employment and Society Conference,* University of Nottingham.

24

MILITARY CONTRIBUTIONS TO ADULT EDUCATION

CHERYL J. POLSON

The fall of the Soviet Union, the rise of globalization, the 9/11 terrorist attacks on the United States, and current ground wars in Afghanistan and Iraq have made education more critical to the armed forces today than ever before. Today's service members find themselves operating in complex and ambiguous environments consistently demanding intellectual agility and critical thinking. Education is central to creating military members who are adaptable and flexible and who can think broadly and contextually to operate effectively in these environments. Not all service members, however, possess the competencies to function at this level of intellectual sophistication (Reoyo, 2002). Preparation for the professional demands confronting soldiers often extends beyond the confines of military education. Numerous adult education providers assist the military in closing the gap between the knowledge soldiers acquire through professional military education and the additional knowledge required to successfully complete their increasingly complex missions.

Throughout this country's history, efforts to train and educate members of the U.S. military have been extensive. Historically, the focus of military adult education has shifted from building soldier morale to preparing members for postservice careers. Adult education has supported the military's efforts to recruit and retain soldiers and to supplement military training, while satisfying the service member's innate desire to continue learning. Today, the promise of educational benefits serves as the military's most potent recruitment tool. Research has validated that voluntary education opportunities not only aid recruitment, but also help reduce personnel attrition by increasing incentives for reenlistment (Sticha et al., 2003).

One of the country's largest providers of adult education, the U.S. Department of Defense (DoD) spent $474.2 million in 2008 to support participation in voluntary education programs (Baker, 2009). For 2009, the DoD budget includes $10.7 billion for military training, recruiting, and retention. This financial investment is designed to maintain a highly educated and trained fighting force of 2.2 million service members and to ensure they possess the critical skills needed to meet tomorrow's defense requirements (Office of the Under Secretary of Defense [Comptroller], 2008).

Stubblefield and Keane (1994) credit military voluntary education programs with having significant impact on the emerging status of adult education as a field of practice and study. Adult education has been instrumental in meeting the voluntary educational needs of service members while also benefiting from the educational innovations pioneered by the military. Equally important, armed forces education has, from its inception, opened doors to previously underserved and, in many

263

instances, unserved adult learners. This chapter will provide a brief glimpse of how military-supported education has expanded access to adult education and been a catalyst for educational and social transformation, while also examining current practices and challenges.

PAVING THE WAY THROUGH LITERACY EDUCATION

Historically, adult education has been viewed as a privilege for a select few. While more widely available today, adult education providers still strive to broaden accessibility. The military has contributed significantly to reducing the gap between the "haves" and the "have-nots" through its focus on literacy education.

Originally, military education was less about preparing soldiers to perform their jobs and more about improving troop morale. The focus was providing soldiers with the literacy skills required to read their Bibles. Military chaplains were the first military adult educators, tasked to provide academic instruction for illiterate convalescing soldiers at Valley Forge (Wilds, 1938). By the end of the 18th century, the Navy employed schoolmasters and teachers to teach reading and writing to seamen (Langley, 1967). The role and scope of literacy efforts expanded as military leaders became increasingly aware of its centrality to effective battlefield communication and to meeting the new demands for increased technical skills (Weinert, 1979).

The military's role in improving access to education continued during the Civil War, when the Union Army specifically assigned lieutenants to assist in eradicating widespread illiteracy among African Americans (Blassingame, 1965). The War Department continued this commitment during Reconstruction, assuming initial responsibility for the creation of the Freedmen's Bureau, which was devoted to the education of former slaves (Sticht, 2002).

The urgency to make education more accessible to previously unserved adults became apparent when the Army called more than 250,000 men to join the "War to End All Wars," or World War I. Literacy levels among many of these draftees were so low that they could not function in the increasingly technical, newly mechanized military. In July 1918, the War Department established a 4-month compulsory course in English. Through the work of development battalions initiated by the Army, almost 25,000 illiterate and non-English-speaking troops received literacy training by February 1919 (Borden, 1989).

The full scope of the military's rich, extensive efforts to address military literacy challenges is beyond the confines of this chapter. For comprehensive reviews, see Anderson's (2006) and Sticht's (2002) insightful summaries.

The military has remained committed to making education more accessible through basic skills development, even if the degree of focus and implementation has shifted considerably. Kime and Anderson (1997, 2000) suggest today's U.S. military-related literacy issues are embedded in the recruitment of what they term "college-capable" soldiers who lack basic literacy skills. They argue the military's education requirement does not guarantee soldiers enter with the basic skills demanded by the military workforce. This issue was originally addressed in 1979, when the Army established its Basic Skills Education Program (BSEP) to help soldiers achieve basic skills proficiency levels required to qualify for military occupational specialties (MOS). Thirty years later, the BSEP continues to fill the gap between soldiers' educational capabilities and occupational requirements.

A related issue is the large number of applicants for enlistment who have not earned the required educational credentials but are otherwise highly qualified for military service. To meet this challenge, in August 2008, the Army piloted a 4-week Army Preparatory School (APS), designed to open the door for deserving applicants to enlist on the condition that they complete their General Educational Development (GED) certificate through the APS (Harlow & Rasmussen, 2008). The program's long-term goal is to offer participants the opportunity to earn a fully accredited high school diploma. While the underlying motivation for creating this program—to increase the eligible recruitment pool—is not necessarily altruistic, it does illustrate the military's continued role in broadening access to adult education.

THE GI BILL—A CATALYST FOR EDUCATIONAL AND SOCIAL TRANSFORMATION

Educational opportunities available to U.S. service members frequently extend beyond active-duty service through a broad range of benefits first introduced in the Servicemen's Readjustment Act of 1944, more popularly known as the GI Bill. The GI Bill is viewed as the most far-reaching piece of legislation—socially, economically, and politically—ever enacted by the federal government. Cited as a primary vehicle for democratizing higher education (Kett, 1994), the GI Bill made college attendance a viable option for a wide range of veterans, including first-generation Americans, individuals from low-income households, and minorities (Bound & Turner, 2002).

By 1956, more than half of returning veterans, 7.8 million in total, used the GI Bill to continue their education at colleges and vocational schools and through participation in on-the-job training. Some believe the bill was the catalyst for the most important educational and social transformation in American history (Burrell, as cited in Bound & Turner, 2002). This legislation not only assisted adults in obtaining education but offered them the possibility of crossing class lines in the process (McBain, 2008). Research indicates that the education and training provisions of the GI Bill are a rare example of a public program that was truly inclusive in terms of its reach among African American veterans (Mettler, 2005). An unexpected by-product of the GI Bill was the disruption of gatekeeping practices previously exhibited by some institutions. Bound and Turner (2002) argue that the most lasting and significant impacts of the GI Bill were in the form of institutional changes that enhanced opportunities for more diverse students to enter once-exclusive elite schools.

Others point to extensive veteran enrollments facilitated by this bill as evidence that adults have an innate desire to learn (Houle, Burr, Hamilton, & Yale, 1947), a fact consistently validated through participation studies (Merriam, Caffarella, & Baumgartner, 2007). It may have been a true lack of awareness about adults' desire to learn that led educational institutions to miscalculate the massive number of service members who would be entering their classrooms and to underestimate the number who were seeking intellectual stimulation versus a vocational curriculum (Kett, 1994). Perhaps more significant, institutions ignored the extent to which this new college student population would require them to reshape their policies and practices.

It was predicted that no more than 150,000 veterans would embark full-time on this educational journey (Kett, 1994). In reality, at the height of GI Bill-supported enrollments, more than half of the higher education student body consisted of veterans. Total enrollments surged from 1,364,815 in 1939 to 2,281,298 in 1950 (Olson, 1974). This emerging adult learner population, with far richer life experiences than the typical entering college student, required institutions to critically examine existing institutional barriers as well as ways to validate college-level learning students had already acquired. While temporary adjustments were made to accommodate veteran college students, many institutions failed to permanently institute adult learner-friendly policies until the traditional-aged college student population pool dwindled and newly recruited adult student populations demanded appropriate institutional practices and policies. Adult learners now comprise a larger percentage of campus enrollments, and some of the institutional barriers once confronted by these learners have diminished. Still, it is uncertain whether higher education is prepared for what is predicted to be yet another influx of veterans onto college campuses.

On June 30, 2008, the Post-9/11 Veterans Educational Assistance Act of 2008 (Post-9/11 GI Bill) was signed into law. While funding for veterans' college attendance has been in place since the mid 1940s, there has been quite a disparity in funds available for past and present educational benefits (McBain, 2008). Over time, the benefits have varied as different versions of the GI Bill have been adopted. Effective August 2009, veterans who have served on active duty for at least 90 days since September 11, 2001, can take advantage of this comprehensive bill, making them eligible for 40% of benefits with 90 days of active-duty service; 3 years active duty is required for 100 percent. Benefits include tuition coverage (up to the cost of in-state tuition at the most expensive public college or university), $1,000 for books and supplies, and a housing allowance. Additional resources, such as educational benefits for dependents or spouses, may be available for soldiers who agree to extended enlistments, but at the time of this writing the exact terms are yet to be finalized.

The bill promises to have a major impact on college campuses, given both its comprehensive nature and the fact that 375,000 service members—many of whom will have access to the funds provided—are leaving the military each year. An additional compounding factor is the fact that a majority of enlisted men and women join the military soon after high school completion and have yet to pursue college degrees (McBain, 2008). As was the case in 1944, American colleges and universities will have to explore ways to accommodate this increasing veteran student population. Fortunately, some critical institutional practices and systems adopted in response to the original GI Bill are still intact.

The magnitude of innovative programs and services implemented in response to increased military student enrollments is impressive. Many of these programs have been institutionalized, and adult education participants continue to benefit from their existence. Their influence is widespread, ranging from the development of new technologies that increase distance learning opportunities, to creation of standardized tests that validate adults' prior learning experiences, and to building institutional networks that support continuing academic pursuits in spite of frequent moves. The innovations explored in the following three sections are far from an exhaustive listing. For a more thorough examination, see Anderson's reviews (2006, 2009).

WORLDWIDE DISTANCE EDUCATION

Military families experience numerous geographic moves as dictated by various duty assignments, some of which are located in highly remote and isolated areas. The DoD has made extensive investments to afford military members and their families access to lifelong learning opportunities regardless of physical location, even in times of war. In the early 1940s, the United States Armed Forces Institute (USAFI) established and coordinated a wide range of wartime correspondence programs. The courses were initially instructed by service personnel of all ranks, teaching whatever they knew, with little relevance to their military assignments. The growing demand for a broader selection of course topics led to soliciting courses from colleges and universities. Later, the course offerings expanded to assist military members transitioning into the civilian workforce. Included were specialized vocational courses geared toward training soldiers for employment, as well as

courses providing the foundation for further academic study. By December 1945, it was reported that sailors had taken a total of 387,586 USAFI correspondence and college extension courses (Anderson, 2006). At one time, USAFI had more than 300,000 annual enrollments through nearly 50 colleges and universities, offering more than 6,000 different correspondence courses (Anderson, 2006).

Individual services have also been proactive in developing distance learning opportunities for their service members. As early as 1914, the Naval War College had a department for correspondence courses (U.S. Naval War College, 2004). More than 4,000 e-learning courses are accessible via Navy Knowledge Online, with more than 600,000 personnel using this delivery system on a daily basis (Barker, 2006). Throughout history, the military has taken the lead in developing the most advanced distance delivery systems. Today, every seven seconds, someone within the Department of Defense completes an online training course (Miles, 2008).

In 1999, President Bill Clinton ordered the establishment of a federal task force to improve and expand the use of technology in training and educating federal government employees (Executive Order 13111). For DoD, the key objective was to establish, by 2012, a new educational framework to meet the contemporary challenges of rapid and frequent military deployments to all corners of the globe. To support this objective, DoD created the Advanced Distributed Learning (ADL) Initiative as a collaborative effort with industry and academia. The ADL Initiative aims to develop common standards for large-scale distributed learning technologies and to make online learning content shareable across all online learning management and delivery systems. This capability will enable worldwide interconnectivity between systems, supporting individually tailored learning that can be delivered "anytime, anywhere" (Office of the Under Secretary of Defense [Personnel and Readiness], 2008b).

Many outside of the federal government, recognizing the value that global integration of learning technologies will have for the broader education and training community, have partnered with DoD to develop common voluntary guidelines for the design and implementation of distributed learning systems. As of December 2008, formal partnerships had been established with more than 70 colleges and universities and more than 200 businesses from around the world. In addition, the ADL Initiative expanded to establish relationships with members of the North Atlantic Treaty Organization (NATO) and the Partnership for Peace (PfP) (Office of the Under Secretary of Defense [Personnel and Readiness], 2008a).

The myriad of distance education options now available to all adult learners can be traced back to armed forces research and development efforts. The distance education delivery systems pioneered by the military have no doubt had a monumental impact in extending adult education's accessibility. Many of the original distance education opportunities afforded military personnel were not formal, credit-bearing courses. This lack of recognition later became the stimulus for identifying methods to validate these college-level learning experiences.

ASSESSING THE EDUCATIONAL VALUE OF MILITARY EXPERIENCE

General Educational Development (GED) Tests

Many veterans returning from World War II were unable to secure employment because they had left the service before their degrees were completed or because they lacked the required high school diploma employers demanded (Sticht, 2002). Others wished to enroll in college-level courses but did not meet entrance requirements. In response to this issue, USAFI created the General Educational Development (GED) tests to quantify the educational value of service members' military experiences. Soldiers could take the exam to qualify for a high school equivalency certificate, or they could earn college credit through the college-level version of the GED (Baldwin, 1995). These tests assisted veterans in securing jobs that required a high school diploma while also allowing them to use the GI Bill to pursue additional adult education options (Olson, 1974).

Although originally designed for use by either active-duty soldiers or veterans, in 1947, the GED was made available to individuals outside the military system. The GED program experienced improvements and expansions throughout the years and has continued to have a significant influence on adult education by enabling those who did not complete high school to resume their formal schooling at a higher level.

Assessment of On-The-Job Training

Adult learners on college campuses today can avail themselves of numerous opportunities to earn college credits for college-level learning acquired outside the classroom. What initially began as a mechanism to help accelerate military veterans' academic progress in postwar higher education has continued to serve adult learners, with or without military service (Stubblefield & Keane, 1994). Military efforts to evaluate on-the-job training in terms of academic credit established the foundation for the process of assessing prior learning. For the implementation of the following varied assessment processes, the overarching stimulus was to allow military members to enter academic programs at the appropriate point based on their prior learning experiences.

American Council on Education's Military Evaluations Program

Since 1945, the American Council on Education (ACE) has served as a critical link between the DoD and higher education. In anticipation of a massive wave of veterans with significant military experience moving into higher education following World War II, ACE recommended the establishment of an evaluation program to help assess educationally significant military experiences (Stubblefield & Keane, 1994). ACE's Military Evaluations Program is responsible for translating military training into appropriate credit recommendations that can be applied to a college degree or a vocational certificate. The *Guide to the Evaluation of Educational Experiences in the Armed Services*, a handbook for educators that describes military courses and credit recommendations, was first published in 1946 and has been continually updated and published ever since (www.militaryguides.acenet.edu).

Credit recommendations are based on a military member's formal service schools, military occupational specialties (MOSs), and college-level standardized tests. Higher education institutions can obtain ACE transcripts that provide official documentation of military experiences and accurate records of applicable ACE credit recommendations. More than 2,300 colleges and universities recognize ACE-endorsed transcripts. Numerous other standardized tests exist for military members to validate experience-based, college-level knowledge, including the College-Level Examination Program (CLEP) and the DSST program (formerly known as the DANTES Subject Standardized Tests). Annually, military members take more than 216,308 standardized college credit exams (Baker, 2009).

College Credit Recommendation Service

An outgrowth of this effort to validate military workplace learning was ACE's College Credit Recommendation Service (CREDIT), previously known as the ACE Program on Non-Collegiate Sponsored Instruction. The program, administered by ACE, assists organizations, professional and volunteer associations, schools, training suppliers, labor unions, and government agencies in validating college-level learning experiences they sponsor. This translation of workplace learning from training and experience into academic credits is yet another far-reaching initiative by the military education community that also directly benefited the broader field of adult education.

GI to Jobs

At times, there has been a direct application of military education initiatives to the civilian world; in other instances, educational approaches created by the military have provided a prototype for non-military institutions to follow. For example, the Army launched the GI to Jobs initiative to help soldiers identify and earn civilian credentials that will benefit them in their military careers as well as when they seek civilian employment. About 94% of the Army's military occupational specialties (MOSs) match civilian jobs that are subject to licensure or certification, and 93% of enlisted soldiers serve in these specialties. To strengthen the soldiers' employability when their service is complete, in 2002, the Army initiated its GI to Jobs Web site, called Credentialing Opportunities On-Line, known as COOL (www.cool.army.mil). This service assists soldiers in evaluating gaps that might exist between their Army training and experiences and the civilian credentialing required for specific careers outside

the military. It appears promising that other adult education providers could replicate this innovative program in fields outside of the military.

While initiatives such as these serve to validate the educational value of service members' real-life experiences, voluntary education programs enable service members to gain additional education that builds on this foundation of professional knowledge.

VOLUNTARY EDUCATION PROGRAMS

All of the aforementioned military innovations continue to be pivotal to the education programs currently offered under the auspices of the Defense Activity for Non-Traditional Education Support (DANTES). This unit provides education support worldwide for the DoD with a mission to support off-duty, voluntary education programs for military members. Funding for voluntary education programs was institutionalized in 1954 when Congress allocated tuition assistance for off-duty civilian education that was distinct from military training (Anderson, 2006). USAFI provided initial program oversight, but due to budget cuts and a desire to streamline processes, it was later replaced by DANTES (Kime & Anderson, 2000).

Army and Navy off-duty education programs were among the first of the large-scale adult education activities (Houle et al., 1947). Service members' participation in voluntary education programs has consistently increased, with more than 400,000 currently participating annually. In 2008, service members earned over 46,569 degrees, diplomas, and certificates (Baker, 2009).

A majority of the voluntary education programs are offered by educational institutions that are members in the Servicemembers Opportunity College (SOC). This is a consortium of national higher education associations and more than 1,800 colleges and universities (www.soc.aascu.org). Participating colleges form networks in which each college accepts credits from the others. Network institutions must agree to reduced residency requirements, maximize transfer of credit from other institutions, recognize evaluated military training and experience, and accept credit from nationally recognized testing. These unique provisions facilitate degree completion for military students whose careers demand frequent relocation and multiple long-term deployments.

As part of its commitment to making learning convenient and accessible to adult learners, in 1947, the armed forces also instituted on-post education providers. In addition to having SOC membership, these adult education providers must meet stipulations outlined in institutional memorandums of understanding (MOU). For example, institutions must provide on-site administrators and support staff. Over time, the mandated requirements for on-post providers have remained largely unchanged; a more in-depth review of education programs offered on military installations is provided by Kime and Anderson (2000).

In 1991, to ensure the quality of on-post voluntary education programs, the DoD, in conjunction with ACE, implemented the Military Installation Voluntary Education Review (MIVER). Although similar to the self-study process required for purposes of accreditation, MIVER reviews are solely focused on quality assessment and enhancement (www.acenet.edu/miver). They ensure quality academic programs are available to service members and encourage installations to evaluate how well their educational needs are being met. With the constantly growing list of skills and capabilities required by modern military operations, it is more important than ever to determine whether service members are getting the kind of education they need to be fully prepared.

COMPLEX MILITARY ENVIRONMENTS AND EVOLVING EDUCATIONAL REQUIREMENTS

Skills that were once seen as mandatory only for key military leaders are now considered essential for all military members regardless of their leadership position, years of service, or rank. Today's military is working in complex strategic environments where the "threats are more diffuse, more difficult to anticipate and to neutralize than ever before" (Paschal, 2006, p. 1). This new atmosphere requires that military education foster critical thinking skills earlier in the careers of all military members (Reoyo, 2002).

Kime and Anderson (1997) suggest that "the lines formerly drawn between those who need 'education' and those who need 'training' have become blurred, if not irrelevant" (p. 7). The

Army posture statement suggests that training prepares soldiers and leaders to operate in relatively certain conditions and focuses them on "what to think." Education, on the other hand, prepares soldiers and leaders to operate in uncertain conditions, focusing more on "how to think" (*Statement on the Posture*, 2008). The military views training as more likely to be reflexive whereas education demands problem-solving. Historically, as individuals progressed in rank, professional development activities would shift from training to education (Tipton, 2006). Currently, a blending of the two is seen as essential for all military members.

Coupled with a need for critical thinking skills, professional military education today must encompass global and cultural awareness (Paschal, 2006). The human dimension has always been a key element of warfare and continues to be a critical component of today's complex military operational environments. Repeatedly, soldiers returning from recent deployments speak of the need for an expanded understanding of language, culture, and customs of the local environment, with a specific focus on religion, political structures, and their impact on a given region. Each individual service is addressing these educational needs differently. For example, Marine Corps junior officers attend the Center for Advanced Operational Culture Learning, leaving with an understanding that handling the cultural and human terrain is equally as challenging and important as navigating the geographic terrain (U.S. Marine Corps Training and Education Command, 2008).

While the services will predominantly serve as a vehicle for fulfilling these educational needs, higher education will also be tapped to assist in this effort (*Statement on the Posture*, 2008). Lewis (2006) argues that Army officer education development should undergo reform. Included in the recommendations is that officers should be afforded time to obtain civilian graduate degrees, which will in turn enhance their intellectual sophistication and better prepare them for today's military challenges. In fact, in 2005, the Army increased the number of Army-sponsored (versus off-duty voluntary education) graduate school opportunities offered to officers, with the goals of developing critical thinking skills and enhancing their cultural awareness, regional knowledge, and foreign language skills.

The armed forces will continue to rely on strong collaborative relations with higher education, requiring institutions to monitor how effectively they address these and other educational needs of military learners. Their success will be determined, in part, by understanding the unique characteristics and concerns of today's service members and veterans who may have experienced repeated and extended deployments.

POSSIBLE CONSEQUENCES OF WAR ZONE EXPERIENCES

It has been estimated that nearly 20% of military service members who have returned from Iraq and Afghanistan—300,000 in all—report symptoms of post-traumatic stress disorder (PTSD) or major depression (Rand Corporation, 2008). Another 19% of returning service members report that they experienced a possible traumatic brain injury while deployed, and 7% report it is highly likely they were experiencing PTSD and had a probable brain injury. Reports on actual numbers of service members impacted by these two conditions vary due to imperfect screening methodology and reliance on self-reporting, but it is clear that adult educators may confront issues that have yet to be identified, confirmed, or treated.

While research reveals that not all veterans are severely impacted by trauma or PTSD (Vasterling & Brewin, 2005), campuses still need to evaluate existing student services in relation to their ability to address the needs of an increasing student population that may exhibit trauma-related learning barriers. Unfortunately, there is limited information pertaining to the impact of these mental health issues as they relate to classroom performance. While neuroscience research findings provide valuable insights, the field of adult education has just begun to examine how these data apply to adult learning.

Along with those suffering from often undetected brain trauma or PTSD combat injuries, a much higher number of severely wounded soldiers are returning from combat than ever before—due to modern life-saving capabilities that were unavailable in past military conflicts. Adult education will be central to their recovery process. As part of their commitment to wounded warriors, the military has pledged, if required, to retrain and educate wounded service members to perform other jobs in the military or to prepare them for transitioning to civilian employment. Higher education institutions are likely to play a pivotal role in helping the military fulfill its commitment to these wounded soldiers.

To better serve service members who have experienced severe injuries, in 2007, ACE initiated the Severely Injured Military Veterans: Fulfilling Their Dreams program, which provides direct support to veterans by aligning their career goals with educational opportunities (American Council on Education, 2009). Within major medical treatment facilities, education advisers tailor comprehensive recovery plans for wounded service members that match their capabilities with available educational programs and services. Developmental academic advising and campus advocacy are two critical components of this program. Once it has been determined where a veteran will continue his or her education, the program matches the veteran with a volunteer from that institution. The volunteer becomes the student's campus advocate, assisting and supporting the student's return to education. While this program is not projected to expand to any large scale, it serves as an innovative model for how institutions can meet the needs of this student population (McBain, 2008).

Institutional responses to wounded veteran students have varied from establishing new programs, as described previously, to awarding scholarships designed to assist recovering service members as they prepare for future employment. Undoubtedly, higher education will continue to be used to assist severely wounded active-duty soldiers and veterans as they transition through role changes precipitated by their injuries. Adult educators will serve as advocates for this growing student clientele, ensuring appropriate institutional policies are in place to accommodate the unique and frequently changing job demands (e.g., being deployed unexpectedly mid-semester) placed on active-duty military learners. They will also be essential to the successful integration and retention of veterans.

THE VETERAN COLLEGE STUDENT

Although data collected on who uses educational benefits and the degree to which these benefits are used are plagued with reporting inconsistencies (Adelman, 2008), it does give institutions cause to reflect on how veterans are integrated into their campuses. For example, on average, service members use only 17 months of the 36 months of VA benefits to which they are entitled, with only 6% using their full VA benefits (Field, 2008). To say these numbers reflect a lack of student retention to graduation would be only speculative, but they do suggest that potential degree-seeking students are not being retained through degree completion. As a result, there appears to be good reason for institutions to examine their practices to ensure they provide supportive campus environments for this student clientele.

Veteran students undergo numerous role changes precipitated by leaving the military. Their transition may be affected by their degree of preparation for their role change and how well they understand the expectations and norms associated with their new roles. Veterans who have successfully negotiated the transition to college may be better poised to respond to transition issues faced by this student and should be asked to participate in college orientation programs.

Soldiers transitioning from combat to college may seek a different kind of support than campus advisers or counselors are equipped to provide. For example, members of the National Guard or the Army Reserve may transition from the combat zone into the civilian community and higher education institutions without the benefit of a local military support system. Having opportunities for new veteran students to interact with those who have experience with this reentry process can potentially impact the veteran's retention. Sachs (2008) reports that during campus-based focus groups, veterans reported feeling stressed and uncomfortable until they were able to connect with other veterans. In response, Montgomery College created a Combat2College program, working collaboratively with a Department of Veterans Affairs Medical Center to assist combat veterans in their transition to higher education.

Once in the classroom, veterans may feel isolated and different from their traditional-aged counterparts, who likely lack both their experience base and an understanding of the experiences veterans endured during their service. To aid in the retention of this clientele, campuses are creating ongoing campus-based opportunities (e.g., campus veterans organization) for student veterans to interact and share concerns with one another. A multidisciplinary veterans committee can be a vital resource for providing ongoing feedback to improve institutional responsiveness.

The Student Veterans of America (SVA), founded in January 2008, may provide campus-based veterans yet another avenue of support. As a coalition of student veteran groups from college campuses across the United States (www.studentveterans.org), the SVA may serve as a valuable resource for institutions with new or growing veteran student populations.

Careful examination of institutional policies and services will be critical to removing potential barriers that may impede the veteran college student's success. Numerous institutions are expanding efforts to respond to and support veteran college students in an effort to facilitate their enrollment and retention (McBain, 2008). Unfortunately, no uniform prescription is available to guide institutional reform; however, the failure to act may result in missed opportunities for both students and higher education.

CONCLUSION

Since the 18th century, the U.S. military has been a leader in making adult education more accessible to service members and, by extension, to the largely underserved adult population as a whole. Though initial efforts focused mainly on improving troop morale, the military's commitment to education has expanded to recruiting and retaining soldiers, preparing them for post-service careers, and satisfying their desire for ongoing learning. As these motivations have shifted, armed forces education has grown from providing literacy education and GI Bill funding, to developing programs for a student clientele that is constantly on the move and that possesses extensive real-life learning experiences. Indeed, the military has pioneered innovations that serve all adult learners well. At the same time, the field of adult education has helped the armed forces supplement military education and training, creating soldiers who are better equipped to deal with the complex realities they face in their profession today. By truly examining the needs and strengths of the adult learner, complete with life experiences that are an education all their own, the military has succeeded in defining and transforming the field of adult education.

REFERENCES

Adelman, C. (2008, June). *What do we know—and not know—about service members as college students?* (PowerPoint slides). Paper presented at the American Council on Education Veteran's Summit, Georgetown University, Washington, DC. Retrieved January 31, 2009, from http://www.acenet.edu/Content/NavigationMenu/ProgramsServices/MilitaryPrograms/Adelman_Cliff(3).pdf

American Council on Education. (2009). *Severely injured military veterans: fulfilling their dreams.* Retrieved February 2, 2009, from http://www.acenet.edu/Content/NavigationMenu/ProgramsServices/MilitaryPrograms/veterans/

Anderson, C. L. (2006). *Remembering those who have made a difference in United States military voluntary education.* Washington, DC: American Association of State Colleges and Universities and American Association of Community Colleges.

Anderson, C. L. (2009). *Annotated bibliography for adult and continuing education in the United States Military.* Unpublished manuscript, Servicemembers' Opportunity Colleges, Washington, DC.

Baker, C. (2009, January 27). *Department of Defense voluntary education.* Presented at the 2009 Council of College and Military Educators (CCME) Symposium, Oahu, HI. Retrieved February 7, 2009, from http://www.ccmeonline.org/sym2009/Carolyn_Baker.ppt

Baldwin, J. (Ed.). (1995). *Who took the GED? GED 1995 statistical report.* Washington, DC: GED Testing Service, Center for Adult Learning and Educational Credentials, American Council on Education.

Barker, E. (2006, June 24). NKO approaches 650,000 user mark. *Navy News Service.* Retrieved November 3, 2008, from http://www.navy.mil/search/display.asp?story_id=24326

Blassingame, J. (1965). The Union Army as an educational institution for Negroes, 1862–1865. *Journal of Negro Education, 34,* 152–159.

Borden, P. (1989). *Civilian indoctrination of the military: World War I and future implications for the military-industrial complex.* Westport, CT: Greenwood Press.

Bound, J., & Turner, S. (2002). Going to war and going to college: Did World War II and the G.I. Bill increase educational attainment for returning veterans? *Journal of Labor Economics, 20*(4), 784–815.

Field, K., (2008, June 9). As Congress prepares to expand GI Bill, colleges reach out to veterans. *The Chronicle of Higher Education Daily News.* Retrieved October 10, 2008, from http://chronicle.com/

Harlow, J., & Rasmussen, C. (2008, August 4). Army opens prep school at Fort Jackson. *Army News Service.* Retrieved September 19, 2008, from http://www.army.mil/-news/2008/08/04/11441-army-opens-prep-school-at-fort-jackson/

Houle, C. O., Burr, E. W., Hamilton, T. W., and Yale, J. R. (1947). *Armed services and adult education.* Washington, DC: American Council on Education.

Kett, J. F. (1994). *The pursuit of knowledge under difficulties: From self-improvement to adult education in America, 1750–1990.* Stanford, CA: Stanford University Press.

Kime, S. F., & Anderson, C. L. (1997). *Education vs training: A military perspective.* Washington, DC: Servicemembers Opportunity Colleges. (ERIC Document Reproduction Service No. ED404452)

Kime, S. F., & Anderson, C. L. (2000). Contributions of the military to adult and continuing education. In A. L. Wilson & E. R. Hayes (Eds.), *Handbook of adult and continuing education* (pp. 464–479). San Francisco: Jossey-Bass.

Langley, H. D. (1967). *Social reform in the United States Navy, 1798–1862.* Urbana: University of Illinois Press.

Lewis, C. T. (2006). *Army officer professional military education system reform to produce leader competency for the future.* Unpublished master's thesis, U.S. Army War College, Carlisle Barracks, PA.

McBain, L. (2008, Summer). "When Johnny [or Janelle] comes marching home": National, state, and institutional efforts in support of veterans' education. *American Association of State Colleges and Universities: Perspectives,* pp. 1–19.

Merriam, S. B., Caffarella, R. S., & Baumgartner, L. M. (2007). *Learning in adulthood: A comprehensive guide* (3rd ed.). San Francisco: Jossey-Bass.

Mettler, S. (2005). "The only good thing was the G.I. Bill": Effects of education and training provisions on African-American veteran's political participation. *Studies in American Political Development, 19,* 31–52.

Miles, D. (2008, April 24). Distributed learning initiative delivers training anywhere, any time. *American Forces Press Service.* Retrieved February 2, 2008, from http://www.defenselink.mil/news/newsarticle.aspx?id=49681

Office of the Under Secretary of Defense (Comptroller). (2008, February 4). *Fiscal year 2009 budget request summary justification.* Retrieved August 7, 2008, from http://www.defenselink.mil/comptroller/defbudget/fy2009/FY2009_Budget_Request_Justification.pdf

Office of the Under Secretary of Defense (Personnel and Readiness). (2008a). *ADL Partners: Advanced distributed learning.* Retrieved

February 2, 2008, from http://www.adlnet .gov/about/partners.aspx

Office of the Under Secretary of Defense (Personnel and Readiness). (2008b). History of ADL. *Advanced distributed learning.* Retrieved February 2, 2008, from http://www.adlnet .gov/about/history.aspx

Olson, K. W. (1974). *The G.I. Bill, the veterans, and the colleges.* Lexington: University Press of Kentucky.

Paschal, D.G. (2006). *Irregular warfare: Impact on future professional military education.* Unpublished master's thesis, U.S. Army War College, Carlisle Barracks, PA.

Post-9/11Veterans Educational Assistance Act of 2008, Pub. L. No. 110–252, 122 Stat. 2323 (2008).

Rand Corporation. (2008, April 19). One in five Iraq and Afghanistan veterans suffer from PTSD or major depression. *ScienceDaily.* Retrieved October 20, 2008, from http://www.sciencedaily .com/releases/2008/04

Reoyo, P.J. (2002). *Professional education: Key to transformation.* Unpublished research report, U.S. Army War College, Carlisle Barracks, PA.

Sachs, R. (2008, June 12). Valuing veterans. *Inside Higher Ed.* Retrieved November 14, 2008, from www.insidehighered.com/views/2008/06/12/c2c

Statement on the Posture of the United States Army 2008: Hearing before the Senate Armed Services Committee, 110th Cong., 2nd Sess. (2008). Retrieved February 21, 2009, from http://www .army.mil/aps/08/APS2008[1].pdf

Sticha, P. J., Dall, T. A., Handy, K., Espinosa, J., Hogan, P. F., & Young, M. C. (2003). *Impact of the Army Continuing Education System (ACES) on soldier retention and performance: Data analyses.* Alexandria, VA: United States Army Research Institute for the Behavioral and Social Sciences.

Sticht, T. (2002). The rise of the adult education and literacy system in the United States: 1600–2000. In J. Comings, B. Garner, & C. Smith (Eds.), *The annual review of adult learning and literacy* (Vol. 3, pp. 10–43). San Francisco: Jossey-Bass.

Stubblefield, H. W., & Keane, P. (1994). *Adult education in the American experience: From the colonial period to the present.* San Francisco: Jossey-Bass.

Tipton, R. A. (2006). *Professional military education for the "pentathlete" of the future.* Unpublished master's thesis, U.S. Army War College, Carlisle Barracks, PA.

U.S. Marine Corps Training and Education Command. (2008). *Center for advanced operational culture learning.* Retrieved February 26, 2009, from http://www.tecom.usmc.mil/caocl

U.S. Naval War College. (2004). *Nonresident graduate degree program, program guide 2004–2005.* Newport, RI: Author. Retrieved January 5, 2009, from http://www.usnwc.edu/admissions/gdp/ documents/GDPguide.pdf

Vasterling, J. J., & Brewin, C. R. (Eds.). (2005). *Neuropsychology of PTSD: Biological and clinical perspectives.* New York: Guilford Press.

Weinert, R. (1979). *Literacy training in the Army.* U.S. Army Training and Doctrine Command. Fort Monroe, VA: TRADOC Historical Office.

Wilds, H. E. (1938). *Valley Forge.* New York: Macmillan.

25

CONTINUING PROFESSIONAL EDUCATION

LAUREL H. JERIS

Newcomers to the field of adult and continuing education are often surprised, perhaps even dismayed, with what may appear to them to be an inability of scholars in the field to define terms, write straightforward histories of important events and movements, and delineate areas of emphasis within the field in unambiguous terms. In response to these frustrations, a few abandon the project entirely, many seek rapprochement—perhaps muttering under their breath, "They really need to get over this." And some embrace the mystery and strive to contribute to it over the long term. Among these newcomers are those who choose to study continuing professional education (CPE); they typically bring with them two additional concerns. First, as practitioners of specific occupational groups, which may be among commonly recognized professions or somewhere along the "professionalizing journey" (Tobias, 2003), they are keenly aware of the boundaries of their group. As such, they believe that the needs for continuing learning and development among their constituents are unique, highly specialized, and not generalizable. Second, there is a shared belief that public recognition of their occupational group as a profession is very desirable and requires vigilance to maintain and develop. Although this chapter will likely contribute to the dilemmas for newcomers noted above, the main purposes are (a) to examine some of the ways in which the notion of a profession conflates with continuing professional education and (b) to highlight historical and contemporary areas of common concerns and responses to those concerns related to the continuing education of professional groups.

The Emergence of Continuing Professional Education

The area of emphasis of adult and continuing education that concerns professional groups and their learning and development beyond initial preparation, typically referred to as continuing professional education (CPE), first appeared as a chapter heading in the 1970 *Handbook of Adult Education* (Smith, Aker, & Kidd, 1970). Previous *Handbooks* (1948, 1960) contained chapters that included discussions of specific professional groups and their needs for learning and development. However, calls for greater public accountability from professional groups, which began in the 1960s (Houle, 1980), were sufficient to suggest to adult education scholars that an interest area of CPE was emerging and that separate consideration of these trends would be useful. Two publications in the early 1980s were significant in codifying those concerns and exploring them in detail.

First, Houle's (1980) book, *Continuing Learning in the Professions*, describes, synthesizes, and to a limited extent critiques the complex issues of CPE. Considering that this book was written 30 years ago, it has an eerily contemporary feel to it. Many of Houle's analyses conclude with several possible scenarios for the future. Later sections of this chapter draw from a number of key contributors to the CPE literature, whose research documents that several of Houle's predictions are apt descriptions of the current state of CPE.

The second publication is found in a volume of the series that comprised the 1980 *Handbook* and focused on controversies in the field (Kreitlow & Associates, 1981). Two chapters were devoted to the issue of mandating continuing education as part of the credentialing renewal process for professional groups, with one author taking the position that this practice increased professional competence, and another arguing against it. This singular focus is indicative of the tremendous growth in mandated CPE that began in the second half of the 1960s and has continued unabated. It has steadily gained momentum and is now the norm for relicensure of state-regulated professional groups; it is also typically required for recertification, largely a function of professional associations.

These two publications, one broadly cast and the other narrowly focused on a single important controversy, contributed enormously to a robust interest in the study of CPE. However, no one has undertaken work with the scope of the Houle (1980) project, which encompassed 20 years of engagement, reflection, and study of 17 occupational groups that represented the range from traditional to emergent professions. This chapter presents a modest opportunity to revisit some of the dilemmas Houle describes and analyzes and to pose some additional concerns.

What Is Continuing Professional Education?

CPE refers to a particular area of interest within adult and continuing education that initially gained traction largely through Houle's work, beginning with articles he wrote in the 1960s. He addresses various issues and needs of post-qualification professionals to keep up with new developments, gain mastery, understand the connections of their field to related disciplines, and grow as people as well as professionals (Houle as cited in Charters, 1970, p. 488). The formally structured approaches to accomplishing at least some of these goals have been described, analyzed, and critiqued by numerous scholars and can be found in the literature using the CPE descriptor. A closely related descriptor, continuing

professional development, is a broader categorization that encompasses formal and informal approaches to continuing learning (Eraut, 1994). It is important to note that in non-U.S. contexts, CPE is generally a category that resides within continuing professional development; this distinction is not as apparent in the United States, where CPE is more commonly used.

Dirkx and Austin (2005) propose a conceptual model of continuing professional development that "characterizes the research and practice . . . in terms of its overall *aims, context* and *focus*" (p. 1). This model came about as a response to the need for graduate students with an interest in the design, delivery, administration, perhaps even accreditation of CPE, to have a common framework for understanding their work regardless of their setting (CPE, training and development, staff development in public school settings, or faculty development in higher education). The model depicts these varied contexts and also builds on Habermas (1971) in terms of delineating possible aims for CPE (technical, practical, and emancipatory) and provides for consideration of these *contexts* and *aims* from the point of view of the *focus* (organization or individual). For example, this model enables us to situate the aims of professional development experiences such as technical updates (new technical procedures to master or regulations to learn); practical approaches to conflict management, better communication, or teambuilding; and more emancipatory learning experiences that increase self-knowledge or the ability to be more critically reflective (as discussed in Dirkx & Austin, 2005, p. 4) within a particular practice arena (context) and focus (organization or individual). Those new to the study of CPE find common ground along the three dimensions of the model, despite what appear at first glance to be dizzying differences in CPE practices, and the model also invites fresh research questions that permit us to compare and contrast these dimensions across professional contexts (Jeris & Daley, 2004).

At first blush, the term CPE may seem accessible, straightforward, and perhaps even uncontroversial. Other chapters in this edition of the *Handbook* contribute to the understanding of the philosophical and political aspects of naming an interest area. A hearty discussion of the dimensions of these arguments is beyond the scope of this chapter; however, brief references to some of the major issues may alert the reader to their "tip of the iceberg" nature and that further study is warranted.

Consider the first and third words together in the CPE descriptor, *continuing* and *education*; they are used in this context to differentiate post-qualification education from initial or pre-qualification preparation. Charters (1970) associated the notion of continuing education with lifelong learning in his handbook chapter on CPE, and it seems to have formed a permanent bond. But several scholars have expressed deep concerns about the notion of and need for lifelong learning. In their view, learning has been insufficiently differentiated from schooling (Illich, 1977; Ohliger, 1981), thus indicating a lifelong need for formal educational intervention as opposed to a more self-directed approach to learning. Perhaps in response to these concerns, the title Houle selected for his book (1980) emphasized continuing learning rather than continuing education because he placed the primary emphasis on one's desire and obligation to continue to learn throughout his/her career and secondary emphasis on the educational systems and processes serving those learning needs. Presumably, this was not an idle concern for Houle, as the rush was well under way as he was writing the book to mandate continuing education for recredentialing (relicensure or recertification).

More recently, typical initial responses from graduate students at the start of a survey course of CPE to Cervero's (2001) question, "What is the problem for which continuing education is the answer?" (p. 25) tend to fall into three categories: (1) relicensure/recertification, (2) quality assurance, and (3) legal compliance and avoidance of litigation of various types. Further probing reveals that improving practice perhaps ought to be the goal, but it is not the problem. Even when the question is posed a different way such as, "What are the goals of CPE?" early responses are much the same, possibly indicating that participation in CPE is viewed as the main vehicle through which members of professional groups remain in good standing. These responses reveal a great deal about the enrollment drivers for CPE, a bit about the expectations of the learners, and even relay a sense of what worries them. These very worries are indicative of Wilson's (2000) concern:

> Professionals are constantly caught up in producing and reproducing the institutional and social mechanisms by which they operate, which in my view is leading to their increasing loss of professional autonomy and corresponding organizational rather than client allegiance. (p. 78)

Consideration of those institutional and social mechanisms that contribute to either the maintenance of professional status or movement toward it inevitably includes CPE.

Alternatively, new research explores learning in the context of professional practice and carefully delineates how members of various professions construct knowledge from formal (Daley, 2001) and informal learning (Eraut, 2004), thus extending the understanding of context on professional development. Dall'Alba and Sandberg (2006) have invigorated the discussion of stage-based models of professional development (e.g., Dreyfus & Dreyfus, 1986) that depict the stages as linear, cumulative, and relatively uniform within a profession, but they fail to describe how professionals move from one stage to the next and what factors influence their development. Dall'Alba and Sandberg propose a more nuanced approach that "calls attention to variation in embodied understanding of practice" (p. 400), which arises in part from the practice context and also from the broader social, cultural, and historical contexts. Thus, two practitioners in the same field, and perhaps even at the same stage of development, are likely to construct quite different knowledge and skills from formal and informal learning opportunities. Recognizing and valuing diverse learning and development trajectories have the potential for improving practice. At the same time, a more pluralistic approach to professional development heightens the difficulties inherent in the current highly standardized approaches to accountability through mandated recredentialing processes.

INTERSECTION OF THE PROFESSIONS AND CONTINUING PROFESSIONAL EDUCATION

Given that practitioners across a broad range of traditional and emerging professions may view the main purpose of CPE as both defensive and developmental, an exploration of the *professional* aspect of the CPE descriptor is warranted. Put another way, what does it mean to be a professional?

The technical/functionalist view, which arose largely from Flexner's work on medical education, completed in the early 1900s (Houle, 1980), lays out any number of traits or characteristics as signifiers of professional status. Although there is no universally accepted set of traits, there are some general areas of agreement, and these typically include a core specialized knowledge/theory base, specific skills and competencies, minimum education requirements, some form of regulation for quality assurance and protection of the public, standards for ethical practice, commitment to continuing learning, and a professional association (Gilley & Eggland, 1989; Houle, 1980; Millerson, 1964). This approach prevailed until the wide circulation of Houle's (1980) work shifted the emphasis from static traits to processes to develop them, opening the door for occupational groups to consider professionalization as a long-term desired goal. This liberalized view, less elitist and restrictive than the trait approach, still draws heavily on particular decontextualized characteristics as markers or milestones for professionalization, and as such, it remains in the functionalist tradition. However, the shift from traits to a process view cemented the connection of the notion of a profession to that of continuing professional education, as CPE was envisioned as a key mechanism for professionalization.

Critics of the functionalist viewpoint are quick to point out that the notion of professionalism (emphasis on the *ism*) is deeply embedded in one's sociocultural location and experience, and the mental models one holds of it cannot be separated from those experiences. Thus, lists of traits or characteristics, or processes used (such as CPE) to acquire and/or strengthen those traits, contribute to reproduction of the existing social order and reinforce asymmetrical power relations. Cervero (1989) classifies this perspective as the conflict viewpoint (p. 518). Along these lines, Cervero, Bussigel, and Hellyer (1985) challenge those adult educators who apply their program planning expertise to the design of CPE "to consider the social function of professionalism in the context of a socially stratified society in which the professions occupy a position of increasing status and power" (p. 22). They introduce a framework through which CPE program planners may critically examine their ideological stance along two continua arranged in a matrix, individual to social/structural, and

traditional to revisionist viewpoints (p. 24). This framework provides a very useful, accessible analytic tool to reflect on practice and to engage in a dialectic that may reveal underlying philosophical meanings and implications. Cervero later captures the essence of this approach to CPE as the critical viewpoint (1989, p. 519). Cervero et al. (1985) and Cervero (1988) were among the first contributors to the CPE literature to name the functionalist and liberal functionalist ideological underpinnings of professionalism and to call attention to the ways in which adult educators who practice within the confines of CPE are obligated to consider the larger political, social, and economic implications of their work. Cervero's work differs substantially in this respect from that of Houle (1980), which does not question the fundamental role of the professions in society. Others certainly have done so, and extensive critiques of the professions reside in the disciplines of history, sociology, philosophy, and anthropology.

Tobias (2003) extends the critique to specifically interrogate the intersection of professionalization and CPE. He takes the liberal functionalist viewpoint to task because it fails to consider the social, political, and economic forces feeding into and flowing out of the professionalization journey of occupational groups. Tobias recognizes that "the professionalization of occupations, and many of the educational processes that have gone along with this professionalization, have served as two-edged swords; they have been riddled with tensions and contradictions" (p. 451). He then proposes that ethics, competence, professional regulation, boundary setting (political and economic), authority, and globalization are salient areas for interrogation of these tensions. For example, in helping professional groups identify, codify, and develop skills training for specific competencies, CPE may also be complicit in "standardizing performance, and limiting creativity and preserving mediocrity" (p. 452). This particular tension is explored below under the broader heading of quality assurance.

QUALITY ASSURANCE

Although consensus has not been achieved on the overall contributions of the professions to the betterment of society, many who study this phenomenon agree that occupational groups that claim this status or strive to achieve it have a special obligation to the public. Their specialized knowledge and sources of expertise set them apart, but they cannot flourish in the absence of trust. Developing and maintaining this trusting relationship with the public is dependent on assuring quality, which encompasses a complex array of decisions, processes, and structures. First, in terms of decisions, who determines quality, at what points is it measured, how is it evaluated and by whom, and what sanctions are appropriate for lapses in it? These decision elements require processes and structures for implementation that are discussed below.

Who determines quality, and at what points is it measured? The key players in determining quality vary by profession or occupational group, but they generally include a mix of stakeholders with an interest in and power to either directly regulate or influence the regulation process. Standards for initial and continuing qualification are heavily leveraged by those who develop and deliver initial professional education, including: faculty and higher education administrators, accrediting bodies of professional preparation programs, professional association leaders, state government regulators, and increasingly, members of the public who are appointed as lay members of various government agencies or citizen watch groups. Involvement of this last stakeholder group was in its infancy when described by Houle (1980), but it is now commonplace for many licensed professions. The most dramatic assessment of quality takes place at the completion of initial professional education requirements, and the outcome of this assessment determines readiness to practice. The range of duties that a newly credentialed practitioner is permitted to undertake without supervision is specific to the profession, as is the nature of subsequent assessments of quality.

What processes and structures are used to assure quality throughout the career lifespan of professionals? Heated calls for public accountability were the precipitating factor in mandating CPE for recredentialing, which grew by leaps and bounds from the mid-1960s through the early 1980s. But according to Cervero (1989), this practice leveled off in the later part of the 1980s. Conversely, Queeney (2000) notes that required

participation in CPE remains a central feature of recredentialing and is a far more appealing alternative than periodic re-examination, a relatively rare choice among a few professions, largely in health care. It is important to differentiate recredentialing from credentialing in specialty areas beyond initial qualification to modify or expand the scope of practice, such as is true, for example, in medical specialties, accounting, and actuarial science.

As administrative practice acts across states call for periodic reviews of the professional regulation rules and regulations of each licensed professional group, demands for quality assurance, protection of the public, and accountability to the public have emerged as prominent features of these reviews. Despite deeply held concerns regarding the ways in which mandating education may alter learners' motivations and outcomes, and the ways in which CP educators then become agents of the state, mandated CPE is unlikely to disappear. Houle (1980) expresses deep concerns regarding this practice and asserts that the leap to requiring CPE prevents vigorous, in-depth study of the recredentialing process and what, if any, educational component is appropriate.

> The full range of evidence on which recredentialing could be based has scarcely been considered. . . . As a result *mandatory continuing education* has incorrectly become a synonym for *relicensure, recertification,* and more generally, the whole concept of recredentialing. The two are separated here because they are essentially distinct from one another. The belief that they are identical prevents the constructive thought that will lead eventually to satisfactory systems whereby all professionals can maintain or improve high levels of performance (italics in original). (p. 281)

As the primary process for recredentialing is mandatory CPE, the providers of CPE serve as key structural components of quality assurance. An early task is to get themselves accredited so they can offer the real deal—continuing education units that count. Accreditation requirements vary by profession and by state, but in many cases, higher education-based providers get virtually an automatic pass, particularly for credit-bearing courses or those that lead to advanced degrees related to the initial qualification. Accrediting CPE providers and programs for requalification has led to the proliferation of associations whose main task is to do just that–case in point, the Association for the Accreditation of Continuing Medical Education (ACCME). And, of course, there is the issue of designing reliable systems for certifying attendance and successful completion of the courses as defined by the particular professional group leadership and its designated accreditors.

It is clear that as CPE has evolved as the key process for recredentialing, which is a central feature of quality assurance, a substantial bureaucratic structure has also evolved to vet and document it. Returning to the tensions mentioned earlier by Tobias (2003), this bureaucratization, with its emphasis on oversight, control, and management of post-qualification eligibility, firmly moves the authority away from the individual practitioner and places it under the purview of regulatory bodies, one of which is likely one's own professional association. Regarding these developments, Houle (1980) notes, "In the course of time it seems likely, therefore, that the various kinds of control and incentive systems, which now operate separately and sometimes at cross purposes, will be brought together into a concerted and highly developed effort to assure quality" (p. x). In contrast to Houle's optimism, Queeney's (2000) assessment is that the systems that have evolved address only superficial aspects of public accountability and that "increased consumer awareness and growing incidence of litigation have made it clear that the appearance of accountability is no longer sufficient" (p. 378). What seems to be getting through loud and clear to individual practitioners is that they not only must be in compliance, but also have the evidence to document that they have attended the required number of continuing education units to remain in good standing in their profession (Jeris & Conway, 2005). This is not surprising, given that their livelihood depends on it.

Professional associations, in no small part to retain the authority to police their membership (Queeney, 2000), have evolved into quasi-governmental regulatory agencies. The tensions inherent in adopting this system are twofold: (1) in providing this system, professional associations have largely been able to avoid broader and possibly more effective forms of accountability and (2) the system deflects attention that is sorely needed to create CPE systems and programs that are grounded in the ways professionals construct knowledge in the context of practice (Daley, 2001).

Issues for Continuing Professional Education Program Design

Cervero (2001, p. 40) vividly describes the ubiquitous informational update course in unmistakable terms. So much so that one can almost feel the need to slip on a jacket in the too chilly hotel conference room, no doubt kept that way to fend off the after-lunch need to snooze as the PowerPoint presentations continue unabated. This particular learning environment is hardly conducive to even the most passive learners, but the larger and more disturbing issue is that of learning transfer. As Daley notes, "the field of adult education can offer few assurances that the knowledge learned in these programs is linked to the context of professional practice" (p. 40). Hence, despite the huge investment in CPE, financed by organizations and individuals, relatively little is understood about how (or if) practitioners integrate new knowledge with their current approaches. The one-size-fits-all appeal of the update model has given it staying power, but there are other models, two of which, the competence and the performance models, have been around for quite some time (Nowlen, 1988, as cited in Mott, 2000). Briefly, what differentiates the competence and performance models from the update model is that they offer more guidance for critical reflection on practice as one aspires to assimilate new knowledge. A vital aspect that is missing from all three models is an emphasis on context. Furthermore, as Woodall and Gourlay (2004, p. 99) point out, how learning programs are designed is heavily influenced by the adult learning theory antecedents of the program developers, which are often accompanied by an implicit assumption that the learning will be classroom based and require a facilitator. These two defining features of CPE indicate the presence of very limited mental models regarding its purposes and possibilities.

Houle's work prominently features common areas of concern among the professions with regard to learning, which he felt could be best addressed by adult educators. But those common concerns have evolved to be heavily related to the regulatory and administrative systems, processes, and structures. Given the highly situated nature of professional groups and their members, much more research is needed to better understand how professionals learn in their context as well as how changes in that context affect their learning needs. Refocusing attention along these lines is likely to be useful in better understanding another fairly recent development, which Cervero (2001) prominently features as "Trend 1: the amount of continuing education offered at the workplace dwarfs that offered by any other type of provider, and probably all other providers combined" (p. 19). Numerous factors have been instrumental in shaping this trend, but one obvious shift is that the era of the independent practitioner has greatly diminished. The advent of third-party payment, which began in health services in the mid-1980s, has dramatically altered the practice environment of the health and human service professions. Once again, as the bureaucracy needed to administer the system has grown to gigantic proportions, practitioners have responded by pooling their resources through large group-practice arrangements, which have also expanded and taken on new forms altogether. In some areas, health professionals continue to serve the public but work for large corporations that assume much of the administrative burden; for example, this arrangement has been true for pharmacists for decades.

A second factor is that many occupational groups have undertaken steps toward professionalization and are somewhere along that journey (Weinstein & Young, 2004; Young, 1998). In many cases, services delivered from these groups (e.g., school teachers, police, allied health service providers) were never designed around the sole practitioner model. They were always part of an organizational entity, underscoring the importance of the focus dimension of the Dirkx and Austin (2005) model (individual or organizational), which merits attention in the design and delivery of CPE.

Disrupting the Status Quo

A contemporary concern, not addressed in the early scholarship of CPE and still neglected today, is that CPE programs and curricula offer cultural texts for interrogating the aspects of professional regulation that are based on a meritocracy that denies difference (Jeris & Armacost, 2002). Current practices regarding both initial and continuing professional education are primarily informed by psychological and behavioral theories of learning. This highly individualistic concentration diverts the focus from the broader social issues. Little attention is devoted to how these approaches fail to take into account their impact on communities of practitioners, the communities they serve, and the communities that must replenish the ranks of service providers (Collins, 1998). Jeris and Armacost (2002) suggest four research propositions that have the potential for shedding light on CPE programs and practices that are reproductive rather than emancipatory. Briefly, they recommend that researchers examine political, cultural, and institutional practices in terms of the ways that they support or injure various groups and examine the structures that house bodies of expert knowledge (hospitals, schools, courts, professional associations, etc.) for the ways in which commitment to social justice is manifested (pp. 94–95). Their findings from a study, which scrutinized annual conference programming decisions by the American Medical Association and the American Bar Association, confirmed that session schedules were more influenced by historical attendance patterns than any other single factor. As a result, topics of particular interest to various marginalized group were often scheduled concurrently with high-demand sessions, resulting in very low attendance or cancellation of special-interest group topics.

Ross-Gordon and Brooks (2004) note that "Although considerable attention has been paid to the diversity of clients by selected professional groups, the topic of positionality of CPE practitioners and scholars has rarely been a focus" (p.79). The findings of the study by Jeris and Armacost (2002), described above, suggest insensitivity at best to the social justice implications of programming decisions of CPE practitioners, supporting Ross-Gordon and Brooks's contention that these issues have been sorely neglected in the practice and scholarship of CPE.

CPE scholars and practitioners are uniquely situated to examine and influence the gatekeeping aspects of professional associations and higher education that negatively impact equal access of marginalized groups to initial and continuing professional education. For example, in their comprehensive study of the consideration of race in college and university admissions, Bowen and Bok (1998) note that "Despite widespread recognition of the value of diversity, efforts to increase the number of minority professionals through race-sensitive admissions policies have never been fully accepted" (p. 13). Even as the traditional professions of law, engineering, and medicine have made progress in diversifying their ranks over the last 50 years (p. 10), membership of less lucrative professions (e.g., allied health practitioners, educators, information technology professionals) largely remain consistent with their traditional demographic profile in terms of race and gender. By the year 2050, people of color will comprise more than half the U.S. population, with little growth in the non-Hispanic, single-race white population (Bernstein & Edwards, 2008). Without a doubt, this is a societal issue. But CPE researchers and practitioners rarely draw attention to the ways in which they are contributing to policy and practice that fails to meet the needs of an increasingly diverse and multiracial population, which includes individuals ready to learn to serve, those who continue to serve, and those in need of services.

Moving Forward

Given that, in practice at least, the predominant aim of CPE has evolved to be recredentialing through technical updates, attention to the ways in which professionals construct knowledge gained through CPE in the context of their practice arenas, as well as their sociocultural histories, has been neglected by all but a handful of scholars. As Fenwick notes, "A particular context of learning presents possibilities from which learners select objects of knowing; thus context influences both the content of experience and the ways people respond to and process it" (2000, p. 250). Furthermore, the instrumental nature of the update model leaves little room for reflection on the special mission of the professions to serve the public interest. At the conclusion on his book, Houle (1980) laments that the vision of what CPE can accomplish is too limited. He charges the next generation of CPE practitioners to "refine their sensitiveness, enlarge their conceptions, add to their knowledge, and perfect their skills so that they can discharge their responsibilities within the context of their own personalities and the needs of the society of which they are a part" (p. 316). Houle's admonition is even more apt today than it was 30 years ago. There is much work to be done.

REFERENCES

Bernstein, R., & Edwards, T. (2008). *An older and more diverse nation by midcentury.* U.S. Census Bureau/Public Information Office/Last revised: November 17, 2008. Retrieved December 18, 2008, from http://www.census.gov/Press-Release/www/archives/population/012496.html

Bowen, W. G., & Bok, D. (1998). *The shape of the river.* Princeton, NJ: Princeton University Press.

Cervero, R. M. (1988). *Effective practice in continuing professional education.* San Francisco: Jossey-Bass.

Cervero, R. M. (1989). Continuing education for the professions. In S. B. Merriam & P. M. Cunningham (Eds.), *Handbook of adult and continuing education* (pp. 513–536). San Francisco: Jossey-Bass.

Cervero, R. M. (2001). Continuing professional education in transition, 1981–2000. *International Journal of Lifelong Education, 20*(1/2), 16–30.

Cervero, R. M., Bussigel, D., & Hellyer, M. (1985). Examining the relationships between continuing educators and the professions. In R. M. Cervero & C. L. Scanlan (Eds.), *Problems and prospects in continuing professional education* (pp. 21–31). New Directions for Continuing Education, No. 27. San Francisco: Jossey-Bass.

Charters, A. N. (1970). Continuing education for the professions. In R. M. Smith, G. F. Aker, & J. R. Kidd (Eds.), *Handbook of adult education* (pp. 487–498). New York: Macmillan.

Collins, M. (1998). *Adult education as vocation: A critical role for the adult educator.* London: Routledge.

Daley, B. J. (1999). Novice to expert: An exploration of how professionals learn. *Adult Education Quarterly, 49*(4) 133–147.

Daley, B. J. (2001). Learning and professional practice: A study of four professions. *Adult Education Quarterly, 52*(1), 39–54.

Dall'Alba, G., & Sandberg, J. (2006). Unveiling professional development: A critical review of stage models. *Review of Educational Research, 76*(3), 383–412.

Dirkx, J. M., & Austin, A.E. (2005). *Making sense of continuing professional development: Toward an integrated vision of lifelong learning in the professions.* Paper presented at the AHRD Preconference on Continuing Professional Education: Exploring a Model of Theoretical Orientations in Professional Development, Estes Park, CO.

Dreyfus, H. L., & Dreyfus, S. E. (1986). *Mind over machine: The power of human intuition and expertise in the ear of the computer.* New York: Free Press.

Eraut, M. (1994). *Developing professional knowledge and competence.* London: Falmer Press.

Fenwick, T. J. (2000). Expanding conceptions of experiential learning: A review of the five contemporary perspectives on cognition. *Adult Education Quarterly, 50*(4), 243–272.

Gilley, J. W., & Eggland, S. A. (1989). *Principles of human resource development.* Reading, MA: Addison-Wesley.

Habermas, J. (1971). *Knowledge and human interests.* Boston: Beacon Press.

Houle, C. O. (1980). *Continuing learning in the professions.* San Francisco: Jossey-Bass.

Illich, I. (1977). Disabling professions. In I. Illich, I. K. Zola, J, McKnight, J. Caplan, & H. Shaiken, *Disabling professions* (pp. 11–39). London: Marion Boyars.

Jeris, L. H., & Armacost, L. K. (2002). Doing good or doing well? A counter-story of continuing professional education. *Learning in Health and Social Care, 1*(2) 94–104.

Jeris, L., & Conway, A. (2005). Time to regrade the terrain of continuing professional education: Views from practitioners. *Adult Learning, 14*(1), 34–37.

Jeris, L., & Daley, B. J. (2004). Orienteering for boundary spanning: Reflections on the journey to date and suggestions for moving forward. *Advances in Developing Human Resources, 6*(1), 101–115.

Kreitlow, B. W., & Associates (Eds.). (1981). *Examining controversies in adult education.* San Francisco: Jossey-Bass.

Millerson, G. (1964). *The qualifying associations.* London: Routledge.

Mott, V. W. (2000). The development of professional expertise in the workplace. In V. W. Mott & B. J. Daley (Eds.), *Charting a course for continuing professional education: Reframing professional practice* (pp. 23–32). New Directions for Adult and Continuing Education, No. 86. San Francisco: Jossey-Bass.

Ohliger, J. (1981). Dialogue on mandatory continuing education. *Lifelong Learning: The Adult Years, 4*(10), 5, 7, 24–26. Occasional Paper. (ERIC Document Reproduction Service NO. EJ246684)

Queeney, D. S. (2000). Continuing professional education. In A. L. Wilson & E. R. Hayes (Eds.), *Handbook of adult and continuing education* (pp. 375–391). San Francisco: Jossey-Bass.

Ross-Gordon, J. M., & Brooks, A. K. (2004). Diversity in human resource development and continuing professional education: What does it mean for the workforce, clients, and professionals? *Advances in Developing Human Resources, 6*(1), 69–85.

Smith, R. A., Aker, G. F., & Kidd, J. R. (Eds.). (1970). *Handbook of adult education.* New York: Macmillan.

Tobias, R. (2003). Continuing professional education and professionalization: Traveling without a map or compass? *International Journal of Lifelong Education, 22*(5), 445–456.

Weinstein, M. B., & Young, W. H. (2004). *Continuing professional education: A historical view of the professions by looking backwards to move ahead for the emerging professions.* Paper presented at the Academy of Human Resource Development Preconference, Continuing Professional Education: Research Implications for Professional Practice Development, Austin, TX.

Wilson, A. L. (2000). Professional practice in the modern world. In V. W. Mott & B. J. Daley (Eds.), *Charting a course for continuing professional education: Reframing professional practice* (pp. 71–79). New Directions for Adult and Continuing Education, No. 86. San Francisco: Jossey-Bass.

Woodall, J., & Gourlay, S. (2004). The relationship between professional learning and continuing professional development in the United Kingdom: A critical review of the literature. In J. Woodall, M. Lee, & J. Stewart (Eds.), *New frontiers in HRD* (pp. 98–111). London: Routledge.

Young, W. H. (1998). *Continuing professional education in transition: Visions for the professions and new strategies for lifelong learning.* Malabar, FL: Krieger.

26

SPIRITUALITY AND ADULT EDUCATION

LEONA M. ENGLISH AND ELIZABETH J. TISDELL

N ot long ago, Irish poet Seamus Heaney (1991) penned the lines, "But then, once in a life-time the longed for tidal wave/of justice can rise up/ and hope and history rhyme" (p. 77). Heaney probably does not identify as an adult educator; yet, he could easily have been speaking of the aspiration of many adult educators to reconnect spirituality to their field, to have its hope and history rhyme. Like all human beings, we want our work to make a difference in the world—in social relations and environmental sustainability. As adult educators, many of us actively work for and teach about social justice, the common good, or civil society (as it is variously known). Furthermore, for some of us, social justice work is intimately connected to spirituality; indeed, history both within and beyond our field has shown that the justice work of many well-known social activists has been fueled by their spiritual commitments. After all, it is through spirituality that many of us engage that sense of hope that keeps us moving forward. But it is in and through acting on that hope in our teaching and social justice work, as Heaney says, that there is a possibility that "hope and history rhyme" (p. 77).

In this chapter, we explore the spirituality-social justice connections where the hope of that rhyme has been present in our field both historically and at present. We begin with a brief discussion to set the context of the religious roots of the field and then move to definitions and descriptions of spirituality and its connection and separations from organized religion present in today's discourse. Then we move toward discussing how spirituality is related to specific areas of research and practice in the field. Finally, we conclude with suggestions for future research and theory building in this area.

SETTING THE CONTEXT: FROM RELIGIOUS ROOTS TO SPIRITUALITY

When Basil Yeaxlee wrote *Spiritual Values in Adult Education* in 1925, his book was well received, in light of the acceptance of how religious values inform education. In fact, at that time, spirituality would have been understood as synonymous with religion. Over the years, adult education interest in *religion* has lessened, although it was still represented in the decennial *Handbook*s, at least until the publication of this present volume, where it is being replaced with *spirituality*. Yet, although it was included in the *Handbook*s, adult educators in the latter part of the 20th century developed suspicion around things religious, perhaps due to the fact that public discussion of religion has, in recent years, often been associated with a right-wing political agenda (particularly in the United States). Shifting to spirituality seemed to be a way to bring attention back to this important issue. But it has not always been that way.

Religious Connections in the Roots of the Field

How it came to be that spirituality was mistrusted is surprising, given that our field, both historically and currently, has been inundated with those who have come from ministry backgrounds (English, 2005a). Indeed, some of the most revered moments in adult education history have been influenced by spirituality, often with connections to religious institutions. Some of these include social justice efforts connected to the Antigonish, Highlander, Chautauqua, and Catholic Worker movements, as well as the civil rights movement. Adult educators who identified most obviously with these movements include Yeaxlee (1925), Lindeman (1926), and Coady (1939). Myles Horton, founder of Highlander Folk School, in New Market, Tennessee, had also studied theology at the radical Union Theological Seminary in New York City (Kennedy, 1981). At Union, Horton had the inspiration of radical and social gospel theologian Reinhold Neibuhr to support his work. Freire (1985), too, was influenced by the left-leaning Roman Catholic liberation theology movement (and influenced it) in South America. Indeed much of Freire's writing is a mixture of Marxism and Christianity, a point that he and Horton (Horton & Freire, 1990) discussed in their time together at Highlander.

But these religious roots were present not only among the men of the field but also among women. Many adult educators who were involved at Highlander on civil rights issues, such as Septima Clark and her work with citizenship schools, as well as Rosa Parks, were also connected to the Southern Christian Leadership Conference. Labor advocate Dorothy Day and several other women were affiliated with the Catholic Worker Movement (Parrish & Taylor, 2007). In Nova Scotia, alongside the male-oriented cooperative movement at Antigonish initiated by Fathers Moses Coady and Jimmy Tompkins in Nova Scotia in the 1930s, there was the very strong Women and Work Program, directed by Sister Marie Michael McKinnon and assisted by a host of women (Neal, 1998). And Chautauqua in upstate New York, which had been founded in 1874 as a summer school for Methodist Sunday School teachers, counts Jane Addams (founder of Hull House, Chicago) and noted suffragettes Susan B. Anthony and Julia Ward Howe among their attendees (Kilde, 1999; Scott, 1999). Even into the 21st century, Chautauqua continues as a meeting place on topics such as religion and public life. The point here is that spirituality has long been part of our field's history in North America, although it has been addressed in a variety of ways over time and has been particularly obvious in the roots of the field in its connection to social justice issues. Admittedly, some of how they defined spirituality is perhaps more obviously influenced by the Christian social gospel than our more secular version today.

The Current Context

When the authors entered the field of adult education in the late 1980s and early 1990s, there had been little overt discussion either of spirituality or of the field's connections to religious institutions through social movements in quite some time. Yet, it was well known that a number of our colleagues had ministry or religious education backgrounds. Both of the authors of this chapter had also come out of theological education and had long histories of working in and with Roman Catholic institutions. The language of spirituality and ties to religion were embedded in us, and neither of us saw this as totally incompatible with our task in adult education. Nevertheless, given the earlier history of the field, we were surprised when our interest in spirituality was met with raised eyebrows, and a mix of interest and suspicion. On the one hand, many of our colleagues seemed to agree with cultural critic bell hooks (2000), who argued that it was time to "break mainstream cultural taboos that silence our passion for spiritual practice" (p. 82). But there were and still are others who wonder, as sociologist of religion Robert Wuthnow (1998) observes, "whether 'spiritual' has become synonymous with 'flaky'" (p. 1). Eventually, our passion on the subject led to books that united our research interests in spirituality with applications for practice (English, Fenwick, & Parsons, 2003; Tisdell, 2003) and continued work in this area (English, 2005a, 2005b; Tisdell, 2007).

Now, with a concomitant sea change and growth of spirituality (as distinct from religion) in the public consciousness generally, adult education is coming to accept spirituality as a category of analysis. Textbooks within the field from Merriam, Caffarella, and Baumgartner (2007) to Hoare (2006) have dedicated space to spirituality. In addition to the authors of this chapter, the number of adult education academics interested in spirituality or soul (Dirkx, 2001) has risen considerably, with works focusing on spirituality in the workplace (Driscoll & Wiebe, 2007; Groen, 2004), community development (Walters & Manicom, 1996), higher education (Groen, 2008; Shahjahan, 2004), indigenous workplaces (Orr, 2000; Papuni & Bartlett, 2006), and church-related institutions as sites of community learning (Findsen, 2006; Parrish & Taylor, 2007). Furthermore, many authors acknowledge the connection of aspects of their own work to some of the more recent discussions of spirituality, as in Kreber, Klampfleitner, McCune, Bayne, and Knottenbelt's (2007) discussion of the authenticity literature.

Higher education has also seen a groundswell of interest in spirituality. Some writers draw on the well-known work of Parker Palmer (1998) and the earlier work of faith development theorist James Fowler to discuss the spiritual development of college students, or to highlight the relevance to teaching (Chickering, Dalton, & Stamm, 2006; Parks, 2000). Furthermore, the Higher Education Research Institute (HERI, 2005a, 2005b) at UCLA published the results of a large research study of the role of spirituality in the lives of students and faculty. In addition, social justice educators in higher education are also discussing the importance of attending to spirituality as well as rationality in social justice and in culturally responsive education, not only for students but also for faculty (Dillard, 2006; Rendón, 2000; Shahjahan, 2004). Laura Rendón (2000), the former president of the Association for the Study of Higher Education (ASHE), refers to this as "blending the scientific mind with the spirit's artistry" (p. 1). Rendón's mention of the "spirit's artistry" hints at the fact that spirituality often connects to a sense of creativity, which is something artists and musicians either intuitively know or have discussed openly (Wuthnow, 2001). On this point, the recent publication of the *International Handbook of Research in Arts Education* (Breslor, 2007) features an entire section made up of nine chapters on the connection between spirituality and the arts, with suggestions for how to facilitate this sense among students. Given these developments, one could argue that we are now beyond the mistrust of spirituality and its role in adult education to the point where it may be moving into the mainstream.

DEFINING SPIRITUALITY IN ITS CURRENT ADULT EDUCATION MANIFESTATIONS

Spirituality has been used and understood in our field in many ways (English et al., 2003; Hunt, 1998; Tisdell, 2003). Thus, here it is important to be as clear as possible what it means in the current context of our field. We divide the discussion into four interrelated primary areas, based on both the wider current literature and our own research, that capture the assumptions and definitions of spirituality: It (1) is different from religion, (2) focuses on individuals' meaning-making processes, (3) contributes to personal values and social action, and (4) relates to symbolic and unconscious knowledge construction processes.

Relationship to Religion

Generally, *religion* in contemporary literature refers to an *organized community of faith*, with an official creed and codes of regulatory behavior (determined by those with the most power in these institutions), as well as formalized ritual and sacred story or text. *Spirituality,* on the other hand, refers to an *individual's* personal experience of making meaning of the sacred, often in relationship to what is perceived as God or an interconnecting life force. Given that one's personal experience of the sacred can happen anywhere, spirituality is not necessarily related to religion.

Yet, it is important to recognize that given that most people are socialized in some sort of religious tradition, their earliest stage of spiritual development often develops in the context of religion. Thus, for many people, it is impossible to *completely* separate spirituality from religion (Tisdell, 2003). Furthermore, *some* spiritual experiences may have taken place in a religious context. It might be through the memory and significance attached to religious ritual of celebrating one of life's important transitions, the quiet of prayer before a service, the power of listening to or participating in the majesty of religious music, or the way we have created meaning through religious and cultural symbols known since childhood. Often, our identities as well as our social support have been partially formed by the religious communities that were a part of our growing up. Concomitantly, these same communities may have been responsible for instilling an importance of working for social justice, at the same time that they may have also contributed to our oppression. Thus, even if we have completely left the religions of our childhood behind, their influence remains, which is why the intersections among spirituality, religion, and culture cannot be completely teased out for most of us, even if we agree that spirituality is largely about an individual's *personal experience* of the sacred.

As many adult educators have noted, while religious groups may have been the standard bearers of rituals and traditions that have supported and nurtured us spiritually, organized religion has also had a history of colonizing the minds, bodies, and spirits and has not always attended to meaning making or to justice (English et al., 2003). This is why some people leave their religious traditions behind; they are attempting to separate spirituality as an experience of the sacred (which can happen anywhere) from the power relations and politics of religious institutions. This is a logical separation, which we recognize. However, it could be argued that in using the term *spirituality,* we mask the very real and contentious issues of religion in international adult education, for instance, where forced marriage, genital mutilation in the name of religion, and the oppression of women by religious fundamentalism are real issues. Spirituality may indeed be a depoliticized term that affects very real life issues for many in education in the Global South, for whom religion and conflict with religion is an everyday issue. Thus, we acknowledge those who suggest that the division between spirituality and religion in the West is somewhat artificial. On this point, even the daily spiritual meditation or body practices popular today of many who might not claim a religious tradition—practices such as mindfulness meditation, yoga, or tai chi—have one or more religious traditions at their root. Nevertheless, the *experience* of engaging in such practices is indeed an individual experience. So, like other contemporary scholars, we do separate religion and spirituality but note that the division is somewhat problematic.

An Individual's Meaning-Making Journey Toward Wholeness

This takes us to the second theme: Nearly all discussions in the literature highlight that spirituality is about an individual's meaning-making journey in dialogue with what is seen as sacred. A participant in one of our studies of the role of spirituality among emancipatory adult educators (Tisdell, 2000, 2003) noted that spirituality is a "journey toward wholeness." This journey was described in relation to seeing the interconnectedness of everything; moving toward/claiming one's more authentic self (deconstructed and reconstructed through analyzing one's socialization processes), often in relation to a perceived higher sense of self, alternatively termed God, higher power, the life force, Great Spirit, or Buddha nature. Significant spiritual experiences along that journey were "shimmering moments" that stood out or, as Sanders (2006) says, those times where people experience "the holy shimmer at the heart of things" (p. 26). The most commonly reported significant spiritual experiences were births, deaths and close brushes with death, dreams and synchronicities, "bliss" experiences in meditation and nature, or human connectedness.

Clearly, it makes sense that experiencing "the holy shimmer at the heart of things" (Sanders, 2006, p. 26) would be an important meaning-making experience. This emphasis on personal meaning making and personal development as part of spirituality is where some adult educators connect it to the humanism in our field (MacKeracher, 2004), and it certainly gels with Knowles's (1968) discussion of andragogy. This stress has connections with the holistic and humanistic education that seemed to predominate earlier on in the field and is still cultivated by faculty writers such as Jack Miller (2000) and his colleagues or students, Janet Groen (2008), Dorothy MacKeracher (2004), and Marie Gillen (English & Gillen 2000), who influenced future scholars as well. But, of course, when the primary or sole emphasis of spirituality in the literature is on the personal meaning-making dimension, when it seems devoid of attention to social responsibility, it falls prey to critique. Critics of the business apprehension of spirituality, for instance, see it as an attempt to colonize the personal self of the worker (Driscoll & Wiebe, 2007) through capitalism in the guise of spirituality. When taken to the extreme or isolated from some of the other dimensions of spirituality, meaning making may lead to a self-serving narcissism. But at its highest level, meaning making through spirituality typically connects to life purpose and social behavior in the world. In speaking to this point, Astin (2004), for example, writes, "Spirituality has to do with the values that we hold the most dear, our sense of who we are and where we came from, our beliefs about why we are here . . . our sense of connectedness to each other and the world around us" (p. 34). This connection to our behavior affecting the world around us is what calls many of us to work for social justice.

Connection to Social Values and Social Transformation

This leads to the third theme: Given the history of the field noted above, there is a clear link between spirituality and working for the common good, social transformation, and care for the world (English & Gillen, 2000). Daloz, Keen, Keen, and Parks (1996) found spirituality to be a strong influence in the motivations of the community leaders in their study. We have also found this link to be strong in our own work and in the lives of the participants in our own studies of the role of spirituality among social justice workers and diversity educators (English, 2005b; Tisdell, 2000, 2003; Tisdell & Tolliver, 2003). But this interest is also strong for those interested in environmental education (O'Sullivan, 1999) and organizational learning (Driscoll & Wiebe, 2007; Groen, 2004). This dimension brings adult educators into the public realm, where spirituality focuses on justice and civil society. There is an intricate cross between spirituality and social justice, and arguably, many have been attracted to adult education because it is concerned about the social good and the promotion of education to address social and economic problems. This is not to suggest, however, that all in the field who are interested in spirituality are necessarily advocates of social justice. Nor are all who are doing social justice work necessarily motivated to do so because of their spirituality. But suffice to say that many in the field doing social justice work

are motivated by their spiritual commitments. For them, their spirituality gives them the hope and the courage to move forward in working for social justice: the blending together of hope and social justice creates the possibility that, as the poet says, "hope and history rhyme" (Heaney, 1991, p. 77).

Symbolic and Unconscious Knowledge Production Processes

Spirituality is also about how people construct knowledge through what faith development theorist James Fowler (1981) referred to as "symbolic processes" and "unconscious structuring processes other than those constituting reasoning" (p. 103). Artist and educator Peter London (2007), in writing about the connection between spirituality and art or creativity, makes a similar point. He notes that the expression of spiritual experiences is often given form through another medium beyond descriptive language. "At these moments," he says, "we spontaneously yield to tears, laughter, silence, and art. In life's high moments we shift inexorably from walking to dancing, and from speech to song" (p. 1480). Similarly, in life's low moments, we might rely on other forms of imaginative or artistic expression "to console us, to hold us fast in trembling times, and carry us closer to the life and world we would prefer . . . We call upon the arts to rejoin our solitary, singular self with the rest of creation" (p. 1480). Clearly, this is a way of creating further meaning and is part of the symbolic and unconscious structuring processes to which Fowler referred. This is part of what it means to be human and explains why people have often created meaning through music, art, poetry, symbol, or ritual in ways they might not be consciously aware of until they find themselves dissolving into tears on hearing a particular song, participating in some ritual, or rediscovering some family religious or cultural symbol. People also give form to spiritual experiences in the creation of art, music, and poetry, which is often why they create it; it also reflects their culture. It is part of the journey toward wholeness; it creates a new order out of chaos. It offers hope. That hope and that sense of spirituality might also be roused in the creative work of others or oneself: through the metaphorical language of poetry, in the vibration of music, the unifying power of song, the creativity of visual art, or through the drum beat of a thousand pairs of feet marching together for a social justice cause. Such expressions are past rational thought and descriptive language; they are given form when hope and history rhyme.

SPIRITUALITY AND ADULT EDUCATION PRACTICE

So what does all this mean for contemporary adult education practice? Interest in how spirituality informs teaching and social action continues today and is present in higher education efforts in many disciplines, from medical education and health care, to education (Puchalski, 2006) for diversity and culturally responsive education (Tisdell, 2007), to education in the arts (Breslor, 2007). It is also present in adult religious education, international adult education (English, 2005b), and workplace settings. Given space limitations, here we focus briefly on some of these settings.

Adult Religious Education

Adult religious education within churches, mosques, synagogues, and temples has been the traditional format for cultivating adult spirituality (e.g., Schuster, 2003). Indeed, all the *Handbooks* have contained chapters on adult religious education through retreats, workshops, and in-service programs. The more recent trend in this area of practice, however, is to sponsor diploma programs in education for the laity. Within Jewish circles, this adult education is typically oriented to ongoing faith or spiritual development, whereas within Christian circles, it has often focused on preparing participants for lay ecclesial ministry or administrative or ministerial roles in the congregation. The Jewish Florence Melton Adult Mini-School, Episcopalian Education for Ministry program (EFM), and the Catholic Loyola Institute for Ministry Extension Program (LIMEX) are examples of these lay ministry programs within different religious groups. Lay ministry programs are often delivered in a partial residential format replete with prayer and education components. While such adult education programs are growing in number, there is scant systematic research to substantiate their effectiveness or contribution to adult education.

International Adult Education

A second place in which spirituality and adult education intersect is in the lives of those working in both domestic and international adult education settings. Many colleagues working in the Global South have known that religion and spirituality are crucial elements of their work, given the strong attachment to religious systems of belief in the South, as compared to the West. Data drawn from a study of 13 women who are international adult educators, conducted by Leona (English, 2005b), draw attention to the spiritual motivations, conflicts, and complexities of negotiating identity in the midst of paradox and inequity. These women were motivated by their religious upbringing and ongoing spiritual practices to work toward promoting justice through education and ultimately to seek opportunities to work internationally. For the four women in the study from Asia and Africa, religion was both a solace and a source of conflict because of local prescriptions around dress, mobility, and the place of women, prescriptions that in some cases were more local than religious. For the nine Western women in the study, religion without justice was empty; subsequently, many of them developed alternative spiritual practices to sustain them. This might suggest, from a practice perspective, that nurturing a sense of spirituality, whether religious or not, might help sustain the hope that is necessary to continue doing justice work.

Higher Education and Culturally Responsive Education

The role of spirituality in culturally responsive adult higher education is another important area of practice that has been a subject of Libby Tisdell's research and practice. In her study of how spirituality informs the work of 31 emancipatory adult educators of different cultural groups dealing with diversity, aspects of which are discussed in detail elsewhere (Tisdell 2003, 2007; Tisdell & Tolliver, 2003), she found that participants highlighted the role of spirituality both in their teaching and in their own lives in four primary ways: (1) through dealing with internalized oppression and reclaiming cultural identity; (2) by mediating among multiple identities (race, gender, class, sexuality); (3) in crossing culture to facilitate spiritual and overall development of a more authentic identity; and (4) and in unconscious knowledge construction processes that are connected to image, symbol, ritual, and metaphor, which are often cultural. This clearly has implications for ways of potentially connecting spirituality to culturally responsive teaching by drawing on cultural imagination and having students work with cultural symbol through art, poetry, music, and story, as well as doing the typical rational work that is part of higher education. This helps connect "the scientific mind with the spirit's artistry" (Rendón, 2000, p. 1). Indeed, both rationality (or the scientific mind) and the hope and inspiration of art and spirituality are necessary for a critical adult education practice that offers hope and sustainable social change.

REFLECTIVE ANALYSIS AND DIALOGUE ON ISSUES

In this chapter, we have drawn, in part, on the journey of adult education from religious influences to humanistic concerns and back to spirituality, albeit in a more secular form, pointing out that over the past 10 years, spirituality has regained legitimacy in our field and is now accepted as a line of inquiry and integration. Despite its ascendancy in adult education, we remain especially concerned with the continuing presence of a noncritical and self-serving spirituality of education. We are reminded that some of the most convincing work in adult education and spirituality is critical in its orientation to race, class, and gender; yet, some remains rooted in humanistic frameworks that pay little attention to the interlocking systems of oppression. Some similar critiques have been made about transformative learning and the tensions between those versions of transformative learning that foreground individual transformation following Mezirow (1995) and those grounded in social transformation following Freire (1971). We challenge the field to simultaneously question and embrace a spirituality of adult education that engages the critical issues of our time.

We also need to avoid any mindless and romantic notions of what spirituality means. Outside the workplace literature and within the traditional canons of Christian spiritual literature, there is some helpful advice on this matter. An ever vibrant and compelling writer on the links

between work and spirituality, Joan Chittister (2004), an American Benedictine nun, warns of the romance and destructive power of spirituality as a place to run away. She notes that the

> thirst for pseudo-contemplation is just as sad. To assume that life is for lounging and then to blame that kind of injustice to others on the search for God is to make a mockery . . . Sloth is not a Christian virtue. Holy leisure was not a license to live irresponsibly. Co-creation is a mandate writ deep in the human heart. Work itself is holy. (p. 11)

Applied to the workplace, community, or higher education, it can mean that spirituality is neither a thing to be manipulated for the bottom line nor an escape.

We remain concerned about these dangers and especially about the power dimensions of incorporating spirituality into our contexts, be they classrooms, clinical settings, or community contexts. The outstanding issues revolve around: Who decides what spiritual practices are important? What are the implications for the workplace of this? Are all discussions of spirituality and work appropriate in all cases? Yet, it is also possible that we have overstated the fears. In all the years that Libby (Tisdell, 2007) has been teaching a class about spirituality in education, or in other classes, drawing on ways of knowing through symbol, story, music, and movement in ways that some connect to as spiritual, nobody has taken it over with a religious agenda. Are kid gloves equally applied to discussions with an economic (capitalist or communist agenda) or historical (patriarchal or traditionalist agenda) perspective? While dealing with such issues in educational activities needs to be handled with care, it is important to consider what is relevant to how learners create deeper knowledge related to the topic.

We end this chapter asking about the future of spirituality and adult education, as well as the ethics of promoting and facilitating it. We have shown how our field has begun in religious impulses and movements and then moved away from this to the now-emergent liaison or conversation with spirituality. As a way forward with spirituality, we have three primary suggestions for areas of research and practice that might be further explored. Building on some of our earlier work, we suggest more development of the cultural imagination and cultural identity.

While the historical examples, for instance, are rooted largely in a white Western context, for many of us, life and work are more diverse. We suggest the deliberate engagement with the cultural symbols that are part of our learners' lives, which may at times be religious but may not be. We also suggest the development of the artistic imagination, which can be cultivated from closer awareness of art and music and media, as well as stories and narratives. Being present to our culture is a way to stimulate spirituality. Third, we suggest the ongoing attention to creating communities of learners who nurture the soul of each one and work for justice together, and, as Heaney (1991) hopes, to help "hope and history rhyme" (p. 77).

REFERENCES

Astin, A. W. (2004). Why spirituality deserves a central place in liberal education. *Liberal Education, 90*(2), 34–41.

Breslor, L. (Ed.). (2007). *International handbook of research in arts education.* Dordecht, The Netherlands: Springer.

Chickering, A. W., Dalton, J. C., & Stamm, L. (2006). *Encouraging authenticity and spirituality in higher education.* San Francisco: Jossey-Bass.

Chittister, J. (2004). *In the heart of the temple: My spiritual vision for today's world.* Ottawa, Canada: Novalis.

Coady, M. (1939). *Masters of their own destiny.* New York: Continuum.

Daloz, L, Keen, C., Keen, J., & Parks, S. (1996). *Common fire: Lives of commitment in a complex world.* Boston: Beacon.

Dillard, C. (2006). On spiritual strivings: Transforming an African American woman's academic life. Albany, NY: SUNY Press.

Dirkx, J. (2001). Images, transformative learning, and the work of the soul. *Adult Learning, 12*(3), 15–17.

Driscoll, C., & Wiebe, E. (2007). Technical spirituality at work: Jacques Ellul on workplace spirituality. *Journal of Management Inquiry, 16*(4), 333–348.

English, L. M. (2005a). Historical and contemporary explorations of the social change and spiritual directions of adult education. *Teachers College Record, 107*(6), 1169–1192.

English, L. M. (2005b). Third-space practitioners: Women educating for civil society. *Adult Education Quarterly, 55*(2), 85–100.

English, L. M., & Gillen, M. A. (Eds.). (2000). *Addressing the spiritual dimensions of adult learning: What educators can do.* New Directions for Adult and Continuing Education, No. 85. San Francisco: Jossey-Bass.

English, L. M., Fenwick, T. J., & Parsons, J. (2003). *Spirituality of adult education and training.* Malabar, FL: Krieger.

Findsen, B. (2006). Social institutions as sites of learning for older adults. *Journal of Transformative Education, 4*(1), 65–81.

Fowler, J. (1981). *Stages of faith: The psychology of human development and the quest for meaning.* San Francisco: Harper and Row.

Freire, P. (1971). *Pedagogy of the oppressed.* New York: Herder & Herder.

Freire, P. (1985). *The politics of education: Culture, power and liberation* (D. Macedo, Trans., introduction by H. Giroux). Hadley, MA: Bergin & Garvey.

Groen, J. (2004). The experience and practice of adult educators in addressing the spiritual dimensions of the workplace. *Canadian Journal for the Study of Adult Education, 18*(1), 72–92.

Groen, J. (2008). Paradoxical tensions in creating a teaching and learning space within a graduate education course on spirituality. *Teaching in Higher Education, 13*(2), 193–204.

Heaney, S. (1991). *The cure at Troy: A version of Sophocles' Philoctetes.* New York: Farrar, Straus & Giroux.

Higher Education Research Institute. (2005a). *Spirituality and the professoriate: A national study of faculty beliefs, attitudes, and behaviors.* Los Angeles: Author.

Higher Education Research Institute. (2005b). *The spiritual life of college students: A national study of college students' search for meaning and purpose.* Los Angeles: Author.

Hoare, C. (Ed.). (2006). *Handbook of adult learning and development.* Oxford, UK: Oxford University Press.

hooks, b. (2000). *All about love.* New York: William Morrow.

Horton, M., & Freire, P. (1990). *We make the road by walking: Conversations on education and social change.* Philadelphia: Temple University Press.

Hunt, C. (1998). An adventure: From reflective practice to spirituality. *Teaching in Higher Education, 3*(3), 325–337.

Kennedy, W. B. (1981). Highlander praxis: Learning with Myles Horton. *Teachers College Record, 83*(1), 105–119.

Kilde, J. H. (1999). The "predominance of the feminine" at Chautauqua: Rethinking the gender-space relationship in Victorian America. *Signs, 24*(2), 449–486.

Knowles, M. (1968). Andragogy, not pedagogy. *Adult Leadership, 16*(10), 350–352, 386.

Kreber, C., Klampfleitner, M., McCune, V., Bayne, S., & Knottenbelt, M. (2007). What do you mean by "authentic"? A comparative review of the literature on conceptions of authenticity in teaching. *Adult Education Quarterly, 58*, 22–43.

Lindeman, E. (1926). *The meaning of adult education.* New York: Continuum.

London, P. (2007). Concerning the spiritual in art education. In L. Bresler (Ed.), *International Handbook of Research in Arts Education* (pp. 1405–1422). Dordecht, The Netherlands: Springer.

MacKeracher, D. (2004). *Making sense of adult learning* (2nd ed.). Toronto, Ontario: University of Toronto Press.

Merriam, S. B., Caffarella, R. S., & Baumgartner, L. M. (2007). *Learning in adulthood: A comprehensive guide* (3rd ed.). San Francisco: Jossey-Bass.

Mezirow, J. D. (1995). Transformation theory of adult learning. In M. Welton (Ed.), *In defense of the lifeworld: Critical perspectives on adult learning* (pp. 39-70). Albany: State University of New York Press.

Miller, J. P. (2000). *Education and the soul: Toward a spiritual curriculum.* Albany: State University of New York Press.

Neal, R. (1998). *Brotherhood economics: Women and cooperatives in Nova Scotia.* Sydney: UCCB Press, Cape Breton Books.

Orr, J. (2000). First Nations education. In L. M. English & M. A. Gillen (Eds.), *Addressing the spiritual dimensions of adult learning* (pp. 59–66). New Directions for Adult and Continuing Education, No. 85. San Francisco: Jossey-Bass.

O'Sullivan, E. (1999). *Transformative learning: Educational vision for the 21st century.* New York: Zed Books; and published in association with University of Toronto Press.

Palmer, P. (1998). *The courage to teach: Exploring the inner landscape of a teacher's life.* San Francisco: Jossey-Bass.

Papuni, H. T., & Bartlett, K. R. (2006). Maori and Pakeha perspectives of adult learning in Aotearoa/New Zealand workplaces. *Advances in Human Resources, 8*(3), 400–407.

Parks, S. D. (2000). *Big questions, worthy dreams: Mentoring young adults in their search for meaning, purpose, and faith.* San Francisco: Jossey-Bass.

Parrish, M. M., & Taylor, E. W. (2007). Seeking authenticity: Women and learning in the Catholic Worker Movement. *Adult Education Quarterly, 57*(3), 221–247.

Puchalski, C. (Ed.). (2006). *A time for listening and caring: Spirituality and the care of the chronically ill and dying.* New York: Oxford University Press.

Rendón, L. (2000). Academics of the heart: Reconnecting the scientific mind with the spirit's artistry. *The Review of Higher Education, 24*(1), 1–13.

Sanders, R. (2006). *A private history of awe.* New York: North Point Press (Farrar, Straus & Giroux).

Schuster, D. T. (2003). *Jewish lives, Jewish learning: Adult Jewish learning in theory and practice.* New York: Union of American Hebrew Congregations Press.

Scott, J. C. (1999). The Chautauqua movement: Revolution in popular higher education. *The Journal of Higher Education, 70*(4), 389–412.

Shahjahan, R. A. (2004). Centering spirituality in the academy: Toward a transformative way of teaching and learning. *Journal of Transformative Education, 2*(4), 294–312.

Tisdell, E. (2000). Spirituality and emancipatory adult education in women adult educators for social change. *Adult Education Quarterly, 50*(4), 308–335.

Tisdell, E. J. (2003). *Exploring spirituality and culture in adult and higher education.* San Francisco: Jossey-Bass.

Tisdell, E. J. (2007). In the new millennium: The role of spirituality and the cultural imagination in dealing with diversity and equity in the higher education classroom. *Teachers College Record, 109*(3), 531–560.

Tisdell, E., & Tolliver E. (2003). Claiming a sacred face: The role of spirituality and cultural identity in transformative adult higher education. *Journal of Transformative Education, 1*(4), 368–392.

Walters, S., & Manicom, L. (Eds.). (1996). Introduction. In *Gender in popular education: Methods for empowerment* (pp. 1–22). London: Zed Books.

Wuthnow, R. (1998). *After heaven: Spirituality in America since the 1950s.* Berkeley: University of California Press

Wuthnow, R. (2001). *Creative spirituality: The way of the artist.* Berkeley: University of California Press.

Yeaxlee, B. (1925). *Spiritual values in adult education* (2 vols.). London: Oxford University Press.

27

ADULT EDUCATION FOR HEALTH AND WELLNESS

LILIAN H. HILL AND LINDA ZIEGAHN

Adult learning is central to health. The correlation between education and health has been well established in population health research, and higher levels of formal education tend to be predictive of better health (Cusack, Thompson, & Rogers, 2003). Health is an individual capacity that is also related to individuals' interactions and day-to-day living practices within their social, cultural, and environmental settings (Daley, 2006). Wellness is a process emerging from a focus on many aspects of a person's life and adoption of health-enhancing behaviors, as opposed to just minimizing conditions of illness (Wurzbach, 2002). These definitions stress interaction and balance, suggesting that health and wellness are activities that do not take place in a vacuum. They depend on individual motivation as well as support from a variety of interpersonal, community, and institutional sources.

At the level of the individual, learning has been shown to mitigate depressive symptoms; reduce stress; improve energy, optimism, and possibly immune function; and, in general, positively affect emotional and psychological well-being regardless of educational context (Cusack et al., 2003; Hammond, 2004). The highly educated will usually find their way to the knowledge they need and have the skills to navigate the health care system to access the answers and treatments desired. However, at the larger societal level, growing inequities in access and opportunities for appropriate health care result in poor health outcomes and increased costs for individuals and society. These inequities, or disparities, can be rooted in a combination of economic, gender, citizenship, rural/urban, and ethnic/racial status. There is a 20-year gap in life expectancy between the most and least advantaged American populations (Murray, Michaud, McKenna, & Marks, 1998), due not only to diseases of poverty but also factors like access to clean water, freedom from violence, Gross National Product, and other social determinants (Marmot, 2005).

Disparities in health care have multiple sources—those listed above as well as genetics, social networks, and human behavior around health—and different populations may be vulnerable to specific diseases for different reasons (Mechanic & Tanner, 2007; Satcher & Higginbotham, 2008). While greater clarity is needed to illuminate the complex interactions around the concept of disadvantage relative to health and health care, it is clear that one of the greatest reasons for vulnerability is poverty (Vladeck, 2007). The field of adult education is critical to the creation of learning environments in which members of communities, poor and rich alike; scientists; and health care providers and policy makers can engage in dialogue at many levels to disentangle the layers of social, economic, and scientific factors that influence health and wellness. Such dialogue can be fostered through collaborations between adult educators and health educators, health care managers, and researchers, among others; all are critical in ensuring that the voices of the disenfranchised are heard and that the various approaches to improving the health status of all citizens are inclusive. Adult educators' concern for diversity and social justice and health educators' interest in alleviating health disparities mean that health education is of concern to both parties. A focus on social, economic, and political forces that contribute to people's health means that health education can be a contributor to social justice (Glanz, Rimer, & Lewis, 2002).

The field of adult education can address several key questions in the area of health and wellness. First, whose responsibility is good health? Second, how can the field of adult education further learning around improved health, at either the level of the individual or society as a whole? The tension that has existed around health care dialogue in the United States for decades mirrors the tension in discussions among adult education practitioners and scholars around adult learning in the service of individual change, along with learning that moves society toward greater inclusivity and awareness of and action toward social justice aims. It is our position that the individual and societal levels are both critical loci for change and that individuals, health professionals, and policy makers would all benefit from a perspective of learning around health and wellness that integrates rather than polarizes the goals of behavioral, individual change and policy change affecting the health of individuals in communities and across the nation.

We would suggest that three primary contexts are useful for an examination of how adult learning can enhance the project of improving the health of citizens, through changes in individual behavior as well as social policy:

1. Individual learning. Individual learners may seek information on health through self-directed learning, and for some, learning will be transformative. People may learn from many sources, including social networks of friends or neighbors, written sources, and electronic references, any of which can help the individual in making decisions about changes in health behavior. Particularly when the source of learning is print-based, adult literacy educators have much to contribute to overall understanding of health.

2. One-on-one interactions between individuals and health professionals. This is the interpersonal realm historically viewed in "top-down" terms within the dyadic context of medical consultations, where physicians were positioned as experts and "patients" encouraged to be compliant recipients of health care. Behavioral change is generally the goal of learning at the individual and interpersonal levels. Literacy is an important interactional setting as health care providers and consumers negotiate the meaning of print, verbal, and other media information.

3. Community health learning in such settings as health fairs and other forums, as well as basic education settings. These contexts tend to stress education, through learning processes that range from information transfer through small- or large-group presentations, to more interactive, collaborative, and relational methods. Learning in these settings may be accompanied by a more activist, advocacy agenda aimed at addressing health disparities and social change.

INDIVIDUAL LEARNING

Many resources are available for adults to learn about their health, ranging from printed patient education brochures and other written materials, recorded information in audio and video formats, computer-mediated information, and information available via the Internet. To gain from information in these formats, adults may take a self-directed learning approach, through which the individual initiates the learning, defines learning goals, seeks learning resources, and evaluates the outcomes. For example, in a study of women with breast cancer, Rager (2003) found three motivations for engaging in self-directed learning: (1) to overcome fear, (2) to understand what was happening, and (3) to make informed health decisions. Learning for health can also involve transformational learning in which people revisit previous health perspectives and/or form new, more inclusive worldviews. Transformational learning may occur in response to illness but is a process that takes more time and involves larger changes in the person than simply gaining information. In a follow-up study of people with HIV/AIDS,

Baumgartner (2002) found that the individuals came to see the disease as a means to make a meaningful contribution to others.

Patient education materials are an important method of health care communications about health behaviors and medical treatments, but their use by individuals is influenced by their readability and cultural sensitivity, and many adults find them inaccessible (Baker, 2006). Information can play an important role in fostering patients' self-care behaviors, yet many health-related materials are written well above the average reading ability of many adults (Paasche-Orlow, Parker, Gazmararian, Nielsen-Bohlman, & Rudd, 2005). Patients who lack the ability to decipher medical terms and educational materials are hindered in understanding information needed to manage illness and negotiate the health care system, engendering nonadherence to prescribed treatment regimens and preventive care, poor health outcomes, and higher health care costs (Baker, 2006).

There are a variety of health-related Web sites, including WebMD and Medline, which are maintained by government organizations such as the Centers for Disease Control, disease-related organizations such as the American Cancer Society, professional organizations like the American Medical Association, and pharmaceutical companies. While health Web sites can provide useful information, adults also need to develop sophisticated skills in discerning the value and usefulness of information they find. Web-based technologies offer individuals opportunities to learn about health conditions and monitor treatment. For example, online programs for health maintenance strategies such as weight management allow individuals to evaluate progress, with optional classroom support (Heetebry, Hatcher, & Tabriziani, 2005). Another Web-based program called REPARERE (learning REsource for PAtients and RElatives during REcovery) is aimed at supporting patients recovering from heart surgery and their families in adjusting after surgery. Textual information, video clips, and illustrations relevant to the course of recovery are included to enable patients to learn about symptom management and self-care while recovering in a way that matches their information and communication needs (Moen & Smørdal, 2006). Ruiter, Kessels, and Jansma (2006) found that personalized nutrition messages provided by computer-tailored health communications increased motivation to change diet behavior more than generalized nutrition messages. In Web-based health learning, adult educators with expertise in distance learning can bring knowledge of adult learning theories and strategies to the design of health information.

It is impossible to discuss learning about health at the individual level without acknowledging the detrimental influence of low health literacy. The Institute of Medicine (2004) defines health literacy as "the extent to which individuals have the capacity to obtain, process, and understand basic health information services needed to make appropriate health decisions" (p. 32). It entails the ability to perform basic reading and numeric tasks including comprehending prescription labels, insurance forms, and other health-related information distributed to patients (Baker, 2006). Zarcadoolas, Pleasant, and Greer (2005) propose an expanded model in which health literacy refers to a "wide range of skills, and competencies that people develop to seek out, comprehend, evaluate and use health information and concepts to make informed choices, reduce health risks, and increase quality of life" (p. 196). Helpful prior knowledge can include health-related vocabulary and conceptual knowledge regarding health (Baker, 2006), both of which tend to correlate with basic literacy skills. However, people who function well in familiar literacy contexts may struggle with decoding health care messages due to the unfamiliar terminology and concepts.

Given that at least a quarter of the North American population experiences difficulties with the literacy and numeracy tasks associated with caring for one's health and negotiating the health care system, adult basic education (ABE) seems a valuable venue for addressing health literacy skills (Baker, 2006; Paasche-Orlow et al., 2005). Similarly, ABE is an important resource for helping adults achieve their goals for health improvement (Golbeck, Ahlers-Schmidt, & Paschal, 2005). Greenberg (2001) suggests that there is insufficient cross-fertilization between the adult literacy and health professional disciplines. She recommends that ABE instructors begin with students' prior knowledge of health topics, discover what adult learners want to learn, provide students with choices especially regarding sensitive health topics, and partner with health care providers.

There is a growing interest in forming partnerships between the health care and adult education sectors to address low health literacy (Rudd, 2007). Cooperative efforts between health care professionals and adult educators to incorporate health topics into literacy or ABE classes would allow adult learners to gain health knowledge and confidence in navigating the complexities of the health care system, while health care providers can develop greater sensitivity to the needs of low literate populations. "Adult educators can help health practitioners understand the underlying assumptions prevalent in public health and in health care, the nature of the demands made on adults, and the need for a better match between these demands and adults' skills" (Rudd, 2007, p. 35). While health literacy is being discussed in the health care sector, it is also of concern to adult educators because it is a social justice issue relevant to concerns regarding diversity and societal inequities (Hill, 2007).

Partnerships can involve literacy educators inviting health providers to address specific issues of concern to class members or working together to create new curricula. Researchers in Illinois created a health education curriculum by bringing together national health experts and adult literacy/ESOL (English for speakers of other languages) teachers. In a well-controlled study, the resulting 42-hour program was used across the state and examined to determine whether it was effective in increasing health knowledge as well as literacy skills in adult literacy and ESOL students. The study's authors concluded that while health content has always been a part of ABE/ESOL, the new curriculum "significantly improved their health knowledge and skills in every literacy level in ABE and ESOL" (Levy et al., 2008, p. 37). While the gains in literacy were not as dramatic, students were also able to progress with their literacy skills.

ONE-ON-ONE INTERACTIONS BETWEEN INDIVIDUALS AND HEALTH PROFESSIONALS

Much of health education takes place in one-on-one consultations between patients and physicians and other health providers such as nurses, pharmacists, or allied health professionals. These communications may involve diagnosis and treatment recommendations, often conveyed in a short time period constrained by health insurance limitations and busy appointment schedules. Young and Flower (2002) suggest that many of these dyadic interactions are characterized by miscommunication caused by an assumption that the interaction involves information transmission with patients as passive recipients with little agency or insight into the causes of their illnesses. Rather than ascertaining patients' explanatory models of illness, physicians and other health providers operate from a biomedical, scientific framework and either fail to inquire about or disregard patients' explanations. Using closed-ended questions that elicit minimal information, providers may not learn about the source of medical problems, the patient's health beliefs, the conditions in which he or she lives, and his or her ability to follow treatment instructions. These failed communications often end with both parties experiencing frustration, the patient feeling misunderstood, and the health provider labeling the patient as uncooperative and noncompliant.

This communication dilemma is echoed by Roter and Hall (2006) in their typology of doctor-patient relationships, in which an excess of patient control in the relationship results in consumer-based interactions, while an excess of physician control is typified by paternalism. More effective in reaching the goal of improved patient health is mutuality, characterized by dialogue and mutual personhood within the consultation context. Using the framework of mutuality, health care workers and patients alike can benefit from dialogue in which each learns from the other, and both lived and scientific experiences are shared and validated.

Research has demonstrated the central role of behavior in the world's major health problems (Clark, 2002) and in achieving and maintaining good health. Yet, people often resist changing health behaviors, and the factors involved are complex. Given the short duration of many one-on-one consultations, the goal of changing health behaviors is difficult to achieve, particularly because many patients often have misconceptions of health and medical treatment that are not adequately addressed by health professionals (Greenberg, 2001). Sources of confusion include the meaning of medical terminology, conversation style and basic communications skills, and the context of the problem, which includes the differing ways that providers and patients conceptualize health problems, treatment plans, and obstacles that patients may have in implementing them (Young & Flower, 2002). "Comprehension is a critical factor in patient decisions to seek care and the patients' ability, once care is sought, to act on the health information or instructions received" (Schwartzberg, Cowett, VanGeest, & Wolf, 2007, p. S97).

Adult educators from a community literacy center and staff and administration of a hospital emergency department collaborated to study problems with patient dissatisfaction and misunderstandings (Young & Flower, 2002). The adult educators conducted an observational study of patient-provider interactions, sought patients' permission to accompany them during their visit to the emergency department, conducted initial and follow-up interviews with the patients, and then later conducted focus groups to analyze the data generated. Sources of confusion included providers' use of medical terminology, patients' reluctance to question physicians' explanations, mismatched frames of reference, failure to inquire about patients' explanations of their health problems, and patients not knowing what information is important to share with providers. The researchers concluded:

> The kinds of information that providers and patients must share is dynamic and multifaceted, requiring an ongoing dialogue with both parties asking questions, listening to answers, and checking interpretations. As this dialogue progresses, patients and providers share, at the most basic level, an understanding of key terms that are used in their dialogue. At a more complex level, they begin to share a common frame of reference around medical problems. Finally, they agree on each person's role in the patient's journey toward wellness. (Young & Flower, 2002, p. 86)

One obstacle to the integrity of health care communications is health care providers' lack of understanding of patients with varying literacy abilities. An alternate perspective to the idea that health literacy is an individual capacity is to consider health literacy in relationship to a person's interactions with the health care system, a more dynamic process in which health literacy may fluctuate depending on the complexity of medical conditions and the interactions between patients, health care providers, and health care systems (Baker, 2006). A study of how health providers adjusted their communication methods for low

literate patients revealed that "using simple language, handing out simplified printed materials to patients, speaking more slowly, reading" instructions out loud, "writing out instructions," and presenting a limited number of concepts at the same time were among the most common strategies employed (Schwartzberg et al., 2007, p. S98). Other techniques are the teach-back method in which patients are asked to repeat in their own words the information that has been conveyed to them and to demonstrate their technique with self-care—for example, how they conduct glucose checks or self-injections. These methods serve to reveal any misunderstandings of health information, which can subsequently be corrected by a health care provider.

Training of medical personnel in community settings is critical to an improvement in the literacy of health care consumers. As an example, a fellowship created by the New York City mayor's office placed first-year medical students in adult literacy classrooms. Medical students were engaged in assisting and learning from trained literacy educators and interacting with adult learners in a sustained way. In contrast to meeting patients briefly in interactions focused solely on treating health problems, fellowship students became familiar with the nature of low-income adults' lives (Tassi & Ashraf, 2008), and the adult learners reported that they would be more comfortable asking doctors for information. This program is expected to have a lasting impact on the practice of the medical students as well as on the adult literacy learners' health care interactions.

Another challenge to effective communication is that health beliefs and practices rooted in culture affect not only people's health, but how they communicate with health care providers and what they will learn. The concept of cultural competence has received a great deal of attention in the health care field, where the need is acute because of increasing patient diversity and differences in health beliefs and practices rooted in culture (Barbian, 2003) and where it has been advocated as a method to counteract health disparities based in ethnic and racial differences, immigration status, and poverty (Betancourt, Green, Carrillo, & Park, 2005). Implications of increased competence extend from more culturally and linguistically appropriate interpersonal interaction to the formulation of policies that ensure that patients will not be marginalized because they deviate from the profile of dominant-culture patients in terms of language ability, education, or economic levels. The system of training for physicians and other U.S. health care providers has long been criticized for assuming that patients are monocultural (Taylor, 2003; Tervalon, 2003; Wear, 2003). Culturally competent health care thus implies a training and educational environment in which changing demographics and cultural diversity are integrated into curriculum (Peña Dolhun, Muñoz, & Grumbach, 2003; Rosen et al., 2004; Whitcomb, 2003). Adult educators who are knowledgeable and experienced in diverse health care settings can lead health personnel training efforts in ways that honor culturally competent care and learning strategies that reflect adult learners' needs and contexts.

COMMUNITY HEALTH LEARNING

The learning that takes place in communities around health may take place at the individual, community, or population levels and is intended to bring about the voluntary, informed behavior change that is central to achieving and maintaining good health (Clark, 2002). People often resist changing health behaviors for a variety of complex reasons. Adult educators, including those in basic literacy or health education, can contribute more sophisticated skills in program planning, delivery, evaluation, and research to create learner-centered programs promoting societal as well as individual change and stimulate more informed, responsible choices (Daley, 2006; Obilade, 2005). The challenge is to reframe health communication and educational programming in a more balanced framework, as a collaborative, shared responsibility between health providers and patients viewed as legitimate sources of information and partners in decision making (Young & Flower, 2002).

Studies in Finland and the United States have shown that when health interventions focus on empowerment at the community level rather than just the individual level, people not only learn about healthier lifestyles and wellness strategies, but feel empowered to make more systemic, health-promoting changes in community and workplace settings (Syme, 2000). Creative efforts have brought health education to churches, health fairs, beauty and barber shops, grocery stores, and shopping malls—in short, places where people gather. For example, health educators at the Mayo Clinic and the University of Pittsburgh collaborated around the offering of an innovative program entitled Take a Health Professional to the People Day, sending physicians, nurses, pharmacists, and health educators to selected beauty salons and barber shops to offer health screenings and convey information to customers receiving haircuts (Taking healthcare to the people, n.d.). A further goal of the program was teaching Mayo Clinic students, faculty, and researchers about the challenges of reaching underserved minority and rural populations.

Classes designed by literacy and health providers are popular learning formats within the context of community learning. For example, a curriculum in Pennsylvania entitled Take Charge of Your Health for mothers of premature infants was created by health and literacy educators to equip mothers with skills in navigating the health environment as well as specific health knowledge. The mothers were selected based on the fact that they scored below the sixth-grade level on the Test of Adult Basic Education (TABE), and the curriculum was delivered through home visits (Bennett, Pinder, Szesniak, & Culhane, 2008). The successful home visits were initiated after an unsuccessful classroom program, and the curriculum was altered to focus on health system navigation skills with less attention paid to developing literacy skills. Similarly, researchers in Illinois worked with national health experts and adult literacy/ESOL teachers to develop a statewide program aimed at improving both health knowledge and literacy skills for adult literacy and ESOL students. The study's authors concluded that while health content had always been a part of ABE/ESOL, the new curriculum "significantly improved their health knowledge and skills in every literacy level in ABE and ESOL" (Levy et al., 2008, p. 37).

A disproportionate share of preventable disease and disability is borne by impoverished and minority groups (House & Williams, 2000). Thus, health education is often coupled with calls for social action (Glanz et al., 2002), with disparities and inequality serving as frameworks for discussion of public health policy. Public health policy and critical adult learning philosophies share several core values, in particular, participation and social justice (Grady & Aubrun,

2008; Marmot, 2005; Mezirow, 1991). An example of health promotion initiatives that aim to bolster social justice objectives include efforts by the National Institute of Health (NIH) to bring together academic health researchers and community members to develop the infrastructure for partnerships around the design and implementation of research projects (Zerhouni, 2003). Through the formation of community advisory boards, increased representation of community interests on institutional review boards, and community engagement training for researchers as well as community residents, the NIH Clinical and Translational Science Awards (CTSAs) seek to break down the traditional power dynamics between academics and ordinary citizens around who has the expertise to identify which public health problems warrant research attention.

The more participatory health promotion approach is distinguished from the information transmission model in health education by its emphasis on "process, autonomy, control, advocacy and action" (Daley, 2006, p. 232). The NIH CTSA network provides another example of how adult and health educators can structure learning experiences to increase participation in the identification of health research topics and curricula. Health researchers from 46 institutions across the United States and their community-based partners, representing nonprofit organizations, tribal agencies, and practitioner networks, came together at regional meetings to identify best practices for breaking down academic-community barriers to collaborative health research (Cook & Community Engagement Steering Committee, 2009). Innovative methods such as open space technology, in which participants come together to set the agenda, then follow through with discussion and, eventually, steps for action, were used in addition to more conventional group needs assessment tools. What emerged were recommendations for actions and strategies around changing the

frame for development of health research studies, forming research partnerships, developing a common language for academic-community research partnerships, and finding new ways in which to analyze data and disseminate findings.

Further examples of forums through which community members can participate in the identification of important health issues are exemplified by the recent national level calls for participation in community-level town hall meetings, aimed at getting public feedback on priorities for national health care reform and recommendations for strategies to improve health care. In a very short time frame, more than 4,200 groups across the nation signed up online to host town hall discussions (Laura G., 2009). The resulting recommendations were sent to all participants, as well as to the health officials in the Obama administration in the hope that programs and policies at both the grassroots and national levels would be influenced by citizen voices.

CONCLUSIONS

Adult learning clearly has a significant affect on health, and adult educators have the knowledge, skills, and motivation to play a positive role. The potential for cooperative working relationships between adult educators and health providers offer new opportunities for understanding and respecting patients in their complexity, including their physical and mental health, literacy capabilities, social conditions, and cultural health beliefs and practices. Adult educators can contribute an integrated vision of learning that encompasses a range of individual, group, and community learning contexts, as well as a range of individual, community, and policy needs. The results for individuals and community can be a greater sense of empowerment around health care needs, and ultimately, better health for all.

REFERENCES

Baker, D. W. (2006).The meaning and the measure of health literacy. *Journal of General Internal Medicine, 21,* 878–883.

Barbian, J. (2003). Moving toward diversity. *Training, 40*(2), 44–46.

Baumgartner, L. M. (2002). Living and learning with HIV/AIDS: Transformational tales

continued. *Adult Education Quarterly, 53*(1), 44–59.

Bennett. I., Pinder, P., Szesniak, R., & Culhane, J. (2008). Taking charge of your health: A collaborative health literacy intervention linking adult education and maternal-infant health care. *Focus on Basics, 9B,* 14–20.

Betancourt, J. R., Green, A. R., Carrillo, J. E., & Park, E. R. (2005). Cultural competence and healthcare disparities: Key perspectives and trends. *Health Affairs, 24,* 499–505.

Clark, N. M. (2002). Foreword. In K. Glanz, B. K. Rimer, & F. M. Lewis (Eds.), *Health behavior and health education: Theory, practice, and research* (3rd ed., pp. xiii-xv). San Francisco: Jossey-Bass.

Cook J., & Community Engagement Steering Committee. (2009). *Researchers and their communities: The challenge of meaningful community engagement.* Washington, DC: Clinical and Translational Science Award Consortium, Center for Disease Control and Prevention, Association for Prevention Teaching and Research Cooperative Agreement No. U50/CCU300860.

Cusack, S. A., Thompson, W. J. A., & Rogers, M. E. (2003). Mental fitness for life: Assessing the impact of an 8-week mental fitness program on healthy aging. *Educational Gerontology, 29,* 393–403.

Daley, B. J. (2006). Aligning health promotion and adult education for healthier communities. In S. B. Merriam, B. C. Courtenay, & R. M. Cervero (Eds.), *Global issues and adult education: Perspectives from Latin American, Southern Africa, and the United States* (pp. 231–242). San Francisco: Jossey-Bass.

Glanz, K., Rimer, B. K., & Lewis, F. M. (Eds.). (2002). *Health behavior and health education: Theory, research, and practice.* San Francisco: Jossey-Bass.

Golbeck, A. L., Ahlers-Schmidt, C. R., & Paschal, A. M. (2005). Health literacy and adult basic education assessments. *Adult Basic Education, 15*(3), 151–168.

Grady, J., & Aubrun, A. (2008). *Provoking thought, changing talk: Discussing inequality.* You *Can* Get There From Here . . ., an occasional paper series from the social equity and opportunity forum of the College of Urban and Public Affairs, Portland State University.

Greenberg, D. (2001). A critical look at health literacy. *Adult Basic Education, 11*(2), 67–79.

Hammond, C. (2004). Impacts of lifelong learning upon emotional resilience, psychological and mental health: Fieldwork evidence. *Oxford Review of Education, 30*(4), 551–568.

Heetebry, I., Hatcher, M., & Tabriziani, H. (2005). Web-based health education, E-learning, for weight management. *Journal of Medical Systems, 29*(6), 611–617.

Hill, L. H. (2007). Health literacy is a social justice issue that affects us all. *Adult Learning, 15*(1/2), 4–6.

House, J. S., & Williams, D. R. (2000). Understanding and reducing socioeconomic and racial/ethnic disparities in health. In B. D. Smedley & S. L. Syme (Eds.), *Promoting health: Intervention strategies for social and behavioral research.* Washington, DC: National Academy Press.

Institute of Medicine. (2004). *Health literacy: A prescription to end confusion.* Washington: National Academies Press. Retrieved Febuary 16, 2009, from http://www.iom.edu/Reports/2004/Health-Literacy-A-Prescription-to-End-Confusion.aspx

Laura G. (2009, February 25, 2009). Obama transition team hears from nurses. Message posted to http://forums.nurse.com/blog.php?b=143

Levy, S. R., Rasher, S. P., Carter, S. D., Harris, L. M., Berbaum, M. L., Mardernach, J. B., Bercovitz, L. S., & Martin, L. (2008). Health literacy curriculum works for adult basic education students. *Focus on Basics, 9B,* 33–39.

Marmot, M. (2005). Social determinants of health inequalities. *The Lancet, 365,* 1099–1104.

Mechanic, D., & Tanner, J. (2007). Vulnerable people, groups, and populations: Societal view. *Health Affairs, 26*(5), 1220–1230.

Mezirow, J. D. (1991). *Transformative dimensions of adult learning.* San Francisco: Jossey-Bass.

Moen, A., & Smørdal, O. (2006). REPARERE; web-based resource to support patients and families in CABG recovery. *European Journal of Cardiovascular Nursing, 5*(Suppl 1), S17–S18.

Murray, C., Michaud, C., McKenna, M., & Marks, J. (1998). *US patterns of mortality by county and race: 1965–94.* Cambridge, MA: Harvard Center for Population and Development Studies.

Obilade, O. O. (2005). Health education. In L. M. English (Ed.), *International encyclopedia of adult education* (pp. 274–277). London: Palgrave Macmillan.

Paasche-Orlow, M. D., Parker, R. M., Gazmararian, J. A., Nielsen-Bohlman, L. T., & Rudd, R. R. (2005). The prevalence of limited health literacy. *Journal of General Internal Medicine, 20,* 175–184.

Peña Dolhun, E., Muñoz, C., & Grumbach, K. (2003). Cross-cultural education in U.S. medical schools: Development of an assessment tool. *Academic Medicine, 78*(6), 615–622.

Rager, K. B. (2003). The self-directed learning of women with breast cancer. *Adult Education Quarterly, 53*(4), 277–293.

Rosen, J., Spatz, E. S., Gaaserud, A. M., Abramovitch, H., Weinreb, B., Wenger, N. S., & Margolis, C. Z. (2004). A new approach to developing cross-cultural communication skills. *Medical Teacher, 26*(2), 126–132.

Roter, D., & Hall, J. (2006). *Doctors talking with patients/patients talking with doctors: Improving communication in medical visits.* Westport, CT: Praeger.

Rudd, R. (2007). Let's become partners: Practitioners in the health and education fields need to cooperate. *Adult Basic Education and Literacy Journal, 1*(1), 32–36.

Ruiter, A. C., Kessels, L. T. E., & Jansma, B. M. (2006). Increased attention for computer-tailored health communications: An event-related potential study. *Health Psychology, 25*(3), 300–306.

Satcher, D., & Higginbotham, E. (2008). The public health approach to eliminating disparities in health. *American Journal of Public Health, 98*(3), 400–403.

Schwartzberg, J. G., Cowett, A., VanGeest, J., & Wolf, M. S. (2007). Communication techniques for patients with low health literacy. A survey of physicians, nurses and pharmacists. *American Journal of Health Behavior, 31*(Supp 1), S96–S104.

Syme, S. L. (2000). Community participation, empowerment, and health development of a wellness guide for California. In M. A. Jamner & S. Arokola (Eds.), *Promoting human wellness: New frontiers for research, practice, and policy* (pp. 78–98). Berkeley: University of California Press.

Taking healthcare to the people: Mayo Clinic, Univ. of Pittsburgh Collaborate to Reach Patients Where They Live and Work (n.d.). Retrieved June 11, 2009, from http://ctsa.mayo.edu/news/healthcare.html

Tassi, A., & Ashraf, F. (2008). Health literate doctors and patients: The New York City Health Literacy Fellowship for first-year medical students. *Focus on Basics, 9B,* 1, 3–8.

Taylor, J. (2003). Confronting "culture" in medicine's "culture of no culture." *Academic Medicine, 78*(6), 555–559.

Tervalon, M. (2003). Components of culture in health for medical students' education. *Academic Medicine, 78*(6), 570–576.

Vladeck, B. C. (2007). How useful is "vulnerable" as a concept? *Health Affairs, 26*(5), 1231–1234.

Wear, D. (2003). Insurgent multiculturalism: Rethinking how and why we teach culture in medical education. *Academic Medicine, 78*(6), 549–554.

Whitcomb, M. (2003). Preparing doctors for a multicultural world. *Academic Medicine, 78*(6), 547–548.

Wurzbach, M. (2002). *Community health education and promotion: A guide to program design and evaluation* (2nd ed.). Gaithersburg, MD: Aspen.

Young, A., & Flower, L. (2002). Patients as partners, patients as problem-solvers. *Health Communications, 14*(1), 69–97.

Zarcadoolas, C., Pleasant, A., & Greer, D. S. (2005). Understanding health literacy: An expanded model. *Health Promotion International, 20*(2), 95–203.

Zerhouni, E. (2003). The NIH Roadmap. *Science, 302,* 63–72.

28

ENVIRONMENTAL ADULT EDUCATION

A Many-Voiced Landscape

ELIZABETH A. LANGE

Many North Americans have a latent sense that all is not well with the Earth, perhaps heightened by public discourse or alarming personal observations of a changing local environment. Now, in support of these sensibilities, there is an overwhelming scientific consensus that we are facing a global ecological crisis (Millennium Ecosystem Assessment Project, 2005; United Nations Intergovernmental Panel on Climate Change, 2007). Environmental educator David Orr (1994) suggests this ecological crisis concerns how we think and thus fundamentally is a learning issue. He believes it compels an examination of the entire fabric of our society and a transformation of cultural values, attitudes, and behaviors. These pressing ecological issues are intertwined with social justice issues, prompting us to rethink the purpose of education as well as the nature of a good society, epistemological and ontological roots of Western society, deeply held notions about the meaning and quality of life, and social constructions of the human-environment relation. Scientists, educators, and UNESCO leaders have underlined that we cannot wait and that adult education, not just K–12 schooling, is urgently needed to promote ecological literacy, foster sustainable behaviors, and revitalize citizen involvement in public decision making and social change (Monroe, 2007; Tilbury & Wortman, 2004; UNESCO, 1997b).

It is intriguing, then, that the theory and practice of environmental education for adults in North America has been so underdeveloped. Despite the relative longevity and visibility of the environmental movement since the 1960s, the vigorous development of K–12 environmental education for 40 years, extensive media coverage of environmental issues, and fervent UN calls for environmental education, environmental concerns did not penetrate the adult education field until the late 1990s. In fact, this chapter will be the first in the *Handbook of Adult and Continuing Education,* since its inaugural issue in 1934, addressing the environment as a theme. Environmental adult education is occurring, but it is dispersed among countless settings—government, postsecondary institutions, community and nonprofit organizations, churches, unions, social movements, and corporate and small business. Yet, these providers do so largely without reference to the theoretical and empirical research provided by the adult education field. It is time to increase our visibility and engagement, for as UNESCO (1997a) asserts, adult education is both a long-term solution and primary lever that can link our existing way of living to a very different future that is ecologically sustainable and socially just.

Since the millennial turn, numerous theorists are now calling for the "greening" or integration of environmental discourse into the adult education field (Hill & Clover, 2003; Hill, 2006; O'Sullivan, 1999; Taylor, 2006). Encouraging adult educators to take up the challenge of environmental education upholds the field's historic responsiveness to society—now that Canadian public polls indicate the environment and climate change to be a top concern (De Souza, 2007) and American polls indicate environmental issues a top concern of the future, with high support for the provision of environmental education (Clover, 2002; Gallup, 2010; National Environmental Education Foundation, 2001; Saad, 2004). Critically minded adult educators have detailed important links between environmental issues, social justice issues, and the international context, notably neoliberal globalization. Together, they are calling for a comprehensive adult education agenda that poses the choice of a sustainable future and a vision of achievable possibilities and that fosters an ecological consciousness and transformative social change (Hill & Clover, 2003; O'Sullivan, 1999).

In this chapter, then, I will argue that environmental adult education and sustainability education for adults are among the newest and most innovative of emerging discourses, challenging orthodoxies and priorities in the adult education field. I will trace the rise of environmental concerns in the field, analyze the historical barriers to its development, introduce environmental discourse, and illustrate how its theoretical contestations are echoed within adult education theory and practice. To conclude, I identify challenges to the larger field and urgently required research at this historical turning point (Korten, 2006).

FERTILE SOIL: EMERGENCE OF ENVIRONMENTAL THEMES IN ADULT EDUCATION

There have been three waves of calls for environmental education in the North American adult education field since 1970, finally falling onto fertile soil in the late 1990s. Rachel Carson's publication of *Silent Spring* in 1962, scientifically documenting the impact of DDT on songbirds, commonly marks the beginning of the environmental movement in North America. By 1970, the first international Earth Day occurred in New York backed by the UN Secretary General, the U.S. Environmental Protection Agency had formed, the Clean Air Act was passed, and Greenpeace was born in Vancouver, Canada, to protest nuclear testing in Amchitka off Alaskan shores. This flurry of activity during the 1960s and 70s touched off the first wave of environmental education in North America as *The Journal of Environmental Education* was launched (1969), the first National Environmental Education Act passed (1970), and the North American Association for Environmental Education formed (1971). At this time, the UN Conference on the Human Environment (1972) recommended that environmental education be recognized and promoted in all countries. These early initiatives coalesced into the Belgrade Charter (UNESCO, 1976) providing the first goal statement for environmental education:

> to develop a world population that is aware of, and concerned about, the environment and its associated problems and which has the knowledge, skills, attitudes, motivations, and commitment to work individually and collectively toward solutions of current problems and the prevention of new ones.

Two years later, the Tbilisi Declaration expanded on various objectives for environmental education. Thus, the early promotion and conceptualization of environmental education came from these national and international level agencies.

While the primary antecedents to environmental education in North America were nature study, outdoor education, and conservation education, environmental education had its strongest initial growth in higher education, quickly dominated by the expansion into K–12 schooling. In particular, the North American Association for Environmental Education began as a professional association to support community college educators looking for instructional materials. However, the term *environmental education* attracted a wide range of professionals—classroom teachers, environmental scientists, naturalists, conservationists, museum and zoo educators, nature center specialists, park interpreters, outdoor educators, government/corporate communication specialists, and activists. Given this, the definition of environmental education has remained highly contested, and the environmental education literature is rife with tensions across dramatically different definitions and perspectives (Heimlich, 2002). These debates revolve around what kind of human-environment relation ought to be fostered and what "education is, is not, should be, and should not be," distinguishing education from communication and interpretation (Disinger, McCrea, & Wicks, 2001, p. 6). Substantial critiques of early environmental education note the problematic affiliation with schooling, the focus on science knowledge and conservation topics, and pedagogies limited to attitude formation and information transmission (Cole, 2007).

Interestingly, these early but dynamic seeds of environmental education both in North America and internationally did not take root in the adult education field during the 1970s and '80s. Only a few lone voices (Emmelin, 1976; Jeske, 1973; Kormondy, 1970) tried "to rally the field of adult education to take up an environmental discourse" (Hill, 2006, p. 265). Hypotheses regarding barriers to the uptake of environmentally oriented education have come from Field (1989), who identifies the dominant individualist focus in the field as discouraging partnership with the environmental movement, and from Boggs (1986), who suggests many adult educators have adopted an apolitical posture uncomfortable with environmentalist intensity. Finger (1989) asserts that adult educators should not emulate the early field of environmental education, given the critiques, but orient it toward transformative learning. Imel (1990) contends that environmental education is political by nature, cautioning that the needs of both the environment and developing nations must be balanced.

A second wave of calls for environmental adult education was stimulated by the 1987 Brundtland Commission Report, *Our Common Future*, positing a global agenda for sustainable development to be achieved by 2000. It introduced the concept of sustainable development, defining it as development that meets the needs of the present without compromising the ability of future generations to meet their own needs (Brundtland, 1987). Shortly thereafter in 1991, the International Council for Adult Education (ICAE) established the Learning for the Environment Programme, which was the "only global network that provided a place of encounter for adult educators who were working within an ecological framework" (Clover, 2004, p. vii). Darlene Clover of Canada and Moema Viezzer of Brazil organized an environmental adult education gathering as part of the 1992 Rio Earth Summit, which produced Agenda 21 as a comprehensive blueprint for a global partnership. Out of this gathering, the first treaty on environmental adult education, Environmental Education for Sustainable Societies and Global Responsibility, was adopted, notable for the profile given to adult education and the use of adult education principles for international policy-making.

In 1989, 1992, 1995, and again in 2000, *Convergence*, the journal of ICAE, published special issues dedicated to environmental themes, the first significant conduit of environmental education messages into the adult education field. Although these developments and the new concept of sustainable development spurred some attention, environmental themes in adult education remained dormant until the late 1990s. Additional hypotheses regarding the lack of engagement include the perceived need for science specialist knowledge (St. Clair, 2003), the lack of institutional structures to support it (McDonald, 2006), and difficulties integrating a wide range of environmental topics and related disciplines into existing programs (Taylor, 2006). Edward Taylor also suggests that a lack of understanding about the philosophical controversies in environmental discourse and a lack of pedagogical material discourage interested educators. He further identifies institutional barriers as a hidden curriculum of inhibiting factors, including architecture that reinforces human-environment separation, anthropocentric and dualist thought forms, and the privileging of industrial capitalist social forms. He depicts this as the "graying" or "polluting" of the academic context (Taylor, 2006, p. 256). Heimlich (2002) alleges that sensationalist media coverage spawns negative connotations of things environmental. Certainly, the overstatement of scientific controversy, the perceived binary dichotomy between economy/jobs and the environment, and intensified ideological polemics in recent years can all be considered nonengagement factors. In a self-reinforcing cycle, the disciplinary silos in environmental research and the paucity of environmental discourse in the adult education field all foster a lack of tradition (McDonald, 2006; Taylor, 2006).

To address this, Clover (2003) echoes Finger, adamant that conventional environmental education models not be adopted in the field, particularly their focus on individual behavior change and information transmission. Rather, she proposes that environmental issues be integrated into adult education discourse, calling this environmental adult education. She further advocates for a critical approach making "concrete links between the environment and social, economic, political, and cultural aspects of people's lives" (Clover, 2003, p. 10).

Finally, in 1997, at the fifth UNESCO international conference on adult education, environmental issues were on the agenda for the first time (Clover, 2006). The resulting CONFINTEA V report, called the *Hamburg Declaration and Agenda for the Future* (UNESCO, 1997a), and the resulting handbook, *Environmental Adult Education: From Awareness to Action,* mark an international watershed. They provide clear principles to guide environmental adult education and propose a working definition:

> a permanent process in which individuals gain awareness of their environment and acquire the knowledge, values, skills, experiences, and also the determination which will enable them to act individually and collectively to solve present and future environmental problems . . . as well as to meet their needs without compromising those of future generations. (UNESCO, 1999, p. 4)

The central focus of this statement is on the building of capacities among adult educators to take up environmentally oriented education for raising environmental awareness; integrating environmental, political, and social issues; and promoting action that respects environmental integrity.

Most recently, adult educators were involved in the Earth Charter process (Clover, 2006) helping create a global consensus around a vision for global sustainability and principles by which to achieve it. As a useful educational framework, curricular resource, and community development tool, the Earth Charter (2000) has been endorsed by the United Nations and thousands of organizations. It challenges the global community:

> As never before in history, common destiny beckons us to seek a new beginning . . . this requires a change of mind and heart. It requires a new sense of global interdependence and universal responsibility. We must imaginatively develop and apply the vision of a sustainable way of life locally, nationally, regionally, and globally. (p. 5)

Frederico Mayor of UNESCO (1997b) concurs: "We must be ready, in all countries, to reshape education so as to promote attitudes and behaviour conducive to a culture of sustainability," (p. 4); this presaged the announcement of the UN Decade of Education for Sustainable Development (2005–2014).

These initiatives in the late 1990s and in the early years of the new millennium culminated in a turning point. A third wave of voices, calling for the integration of an ecological lens into adult education, finally fell onto fertile soil, stimulating a landscape of diverse theoretical voices.

A MANY-VOICED LANDSCAPE: MAPPING THEORETICAL PERSPECTIVES IN ENVIRONMENTAL DISCOURSE

Environmental discourse is a many-voiced landscape (Abram, 1996) linking scientific, political, economic, and ethical thought. Yet, in environmental adult education, the theoretical foundations and principles for practice are still in development. Thus, a brief introduction to environmental thought, particularly deep ecology, spiritual ecology, social ecology, environmental justice, ecofeminism, sustainable development, and sustainability (Merchant, 2005) is necessary as discursive groundwork for understanding the approaches taken in the adult education field.

For all its shortcomings, extremist versions, and eclectic mix of influences, one of the most influential approaches is *deep ecology.* Deep ecology (Naess, 1973) considers mainstream environmentalism as shallow, piecemeal, and reformist, not capable of spawning the deep changes necessary to replace the Western mechanistic paradigm. Deep ecology seeks to catalyze an ecological consciousness and a culture shift based on the nonanthropocentric premise that humans are only one among many species, not exempt from but dependent on ecological laws and natural processes. A biocentric ethic places a moral duty on humans to maintain ecosphere integrity, adapt to natural world processes, and live within rather than technologically manipulate bioregional limits. It fosters the view that each person is part of the universal fabric of wholeness, often drawing from Eastern spiritualities and New Science. Capra (1992) elaborates that relativity theory, quantum mechanics, process physics, complexity theory, and Gaia theory all support a holistic worldview for living sustainably. Deep ecology purports that social change occurs as it does in complex living systems—by reaching bifurcation points where the forces of order and chaos create many possibilities and small factors can create a tipping point for sudden, rapid change.

Deep ecology is critiqued for the lack of any structural analysis of capitalist production, patriarchy, social class, and race and thus its inability to fully understand the origins of cultural ideas and the pathologies of industrialism (Bookchin, 1995). Furthermore, Bradford (1989) says deep ecologists mask social stratification, conflict, and injustice and contradict their own espousal of species equal rights, particularly when privileging wilderness preservation over human welfare.

Spiritual ecology reclaims nature-based spiritualities that have been lost or suppressed historically. Ancient goddess worship and neo-pagan rituals have been revived as Earth-based spiritualities predicated on feminine and partnership principles. Indigenous spiritualities provide ethical guidance and healing rituals for a new relationship with the Earth, and many world religions are now reviewing and reinterpreting their sacred writings through an ecological lens (Kinsley, 1995). Christian process theology, Buddhism, and complexity science have been linked to give nourishment for new approaches to educational, political, and protest work (Cobb, 1982). Yet, spiritual ecology is critiqued for lacking a power and economic analysis, for ignoring the negative histories of some spiritualities, and for assuming that they necessarily lead to environmental protection or female equality (Merchant, 2005).

Social ecology examines the ecological ramifications of capitalism, specifically for appropriating the Earth as property and promoting its despoilation, embracing progress as mastery over natural laws and limits, and exploiting and dispossessing indigenous people and other vulnerable groups from traditional lands and ways of life. Social ecologists suggest that a mere shift in values and worldview will not create the fundamental economic transformation needed to create sustainable, just, and economically democratic societies (Bookchin, 1995). They argue that the physical and spiritual life of humans is intimately linked to the natural world. The anarchist strand calls for egalitarian face-to-face democratic self-governing communities. The socialist strand calls for a postcapitalist society, beyond the failures of both state socialism and industrial capitalism, predicated on ecological socialism. The radical ecology strand perceives all current crises as manifesting one system of injustice and domination. It integrates a race, class, and gender analysis and advocates for the transformation of both structures of thought and socioeconomic structures. Social ecology has been critiqued for using outdated Marxist theory, a homocentric ethic, and utopianism (Merchant, 2005).

Environmental justice is "the principle of equitable protection from environmental hazards for all races, ethnicities, and socioeconomic groups and the preservation of natural resources of the people, including indigenous communities" (Hill, 2003, p. 27). The environmental justice movement arose in the 1970s as it became clear that people of color and lower income unfairly bore the brunt of environmental consequences—whether the siting of landfills, nuclear plants, or extractive industries; the dumping of toxic waste; or harmful exposure at work sites. Early environmental movements were also racially exclusive in membership and practices, tending to focus on middle-class consumption and conservation issues with little concern for the health, livelihood, and survival of marginalized groups. Critiques identify a homocentric approach and inadequate attention to changing the human-ecology relation (Merchant, 2005).

Ecofeminism adds reproduction to an analysis of production and consciousness, recognizing the intertwined domination of women and the natural world. The strands of ecofeminism parallel the strands of feminism but generally are committed to life-giving principles. They address the assault on women's and children's bodies and the societal necessity of providing for the basics of life as necessary conditions for human survival. Liberal ecofeminism aligns with mainstream environmentalism; cultural ecofeminists critique patriarchy choosing to valorize women's inherent biological and spiritual connection to the Earth; and socialist ecofeminism critiques the links between global capitalist production, postcolonial realities, gender, and race. Radical ecofeminists blend these critiques, advocate for the nongendering of the natural world (i.e., Mother Earth) while proposing a partnership ethic that treats male, female, and nonhuman species as partners, each needing sufficient room for life-generating processes.

A core contention is whether an ethics of care and nurture is part of women's nature, an essentialist stance within dualist rationality, or an idea constructed by a patriarchal, capitalist culture (Merchant, 2005).

The *sustainable development* discourse aligns with mainstream environmentalism in the goal of making existing production systems more ecologically sustainable. This conventional "greening" discourse attempts to reconcile the differences between environmentalists and corporate business while maintaining rapid economic growth, increased consumption, and technological innovation. These approaches are often promoted by global institutions and are reflected in policies that attempt to measure environmental carrying capacity, design more accurate resource pricing, measure the capital worth of services provided by the natural world, and put in place a global system of pollution tradeoffs. Although some of these policy adjustments, technological fixes, market solutions, and managerial processes might be important short-term initiatives, they are criticized for not addressing deeper causes of poverty and environmental degradation and maintaining the anthropocentric, resourcist, developmentalist, social engineering paradigm (Orr, 1992).

Edwards (2005) contrasts sustainable development with what he considers the *sustainability revolution* and its characteristics: a large number of grassroots groups prevalent globally; uncentralized multiple nodes of independent activity addressing diverse issues with remarkably similar values and intentions; leadership by decentralized visionaries; and varying modes of social action from oppositional to alternative. Hawken (2007) suggests this is likely the largest movement ever, and he estimates there are at least 30,000 sustainability groups in the United States alone. The sustainability or sustainable communities approach is based on specific principles, such as *localization* and *bioregionalism,* where self-sufficient communities meet their own needs largely from within their own bioregion with locally appropriate technology; *restoration ecology,* which restores ecosystems and establishes no-waste and renewable energy policies; *indigenous sustainability,* which preserves traditional lands and ways of knowing, *restorative economics,* where commerce is redesigned to give back as much as is taken; and *participatory democracy.* The sustainability approach engages grassroots populations in transforming Western ways of thinking as well as economic and political systems toward life-giving values where societal interactions flow with the biological, life-preserving systems of Earth (Korten, 2006).

UNFURLING LEAVES: ENVIRONMENTAL DISCOURSE IN ADULT EDUCATION

Just as there is a many-voiced natural landscape, so these voices are now unfolding within adult education discourse; just a sampling of voices is highlighted here. Two seminal theorists of environmental adult education, whose publications represent the turning point, are Edmund O'Sullivan and Darlene Clover. O'Sullivan (1999) merges deep ecology to critical ecopsychology, ecospirituality, and ecofeminism to build a comprehensive vision for adult education. He advocates for an *ecozoic* educational vision that transcends modernity through deep cultural therapy—transforming the dream structures that fuel industrial society and its dominator hierarchies. He describes a new cosmological story (Swimme & Berry, 1992) around which to educate for a full planetary consciousness, so that humans can situate themselves within the unfolding universe story and reclaim a sense of purpose. For him, transformative learning practices foster a critique of the interlocking power relations of class, race, and gender and incorporate visions of alternative ways of living that manifest sustainability, social justice, and personal joy. He details practices for forming an ecological consciousness in an edited collection with Marilyn Taylor (O'Sullivan & Taylor, 2004). This volume includes Kovan and Dirkx's research on how long-time environmental activists sustain their commitment through self-reflexivity, a sense of calling, and soul work and Daloz's research on the seven factors that can foster a sense of bioregional citizenship and a consciousness of interdependence (O'Sullivan & Taylor, 2004).

From a critical ecofeminist position, Darlene Clover (1995) has been developing the theoretical and pedagogical foundations for a critical environmental adult education. Clover (2004) defines the environment holistically as "an integrated human and non-human context or space within which all thought, emotion and activity must also be situated" (p. ix). She argues that the rationale for a critical approach is to move beyond conventional, one-time, instrumental forms into a critical and lifelong learning process (Clover, 1995). Pedagogy must critique the structures of globalization—including war, production, consumption, corporatization—and surface the implications, such as environmental racism and sexism (Clover, 2003). Clover, Follen, and Hall (1998) suggest the practice of environmental adult education should be community-based; begin from learners' lived experience; facilitate a root cause analysis; offer participatory, democratic, creative, and collaborative learning processes; and catalyze links to local, national, or global activism. Finally, environmental adult education should teach key ecological principles, such as interdependence, interconnectedness, and diversity, as well as understand the natural world as a site of experiential learning and as a teacher in its own right.

Beyond these key theorists, many other adult educators and researchers are now taking up various paradigms of environmental discourse. Lilian Hill and Julie Johnston (2003) draw attention to the emotional manifestations of human alienation from the Earth. From a deep ecology and ecospiritual perspective, they encourage a critique of socially constructed meanings about human-environment relations and promote actions that restore human and Earth well-being, as a spiritual act (Hill & Johnston, 2003). Robert Hill (2003) takes up the environmental justice approach and advocates for a broad social agenda that addresses the confluence of racism, white privilege, sexism, class advantage, and other forms of oppression. He insists that adult educators need to be involved among communities that face environmental and social justice dilemmas, drawing on popular education, community organizing, alliance building, participatory research, and problem-solving activism. Tan (2004) highlights how often mainstream environmental leadership lacks alliance building with immigrant and multicultural communities, and she too advocates for an inclusive anti-racist environmental discourse and the integration of the ecological wisdom of newcomers. Bowles (2007) has been theorizing Black women's learning in the environmental justice movement, and Feinstein (2004) draws on Hawaiian traditional ecological knowledge as a form of transformative environmental education. Cajete (2004) of the Pueblo peoples in New Mexico illustrates how their guiding sacred story connects the people to the land. This story is encoded in art, dance, and language and is a source of ecologically and life-oriented learning to ensure the sustainability of indigenous societies.

Taking up the sustainability discourse, Sumner (2005) redefines community sustainability to be the structures and processes that build the civil commons and its cooperative basis, rather than those that support economic growth. She identifies various entry points for sustainability education, including among rural farmers as they learn their way into sustainability. Other community-based entry points for sustainability education include the struggle for clean water, breathable air, intact forests, nonengineered and uncontaminated food and clothing, and meaningful work. My own scholarship (Lange, 2004, 2009) merges radical ecology and critical transformative learning into sustainability education, identifying the importance of restorative learning as a companion to transformative learning. Pedagogies that nourish life-affirming changes in ways of being and thinking can often generate new energy for civic involvement. Duguid, Mundel, and Schugurensky (2007) examine the importance of informal learning within community volunteerism and activism related to sustainability, noting increasingly complex environmental understandings and skills that augment the functioning of a sustainable community.

Belanger (2003) integrates environmental discourse with lifelong learning, promoting a synergy between formal, nonformal, and informal learning. Using an "open your eyes" approach, Belanger suggests practices where learners unveil architectural, institutional, and cultural structures that are in tension with or negate interdependence relationships with local environments. St. Clair (2003) integrates deep ecology with critical literacy, considering environmental literacy integral to functional literacy, where being "competent as a citizen would involve recognizing the state of environmental systems and being prepared to address problems within them" (p. 70). Finally, there is an active "green campus" movement in higher education, which promotes the green retrofitting of buildings, ethical purchasing/cleaning/waste/energy practices, university-wide ethics dialogue, interdisciplinary curriculum development, collaborative research, and policies addressing justice issues embedded in corporate sponsorships, not yet extensively discussed in the adult education field (Fein, 2002; Lange & Chubb, 2009; Sibbel, 2009).

ALL OUR RELATIONS: AN INTEGRATED AGENDA FOR ENVIRONMENTAL ADULT EDUCATION

In sum, environmental adult education is one of the most innovative and challenging of the emerging discourses in the field of adult education. It involves a fundamental rethinking of the purpose of adult education and its role in the human and more-than-human world. Asking the question "what is adult education for?" represents a revolution of reconsideration—what is worth educating for; what knowledge, values, insight, and wisdom are worth reproducing; and what form of collective life is worthy of our dedicated energies? This questions the cosmological, epistemological, and ontological roots of the Western intellectual tradition as much as it questions the way our daily living and yearning has been structured. David Orr (1994), inspired by Thomas Merton, challenges us,

> The plain fact is that the planet does not need more successful people. But it does desperately need more peacemakers, healers, restorers, storytellers, and lovers of every kind. It needs people who live well in their places. It needs people of moral courage willing to join the [struggle] to make the world habitable and humane. (p. 12)

Examining all of our relations, natural and social, as entwined in a life-giving web and exploring the possibilities emanating from precepts of nonharming, dynamic balance and beingness (not havingness) can move environmentally oriented education beyond ideological polemics. However, this also implies a broad critique of politico-economic structures and of cultural constructions manifested in space, time, body, language, and narrative, as well as consideration of possible alternatives, welcoming non-Western ways of knowing and being that are life affirming.

Environmental adult education also urges the field back to its social purpose roots, given that the primary engagement node is local communities—their concerns, vulnerabilities,

perpetrated injustices, and bioregional context. It returns to the basics of life—air, food, water, shelter, clothing, sleep, safety, love, and belonging—and encourages adult educators to provide spaces to stop frenzied lives long enough to critique lived societal practices and consider individual, global, and Earth implications. It expands the educative entry points for engaging adults and returns to the historic role of empowering folks to become informed, deliberative, and active in challenging the life-negating forces around them. It integrates a critique of global, market-driven, corporatized structures with a vision of learning for sustainable societies. No matter the social location of participants by gender, race/ethnicity, class, sexual orientation, ability, or nationality—adults are embedded in an evocative living world that restores a sense of balance, mental clarity, physical health, and a sense of peace. The loss of natural spaces for (re)discovering this relationship has caused our moral and spiritual knowledge to shrivel, collapsed our sense of wildness in favor of domestication, dulled our creative and self-healing capacities, and reduced our ability to participate in and preserve the natural conviviality that surrounds us (Abram, 1996; Louv, 2005).

To conclude, a tremendous paucity of theoretical and empirical research must be rectified to bring environmental adult education to fruition and, more important, to societal relevance. Examining pedagogical entry points, catalytic factors moving people to action, effective environmental learning processes across the lifespan, potential of intergenerational learning, comparisons of paradigmatic approaches, expansions beyond Western epistemologies and ontologies, and interdisciplinary issues are all areas of research need. Furthermore, educational and research links with local and global movements can broaden our identity, heighten the visibility of adult education, make vital interdisciplinary contributions, and spawn locally rooted leaders. Adult educators need to increase their ecological and political literacy at local, regional, and global levels as well as learn to build social capital and citizen science among local communities. We are challenged to learn and integrate ecological knowledge with respect for the spirit of the land. Then, as governments, businesses, and citizen groups take up the sustainability challenge, adult educators can be there, facilitating and sharing our unique and relevant body of theory and practice developed over the history of our field. As Benavides (1992, p. 43) has said, the challenge for adult education is to become "environmental and just in its essence, spirit, and practice."

REFERENCES

Abram, D. (1996). *The spell of the sensuous.* New York: Vintage Books.

Belanger, P. (2003). Learning environments and environmental education. In L. Hill & D. Clover (Eds.), *Environmental adult education: Ecological learning, theory, and practice for socioenvironmental change* (pp. 79–88). New Directions for Adult and Continuing Education, No. 99. San Francisco: Jossey-Bass.

Benavides, M. (1992). Lessons from 500 years of a "New World Order"—Towards the 21st century. *Convergence, 25*(2), 37–45.

Boggs, D. (1986). A case study of citizen education and action. *Adult Education Quarterly, 37*(1), 1–13.

Bookchin, M. (1995). *The philosophy of social ecology.* Montreal: Black Rose Books.

Bowles, T. (2007). The dimensions of black women's learning in the environmental justice movement in the southeastern U.S. In L. Servage & T. Fenwick (Eds.), *Proceedings of the Joint International Conference of the AERC* (pp. 55–60). Halifax, Nova Scotia: Mount St. Vincent University.

Bradford, G. (1989). *How deep is deep ecology?* New York: Times Change Press.

Brundtland, G. H. (1987). *The Brundtland report to the World Commission on Environment and Development (Our common future).* Oxford, UK: Oxford University Press.

Cajete, G. (2004). A pueblo story for transformation. In E. O'Sullivan & M. Taylor (Eds.), *Learning toward an ecological consciousness* (pp. 103–114). New York: Palgrave Macmillan.

Capra, F. (1992). *The web of life.* New York: Anchor Books.

Clover, D. (1995). Theoretical foundations and practice of critical environmental adult education in Canada. *Convergence, 28*(4), 44–54.

Clover, D. (2002). Environmental adult education. *Adult Learning, 13*(2/3), 2–6.

Clover, D. (2003). Environmental adult education: Critique and creativity in a globalizing world. In L. Hill & D. Clover (Eds). *Environmental adult education: Ecological learning, theory, and practice for socioenvironmental change* (pp. 5–16). New Directions for Adult and Continuing Education, No. 99. San Francisco, CA: Jossey-Bass.

Clover, D. (Ed.). (2004). *Global perspectives in environmental adult education.* New York: Peter Lang.

Clover, D. (2006). Policy development, theory, and practice in environmental adult education. *Convergence, 39*(4), 51–54.

Clover, D., Follen, S., & Hall, B. (1998). *The nature of transformation: Environmental, adult and popular education.* Toronto, Ontario: University of Toronto.

Cobb, J. (1982). *Process theology as political theology.* Philadelphia: Westminister Press.

Cole, A. G. (2007). Expanding the field: Revisiting environmental education principles through multidisciplinary frameworks. *Journal of Environmental Education, 38*(2), 35–44.

De Souza, M. (2007). *Environment biggest public concern, poll finds.* Retrieved August 6, 2008, from http://www.canada.com/ edmontonjournal/news/story.html?id= 802cac42-dfe5–4c5a-965f-d5ddd3f37067

Disinger, J., McCrea, E., & Wicks, D. (2001). *The NAAEE thirty years of history 1971–2001.* Washington, DC: NAAEE. Retrieved July 30, 2008, from www.naaee.org

Duguid, F., Mundel, K., & Schugurensky D. (2007). Volunteer work, informal learning, and the quest for sustainable communities in Canada. *Canadian Journal for the Study of Adult Education, 20*(2), 41–56.

Earth Charter. (2000). Available at www .earthcharter.org

Edwards, A. (2005). *The sustainability revolution.* Gabriola Island, BC: New Society Publishers.

Emmelin, L. (1976). The need for environmental education for adults. *Convergence, 9*(1), 45–53.

Fein, J. (2002). Advancing sustainability in higher education: Issues and opportunities for research. *International Journal of Sustainability in Higher Education, 3*(3), 243–254.

Feinstein, B. (2004). Learning and transformation in the context of Hawaiian traditional ecological knowledge. *Adult Education Quarterly, 54*(2), 105–120.

Field, J. (1989). Is the future of adult education green? *Adult Learning, 1*(1), 24–26.

Finger, M. (1989). Environmental adult education from the perspective of the learner. *Convergence, 22*(4), 25–32.

Gallup. (2010). Environmental polls. Retrieved January 2, 2010, from http://www.gallup.com/ poll/1615/Environment.aspx

Hawken, P. (2007). *Blessed unrest.* New York: Viking.

Heimlich, J. (2002). *Environmental education.* Bloomington, IN: Phi Delta Kappa Educational Foundation.

Hill, L., & Clover, D. (2003). Editors notes. In L. Hill & D. Clover (Eds.), *Environmental adult education: Ecological learning, theory, and practice for socioenvironmental change* (pp. 1–3). New Directions for Adult and Continuing Education, No. 99. San Francisco: Jossey-Bass.

Hill, L., & Johnston, J. (2003). Adult education and humanity's relationship with nature reflected in language, metaphor, and spirituality. In L. Hill & D. Clover (Eds.). *Environmental adult education: Ecological learning, theory, and practice for socioenvironmental change* (pp. 17–26). New Directions for Adult and Continuing Education, No. 99. San Francisco: Jossey-Bass.

Hill, R. (2003). Environmental justice: Environmental adult education at the confluence of oppressions. In L. Hill & D. Clover (Eds). *Environmental adult education: Ecological learning, theory, and practice for socioenvironmental change* (pp. 27–38). New Directions for Adult and Continuing Education, No. 99. San Francisco: Jossey-Bass.

Hill, R. (2006). Environmental adult education. In S. Merriam, B. Courtenay, & R. Cervero (Eds.), *Global issues and adult education.* San Francisco: Jossey-Bass.

Imel, S. (1990). *Environmental adult education: Trends and issues alerts.* (ERIC ED 321154). Retrieved January 13, 2010, from http://www.eric.ed.gov/ERICDocs/data/ericdocs2sql/content_storage_01/0000019b/80/20/8c/b8.pdf

Jeske, W. (1973). Should adult education programs include courses relating to environmental concerns? *Adult Leadership, 21*(9), 283–284, 307–308.

Kinsley, D. (1995). *Ecology and religion.* Englewood Cliffs, NJ: Prentice Hall.

Kormondy, E. J. (1970). *Environmental education: The adult public.* Washington, DC: American Institute of Biological Sciences.

Korten, D. (2006). *The great turning.* San Francisco: Berrett-Koehler.

Lange, E. (2004). Transformative and restorative learning: A vital dialectic for sustainable societies. *Adult Education Quarterly, 54*(2), 121–139.

Lange, E. (2009). Fostering a learning sanctuary for transformation in adult sustainability education. In J. D. Mezirow & E. Taylor (Eds.), *Transformative learning in practice.* San Francisco: Jossey-Bass.

Lange, E., & Chubb, A. (2009). Critical environmental adult education in Canada:

Student environmental activism. In P. Cranton & L. English (Eds.), *Reaching out across the border: Canadian perspectives in adult education* (pp. 61–72). New Directions for Adult Continuing Education, No. 124. San Francisco: Jossey-Bass.

Louv, R. (2005). *Last child in the woods.* Chapel Hill, NC: Algonquin Books of Chapel Hill.

McDonald, B. (2006). Adult education on the environmental margin. In S. Merriam, B. Courtenay, & R. Cervero (Eds.), *Global issues and adult education.* San Francisco: Jossey-Bass.

Merchant, C. (2005). *Radical ecology.* New York: Routledge.

Millennium Ecosystem Assessment Project. (2005). Retrieved September 11, 2008, from http://www.millenniumassessment.org/en/index.aspx

Monroe, M. C. (2007). A priority for ESD research: Influencing adult citizens. *Journal of Education for Sustainable Development, 1*(1), 107.

Naess, A. (1973). The shallow and deep, long-range ecology movements. *Inquiry, 16,* 95–100.

National Environmental Education Foundation. (2001). Ninth annual national report card: Summary of environmental readiness for the 21st century. Retrieved August 6, 2008, from http://neefusa.org/resources/roper_99.htm

Orr, D. (1992). *Ecological literacy.* Albany: State University of New York.

Orr, D. (1994). *Earth in mind.* Washington, DC: Island Press.

O'Sullivan, E. (1999). *Transformative learning: Educational vision for the 21st century.* London: Zed Books.

O'Sullivan, E., & Taylor, M. (Eds.). (2004). *Learning toward an ecological consciousness.* New York: Palgrave Macmillan.

Saad, L. (2004). *Environment not a pressing concern* (Gallup News Service). Retrieved January 2, 2010, from http://www.gallup.com/poll/11380/Environment-Pressing-Concern.aspx

Sibbel, A. (2009). Pathways towards sustainability through higher education. *International Journal of Sustainability in Higher Education, 10*(1), 68–82.

St. Clair, R. (2003). Words for the world: Creating critical environmental literacy for adults. In L. Hill & D. Clover (Eds). *Environmental adult education: Ecological learning, theory, and practice for socioenvironmental change* (pp. 69–78). New Directions for Adult Continuing Education, No. 99. San Francisco: Jossey-Bass.

Sumner, J. (2005). *Sustainability and the civil commons.* Toronto, Ontario: University of Toronto Press.

Swimme, B., & Berry, T. (1992). *The universe story.* San Francisco: Harper.

Tan, S. (2004). Anti-racist environmental adult education in a trans-global community. In D. Clover (Ed.), *Global perspectives in environmental adult education.* New York: Peter Lang.

Taylor, E. (2006). The greening of the adult education academy. In S. Merriam, B. Courtenay, & R. Cervero (Eds.), *Global issues and adult education.* San Francisco: Jossey-Bass.

Tilbury, D., & Wortman, D. (Eds.). (2004). *Engaging people in sustainability.* Cambridge, UK: International Union for Conservation of Nature and Natural Resources.

UNESCO. (1976). The Belgrade charter: A global framework for environmental education. *UNESCO-UNEP Environmental Education Newsletter, 1*(1), 1–4.

UNESCO. (1997a). Adult education: The Hamburg declaration and the agenda for the future. *Proceedings from CONFINTEA V: The Fifth International Conference on Adult Education.* Hamburg, Germany: Author.

UNESCO. (1997b). *Educating for a sustainable future.* Retrieved from http://www.unesco .org/education/tlsf/TLSF/theme_a/mod01/ uncom01t05s01.htm

UNESCO. (1999). *Adult environmental education: Awareness and environmental action.* Adult Learning and the Challenges of the 21st Century, Booklet 6a. Hamburg, Germany: UNESCO, Fifth International Conference on Adult Education (CONFINTEA V).

United Nations Intergovernmental Panel on Climate Change. (2007). *Climate change 2007: Synthesis report.* Retrieved August 6, 2008, from http://www.ipcc.ch/pdf/assessment-report/ar4/syr/ar4_syr.pdf

29

DISTANCE EDUCATION IN THE AGE OF THE INTERNET

WALTER ARCHER AND D. RANDY GARRISON

D istance education originated in a social justice context, as a way to provide access to learning opportunities to those unable to access the usual face-to-face settings because of distance, time, physical handicap, or other barriers. In this chapter, we will present a brief account of how distance education has evolved and continues to evolve in an attempt to address these barriers.

Overcoming barriers of distance, time, or both necessarily requires use of some form of communications technology. We will not attempt a detailed discussion of the many specific technologies that have been used in support of distance education, partly because they are currently changing so rapidly. Instead, we will present the history of distance education in terms of the *types* of two-way communication that have been used to support it, rather than focusing on specific technologies of each type.

This framing of the evolution of distance education in terms of the types of technologies that have been used to support it will be followed by short summaries of several of the theories of distance education that have been developed to explain the distinctive characteristics of this field. We will conclude by revisiting the social justice function of distance education and suggest how this social justice function may now be eroding in developed countries.

WHAT IS DISTANCE EDUCATION?

There are many definitions of distance education, just as there are many definitions of adult education. A succinct definition that is easy for nonspecialists to understand is offered in Moore and Kearsley (2005):

> Distance education is all planned learning that normally occurs in a different place from teaching, requiring special techniques of course design and instruction, communication through various technologies, and special organizational and administrative arrangements. (p. 2)

This is our understanding of what we will be discussing in this chapter. Although this definition is quite clear by itself, we would like to highlight two of its assumptions. The first is the assumption that distance education includes teaching—that is, the intervention of an educator. Therefore, self-directed learning, an important and interesting form of learning, will not be discussed here. For a discussion of self-directed learning and distance education, see the chapter by Garrison (2003) in the first edition of the *Handbook of Distance Education* edited by Michael Grahame Moore and William G. Anderson.

The second assumption is that teaching and learning "normally" occur in different places. This proviso allows for the occasional face-to-face meetings that occur in many experiences that we wish to refer to as distance education. However, it excludes courses that are largely face-to-face but have a Web-based component as an "add-on," as is now the case with many of the face-to-face courses that occur in colleges and universities, as well as in some secondary and even primary schools.

A final point related to definitions is that the term *open learning*, which occurs in the names of many institutions specializing in distance education, is not a synonym for distance education. An institution that uses *open learning* in its name thereby states its intention to remove as many barriers to learning as possible—but not necessarily including the barrier of distance. Therefore, some open learning institutions and agencies operate entirely face-to-face; on the other hand, many distance education programs and even institutions maintain substantial barriers to learners (e.g., high fees, high entrance requirements) despite having addressed the barrier of distance.

Why Distance Education?

Distance education has a long and strong connection to adult education. It developed primarily as a way to address the geographic barriers that hinder some adults' access to learning opportunities—a subset of what Patricia Cross (1981, p. 99) described as the "situational barriers" faced by adult learners. In addition to this geography-spanning function, some forms of distance education also address the barrier of time—also one of the most significant barriers Cross describes. Although distance education for children facing geographic and other barriers does take place, most distance education has always been for the benefit of adults. Therefore, the theory and practice of distance education are very largely a subset of the theory and practice of adult education.

One aspect of distance education that is obviously more problematic than in most adult education is the issue of communication between teacher (facilitator) and learner and, in some forms of distance education, among learners. In adult education that takes place in face-to-face settings, communication among those involved can almost be taken for granted and does not often become the focus of particular attention; that is not the case when the participants are in different places, and communication among them must occur through the use of some kind of technology.

For this reason, distance education scholars have paid a great deal of attention to communication and have built models of distance education and education in general around this focus. As one example among many, Garrison (1989) contained a clear statement of the importance of two-way communication for quality distance education. Garrison and Archer (2000) expanded this statement to the fields of adult and higher education in general. In this chapter, we would like to use this concept of "education as communication" as an organizing principle to explain how and why distance education has evolved over the past two centuries.

The Generations Metaphor in Distance Education

We will sketch the history of distance education by dividing this history into three generations. Over two decades ago, Garrison (1985, modified slightly in Garrison, 1989) became the first to use the "generations of distance education" metaphor. The three generations were defined by the different modes of two-way communication that they employed. Various forms of this metaphor, some describing four or five generations, have since been put forward by other scholars. However, those later versions of the metaphor are all linked to changes in the *specific technologies* used in distance education or to ways in which different forms of distance education are *administered*, rather than to the *modes of two-way communication* that we regard as crucial in distance education. For present purposes, we will outline a compressed version of Garrison's concept similar to that published in Archer (2001), as this version very strongly stresses *types of communication*, and is, therefore, a framework that links clearly to andragogical issues.

We should add that the metaphor of historical generations of distance education could be somewhat misleading if it were taken to imply that each succeeding generation entirely supplants the previous one. That is definitely not the case. While they emerged at different times over the past two centuries, all three generations currently coexist and are used for different purposes in different places around the world.

GENERATION 1: SLOW ASYNCHRONOUS DISTANCE EDUCATION

The earliest form of distance education involved communication or correspondence between teacher and learner via the postal system. It became feasible in the 19th century with the development of efficient and reliable postal systems in a number of countries. What is often cited as the first example of correspondence education was Isaac Pitman's use of the British postal system to teach his system of doing shorthand. Probably the first instance of an entire program being delivered by correspondence originated from the Chautauqua Institute, which in 1878 created a 4-year correspondence course to supplement its summer schools for Sunday school teachers (Moore & Kearsley, 2005, p. 25). The first formal correspondence program at an American university was set up at the University of Chicago in 1892 (Moore & Kearsley, 2005, p. 26). Correspondence education also became an integral part of the North American version of university extension, which developed mainly at U.S. land grant institutions and some of the Canadian provincial universities from about the beginning of the 20th century. Correspondence education expanded rapidly among both public and private providers of adult education during the early 20th century.

A major advantage of Generation 1 distance education is the obvious one that it addresses the barrier of distance—that is, adult learners do not have to live near a campus or other provider to take part. They only have to have postal service and be able to read. A second major advantage is that this form of distance education addresses the barrier of time. Correspondence education is asynchronous—that is, the learner and facilitator

do not have to participate at any particular time of the day or week but can engage in their learning activities at times of their own choosing.

A major disadvantage of this type of distance education is its relatively high dropout rate. This is particularly problematic when the *only* communication between learner and facilitator is the rather slow exchange of assignments and feedback through the postal system, sometimes resulting in a lag of several weeks before the learner receives the tutor/facilitator's comments. This is andragogically unsound and undoubtedly reduces learner satisfaction with this mode of learning. However, completion rates can be much improved when this form of interaction is supplemented by others, such as telephone calls or occasional face-to-face meetings, perhaps involving groups of learners (Garrison, 1987).

After rapid expansion of correspondence education during the first decades of the 20th century, severe criticism of its quality led to dropping of correspondence programs at some universities, including the University of Chicago. This intense bout of criticism of distance education can be seen as the beginning of a persistent credibility problem, which distance education has never quite been able to shake off. In addition to the withdrawal from distance education by some universities, one reaction to this criticism was that the more quality conscious practitioners in the field began organizing quality control mechanisms. By 1924, the universities still practicing distance education had formalized their standards under the auspices of the National University Extension Association, now the University Continuing Education Association (Moore & Kearsley, 2005, p. 27). The for-profit schools, some of which had engaged in marketing practices that had largely provoked the adverse reaction to correspondence education, created their own organization in 1926. This organization is now known as the Distance Education and Training Council (http://www.detc.org/).

Beginning in the early decades of the 20th century, new technologies besides the postal system were added as means through which distance education could be conducted. Radio and later television broadcasting was used to transmit educational material to adults in North America and elsewhere. Although some scholars (including Moore & Kearsley, 2005, pp. 31–33) refer to this one-way provision of material as a separate generation of distance education, we consider it to be simply ancillary material added onto Generation 1 because it did not involve two-way interaction between facilitator/teacher and learner or among learners. However, it did prove to be a valuable supplement to what was essentially correspondence education.

We should also mention, in this context, what is probably the most famous distance education institution in the world, the British Open University (UKOU or BOU), founded in 1969. This is a single-mode institution—that is, one engaged only in distance education, with no primarily face-to-face programs. Some scholars identify its use of combinations of modern media (broadcast television, audio and video recordings supplied to learners, and elaborate print packages produced by teams of academic experts, instructional designers, and graphics designers) as marking the beginning of a new generation of distance education. Moore and Kearsley (2005) refer to it as such for a somewhat different reason—because it was the first institution to make extensive use of what they call the "systems approach" to distance education, including teams of specialists, each attending to a different aspect of the entire process, pioneered on a much smaller scale by Wedemeyer (1981) at the University of Wisconsin. This more attractive form of distance education pioneered by the UKOU certainly raised the profile of distance education and helped to address its credibility problem. However, the changes made by the UKOU, as compared with previous forms of correspondence education, were mainly from the point of view of the administrator and providing institution, not so much the learner. The latter still communicated with the facilitator mainly or entirely through the postal system, even though the materials provided to the learner were now much more varied and attractive. Therefore, we consider the form of distance education provided by UKOU and its many imitators around the world to be still a form of Generation 1 distance education, albeit a very sophisticated one.

GENERATION 2: SYNCHRONOUS DISTANCE EDUCATION

This form of distance education has more resemblance to regular classroom instruction than do other forms. It involves students and instructor/facilitator all participating at the same time (hence, synchronous) but from different places. The two-way communication takes place through audio, sometimes supplemented by video images transmitted via telecommunications systems of various kinds. Early experiments used only voice communication over regular telephone lines. As this form of distance education became more popular, educational institutions often purchased or leased special pieces of equipment to support it, including bridges to connect a number of telephone lines easily and reliably and conveners to connect the individual microphones used by students at a given site.

After several decades of experiments with audioconferencing, a number of educational institutions and corporations moved on to videoconferencing, which uses similar sorts of bridging equipment to transmit video signals in addition to audio ones. Many participants found that the ability to see other participants added considerably to the value of their educational experience. However, videoconferencing equipment suitable for use by at least small groups of people at each of a number of different sites tended to be very expensive.

More recently, both audioconferencing and videoconferencing have to a considerable extent migrated onto the Internet. This has been facilitated by the development of a number of proprietary products that permit individuals, from their own computers, to take part in either audioconferencing sessions with added graphics and other useful features or else videoconferencing. This has tended to make Generation 2 distance education both more convenient and less expensive. Variants of synchronous group interaction via the Internet are now often termed *web conferencing* or "webinars."

Despite all the changes in the technologies underlying Generation 2 distance education, its advantages and disadvantages have remained relatively constant. They are similar to the advantages and disadvantages of face-to-face education, which this generation of distance education resembles much more closely than do Generations 1 and 3.

The first advantage of Generation 2 distance education is that, because the two-way communication is mostly by voice and in "real time," facilitators and students have less of an adjustment to a new context than in either of the asynchronous forms of distance education.

Second, group interaction among the members of the class is possible, which is not the case in Generation 1 distance education. This has become particularly significant, given the increasing influence of constructivist theories of adult learning.

Third, this mode of distance education requires much less lead time on the part of the instructor and the institution, particularly now that reading materials can often be transmitted electronically to the students rather than having to be mailed to them. This compares very favorably to the months of lead time needed to prepare and distribute the often elaborate print packages and other materials used in Generation 1 distance education.

Student (and facilitator) satisfaction with this form of distance education is often very high, particularly as compared with Generation 1 distance education, where course completion rates are sometimes as low as 10%. The addition of telephone tutoring (i.e., an individualized form of Generation 2 distance education) to correspondence courses raised completion rates substantially. The addition of audioconferences (i.e., group-based Generation 2 distance education) further raised completion rates to the 90% to 95% range, comparable to face-to-face courses (Garrison, 1987; Poellhuber, Chomienne, & Karsenti, 2008).

Because of these advantages, Generation 2 distance education is often employed by dual mode institutions, as it can be treated as just an "add-on" to their regular face-to-face offerings, requiring relatively small adjustments on the part of instructors, students, and administrators. For similar reasons, it is often employed in the corporate sector when "just in time" training has to be delivered to a dispersed workforce.

The disadvantages of Generation 2 distance education are also related to its similarities to face-to-face instruction. The most obvious of these is that everyone involved has to be available to participate at the same time. This is often a serious barrier to participation by adult learners, for whom scheduling can be as serious a barrier as is distance from a campus.

A second disadvantage, from the point of view of the delivering institution, is that the cost structure is similar to that of face-to-face instruction in that it does not "scale" very well. That is, although the initial cost of beginning use of this form of distance education may be quite low (unless expensive room-scale video-conferencing equipment is purchased), the per-student continuing costs are usually quite high. One reason is that the student/instructor ratio has to be kept fairly low to allow for student-instructor and student-student interaction during class sessions. The administrative cost of close coordination of activities at multiple sites can also be considerable.

For these reasons, Generation 2 distance education is often used by "dual mode" institutions as an add-on to the face-to-face versions of the same courses and programs, but it is not much used by the single-mode distance education institutions such as the many open universities around the world that have been created on the model of the UKOU. The latter type of specialized institution has often been created, mostly by governments in developing countries, for the specific purpose of providing access to university education to large numbers of adult learners at relatively low cost—that is, for purposes of promoting social justice. They usually succeed in attaining this goal: Daniel (1996, p. 31) reports that these generally very large (some with more than a million students each), single-mode institutions operate with per-student costs of between 5% and 50% of those incurred by conventional universities in the same countries. But they accomplish this feat by relying almost exclusively on Generation 1 distance education techniques. Generation 2 distance education, which is truly interactive (rather than just one-way broadcasting), does not generate this sort of cost savings.

GENERATION 3: FAST ASYNCHRONOUS DISTANCE EDUCATION

Generation 3 distance education, particularly in its recent variants often referred to as "e-learning," has attracted a great deal of mostly favorable attention in the general field of education beyond the rather small group of distance education scholars. It has also attracted considerable attention in the mainstream media. This may be because, to a considerable extent, it combines the advantages of both Generation 1 and Generation 2 distance education while eliminating some of their disadvantages.

Generation 3 distance education involves electronic transmission of learners' and facilitators' contributions to a learning event to a central server, where they are stored in a systematic way so that they can be accessed easily by other participants at any time. This process is sometimes referred to as *computer conferencing,* by analogy to audioconferencing and videoconferencing. Whereas early examples of this form of distance education, involving mainframe computers in the 1970s, allowed transmission of only text messages and still images, current forms may involve transmission of voice and video files as well.

Distance educators made steadily increasing use of Generation 3 distance education throughout the 1980s and 1990s, first on mainframe computers and later on microcomputers linked via the Internet. This generated a considerable amount of research and scholarly discussion within the community of distance education specialists. However, with the development of the World Wide Web in the mid to late 1990s, making the Internet much easier to use, this form of education suddenly expanded outside the traditional distance education community and became increasingly popular in the education community generally, both in the formal system at all levels and in the private sector. It even acquired a new name—"e-learning."

The enthusiasm that surrounded e-learning from the late 1990s until recent years has certainly given another boost to the visibility and reputation of distance education. On the other hand, e-learning may to some extent have fallen victim to the overinflated expectations or "hype" with which it has been greeted, much as overinflated expectations damaged the reputation of correspondence education in the 1920s. While e-learning continues to advance in all sectors of adult education, some sober second thought is occurring about the extent to which it will transform the entire field. One indicator of this increasing realism is the inclusion, in *The E-Learning Handbook: Past Promises, Present Challenges* (Carliner & Shank, 2008), of an entire section, consisting of three chapters, with the heading "The Reality Versus the Hype of E-Learning."

THEORIES OF DISTANCE EDUCATION

We have presented the brief sketch of the history of distance education, above, as one way in which many people gain a general understanding of a field. However, other individuals find that they gain a better understanding of a field by having someone explain it conceptually—that is, by presenting a theory. Therefore, we will now sketch, again very briefly, several theories of distance education that have been developed over the past several decades by individuals knowledgeable about the field. The four theories we have selected are frequently referenced by scholars of distance education. Readers of this chapter who wish to examine these theories in more depth may wish to consult the *Handbook of Distance Education* edited by Michael Grahame Moore (2007a), where each is described in a full chapter.

Otto Peters: The Most Industrialized Form of Education

The German scholar Otto Peters was probably the first to articulate a coherent theory of distance education, beginning in the 1960s but continuing to take account of developments in the field up to the present. Peters (2007) noted that distance education is facilitated by teams of educators, sometimes quite large teams, each member of which performs a specific function that contributes to the learning of usually quite large numbers of students. This contrasts with most face-to-face instruction, in which one teacher facilitates the learning of one student or a small group of students. Distance education is, therefore, an industrial process, involving systematic planning, division of labor, automation, mass production, and economies of scale. Peters (2007, p. 58) notes that due to this industrialized nature, distance education has a close affinity with business and advances the commercialization of education. This compares to the essentially craft enterprise of face-to-face education. According to Peters, distance education is, therefore, a more modern and progressive form of education, as contrasted with face-to-face education, which has not changed a great deal since the time of Socrates.

The theory developed by Peters did not attract much attention until some of his writing was translated into English in the 1980s and widely disseminated in publications such as Sewart, Keegan, and Holmberg (1983) and Keegan (1986). By that time, educators and administrators working in the many new single-mode distance education institutions being created around the world on the model of the UKOU found that Peters's theory corresponded very closely to the context in which they were working and was very useful in clarifying their thinking.

Peters's theory was created during the era when Generation 1 distance education totally dominated the field and was not yet overlain by a significant presence of Generation 2 or Generation 3 distance education. Although Peters has recently elaborated his theory to take more account of what we term Generation 3 distance education, it has never applied very well, or at all, to Generation 2.

Holmberg's Theory of Teaching-Learning Conversations

Another theory of distance education was put forward as early as the 1960s by Börje Holmberg. This theory, as with Peters's theory, originated at a time when only Generation 1 distance education was being done on any significant scale. In this form of distance education, as contrasted with the Generation 2 form that was just beginning to make an impact, the quality of communication between the tutor and the organization delivering the education and its students is particularly problematic, given that it occurs mainly through instructional materials prepared through the industrial process described by Peters, supplemented by slow exchanges of written and printed messages via the postal system.

Holmberg (2007) now refers to his theory as "a theory of teaching-learning conversations." He states that this theory is "based on the very general observation that feelings of empathy and personal relations between learner and teacher support motivation for learning and tend to improve the results of learning" (p. 69).

Holmberg's theory has been characterized by a number of scholars (including both Moore, 2007b, and Peters, 2007) as describing a very important aspect of distance education—the desirability of ensuring that the necessarily mediated communication that occurs in distance education be sufficiently "empathetic"—but as being too narrowly focused to serve as an overall theory of distance education.

Moore's Theory of Transactional Distance

The most cited theory of distance education is the one developed by Michael Grahame Moore in his many publications from the early 1970s to the present. It is based on a concept that he eventually named *transactional distance*. This concept is seen by its developer as "a theory of the pedagogy of distance education, not a theory of its organizations" (Moore, 2007b, p. 91).

According to this theory, each educational transaction has a relative transactional distance calculated on two intersecting axes of structure and dialogue. The component of structure in a given course is a measure of how tightly the instructional designer has specified what the instructor and the student(s) are to do. "Since structure expresses the rigidity or flexibility of the course's educational objectives, teaching strategies, and evaluation methods, it describes the extent to which a course can accommodate or be responsive to each learner's individual needs and preferences" (Moore, 2007b, p. 92). The component of dialogue refers to the amount of constructive interpersonal communication between instructor and learner(s). The degree of dialogue can vary from almost continuous, as in one-to-one telephone tutoring, to almost none, as in self-instructional books or other materials.

These two components can be used to assign a relative transactional distance to each distance education course or event. More structure produces more transactional distance, while more dialogue reduces the transactional distance.

Distance education courses or events that are designed so as to have a high degree of transactional distance (i.e., high structure and low dialogue) require a high degree of learner autonomy to be effective. That does not mean that a high degree of transactional distance is necessarily a good thing. As Moore (2007b) notes, some learners are able to function with more autonomy than others (p. 95).

While Peters's theory of distance education as an industrialized process is closely linked to Generation 1 distance education, as is Holmberg's theory, Moore's theory of transactional distance can be and has been applied to all forms of distance education.

The Community of Inquiry Theory

A theory of distance education that has appeared much more recently is the "community of inquiry" theory developed in the late 1990s by a group of scholars including Terry Anderson, Liam Rourke, and this chapter's two authors. The theory has since been applied and in some cases modified by a number of other scholars and practitioners of distance education (Garrison & Arbaugh, 2007; Garrison & Archer, 2007).

Unlike the earlier theories, which were developed primarily to describe Generation 1 distance education (although Moore's theory obviously took account of Generation 2 as well), this theory is focused primarily on Generation 3, with particular attention to the fast asynchronous online discussions that take place in this form of distance education. However, its authors consider it to be a general theory of teaching and learning, which has also been applied to blended learning (Garrison & Vaughan, 2007) and to face-to-face learning contexts (Archer et al., 2008).

The name *community of inquiry* refers to the possibility of using constructivist learning techniques in Generation 3 distance education, something that is not possible in the necessarily individualized Generation 1. This theory posits three intersecting elements in the teaching and learning transaction: social presence, teaching presence, and cognitive presence. The social presence element refers to the importance and difficulty (also noted by Holmberg) of participants projecting themselves as "real people" into learning transactions that occur without benefit of the visual and voice contact, which is such an important part of face-to-face teaching/learning transactions. The cognitive presence element refers to the ability to realize the cognitive domain goals of higher education—that is, knowledge generation and critical thinking. The third element, teaching presence, describes the techniques facilitators use to ensure that the proximate goals (social presence) and ultimate goals (cognitive presence) are attained.

The transformation of distance education resulting from the introduction of online learning is a result of the convergence of constructivist ideas and the enormous potential of new and emerging technologies to bring people together. Social presence contributes to the creation and sustainability of the community. This is consistent with the practice of adult and continuing education, in that context and cooperation have historically been trusted principles as participants reconstruct experience (Lindeman, 1926/1989). At the same time, an adult education experience is a purposeful learning experience. The nature of this experience is associated with critical thinking, a hallmark of adult and higher education (Brookfield, 1987). It is grounded in collaborative constructivist principles and the importance of integrating reflection and discourse. Teaching presence in the form of design, facilitation, and direction is essential to achieve purposeful goals in a quality and timely manner.

PARTICIPATION IN DISTANCE EDUCATION IN THE 21ST CENTURY

In developed countries such as the United States, participation in online learning or e-learning has now pervaded higher education. A recent major survey carried out by the Sloan Consortium (Allen & Seaman, 2008) reports that more than 3.9 million college and university students in the United States were taking at least one online course during the Fall 2007 term—about 20% of all higher education students. This was a 12% increase over the previous year, a rate of growth that far exceeded the 1.2% growth in the overall number of students in higher education. As a point of comparison, in 2002, the first of this series of annual surveys reported only 1.6 million students taking at least one online course.

The story in underdeveloped countries is rather different. Online (Generation 3) distance education requires access to technology and infrastructure. Daniel, Kanwar, and Uvalic-Trumbic (2006) report that the proportion of people online in that year was only 4% in India, 1% in Africa, and 0.1% in Bangladesh. This situation may change rapidly if those areas are able to "leapfrog" generations of technological infrastructure and move straight into wireless digital infrastructure. However, at present, distance education in those areas, although serving many millions of learners, is necessarily dominated by Generation 1 provision.

DISTANCE EDUCATION FOR SOCIAL JUSTICE REVISITED

We began this chapter by pointing out that distance education for adults has historically had a strong social justice function in that it gave access to learning to those who would otherwise have been excluded because of geographic location or other barriers. That remains generally true throughout the underdeveloped world, where factors of distance and cost still result in many being excluded from standard face-to-face provision. It also remains true for many people in developed countries as well. However, Generation 2 and Generation 3 distance education have, in recent decades, become such attractive modes of learning that they are often taken up by people in developed countries who also have easy access to regular face-to-face provision and are not facing unusual barriers to learning.

This mainstreaming and increased respectability of what has traditionally been a very marginalized form of adult learning, sometimes seen as a "second class" form of learning to be resorted to only when absolutely necessary, is tending to turn at least the e-learning segment of distance education into just another option at the disposal of already privileged learners. It remains to be seen whether or not this development will tend to erode the traditional devotion of distance educators to issues of social justice. This is clearly not happening among those serving distant learners in the underdeveloped world, but there are signs that it may be doing so in more developed countries.

References

Allen, I. E., & Seaman, J. (2008). *Staying the course: Online education in the United States, 2008.* Needham, MA: Babson Survey Research Group (Sloan Consortium).

Archer, W. (2001). Distance education for adults. In D. Poonwassie & A. Poonwassie (Eds.), *Fundamentals of adult education: Issues and practices for lifelong learning* (pp. 286–298). Toronto, Ontario: Thompson Educational Publishing.

Archer, W., Wallace, R., Dunwoody, A., Finlayson, H., Morrison, D., & Wong, A. (2008, October). *Critical thinking by students in service learning placements: The Community of Inquiry Model extended.* Presented at the International Society for the Study of Teaching and Learning conference, Edmonton, Alberta.

Brookfield, S. D. (1987). *Developing critical thinkers.* San Francisco: Jossey-Bass.

Carliner, S., & Shank, P. (Eds.). (2008). *The e-learning handbook: Past promises, present challenges.* San Francisco: Pfeiffer.

Cross, K. P. (1981). *Adults as learners: Increasing participation and facilitating learning.* San Francisco: Jossey-Bass.

Daniel, J. (1996). *Mega-universities and knowledge media: Technology strategies for higher education.* London: Kogan Page.

Daniel, J., Kanwar, A., & Uvalic-Trumbic, S. (2006, July/August). A tectonic shift in global higher education. *Change.*

Garrison, D. R. (1985). Three generations of technological innovation in distance education. *Distance Education, 6,* 235–241.

Garrison, D. R. (1987). Researching dropout in distance education. *Distance Education, 8,* 95–101.

Garrison, D. R. (1989). *Understanding distance education: A framework for the future.* London: Routledge.

Garrison, D. R. (2003). Self-directed learning and distance education. In M. G. Moore & W. G. Anderson (Eds.), *Handbook of distance education* (pp. 161–168). New York: Lawrence Erlbaum.

Garrison, D. R., & Arbaugh, J. B. (2007). Researching the community of inquiry framework: Review, issues, and future directions. *Internet and Higher Education, 10*(3), 157–172.

Garrison, D. R., & Archer, W. (2000). *A transactional perspective on teaching and learning: A framework for adult and higher education.* Oxford, UK: Pergamon.

Garrison, D. R., & Archer, W. (2007). A theory of community of inquiry. In M. G. Moore (Ed.), *Handbook of distance education* (2nd ed., pp. 77–88). Mahwah, NJ: Lawrence Erlbaum.

Garrison, D. R., & Vaughan, N. (2007). *Blended learning in higher education.* San Francisco: Jossey-Bass.

Holmberg, B. (2007). A theory of teaching-learning conversations. In M. G. Moore (Ed.), *Handbook of distance education* (2nd ed., pp. 69–75). Mahwah, NJ: Lawrence Erlbaum.

Keegan, D. (1986). *The foundations of distance education.* London: Croom Helm.

Lindeman, E. C. (1989). *The meaning of adult education* (4th printing). Norman: The University of Oklahoma. (Original work published 1926)

Moore, M.G. (Ed.). (2007a). *Handbook of distance education* (2nd ed.). Mahwah, NJ: Lawrence Erlbaum.

Moore, M. G. (2007b). The theory of transactional distance. In M. G. Moore (Ed.), *Handbook of distance education* (2nd ed., pp. 89–105). Mahwah, NJ: Lawrence Erlbaum.

Moore, M. G., & Kearsley, G. (2005). *Distance education: A systems view* (2nd ed.). Belmont, CA: Thomson Wadsworth.

Peters, O. (2007). The most industrialized form of education. In M. G. Moore (Ed.), *Handbook of distance education* (2nd ed., pp. 57–68). Mahwah, NJ: Lawrence Erlbaum.

Poellhuber, B., Chomienne, M., & Karsenti, T. (2008). The effect of peer collaboration and collaborative learning on self-efficacy and persistence in a learner-paced continuous intake model. *Journal of Distance Education, 22*(3), 41–62.

Sewart, D., Keegan, D., & Holmberg, B. (Eds.). (1983). *Distance education: International perspectives.* Beckenham, Germany: Croom Helm.

Wedemeyer, C. (1981). *Learning at the back door: Reflections on non-traditional learning in the lifespan.* Madison: University of Wisconsin Press.

30

ADULT EDUCATION IN CULTURAL INSTITUTIONS

Libraries, Museums, Parks, and Zoos

EDWARD W. TAYLOR, MARILYN MCKINLEY PARRISH, AND RICHARD BANZ

M illions of adults can be found gathering in person and online at libraries, parks, zoos, and museums across North America every week. As cultural institutions and as sites of adult education, these locations of learning fall within an inclusive frame. "They are similarly founded and driven, and . . . inspire similar cognitive acts. Perhaps they are treasuries of a culture, but they are not passive" (Carr, 1991, p. 81). They are contested and dynamic repositories of knowledge where lifelong education of adults is inherent to their mission (Chadwick & Stannett, 2000). Rooted in the idea of free choice (e.g., Falk & Storksdieck, 2005), they are similar in many ways: social and historical development, community of practice, epistemological tensions and contestations, and challenges associated when attracting and educating adult visitors. Most significantly, these "cultural institutions—libraries, museums, historical societies, botanical gardens, archives, zoos, parks—are grounded in the idea that a culture requires places, forums, working laboratories for cognitive change" (Carr, 2000, pp. 117–118). As public places of adult learning and teaching, they yield a perspective of the field that has been historically overlooked and poorly understood (Bekerman, Burbules, & Silberman-Keller, 2006).

Previous editions of the handbook have explored these institutions narrowly, as separate entities, with a focus primarily on adult programming. Other related sites (parks, zoos, aquariums) have been overlooked, as has the complex nature of adult teaching and learning. Furthermore, there has been a lack of academic engagement between scholars of cultural institutions and adult education. In response, this chapter provides a more integrated perspective of the role of cultural institutions in society and their significance to the lifelong education of adults. These institutions are explored, not as silos, but within a shared framework as distinct sites of learning, to better understand adult education in similar locations, provide guidance for future research, and offer insight for pedagogy in more formal settings. This chapter challenges the field to simultaneously question and embrace cultural institutions as viable forms of adult education, while engaging critical educational issues.

To foreground cultural institutions as public locations of adult education, this chapter is broken into two sections. The first section illustrates the commonalities among these institutions as sites of adult education, through an exploration of the following themes: cultural heritage, cultural commons, repositories of knowledge, structures for cognitive change, digital conversations, and facilitators of change. A second section identifies current challenges facing these institutions most relevant to the field. It is important to note that literature from the field of adult education about zoos, museums, libraries, and parks is disparate, offering an opportunity for an interdisciplinary perspective in the development of this chapter.

Cultural Heritage

Libraries, museums, zoos, and parks are places associated with a community's cultural heritage—the sites, objects, and specimens that are socially valued by a particular community. These institutions were created to preserve history that is passed on to future generations, to provide public places for learning and recreation, to offer educational resources for both formal education and the promotion of lifelong learning (Carr, 1991; McCook & Jones, 2002).

Like the field of adult education, cultural institutions have chartered a dynamic course that is increasingly socially inclusive and learner focused. In the United States, they evolved from prestigious individual collections and elite private societies, experiencing monumental growth during the 19th century. As attractions for the upper class, these centers mirrored the lyceum movement in adult education (Knowles, 1977). While not necessarily viewed as places of learning for the general public, cultural institutions were also considered laboratories of learning to be used by scholars (Grinder & McCoy, 1985). With the dawn of the 20th century, attitudes toward social inclusion changed and cultural institutions began to reach out to a wider audience. Libraries emerged as centers for community learning as this growing appreciation for the adult visitor developed. "Like department stores, libraries would offer something for everyone, particularly information for specific occupational groups" (Kett, 1994, p. 220). During the same period, museums became more reliant on public support as wealthy donors decreased contributions. Much of the newly focused attention on adults mirrored the rise of the adult education movement. The American Association for Adult Education initiated several studies of social significance about these institutions for adults, including T. R. Adam's 1937 *The Civic Value of Museums*. Furthermore, the Adult Education Act

of 1966 underscored libraries' roles in adult education, fostering greater inclusiveness and dedicating resources toward basic adult literacy services and programs (Monroe, 1991).

Recently, cultural institutions have become conduits through which the mainstream narratives are challenged. For example, zoos are embracing the need to become proactive voices for a rapidly decreasing wildlife population (Conway, 2003). Similarly, the growing appreciation of cultural differences among learners has been paramount in changing how these institutions portray cultural heritage. Whereas these institutions have traditionally viewed the visiting public as homogeneous (Kavanagh, 1995), they are developing a greater appreciation for diverse patrons (O'Neill, 2002). The challenge for these institutions is engaging their cultural heritage as an educational medium while fostering greater equity within communities.

Cultural Commons

Cultural institutions such as libraries, museums, parks, and zoos serve as commons (Daloz, Daloz, Keen, & Keen, 1996) for their communities. Commons represent the desire of the community to work toward the common good, despite the fact that historically not all members of a community were welcome to participate, particularly marginalized groups. Nevertheless, commons of old were "public space[s] that anchored the American vision of democracy," the places "where diverse parts of a community could come together and hold a conversation within a shared sense of participation and responsibility" (Daloz et al., 1996, p. 2).

Similarly, cultural institutions act as "third places," which are public settings that meet the human need to connect with others in settings that are neither work nor home (Harris, 2007; Oldenburg, 1989). Third places bring "together communities of interest to peruse, discuss, debate, and celebrate the world of learning and the creative arts" (Demas & Scherer, 2002, p. 67). For example, Seattle Public Library (http://www.spl.org/) invites visitors to explore programming and resources for adult, English as a Second Language, Chinese, Russian, and Vietnamese learners. From author readings, book groups, and writing workshops to opera performances, the library is a location of cultural celebration and community connection.

Cultural institutions serve as commons in terms of collaboration within communities, which is crucial for both institutions and learners. Learning takes place in collaboration with others seeking to understand local knowledge as represented in text or artifact held in repositories. Furthermore, due to limited resources, cultural institutions seek partners for exhibits, technology, and digitization efforts and to offer greater resources to the learners they serve (Schull, 2007). For example, the Lancaster County Digitization Project (2010) is a consortium of cultural institutions initiated to share expertise and to encourage the digitization of rare historical materials unique to the area, increasing access to local history and culture for researchers of all ages.

Cultural institutions are also locations of contestation, spaces "where cultures meet, clash, and grapple with each other, often in contexts of highly asymmetrical relations of power" (Pratt, 2002, p. 4). Institutions seeking to present multiple viewpoints on certain events can face public backlash for disrupting dominant narratives of the larger America story. For example, the controversy surrounding the Smithsonian Enola Gay exhibit about the dropping of the atomic bomb on Hiroshima (Yakel, 2000) raises questions about whose story is told. Similarly, in response to community challenges over specific books on library shelves, staff across the country celebrate Banned Books week each September, educating community members about their constitutional rights "to both seek and receive information from all points of view without restriction" (Intellectual Freedom Basics, 2010, p. 1).

Learners bring their own positionality and contextually situated perspectives when interacting with other learners and with the local narratives located in the commons offered by cultural institutions. The awareness of a multiplicity of voices (Bakhtin, 1981) creates opportunity to question dominant narratives that are used to "control dangerous social disruptions" (Elmborg, 2006, p. 58). The experiences of adult learners in cultural institutions are thus shaped by hegemonic structures expressed through narratives, their relationship to those structures and stories, and the interaction with other voices comprising their shared cultural story.

Commons or third places are underappreciated and marginally explored as sites of learning and teaching by the field of adult education.

Also, the field has much to contribute in helping learners become critical consumers of cultural institutions, challenging dominant narratives.

Repositories of Knowledge

A cultural institution is a repository that focuses on collecting, preserving, and/or presenting a body of knowledge. Manuscripts, artifacts, documents, animals, plants, natural or historical landmarks, and unique objects form the heart of the cultural institution and serve as the content for all educational activities. The adult education field itself has a significant repository at Syracuse University library, The Alexander N. Charters Library Resources for Educators of Adults, which is "the largest and most comprehensive compilation of English-language materials in the field of adult and continuing education" (Syracuse University Library, 2008, p. 1).

The content of repositories is what often attracts learners to cultural institutions. For example, an individual may study the Civil War in a history class; however he or she will visit the appropriate library to find more specific content relevant to the subject; tour a museum exhibit to visually observe actual objects from the period; or walk a park or battlefield site like the one at Gettysburg, Pennsylvania, to witness firsthand where events actually occurred.

Cultural institutions are also continually looking for ways to improve programming and reach a larger audience of adult learners (Sachatello-Sawyer et al., 2002). The use of technology is one such effort and it has greatly changed the manner which institutions can store and present their content (Brantley, 2008). It has increased the use of interactive components, virtual tours, and digital exhibits and provided greater accessibility to the content. In libraries, these initiatives are similar to bookmobiles and other outreach efforts of past eras. For example, in the 1930s, the Harry Lasker Library at the Highlander Research and Education Center in Knoxville, Tennessee, sponsored a traveling library program out of the back of a station wagon, making books available to people throughout the mountains of Tennessee (Loveland, 1999).

Exhibitions are also commonly used to educate individuals about specific content. In museums and zoos, each object or specimen exhibited has its own complex presence, offering the learner the possibility of multiple interpretations

(Smith, 1989). From the standpoint of learning, the information associated with objects can be as important as the actual preservation of the objects themselves (Fahy, 1995). The exhibition is a changing or false reality—a depiction of circumstance where objects and messages from one time and culture are brought into contact with learners from another specific time and culture (Maroević, 1995). A zoo, for instance, is a human-friendly depiction of animals in their exotic habitat; in reality, the zoo is not the natural habitat for these creatures. Often, objects in museums and libraries have been altered or restored, therefore masking messages of their journey through space and time (Rothfels, 2002). In response, institutions need to routinely re-examine their mission and collections, removing objects or material no longer deemed relevant.

Furthermore, the presentation of the content (through exhibits and instruction) reflects a particular viewpoint often from those with the most authority, raising the question as to whose story is being told. Traditionally, such presentations had a strong Western European influence (Rothfels, 2002). As collection objects yield their own relevance (e.g., political, sociocultural) (Chung, 2003), the mere decision of what to include can significantly impact the meanings of any exhibition or presentation. Informed by cultural theory, Hooper-Greenhill (2007) posits that "the displays of artefacts [sic] and the visual and textual narratives produced and reproduced in museums have the power to produce meanings that work towards constructing specific social formations" (p. 41). Learners therefore need to be critical consumers of information located in cultural institutions, developing an awareness of embedded agendas.

Digital Conversations

Cultural institutions are responding to and being shaped by emerging technology. They are evolving from physical commons to digital commons, providing new avenues for learning (Seely Brown & Adler, 2008). Many institutions offer Web sites that extend teaching and learning beyond a physical location, such as Jefferson's blog at Colonial Williamsburg (2009) and iZoofari Chats at the San Diego Zoo (2008). Social networking tools allow learners opportunities to seek out alternate perspectives, contribute to collaborative discussions, and personalize the content they uncover. In addition, the open source movement, emphasizing transparency and participatory knowledge creation, has resulted in "content and the process by which it is created [made] equally visible" (Seely Brown, & Adler, 2008, p. 20). Examples of Web sites where learners can engage interactive exhibits are varied, including Second Life (Diehl, 2008), the Long Island South Shore History (2008), and "Race: Are We so Different?"(American Anthropological Association, 2008). Furthermore, both libraries and museums are increasing the use of gaming (e.g., Smithsonian American Art Museum) to fostering learning among adults (Lipschultz, 2009).

Within museums, conversations among learners constitute the "real moment of co-construction of meaning . . . dialogue [that] both mediates and contributes to learning" (Leinhardt & Knutson, 2004, p. xv). Similarly, conversation theory can be used to explore libraries' roles in promoting processes of metacognition for learners through information literacy and critical thinking skills. Libraries and other cultural institutions can serve as memory keepers, "documenting agreements and outcomes to facilitate future conversations" within the community and fostering exchange of ideas around specific digital content (Lankes, Silverstein, Nicholson, & Marshall, 2007, p. 3)

Among cultural institutions, there is a great range in scope and size of available technology, challenging smaller institutions to create common digital spaces. Nevertheless, efforts supported by the Institute of Museum and Library Services (http://www.imls.gov/) and other agencies to fund the preservation and digitization of local resources have increased the availability of online cultural heritage materials for learners nationwide. In 2009, more than 624 cultural and educational institutions and consortia, state libraries, and Native American tribes received grants ranging from $1,400 to nearly $1 million for cultural heritage projects from the Institute for Museum and Library Services.

As cultural institutions offer opportunities for adult learners to create knowledge around unique content online, they facilitate sharing of this knowledge with broader audiences. Technology challenges facing cultural institutions and learners include access, funding, authenticity, and privacy. Also, despite the marked increase in digital conversations, learners continue to seek collaborative learning within social spaces in physical settings (Fried-Foster & Gibbons, 2007).

Structures for Cognitive Change

Cultural institutions such as zoos, libraries, and museums are not passive repositories, they are organized environments of knowledge with intentional structures designed to foster learning (Carr, 1991). Typically, adult education has attempted to make sense of these nonformal institutions through a comparison to education in more formal institutions (e.g., Livingstone, 2006; Schugurensky, 2000). For example, learning outcomes in formal institutions are often standardized, defined in advance, and revisited throughout the course. On the other hand "many visitors to museums, and users of archives and libraries . . . have their own agendas for learning (some of which are very unfocused and undeveloped), and they are not required to disclose these in advance" (Hooper-Greenhill, 2007, p. 32). Furthermore, in concert with their agenda (e.g., research, edutainment), visitors to cultural institutions also make their own assessment of their learning experience, which further complicates the goal of measuring outcomes. Assessment and other challenges highlight the complexities of learning and teaching in cultural institutions and bring meaning to nonformal education.

Concepts more specifically associated with learning in these institutions include informal learning, self-directed learning, and free-choice learning. Informal learning is the broader term often used to explain incidental unintentional learning both in and outside cultural institutions. Similarly, self-directed learning is considered more goal-directed and is often overlooked by cultural institutions to explain learning. An alternate concept to self-directed learning, which emerged from museum education, is "free choice," which refers to learning when individuals have significant control over their learning (Banz, 2008). It is "non-sequential, self-paced, and voluntary . . . that is primarily driven by intrinsic needs and interests of the learner" (Falk, 2005, p. 272). Directly related to the voluntary nature of cultural institutions is the role of the affective, where learners often have a heightened sense of curiosity and attention to newness. For example, in a tour of a park

it is the selective attention and emotive valence of learners that determines if they will view particular panorama or pay mind to the guide's tour. It is the affective domain that advantages learning in nonformal settings (Taylor, 2008).

Theoretically framed research concerning adult learning in cultural institutions is limited (Dudzinska-Przesmitzki & Grenier, 2008). The predominant focus has been on visitor outcomes and perceptions of exhibits (e.g., Falk & Storksdieck, 2005; Sachatello-Sawyer et al., 2002). Furthermore, research tends to be site specific, focusing on a particular zoo, park, or library as opposed to studies that transcend location and type. Despite these shortcomings, over the last decade, constructivism (e.g., Hein, 1998; Roy & Novotny, 2000) has emerged as the most relevant theory for making sense of learning in cultural institutions. For example, the reference desk in the library has been referred to as the "most natural constructivist teaching environment . . . a staging area from which to launch into the multivoiced, multigenred array of resources that can be used to create knowledge" (Elmborg, 2002, p. 463). Offering further insight into this constructivist approach is the contextual model of learning, which sees the inquiry process as a dialogue between the individual and the environment of the institution (Brody, Tomkiewicz, & Graves, 2002). More specifically, learning is seen as "interactions between an individuals' *personal* [motivation, prior experience], *sociocultural* [relationships with others], and *physical* [space, lighting, sound, color, etc.] context over time" (Falk & Storksdieck, 2005, p. 745). Unfortunately, this model overlooks "specificities of learning in relation to class, gender or ethnicity" (Hooper-Greenhill, 2007, p. 40) and does not consider the contested nature of repository-based narratives.

Historically, a critical perspective of learning has received scant attention in cultural institutions. A critical lens recognizes that knowledge within these sites of learning is not just an individual construct, but also an ideological tool, "that social processes are not equal . . . and that [for example] museum education is not ahistorical, apolitical . . . it is substantially affected . . . by the wider political, economic and educational policy agendas" (Grek, 2007, p. 179). For example, Borg, Cauchi, and Mayo (2006) rejected the notion of museums as neutral sites of historical display, exploring how the Malta Maritime

Museum constructed its narrative in relationship to the local community. They found that situations of limited resources and trained personnel resulted in what Bourdieu refers to as "cultural arbitrary." This is where legitimacy is given "to certain forms of knowledge and representations at the expense of others rendering the former . . . 'official knowledge'" (p. 83). Much more research is needed to better understand what promotes cognitive change in cultural institutions and how it informs learning and teaching in both informal and formal settings.

Facilitators of Change

Facilitators of cognitive change working in cultural institutions are quite diverse when compared to more formal institutions. They include the educator (e.g., librarian, curator, docent, naturalist, zoo keeper), the content (exhibits, books, animals), and for some institutions the natural setting itself. It is the interrelationship between these different facilitators that make teaching within cultural institutions challenging and complex. Research concerning the educator is limited. However, it is apparent, that a similar community of practice exists across varied institutions (e.g., museums, parks) reflected in shared beliefs about teaching and learning (Taylor, 2006). For example, a national survey of museum docents revealed that they see themselves as facilitators of learning who encourage hands-on participation, convey a sense of fun, are knowledgeable about subject matter, and seek to actively engage participants in learning (Sachatello-Sawyer et al., 2002). Similarly, librarians are seeing a shift from the traditional provision of reference services to a more instruction-centered role (Elmborg, 2006).

In addition to shared conceptions of teaching, there are similar contextual factors influential in shaping practice within these institutions; they include the novel setting, voluntary participation, heterogeneity of learners (e.g., age, class, social background), and the limited time to engage visitors. In response to these factors, educators often place a priority on establishing a rapport with visitors, exploring visitors' interest, emphasizing a content-driven teaching couched within a narrative format, encouraging dialogue, and providing a pleasurable experience (Taylor, 2006; Taylor & Neill, 2008).

The setting and constructed exhibits within the museum or historical society serve as additional elements in facilitating cognitive change. Such exhibits may include both the static and interactive displays found in museums and science centers, as well as wildlife displays in zoos and arboretums (Falk, Scott, Dierking, Rennie, & Jones, 2004; Lindemann-Matthies & Kamer, 2005). Exhibits transmit information and generate meaning mediated through the visitors' experiences, particularly in settings where the exhibit is free of direct engagement, allowing for shared authority and the creation of cultural capital (Rowe, 2002). This is particularly the case in museums and parks where there are opportunities to learn *in situ* (the original or a close fabrication of the setting), which evokes an authentic learning experience. In these settings, the context often speaks for itself, mediated by the visitor placing the nonformal educator in a secondary role (Courtney, 1995; Taylor, 2008).

CURRENT CHALLENGES

Several challenges for the study of adult education in cultural institutions emerge from this chapter. Three issues in particular require greater attention by scholars in the field: the continuing need to highlight diversity and equity (e.g., competing and marginalized narratives, reaching out to diverse audiences), the need for collaborative interdisciplinary conversations between scholars of the field of adult education and cultural institutions, and the need to recognize these institutions as viable sites for fostering social justice and change

The first challenge for the field is to develop a better understanding of how to critically engage the ordinary everyday narratives, texts, landscapes, and objects located in cultural institutions. Questions of whose stories are told are answered against a backdrop of competing interests of community members, donors, volunteers, and professional staff. Are members of marginalized racial and ethnic groups represented in the development of stories? Who makes the decisions about selection and presentation of content for exhibits? How are narratives constructed so they capture with integrity of ever shifting stories of a community?

Adult educators can play a role in assisting learners in common spaces as they engage in critical analysis of cultural narratives. More specifically, they can create intentional communities of practice (Seely Brown & Adler, 2008, p. 20) that foster transparency in the creation of local knowledge and develop new technology that helps facilitate the engagement among diverse learners. As learners are invited into conversations with cultural institutions, it increases the likelihood that new understandings about the unique intellectual and cultural heritage embedded in communities will emerge. Alongside the educator and the learner, the task of the cultural institution is to facilitate the development of local knowledge that represents the diversity of the community in terms of race, gender, class, and sexual orientation.

A second challenge is fostering interdisciplinary conversations between scholars in cultural institutions and adult education. Significant gaps exist between the disciplines due to a lack of dialogue; each has developed its own discourse and overlooked important research contributions, such as the isolation of "free choice learning" explored within museums versus self-directed learning explored within informal settings (Banz, 2008). Fortunately, dialogue is occurring among cultural institutions. For example, the Institute of Museum and Library Services has established a library-museum collaboration program seeking to understand how these two cultural institutions can improve services to the public through mutual cooperation (McCook & Jones, 2002). What is missing is active engagement by the field of adult education with cultural institutions. One avenue to address this concern would be to invite scholars of cultural institutions and adult education to give joint presentations at national conferences in both fields. Better understanding of teaching and learning within cultural institutions could lead to more effective practices for both formal and informal settings, in turn better addressing the needs of lifelong learning within communities.

A third challenge is the need for the field of adult education to recognize cultural institutions as viable sites for fostering social justice and change. Parks, libraries, museums, and zoos represent public spaces where adults come together to question and critique the ideologies on display. Furthermore, some of these institutions see themselves primarily as instruments of social change. For example, the Caracas Declaration (mission of museums in Latin America) evolved from a UNESCO initiative where museums were seen as having potential for fostering development by

representing the needs of the disenfranchised. One such endeavor is the "Pinacoteca do Estdo de São Paulo" art museum, which "set up the Social-Cultural Inclusion Programme." Its aim is to increase accessibility for certain groups that suffer exclusion, such as sex workers, the homeless and young children in risk situations" (Cabral, 2005, p. 12).

The recognition of cultural institutions as vehicles for social change is not an isolated event; it is indicative of the historical evolution of these institutions. As sites of competing narratives, they provide an untapped resource for better understanding how to foster social change outside formal institutions. Zoos, for example, have become highly contested places, where there is growing emphasis on environmental activism, educating the public about biological diversity and sustainability while at the same time needing to remain a place for leisure for adults and children. Scholars reflect: "Is the zoo a restorative landscape of leisure and passive contact with nature or is it a tangible expression of, and agent for, espousing cultural values such as conservation, environmental protection and sustainability?" (Hallman & Benbow, 2006, p. 263). By exploring cultural institutions as sites of social change, the field of adult education can both contribute to and learn from new approaches to engaging adults in fostering a more equitable society.

CONCLUSION

In reflecting back, it is apparent that the field of adult education can learn from and contribute significantly to the study of cultural institutions. As sites of learning, they are ubiquitous in the cultural landscape, easily accessible and decentralized; they attract a highly motivated and diverse group of adult learners. They are ideal sites for in-depth exploration of key constructs central to the field, such as informal and self-directed learning, and offer a significant venue for better understanding of teaching and learning in nonformal settings. They far surpass formal institutions of learning in number and variety, challenging the field to take a more active role in better understanding how these sites are structures of cognitive change and the role adult educators can play in facilitating change, both on personal and social level. Zoos, museums, libraries, and parks are cultural landscapes of learning shaped by a shared purpose of providing a storehouse of a community's cultural heritage within a public space. It is these public spaces, the commons, as sites of collaboration and contestation, that create a community of practice of teaching and learning unique

to these institutions. Bringing this community of practice to life through research provides a venue for adult education as a field of study, both to broaden its reach and give it a greater purpose, strengthening its professional identity as it explores learning beyond the confines of the classroom.

REFERENCES

Adam, T. R. (1937). *The civic value of museums.* New York: American Association for Adult Education.

American Anthropological Association. (2008). *Race: Are we so different?* Retrieved July 13, 2008, from http://www.understandingrace.org/home.html

Bakhtin, M. (1981). *The dialogic imagination: Four essays.* Austin: University of Texas.

Banz, R. (2008). Self-directed learning: Implications for museums, *Journal of Museum Education, 33*(1), 43–54.

Bekerman ,Z., Burbules, N. C., & Silberman-Keller, D. (2006). Introduction. In Z. Bekerman, N. C. Burbles, & D. Silberman-Keller (Eds.). *Learning in places* (pp. 1–8). New York: Peter Lang.

Borg, C., Cauchi, B., & Mayo, P. (2006). Museum education as cultural contestation. In C. Borg & P. Mayo (Eds.). *Learning and social difference* (pp. 75–89). London: Paradigm.

Brantley, P. (2008). Architectures for collaboration: Roles and expectations for digital libraries. *Educause Review, 43*(2), 31–38.

Brody, M., Tomkiewicz, W., & Graves, J. (2002). Park visitors' understandings, values, and beliefs related to their experience at Midway Geyser Basin, Yellowstone National Park, USA. *International Journal of Science Education, 24*(11), 1119–1141.

Cabral, M. (2005). Democratisation and access to cultural heritage in Brazil. In J. Thinesse-Demel (Ed.), *Museums, libraries, and cultural heritage.* Report on the Workshop held at CONFINTEA V Mid-term Review Conference, Bangkok, Thailand: UNESCO.

Carr, D. (1991). Minds in the museums and libraries: The cognitive management of cultural institutions. *Teachers College Record, 93*(1), 6–25.

Carr, D. (2000). In the contexts of the possible: Libraries and museums as incendiary cultural institutions. *RBM: A journal of rare books, manuscripts, and cultural heritage, 1*(2), 117–134.

Chadwick, A., & Stannett, A. (Eds.) (2000). *Museums and the education of adults.* Leicester, UK: NIACE.

Chung, S. K. (2003). The challenge of presenting cultural artifacts in a museum setting. [Electronic Version]. *Art Education, 56*(1), 13–18.

Colonial Williamsburg. (2009). Jefferson's blog. Retrieved January 18, 2009 from http://jeffersonblog.history.org/

Conway, W. (2003). The role of zoos in the 21st century. *International Zoo Yearbook, 38,* 7–13.

Courtney, S. (1995). *The sixth floor: Museum experiences as learning environments.* (ERIC Document Reproduction Service No. ED413517)

Daloz, L. P., Daloz, S., Keen, C. H., & Keen, J. P. (1996). *Common fire: Lives of commitment in a complex world.* Boston: Beacon Press.

Demas, S., & Scherer J.A. (2002). Esprit de Place: Maintaining and designing library buildings to provide transcendent spaces. *American Libraries, 33*(4), 65–68.

Diehl, W. C. (2008). Formal and informal learning experiences in Second Life: An overview. *Proceedings of the 49th Annual Adult Education Research Conference,* pp. 90–95. St. Louis, MO: University of St. Louis.

Dudzinska-Przesmitzki, D., & Grenier, R. (2008). Nonformal and informal adult learning in museums: A literature review. *Journal of Museum Education, 33*(1), 9–22.

Elmborg, J. (2002). Teaching at the desk: Toward a reference pedagogy. *Libraries and the Academy, 2*(3), 455–464.

Elmborg, J. (2006). Libraries in the contact zone: On the creation of educational space. *Reference & User Services Quarterly, 46*(1), 56–64.

Fahy, A. (1995). New technologies for museum education. In E. Hooper-Greenhill (Ed.), *Museum, media, message* (pp. 82–96). London: Routledge.

Falk, J. H. (2005). Free-choice environmental learning: Framing the discussion. *Environmental Education Research, 11*(3), 265–280.

Falk, J. H., & Storksdieck, M. (2005). Using the contextual model of learning to understand visitor learning from a science center exhibition. *Science Learning in Everyday Life.* Published online 18 July 2005 in Wiley InterScience (www.interscience.wiley.com).

Falk, J. H., Scott, C., Dierking, L., Rennie, L., & Jones, M. C. (2004). Interactives and visitor learning. *Curator, 47*(2), 171–198.

Fried-Foster, N., & Gibbons, S. (2007). *Studying students: The undergraduate research project at the University of Rochester.* Chicago: Association of College and Research Libraries. Retrieved from http://tinyurl.com/f63dj

Grek, S. (2007). Adult education, museums, and critique. In C. Borg & P. Mayo (Eds.). *Learning and social difference* (pp. 178–191). London: Paradigm.

Grinder, A. L., & McCoy, E. S. (1985). *The good guide: A sourcebook for interpreters, docents, and tour guides.* Scottsdale, AZ: Ironwood Press.

Harris, C. (2007). Libraries with lattes: The new third place. *Aplis 20*(4), 145–152.

Hallman, B. C., & Benbow, M. (2006). Cultural human landscapes examples. *The Canadian Geographer, 50*(2), 256–264.

Hein, G. E. (1998). *Learning in the museum.* New York: Routledge.

Hooper-Greenhill, E. (2007). *Museums and education: Purpose, pedagogy, performance.* New York: Routledge.

Intellectual Freedom Basics. (2010). *Intellectual freedom and censorship Q & A.* Retrieved January 6, 2010, from http://www.ala.org/ala/aboutala/offices/oif/basics/ifcensorshipqanda.cfm, P. 1

Kavanagh, G. (1995). Museums in partnership. In E. Hooper-Greenhill (Ed.), *Museum, media, message* (pp. 124–134). London: Routledge.

Kett, J. F. (1994). *The pursuit of knowledge under difficulties.* Stanford, CA: Stanford University Press.

Knowles, M. (1977). *A history of the adult education movement in the United States* (Rev. ed). Malabar, FL: Krieger. (Original work published in 1962 as *The adult education movement in the United States*)

Lancaster County Digitization Project. (2010). Retrieved February 13, 2010 from: http://lcdp.wetpaint.com

Lankes, R. D., Silverstein, J., Nicholson, S., & Marshall, T. (2007). *Participatory networks: The library as conversation.* Information Institute of Syracuse, Syracuse, NY: Syracuse University School of Information Studies. Retrieved January 5, 2010 from: http://ptbed.org/ readings.php

Leinhardt, G., & Knutson, K. (2004). *Listening in on museum conversations.* Walnut Creek, CA: AltaMira Press.

Lindemann-Matthies, P., & Kamer, T. (2005). The influence of an interactive educational approach on visitors learning in a Swiss Zoo. *Science Learning in Everyday Life, 2*(90), 296–315.

Lipschultz, D. (2009). Gaming @ your library. *American Libraries, 40*(1 & 2), 40–43.

Livingstone, D. W. (2006). Informal learning: Conceptual distinctions and preliminary findings. In Z. Bekerman, N. C. Burbles, & D. Silberman-Keller (Eds.). *Learning in places* (pp. 203–228). New York: Peter Lang.

Long Island South Shore History. (2008). Retrieved July 13, 2008, from http://www.dowling.edu/wikis/pmwiki.php/LISSHistory/LISSHistory

Loveland, G. (1999). Educating for social justice: The Harry Lasker library at Highlander. *Journal of Appalachian Studies, 5*(2), 181–195.

Maroević, I. (1995). The museum message: Between the document and the information. In E. Hooper-Greenhill (Ed.), *Museum, media, message* (pp. 24–36). London: Routledge.

McCook, K., & Jones, M. (2002). Cultural heritage institutions and community building. *Reference and User Services Quarterly, 41*(4), 326–329.

Monroe, M. E. (1991). Beginnings: Public libraries and adult education from 1900 to 1966. In M. E. Monroe & K. M. Heim (Eds.), *Partners for lifelong learning: Public libraries and adult education* (pp. 3–20). (ERIC Document Reproduction Service No. ED341393)

Oldenburg, R. (1989). *The great good place: Cafes, coffee shops, bookstores, bars, salons, and other hangouts at the heart of a community.* Cambridge, MA: DaCapo Press.

O'Neill, M. (2002). The good enough visitor. In R. Sandell (Ed.), *Museums, society, inequality* (pp. 24–40). London: Routledge.

Pratt, M. L. (2002). Arts of the contact zone. In J. M. Wolff (Ed.), *Professing in the contact zone* (pp. 1–18). Urbana, IL: NCTE.

Rothfels, N. (2002). *Savages and beasts: The birth of the modern zoo.* Baltimore: The Johns Hopkins University Press.

Rowe, S. (2002). The role of objects in active, distributed meaning-making. In S. G. Paris (Ed.), *Perspectives on object-centered learning in museums* (pp. 19–36). Mahwah, NJ: Lawrence Erlbaum.

Roy, L., & Novotny, E. (2000). How do we learn? Contributions of learning theory to reference service and library instruction. In K. Sarkodie-Mensah (Ed.), *Reference services for the adult learner: Challenging issues for the traditional and technological era* (pp. 129–140). New York: Haworth Press.

Sachatello-Sawyer, B., Fellenz, R. A., Burton, H., Gittings-Carlson, L., Lewis-Mahony, J., & Woolbaugh, W. (2002). *Adult museum programs: Designing meaningful experiences.* Walnut Creek, CA: Alta Mira Press.

San Diego Zoo. (2008). iZoofari Chats. Retrieved June 30, 2008, from http://www.sandiegozoo.org/wordpress2/category/izoofari-chats/

Schugurensky, D. (2000). *The forms of informal learning: Towards a conceptualization of the field* (NALL Working Paper 19). Retrieved April 12, 2008, from http://www.oise.utoronto.ca/depts/sese/csew/nall/res/19formsofinformal.htm

Schull, D. D. (2007). *Libraries and place-making: Libraries are the new commons for the 21st century.* Retrieved July 3, 2008, from: http://www.pps.org/info/newsletter/april2007/library_placemaking

Seely Brown, J., & Adler, R. P. (2008). Minds on fire: Open education, the long tail and learning 2.0. *Educause, 43*(1), 17–32.

Smith, C. S. (1989). Museums, artifacts, and meanings. In P. Vergo (Ed.), *The new museology* (pp. 6–21). London: Reaktion Books.

Smithsonian American Art Museum. *Ghost of a chance.* Retrieved February 13, 2010, from: http://www.americanart.si.edu/calendar/activities/ghosts/

Syracuse University Library, The Alexander N. Charters Library of Resources of Educators for Adults Retrieved July 10, 2008, from: http://library.syr.edu/digital/guides/a/AlexanderNCharters/flyer/chartersflyer.htm

Taylor, E. W. (2006). Nonformal education: Practitioner's perspective. *Adult Education Quarterly, 56,* 291–307.

Taylor, E. W. (2008). Teaching and emotions in a nonformal educational setting. In J. Dirkx (Ed.), *Adult learning and the emotional self* (pp. 79–87). New Directions in Adult and Continuing Education, No. 120. San Francisco: Jossey-Bass.

Taylor, E. W., & Neill, A. (2008). Museum education: Nonformal adult educator's perspective. *The Journal of Museum Education, 33*(1), 23–32.

Yakel, E. (2000). Museums, management, media, memory: Lessons from the Enola Gay Exhibition. *Libraries & Culture 35*(2), 278–310.

PART V

CENTRALITY OF SOCIAL JUSTICE

31

SOCIAL JUSTICE IN ADULT AND CONTINUING EDUCATION

Laboring in the Fields of Reality and Hope

JUANITA JOHNSON-BAILEY,
LISA M. BAUMGARTNER, AND TUERE A. BOWLES

There are deep and rich social justice roots in adult education. These foundational origins of social justice can be traced to the establishment of adult education as a field of study in the early 1920s. A primary mission of this new educational area was to provide an education that would enhance lives, affording adults an opportunity for instruction that would license them to fully participate in a capitalistic democracy (Cunningham, 1988, 1996). Noted adult educator Alain Locke (1947, 1948) directly challenged adult education to equalize the wrongs of society by providing an education to an adult populace that did not receive the basics through traditional education. This equality-based form of distributive and procedural justice says that resources must be allocated equally, and procedures for assigning outcomes must be fair. Equality is concerned with the same treatment in dealings, quantities, or values (Miller, 1999). Because a broad definition of social justice rests on the premise of the equitable distribution of rights, responsibilities, and assets (Vera & Speight, 2003), the embodiment of social justice in the field of adult education seems implicit, and this explains why social justice is embedded in the current writings by many adult education scholars.

However, a close examination of the family pedigree shows that the yield harvested from the field's social justice tree may in fact be heavier with the fruit of critique and theoretical abstraction than with activism. After all, education was established to transmit cultural messages and to maintain the status quo, and in the capitalistic societies of North America, this purpose translates into educative efforts that mirror the hierarchical systems of Western society, which privilege some people and deny others (Johnson-Bailey & Cervero, 2000; Nesbit, 2006). Within adult education, social justice seems confined to either theoretical discussions of social justice or descriptions of adult education programs that use social justice as one of their guiding principles. Theorists classify this division as recognition and redistribution (Fraser & Honneth, 2004; Huttunen, 2007). The majority of the writings on social justice by adult educators fit into the first grouping, with the assumption being that if learners, policy experts, and teachers understand society's inequities, they will use their personal and collective agency to eliminate wrongs. A smaller body of the literature describes programs and classroom environments where efforts are being made to put social justice into practice, providing examples of and encouraging activism.

Subsequently, let us also clarify that there are two broad perspectives across all of the social justice literature. One prominent social justice perspective declares that there is a right and moral position that should direct our society. The second category adds an activist component, addressing the differences between groups and highlighting how power is exercised in favor of one group to the detriment of others. This equity-based perspective refers to fairness, which may require different treatment or special measures for some people or groups. Hence, each group might not have the same outcome.

Despite the adult education legacy of initiatives like the Highlander Folk School and the Freedom Schools, the field has fallen short of its stated goals of leveling the playing field for all adults through educational opportunities. Most educational programs for adults in the United States, Europe, Australia, Japan, and other heavily industrialized settings involve continuing education and human resource development programs in business and industry (Allman, 2001; Levin, 2001; Luke, 2001; Singh, 2004).

As a field, we consider our definition of social justice is reflected in how we write, research, and teach. A key idea in the social justice literature is the belief that the purpose of education is to develop democratic citizens who possess a strong sense of agency, able to ask critical questions, derive their own conclusions, and engage in participatory processes to the betterment of society. How can we teach for change when for the most part, the adult education writings, especially work from North America and Europe, have encompassed an implicit cultural hegemony? Regardless of intentions, the adult education literature centers the dominant White majority as the norm, empowering this one group while disempowering other groups in the United States. As such, in teaching for social justice, it is inadequate to simply point out injustices; rather, educators must invite the learners to discuss and explore these injustices using their own perspectives and experiences so that they may fully understand them and enact change (Ayers, Hunt, & Quinn, 1998; Goodman, 2001). Furthermore, adult educators must seek and include disparate and marginalized voices, including the stories, contributions, and histories of the "others" who often are omitted from our texts. Thus, teaching

for social justice, as Ayers aptly puts it, "arouses [learners], engages them in a quest to identify obstacles to their full humanity, to their freedom, and then to drive, to move against those obstacles" (Ayers, 1998, p. xvii).

In this chapter, we unearth the lived and the longed-for social justice high ground within adult education. First, we discuss adult educators' personal commitments to social justice. Next, we explore the philosophical underpinning to social justice initiatives, including both the progressive and radical philosophies, before moving on to examine social justice perspectives and their application to race, class, gender, and sexual orientation. In attempting to provide a view beyond the academic and theoretical domains of social justice, we next include information on international and domestic social justice movements and programs. The chapter concludes with a look toward the future of social justice in adult education.

PERSONAL AND DISCIPLINE-INSPIRED COMMITMENTS TO SOCIAL JUSTICE

Since the 2000 edition of the *Handbook of Adult and Continuing Education,* there has been a yearning for social justice among many adult educators as evidenced by the titles of New Directions (e.g., *Embracing and Enhancing the Margins of Adult Education, Class Concerns, Teaching for Change, Promoting Critical Practice in Adult Education, Environmental Adult Education, Learning and the Sociocultural Contexts*) and the plethora of social justice articles in *Adult Education Quarterly* and the *International Journal of Lifelong Education.* This desire is openly manifested in the writings of adult educators, who describe how they attempt to make a difference in their pedagogical practices and through their research (e.g., Alfred, 2003; Grace & Wells, 2007; Guy, 1999; Sheared & Sissel, 2001). To varying degrees, most adult educators embrace social justice principles and as a group have incorporated social justice tenets into the platforms of the Adult Education Research Conference (AERC), the American Association for Adult and Continuing Education (AAACE), and the Standing Conference on University Teaching and Research in the Education of Adults (SCUTREA).

Regardless of our particular commitments in adult education, we work in multiple contexts (formal, nonformal, informal) and serve a host of populations/audiences (many who are disenfranchised); our jobs tend to be in the public and nonprofit sectors and mostly work on fostering change at the individual, organizational, and societal levels.

To demonstrate further that a yearning for social justice among adult educators defines our professional identity, we need only to examine a broad swath of what we do in practice to unearth our social justice dispositions and commitments. As Basic Skills/General Education Development (GED)/English as a Second Language (ESL) teachers, literacy volunteers, community organizers, and nonprofit leaders, adult educators work overtime for little or no compensation and often personally sponsor programmatic events that other state/federal agencies or entities no longer support. We find ways or make ways when paths do not exist. We show up early and stay late until everyone has been helped, the issue resolved, or the policy implemented. We do all of this with a scarcity of resources, limited time, and slight regard for balancing our life and work commitments because we yearn to make a difference in the lives of individuals and be a benefit to society.

COMMITMENTS TO SOCIAL JUSTICE: THE PROGRESSIVE PHILOSOPHY

Social justice both critiques and redresses sources of societal oppression that have disadvantaged social groups according to race, class, gender, sexual orientation, ability, and so forth. Consequently, the concepts of social justice intentionally align with the progressive and radical strands of adult education.

Early 20th-century, reform-minded thinkers and writers, such as Lindeman (1926/1989) and Dewey (1938), contributed to a philosophical understanding of education as an instrument for social change. Lindeman's text (which was originally published in 1926), *The Meaning of Adult Education* (1989), portrayed an emerging vision of adult education as a field of practice and study that was tied to the progressive philosophy that discussed social change. A man of his times, Lindeman was influenced by progressivism's tenets (Long, 1989). These principles included (a) education extends beyond schooling to socialization, (b) education is lifelong, (c) education should include the practical and pragmatic, (d) experience is central to the learning that occurs

in the educative process, and (e) learning should be student centered (Lindeman, 1926/1989).

Lindeman, like John Dewey, believed there was a middle ground between preserving the status quo and focusing solely on personal uniqueness and individuality (Heaney, 1996). This middle ground, lauded by progressive educational reconstructionists George Counts and Theodore Brameld, included the idea that "individual growth is possible only with a concomitant modification and development of society and the purpose of adult education is both to announce and transform the world (Heaney, 1996, pp. 9–10). Lindeman noted that power over others was to be avoided (1926/1989) and that "all successful adult education groups sooner or later become social action groups" (Lindeman, 1945, p. 12).

COMMITMENTS TO SOCIAL JUSTICE: THE RADICAL PHILOSOPHY AND CRITICAL SOCIAL THEORY

Most progressives wanted to reform society by working within established social structures. Brazilian literacy educator Paulo Freire (2000), who espoused a more radical philosophy, sought to make profound changes in society. Radicalism arises from the traditions of anarchism, which champions personal autonomy and eschews government-sponsored educational systems (Suissa, 2001). A second influence on the radical philosophy is the Marxist/socialist tradition, which believes socialist doctrine will produce free learners (Suissa, 2001).

Freire (2000) espoused education should be about political action and that the social context influences individuals' ideas and thinking. He also believed that every person is a teacher and learner and that problem-posing education, where the student and teacher learn and teach each other through dialogue, was preferable, moving them toward a critical consciousness by means of conscientization (Freire, 1985).

In studying the notable radical adult educator-activists, Freire (2000), Horton (Horton & Freire, 1990), and Illich (1973), we see how social justice adult education historically has manifested itself via community and civic engagement programs. For specific examples, we note programs established or stewarded by educator-activists, such as Jane Addams at Hull House; the modern civil rights era; the feminist agendas; the peace movement; environmentalism; and the struggles for lesbian, gay, bisexual, transgendered, and disability rights (Finger, 1989; Holford, 1995; Spencer, 1995; Welton, 1993).

Like radical theory, critical social theory examines "structural conditions and human agency" (Leonardo, 2004, p. 11). Critical social theory as applied to adult education is concerned with issues of power, knowledge, cultural reproduction, and hegemony in education and is influenced by critical theorists such as Habermas and Horkheimer (Leonardo, 2004). Through critique, a more just and free society will emerge (Collins, 1998). Critical social theory is evident in the works of Collins (1998), Griffin (1983), and Welton (1993).

SOCIAL JUSTICE PERSPECTIVES AND THE SOCIAL LOCATIONS OF RACE, GENDER, CLASS, AND SEXUAL ORIENTATION

The contemporary equity-based writings use this approach to address all societal hierarchies constructed to serve one group while disenfranchising another. For example, scholars of critical race theory, such as Derrick Bell, explore how the systems and structures of White supremacy, which subordinate people of color, have been created and are maintained in U.S. society as well as how to change the relationship between the law and racial power (Bell, 1992).

Race—An important part of fostering diversity and multiculturalism in adult education means discussing the elements of power and privilege accorded along the postionalities of race and ethnicity and the effects of this privilege on those from such marginalized postionalities. Unfortunately, conversation on race and multiculturalism in adult education has been confined to a conversation on Black and White, with only a recently developing examination of Latino/as.

In the last decade, another important aspect of discussing race and ethnicity has been an examination of how Whites construct their racial identity and how the social construction of Whiteness affects educational systems. When the discourse on Whiteness or privilege occurs in the adult education literature, it usually involves the following: recognition of privilege and of underprivilege (Barlas, 1997; Colin & Preciphs, 1991), an examination of classroom practices (Johnson-Bailey & Cervero, 1998; Shore, 2000), examples of curricula or texts that reproduce privilege (Colin & Preciphs, 1991), and various anecdotal examples of how privilege operates in society (Johnson-Bailey & Cervero, 2008). Although the multicultural literature and critical race literature acknowledge that the power lies in the hands of a dominant White majority, writings in these areas often refrain from saying that the concentration of power is deliberate and that the intent is to maintain the status quo. It is the proponents who produce the social justice literature on race that encourage and ask for a renegotiation of the balance of power.

Gender—The focus on social justice in education has more often than not focused on either race or its tandem compatriot, Whiteness, while the most universal of oppressions, gender, has remained largely unexamined. Only the UNESCO proclamation has major statements or a deliberative focus on gender oppression as the most major of human rights issues. UNESCO places women's education in the context of a larger adult education dialogue, framing it in terms of literacy, poverty, fundamental schooling, economic equity, and human rights. This declaration, entitled the Convention on the Elimination of All Forms of Discrimination Against Women (CEDAW, 1981), was proposed in 1979 and ratified in 1981 and includes a preamble or a bill of rights for women and 30 articles defining and describing inequities against women.

The adult education field must move its discussion of gender past how gender functions in classrooms and our praxis to recognizing the enormity of global gender oppression. Such an expanded focus seems compulsory, given that the expressed mission of the field of adult education is the democratization of the citizenry, and women are more than 50% of the world population and remain the most subliterate and the poorest.

Gender must be recognized as a social construct that affects the distribution of power and privilege in society. Therefore, the ways in which adult educators construct practices around gender defines communities locally and globally with real consequences accorded along queues of privilege and disadvantage. Adult education cannot continue to add gender as an afterthought in research and praxis, but must focus on gender as the field continues to fulfill the mission of democratizing the adult citizenry.

Class—Overall, the issue of class is primarily addressed when the field turns its attention to literacy, assuming a direct causal link between literacy and poverty, joblessness, underemployment, and possibly homelessness (Nesbit, 2006). The majority of programs, therefore, focus on job training and work skills. Such programs and the research on these programs have traditionally refrained from critiquing the root causes of poverty, underemployment, and low literacy, opting instead to concentrate on employment goals.

However, class is more a consideration when the discussion has an international focal point other than the United States and Canada. Issues of class are more prominent topics for discussion in the British-based journal, *The International Journal of Adult Education,* and the proceedings of the Standing Conference on University Teaching and Research (SCUTREA). However, to speak of adult education and social justice in reference to the northern and southern hemispheres is to speak of nationality, indigenous peoples, poverty, globalization, and literacy, more than to speak of race and ethnicity. Although race and ethnicity are tied to these issues and are especially linked to poverty and low levels of literacy in the southern hemisphere, and even though literacy and literacy initiatives dominate the southern adult education literature, the central focus is more often indigenous peoples' knowledge and culture. The topic of indigenous knowledge includes honoring the oral traditions and languages of native populations amid the emerging push to use Western languages to accommodate commerce (Walters & Watters, 2001).

The focus on literacy in the southern hemisphere seems driven by the global economic market, as African nations, India, and China, the fastest-growing and more populous world areas, are thought to lag behind industrialized nations due in part to large segments of their citizens being undereducated (Singh, 2004). The purpose of the literacy exchange is twofold: It advances economic initiatives for the south and develops and advances a labor pool for the north. However, when economics drive the market and dictate policies, individual nations and groups of people are inevitably disenfranchised because the idea of

equality and other democratic ideals are inextricably tied to governments and social movements and not to economies. The capitalistic process and the phenomenon of globalization disempower countries, their people, and any claims for rectifying any social ills that might have occurred within national borders (Singh, 2004).

Sexual orientation—Writings concerning sexual orientation in the field of adult education have increased over the past 15 years. In the 1990s, writings of note that addressed sexual orientation were Edwards and Brooks (1999) on sexual identity development and queer theory; Nelson (1999) on sexual orientation issues in ESL classrooms; and Sanlo (1998) and Tisdell and Taylor (1995) on higher education. The amount of scholarship and research concerning lesbian, gay, bisexual, transgender, two-spirited, and queer (LGBTTQ) issues and adult education has increased since the publication of the *Handbook of Adult and Continuing Education* in 2000. Topics now include queer cultural studies in adult education (Grace, 2001). Not routinely included, however, are the intersection of sexual orientation and other postionalities, such as students with disabilities (Harley, Nowak, Gassaway, & Savage, 2002); race and sexual orientation in adult and higher education (Misawa, 2005, 2009); and gender and sexual orientation in the workplace (Gedro, Cervero, & Johnson-Bailey, 2004). The perspective of focusing on one social location to the exclusion of additional postionalities that may intersect is a critique that has been leveled against all standpoint literature. Other topics include revealing one's sexual minority status in the higher education classroom (Toynton, 2006); resistance and learning in the lives of gay male activists (Wells, 2006); gay midlife men and adult learning (Bettinger, 2007); empowerment of sexual minorities through pod-casting (King & Sandquist, 2008); and "critical social learning in arts-informed community education for sexual minorities" (Grace & Wells, 2007, p. 95).

Scholars have emphasized the dearth of literature on the LGBTTQ issues in adult education, (Gedro, 2007), the need to challenge the heteronormative (Grace & Wells, 2007), a call for inclusion of LGBTTQ issues in various contexts including the adult education classroom and curriculum (e.g., Misawa, 2005), sexual difference as a learning opportunity (e.g., Gedro et al.,

2004), and strategies used to counter heteronormativity (Wells, 2006) and to create more inclusive environments for LGBTTQ individuals (Harley, Nowak, Gassaway, & Savage, 2002). These themes of marginalization and petitions for resistance and inclusion reverberate throughout the literature of other oppressed minorities.

The adult education field needs to continue to open spaces and encourage dialogue regarding heterosexism/heteronormativity for some of the same reasons that gender needs to be discussed in the adult education field. Namely, democratization of society cannot be achieved when LGBTTQ voices are not included in the adult education curriculum and when individuals who are LGBTTQ fear for their safety in the classroom and larger society. The specific experiences of multiple oppressed groups, such as lesbians and gay men of color, and more literature concerning the experiences of transgender individuals within and outside of the LGBTTQ community is needed.

POPULAR ADULT EDUCATION AND SOCIAL JUSTICE MOVEMENTS IN THE UNITED STATES

Another focal point in the social justice dialogue is education for the masses or population education or education that most often occurs outside of the academic classes and is not degree- or credential-seeking. Popular adult education occurred before and after the field of adult education existed in the United States. Examples include the German American workers' movement in the late 19th and early 20th centuries (Shied, 1993), the education of the freedmen after the Civil War, and the independent educational equity efforts for African Americans between 1920 and 1945 (Johnson-Bailey, 2006). A well-known example of efforts in the field toward promoting the democratization of society through the education of adults was the Highlander Folk School (now called the Highlander Research and Education Center), an organization established in 1932 (Adams, 1975). From 1932 until the mid-1940s, Highlander Folk School served its Tennessee neighbors, the mountain poor: the coal miner labor movement centered in Monteagle and extended to Wilder; the woodcutters in

Grundy County; and the textile workers and farmers across Tennessee (Horton, 1989).

Highlander shifted its focus to meetings regarding school desegregation and the civil rights movement in 1953 (Horton, 1989). In 1957, Highlander's summer workshop director, Septima Clark, and Esau Jenkins, a community leader on Johns Island, South Carolina, as well as Bernice Robinson, were instrumental in starting the first citizenship school on Johns Island. An integral part of the civil rights movement, by 1961, the citizenship school initiative expanded and eventually came under the leadership of Dr. Martin Luther King, Jr., and the Southern Christian Leadership Conference. By 1970, 897 citizenship schools were open across the southern United States (Clark, 1986).

In the 1970s, Highlander returned its focus to the Appalachian community. "Highlander reached out to groups organizing around issues such as banning strip-mining, improving healthcare in the coalfields, and eliminating toxic pollution in their communities" (Highlander Education and Research Center, 2008a, paragraph 2). Highlander rebuilt connections with community organizers in the Deep South and sought connections with activists around the globe to grapple with problems created by global economic forces in the 1980s (Highlander Education and Research Center, 2008a). In the 1990s, Highlander supported the efforts of environmental organizations and addressed economic issues for its rural constituents in Appalachia and the Deep South. Currently, Highlander initiatives include for the rights of the young, the working poor, people of color, and the lesbian and gay communities (Highlander Research and Education Center, 2008b).

Grassroots movements concerning environmental justice remain popular. Bullard and Johnson (2000) notes that the environmental justice movement began in Warren County, North Carolina, in 1982 where "a PCB landfill ignited protests and over 500 arrests" (p. 556). A subsequent study revealed that most hazardous waste landfills in the South were located in African American neighborhoods. Grassroots efforts occurred in a variety of communities as a result of environmental racism. Bullard defines environmental racism as "any policy, practice, or directive that differentially affects or disadvantages individuals, groups or communities on the basis of race or color, whether the differential effect is intended or unintended" (pp. 33–34).

INTERNATIONAL POPULAR EDUCATION AND SOCIAL JUSTICE MOVEMENTS

The United Nations Educational and Scientific Cultural Organization (UNESCO), which was established in 1945, is widely acknowledged as the international voice of adult education, representing global causes and concerns rather than those of any one country. UNESCO's declarations, program, and initiatives challenge racism, sexism, and any discrimination that contributes to or interrupts education and development. Important examples of this would be the Declaration on Race and Racial Prejudice, which was adopted in 1978. The preamble noted that racism, racial discrimination, colonialism, and apartheid continue to afflict the world in ever changing forms, and the United Nations declared a desire to play a vigorous and constructive part in implementing the program of a Decade for Action to Combat Racism and Racial Discrimination, as defined by the General Assembly of the United Nations at its 28th session. The 10 Articles of the Declaration encouraged the countries of the world to eliminate discrimination, adapt policies to improve the lives of their citizens of color, and respect cultural differences.

For the most part, any discussion of adult education in the southern hemisphere occurs against the backdrop of UNESCO, its conferences, and programs. For many nations in the southern hemisphere, adult education is a matter of redress as many southern nations did not have free mandatory children's education; also, an agriculture-based economy necessitated the involvement of all members of the family, including children. The UN Literacy Decade, 2003–2012, emphasizes the importance of honoring indigenous knowledge as a means of promoting education. Important adult education enterprises spearheaded by UNESCO are Education for All (EFA) and International Adult Learners' Week. Adult Learners' Week was first held in the United Kingdom in 1992 and was formally endorsed by UNESCO in 1999 (UIL Nexus, 2007). Since that time, more than 40 countries have joined in the annual participation of Adult Learners' Week. The week's purpose is to impact policy, promote access to existing adult education programs, and increase literacy. Another cornerstone program that redressed issues inequity is the Education for All movement, which began in 1990 at the World Conference in Jomtien, Thailand, setting as its universal goal education for all children and adults and pledging to attempt to cut the 1990 rate of illiteracy 50% by 2000. By the 2000 World EFA Conference in Dakar, Senegal, 180 countries had signed on to promote basic education for all citizens (UIL Nexus, 2008).

The region of southern Africa provides an opportunity to look at adult education in a southern setting. Prior to the emancipation of many nations in southern Africa, adult education was recognized by the 14 nations in the region as an essential and necessary part of liberation struggles. This is aptly illustrated by the underground educational plan that was led by the Black South Africans interned at Robben Island. The literate and educated prisoners worked in secret during their lunch breaks to tutor the less literate and undereducated inmates (Buntman, 2003).

Southern African nations came together to form the Southern African Development Community (SADC) in 1992. This coalition of 14 countries, which include Botswana, South Africa, Zambia, and Mozambique, expresses the importance of educating the citizenry as a means of encouraging full participation and exercise of rights, with most countries in the pact spending 20% of their budgets on education. Given the homogeneity of member countries and the legacy of colonization, the SADC focuses on indigenous knowledge as a bridge between organic knowledge and formal knowledge. The concept of knowledge from the people is particularly important in health education. The low life expectancy of the region has been compounded by the HIV/AIDS pandemic. While championing the importance of local knowledge, the adult health educators are faced with the challenge that at times religious, gender, cultural, and tribal-based behavior, practices, and traditions may conflict with modern medical practices.

OUR GLORIOUS PAST AND OUR HOPEFUL FUTURE

On the surface, it seems that we all know what we are talking about when we reference social justice by pointing to a host of social injustices such as racism, sexism, classism, heterosexism, able-ism, and so on. Yet, the depth and contours of the term are not easily untangled. However, in these early years of the 21st century, we are facing widening gaps economically and educationally between the haves and the have nots. Rather than bringing cultures closer and diminishing societal inequities, globalization, the exportation of and adoption of capitalization and the introduction of competing industrialized markets, has actually exacerbated world economics, while providing new markets and new resources of undereducated vulnerable laborers. With the effects of globalization come the increased necessity of adult education and the need for social justice in adult education to rise to the top and become more prominent rather than remain the undercurrent of our professional practice, which ebbs and flows ubiquitously. Specifically, the global world in which we live is ever changing, dictating that we immediately engage our problem-solving expertise in solving extremely complex issues; and, as educators of adults, we can no longer afford to possess a silent longing for social justice that has been subdued because of a need to appear neutral or objective. Nor should we simply embrace a yearning for social justice without concerted efforts to affect societal change.

For various reasons, however, our efforts regarding social justice often are not as sustained. Sometimes, educators of adults merely are responding to a crisis; our participation in historical social justice movements, as well as contemporary issues or new social movements, evidences this level of societal involvement. Sometimes, social justice projects get little in the way of financial support from government, grants from foundations, or other sources of support earmarked for social justice adult education.

As scholars and practitioners, we may often invoke the concept of social justice or reference a wide variety of social justice issues, yet we all have varying understandings and several different points of departure (based on our context of practice). The yearning for social justice is often expressed during common conversation and in adult education discourse. Yet, untangling the exact ways it is understood as well as the meanings folks derive from the concept may prove quite challenging.

To quickly illustrate, in preparing for an adult education miniconference on social justice a few years ago, the planning committee quickly realized the urgent need to explicitly define *social justice*. As a planning committee of practitioners representing nonprofit organizations, civic groups, government, and faculty in adult education, we were collectively at a loss in (de)constructing language to capture the meaning of social justice. As a group, however, we were actively engaged in multiple social justice projects such as redressing health and environmental disparities, equalizing the digital divide in rural areas, and organizing relief efforts for victims of Hurricanes Katrina and Rita on the Gulf Coast. This vignette speaks to a seemingly common commitment to social justice, while at the same time it documents the challenges of achieving unanimity in understanding the concept of social justice, given that the committee came together with the explicit purpose of focusing on social justice in adult education practice. Yet, the need to meld together diverse bodies of literature to map out the contours of social justice is quite evident.

The overarching framework of social justice adult education simultaneously explores multiple forms of oppression with the aim of eliminating societal–isms. Although there is no one set of tenets to which all adult educators will subscribe, we offer the following:

1. employing interdisciplinary perspectives

2. recognizing the importance of reflexivity/ reflective practice

3. encouraging collaboration/collaborative inquiry

4. valuing experiential ways of knowing/doing

5. stipulating the importance of social context

6. engaging in social justice projects/movements

This framework, then, emphasizes six major tenets to provide a lens for understanding our teaching, program planning, research, and policy making.

REFERENCES

Adams, F. (1975). *Unearthing seeds of fire*. Winston-Salem, NC: John F. Blair.

Alfred, M. V. (2003). Sociocultural contexts and learning: Anglophone Caribbean immigrant women in US Post-Secondary Education. *Adult Education Quarterly, 53*(4), 242–260.

Allman, P. (2001). *Critical education against global capitalism*. Westport, CT: Bergin and Garvey.

Ayers, W. (1998). Foreword: Popular education—teaching for social justice. In W. Ayers, J. A. Hunt, & T. Quinn (Eds.), *Teaching for social justice* (pp. xvii–xxv). New York: Teachers College Press.

Ayers, W., Hunt, J. A., & Quinn, T. (Eds.). (1998). *Teaching for social justice*. New York: Teachers College Press.

Barlas, C. (1997). Developing White consciousness through a transformative learning process. *Proceedings of the 38th Annual Adult Education Research Conference* (pp. 19–24). Stillwater: Oklahoma State University.

Bell, D. A. (1992). *Faces at the bottom of the well: The permanence of racism*. New York: Basic Books.

Bettinger, T. V. (2007). Gay men at midlife and adult learning: An uneasy truce with heteronormativity. In L. Savage & T. Fenwick (Ed.), *The 48th Annual Adult Education Research Conference Proceedings/ (48th National Conference) and the Canadian Association for the Study of Adult Education (CASAE)/l'Association Canadienne pour l'Étude de l'Éducation des Adultes (ACÉÉA) (26th National Conference)* (pp. 43–48). Halifax, Nova Scotia: Mount Saint Vincent University.

Bullard, R. D., & Johnson, G. S. (2000). Environmental justice. Grassroots activism and its impact on public policy decision-making. *Journal of Social Issues, 56*(3), 555–578.

Buntman, L. (2003). *Robben Island and prisoner resistance to apartheid*. Cambridge, UK: Cambridge University Press.

Clark, S. P. (Ed.). (1986). *Ready from within: Septima Clark and the civil rights movement*. Navarro, CA: Wild Tree Press.

Colin, S. A. J., III., & Preciphs, T. (1991). Perceptual patterns and the learning environment: Confronting white racism. In R. Hiemstra (Ed.), *Creating environments for effective adult learning* (pp. 61–70). San Francisco: Jossey-Bass.

Collins, M. (1998). *Critical cross-currents in education*. Malabar, FL: Krieger

Convention on the elimination of all forms of discrimination against women, UNESCO Constitution, UNESCO General Assembly Resolution, 34/80. (1981). Retrieved January 18, 2009, from: http://portal.unesco.org/ shs/en/ev.php-

Cunningham, P. M. (1988). The adult educator and social responsibility. In R. G. Brockett (Ed.), *Ethical issues in adult education* (pp. 133–145). New York: Teachers College Press.

Cunningham, P. M. (1996). Race, gender, class, and the practice of adult education in the United States. In P. Wangoola & F. Youngman (Eds.), *Towards a transformative political economy of adult education: Theoretical and practical challenges* (pp. 139–159). De Kalb, IL: LEPS Press.

Declaration on Race and Racial Prejudice, UNESCO Constitution. (1978). Retrieved January 18, 2009, from: http://portal.unesco.org/en/ev.php-

Dewey, J. (1938). *Experience and education*. New York: The Macmillan Company.

Edwards, K., & Brooks, A. K. (1999). The development of sexual identity. In M. C. Clark & R. S. Caffarella (Eds.), *An update on adult development theory* (pp. 49–57). New Directions for Adult and Continuing Education, No. 84. San Francisco: Jossey-Bass.

Finger, M. (1989). New social movements and their implications for Adult Education. *Adult Education Quarterly, 40*(1), 15–22.

Fraser, N., & Honneth, A. (2004). *Redistribution or recognition? A political-philosophical exchange*. New York: Verso.

Freire, P. (1985). *The politics of education: Culture, power, and liberation*. New York: Bergin & Garvey.

Freire, P. (2000). *Pedagogy of the oppressed* (30th anniversary ed.). New York: Continuum.

Gedro, J. (2007). Conducting research on LGBT issues: Leading the field all over again. *Human Resource Development Quarterly, 18*(2), 153–158.

Gedro, J., Cervero, R. M., & Johnson-Bailey, J. (2004). How lesbians learn to negotiate the heterosexism of corporate America. *Human Resource Development International, 7*(2), 181–195.

Goodman, D. J. (2001). *Promoting diversity and social justice: Educating people from privileged groups*. Thousand Oaks, CA: Sage.

Grace, A. P. (2001). Using queer cultural studies to transgress adult educational space. In V. Sheared & P. A. Sissel (Eds.), *Making space: Merging theory and practice in adult education* (pp. 257–270). Westport, CT: Bergin & Garvey.

Grace, A. P., & Wells, K. (2007). Using Freirean pedagogy of just IRE to inform critical social learning in arts-informed community education for sexual minorities. *Adult Education Quarterly, 57*(2), 95–114.

Griffin, C. (1983). *Curriculum theory in adult and lifelong learning*. New York: Nickols Publishing.

Guy, T. C. (1999). Culture as context for adult education: The need for culturally relevant adult education. In T. C. Guy (Ed.), *Providing culturally relevant adult education: A challenge for the twenty-first century* (pp. 5–18). New Directions for Adult and Continuing Education, No. 82. San Francisco: Jossey-Bass.

Harley, D. Λ., Nowak, T. M., Gassaway, L. J., & Savage, T. A. (2002). Lesbian, gay, bisexual, and transgender college students with disabilities: A look at multiple cultural minorities. *Psychology in the Schools, 39*(5), 525–538.

Heaney, T. (1996). *Adult education for social change: From center stage to the wings and back again.* Columbus, OH: ERIC Clearinghouse on Adult, Career and Vocational Education. (Information Series No. 365)

Highlander Education and Research Center. (2008a). *History—1970–1990: Appalachian people's struggles & supporting local communities in a global context.* Retrieved December 1, 2008, from: http://www.highlandercenter.org/a-history4.asp

Highlander Education and Research Center. (2008b). *History—1990s–Today: The 21st-century Highlander.* Retrieved December 1, 2008, from: http://www.highlandercenter.org/a-history5.asp

Holford, J. (1995). Why social movements matter: Adult education theory, cognitive praxis, and the creation of knowledge. *Adult Education Quarterly, 45*(2), 95–111.

Horton, A. I. (1989). *The Highlander Folk School: A history of its major programs, 1932–1961.* Brooklyn, NY: Carlson.

Horton, M., & Freire, P. (1990). *We make the road by walking: Conversations on education and social change.* Philadelphia: Temple University Press.

Huttunen, R. (2007). Critical adult education and the political philosophical debate between Nancy Fraser and Axel Honneth. *Educational Theory, 57*(4), 423–433.

Illich, I. (1973). *Tools for conviviality* (1st ed.). New York: Harper & Row.

Johnson-Bailey, J. (2006). African Americans in adult education: The Harlem renaissance revisited. *Adult Education Quarterly, 56*(2), 102–118.

Johnson-Bailey, J., & Cervero, R. (1998). Power dynamics in teaching and learning practices: An examination of two adult education classrooms. *International Journal of Lifelong Education, 17,* 389–399.

Johnson-Bailey, J., & Cervero, R. M. (2000). The invisible politics of race in adult education. In A. L. Wilson & E. R. Hayes (Eds.), *Handbook of adult and continuing education: New edition* (pp. 147–160). San Francisco: Jossey-Bass.

Johnson-Bailey, J., & Cervero, R. (2008). Different worlds and divergent paths: Academic careers defined by race and gender. *Harvard Educational Review, 78*(2), 311–332.

King, K. P., & Sandquist, S. R. (2008). Case study of empowerment through new media among underrepresented groups: GLBT adults gain dominant voice in the first wave of podcasting. In S. L. Lundry & E. P. Isaac Savage (Eds.), *The 49th Annual Adult Education Research Conference Proceedings* (pp. 210–215). St. Louis: University of Missouri at St. Louis.

Leonardo, Z. (2004). Critical social theory and transformative knowledge: The functions of criticism in quality education. *Educational Researcher, 33*(6), 11–18.

Levin, J. S. (2001). *Globalizing the community college: Strategies for change in the twenty-first century.* New York: Palgrave.

Lindeman, E. C. (1945). The sociology of adult education. *Journal of Education Sociology, 19,* 4–13.

Lindeman, E. C. (1989). *The meaning of adult education.* New York: New Republic. (Original work published 1926)

Locke, A. (1947). Education for adulthood. *Adult Education Journal,* 104B–107.

Locke, A. (1948). Foreword. In *Handbook of adult education in the United States* (pp. ix–x). New York: Teachers College Press.

Long, H. B. (1989). Editor's preface. In E. C. Lindeman (1926/1989), *The meaning of adult education* (pp. xiii–xxii). New York: New Republic.

Luke, C. (2001). *Globalization and women in academia: North/west, south/east.* Mahwah, NJ: Lawrence Erlbaum.

Miller, D. (1999). *Principles of social justice.* Cambridge, UK: Harvard University Press.

Misawa, M. (2005). The intersection of race and sexual orientation in adult and higher education. In R. J. Hill & R. Kiely (Eds.), *Proceedings of the 46th Annual Adult Education Research Conference* (pp. 307–312). Athens: University of Georgia.

Misawa, M. (2009). The intersection of homophobic bullying and racism in adulthood: A graduate school experience. *Journal of LGBT Youth, 6,* 47–60.

Nelson, C. (1999). Sexual identities in ESL: Queer theory and classroom inquiry. *TESOL Quarterly, 33*(3), 371–391.

Nesbit, T. (2006). What's the matter with social class? *Adult Education Quarterly, 56*(3), 171–187.

Sanlo, R. L. (Ed.). 1998. *Working with lesbian, gay, bisexual, and transgender college students: A handbook for faculty and administrations.* Westport, CT: Greenwood Press.

Sheared, V., & Sissel, P. A. (2001). *Making space: Merging theory and practice in adult education.* New York: Bergin & Garvey.

Shied, F. (1993). *Learning in social context: Workers and adult education in nineteenth century Chicago.* DeKalb, IL: LEPS Press.

Shore, S. (2000). "White practices" in adult education settings: An exploration. *Proceedings of the 41st Annual Adult Education Research Conference* (pp. 423–427). Vancouver: University of British Columbia, Department of Educational Studies.

Singh, P. (2004). Globalization and education. *Educational Theory, 54*(1), 103–115.

Spencer, B. (1995). Old and new social movements as learning sites: Greening labor unions and unionizing the greens. *Adult Education Quarterly, 46*(1), 31–42.

Suissa, J. (2001). Anarchism, utopias, and philosophy of education. *Journal of Philosophy of Education, 35*(4), 627–646.

Tisdell, E. J., & Taylor, E. W. (1995). Out of the closet: Lesbian and gay adult education and sexual orientation issues in the university learning environment. In P. Collette, B. Einsiedel, & S. Hobden (Eds.), *36th Annual Adult Education Research Conference Proceedings.* Edmonton: University of Alberta.

Toynton, R. (2006). "Invisible other": Understanding safe spaces for queer learners and teachers in adult education. *Studies in the Education of Adults, 38*(2), 178–194.

UIL Nexus, 2(3). (2007). Retrieved January 18, 2009, from: http://www.nald.ca/library/newsletter/unesco/07Oct.pdf

UIL Nexus, 3(3). (2008). Retrieved January 18, 2009, from: http://www.nald.ca/library/newsletter/unesco/08Oct.pdf

Vera, E., & Speight, S. (2003). Multicultural competence, social justice and counseling psychology: Expanding our roles. *The Counseling Psychologist, 31*(3), 253–272.

Walters, S., & Watters, K. (2001). Twenty years of adult education in Southern Africa. *International Journal of Lifelong Education, 20*(1), 100–113.

Wells, K. (2006). Learning to transgress: Queer young adults, emotional resilience, and intellectual resistance as impetus for lifelong learning for social justice. In M. Hagen & E. Goff (Eds.), *Annual Adult Education Research Conference proceedings* (pp. 458–464). Minneapolis: University of Minnesota.

Welton, M. (1993). Social revolutionary learning: The new social movements as learning sites. *Adult Education Quarterly, 43*(3), 152–164.

32

STRUGGLES FOR UTOPIA(S)?

Gender and Sexuality in Adult and Continuing Education

SUSAN J. BRACKEN AND HEATHER NASH

Gendered scholarship is deeply personal because we cannot escape ourselves in our own projects; it is what we study and analyze, but it also *who we are*. Thus, it adds a dimension of emotional labor to our work lives (Omolade, 2002), irrespective of our viewpoints. Arguably, this is also similar to other forms of adult education scholarship where we cannot escape our own informal, ongoing experiences as learners, which are bound up with whatever we are investigating, teaching, or writing about. It's at once exciting and suffocating. Margaret Atwood in the 1980s wrote about feminist dystopia in *The Handmaid's Tale* (Atwood, 1986). It was written during a time (Tolman & Brydon-Miller, 2001) when women's studies scholarship had an incredible trajectory in universities and internationally; the women's movement had an optimism and momentum that was very intoxicating. Written as science fiction, *The Handmaid's Tale* explores several female characters' differential approaches to seeking agency, freedom, and a just society. Each of their experiences, philosophies, strategies, and actions were different. Yet, their goals were shared: to create a space within social structures that allowed freedom, and perhaps even happiness, although this wasn't guaranteed. As a dystopia, the hinge in the story is that by pursuing utopia, the characters become so extreme that they oppress themselves and each other. This classic theme has been explored in virtually every type of activist or social justice venue.

This chapter represents a modest, albeit temporary struggle for gendered utopia with an underlying caution that in doing so, our field, like others, is susceptible to a dystopian environment. The chapter includes past and present as well as a vision for the future contributions of women's and gender studies for the field of adult education. We've organized the writing around only a few core assumptions. First is the assertion that gender as a category of analysis *matters* and that it matters to *all of us*. Our human experiences, the way we see the world and the world sees us, our identities in whatever form we believe they take, and the societal and organizational structures we design, promote, and even resist—all these are influenced by gendered constructions. There is no such thing as gender neutral, just as there is no neutrality regarding race (Johnson-Bailey & Cervero, 2000). The second assumption is that lack of perfection should not be a barrier to continued gendered scholarship. Historically, different waves of feminist thought have been criticized for being largely White, heterosexual, middle class, or narrowly focused. Some of that criticism is well deserved. There have been great strides in postcolonial, Black feminist thought and queer theories, among other areas, that address problems and move in new directions. Furthermore, we choose to define feminist or gendered work based on cross-cutting general criteria:

1. Gender is a socialized construct, and it influences who we are, how we change and grow, how we perceive others, and how they perceive us; in other words, we can learn about ourselves and others by thinking about "gender."

2. There are demonstrable patterns of structural inequity and decreased material living conditions based on gender.

3. As scholars and practitioners, we share a commitment to identifying, understanding, and addressing the root causes behind those patterns.

Just as *The Handmaid's Tale's* characters have unique approaches, the scholarship, activism, and constructions presented in this chapter are full of twists and turns, and it is up to readers to write and rewrite the stories.

Adult education, as a field, does not have a coherent, easy to find history of gendered scholarship and participation. This creates a daunting challenge—how do we, then, cultivate a habit of considering and including women, gender, and sexuality as categories of analysis in our work? How do we know what has been done in the past, thus avoiding "re-creating the wheel" and, at the same time, how do we also approach our work in a way that allows us to be free from past ways of gendered scholarship? This chapter is an introduction to a few basic starting points. First, what are some of the past contributions in the adult education field? How have associations, interest groups, and scholars created a space that allows for gender studies within the field? Next, what are some key features of contemporary U.S. feminist movements within and outside of the academy? And finally we make comparisons between adult education literature and the curricular change process as described by Marilyn Jacoby Boxer in her analysis of the history of women's studies in higher education.

PAST CONTRIBUTIONS IN THE FIELD

The adult education handbooks date back to 1934. This was a very exciting time period for women, and for discussions and study of how gender influences and is influenced by every aspect of our social, political, intellectual, and practical lives. A few events or issues relevant to women were mentioned in the 1930s handbooks. For example, there were chapters on men's and women's clubs, settlement houses, and summer school. Then, a significant time lapse occurs, and the next prominent discussion of gender, in any form, appears in the 1980 and 1989 handbooks.[1] In those, there are brief discussions of women's issues in continuing education. There are no previous handbook chapters dedicated to those interested in issues and theories of sexuality and sexual orientation in relation to adult education.

In 1991 Jovita Ross-Gordon (1991) wrote a brief article detailing how adult education needed to shift to the 21st century with a multicultural perspective. While the focus of the article was on the limited attention to race and ethnicity within the discourse of adult and continuing education, it also pointed to an emerging body of work within the field reflecting feminist analyses. At the same time, an additional text, *Adult Education: Evolution and Achievements in a Developing Field of Study* (Peters, Jarvis, & Associates, 1991), known as the "blue" book for its blue cover, followed the "black" book, *Adult Education: Outlines of an Emerging Field of University Study* (Jensen, Liveright, & Hallenbeck, 1964). The two books were intended to celebrate and assess the state of the adult education field as it was practiced in university settings. It was, according to Phyllis Cunningham, supposed to be a reflection on the accomplishments of the field in a quarter century as well as a space in which to consider its future (in Sheared & Sissel, 2001, Foreword). The blue book was the subject of a heated debate in 1992 at the Adult Education Research Conference (AERC), accused of "being Eurocentric, racist, gender insensitive, elitist, and exclusionary" (Cunningham, in Sheared & Sissel, 2001, p. xii). After the debate, the book came to be referred to as the "black and blue" book. In response, a new approach was called for, and eventually *Making Space* (Sheared & Sissel, 2001), known informally as the "pink and purple" book, was published. Its contents were planned in 1993 at AERC in the feminist caucus. The Sheared and Sissel text has had an enormous impact—but it is possible the entire process, debate, and response had as much of an impact on the adult education field as the chapters themselves. At that feminist caucus, questions were raised about inclusion, gatekeeping, marginal groups, a wide range of voices, and social movements. The table of contents in the Sheared and Sissel book includes words like hegemony, feminist, Whiteness, African American, workers, ageism, queer, and inclusion. This made a strong statement that resonates through the fabric of the field to this day.

Recent scholarship that examines women's experiences as postsecondary learners or postsecondary workers (or both) examines student learning experiences and issues relevant to women staff, faculty, or administrators and argues that we have reached a plateau; the notion of gender equity is not an outdated or unnecessary goal. The feminist agenda, which arguably also includes issues of equity surrounding gender, sexuality, class, and race, is indeed unfinished (Glazer-Raymo, 2008). In her book, *Unfinished Agendas: New and Continuing Gender Challenges in Higher Education,* Glazer-Raymo presents demographic data and discussion surrounding hiring, promotion, and pay equity patterns; access and degree (study) participation patterns; campus activism related to women and gendered issues; and the nature of gendered experiences on a college campus. Bracken, Allen, and Dean's (2006) book, *The Balancing Act,* delves into faculty members' gendered experiences and challenges relating to balancing work and home lives. Hayes and Flannery (2000) provide an introduction and overview of women as *learners,* serving as a resource for graduate students, practitioners, and faculty members within the field of adult education and beyond. Taken together, these books offer an overview of gendered patterns and the nature of participation in formal postsecondary and informal adult education contexts.

FEMINIST MOVEMENTS WITHIN AND OUTSIDE OF THE ACADEMY

The 1960s were a period of intense radical activism for civil rights in the United States. One of the movements sweeping communities and universities was the women's movement. During the late 1960s and early 1970s, women's groups on campus formed and began to challenge many facets associated with higher education. At first, they advocated for basic issues of campus safety, adequate access, unfair conditions for female students and university employees, and access to health care. This quickly turned to scrutiny of the academic disciplines and the absence of women's voices or gendered perspectives in curricula across virtually all fields (Boxer, 1998; Bracken et al., 2006; Fish & Lin, 2002; Fox O'Barr, 1994; Morgen, 2002). The energy and the momentum associated with the 1960s and 1970s era certainly led to the label *radical feminism* and a radical feminist school of thought. In contrast to liberal feminists views of women as being separate (different than men) but equal, radical feminists pushed against interpretations that cast women into prescribed roles based on biology and moved toward social and sociocultural understandings of women and gender. Women's bodies, their health care, and outrage with racism, sexism, and other forms of discrimination were analyzed based on gender awareness or consciousness and social structures, although the participants and perspectives most frequently examined were arguably White, middle class, and heterosexual (Bracken et al., 2006; Morgen, 2002; Steinem, 1994). During this time period, concepts such as oppression, power, patriarchy, and women's liberation were broadly debated and introduced into academic scholarship. The Boston Women's Health Collective issued *Our Bodies, Ourselves* (Birden 2004; Morgen, 2002), which was a huge step forward in improving women's opportunities to take ownership of their own learning regarding health care and sexuality. Susan Birden's 2004 *Adult Education Quarterly* article analyzes the Boston Women's Health Collective as a form of coalition-engendered learning. Drawing on Phyllis Cunningham and Paulo Freire, she systematically deconstructs the informal adult learning processes in relation to the concepts of agency and gender.

Second wave or radical feminism is also the strain of feminism that has been referred to both lovingly and angrily as the "f word." Certainly, the story of the black and blue book in adult education and a review of past literatures illustrate the challenges, the emotions, and the types of topics, methodologies, and awareness (or lack of) that permeated the field during the 1960s and 1970s. One of the challenges that is difficult to overcome is that our own contemporary positionalities risk a distorted view of how serious the material and fundamental issues were for the field during this debate, and how personally difficult employing different categories of analysis can be to enact.

The narratives that dominate many feminist writings assert that other feminisms beyond middle-class white feminisms developed after the second wave. Counternarratives that expand the interpretations of radical feminism(s) need to be incorporated *specifically into the adult education literature.* The radical movement had two branches, one more middle class (think of the National Organization for Women [NOW] and its roots) and the other politically to the left and more collectivist. Second-wave feminist thought often focused on material working conditions and experiences for women in the workplace: issues of access, pay, climate, and so on. Roth (2004) traces the emergence of Black and Chicana feminism(s), for example, to the early *left second wave* and the integral presence of black women in the formation of NOW. Roth's thesis that the second wave has been historically "whitewashed" (p. 7) is an important one. On the one hand, the women's movement at that time was largely White, and on the other hand, by disproportionately repeating and featuring this narrative, the contributions, activism, and emergence of feminists of color are virtually undiscussed until later time periods. For readers seeking a deeper understanding, Frances Beal (1970) explicates this irony further in *Double Jeopardy.*

Frameworks can be blended and perspectives combined, as can be seen in numerous cases within adult education literature. An example of this is Mary Alfred's (2001) article on Black women's experience in the White academy. In the article, she explores how race, culture, and identity play a role in Black women's experiences within majority organizations, in this case, universities. Using an interpretive interactionist frame, there are hints of second-wave, postmodern, poststructuralist, and bicultural theories, along with Black feminist thought, woven together.

Patricia Hill Collins's (2000) book includes a preface and an early chapter on the politics and social construction of Black feminist thought. It theorizes that sexism, racism, and classism are intertwined and cannot be resolved on an individual basis and that oppression has an interlocking nature. This isn't a conceptual add-on: It is a form of analysis that looks at the connections, overlaps, and activist possibilities that exist between multiple oppressions, as well as bringing to the forefront expressions and understandings of African American women's culture (Hill Collins, 2004).

In the late 1970s through the 1990s, many other schools of feminist thought spun out, and since that time, there has been a waxing and waning of theoretical approaches to gender and women as a legitimate category of analysis. As critical and diverse discourse swept the academy, feminist and other gendered analytical frameworks multiplied. Marxist feminist frameworks that focus on work, labor, and class have appeared within adult education, although not often. One key work that serves as a good beginning point for newcomers to Marxist feminist analyses is an article on learning organizations and women's consciousness written by Shahrzad Mojab and Rachael Gorman in 2003. Their framework defines historical, materialist, dialectical, and gender critical terms, juxtaposed with learning organization literatures, applied toward uncovering women's consciousness in their roles as workers in relation to learning organization models. Mechtild Hart's (1992) book on labor, women, and the future of work allows readers to connect the feminist, Marxist, and adult education issues and literatures as a way of developing "education for life"; it provides a deeper and more in-depth discussion.

Issues of globalization and international or non-Western ways of knowing are increasingly studied by those focusing on gender within the field of adult education. *Under Western Eyes,* a well-known postcolonial feminist essay now considered a classic (Mohanty, 1991), was a crucial and highly visible beginning step in urging feminists and those interested to consider the implications of a postcolonial or north-south politics and to open discourses beyond nationalities, races, and ethnicities while simultaneously rooting analysis, activism, and scholarship in the localized contexts within which they are embedded. Mohanty's key argument is that issues of equity are inescapably intertwined, and we all have a shared interest in understanding and resolving issues regarding human freedoms and equity. Later work increasingly ties analyses of global economy and consumerism to feminist postcolonial theories and practicalities: How do we find ways to create better living conditions and participatory societies in an age of devolving notions of community and solidarity (Calás & Smircich, 2006; Mohanty, 2003)?[2]

Using a postcolonial framework, Leona English (2005) adopts the concept of Global South as a way to explore women's participation in international adult education. She manages to incorporate discussions of power and inequity with postcolonial dynamic or fluid concepts in a way that gives the participants the predominant voice, intimately connected to both their local and global contexts. The March/April 2008 issue of the *International Journal of Lifelong Education* features a thematic discussion of women and wartime, geographically focused in the Middle East and Asia. These types of works are being published in adult education more often and are increasingly incorporating postcolonial and poststructuralist perspectives, a step in a positive direction.

Feminist scholars often struggle with how to sustain congruence yet combine the elements of frameworks that are useful or meaningful to our research studies. For example, contemporary feminist scholars often use poststructural or postcolonial approaches, yet some also see a value in critical theory, which is distinctly modernist conceptually and has many contradictions with feminist or gendered work. Interestingly enough, Patti Gouthro (2005) combines critical feminist analysis and an examination of masculine frameworks with critical Habermasian approaches. This pairing is quite interesting, intellectually speaking, in its juxtaposition of intersubjectivity with rationality. Meehan (1995) begins her book of feminist critiques on Habermas with the question of "why feminists *should* read Habermas at all?" (p. 1) In the end, even though the political theories and ethical frameworks used are not compatible with most feminist or gendered frameworks, Habermas's discourse theory is incredibly useful to understanding how societally mediated learning and systems converge to produce and reproduce our worlds. For those scholars who are interested in the public and private spheres, in discourse theory or critical theory, it is a worthwhile investment to read Meehan's book and to work through the ways in which feminist critiques can stretch, alter, and render notions of identity, learning, the public, the private, consumerism, communication, social structures, ethics, and difference. This book suggests that perspectives as diverse as postmodern and poststructural feminist frames can be reconciled with critical theory. One important contribution for practitioners and scholars alike is the influence of gendered scholarship on philosophy, epistemology, and research methods.

ADULT EDUCATION, QUEER THEORY, AND SEXUALITY STUDIES

At the same 1993 AERC conference where the women's caucus met for the first time, the caucus for sexual minorities and their allies held its first meeting. Ten years later, the Lesbian, Gay, Bisexual, Transsexual, Queer, and Allies (LGBTQ&A) preconference to the AERC conference was first offered (Hill, 2007b), and the movement has flourished ever since. Bob Hill (2007b) identified three pivotal moments for queer studies in adult education. The first is the formation of the caucus, which is now 16 years old. The second moment he identifies as critical is the first scholarly presentation with an LGBTQ focus, made at the 1994 conference. And finally, he cites the inaugural preconference meeting held in San Francisco in 2003. In a recent presentation, Hill (2008) also presented a summary of a basic keyword search from 2003 to 2008 in the AERC proceedings. The search was done on titles and abstracts only and looked for nine keywords: bisexual, gay, heterosexism, homophobia, lesbian, queer, sexual orientation, transgender, and transsexual. In total, across a five-year time period, the nine words were cited 20 times. Standing in contrast to the dozens or hundreds of times that other diversity or gendered terms have appeared in the adult education conference proceedings, this is a telling snapshot.

Of note, the *New Directions* series featured an edited 2007 volume on LBGTQ issues within adult and continuing education (Hill, 2007a), which included several chapters based on papers previously shared at the LGBTQ&A preconference of AERC. The volume editor, Robert Hill, asks the question, "What's it like to be queer here?" and has organized chapters that address different perspectives on sexual minorities in adult education settings. The authors explored topics such as transformative learning perspectives, straight privilege, the double bind of sexual orientation and gender in organization settings, the meaning and the dynamics of being out in the classroom, and policies that could drive organizational change. These chapters represent a step toward incorporating sexual orientation and sexual minority scholarship into a field where it has been largely absent, as do recent writings by Grace and Hill (2004) and Nelson (2004). Yet, they remind also us that our use of language and our inability to see what is before us can be incredibly incongruent with the social justice and social equity goals that are a part of the adult education tradition (Hill, 2007a).

Concluding Discussion

Marilyn Jacoby Boxer (1998) uses a framework, originally by McIntosh, which discusses the progression of university curriculum in terms of gender awareness. Her theory is that we move from teaching history first as "womanless history" with a virtual absence of women as authors or actors. Then, we begin to problematize and the absence of gender is constructed as a problem; eventually, we move through phases that reconstruct history to include us all (Boxer, 1998, p. 62). If we conceptualize the adult education literature in a broad sense as a curriculum, it is easy to see that we are in many different overlapping phases simultaneously. For instance, certain works or examples are used repeatedly within the field—attempts to avoid a womanless or genderless history. The Bryn Mawr Summer School for Women Workers, credited as a key force in the early worker education movement (Heller, 1986), and the Jane Addams Hull House (Addams & Hurt, 1990) both present opportunities for discussion and analysis of adult education, learning, gender, class, and social participation. Both translate well in terms of past, present, and future. Many scholars also include Ida B. Wells as a part of our teaching and writing. Ida B. Wells was a post-Civil War and early 20th-century African American activist, who was prominent in both the black and women's rights communities. Her activism is very instructive in studying the intersections of race, class, and gender and also in examining the dualities that women activists face in claiming or being labeled

with a particular role or identity (Bogues, 2003; Schecter, 1998).

Further along Boxer's continuum (1998), Margaret Urban Walker's scholarship (1998) discusses something she calls "testing sight lines." Walker writes about the issues involved in moral authority, representation, and acting and persuading others as we balance uniquely socially constructed perspectives and frameworks. She argues that while we need to be responsible and continually thoughtful in considering issues of representation[3] and power and we are doing this within changing cultural contexts, we still have defined responsibilities of critical practice.

Extending Walker's argument, we are educational actors, and as such, we carry responsibilities for being thoughtful, reflective, ethical, and well-informed about issues of power, equity, and difference; and, in turn, our actions influence and shape our various arenas of participation. This is a not a new general argument within adult education, but regarding gender analyses, perhaps it is. For those of you who already participate in the field: When attending scholarly sessions that are inclusive of philosophical, epistemological, and practical gender discussions, do you observe the same subset of scholars appear and re-appear? Do you tend to read or avoid reading scholarship focusing on gender or sexuality? Do you or others around you consistently look to see if issues of gender and sexuality, and their intersections with class and race, are included in your teaching? Are you aware of issues related to gender and sexuality that may play a significant role in your area of practice? Authors cited in this chapter remind us that gender is relevant to the practice of adult and continuing education across settings and contexts, whether we are conscious of this or not. In the 21st century, one challenge facing adult and continuing educators who are concerned with social justice is to build on the progress made over recent decades, without taking the proverbial "two steps back" sometimes historically observed in times of economic instability and rapid social change.

Notes

1. One way to track these conversations is to consult the 2000 *Handbook of Adult Education*'s Wilson and Hayes chapter, which lists the table of contents for all previous handbooks.

2. For detailed discussion of feminist organizational studies, the Calás and Smircich handbook chapter provides an excellent discussion. Thank you

to Julia Storberg-Walker for drawing the lead author's attention to this publication.

3. For further foundational reading on feminist scholarship's contributions to philosophical or methodological advances, we recommend reading Patti Lather's 1992 "Critical Frames in Educational Research: Feminist and Poststructuralist Perspectives" and Acker, Barry, and Essevald's 1983 article on Objectivity & Truth in Feminist Research.

REFERENCES

Addams, J., & Hurt, J. (1990). *Twenty years at the Hull-House, with autobiographical notes.* Urbana: University of Illinois Press.

Alfred, M. V. (2001) Expanding theories of career development: Adding voices of African American women in the White academy. *Adult Education Quarterly, 51*(2), 108–127.

Atwood, M. (1998). *The handmaid's tale.* New York: Anchor Books.

Beal, F. (1970). *Double jeopardy: To be Black and female.* In T. Cade (Ed.), *Black woman: An anthology.* New York: New American Library.

Birden, S. (2004). Theorizing a coalition engendered education: The case of the Boston women's health book collective's body education. *Adult Education Quarterly, 54*(4), 257–272.

Bogues, A. (2003). The radical praxis of Ida B. Wells Barnett: Telling the truth freely. In A. Bogues (Ed.), *Black heretics, Black prophets: Radical political intellectuals.* New York: Routledge.

Boxer, M. J. (1998). *When women ask the questions: Creating women's studies in America.* Baltimore: The Johns Hopkins University Press.

Bracken, S. J., Allen, J. K., & Dean, D. (Eds.). (2006). *The balancing act: Gendered perspectives in faculty roles and work lives.* Sterling VA: Stylus.

Calás, M. B., & Smircich, L. (2006). Feminist organization theory: Hierarchies, jobs, bodies: A theory of gendered organizations. In B. Czarniawska, *Organization theory.* Northampton, MA: Cheltenham.

English, L. (2005). Third-space practitioners: Women educating for justice in the Global South. *Adult Education Quarterly, 55*(2), 81–100.

Fish, C. J., & Lin, Y. T. (Ed.). (2002). Women's studies then and now. [Special issue]. *Women's Studies Quarterly, 30*(3/4).

Fox O'Barr, J. (1994). *Feminism in action.* Chapel Hill: North Carolina University Press.

Glazer-Raymo, J. (2008). *Unfinished agendas: New and continuing challenges in higher education.* Baltimore: The Johns Hopkins University Press.

Gouthro, P. (2005). A critical feminist analysis of the homeplace as learning site: Expanding the discourse of lifelong learning to consider adult women learners. *International Journal of Lifelong Education, 24*(1), 5–19.

Grace, A., & Hill, R. (2004). Positioning queer in adult education: Intervening in politics and praxis in North America. *Studies in the Education of Adults, 36*(2), 167–189.

Hart, M. (1992). *Working and educating for life: Feminist and international perspectives on adult education.* London: Routledge.

Hayes, E. R., & Flannery, D. D. (2000). *Women as learners: The significance of gender in adult learning.* San Francisco: Jossey-Bass.

Heller, R. (1986). The women of summer: The Bryn Mawr summer school for women workers, 1921–1938. *Dissertation Abstracts International,* ATT 8620038.

Hill, R. (Ed.). (2007a). *Challenging homophobia and hetersoexism: Lesbian, gay, bisexual, transgender, and queer issues.* New Directions for Adult and Continuing Education, No. 112. San Francisco: Jossey-Bass.

Hill, R. (2007b). What's it like to be queer here? In R. Hill. *Challenging homophobia and hetersexism: Lesbian, gay, bisexual, transgender, and queer issues* (pp. 7–16). New Directions for Adult and Continuing Education, No. 112. San Francisco: Jossey-Bass.

Hill, R. (2008). A retrospective on the LGBTQ&A Caucus/SIG and Pre-Conference) Hidden & displayed: Queer memory work revisited. *Proceedings of the LBGTQ&A Preconference of the Adult Education Research Conference* (pp. 09–37), St. Louis, MO. (ERIC Document Reproduction Service No. 503480)

Hill Collins, P. (2000). *Black feminist thought: Knowledge, consciousness, and the politics of empowerment* (2nd ed.). New York: Routledge.

Hill Collins, P. (2004). Learning from the outsider within: The sociological significance of Black feminist thought. In S. Harding (Ed.), *The feminist standpoint theory reader: Intellectual and political controversies* (pp. 103–126). New York: Routledge.

Jensen, G., Liveright, A., & Hallenbeck, W. (1964). *Adult education: Outlines of an emerging field of university study.* Washington, DC: Adult Education Association of the USA.

Johnson-Bailey, J., & Cervero, R.M. (2000). The invisible politics of race in adult education. In A. L. Wilson & E. R. Hayes (Eds.), *Handbook of adult and continuing education.* (New edition). San Francisco: Jossey-Bass.

Meehan, J. (Ed.). (1995). *Feminists read Habermas: Gendering the subject of discourse.* New York: Routledge.

Mohanty, C. T. (1991). Under Western eyes: Feminist scholarship and colonial discourses. In C. T. Mohanty, A. Russo, & L. Torres (Eds.), *Third world women and the politics of feminism.* Indianapolis: Indiana University Press.

Mohanty, C. T. (2003) *Feminism without borders: Decolonizing theory, practicing solidarity.* Durham, NC: Duke University Press.

Mojab, S., & Gorman, R. (2003). Women's consciousness in the learning organization: Emancipation or exploitation. *Adult Education Quarterly, 53*(4), 228–241.

Morgen, S. (2002). *Into our own hands: The women's health movement in the United States, 1969–1990.* New Brunswick, NJ: Rutgers University Press.

Nelson, C. D. (2004). A queer chaos of meanings: Coming out conundrums in globalized classrooms. *Journal of Gay and Lesbian Issues in Education, 2*(1), 27–46.

Omolade, B. (2002). Women and work: Class within the classroom. *Women's Studies Quarterly, 30*(3/4), 284–293.

Peters, J. M., Jarvis, P., & Associates. (1991). *Adult education: Evolution and achievements in a developing field of study.* San Francisco: Jossey-Bass.

Ross-Gordon, J. (1991). Needed: A multicultural perspective for adult education research. *Adult Education Quarterly, 42*(1), 1–16.

Roth, B. (2004). *Separate roads to feminism: Black, Chicana, and White feminist movements in America's second wave.* Cambridge, UK: Cambridge University Press.

Schecter, U. T. (1998). The historical evolution of Black feminist theory and praxis. *Journal of Black Studies, 29*(2), 234–253.

Sheared, V., & Sissel, P. (2001). *Making space: Merging theory and practice in adult education.* Westport, CT: Bergin & Garvey.

Steinem, G. (1994). *Moving beyond words: Age, rage, sex, power, money, muscles: Breaking boundaries of gender.* New York: Simon & Schuster.

Tolman, D. L., & Brydon-Miller, M. (Eds.) (2001). *From subjects to subjectivities: A handbook of interpretive and participatory methods.* New York: New York University Press.

Walker, M. U. (1998). *Moral understandings: A feminist study in ethics.* New York: Routledge.

33

CHASING THE AMERICAN DREAM

Race and Adult and Continuing Education

E. PAULETTE ISAAC, LISA R. MERRIWEATHER,
AND ELICE E. ROGERS

T he American dream is a prevalent concept in American society. A significant belief related to the dream is that America will deliver on its greatest promise—that every adult is entitled to "life, liberty, and the pursuit of happiness." However, we find that the American dream is flawed. West (1993) contends that the flaws are rooted in "historic inequalities and longstanding cultural stereotypes" (p. 6). They are consistent with the American dilemma or paradox (Herrnstein, 1990; Myrdal, 1944). The American dilemma names race and ethnicity as being the most critical factors (Ferrouillet Kazi, 1993) in assessing the degree of leverage on the "playing field," such that European Americans are distinctly advantaged. Members of this racial group claim privileges for themselves while denying privileges to racialized minorities, resulting in inequities (Akintunde, 1999; Fish, 1993). This is a major feature in the makeup of the American dilemma. W. E. B. Du Bois (1944) characterized this dilemma as the problem of the color line, which he asserted was the greatest problem faced in America.

Race in the United States has been a contentious subject that has resulted in spirited discussions across all levels of education. Race, according to Mitchell and Salsbury (1999), refers to the presupposition that humans can be grouped according to their overt biological characteristics and postulates that members of individual racial groups automatically inherit such preordained characteristics as intelligence and other traits. Unfortunately, the biological origin of race is commonly accepted, but most social scientists suggest that race is not biological but rather its roots are "the result of social and historical processes" (Andersen & Collins, 2007, pp. 62–63).

Any discussion of race should begin only after there has been an examination of the flaws in our society (West, 1993). According to West, "How we set up the terms for discussing racial issues shapes our perceptions and response" (p. 6) to the issues. Appreciating the social constructedness of race and the importance of not reducing "race to a mere manifestation of other supposedly more fundamental social and political relationships such as ethnicity or class" (Omi & Winant, 1994, p. 2) are the terms by which we have developed our analysis of race and ethnicity within adult education.

Throughout history, race has been a problem in America, and it is also a problem in adult education. We must engage in a praxis that entertains ways to level the playing field. In this chapter, we interrogate race and its import to the field of adult education. We begin by offering a critique of contemporary race-based theories, which we believe should inform adult education practice and research. Second, we outline the degree to which graduate programs and scholar/researchers are involved in race-centered dialogues. Last, we address the ways adult education plays a role in either mitigating or exacerbating inequities related to race and ethnicity.

CRITIQUE OF CONTEMPORARY RACE-BASED THEORIES

After the civil rights era, we saw a rise in the research exploring race and ethnicity within the educational context. In the United States, this proliferation fueled a number of theories and models. Many of these theories and paradigms transcend educational contexts. Although space limitations do not allow us to address every theory, we examine a few that have surfaced in adult education. They include multiculturalism, Black feminist thought, critical race theory, and Africentrism.

Multiculturalism

Toward the end of the 20th century, race-oriented theories began to gain traction. One of the precursors used to describe the diversity in our society was multiculturalism. The term in and of itself has different meanings to different people. Many people mistakenly use a myopic lens and limit multiculturalism to race or ethnicity. Grant and Ladson-Billings (1997) define multiculturalism as a philosophical position and movement that assumes that the gender, ethnic, racial, and cultural diversity of a pluralistic society is reflected in all of its institutionalized structures but especially in educational institutions, including the staff, norms and values, curriculum, and student body. A "central idea that is shared by all types of multiculturalism is that one culture is seen as dominant and therefore the educational need is to teach the importance of values and beliefs that are held by other cultures" (Johnson-Bailey & Cervero, 2000, p. 155).

Because many people limit multiculturalism to race, often its definition becomes dichotomous and leads only to discussions of Black and White binaries. Thus, instructors who incorporate some aspect of race in the curriculum assume that multiculturalism has been adequately addressed. Sleeter and Grant (1987) identified

five approaches to multiculturalism, which we believe still exist today. They consist of (1) teaching to those who are culturally different and helping them to assimilate to mainstream culture; (2) helping students get along with and appreciate one another; and (3) "teaching courses about the experiences, contributions, and concerns of distinct ethnic, gender, and social class groups" (p. 139). They identified more advanced and inclusive approaches such as (4) reforming institutions to reflect the diversity of the student population; and (5) preparing "students to challenge social structural inequality and to promote cultural diversity" (p. 139). Multiculturalism has served as the impetus for the more contemporary theories such as Africentrism, Black feminist thought, and most recently, critical race theory.

Africentrism

Unlike multiculturalism and Black feminist thought, Africentrism and critical race theory use race exclusively as a lens. Colin and Guy (1998) were among the early scholars in adult education to write and research from an Africentric framework. Asante (1988) articulates an Africentric theoretical framework in which race is central. He asserts the importance of centering people of African descent within an African cultural frame consistent with their sociohistorical standpoint and warns of the danger of working from a standpoint alien to their own.

> Our relationship to the culture that we have borrowed defines what and who we are at any given moment. By regaining our own platforms, standing in our own cultural spaces and believing that our way of viewing the universe is just as valid as any, we will achieve that kind of transformation that we need to participate fully in a multicultural society. (p. 8)

People of the African diaspora stand on their own platforms when they allow core principles such as communalism, holism, and spirituality to guide their actions. Africentrism also stresses the importance of agency for eradicating racism.

Black Feminist Thought

Women have been fighting for equal rights in every arena of life. During the last century, feminists and subsequently feminist works permeated dialogue relative to literature, research, and learning. These women and the studies they presented assumed that women from all walks of life and cultural groups were equally and fairly represented. However, just as African Americans as a whole are marginalized, many women of color believed that the thrust of feminists and feminist literature did not adequately reflect their cultural issues and overlooked their voice.

As a result of this exclusion, many women of color sought a more inclusive reflection. According to Collins (1996), in the 1980s and '90s, African American women "developed a 'voice,' a self-defined collective black women's standpoint about black womanhood" (p. 9). As the following discussion suggests, Black feminist thought (Collins, 1990) was birthed to address the lack of attention to African American women's experiences.

Although some African American women have rejected the term *feminism* (Collins, 1996), many have adopted the use of *Black feminist thought*. According to Johnson-Bailey and Cervero (2000), "Black feminist thought extends from Black feminism which is a movement that addresses issues of race, gender, class, and color as they pertain to Black women" (p. 144). It acknowledges Black women's knowledge and experiences and plays "an integral role in their empowerment" (Williams, Brewley, Reed, White, & Davis-Haley, 2005, p. 182) because it enables them to create new knowledge from their own experiences and those that they learn from other Black women, who also share their knowledge, which ultimately derives from their experiences.

As with other theories, Black feminist thought "encourages new techniques to study Black females because their experience cannot be studied using the standard techniques of dominant practice" (Williams et al., 2005, p. 183). These new techniques enable women to build critical awareness of images that are often false and misleading. In addition, they open the door for new and empowering knowledge to emerge (Clayborne & Hamrick, 2007). Hence, Black feminist thought challenges traditional approaches to obtained knowledge (Harris, 2007).

Critical Race Theory

More recently, adult educators have used critical race theory (CRT) to inform both their research and pedagogy. Pioneered in the field of law, CRT (Crenshaw, Goutanda, Peller, & Thomas) was popularized in education by Ladson-Billings and Tate (2006) and was introduced into the field of adult education by Elizabeth Peterson (1999). Throughout the beginning of the 21st century, other adult educators have used the theory to frame their work (Bowman, 2005; Merriweather Hunn, Manglitz, & Guy, 2006; Peterson, Bowman, Rocco, & Adker, 2008). CRT amalgamates several elements from the aforementioned race-based theories and offers to adult education a unique lens with which to view practice and work toward social justice. Like critical theory, CRT's end goals are activism and change. Educators using it seek to cure inequities in education based on race. CRT goes beyond a critique of civil rights legislation aimed at redressing inequality to address extreme cases of inequality as well as the everyday microaggressions that racialized minorities encounter (Sue et al., 2007).

The primary aim is "to provide a more cogent analysis of 'raced' people and move discussions of race and racism from the margins of scholarly activity to the fore of educational discourse" (Ladson-Billings & Tate, 1995, p. 196). The basic five tenets of CRT provide an operational framework for achieving that end. They include (1) racism is endemic in our society; (2) CRT is not bound to any one academic discipline; (3) it recognizes that civil rights law and educational theories are limited by their lack of attentiveness to race-based issues; (4) commonly accepted ideas, such as meritocracy and color blindness, serve the interest of those in power; and (5) credence must be given to the experiences of racialized groups, and they must be situated in both a social and historical context. This body of literature holds great promise for adult education because a number of race-centric theories sprang from CRT such as LatCrit, Asian Crit, and Tribal Crit.

Many of the theoretical underpinnings of Africentricism, Black feminist thought, and CRT can be traced back to the theories of multiculturalism, which acknowledges and honors the diversity of people of all races and ethnicities. Yet, for all of its contributions, theories of multiculturalism did not challenge the influence of institutional and systemic racism and inequality within the lives of people of color, as later theories did. Each of these concepts can transcend to ethnic minorities and better inform practice in diverse settings. Given the narrow conception of race present in the current body of adult education literature, this line of scholarship offers a wide range of options for those wishing to conduct research, plan curricula, and advise students in ways that privilege all voices.

Program and Practitioner Dialogues

Race is not an issue that has been adequately addressed by researchers and practitioners of adult education. According to Johnson-Bailey (2001), "Historically, the field of Adult Education, in practice and in programming, in both formal and informal education, has been silent on issues of race and ethnicity" (p. 89). This silence was manifested by avoidance of racially oriented topics and a narrow conception of race in terms of Black and White. Franklin (1992) called this the "conspiracy of silence" (p. 44)—a term used to describe the absence of African Americans from history. He further suggested that this absence was not accidental but rather was a deliberate ploy by hegemonic systems.

Near the end of the last century, adult education witnessed an apparent metamorphosis from European American domination to participation of greater numbers of scholars considered as racialized minorities. The entrance of these scholars, the authors of this chapter included, ushered in increased attention to race within the field (Johnson-Bailey, 2001). As a result of our educational experiences, we understood and appreciated the significance of different perspectives and naturally incorporated race into our respective courses. However, our experiences are not representative of the field at large.

Baumgartner and Johnson-Bailey (2008) argue that "race and ethnicity affect the educational process in the adult education classroom" (p. 45) and remind adult educators that our "multicultural classroom can be an uncomfortable place for students of color" (p. 50). When we consider how graduate programs in adult education prioritize race and racism, it becomes apparent that, by virtue of their training, practitioners at all points of entry for adult learners—adult basic education, community education, human resource development, and higher education—are ill equipped to create inclusive spaces.

An examination of adult education graduate programs reveals some diversity in curricular offerings. Nonetheless, most curricular requirements of adult education graduate programs deem program planning, adult learning, and administration as canonical, but none bestow the status of "canon" on a course that exclusively focuses on race. A small number of programs include, as part of the core, courses on diversity or multiculturalism. A larger number of programs feature elective courses that examine race and gender, multiculturalism, or social context. The African proverb, "Wherever man goes to dwell, his character goes with him" (Thinkexist.com, 2008) says it best. If we assume that programs require what is important (where they dwell) then race would be considered unimportant to the development (character) of adult education. The implicit message sent is that race is not integral to the practice and theoretical development of this academic discipline. Scholars such as Colin and Guy (1998), Guy (1999), and Peterson (1999) recognized the integral role that graduate programs played as arbiters of knowledge and influencers of public policy; they challenge the community of practice and research to address race and consider theories and practices not built on Eurocentric worldviews.

The conspicuous absence of attention to race and racism clearly infiltrates the field of practice. Sheared (1999) notes, educators do not "give much thought to how their race, gender, class, or language influences their philosophy and what they do in the classroom" (p. 35). She employs the notion of polyrhythmic realities as a device to highlight the significance of race in adult basic education classrooms. These realities require that adult educators give "voice to learners' lived experience" (Sheared, 1999, p. 40), which means that educators must attend to race as a dimension of the teaching-learning transactions in adult basic education classrooms.

Rocco and Gallagher (2004) illustrate the importance of integrating race, as well as other categories of difference, into the dialogue in urban adult education. In describing the significance of discriminative action for adult educators, they write,

> Discriminative action is good when it reveals processes of oppression and privilege in classrooms, funding, and policies. Adult educators must struggle to recognize the small things we do that honor this system that privileges some and marginalizes others. We should attempt to deconstruct the dynamics in the classroom and in the boardroom that replicate oppression. (p. 39)

In some adult literacy programs, which often use volunteers, it is not unusual for the volunteers' racial background to be in stark contrast to that of the learners. In addition, these programs, "Workbooks and other texts often reflect knowledge and behaviors that are valued primarily by educators and mainstream white, middle-class culture" (Fingeret & Drennon, 1997, p. 87). Thus, adult literacy programs as well as other community programs should adequately prepare participants (educators) for working with diverse learners. Discriminative action by default requires that we take note of the diversity that exists in our adult education venues. Race is one of the dimensions that is most visible and has been historically and contemporaneously shaped by hierarchical systems of prejudice and privilege that favor White Americans.

Practitioners and academicians alike must be aware of how interactions in adult education are impacted when race is negated or dismissed as a pivotal factor. Failure to do so impacts access to learning, quality of instruction, feelings of being unwelcomed, and the ability to persist. The effects of the conspiracy of silence reverberate throughout the whole of the adult education enterprise. For example, if practitioners fail to acknowledge the experiences of learners in the classroom, the learners could feel those experiences are less valuable or insignificant, thus withdrawing mentally from the course.

The body politic of adult education has not named race as an issue of primary importance to the field. An analysis of journals and conferences affiliated with the discipline suggest that there are two broad categories that describe how race and racism are approached in adult education: (1) racialized minorities as subject and (2) interrogation of race and racism at the theory level.

Most research that considers either race or racism falls into the first category and, as noted by Johnson-Bailey (2001), reflects a binary of Black and White. There is clearly a need to extend the dialogue to include other racialized minority groups. Undoubtedly, research that focuses on racialized minorities is necessary to stretch our understanding of adult education by decentering adult learners of European descent, thus widening the circle of who counts in adult learning, development, and leadership. But adult educators must not become complacent with just researching racialized minorities and becoming lulled into a false sense of security

about the progress made by having these works (limited as they are) represented in our educational journals and conferences. We must move beyond this and engage in more research that directly interrogates race and racism as theoretical constructs.

In Brookfield's (2003) *Racializing Criticality in Adult Education* and Manglitz's (2003) *Challenging White Privilege in Adult Education,* an example of this type of interrogation can be seen. Both force the reader to make race central as opposed to a peripheral discussion. Although some of the research featuring racialized minorities as primary subjects included connections to racism or race, it is also necessary to consider these constructs as starting points as opposed to ending points. These starting points reframe the research inquiry and squarely position race and racism at the forefront. This becomes a precondition to race and racism being legitimated as worthwhile research interests in adult education. Unfortunately, articles and presentations of this nature are not prevalent in journals and conference proceedings. This type of research and its subsequent dissemination across the expanse of the landscape are critical to igniting dialogue among practitioners and beginning the process of developing adult educators who recognize the import of race in their practice and research.

ADULT EDUCATION AND INEQUITIES RELATED TO RACE AND ETHNICITY

The challenge for the field as the dialogues indicate is both immediate and urgent regarding exacerbating inequities related to race and ethnicity. To better understand the current state of the field, we present a candid and genuine discussion about the realities of race-based inequity in adult education. We argue that adult education has for the most part remained virtually silent on its failure to (a) aggressively move outside of its comfort zone to the margins in an effort to reach racial ethnic minorities; (b) address individual racism, privilege, and power; and (c) acknowledge old racism in new attire.

Failure to Retreat to the Margins

Adult education, as a field, is not aggressive in retreating to the margins, where diverse adults in the social context and community can be better understood, where we learn more about how macrostructures influence adults, and where we learn about factors that influence adult development, motivational patterns, learning styles, and learning preferences of adults and the role that community plays in the social context (Rogers & Hansman, 2004). When we remove ourselves from our ivory towers, classrooms, and offices and go to where the people are, we will discover that the social context embodies elements, such as race and racism, that shape the nature, character, and practice of adult education. We also gain more knowledge about how the sociocontextual landscape influences the delivery of adult education programs (Martin & Rogers, 2004). Critically reflective practitioners retreat to the margins to obtain a glimpse of the world from different racial/ethnic perspectives, enabling them to radically alter the paradigms that inform practice.

White Privilege

White privilege (McIntosh, 1990, 2007) or "Whiteness" and its impact are rarely acknowledged within adult education. Some adult educators have acknowledged their privilege and theorized how it affects their practice, research, and relationships with others (Brown, Cervero, & Johnson-Bailey, 2000; Johnson-Bailey & Cervero, 2000; Manglitz, 2003). The majority, however, do not question their Whiteness and the unearned advantage that accompanies it. Furthermore, they do not recognize how that privilege operates at the expense of racial/ethnic minorities. These educators wear clever masks that cloak their racist behaviors while engaging in the politics of race. For example, one might serve as chairperson of a university-wide task force commissioned to hire diverse faculty, while simultaneously working to ensure that a Native American junior faculty member, who happens to be a woman, is denied tenure. Within the community, an adult educator might volunteer at the local homeless shelter while working at the planning table to limit the numbers of racial/ethnic minorities who can qualify to receive those services. These examples illustrate how White privilege operates at the microlevel in our work as adult educators. Failure to address this results in the insidious presence of White privilege that propels racial ethnic minorities to the margins of our discourse and practice.

Racism: Same Name, New Game

The historical transcript of racism in adult education has an attire indicative of silence as evidenced by the absence of racial/ethnic minorities in the field, the limited discussion and inclusion of racial/ethnic minorities in the curricula, de facto and de jure segregation and discrimination seen in gatekeeping practices, an emphasis on Whiteness as the normative experience, and dismissal of polyrhythmic realities (Sheared, 1999), inequity, and oppression. This transcript unveiled itself in four *New Directions for Adult and Continuing Education* sourcebooks on culture, diversity, race, and the urban context (Guy, 1999; Hayes & Colin, 1994; Martin & Rogers, 2004; Ross-Gordon, Martin, & Buck Briscoe, 1990). Researchers (Jensen, Liveright, & Hallenbeck, 1964; Johnson-Bailey & Cervero, 2000; Peters, Jarvis, & Associates, 1991; Sheared & Sissel, 2001) have pointed to the racism that existed in adult education handbooks that were published between 1934 and 1989. In many instances, there were no discussions of race in these publications. Today, racism in adult education is wearing new robes. The most interesting of these is "managing diversity."

Managing diversity is reflective of the cultural, sociopolitical contextual climate inside an institution designed to meet the needs of the center and its interests. On the one hand, this strategy appears genuine as we find technical rationality and discourse such as target ratio, representative ratio, institutional diverse readiness and responsiveness, designs for diversity, and variability in human capital utilization. Under the existing paradigm, managed diversity says that we can define, objectify, determine, and exercise the economy of power relations (Collins, 1991; Foucault, 2003), but we find that in reality, spaces are not substantively made more diverse due to two primary factors.

First, the cultural milieu is such that diversity is managed through numbers. From this vantage point, most racial/ethnic minorities find themselves operating in environments on a daily basis without "self-ethnic" reflectors (Colin, 1989) with whom they can share intellectual, political, social, and work-related experiences.

Second, a managed diversity strategy promotes invisibility through conformity. That is, diverse people adhere to a notion of professionalism that is aligned with the experience of Whiteness and White privilege. To remain competitive and accepted, racialized minorities suppress their "voice" (Foucault, 2003) and conform to the norm by acting in ways that enhance their images as good professionals who are good citizens that go-along-to-get along, thus remaining culturally invisible but counted in the diversity ratio.

By failing to retreat to the margins and by acknowledging White privilege and the new face of racism, adult educators play an active role in exacerbating inequities related to race. We argue that mechanisms that address power and its misappropriation must be created. A sense of immediate agency and cogency exist and require adult educators to engage in radical mutuality and communicative action such that we can focus on our common destiny and cultivate an authentic multiracial democracy that will sustain our union as well as enhance our global relationships (Baumgartner, 2006; Freire, 1993; Rossiter, 2006). Two ways radical mutuality and communicative action are achieved are through increased diversity among educators and adult learners and through ethnic-oriented activities. For example, a number of adult education conferences (Commission on Adult Basic Educators, Adult Education Research Conference, American Association for Adult and Continuing Education) are held throughout the year. Many of these conferences now offer educational opportunities for ethnic minorities to have voice. These are prime examples of how the field of adult education works to close the gap in inequities related to race and ethnicity.

OPENING UP THE GATES: ACCESS AND OPPORTUNITY IN ADULT EDUCATION

Racial minorities have been active participants in adult education since the 1920s, and the field continues to diversify to mirror contemporary society. Sheared and Sissel (2001) and Guy (1999) expose the field to the rich "voices" of those historically marginalized in adult education such as African Americans, Asian Americans, Hispanic Americans, and Native Americans. Through these works and the increasing presence in the field as learners, educators, and policy makers, these racialized minorities have become more visible and are making contributions to adult education. Specifically the numbers of racial ethnic minorities in the adult education professoriate continue to increase due in large part to a small number of trailblazing African American faculty who used their voices as authors, editors, teachers,

policy makers, tenured and full professors, researchers, and administrators to make critical decisions at the planning tables of higher education (Cervero & Wilson, 1996) and encouraged junior scholars of color to enter the field.

An enhanced presence of racialized minorities has ushered in an increased awareness of ways of knowing that diverge from the hegemonic normative experience of Whiteness. These scholars] validated the lived experiences of ethnic minorities and in doing so influenced pedagogy, shaped research agendas, and created new paradigms of understanding (Smith & Colin, 2001). These new paradigms are encapsulated in race-based theories and have been employed by contemporary adult educators.

CONCLUSION

Clearly adult educators are engaging in dialogues about race more frequently now than in the past, but we need to expand the discourse to include more analyses of race at the theory level. These dialogues have worked in some cases to close the gap as the professoriate becomes more diverse, and conference venues create spaces for racialized minorities to highlight issues of relevance to their experience. More often than not, dialogues in adult education exacerbated inequities based on race through its failure to retreat to the margins and to acknowledge white privilege and the new look of racism. Finally, through the use of race-based theories such as CRT and Black feminist thought, adult educators have great opportunities to expand the dialogue on race and continue to close the gap. One of the challenges now lies in merging theory and practice so that regardless of the learning contexts, all learners, regardless of their ethnic identity, are reflected in the curriculum. If we truly believe in the education and empowerment of adults, then we need to look at who we are and unpack the knapsack of special provisions, interrogate our interests, and address how we use our power to help and not harm others in our enterprise. If we replace racial reasoning with moral reasoning and choose ethical principles over racial phenotype and wise politics over the hegemonic grip, then in the struggle together we stand the chance in the 21st century to make a great contribution in strengthening civil society (Cunningham, 1996; Ferrouillet Kazi, 1993).

REFERENCES

Akintunde, O. (1999, Winter). White racism, white supremacy, white privilege, and the social construction of race. *Multicultural Education, 7*(2), 2–8.

Andersen, M. L., & Hill Collins, P. (2007). *Race, class, and gender: An anthology* (6th ed.). Belmont, CA: Wadsworth.

Asante, M. K. (1988). *Afrocentricity.* Trenton, NJ: Africa World Press.

Baumgartner, L. (2006). Breaking down barriers. Challenging the hegemony of privileged personalities. In S. B. Merriam, B. C. Courtney, & R. M. Cervero (Eds.), *Global issues and adult education: Perspectives from Latin America, Southern Africa, and the United States* (pp. 193–204). San Francisco, CA: Jossey-Bass.

Baumgartner, L., & Johnson-Bailey, J. (2008). Fostering awareness of diversity and multiculturalism in adult and higher education. In J. Dirkx (Ed), *Adult learning and the emotional self* (pp. 45–53). New Directions for Adult & Continuing Education, No. 120. San Francisco: Jossey-Bass.

Bowman, L. (2005). Race and continuing legal education: From the functionalist approach to the critical approach. *Adult Learning, 16* (3&4). 14–17.

Brookfield, S. (2003). Racializing criticality in adult education. *Adult Education Quarterly, 53*(3), 154–170.

Brown, A., Cervero, R., & Johnson-Bailey, J. (2000). Making the invisible visible: Race, gender, and teaching in adult education. *Adult Education Quarterly, 50*(4), 273–288.

Cervero, R. M., & Wilson, A. L. (Eds.). (1996). *What really matters in adult education program planning: Lessons in negotiating power and interests.* New Directions for Adult and Continuing Education, No. 69. San Francisco: Jossey-Bass.

Clayborne, H. L., & Hamrick, F. A. (2007). Re-articulating the leadership experiences of African American women in midlevel student affairs administration. NASPA, *44*(1), 123–146.

Colin, S. A. J., III. (1989, November). Cultural literacy: Ethnocentrism versus self-ethnic reflectors. *Thresholds in Education, 15*(4), 16–20.

Colin, S. A., J., & Guy, T. (1998). An Africentric interpretive model of curriculum orientations for course development in graduate programs in adult education. *PAACE Journal of Lifelong Learning, 7*, 43–55.

Collins, M. (1991). *Adult education as vocation.* New York: Routledge.

Collins, P. H. (1990). *Black feminist thought: Knowledge, consciousness, and the politics of empowerment.* New York: Routledge.

Collins, P. H. (1996). What's in a name? Womanism, black feminism, and beyond. *The Black Scholar, 26*(1), 9–17.

Crenshaw, K., Goutanda, N., Peller, G., & Thomas, K. (Eds.). (1995). *Critical race theory: The key writings that formed the movement.* New York: The New Press.

Cunningham, P. (1996). Race, gender, and class, and the practice of adult education in the United States. In P. Wangoola & F. Youngman (Eds.), *Towards a transformative global economy of adult education* (pp. 139–159). De Kalb, IL: LEPS Press.

Du Bois, W. E. B. (1944). Prospect of a world without racial conflict. *The American Journal of Sociology, 49*(5), 450–456.

Ferrouillet Kazi, K. (1993, September/October). Interview: Cornel West talking about race matters. *The Black Collegian*, pp. 24–35.

Fingeret, H. A., & Drennon, C. (1997). *Literacy for life: Adult learners, new practices.* New York: Teachers College Press.

Fish, S. (1993, November). How the pot got to call the kettle black. *The Atlantic Monthly.* pp. 128–136.

Foucault, M. (2003). The subject and power. In P. Rabinow & N. Rose (Eds.), *The essential Foucault: Selections from essential works of Foucault, 1954–1984* (pp. 126–144). New York: New Press.

Franklin, J. H. (1992). *Race and history: Selected essays, 1938–1988.* Baton Rouge: Louisiana State University Press.

Freire, P. (1993). *Pedagogy of the oppressed* (20th anniversary ed.). New York: The Continuum Publishing.

Grant, C. A., & Ladson-Billings, G. (Eds.). (1997). *Dictionary of multicultural education.* Phoenix, AZ: Oryx Press.

Guy, T.C. (Ed.). (1999). *Providing culturally relevant adult education: A challenge for the twenty-first century.* New Directions for Adult and Continuing Education, No. 82. San Francisco: Jossey-Bass.

Harris, T. M. (2007). Black feminist thought and cultural contracts: Understanding the intersection and negotiation of racial, gendered, and professional identities in the academy. In K. G. Hendrix (Ed.), *Neither white nor male: Female faculty of color* (pp. 55–64). New Directions for Teaching and Learning, No. 110. San Francisco: Jossey-Bass.

Hayes, E. R., & Colin, S. A. III (Eds.). (1994). *Confronting racism and sexism.* New Directions for Adult and Continuing Education, No. 61. San Francisco: Jossey-Bass.

Herrnstein, R. (1990). Still an American dilemma. *Public Interest, 98,* 3–17.

Jensen, G., Liveright, A., & Hallenbeck, W. (1964). *Adult education: Outlines of an emerging field of university study.* Washington, DC: Adult Education Association of the U.S.A.

Johnson-Bailey, J. (2001). The road less walked: A retrospective or race and ethnicity in adult education. *International Journal of Lifelong Education, 20*(1/2), 89–99.

Johnson-Bailey, J., & Cervero, R. (2000). The invisible politics of race in adult education. In A. L. Wilson & E. R. Hayes (Eds.), *Handbook of adult and continuing education* (pp. 147–160). San Francisco: Jossey-Bass.

Ladson-Billings, G., & Tate, W. F. (1995). Toward a critical race theory of education. *Teachers College Record, 97*(1), 47–68.

Ladson-Billings, G., & Tate, W. F. (2006). Toward a critical race theory of education. In A. D. Dixson & C. K. Rousseau (Eds.), *Critical race theory in education: All God's children got a song* (pp. 11–30). New York: Routledge.

Manglitz, E. (2003). Challenging white privilege in adult education: A critical review of the literature. *Adult Education Quarterly, 53*(2), 119–135.

Martin, L. G., & Rogers, E. E. (Eds.). (2004). *Adult education in an urban context: Problems, practices, and programming for inner-city communities.* New Directions for Adult and Continuing Education, No. 101. San Francisco: Jossey-Bass.

McIntosh, P. (1990, Winter). Unpacking the knapsack of white privilege. *Independent School,* pp. 52–56.

McIntosh, P. (2007). White privilege: Unpacking the invisible knapsack. In M. L. Andersen & P. H. Collins (Eds.), *Race, class, and gender: An anthology* (6th ed., pp. 98–105). Belmont, CA: Thompson Wadsworth.

Merriweather Hunn, L., Manglitz, E., & Guy, T. C. (2006). *Who can speak for whom? Using counter-storytelling to challenge racial hegemony.* Paper presented at the Adult Education Research Conference, University of Minnesota, MN.

Mitchell, B. M., & Salsbury, R. E. (1999). *Encyclopedia of multicultural education.* Westport, CT: Greenwood Press.

Myrdal, G. (1944). *An American dilemma: The Negro problem and modern democracy.* New York: Harper.

Omi, M., & Winant, H. (1994). *Racial formation in the United States: From the 1960s to the 1990s.* New York: Routledge.

Peters, J. M., Jarvis, P., & Associates. (Eds.). (1991). *Adult education: Evolution and achievements in a developing field of study.* San Francisco: Jossey-Bass.

Peterson, E. A. (1999). Creating a culturally relevant dialogue for African American adult educators. In T. C. Guy (Ed.), *Providing culturally relevant adult education: A challenge for the twenty-first century* (pp. 79–91). New Directions for Adult and Continuing Education, No. 82. San Francisco: Jossey-Bass.

Peterson, E. A., Bowman, L., Rocco, T. S., & Adker, W. (2008). Dismantling the myth of "the end of racism": The use of CRT to analyze stories of race. In M. L. Rowland (Ed.), *Proceedings of the 27th Annual Midwest Research-to-Practice Conference* (pp. 176–181). Bowling Green: Western Kentucky University.

Rocco, T., & Gallagher, S. (2004). Discriminative justice: Can discrimination be just? In L. G. Martin & E. E. Rogers (Eds.), *Adult education in an urban context: Problems, practices, and programming for inner-city communities* (pp. 29–42). New Directions for Adult and Continuing Education, No. 101. San Francisco: Jossey-Bass.

Rogers, E. E., & Hansman, C.A. (2004). Social and cultural issues in urban communities. In L. G. Martin & E. E. Rogers (Eds.), *Adult education in an urban context: Problems, practices, and programming for inner-city communities* (pp. 17–28). New Directions for Adult and Continuing Education, No. 101. San Francisco: Jossey-Bass.

Ross-Gordon, J. M., Martin, L. G., & Buck Briscoe, D. (Eds.). (1990). *Serving diverse populations.* New Directions for Adult and Continuing Education, No. 48. San Francisco: Jossey-Bass.

Rossiter, M. (2006). Radical mutuality and self-other relationship in adult education. In S. B. Merriam, B. C. Courtney, & R. M. Cervero (Eds.), *Global issues and adult education: Perspectives from Latin America, Southern Africa, and the United States* (pp. 387–398). San Francisco: Jossey-Bass.

Sheared, V. (1999). Giving voice: Inclusion of African American students' polyrhythmic realities in adult basic education. In T. C. Guy (Ed.), *Providing culturally relevant adult education: A challenge for the twenty-first century* (pp. 33–48). New Directions for Adult and Continuing Education, No. 82. San Francisco: Jossey-Bass.

Sheared, V., & Sissel, P. A. (Eds.). (2001). *Making space: Merging theory and practice in adult education.* Westport, CT: Bergin & Garvey.

Sleeter, C., & Grant, C. (1987). An analysis of multicultural education in the United States. *Harvard Educational Review, 57*(4), 138–161.

Smith, S. E., & Colin, S. A. J., III. (2001). An invisible presence, silenced voices: African Americans in the adult education professoriate. In V. Sheared & P. A. Sissel (Eds.), *Making space: Merging theory and practice in adult education* (pp. 57–69). Westport, CT: Bergin & Harvey.

Sue, D. W., Capodilupo, C. M., Torino, G. C., Bucceri, J. M., Holder, A. M. B., Nadal, K. L.; & Esquilin, M. (2007). Racial microaggressions in everyday life: Implications for clinical practice. *American Psychologist, 62*(4), 271–286.

Thinkexist.com (2008). *African proverb quotes.* Retrieved May 30, 2008, from: http://think exist.com/quotes/africanproverb/

West, C. (1993). *Race matters.* Boston: Beacon Press.

Williams, M. R., Brewley, D. N., Reed, R. J., White, D. Y., & Davis-Haley, R. T. (2005). Learning to read each other: Black female graduate students share their experiences at a white research institution. *The Urban Review, 37*(3), 181–199.

34

Adult and Continuing Education for an Aging Society

Mary Alice Wolf and E. Michael Brady

The purpose of adult education is to put meaning into the whole of life.

Eduard Lindeman (1961)

Why Learn in Old Age?

Any discussion of theory and research on older adult learners (50 and older) begins with an understanding of the role of education and construct of learning. For many adults—whether it be for meaning making, vocation, literacy, socialization, or personal development—learning is a voluntary, often need-driven activity. Older people make an active decision to embark on this quixotic and dynamic path: to partake as learners of a variety of personal, programmatic, and social endeavors. The framework of this chapter is the aging process itself and the definition of lifelong learning given by older people themselves. For older adults, this is both a process of understanding and influencing the world and an important life course goal, a way of living in community and understanding the contradictions of a lifetime of experience.

Paulo Freire (1970/1992) described the process of *praxis* as naming, reflecting, acting, and re-evaluating one's own world. He observed, "Concern for humanization leads at once to the recognition of dehumanization, not only as an ontological possibility but as an historical reality" (p. 27). Therefore, too, an understanding of older adult learning lies in the struggle to experience a significant awareness of growth: ontological and human. Unfortunate ageist stereotypes often cloud older adults' self-esteem, and greeting cards reinforce this phenomenon. Many fear that they are cognitively deficient and lack the "modern" tools of learning. Sadler and Krefft (2008) describe negative and ageist tendencies in society as the dreaded 'D' words: difficulty, decline, degeneration, decrement, disease, disengagement, depression, dependency . . . and the last D-word that marks the end of the line" (p. 18). Elder learning is all about reversing the messages communicated by this litany of Ds while instilling growth, hope, community, and enhanced spirit. For many older people, learning is an opportunity to address environmental indignities and participate in social reform. In every way, learning is a process—actively sought, aggressively pursued—of meaning making. This process is finding a lifelong connection to learning.

Older people know that their future is limited and therefore choose to exercise their capacity for wonder and hope. It is essential that learning environments provide opportunities for intergenerational legacies—whether they are cultural, poetic, or self-advocacy. Later life is a time of generativity and integrity, a means of connecting with others (Cohen, 2005; Erikson, Erikson, & Kivnick, 1986; Wolf, 2007). The process of learning is tied to the human need to make sense and to adapt, to understand, and to change one's world. For many older adults, the opportunity to learn is a lifelong wish—often deferred by economic circumstances and family/work obligations. Of the current population of older people (over 55 years of age), 9.4 % have less than a ninth-grade education; nearly 20% have not completed high school, and 34.5% have only a high school education (U.S. Census Bureau, 2007). Learning as a lifelong process is valuable to the culture; adult and continuing education is essential for an aging society.

HISTORICAL AMERICAN ROOTS

A brief history of the phenomenon of late-life learning sets the stage for an overview of current learning and programs for older people. While, historically, older adults have not participated in either formal or nonformal adult education programs to the same degree as younger adults, there have been increases in participation in recent years. Manheimer (2007a) reported that adult education participation rates among people age 55 and older have climbed steadily since the 1970s (the decade in which interest in older adult education began in earnest and the subspecialty of educational gerontology was created). Courtenay (1989) observed of the field:

> While educational gerontology may have other geneses, it is reported to have been used first in the United States in a doctoral program initiated at the University of Michigan in 1970 by Howard McClusky, who is often referred to as the father of educational gerontology. (p. 526)

Major contributors to the field include, among others: Paulette T. Beatty, James Birren, Bradley C. Courtenay, James E. Fisher, Michael Galbraith, Roger Hiemstra, Peter Jarvis, JoAnn Luckie, D. Barry Lumsden, R. J. Manheimer,

H. R. Moody, and David A. Peterson. In the past 30 years, there has been a growing body of gerontological theory and research, practice and analysis, and participation of older learners. These adult educators have explored cognitive and affective dimensions of development through research and theory, defining the need to learn and the pragmatics for practitioners and curriculum development. Several journals focus entirely on learning theory and research, as well as applied curricula and interventions designed for late-life learners. These include *Educational Gerontology; Geriatrics and Gerontology for Education; Older Learners; The LLI Review: The Annual Journal of the Osher Lifelong Learning Institutes;* and *The International Journal of Lifelong Learning;* as well as *The Older Learner,* a newsletter of the American Society on Aging. In the United States, the Libraries of the Future has begun training librarians across the country to develop outreach for older people, particularly that behemoth: the Baby Boomer generation.

THEORETICAL PERSPECTIVES

One theorist who has influenced our work is the psychosocial developmentalist, Erik Erikson (1968, 1978, 1982, 2001; Erikson et al., 1986). Erikson focused on understanding the inner life of older people. In his eight-stage theory of psychosocial development, he pointed out that older adults also have mandated tasks to achieve fullness and to grow as human beings. *Integrality* was his term for the wisdom and perceptions that are uniquely available to older people (Erikson, 1982). He wrote,

> This we have described as a kind of "informed and detached concern with life itself in the face of death itself," as expressed in age-old adages and yet also potentially present in the simplest references to concrete and daily matters. (p. 62)

We can well use his assertion of growth in old age as a rationale for advances in education for elders. Erikson (1982) asked,

> What is the last ritualization built into the style of old age? I think it is *philosophical:* for in maintaining some order and meaning in the disintegration of body and mind, it can also advocate a durable hope in wisdom. (pp. 62–64)

In light of Erikson's ontological model of development and Freire's assessment of the need to achieve "selfhood" (1970/1992, p. 22), we might assert that education for older people is *essential* for the civilization. For those who seek it, the learning process enables the older adult to develop integrality, achieve well-being, and make genuine contributions to the culture. Research points out that active elders seek medical care less frequently (Cohen, 1992, 2001; Rowe & Kahn, 1998; Vaillant, 2002), and participation in adult education experiences is considered a developmental opportunity (Beatty & Wolf, 1996; Wolf, 2005, 2009). Older adults can be fully integrated into the everyday changes experienced by younger cohorts. They will not be isolated, marginalized, or "fogies" to be tolerated. Learning for lifelong development and a recognition that *all* human beings change, grow, and develop is an international educational perspective (Jarvis & Parker, 2005). Education can be the hallmark of the search for hope, meaning, and connection for all other generations.

PARTICIPATION IN LEARNING PROGRAMS

By 1999, the percentage of people in the United States ages 66 to 74 who took at least one adult education course in a school or postsecondary institution more than doubled from what it had been at the start of the decade. There were similarly strong increases in participation among older learners in community-based (nonformal) programs. A recent report issued by the American Council on Education shows these growth trends in participation among learners over the age of 55 continuing into the first decade of the 21st century (Robinson & Lakin, 2007).

Fisher and Wolf (2000) cited several needs for education: These continue to drive older learners into educational experiences. Today, they include learning as meaning making, for employment, inclusion, literacy, self-efficacy, spiritual development, leisure and travel, socialization, the desire for intellectual maintenance, personal development, care giving, and health and wellness. The organization Libraries for the Future has created the format for a wide variety of outreach activities. Funded by The Atlantic Philanthropies, it is

dedicated to bringing about lasting changes in the lives of disadvantaged and vulnerable people . . . [It]

seeks to bring about lasting improvements in the lives of older adults, transform how ageing is viewed within society and improve the way older persons are treated by society. (Americans for Libraries Council, 2007, p. 2)

Libraries for the Future has provided leadership training for mid-career librarians to learn about "aging, the brain, multigenerational activities, civil society, and lifelong learning" (Americans for Libraries Council, 2007; Libraries for the Future, 2007). The results have been impressive, including programs for disadvantaged older people; architectural changes to existing library structures to enhance access; technological resources; informational and volunteer resources for caregivers, African Americans, and elder Native Americans; civic and health education; and equal access programming. This outreach is phenomenal, as the town librarian is a most trusted icon for midlife (aka Baby Boomers) and older adults. Libraries can be central to the health and security of seniors by providing safe and regular outreach to previously marginalized populations: They might have a regular tax consultant, citizenship adviser, translator of government correspondence and paperwork advisories, for example.

Programs for older learners are proliferating. In the United States, they include The Third Age Initiative, Civic Engagement, Encore Careers (Reserve), New Chapters Centers, Older Adult Service and Information Systems (OASIS), The Osher Lifelong Learning Institutes, The Second Journey, The University without Walls, The Shepherd's Centers, Transitional Keys, Exploritas (formerly Elderhostel), Roads Scholars, and Centers for Creative Retirement (NCCR). Pruchno and Smyer (2007) explored the challenges of an aging society and concluded that education is an integral part of the themes of "autonomy, responsibility, and distributive justice . . . that resonate in personal and public life" (p. 14).

However, not all older learners participate equally. People of lower socioeconomic status, racial minorities, residents of rural areas, and those with comparatively low levels of formal education historically participate at lower rates than other older people, but recent data show that the gap has been closing (Merriam, Caffarella, & Baumgartner, 2007). Reasons for this include a recent increase in outreach activities among nonformal educational providers and a substantial growth of interest in older adult education among formal providers, especially institutions of higher education. (The specific example of lifelong learning institutes is explored in depth later in this chapter.)

A good example of noneducational institutions' involvement as providers of adult education involves religious organizations. Faith-based programs offer numerous educational opportunities, which often reach otherwise underserved elders. For example, Shepherd's Centers, which are nonprofit community organizations sponsored by a coalition of religious congregations, are committed to the delivery of a wide range of programs and services including adult education. Begun in 1972 in Kansas City, when 23 churches and synagogues joined in an interfaith effort, today more than 75 Shepherd's Centers in 20 states comprise a network of 15,000 volunteers serving more than 250,000 older adults. While offering a wide range of programs designed to empower older adults to lead creative and productive lives, Adventures in Learning uses elders as both teachers and learners. Classes in a wide array of subjects—art, music, science, current events, history, health, religion—provide an environment in which older adults may share their knowledge, skills, and new interests with each other (Manheimer, 2007a). Individual workshops are also abundant, such as the Confident Living Program for Senior Adults Who Are Hard of Hearing and Blind or Visually Impaired.

In his book *Learning Later*, Brian Findsen (2005) writes from an international perspective about religious institutions serving as a pathway to adult education. He discusses how churches, synagogues, and mosques throughout the world not only meet religious and spiritual needs but also can be a locale of social networks and learning.

> Churches are underrated places for adult learning to occur. On the one hand, a sensitive spiritual leader/teacher can help older adults to retain knowledge of a religious kind, challenge people's beliefs about life, and provide encouragement in social action to improve the world. On the other, effective leaders can also foster a learning community and be a facilitator to spearhead collaborative learning. (p. 104)

A recent student project in Hartford, Connecticut, explored the use of music in a church setting. Golaski (2007) found that inner-city elders recalled the power of certain hymns—unknown to the mid-life choir director—as impetus for reminiscence and life review. Teaching them to youngsters developed into an intergenerational activity. Faith-based programs can be a gathering place for intergenerational adult education, a phenomenon that requires greater attention in both adult education and gerontology.

Another domain, which has created greater access, yet simultaneously has accentuated the gap between adult education "haves" and "have-nots," is information technology. It is clear that older adults are using computers and the Internet at ever-increasing rates. For example, Ownby (2006) reported that 31% of people age 65 and older have used the Internet for searching information and e-mail communication while an even larger proportion (70%) of adults age 50 to 64 are Internet users. Several demographic factors have been found to be associated with use of computers and the Internet, including age, educational level, participation in the workforce, type of occupation, and type of household (e.g., having a skilled user of computers and/or a younger person in the same household.)

In recent years, attempting to decrease the digital divide between computer users and nonusers, local and state governments have striven to increase public access by way of buying and installing computers in libraries, post offices, and other public facilities. Creating access to technology does not necessarily, however, automatically translate into educational activity. Selwyn, Gorard, and Furlong (2006) stressed that access to information technology is one thing while "meaningful use" is quite another. Willis (2006) has argued that among the significant challenges faced by older people who want to use computer technology for learning is obtaining skills to learn how to use computers effectively.

> Research on the most effective training methods supports the importance of hierarchically organizing the information to be learned, proceeding in training from simple to more complex concepts and skills, and highlighting for the older learner the most salient information and skills to be required. (p. 46)

A creative strategy that has been developed to help train previously uninitiated older people to use computers engages traditionally aged under-graduate students in an intergenerational men-toring program. Shedletsky (2006) describes one such course in which third-year communication majors at a public university learn about geron-tology and the realities of aging through read-ings and discussion while they provide one-on-one mentoring to older learners in an experiential component of the course. Research conducted on the efficacy of this model revealed that substantial learning took place on the part of the undergraduate students (about aging) and the elders (about computers). Other com-puter training programs that have achieved suc-cess and have won national recognition for their work with older learners are *SeniorNet* and *CyberSeniors*. Fitzpatrick (2003) found an impres-sive rise in self-esteem among women religious (Catholic nuns) who mastered computer skills. And, at a rural community center, one retired senior announced that he spent 40 hours per week sending jokes to Army buddies all over the world. Now he has a plan to interact with service men and women abroad. "I have no time to nurse my arthritis," he claims.

FURTHER PERSPECTIVES

While much of what takes place in older adult education is based on a consumer-driven provi-sion of programs (i.e., meeting coping or expres-sive needs), there are voices calling for a more critical approach. The concept of lifelong learn-ing provides a basis for arguing that learning for older adults is an essential element of modern life and that adult education should be justified as a basic human right (Cohen, 2005; Manheimer, 2007b). Age, economic status, or other traditional barriers to participation should have nothing to do with one's access to education. The challenge is to move beyond traditional models to incorpo-rate a more participatory, collaborative system of adult education in which older adults are the principle stakeholders in the goals, processes, and outcomes of their own learning. If we can move in such a direction, while individual older adults will continue to fulfill their personal needs through adult education, they will "more impor-tantly be contributing through social action to improving the predicaments of disenfranchised older adults and to society more generally" (Findsen, 2005, p. 141).

INDIVIDUAL VARIATIONS

A recent study undertaken in Portland, Maine, which is a government-designated refugee reset-tlement city, investigated barriers to participa-tion in adult education programs among older immigrants and refugees from Southeast Asia and Africa. Pejic (2008) found that traditional attitudes about aging held by people who grew up in Vietnam and Cambodia served as a barrier to participation in adult education. Growing up in Southeast Asia, many people were taught that attending school is for early in life. This stage of preparation is then followed by work (young adult and middle years) and finally old age. To quote one of the study participants: "In Asia it is not expected that one would start learning new things in the elder years" (Pejic, 2008, p. 3).

Moreover, research among older people from Africa but now living in Maine revealed a differ-ent set of barriers. Subjects came from a variety of nations including the Democratic Republic of the Congo, Rwanda, Ethiopia, Burundi, Sierra Leone, Somalia, and The Sudan. It was discovered that great diversity in educational backgrounds exists among African immigrants, ranging from total illiteracy (i.e., people who had never spent a day in a formal school and, in fact, had not even held a pencil) to those with graduate degrees earned in their native country (Pejic, 2008). Because obtaining language skills is important for sur-vival, many African immigrants and refugees enroll in English for speakers of other languages (ESOL) classes in the local public school adult education program. Attracting them to the more liberal arts-oriented lifelong learning institute is far more problematic, however, especially in light of immigrants' and refugees' basic survival and coping needs.

MODELS FOR PRACTICE

Learning Through Peers: The LLI Movement

In 1962, a group of retired New York City public school teachers approached what was at the time the New School for Social Research (now New School University) in Greenwich Village to ask if the university would assist them in creating an adult learning program. The group was dissatisfied with unchallenging edu-cational programs they were getting from their union and wanted the New School to help them create something more intellectually rigorous. This program became the Institute for Retired Professionals and in effect the first lifelong learning institute (LLI) in the United States.

LLI has recently become the generic term for a range of adult education programs created by and for people age 50 and older. (Some LLIs vary the minimum age for membership, but most commonly, it is 50.) Less than a decade ago, other generic names were employed to describe the same type of program including Institute for Learning in Retirement, Academy for Lifelong Learning, and Senior College. However, the consensus today is to call these LLIs.

Today, there are more than 400 LLIs in the United States and Canada and hundreds more Universities of the Third Age (U3A) in Europe, Australia, Asia, and elsewhere. (Although differentiated from LLIs in several ways, U3As share the same basic mission as their North American counterparts.) While no two LLIs are alike, they tend to have a number of common characteristics:

- Some level of self-governance, on a continuum from groups with complete autonomy as 501c3 nonprofit organizations to groups with a strong advisory role in the planning of courses and activities that are nevertheless managed by staff in a college or university.

- Affiliation with an institution of higher education. Although some LLIs are affiliated with K–12 public schools or other agencies, the vast majority align administratively with continuing education units of colleges and universities.

- Member-based. People join LLIs by paying what is usually a modest membership fee (although fees in some cases will range dramatically.) This is an important distinction from other adult education programs, in which learners simply pay tuition or a fee and take courses. Membership implies a deeper commitment to the ongoing activities and governance of the program.

- A curriculum that is heavily focused on the liberal arts. Some LLIs include technical and applied courses in the curriculum, and there is also a recent trend toward offering community-based service learning opportunities.

- Teachers/facilitators are members of the LLI and educate their peers. While selected LLIs hire full-time faculty from their affiliating college or university to teach courses, the dominant model is to have member-led facilitation. (In some cases, these peer teachers are paid, and in other cases, they are volunteers.)

- A student body that on the whole is better educated and more affluent than the general population age 50 and older. (Lightfoot & Brady, 2005)

This last common factor is worthy of more reflection, especially in light of the previous section on older adult education participation and access. While most LLIs in fact do attract the more highly educated and affluent elder, conscious efforts are made to recruit a broader membership. The vast majority of LLIs offer scholarships that pay most or all of the membership costs. (It also should be said that those programs run with all-volunteer faculty charge modest fees anyway, often in the $25 to $50 range.) Some programs have specifically included outreach to underrepresented groups as part of their strategic planning and research agendas (Pejic, 2008). The barriers to participation in LLIs in many cases are more attitudinal than structural (Robinson & Lakin, 2007). In 2000, the work of LLIs caught the attention of a philanthropist from California, whose foundation had a long record of making generous gifts to the arts and education. The first major endowment of an LLI occurred that year (University of Southern Maine) and was followed by more than 120 endowments to colleges and universities to create or in some cases grow previously established institutes. Today, these Osher Foundation-supported lifelong learning institutes, or OLLIs, involve more than 75,000 older adult learners.

INTERGENERATIONAL CONNECTIONS

Efforts to develop programming for children, young people, and older adults have led to some powerful learning opportunities (Barton, 2000; Brabazon, 2007; Henkin & Zapf, 2007; Kaplan, 2008; Newman, Ward, Smith, McCrea, & Wilson, 2008; Strom & Strom, 1995). Many of these activities have been facilitated in areas with high rates of poverty for both elders and children or in rural communities lacking in technological resources; several pair incarcerated youngsters and long-term-care residents. Mutual support and caring communities of foster grandparents, Third Age resettlement sponsors, and grandparents who are raising grandchildren are increasing.

An important way LLIs try to give back to the institutions and communities in which they are located is through civic engagement and service learning programs. Service learning involves offering courses in partnership with local agencies in which older individuals learn new knowledge and skills that they can later apply in volunteer service. For example, one successful model in Portland, Maine, has OLLI students working with the public school adult education program in ESOL courses. OLLI students take a course offered by a team of ESOL teachers and learn about how to teach English to people who have come to the United States as refugees or immigrants. On successful completion of the course, the OLLI students volunteer as teacher aides in regular ESOL classes. Other successful service learning collaborations have occurred with hospitals, historical societies, hospices, nursing homes, and a range of community-based organizations.

Glasser (2008) taught an intergenerational American history course that included traditional undergraduate students earning three academic credits and a group of older adults who were members of the LLI at the same university. Although much of the course was classroom-based, an important module involved having everyone read about the Five Points neighborhood in Lower Manhattan (made famous by the Martin Scorsese movie, *Gangs of New York*) and making a field trip by bus to that location. One observation made was that the older students "felt invigorated by being surrounded by young people while the traditional students enjoyed the insights and memories of the older adults" (Glasser, 2008, p. 66). Brady (2006) reports having had similarly successful intergenerational educational experiences in a travel-based course he facilitates each summer entitled, Baseball and American Society: A Journey.

Kaplan (2008) describes international programs in the United Kingdom, including dance, film, and a city-sponsored intergenerational champion mentoring project. Young and Rosenberg (2006) explore Japanese models. Both the University of Pennsylvania and the University of Pittsburgh have established resource banks, primary research, curricula, specific funding, and support for intergenerational programming (Kaplan, 2008; Newman, Ward, Smith, McCrea, & Wilson, 2008).

EMERGING ISSUES AND CONTROVERSIES IN THE FIELD

It should be noted that educational programming and learning for older adults is a fluid, not crystallized venture (Wolf, 1994, 2007). Despite a general agreement that learning contributes to well-being for older people, several current debates and disagreements among practitioners can be cited:

• Who should teach or administer programs for older adults? Should LLIs, for example, have paid and professional faculty or keep with the mainstream practice of using volunteers? Paid professional teachers can help to ensure quality, but member fees and overall program costs go up. While most volunteer peer instructors seem to be doing a good job, there can be uneven quality when people who think they can teach and want to teach have unproven track records.

• To what degree are program initiators obligated to seek out isolated or disengaged elders so as to provide socialization for these individuals?

• How will programs be funded? At a recent seminar in England, a representative of Learning Over 50 reflected, "Older people have paid for education all their lives, now they want to have it for themselves" (Benyon, 2008).

• To what degree will elder learning provide support to the community (i.e., to ameliorate poverty) (Eisen, 2005).

• What platform will exist to track advances in research, programmatic delivery, and technology to benefit this constituency?

• As greater numbers of Americans age, our field will grow exponentially. What paradigms will shift? What priorities will prevail in the development of theory and practice?

• Where will the resources come from to provide safe environments for elders who are vulnerable to crime and abuse? What role will older adult education take in leading this area of concern? Will transportation services be added? Will rural centers be developed?

- Will older adult programs be available for prisoners? To train in literacy, numeracy, basic skills?

- What is the role of lifelong learning in U.S. citizenship? In belonging? A noted researcher observed that "the potential of lifelong learning helps cut the dependency of individuals on other often costly state-funded support services" (Inquiry into the Future for Lifelong Learning, 2009).

THE OLDER LEARNER AS A UNIQUE INDIVIDUAL

Sometimes, in our zeal as educational gerontologists, we err on the side of stereotyping older people (Alemon & Fitzpatrick, 2000; Wolf, 1994). We think of homogeneity and not of heterogeneity. Obviously, this is a miscarriage of well wishing. In addition, it is a barrier to educational connection. Each person is unique, often having meaningful connection to a particular cohort or region. Each of us is awed when we meet an older adult learner. For example, this is a small cross-section of folks we have encountered in the past year:

- A retired Marine (male) taking a ballet class in Cambridge, Massachusetts

- A wheelchair-bound 81-year-old in California who wants to complete a Certificate in Gerontology online so that she can provide advocacy for the elderly

- A 74-year-old who hopes to work with autistic children

- A former U.S. Army chaplain (male) who wants to teach junior high school home economics

- A rabbi in need of information about aging so he can counsel and also age well

- A victim of spousal abuse who hopes to work in social work

- An incarcerated woman planning to open a beauty parlor when she is paroled

- A 60-year-old taking a mandated DUI course

- A lawyer hoping for a new career

- A woman (age 80) who hopes to collect reminiscences of seniors in long-term care

- An immigrant (age 66) with a dental degree who is driving a taxi

- An illiterate grandmother who is caring for her grandchildren

- An American Indian who hopes to provide Medicare and Medicaid advice to tribal cohorts

- An isolated 70-year-old caregiver who writes poetry

- A Somali refuge (age 61) who hopes to bring his family to the United States

- An instructor in motorcycle safety who wants to write a book

How do we prepare for such a diverse population? We stop, we assess, and we listen. Often, our older adult learners will identify where they are going; sometimes they will need to explore and experiment with various modalities in adult education. There is a story everywhere: Opening our senses and honoring these stories will guide us to programming and inform our hearts about the nature of aging and learning. If we truly believe that every individual in every generation deserves to grow and develop to his or her greatest potential, then we are awed and inspired by the opportunity to create learning environments that allow for enhancement and cultural connection.

CONCLUSION

Times change. We build our classrooms—the *classroom* is an enormous metaphor for the myriad ways of education—to provide for the learners who come to us. Now an aging society, we begin to hear the voices of our new constituents. Who they are and what will work for them is still in flux (Administration on Aging, 2006). Whereas one set of older adults wants a course in Shakespeare, another needs workforce training (New York State Office for the Aging, 2008), and still another wants literacy and advocacy training, and another seeks to be thoroughly involved with the next generations. Freire (1970/1992) framed his theory of learning on the morality of an educational system that is underpinned by "a quality of consciousness by which men and women, together, critically perceive, and name their reality" (pp. 5–6). As we reflect on the peoples coming into our view and honor those who have arrived at integrity, we can respond creatively to an aging society.

REFERENCES

Administration on Aging. (2006, October). Statistics, profiles of older Americans. Retrieved July 29, 2008, from http://www.aarp.org/research/reference/statistics/aresearch-import-519.html

Alemon, S., & Fitzpatrick, T. (2000). *Therapeutic interventions with ethnic elders: Health and social issues.* New York: Haworth Press.

Americans for Libraries Council. (2007). *Libraries for the future.* New York: Americans for Libraries Council, Lifelong Access Libraries Leadership Institute.

Barton, H. (2000). *Junior Republic and elders.* Presentation to the Gerontological Society of America, Phoenix, AZ.

Beatty, P. T., & Wolf, M. A. (1996). *Connecting with older adults: Educational responses and approaches.* Malabar, FL: Krieger Press.

Benyon, J. (2008). *Older people, learning, and society* (research seminar). University of Leicester, United Kingdom.

Brabazon, K. (2007). Innovative intergenerational curriculum enhances learning at Bronx high school. *The Older Learner, 15*(4).

Brady, E. M. (2006). Journal of a journey—Teaching baseball on the road. In E. J. Rielley (Ed.), *Baseball in the classroom: Essays on teaching the national pastime.* Jefferson, NC: McFarland & Co.

Cohen, G. D. (1992). *The brain in human aging.* New York: Springer.

Cohen, G. D. (2001). *The creative age: Awakening human potential in the second half of life.* New York: Harper & Collins.

Cohen, G. D. (2005). *The mature mind: The positive power of the aging brain.* New York: Basic Books.

Courtenay, B.C. (1989). Education for older adults. In S. B. Merriam & P. M. Cunningham (Eds.), *Handbook of adult and continuing education.* San Francisco: Jossey-Bass.

Eisen, M. J. (2005). Shifts in the landscape of learning: New challenges, new opportunities. In M. A. Wolf (Ed.), *Adulthood, new terrain.* New Directions for Adult and Continuing Education, No. 108. San Francisco: Jossey-Bass.

Erikson, E. H. (1968). *Identity: Youth and crisis.* New York: W. W. Norton.

Erikson, E. H. (Ed.). (1978). *Adulthood.* New York: W. W. Norton.

Erikson, E. H. (1982). *The life cycle completed* (2nd ed.). New York: W. W. Norton.

Erikson, E. H. (2001). Reflections on the last stage—And the first. In R. Diessner & J. Tieggs (Eds.), *Notable selections in human development* (2nd ed., pp. 340–347). Guilford, CT: McGraw-Hill.

Erikson, E. H., Erikson, J. M., & Kivnick, H. (1986). *Vital involvement in old age.* New York: W. W. Norton.

Findsen, B. (2005). *Learning later.* Malabar, FL.: Krieger.

Fisher, J. C., & Wolf, M. A. (Eds.). (1998). *Using learning to meet the challenges of older adulthood.* San Francisco: Jossey-Bass.

Fisher, J. C., & Wolf, M. A. (2000). Older adult learning. In A. L. Wilson & E. R. Hayes (Eds.), *Handbook of adult and continuing education* (pp. 480–492). San Francisco: Jossey-Bass.

Fitzpatrick, T. (2003). Computer attitudes and life satisfaction among older religious women. *Journal of Religious Gerontology, 15*(4), 57–78.

Freire, P. (1992). *Pedagogy of the oppressed* (M. B. Ramos, Trans.). New York: Continuum. (Original work published 1970)

Glasser, R. (2008). WOW!—An intergenerational OLLI experience in Waterbury, Connecticut. *The LLI Review, 3,* 62–66.

Golaski, A. (2007). *Musical interventions with older adults.* Unpublished master's research, Saint Joseph College, West Hartford, CT.

Henkin, N., & Zapf, J. (2007). How communities can promote civic engagement of people age 50-plus. *Generations,* pp. 72–77.

Inquiry into the Future for Lifelong Learning (IFLL). (2009). Retrieved February 1, 2009, from http://www.niace.org.uk/lifelonglearninginquiry/news.htm

Jarvis, P., & Parker, S. (Eds.). (2005). *Human learning: From the biological to the spiritual.* London: Routledge.

Kaplan, M. (2008). An American werewolf in London. In *Grow,—intergenerational bonds* (pp. 2 & 4). University Park, PA: Penn State Extension. http://intergenerational.cas.psu.edu/Newsletters.html Retrieved August 3, 2008

Libraries for the future. (2007). *Lifelong access libraries leadership institute.* New York: Americans for Libraries Council.

Lightfoot, K., & Brady, E. M. (2005). Transformation through teaching and learning: The story of Maine's Osher Lifelong Learning Institute. *Journal of Transformative Education, 3*(3).

Lindeman, E. (1961). *The meaning of adult education.* Norman: Oklahoma Research Center for Continuing, Professional, and Higher Education.

Manheimer, R. (2007a). Adult education. In J. Birren (Ed.), *Encyclopedia of gerontology* (2nd ed.). New York: Academic Press.

Manheimer, R. (2007b). Allocating resources for lifelong learning for older adults. In R. A. Pruchno & M. A. Smyer (Eds.), *Challenges of an aging society, ethical dilemmas, political issues* (pp. 217–237). Baltimore: The Johns Hopkins University Press.

Merriam, S., Caffarella, R., & Baumgartner, L. (2007). *Learning in adulthood: A comprehensive guide* (3rd ed.). San Francisco: Jossey-Bass.

Newman, S., Ward, C., Smith, T., McCrea, J., & Wilson, J. (2008). *International programs: Past, present and future.* London: Taylor and Francis.

New York State Office for the Aging. (2008). *Working with older adults: Charting the future of workforce training and education in New York.* Retrieved January 6, 2010, from http://www.aging.ny .gov/ReportsAndData/WorkforceEducation/ WorkforceEducationAndTrainingListening SessionsReport2008.pdf

Ownby, R. L. (2006). Making the Internet a friendlier place for older people. *Generations, 3*(2).

Pejic, B. (2008). Culture, community, and diversity in OLLI: A case study. *The LLI Review, 3,* 1–10.

Pruchno, R. A., & Smyer, M. A. (Eds.). (2007). *Challenges of an aging society, ethical dilemmas, political issues.* Baltimore: The Johns Hopkins University Press.

Robinson, S. P., & Lakin, M. B. (2007). *Framing new terrain: Older adults and higher education.* Washington, DC: American Council on Education.

Rowe, J. W., & Kahn, R. L. (1998). *Successful aging.* New York: Pantheon.

Sadler, W. A., & Krefft, J. H. (2008). *Changing course: Navigating life after fifty.* Centennial, CO: The Center for the Third Age Leadership Press.

Selwyn, N., Gorard, S., & Furlong, J. (2006). *Adult learning in the digital age: Information technology and the learning society.* London: Routledge.

Shedletsky, L. (2006). Internet training for older adult learners: An intergenerational mentoring approach. *The LLI Review, 1,* 34–43.

Strom, R. D., & Strom, S. K. (1995). Intergenerational learning: Grandparents in the school. *Educational Gerontology,* pp. 321–335.

U.S. Census Bureau, Current Population Survey. (2007, July 27). *Educational attainment of the population 55 years and over by sex and age.* Retrieved July 29, 2008, from http:///www .census.gov/population/socdemo/age/20060lder_ table3.xls Accessed July 29, 2008.

Vaillant, G. E. (2002). *Aging well.* Boston: Little, Brown.

Willis, S. (2006). Technology and learning in current and future generations of elders. *Generations, 30*(2).

Wolf, M. A. (1994). *Older adults: Learning in the Third Age.* ERIC Center on Education and Training for Employment. Information Series No. 358.

Wolf, M. A. (Ed.). (2005). *Adulthood: New terrain.* New Directions for Adult and Continuing Education, No. 108. San Francisco: Jossey-Bass.

Wolf, M. A. (2007). *Profiles in older adult learners for 2010.* Chapel Hill, NC: Annual Lifelong Access Libraries Leadership.

Wolf, M. A. (2009). Learning in older adulthood. In P. Jarvis (Ed.), *The Routledge international handbook of lifelong learning.* London: Routledge.

Young, K., & Rosenberg, E. (2006). Lifelong learning in the United States and Japan. *The LLI Review, 1,* 69–85.

35

PERSPECTIVES ON DISABILITY IN ADULT AND CONTINUING EDUCATION

TONETTE S. ROCCO AND SANDRA L. FORNES

The estimated number of people with disabilities in the United States is 43 million (Colker, 2005). Fewer than 15% of people are born with disabilities (Shapiro, 1993). Any person regardless of education, socioeconomic status, race, ethnicity, or gender can become disabled throughout the lifespan. People with disabilities constitute possibly the largest minority group whose access to public places, education, and the political sphere has been limited.

In 1962, Ed Roberts began the civil rights movement of people with disabilities when he entered the University of California at Berkeley in a wheelchair (Shapiro, 1993). Accessibility was his first concern when considering what university to attend instead of academics; the University of California at Los Angeles was accessible because of an influx of veterans. UCLA, however, did not offer the program Roberts wanted to pursue. His community college adviser suggested the least restrictive environment should not be the deciding factor; instead, he should pursue his academic interests (Shapiro, 1993). Roberts's pursuit of his academic interest required UC Berkeley to provide accommodations. Roberts's insistence on being accommodated at the university of his choice was a turning point for adult, continuing, and higher education institutions, which now must consider the relationship of disability to adult learning and education.

This chapter attempts to represent the worldview of people with disabilities through use of the literature of disability studies; it is written from the perspective that people with disabilities compose a minority group struggling for civil rights. The chapter is organized in four parts: perspectives on disability, access and accommodation, considerations for instructors and program planners, and implications.

PERSPECTIVES ON DISABILITY

This section includes the medical and economic perspective, sociopolitical perspective, and disability studies. Each section contains the relevant academic and professional field, description, and definition of disability.

Medical and Economic Perspective

Special education, rehabilitation, vocational education, and allied health are some of the fields that view disability from a medical and economic perspective. Prior to 1970, the medical and economic perspectives were dominant (Engel, 1977). These perspectives focus on people's disabilities rather than on their abilities, which stereotypes individuals with disabilities as second-class citizens unable to make competent decisions or perform job duties (Boyle, 1997). Often, individuals with disabilities are seen as "owning" the problem rather than having limitations caused by environmental restrictions such as discrimination (Kaplan, 2000).

The medical perspective is based on clinical examinations and medical remedies of a person's handicap and aims to restore abilities or "fix" supposed bodily defects or deficiencies (Tate & Pledger, 2003). To be recognized as a disability, a medical condition must be identified and given a diagnosis, defining disability as a condition of impairment (Hahn, 1988). This medical perspective constructed images of people with disabilities as deviants, menaces, angelic innocents, and poor unfortunates (Shapiro, 1993).

The medical perspective has often been joined with an economic perspective. The economic perspective defined disability as an inability to work (Hahn, 1985, 1999) and aimed at enhancing individuals' occupational capacities and talents to overcome their vocational limitations (Verbrugge & Jette, 1994). Under this perspective, logic exists that disabled people are less productive than able-bodied people, so paying less for their work is permitted (Gorman, 2000). Worker productivity is measured against accommodation costs to determine the feasibility of employment of the person (Engel & Munger, 2003). Disability is viewed as a commodity (Albrecht, 1992; Barnes, 1998) that "acquires an exchange value that a few people profit from" (Charlton, 1998, p. 47). An industry has developed to serve the needs of people with disabilities in institutions such as nursing homes, with an average annual cost of $40,784. Allowing someone to live independently with personal assistance services costs only $9,692 (*Mouth Magazine*, 1995).

There are five main classifications of disability: developmental, cognitive, mental, physical, and sensory. A disability can be in more than one category, and an individual can have multiple disabilities. Developmental disabilities are substantial, originate before the age of 18, and are expected to continue indefinitely (Wright, 1980). This classification includes mental retardation, epilepsy, cerebral palsy, and other conditions such as traumatic brain injury (TBI) acquired before the age of 18. Cognitive disabilities affect "the ability to think, understand, learn about, and be aware of the environment through the senses" (Wright, 1980, p. 96). Mental retardation, learning disabilities, autism, and TBI are examples of cognitive disabilities. Cognitive disabilities can range "from mild conditions to severe dysfunction" (Brodwin, Parker, & DeLaGarza, 1996, p. 199). Mental disabilities or disorders are psychological or behavioral patterns that occur and cause distress that is not expected as part of normal development or culture. These can include schizophrenia, bipolar disorder, obsessive compulsive disorder (OCD), panic disorder, post traumatic stress disorder (PTSD), and borderline personality disorder, emotional dysfunction due to substance abuse or TBI, depression, and other conditions. Physical disabilities are limitations in mobility, use of limbs, disfigurement, and pain caused by injury or chronic condition. One type of physical disability is paralysis requiring a person to use a wheelchair for mobility. Sensory disabilities are related to a loss of an external sense such as seeing, hearing, smelling, tasting, or touching (Wright, 1980). Vision and hearing are the most common sensory disabilities. Degrees of sensory loss range from meeting the legal measure (legally blind) to total loss. Communities and cultures exist around these disabilities known as "the blind" and "the deaf" (Clark, 2002; Shapiro, 1993). Individuals who identify with Deaf as a culture have a fierce pride in their deafness, language, and social system. Adult educators should be aware that adults classified as disabled may not view themselves as anything other than a member of another culture or oppressed group.

Sociopolitical Perspective

Sociology, history, political science, and literature are some of the fields where the sociopolitical perspective originated. In the 1970s, the traditional medical and economic perspectives were challenged first by the minority group model and then by the sociopolitical perspective on disability (Hahn, 1988). This perspective is based on four traditions: American functionalism, social constructionism, historical materialism, and alienation (Rocco, 2006). American functionalism sees people with disabilities as having diminished capacity to make decisions and to contribute to an industrialized system where workers are seen as individual units of production (Barnes, 1998). Social constructivism is the notion that concepts or practices are normal even though they are artifacts of specific cultures and contexts. Historical materialism argues that disability is socially constructed, emerging from the explicit ways society organizes basic and necessary activities such as work, leisure, education, domestic life, and citizenship (Gleeson, 1999). Alienation is internalizing oppression to the point that individuals feel isolated from similar others and powerless to change their condition. Society's attitudes and structures are the cause of handicaps, not individual biological or cognitive differences (Bogdan & Taylor, 1976, 1982; Oliver, 1996). Under this perspective, society's attitudes based in the personal tragedy, social deviant, and shirker views (Goffman, 1963) sustain another categorization system for defining disability—people with visible and invisible disabilities (Rocco, 1997, 2001b). A visible disability is readily seen by an observer, and the person is recognized and accepted as having a disability. Invisible disabilities cannot be seen, and after disclosure, the person with an invisible disability is frequently thought to be lying or shirking responsibility (Rocco, 2000).

Disability Studies

Disability studies is an interdisciplinary field based on a sociopolitical analysis of disability reframed as a designation with political and social significance. The critical divisions in society are explored, such as "normal vs. pathological, the insider vs. the outsider, or the competent citizen vs. ward of the state" (Linton, 1998, p. 2), along with the question of who decides a person is disabled, the person or society. Under investigation are variations in behavior, appearance, and function, with a resistance to reducing disability to categories to be counted and defined (Linton, 1998).

Disability studies scholars argue that disability, impairment, and oppression of the disabled are underconceptualized and theorized (Charlton, 1998; Linton, 1998; Oliver, 1990). In response, Charlton (1998) proposed a comprehensive theory of disability oppression. Oppression is "when individuals are *systematically* subjected to political, economic, cultural, or social degradation" because of group membership (Charlton, 1998, p. 8). The theory is composed of these concepts: (a) political economy, (b) culture(s) and belief systems, (c) (false) consciousness and alienation, and (d) power and ideology. Political economy has at its core issues of class and who "control[s] the means of production and force" (Charlton, 1998, p. 23). Culture and belief systems include attitudes which "are almost universally pejorative" (Charlton, 1998, p. 25). Culture is not static and is influenced continually by history, politics, economy, and institutions. False consciousness and alienation are the third concepts. Alienation is the internalization of the image of being less normal and capable than others (Charlton, 1998). Authentic consciousness informs being when an individual becomes critically aware of the social conditions, opportunities, and oppressive forces that exist. Power and ideology organize the way in which the world is experienced through social, political, and economic systems.

The definition of disability is terrain contested by people with specific disabilities (such as the Deaf) and their organizations (Thomas, 2003). Scholars use three meanings, "disability as restricted activity" (Thomas, 2003, p. 2), disability as a form of social oppression (Oliver, 1990, 1996), and disability as socially constructed. An example is the United Nations definition of disability, "Society creates a handicap when it fails to accommodate the diversity of all its members"; it argues that attitudinal and environmental barriers prevent "full, equal and active participation in society" (United Nations, 1994, paragraphs 3 and 4, cited in Priestly, 2001).

ACCESS AND ACCOMMODATIONS

Students eligible for services under the Individuals with Disabilities Education Act (IDEA) are not automatically eligible for accommodations at work or university under Section 504 and the Americans with Disabilities Act (ADA) (Gormley, Hughes, Block, & Lendman, 2005). IDEA provides a free and appropriate public education to qualifying students up to age 21 and focuses on educational outcomes and success, whereas Section 504 and ADA are civil rights mandates that ensure opportunity and equal access and prevent discrimination (Gormley et al., 2005). Section 504 and the ADA require that a specific diagnosis with an established functional limitation in a major life activity be present (Gormley et al., 2005). In this section, the legal responsibilities of educational and employing institutions, the adult learner, and the worker are discussed.

Legal Responsibilities of Educational and Employing Institutions

Federal laws were enacted to protect people with disabilities from discrimination (Clark, 2006; Thomas, 2000), based on the premise that disability is a natural part of the human experience and that individuals have the right to live independently, pursue meaningful careers, and enjoy full inclusion in society (Milani, 1996). These laws include the Rehabilitation Act of 1973, Section 504, and the ADA (Thomas, 2000). The ADA is aimed at integrating individuals with disabilities into society and the workforce.

Section 504 "stipulates that no qualified person with a disability may be denied participation in, be denied the benefits of, or be subjected to discrimination under any program or activity receiving federal financial assistance" (Thomas, 2000, p. 249). Section 504 applies to organizations receiving federal funds. The ADA is modeled after Section 504 and extends protection of people with disabilities to work, nonformal education venues, and other organizations. The law applies to employers of 15 or more. Title II forbids discrimination by an employer if the applicant or employee can perform the essential functions of the job with "reasonable proficiency." The employer is obligated to eliminate nonessential duties from a position when hiring a worker with a disability (Kemp, 1994). The ADA further prohibits entities that operate places of public accommodation from discriminating against people with disabilities by denying them full and equal enjoyment of the goods, services, facilities, privileges, advantages, or accommodations provided.

In the last 20 years, there has been a 32% increase in students with disabilities enrolling in postsecondary education (National Council on Disability, 2003); however, more than half of these students are at risk of failure (National Council on Disability, 2003). Court decisions have shaped access and accommodations in postsecondary settings (Brinkerhoff, McGuire, & Shaw, 2002), which impacts the adult learner, the university, and instructors.

Title II of the ADA prohibits public entities such as adult basic education venues and colleges from denying qualified people with disabilities the right to participate in or benefit from the services or programs provided and from subjecting such individuals to discrimination due to having a disability (42 U.S.C. § 12132). Whether providing postsecondary education, adult basic education, literacy education, or continuing professional education, the institution has an obligation to administer tests such as the General Education Development (GED) tests, finals, or certification exams "in a place and in a manner that ensures the testing reflects an individual's aptitude, achievement level, or other factors the test is designed to measure" (Sturomski & Auchter, 2001, p. 13).

Once a student or employee has documented a qualifying disability, the organization is responsible for providing reasonable accommodations or modifications that would allow the person to participate in programs and be a productive member of the organization. Accommodations must be provided on a nondiscriminatory basis and cannot result in unfair advantage, require significant alteration to the program or activity, result in the lowering of academic or technical standards, or cause the college or employer to incur undue financial hardship (*Nathanson v. Medical College of Pennsylvania*, 1991; *Wynne v. Tufts University School of Medicine*, 1992). When accommodations are necessary, they must be provided in a timely fashion (*Smith v. State University of New York*, 1997) and include (but are not limited to) adjustments in timelines for the completion of degree requirements and substitutions for course requirements. Other accommodations include adaptation of course delivery, the use of tape recorders (Braddock, 2002), auxiliary aids such as interpreters (*Indiana Department of Human Services v. Firth*, 1992) or readers in libraries, classroom equipment adapted for use by students with manual impairments, and the use of service dogs (34 C.F.R. § 104.44[b]). In addition, work accommodations also include job reassignment or restructuring and policy and work schedule modifications.

Legal Responsibilities of the Adult Learner and Worker

Many variables affect the successful transition of students with disabilities into postsecondary education or, if leaving secondary education, to seek adult basic education or literacy services. The disability documentation purpose changes from IDEA's requirements for instruction and intervention at the primary and secondary levels to the ADA's and Section 504's requirements of documentation to verify eligibility at a postsecondary level (Shaw, 2006) or for work. Students and secondary school personnel involved in the transition need to recognize that postsecondary service providers require information addressing key legal questions such as: Does the student have a disability as defined by Section 504 and ADA? Is the disability substantially limiting? and What accommodations should be provided to effectively address these functional limitations in the postsecondary context (Brinkerhoff et al., 2002)? Adult learners and workers have the burden of proof to document that function is "substantially limited" and that they are "otherwise qualified" before the university or workplace is required to make "reasonable accommodations" (Brinkerhoff et al., 2002).

The U.S. Supreme Court ruled that it is insufficient for individuals attempting to prove disability status to submit only evidence of a medical diagnosis (Thomas, 2000). The ADA requires evidence that the extent of the limitation caused by impairment is "substantially limiting" (*Toyota Motor Manufacturing, Kentucky, Inc. v. Williams*, 2002). This means that life activities are restricted as to the conditions, manner, or duration under which they can be performed in comparison to most people (28 C.F.R. App. B to Part 36). A condition may be substantially limiting under ADA even though it has not been rated as permanent (*Aldrich v. Boeing Co*, 1998). Once it is determined that a person's impairment is substantially limiting, it then is necessary to ascertain whether the individual is "otherwise qualified." Otherwise qualified means that the person must be able to meet the essential eligibility requirements of a program, with or without reasonable accommodation, in spite of the restrictions imposed by the disability (42 U.S.C. § 12112).

CONSIDERATIONS FOR INSTRUCTORS AND PROGRAM PLANNERS

Instruction in college classrooms and workplace training is at a faster pace and requires more reading, more independent problem-solving, higher order thinking, and self-empowerment strategies (Rosenbaum & Person, 2003). However, people do not learn at the same pace (Tincani, 2004). People with learning or cognitive disabilities are likely to require additional instruction and practice (Tincani, 2004). Poor note-taking skills, limited participation opportunities, infrequent assessment, nonindividualized instruction (Tincani, 2004), and lack of self-determination skills (Hong, Ivy, Gonzalez, & Ehrensberger, 2007) contribute to academic failure. All of these factors create barriers and frustration for students with disabilities (National Council on Disability, 2003). When instructors make an effort to promote barrier-free learning environments and encourage self-determination skills and honest communication, as well as using teaching strategies to benefit people with disabilities, all learners will become more engaged in learning (Tincani, 2004).

Barrier-Free Learning Environments

The external environment contributes to successful learning. In the case of students with disabilities, elements in the environment can aggravate a condition. These elements include appropriate lighting for students with visual impairments or light sensitivities, adequate ventilation and temperature regulation for students with health impairments (e.g., asthma, allergies), and nonencumbered access to the door for students who need to use the restroom frequently (Hong et al., 2007). "White noise" from overhead projectors and other equipment, hallway noise, or activity outside the classroom (Hong et al., 2007) can be distracting to all students. Students with cognitive and mental disabilities are more easily distracted, losing concentration. Students who are hard of hearing may become totally confused and frustrated because of background noise. While the instructor does not have total control over the environment, a change of room or other adaptations can be requested to reduce environmental distractions, which benefits all learners (Hong et al., 2007).

Self-Determination

Helping learners with disabilities develop vital self-determination skills will enhance learners' success in postsecondary education, adult basic education, and work. Self-determination refers to actions that are identified by four essential characteristics: (1) autonomous actions, (2) self-regulated behaviors, (3) empowered manner, and (4) self-realizing manner (Wehmeyer, 2001). Self-determination skills have been shown to be the primary factor in improving employment retention for individuals with disabilities (Fornes, Rocco, & Rosenberg, 2008). Self-determination emerges from learning across the lifespan and empowers individuals to plan and make choices about their careers, work, and life.

Communication

Open and honest communication must be established. Communication is complicated by the knowledge that many adults become disabled as adults; disability and chronic illness are private matters, disability affects communication skills, and learning about the disability is a process (Rocco, 2001a). Adults with cognitive disorders may go undiagnosed until their compensation skills are no longer enough (Jordan, 1996) for success at work or in higher education. Being diagnosed with learning disabilities after being successful is a disconcerting experience. Adults may fear discrimination and other negative reactions after disclosing disability status and requesting an accommodation (Rocco, 2000, 2001a). The disability may affect the ability to communicate effectively and in a timely manner. Service providers may be late with documentation.

On the instructor's and employer's sides, little experience with disability, the suspicion that accommodations provide an unfair advantage, and the frustration of already being overworked interfere with effective communication. The best course of action is to schedule an appointment to discuss the accommodations and the disability prior to the start of an academic term or as soon as a worker or student is diagnosed. When this does not happen, the instructor or employer should not assume negligence or lack

of responsibility on the part of the adult. Rather, the instructor or employer should try to alleviate fear of a negative reaction by leading a proactive discussion.

Teaching Strategies for Instructors

When instructors use teaching strategies and good principles of learning and motivation, they create a learning environment effective for all learners. Universal instructional design is based on the principle that learning can and should be made accessible to all students, regardless of their need or learning ability (Battle, 2002). Another principle is that curriculum should be based on multiple means of representation, expression, and engagement to expand learning opportunities "for individuals with different backgrounds, learning styles, abilities, and disabilities in widely varied learning contexts" (Center for Applied Special Technology, 2001).

For all students, universal instructional design starts with universal environmental design, which improves physical spaces in the community (i.e., building, transportation systems, and other systems) and incorporates accommodations and access strategies that increase learning. For example, putting course materials on an accessible Web site (see http://people.rit.edu/easi/) increases access for students with disabilities, English as a Second Language (ESL) learners, older learners, and others. Instructors should clarify the course's essential components (Hong et al., 2007). Essential components are the outcomes (including skills, knowledge, and attitudes) all students must demonstrate. Instructors can use multiple assessment approaches to evaluate learning outcomes, such as multiple choice questions, written essays, group assignments, class presentations, and portfolios (Carlson, 1980). An accessible syllabus contains (a) learning objectives; (b) schedule of events, discussion topics, exam dates, assignments, and readings; (c) assignments and grading rubrics; and (d) details on academic misconduct such as tardiness, absences, late assignments, and test and assignment makeups (Ohio State University Office for Disability Services, 2000). Listing study objectives for each unit will help learners (Malott, 1984) organize content, gain time management skills, and remind them of techniques they previously used, improving student efficiency. Instructors should increase the frequency of tests and quizzes at regular intervals throughout the course (Polson, 1995).

A positive relationship exists between academic achievement, student engagement (Greenwood, Delaquardi, & Hall, 1984), and self-empowerment. Ways to increase learner engagement in lectures are guided notes, response cards, and peer tutoring (Tincani, 2004). Guided notes are handouts that provide basic information about the lecture, with spaces for students to write key points (Barbetta & Skaruppa, 1995). For students with note-taking difficulties, guided notes help them to identify what to write and to organize information. "Response cards are cards or signs that are held up simultaneously by all students to display their response to a question or problem presented" (Heward, 1994, p. 299). In peer tutoring (DuPaul, Ervin, Hook, & McGoey 1998; Gumpel & Frank 1999), students break off into small groups and take turns teaching each other. The tutor provides feedback to responses.

IMPLICATIONS AND FUTURE RESEARCH

Little work from a critical perspective or that includes the voice of the disabled has been published in adult education literature outside of conference proceedings. In all of the *Handbooks* starting with Knowles (1960), and including the two books attempting to be more inclusive than the *Handbooks* (Peters, Jarvis, & Associates, 1991; Sheared & Sissel, 2001), only one chapter on disabilities was evident (Klugerman, 1989). From 1984 to 2005, seven articles were published on disability in *Adult Education Quarterly,* and five of these are on issues surrounding HIV/AIDS. "At issue here is who speaks, under what conditions, for whom, and how knowledge is constructed and translated within and between different communities located within asymmetrical relations of power" (Giroux, 1992, p. 26). The field of adult education maintains this asymmetrical power relationship with people

with disabilities by centering on issues of disease and health and not on the experiences of adults with disabilities as a social justice issue.

Certainly, there are venues where adult educators train people with disabilities, and the delivery systems are based in the medical or economic perspective. Recognizing this is a first step toward "creating a new learning alternative" (Ohliger, 1975, p. 38) for people with disabilities from the perspective of education as a civil right. In 1989, Ross-Gordon suggested a need for research on individuals with learning disabilities at different points in their development and educational settings from an interdisciplinary approach. In 1998, Gadbow and DuBois suggested increasing awareness of all disabilities, creating diversity efforts inclusive of people with disabilities in all types of organizations, and increasing collaboration with business. We would agree with this and suggest that the multifaceted experience of disability, and the many disabilities people live with, should be of increasing concern for adult educators. As Clark (2006) suggests, we need to make visible the "elements obscure[ing] disability as a social phenomenon" (p. 318). We conclude with some questions to consider when creating programs or conducting research on/about/with people with disabilities:

1. Does adult education play a role in mitigating or exacerbating inequities faced by individuals with disabilities?

2. When designing and implementing programs and practices, are individuals with disabilities considered in terms of accommodations and equity?

3. Is the experience of disability looked at as limiting educational options, or is access to education a civil rights concern?

4. What influence has disability studies or disability theory had on adult education research?

REFERENCES

Albrecht, G. L. (1992). *The disability business: Rehabilitation in America.* Sage Library of Social Research, No. 190. Newbury Park, CA: Sage.

Aldrich v. Boeing Co, 146 F, 3d 1265 (10th Cir, 1998).

Americans with Disabilities Act of 1990, Pub. L. No. 101–336, § 2, 104 Stat. 328 (1991).

Barbetta, P. M., & Skaruppa, C. L. (1995). Looking for a way to improve your behavior analysis lectures? Try guided notes. *Behavior Analyst, 18,* 155–160.

Barnes, C. (1998). The social model of disability: A sociological phenomenon ignored by sociologists? In T. Shakespeare (Ed.), *The disability reader: Social science perspectives.* (pp. 66–78). London: Cassell.

Battle, D. E. (2002). Laws impacting on higher education. In K. B. Butler & E. R. Silliman (Eds.), *Speaking, reading, and writing in children with* language learning disabilities: New paradigms in research and practice (pp. 316–336). Mahwah, NJ: Lawrence Erlbaum.

Bogdan, R., & Taylor, S. (1976). The judged not the judges: An insider's view of mental retardation. American Psychologist, 31(1), 47–52.

Bogdan, R., & Taylor, S. (1982). Inside out: The social meaning of mental retardation. Toronto, Ontario: University of Toronto Press.

Boyle, M. (1997). Social barriers to successful reentry into mainstream organizational culture: People with disabilities. Human Resource Development Quarterly, 8, 259–269.

Braddock, D. L. (2002). Public financial support for disability at the dawn of the 21st century. American Journal on Mental Retardation, 6(107), 478–489.

Brinkerhoff, L. C., McGuire, J. M., & Shaw, S. F. (2002). Postsecondary education and transition for students with learning disabilities (2nd ed.). Austin, TX: Pro-ed.

Brodwin, M., Parker, R. M., & DeLaGarza, D. (1996). Disability and accommodations. In E. M. Szymanski & R. M. Parker (Eds.), Work and disability: Issues and strategies in career development and job placement (pp. 165–208). Austin, TX: PRO-ED.

Carlson, N. A. (1980). General principles of learning and motivation. Teaching Exceptional Children, 12, 60–62.

Center for Applied Special Technology. (2001). Universal design for learning. Retrieved July 25, 2008, from http://www.cast.org/udl/

Charlton, J. I. (1998). Nothing about us without us: Disability oppression and empowerment. Berkeley: University of California Press.

Clark, M. (2002). Do you hear what I see: Learning experiences of black men who are Deaf or hard of hearing. In J. M. Pettitt (Ed.), Proceedings of the 43rd Annual Adult Education Research Conference (pp. 79–84). Raleigh: North Carolina State University.

Clark, M. (2006). Adult education and disability studies, an interdisciplinary relationship: Research implication for adult education. Adult Education Quarterly, 56(4), 308–322.

Colker, R. (2005). The disability pendulum: The first decade of the Americans with Disabilities Act. New York: New York University Press.

DuPaul, G. J., Ervin, R. A., Hook, C. L., & McGoey, K. E. (1998). Peer tutoring for children with attention deficit hyperactivity disorder: Effects on classroom behavior and academic performance. Journal of Applied Behavior Analysis, 31, 579–592.

Engel, D. M., & Munger, F. W. (2003). Rights of inclusion: Law and identity in the life stories of Americans with disabilities. Chicago: University of Chicago Press.

Engel, G. (1977). The need for a new medical model: A challenge to biomedicine. Science, 196, 129–136.

Fornes, S. L., Rocco, T., & Rosenberg, H. (2008). Connecting human resource development to vocational rehabilitation: Improving outcomes for workers with mental retardation. Human Resource Development Quarterly, 19(4), 373–395.

Gadbow N. F., & DuBois, D. A. (1998). Adult learners with special needs: Strategies and resources for postsecondary education and workplace training. Melbourne, FL: Krieger.

Giroux, H. A. (1992). Border crossings: Cultural workers and the politics of education. New York: Routledge.

Gleeson, B. (1999). Geographies of disability. London: Routledge.

Goffman, E. (1963). Stigma: Notes on the management of spoiled identity. New York: Touchstone.

Gorman, R. (2000). Research that hurts or research that helps? A critical framework for adult education inquiry and people with intellectual disabilities. In T. J. Sork, V-L. Chapman, & R. St. Clair (Eds.), Proceedings of the 41st Annual Adult Education Research Conference (pp. 129–133). Vancouver: University of British Columbia.

Gormley, S., Hughes, C., Block, L., & Lendman, C., (2005). Eligibility assessment requirements at the postsecondary level for students with learning disabilities: A disconnect with secondary schools? Journal of Postsecondary Education and Disability, 18(1), 63–70.

Greenwood, C. R., Delaquardi, J. C., & Hall, R. V. (1984). Opportunity to respond and student academic performance. In W. L. Heward, T. E. Heron, D. S. Hill, & J. Trap-Porter (Eds.), Focus on behavior analysis in education (pp. 58–88). Columbus, OH: Merrill.

Gumpel, T. P., & Frank, R. (1999). An expansion of the peer-tutoring paradigm: Cross-age peer tutoring of social skills among socially rejected boys. Journal of Applied Behavior Analysis, 32, 115–118.

Hahn, H. (1985). Changing perceptions of disability and the future of rehabilitation. In L. G. Perlman & G. F. Austin (Eds.), Societal influences in rehabilitation planning: A blueprint for the 21st century (pp. 53–64). Alexandria, VA: National Rehabilitation Association.

Hahn, H. (1988). The politics of physical differences: Disability and discrimination. Journal of Social Issues, 44(1), 39–47.

Hahn, H. (1999). Foreword. In R. P. Marinelli & A. E. Dell Orto (Eds.), *The psychological and social impact of disability* (pp. xv–xvii). New York: Springer.

Heward, W. L. (1994). Three low-tech strategies for increasing the frequency of active student response during group instruction. In R. Gardiner III, D. M. Sainato, J. O. Cooper, T. E. Heron, W. L. Heward, J. Eshleman, & T. A. Grossi (Eds.), *Behavior analysis in education: Focus on measurably superior instruction* (pp. 283–320). Pacific Grove, CA: Brooks/Cole.

Hong, B. S. S., Ivy, W. F., Gonzalez, H. R., & Ehrensberger, W. (2007). Preparing students for postsecondary education. *Teaching Exceptional Children, 40*(1), 32–38.

Indiana Department of Human Services v. Firth, 590 N.E. 2d 154 (Ind Ct. App.1992).

Jordan, D. (1996). *Teaching adults with learning disabilities.* Malabar, FL: Krieger.

Kaplan, D. (2000). The definition of disability: Perspective of the disability community. *Journal of Health Care Law & Policy, 3,* 352–364.

Kemp, D. R., (1994). *Mental health in the workplace: An employer's and manager's guide.* Westport, CT: Quorum Books.

Klugerman, P. B. (1989). Developmentally disabled adult learners. In S. Merriam & P. Cunningham (Eds.). *Handbook of adult and continuing education* (pp. 599–610). San Francisco: Jossey-Bass.

Knowles, M. (1960). *Handbook of adult education in the United States.* Chicago: Adult Education Association of the U.S.A.

Linton, S. (1998). *Claiming disability: Knowledge and identity.* New York: New York University Press.

Malott, R. W. (1984). In search of human perfectibility: A behavioral approach to higher education. In W. L. Heward, T. E. Heron, D. S. Hill, & J. Trap-Porter (Eds.), *Focus on behavior analysis in education* (pp. 218–45). Columbus, OH: Merrill.

Milani, A. A. (1996). Disabled students in higher education: Administrative and judicial enforcement of disability law. *Journal of College and University Law, 22*(4), 989–1043.

Mouth Magazine. (1995). *What would you choose for this child?* Rochester, NY: Free Hand Press.

Nathanson v. Medical College of Pennsylvania, 926 / f, 2d 1368 (3d Cir.1991)

National Council on Disability. (2003). *People with disabilities and postsecondary education* (Position paper). Retrieved July 12, 2008, from http://www.ncd.gov/newsroom/publications/2003/education.htm

Ohio State University Office for Disability Services. (2000). *Instructor handbook: Teaching students with disabilities.* Columbus: Ohio State University.

Ohliger, J. O. (1975). Prospects for a learning society. *Adult Leadership, 24*(1), 37–39.

Oliver, M. (1990). *The politics of disablement.* New York: St. Martin's Press.

Oliver, M. (1996). *Understanding disability: From theory to practice.* New York: St. Martin's Press.

Peters, J. M., Jarvis, P., & Associates (Eds.). (1991). *Adult education: Evolution and achievements in a developing field of study* (pp. 97–120). San Francisco: Jossey-Bass.

Polson, A. D. (1995). Fostering multiple repertoires in undergraduate behavior analysis students. *Behavior Analyst, 18,* 239–299.

Priestly, M. (2001). Introduction: The global context of disability. In M. Priestly (Ed.), *Disability and the life course: Global perspectives* (pp. 3–14). Cambridge, UK: Cambridge University Press.

Rocco, T. (1997). Hesitating to disclose: Adult students with invisible disabilities and their experiences with understanding and articulating disability. In S. J. Levine (Ed.), *Proceedings of the 16th Annual Midwest Research-to-Practice Conference in Adult, Continuing, and Community Education* (pp. 157–163). Lansing: Michigan State University.

Rocco, T. (2000, June). Making assumptions: Faculty responses to students with disabilities. In T. J. Sork, V.-L. Chapman, & R. St. Clair (Eds.), *Proceedings of the 41st Adult Education Research Conference* (pp. 387–391). Vancouver: University of British Columbia.

Rocco, T. S. (2001a). Helping adult educators understand disability disclosure. In J. Ross Gordon (Ed.), *Adult learners with disabilities: An overlooked population* [Special Issue]. *Adult Learning, 12*(2), 10–12.

Rocco, T. (2001b, June). "My disability is part of me:" Disclosure and students with visible disabilities. In R. O. Smith, J. M. Dirkx, P. L. Eddy, P. L. Farrell, & M. Polzin (Eds.), *Proceedings of the 42nd Adult Education Research Conference* (pp. 319–324). East Lansing: Michigan State University.

Rocco, T. S. (2006). Disability as an issue of marginalization. In S. Merriam, B. Courtenay, & R. Cervero (Eds.), *Global issues in adult education: Perspectives from Latin America, Southern Africa, and the United States* (pp. 169–181). San Francisco: Jossey-Bass.

Rosenbaum, J. E., & Person, A. E. (2003). Beyond college for all: Policies and practices to improve transitions into college and jobs. *Professional School Counseling, 6*(4), 252–260.

Ross-Gordon, J. M. (1989). *Adults with learning disabilities: An overview for the adult educator* (Information Series No. 337). Columbus, OH: ERIC Clearinghouse on Adult, Career, and Vocational Education. (ERIC No. ED315 664)

Shapiro, J. P. (1993). *No pity: People with disabilities forging a new civil rights movement.* New York: Random House.

Shaw, S. F. (2006). Legal and policy perspectives on transition assessment and documentation. *Career Development for Exceptional Individuals, 29*(2), 108–113.

Sheared, V., & Sissel P. A. (Eds.). (2001). *Making space: Merging theory and practice in adult education.* Westport, CT: Bergin & Garvey.

Smith v. State University of New York, No. 95-CV-0477E(H), 1997 U.S. Dist. LEXIS 20782 (W.D. N.Y., December 30, 1997).

Sturomski, N., & Auchter, J. (2001). Providing accommodations on the GED test. In J. Ross Gordon (Ed.), *Adult learners with disabilities: An overlooked population* [Special Issue]. *Adult Learning, 12*(2), 13–18.

Tate, D. G., & Pledger, C. (2003). An integrative conceptual framework of disability. *American Psychologist, 58,* 289–295.

Thomas, S. B. (2000). College students and disability law. *The Journal of Special Education 33*(4), 248–257.

Thomas, C. (2003). *Defining a theoretical agenda for disability studies.* Keynote presented at Disability Studies: Theory, Policy and Practice, Inaugural Conference of the Disabilities Studies Association, University of Lancaster, United Kingdom.

Tincani, M. (2004). Improving outcomes for college students with disabilities. *College Teaching 52*(4), 128–132.

Toyota Motor Manufacturing, Kentucky, Inc. v. Williams, 534 U.S. 184 (2002).

United Nations. (1994, September). *Towards a society for all: Long-term strategy to implement the world programme of action concerning disabled persons to the year 2000 and beyond* (Report of the Secretary-General). New York: Author.

Verbrugge, L. M., & Jette, A. M. (1994). The disablement process. *Social Science Medicine, 28,* 1–14.

Wehmeyer, M. L. (2001). Self-determination and mental retardation. In L. M. Glidden (Ed.), *International review of research in mental retardation* (Vol. 24, pp. 1–48). San Diego, CA: Academic Press.

Wright, G. N. (1980). *Total rehabilitation.* Boston: Little, Brown.

Wynne v. Tufts University School of Medicine, 976 F.2d 791 (1st Cir. 1992).

36

CLASS AND PLACE IN ADULT AND CONTINUING EDUCATION

TOM NESBIT AND ARTHUR L. WILSON

Class and place are increasingly recognized as major influences on the policies and practices of adult and continuing education. Whatever its particular focus, approach, setting, or clientele, adult and continuing education (ACE) is involved with personal and social change: an essentially social endeavor with struggles for power—who has it, how they use it, where, and in whose interests—at its heart. As class and place play a significant role in the mediation, production, and reproduction of power relations, they heavily influence the knowledge, skills, attitudes, and learning of people involved with adult education. They also impact its curricula, pedagogy, sites, processes, and policies. Although not always obvious, class and place matter.

The relationships between ACE, class and place are fundamentally reflexive. Examining them does three things. First, it draws clear links among adult learners, educational institutions, and processes; the social worlds of work, family, and community; and the socioeconomic and spatial systems that underpin them. Second, it makes visible the struggles of those who are poor, excluded, or dispossessed and the educational resources on which they can draw. Third, it highlights how educational institutions and processes inculcate and maintain dominant ideologies and values. As ACE is a moral and political endeavor as well as a technical practice, it has a role in maintaining or challenging the social order. Do its policies, discourses, and practices reproduce existing relations of dominance and oppression? Alternatively, do they contribute to lasting social as well as personal change that challenges and alters relations of dominance and oppression?

Although class and place matter, their applications to ACE have yet to attract the attention afforded other markers of social division. We wish to redress this by introducing the broad scope of this body of work, exploring and analyzing recent developments in research and delineating several of the larger contextual trends and issues. By coming to better understand the relationships among class, place, and power, adult and continuing educators will better comprehend the conditions in which they work and perhaps better appreciate the possibilities of changing those conditions. We first introduce key theories of class and place and discuss the approaches of several prominent theorists. Then, we explore the effects of class and place on the forms, structures, policies, and practices of ACE. As issues of class and place rarely act independently of other social forces, we next discuss the relationships between them and other major markers of social division. Finally, we reflect on some current issues and trends of research in relation to class, place, and ACE.

What Is Class?

The concept of class is indispensable yet elusive. Notions of class are deeply embedded within broader beliefs about society and history and endure as a way of explaining continuing inequalities in opportunities and standards of living and the social divisions they foster. However, class remains an ambiguous concept, threatened by the lack of a commonly accepted definition, new forms of social stratification, and the rise of identity and other subjective politics.

The modern concept of class dates from the mid-19th century when it was used as a foundational idea for understanding social organization. Karl Marx (Marx & Engels, 1845/1970) claimed that societies essentially consisted of two classes with differing interests and power: those who owned and controlled the means of production and workers who sold their labor for wages. The relationship between these two was basically unequal, exploitative, and of major benefit to owners. Although workers create surplus wealth, they do not equally share in its benefits, and this, in turn, generates the tensions that produce class oppression and conflict.

As modes of production and types of work became more complex, understanding society as essentially two opposing classes became seen as overly reductionist and outmoded. Industrial societies have shifted from principally manufacturing toward more service- and knowledge-based industries. As forms of work became more elaborate, intermediate class positions developed, and European societies soon settled into the now more familiar structuring of three classes—upper, middle, and lower—although still largely related to occupation and income. Recently, the concept of an underclass has arisen, one that consists of those largely excluded from established economic systems (Morris, 1994).

Others regard class in less materialistic or deterministic ways. The work of Max Weber (1920/1968), for instance, marked a shift away from a purely economic toward a more social perspective. He argued that class is better defined by including notions of culture, values, politics, and lifestyle and by placing greater emphasis on individuals' situations, attributes, autonomy, and engagement in meaningful action. Pierre Bourdieu (Bourdieu & Passeron, 1977) regarded class as groups of individuals sharing similar conditions of existence and dispositions. Equally important as one's location in an economic order is the possession of various forms of capital—economic, cultural, social, or symbolic—that can constellate differently in different societies. Most recently, scholars have challenged the depiction of class as essentially static and refer to it more as a dynamic relationship between groups of people. However, although recent approaches to the study of class allow more scope for human agency than did Marx, they still assume that society is made up of relatively constant but unequal class relationships that transcend the individual.

These broad approaches have shaped the understanding of class in most industrial societies. However, North American countries tend to see themselves as relatively free from historical understandings and resist simplistic polarizations between exploiters and exploited. So, especially in the United States, one commonly hears either that class has ceased to exist or, alternatively, that everyone is middle class. Instead, the ethics of self-reliance, personal transformation, and mobility and the ideologies of individualism, egalitarianism, and meritocratic achievement have had a more powerful effect on American society than class solidarity. Nowadays, existential rather than social factors tend to influence Americans' view of themselves. The more complicated systems of stratification in modern society are now maintained by ideological and economic factors, and constructs such as class, race, and gender are commonly seen as interrelated and overlapping—an issue we return to below.

Curiously, even though vast institutionalized social inequalities still persist, the discussion of class remains relatively ignored. Of course, the explanatory and analytic power of the concept of class relates more to the notion that society is still stratified in ways that link individuals and groups with the economic order of production than it does to the specific number of different classes, their definition, or even the people who form them. So whether there are two, three, four, or more classes, every division of society by class continues to stigmatize the less well-off and to hold them responsible for their own situation. Class still exists. As in Marx's time, all social life continues to be marked by the struggles and conflicts over access to the generation and distribution of wealth and status.

What Is Place?

Place is usually assumed to require no explanation; it just is. Alternatively, it is often regarded as a container (Edwards, 2005) in which social action unfolds but which has little to no actual presence or effect in itself. Neither assumption is particularly sustainable. Even though we have conflated them here for brevity, place and space differ. Essentially, place is a less abstract notion: "Place is space to which meaning has been ascribed" (Carter, Donald, & Squires, 1993) and a location of (and influence on) direct experience rather than merely an objective backdrop. Finally, Western understandings of place and space, which stipulate them as Cartesian or Euclidean constructs, are too restrictive for understanding their role in educational settings. So, with those caveats, the question becomes: How is social place produced or constructed and to what ends (Unwin, 2000)? Because place can mean different things (Gruenewald, 2003; Soja, 1989), we will clarify some of the major interpretations.

Kipfer, Goonewardena, Schmid, and Milgrom (2008) argue that there are three waves to the recent study of space/place. All commentators start with the same source: Henri Lefebvre, a Marxist scholar who contributed widely to various areas of critical inquiry, especially the spatial disciplines of architecture, geography, city and regional planning, and urban studies. His best-known work, *The Production of Space* (Lefebvre, 1974/1991), was "committed to rectifying the undertheorization of space in Marxist traditions. . . . The emphasis lay for him not on space as an a priori or ontological entity, but on the processes and strategies of producing space" (Kipfer et al., 2008, p. 9). Lefebvre analyzed how spatial and temporal practices are "implicated in processes of reproduction and transformation of social relations" (Harvey, 1990, p. 218), and this led to his triadic analysis of spatial practices as experienced, representations of space as conceived, and spaces of representations as imagined. Lefebvre's analysis, bringing space into a dialectic relationship with historical materialism, articulated the ways in which space and time co-produce capitalist society and demonstrated how the production of social space serves to advantage some social classes while disadvantaging others.

The first wave of scholarly interpretation is exemplified by the work of David Harvey (1990, 1996), who examines changing cultural practices as new forms of capitalism develop. The second wave is typified by the work of Edward Soja (1989, 1996), who critiques the dominance of time over space in social analysis. Kipfer et al. (2008) suggest a third wave that does not succumb to such bifurcation. Their more nuanced understanding of the role of place and space argues that analyses of postmodern problems of identity, language, and difference can be conducted in materialist and dialectical ways which lead to a "heterodox and open-ended historical materialism . . . committed to an embodied, passionately engaged, and politically charged form of critical knowledge" (p. 3). This approach holds much promise for better understanding the socially complex interactions of educational endeavors, themselves often affected by issues of class, race, gender, place, and so on.

In sum, examining the divisions that class and place produce and maintain thus invites a stronger understanding of the production and reproduction of power. Such analyses also help illuminate how educational activities and policies produce differences that benefit some and disadvantage others; produce and reproduce various aspects of class, place, and other markers of social division; and highlight how educational practices might enliven or dampen democratic transformation.

CLASS, PLACE, AND ADULT AND CONTINUING EDUCATION

Together with its K–12 and higher education counterparts, ACE is now firmly established as central to the smooth functioning of economic systems and societies. As concepts such as lifelong learning and the knowledge society gain prominence, ACE is integral to the process whereby people adapt to economic and cultural changes in society. Clearly, mainstream approaches to education are generally intended to inculcate dominant values, not confront them. And because educational institutions are generally a middle-class domain, their policies and practices are weighted strongly in favor of middle-class values. So, capitalist societies, in which class and place operate as key indicators of social inequality, usually ignore or disguise class and place perspectives. Consequently, many adult educators are uncertain about how their work reflects underlying political structures and economic and spatial systems—especially as they are rarely encouraged to do so. Hence, we now explore some ways in which class and place contribute to reproducing existing patterns of power and privilege in educational settings.

Class and Education

As suggested earlier, class is less an individual attribute than a structural dynamic: a relationship between different people and groups arrayed across relations of power and privilege. Adult education plays a critical role in forming and mediating these relations: providing opportunities for personal mobility while legitimating social inequality. Thus, adopting a class perspective on ACE does two things: It draws clear links between educational institutions, the world of work, and the economic system that underpins them; and it highlights how educational institutions function to maintain and inculcate societal ideology and values.

Much of the foundation of this work comes from outside mainstream adult education. Social theorists like Louis Althusser (1971) and economists Samuel Bowles and Herb Gintis (1976) showed how educational systems are one part of a system of broader capitalist class relations. Bowles and Gintis's correspondence theory explains how educational institutions reproduce the social relations that capitalist societies need by producing (a) workers of specific types and with specific competencies and (b) relative social stability and ideological acceptance of existing class relations. For them, the capitalist class has a comparatively cohesive and broadly shared set of interests in educational systems and practices and, crucially, the capacity to promote its interests. Similarly, Bourdieu and Passeron (1977) suggest that education serves the interests of the privileged by structuring learners' access to and uses of various forms of social and cultural capital. Of course, education is not just a unitary or unidirectional endeavor devoid of human agency or possibility. Others have introduced notions of struggle and resistance into this process. For example, Willis (1977), McLaren (1995), and Apple (1996) document the complex relationships between cultural reproduction and economic reproduction

and explore how class interrelates with the dynamics of race and gender in education.

Most of the 100 or so documents in the ERIC database that link adult education with social class explore the consequences or experiences of class and examine such issues as the participation, access, and attainment of different groups. Those studies consistently underscore how social class remains a key determinant of adult participation in organized learning. In addition, Paula Allman (2001) and Frank Youngman (2000) explore how adult education practices are linked to social class and the increasingly globalized nature of capitalism. Appreciating that class is understood and experienced differently around the world, Nesbit (2005) gathers several adult educators from different countries to explore how the complex relationships between class, gender, and race play out in ACE's policies, practices, and discourses.

These studies indicate the essential role of ACE in promoting and maintaining the social relations required for capitalist production. Furthermore, they suggest that we more fully understand education only if it is seen as part of a broader capitalist class system. Although we now recognize that the relationships between educational practices and political structures are much more complex than correspondence theory suggests, adult educators who work in such areas as adult basic education, literacy, vocational education, and welfare-to-work programs will recognize how often their work, the policies about it, and the textbooks and curricula they use are still much more closely tied to employers' needs than to their adult learners' interests.

Place and Education

There are at least two very broad educational traditions that consider the importance of place: the movement to "situate" learning and place-conscious education. Efforts to situate learning are complex, multidisciplinary, and difficult to adequately summarize here. Most important, situated learning removes the notion of learning from the neurological and psychological confines of the human mind and imbricates it in the living conditions of human and cultural interaction (Lave, 1988). Rather than being contained within the mind, learning is thus seen as inseparable from its cultural and social contexts. Place-conscious education, by contrast, includes theories and practices that "enlist teachers and students in firsthand experience of local life and in the political process of understanding and shaping what happens there" (Gruenewald, 2003, p. 620). Both traditions depend on the notion that there is no way ever to be outside of the places we inhabit nor outside of the power relations in which we participate:

> Places are profoundly pedagogical . . . as centers of experience, places *teach* us about how the world works and how our lives fit into the spaces we occupy. Further, places *make* us: As occupants of particular places with particular attributes, our identity and possibilities are shaped.
> (Gruenewald, 2003, p. 621; original emphasis)

Regrettably, ACE has yet to generate much research that employs such wide-ranging social, political, economic, ideological, and spatial analyses. Of course, adult educators have long promoted such place-based pedagogies as experiential learning, problem-posing education, service learning, critical pedagogy, and community-based learning. But their theoretical justifications are typically dependent on either psychological understandings of human learning and development or various critical structuralist analyses. Yet, notable examples of a place-based approach to ACE do exist. First, the burgeoning discussion and analysis of social capital and lifelong learning are often based on understandings of the role of place in the production of social networks, difference, and identity (Field, 2005; Osborne, Sankey, & Wilson, 2007). Second, there are a proliferating number of spatial metaphors with which to contemplate adult education practice. Richard Edwards's (1997) notion of "changing places" is about the "closed field" of adult education turning into a "moorland" of adult learning as learners find new places for learning. In a similar vein, ACE researchers have considered the "boundaries of adult learning" (Edwards, Hanson, & Raggatt, 1996), "learning beyond the limits" (Usher, Bryant, & Johnston, 1997) or "learning our way out" (Finger & Asun, 2001).

Third, there has been growing interest in theorizing place and examining its role in practice in ACE. British scholar Richard Edwards, together with various associates, has probably contributed more to theorizing space/place in adult education than anyone else. Beyond re-imagining the practice of adult education in terms of boundaries and terrain, he has grappled with major intellectual themes such as postmodernism, post-structuralism, globalization, and neoliberalism in adult education theory and practice. For example, in their edited collection, Edwards and Usher (2003) gather together several studies and analyses from the broader traditions referred to earlier but conducted specifically in ACE settings. Then, in a later work (2008), they present a series of "glimpses" of globalization and pedagogy that examine themes of place, space, and the formation of identity. Within the United States, Wilson (1993, 2000; Wilson & Hayes, 2000) has long argued for a more situated understanding of and approach to adult education.

CLASS, PLACE, AND OTHER MARKERS OF SOCIAL DIVISION

ACE is generally intended to ameliorate the personal and social disadvantages created by circumstance and background. However, although its history bears testament to some remarkable educational achievements, too often, ACE merely serves to clarify or, worse, exacerbate existing disadvantages. So it is not surprising that social divisions and the tensions they bring about are seen as critical issues. In fact, the ACE literature contains several trenchant analyses of the educational approaches, structures, and activities that perpetuate the silence and invisibility of marginalized and disenfranchised groups. Unsurprisingly, this literature is also permeated with regular exhortations to consider class, race, and gender (and more latterly, sexual orientation, age, and place) as prime markers of social division.

As suggested earlier, the constructs of class, race, and gender are now commonly seen as interrelated and overlapping. In particular, older depictions of class are now regarded as too simplistic for heterogeneous countries like the United States. The civil rights and women's movements of the 1960s and '70s underscored that racial and gender inequality could neither be ignored nor treated as secondary to class inequality. Focusing specifically on how such forces play out in educational systems, Weis (1988) provides a comprehensive overview of the major theoretical approaches linking class, race, and gender and shows the inadequacy of explaining problems of racial, class, and sexual oppression in terms of attitudes, values, and psychological differences. Hart (2005), Mojab (2005), Thompson (2000), and Tisdell (1993) further illuminate these various intersections in adult education and show how class, race, and gender are interlocking elements within one overarching system of social power and stratification.

Yet in comparison with its counterparts, the study of social class remains underexplored, especially by American adult educators. Why is this? Why has class been so underrepresented in social and educational theory? To respond with an example, consider the notion of identity—a significant aspect of the individualistic U.S. society and a major focus in its adult education literature. One of the effects of capitalist ideology has been to reinforce the notion that individual identity is unrelated to such supposedly hidden forces as class and place. Identity politics, usually based on claims of individual importance, represents the success of this misconception. Identity and other subjective politics are generally less overtly opposed to capitalism and portrayed as more logical and commonsensical. In the absence of any alternatives, they therefore attract greater interest. So even though vast institutionalized social inequalities persist in the United States, any discussion of class is downplayed.

In addition, when compared with other categories such as race or gender, class appears invisible. Of course, it is precisely this invisibility that, when linked with its apparent naturalness, allows an unfair class system to regularly reproduce itself (Gramsci, 1971). In hierarchical systems people tend to internalize the conflicts they face. This is especially true for those without much power, who often experience class at the same time as other forms of oppression. These factors, when combined with the public scarcity of class scrutiny, ensure that people do not always have readily available concepts to identify—let alone analyze—the class aspects of their experiences. Even when it is acknowledged, class still tends to be regarded as an individual characteristic or entity rather than a constituent social relationship. So, the tendency of many adult education researchers to assume a strong individual orientation further diverts attention away from class perspectives. ACE practitioners remain focused on the psychological aspects of their work, and scholars continue to overlook class in their theoretical lexicon.

Place is also a significant contributor to interlocking systems of domination and also needs to be understood relationally. Harvey (1992) argues that people "invest places" with power, and such "geographies of social action" need to be interrogated for how power is produced and to what purpose. Foucault (1980) has commented similarly that "a whole history remains to be written of spaces—which would be at the same time the history of powers" (p. 149). Keith and Pile (1993) argue that essentialist and individualistic notions of identity as "formed" have been shunted aside by post-structuralist notions of identity as variously fluid, developing, or becoming in which subjects become "surfaces of inscription" (p. 27). Again, this is deceptive. Such inscription is profoundly spatial: Identity and location are inseparable, and there is no way to consider identity outside the context of its production. So, to understand the relations among interlocking definers of difference, we need to map geographies of power as definers of unequal difference via an identity politics of place and a spatialized politics of identity (Wilson, 2001).

RESEARCH ISSUES AND TRENDS

In this section, we reflect on some current issues and trends of research in relation to class, place, and ACE. We first consider class. Given the different perspectives and ambiguities about it, class can often be difficult to analyze. It can mean different things to different people: a theoretical device for analyzing the social world; shared social conditions; or a set of particular orientations, beliefs, and life practices. Popular understandings of class still describe it in terms of jobs, income, wealth, the lifestyles that people can buy, or the power that accrues from ownership. One of the leading class scholars, Eric Olin Wright (1979), identifies four major approaches to its understanding: a functional differentiation of positions within a society, groups unified by their common position in a hierarchy of power or authority, groups with different market capacities that result in different life chances, and a shared location in the social organization of production. These approaches offer significant opportunities for adult education researchers.

To identify some of these opportunities, we first explore how class has been used in different arenas of adult education practice: its approaches to learning and its role in social movements. One distinguishing feature of adult education is its close attention to learning. In their studies of working people's intelligence and learning, both Rose (2004) and Sawchuk (2003) provide two of the best recent analyses of the interrelationships of class and adult learning. Both identify a distinctive working-class learning style that operates independently of formal training and centers on informal workplace and community networks. This learning style is collective, mutual, and solidaristic: People exchange knowledge and skills, hardware and software, and draw on each other's different expertise to develop group resources for anyone to use. And so they develop an expanding learning network: a powerful working-class resource that stands opposed to the trajectory of dominant forms of workplace and institutionalized education, which individualize and commodify learning.

Adult education deliberately seeks to link personal with social change, and much of its historical development and traditions are linked with movements for social justice and equity. Considering adult education's role in social movements underscores that lasting social change comes about through people learning how to act together to challenge inequality and oppression. Altenbaugh (1990), Schied (1993), and Walters (2005) provide compelling accounts of the ways that class affects the educational activities of those who are active in labor and workers' movements or who struggle for social justice. As Walters shows, learning about and discussing earlier battles for social justice can provide resources and hope to those involved in current struggles. Holst (2002) and Foley (1999) also discuss the role of adult learning and education in social movements. Basing their work on the ideas of Freire, Gramsci, and Marx, they each explore how radical adult educators can help build civil society through social movements.

As for place, Edwards, Usher, and others have demonstrated that the analysis of place is not only important to adult education but also both doable and consequential. Also, a considerable amount of intellectual analysis and empirical examination emanates from other disciplines like geography and sociology (e.g., Crang & Thrift, 2000; Friedland & Boden, 1994; Harvey 1996). But as with class, questions of place have yet to gain much purchase in ACE research. Both are hard to discern, but questions of place raise additional complications. Where class can be subtle

and nuanced, place is considered obvious but unaffecting, not needing any further explanation. For example, efforts to situate adult learning as embodied and inseparable from social interaction have been reduced to "context-based learning," in which space/place becomes a container but not contributor (Niewolny & Wilson, 2009). As with class, efforts to promote research on place are often met with resistance. Whereas the social movement and social action orientations in ACE have little trouble understanding the historical role of place in producing identity and relations of power, the more dominant professionalized approach does not. The issue here is one of purpose. Whereas the former see ACE as an essential part of a social movement dedicated to the struggle to create a fairer and more just society, the latter's interests chiefly lie in a more ameliorative approach: social reform rather than social transformation. Although much adult education theory is willing to accommodate the notion of context, such concepts are typically regarded only functionally because they recognize place as a container, not as an enabler or producer of difference and power relations.

As we identified earlier, other academic disciplines provide greater theoretical richness about the idea that place is neither a self-evident concept nor a transparent metaphor. In particular, Unwin (2000) presents a number of issues about the "social production of space," located around the intersecting themes of language and meaning, the separation of space and time, the processes of production and construction, empowerment and value, and space and place. More expressly related to education, Gruenewald (2003) describes what he calls the "pedagogical pathways" and "institutional challenges" to engendering "place-conscious" educational theory and practice. As he argues, we must become more conscious and critical of our "place making" for it has real consequences for who we are, have become, or may become.

Conclusion

Adult educators are pragmatic people, and the practical implications of a concern for class and place lie in deepening understandings of the production and reproduction of power relationships. As we have shown, ideas of class and place theoretically underpin educational practices that challenge relationships of domination and subjugation and promote equality, fairness, and justice. Whether we choose to recognize it or not, our practices as adult educators variously produce, reproduce, or alter relations of power. So we have a professional responsibility to become knowledgeable about how class and place affect difference and power. We need to understand the roles of class and place in producing and reproducing inequality. We need to expand our understandings of the semiotic and ideological significance of what we often take to be routine technical effort. This can be challenging. Many adult educators are reluctant to ask critical questions or confront commonly held assumptions or deeply embedded cultural practices. However, if we are to grasp the "geography of difference" (Harvey, 1996), then we must ask how does difference get produced, whose interests do such differences serve, what roles do we play in producing difference, and what are our responsibilities to confront and change unjust power relations?

Although studies of class and place in adult education are still too infrequent, the value of such work cannot be overstressed. There is no space to go into further detail here but more practical examples can be gleaned from Edwards and Usher (2003), Nesbit (2005), or Wilson (2001). Such studies illuminate the dynamics between educational activities and their wider cultural and political contexts. They also expose the superficiality of various currently prescribed educational reforms: the individualizing of educational opportunities, increased commercial involvement and managerialism, privatization of schools and colleges, a return to so-called basics, the reduction of learning to cultural and functional literacies or core competencies, and the increasing pressures to work harder and longer for fewer benefits or less reward (Aronowitz, 2008).

Whether teaching, administering, or conducting research, adopting class and place perspectives on ACE makes clear that its policies, practices, and situations are far from context-free but, instead, are part of a larger and complex structure of social relations. Such perspectives also help adult educators resist what Paula Allman (2001) calls the postmodern condition of "skepticism, uncertainty, fragmentation, nihilism, and incoherence" (p. 209). Finally, we believe wholeheartedly that the practical worth of class and place perspectives aids "the task of critical analysis [which] is not . . . to prove the impossibility of foundational beliefs (or truths), but to find a more plausible and adequate basis for the foundational beliefs that make interpretation and political action meaningful, creative, and possible" (Harvey, 1996, p. 2).

REFERENCES

Allman, P. (2001). *Critical education against global capitalism.* New York: Bergin & Garvey.

Altenbaugh, R. J. (1990). *Education for struggle: American labor colleges of the 1920s and 1930s.* Philadelphia: Temple University Press.

Althusser, L. (1971). Ideology and ideological state apparatuses. In B. Brewster (Ed.), *Lenin and philosophy.* London: New Left Books.

Apple, M. W. (1996). *Cultural politics and education.* New York: Teachers College Press.

Aronowitz, S. (2008). *Against schooling: For an education that matters.* Boulder, CO: Paradigm.

Bourdieu, P., & Passeron, J. C. (1977). *Reproduction in education, society, and culture.* Thousand Oaks, CA: Sage.

Bowles, S., & Gintis, H. (1976). *Schooling in capitalist America.* New York: Basic Books.

Carter, E., Donald, J., & Squires, J. (1993). *Space and place: Theories of identity and location.* London: Routledge & Kegan Paul.

Crang, M., & Thrift, N. (Eds.). (2000). *Thinking space.* London: Routledge.

Edwards, R. (1997). *Changing places? Flexibility, lifelong learning and a learning society.* London: Routledge.

Edwards, R. (2005, September 14–17). *Contexts, boundary zones and boundary objects in lifelong learning.* Paper presented at the British Educational Research Association Annual Conference, University of Glamorgan.

Edwards, R., Hanson, A., & Raggatt, P. (Eds.). (1996). *Boundaries of adult learning.* London: Routledge.

Edwards, R., & Usher, R. (Eds.). (2003). *Space, curriculum, and learning.* Greenwich, CT: Information Age Publishing.

Edwards, R., & Usher, R. (2008). *Globalisation & pedagogy: Space, place and identity* (2nd ed.). London: Routledge.

Field, J. (2005). *Social capital and lifelong learning.* Bristol, UK: Policy Press.

Finger, M., & Asun, J. (2001). *Adult education at the crossroads: Learning our way out.* London: Zed.

Foley, G. (1999). *Learning in social action.* London: Zed.

Foucault, M. (1980). *Power/knowledge: Selected interviews and other writings, 1972–1977* (C. Gordon, Ed.). New York: Pantheon.

Friedland, R., & Boden, D. (Eds.). (1994). *NowHere: Space, time and modernity.* Berkeley: University of California Press.

Gramsci, A. (1971). *Selections from the prison notebooks.* London: Lawrence & Wishart.

Gruenewald, D. (2003). Foundations of place: A multidisciplinary framework for place-conscious education. *American Educational Research Journal, 40*(3), 619–654.

Hart, M. (2005). Class and gender. In T. Nesbit (Ed.), *Class concerns: Adult education and social class* (pp. 63–72). San Francisco: Jossey-Bass.

Harvey, D. (1990). *The condition of postmodernity: An inquiry into the origins of cultural change.* Oxford, UK: Blackwell.

Harvey, D. (1992). From space to place and back again: Reflections on the condition of postmodernity. In J. Bird et al. (Eds.), *Mapping the futures* (pp. 3–30). London: Routledge.

Harvey, D. (1996). *Justice, nature & the geography of difference.* Oxford, UK: Blackwell.

Holst, J. D. (2002). *Social movements, civil society, and radical adult education.* New York: Bergin & Garvey.

Keith, M., & Pile, S. (Eds.). (1993). *Place and the politics of identity.* London: Routledge.

Kipfer, S., Goonewardena, K., Schmid, C., & Milgrom, R. (2008). On the production of Henri Lefebvre. In K. Goonewardena, S. Kipfer, R. Milgrom, & C. Schmid (Eds.), *Space, difference, everyday life* (pp. 1–23). New York: Routledge.

Lave, J. (1988). *Cognition in practice.* Cambridge, UK: Cambridge University Press.

Lefebvre, H. (1991). *The production of space* (D. Nicholson-Smith, Trans.). Oxford, UK: Blackwell. (Original work published 1974)

Marx, K., & Engels, F. (1970). *The German ideology* (C. J. Arthur, Trans. & Ed.). London: Lawrence & Wishart. (Original work published 1845)

McLaren, P. L. (1995). *Critical pedagogy and predatory culture.* New York: Routledge.

Mojab, S. (2005). Class and race. In T. Nesbit (Ed.), *Class concerns: Adult education and social class* (pp. 73–82). San Francisco: Jossey-Bass.

Morris, L. (1994). *Dangerous classes: The underclass and social citizenship.* London: Routledge.

Nesbit, T. (Ed.). (2005). *Class concerns: Adult education and social class.* San Francisco: Jossey-Bass.

Niewolny, K. L., & Wilson, A. L. (2009). What happened to the promise? A critical (re)orientation of the sociocultural learning tradition. *Adult Education Quarterly, 60*(1), 26–45.

Osborne, M., Sankey, K., & Wilson, B. (Eds.). (2007). *Social capital, lifelong learning, and the management of place: An international perspective.* London: Routledge.

Rose, M. (2004). *The mind at work.* New York: Viking Books.

Sawchuk, P. H. (2003). *Adult learning and technology in working-class life.* New York: Cambridge University Press.

Schied, F. M. (1993). *Learning in social context.* DeKalb, IL: LEPS Press.

Soja, E. (1989). *Postmodern geographies: The reassertion of space in critical social theory.* London: Verso.

Soja, E. (1996). *Thirdspace: Journeys to Los Angeles and other real-and-imagined places.* Oxford, UK: Blackwell.

Thompson, J. (2000). *Women, class, and education.* New York: Routledge.

Tisdell, E. (1993). Interlocking systems of power, privilege, and oppression in adult higher education classrooms. *Adult Education Quarterly, 43*(4), 203–226.

Unwin, T. (2000). A waste of space? Towards a critique of the social production of space. *Transactions of the Institute of British Geographers* (New Series), *25*(1), 11–29.

Usher, R., Bryant, I., & Johnston, R. (1997). *Adult education and the postmodern challenge: Learning beyond the limits.* London: Routledge.

Walters, S. (2005). Social movements, class, and adult education. In T. Nesbit (Ed.), *Class concerns: Adult education and social class* (pp. 53–62). San Francisco: Jossey-Bass.

Weber, M. (1968). *Economy and society: An outline of interpretive sociology.* New York: Bedminster Press. (Original work published 1920)

Weis, L. (Ed.). (1988). *Class, race, and gender in American education.* Albany: State University of New York Press.

Willis, P. (1977). *Learning to labour.* Farnborough, UK: Saxon House.

Wilson, A. L. (1993). The promise of situated cognition. In S. Merriam (Ed.), *An update on adult learning theory* (pp. 71–80). San Francisco: Jossey-Bass.

Wilson, A. L. (2000). Place matters: Producing power and identity. In T. Sork, V. Chapman, & R. St Clair (Eds.), *Proceedings of the 41st Adult Education Research Conference* (pp. 502–506). Vancouver: University of British Columbia.

Wilson, A. L. (2001). The politics of place: Producing power and identity in continuing education. In R. M. Cervero, A. L. Wilson, & Associates, *Power in practice: Adult education and the struggle for knowledge and power in society* (pp. 226–246). San Francisco: Jossey-Bass.

Wilson, A. L., & Hayes, E. R. (Eds.). (2000). *Handbook of adult and continuing education.* San Francisco: Jossey-Bass.

Wright, E. O. (1979). *Class structure and income determination.* San Diego: Academic Press.

Youngman, F. (2000). *The political economy of adult education.* London: Zed Books.

PART VI

THE FUTURE OF ADULT AND CONTINUING EDUCATION WITHIN A GLOBAL CONTEXT

37

GLOBALIZATION AND THE ROLE OF ADULT AND CONTINUING EDUCATION

Challenges and Opportunities

SHARAN B. MERRIAM

Not too long ago, I received an invitation over e-mail to give a keynote address at an adult education conference in Istanbul. Communication between myself and conference organizers thousands of miles away was via e-mail as we worked out the details of my visit. I also went to the Internet for information about adult education and lifelong learning in Turkey and met with one of our graduate students from Turkey. While driving to my office shortly after accepting the invitation, I just happened on a National Public Radio interview with Turkish Nobel Prize author Orhan Pamuk and immediately bought his book *Istanbul* (through Amazon.com). And, on a lighter note, as I was leisurely reading the *International Herald Tribune* on an airplane to another part of the world, I came across a little article about "An Empire's Drink" or *boza*, available from vendors in Istanbul and definitely "worth trying." My experience has all the earmarks of globalization—the merging of technology, travel, education, and culture across and between borders.

The movement of people, services, goods, and ideas across national borders is, in fact, one of the characteristics of globalization. Historically, nation-states have always related to each other, but globalization "is new in the sense of the growing extensiveness of social networks involved, the intensity and speed of flows and interconnections within these networks, and the reach of its impact" (Glastra, Hake, & Schedler, 2004, p. 292). Globalization is more than movement across borders; globalization is an intensely complex phenomenon with both positive and negative characteristics. It is both a challenge and an opportunity for the field of adult education.

UNRAVELING THE PHENOMENON OF GLOBALIZATION

Often associated with the outsourcing of manufacturing to low-wage, labor-intensive developing countries, and with transnational companies that operate across and outside the control of nation-states, globalization is intricately interwoven with the market economy. What drives this market economy is the desire to make a profit. To make a profit, corporations need to create a market for their products. Thus, "corporations not only control the means of production—both economic and technological—but they also control the means of spreading knowledge about their products as they seek to convince the public to purchase what they produce" (Jarvis, 2008, p. 20). Thus, the market economy involves more than production and distribution of goods; information and knowledge are equally brokered across the globe. Law offices in the United States are using legal consulting companies in India for what is now being called "knowledge processing outsourcing" or KPO (Baryln, 2008). Parents in the United States can have their children tutored after school in math and science by teachers sitting at a computer in India (Friedman, 2005). Even culture and education have become commodities in the globalized market economy: "In market terms, culture is an industry that involves producing and exchanging cultural goods and services for profit; education is an industry that involves producing and exchanging educational goods and services for profit" (Merriam, Courtenay, & Cervero, 2006, p. 2).

Globalization can thus be conceptualized as the movement of goods, services, and information across national boundaries and as a borderless marketplace shored up by what is being called the knowledge economy. This borderless marketplace is a shift from the mid-1960s to the mid-1980s thinking in which the role of the nation-state was central to the process of economic development and modernization, especially in underdeveloped countries. Known as modernization theory,

> the proposed economic strategy was . . . to develop a "modern" sector based on industrialization and commercial agriculture by mobilizing the underemployed labour in the "traditional" rural sector. Development was seen essentially in terms of economic growth based on the expansion of the modern sector and the export of primary products. . . . The fundamental premise of modernization theory was that there is a single process of social evolution, the highest stage having been reached by the USA. (Youngman, 2000, p. 53)

In contrast to modernization theory, "the essence of globalization is . . . cross-border economic activity and the decreased significance of national boundaries. . . . The bottom line is capital's search for maximum returns on its investment" (Youngman, 2000, p. 95). Wealth is tied to those with knowledge and the educational systems that produce these knowledge workers.

Profit is sustained by the knowledge base that underlies it. This is a battle fought on the global stage as captured in a special edition of *Newsweek* (2006), on "The Knowledge Revolution: Why Victory Will Go to the Smartest Nations & Companies."

In a review of the research on globalization and education, Spring (2008) identifies three fallouts from the knowledge economy, each of which has implications for education. First is the global migration of workers from poorer to wealthier nations or in some situations within country from rural to urban areas. Part of China's learning society agenda, for example, is to enable migrants from rural areas to become integrated into urban city cultures. The learning city of Zhabei District in Shanghai sponsors a club for migrants to teach them Shanghai ways (Chang, 2009). A second fallout of the global knowledge economy is a move from a "brain drain" to "the developing phenomenon of 'brain circulation' where skilled and professional workers move between wealthy nations or return to their homelands after migrating to another country" (Spring, 2008, p. 341). Several countries are now offering enticing opportunities to encourage their educated workers to return home. The third factor Spring (2008) identifies is an increase in multicultural populations as workers move around the globe. Aside from stimulating multicultural education research, these movements result in "concerns about cultural and religious conflicts" and social cohesion (p. 342). Cultural integration brings down barriers among people at the same time that its homogenization of traditions and customs can lead to loss of identity.

The Downside of Globalization

The market economy dimension of globalization has its negative side. Globalization seems to benefit those countries that are already economically developed, while others "like Zambia are virtually excluded from the market" (Jarvis, 2004, p. 5). In fact, as Jarvis (2008) points out, "even in the first world, the poor continue to be excluded and get poorer" with, for example, "16.5% in the U.S. living in poverty and 17% of the population of the UK living below the low income threshold" (p. 18). As the gap between the growing rich and the very poor widens, the world is destabilized, creating factional and ideological conflicts. The United States, with only 4% of the world's population, is "seen everywhere as the principal engine and principal beneficiary of global capitalism. We are also seen as 'almighty,' 'exploitative,' and 'able to control the world,'" (Chua, 2003, p. 16), emotions generating resentment, often with deadly consequences. People are resisting "the 'converging powers' of globalization, as exemplified in social and popular movements around the struggle for national, regional, ethnic, or religious identities" (Glastra et al., 2004, p. 293). Furthermore, "the instability of impoverished and water-stressed countries has ignited a swath of violence across the Horn of Africa, the Middle East, and Central Asia," Sachs (2008) writes in a recent issue of TIME magazine. "What we call violent fundamentalism should be seen for what it really is: poverty, hunger, water scarcity and despair" (p. 38).

The intertwining of the market economy and the social and technological dimensions of globalization have marginalized certain groups of people and also brought attention to health and environmental issues on a scale never before realized. Throughout the world, certain groups of people live on the margins of society, without full access to the social and economic institutions and opportunities in the community. Gender, race or ethnicity, disability, age, and sexual orientation are some of the common bases for being denied rights and benefits that those in the mainstream take for granted. Indigenous groups, migrants, and refugees are other marginalized groups.

The situation for many marginalized groups has been exacerbated by uneven economic development tied to globalization. The market economy in China, for example, has created a well-to-do upper class able to buy cars and homes, while the rural poor barely subsist. As another example, migrants and immigrants often find themselves in training that "prepares them for occupations which the host population would not want to occupy themselves, and consequently serves to further marginalize [them]" (Medel-Anonuevo, 1997, p. 167). Gender intersects with most categories of marginalization. For example, "women make up 70 percent of the 1.3 billion absolutely poor, more than half the population of women over age fifteen worldwide are illiterate, and 75 percent of the refugees and internally displaced are women" (Merriam et al., 2006, p. 92).

Health and the environment are also coming to our attention because of and due to globalization. The HIV/AIDS pandemic, from which no part of the world is exempt, is a good example of the interaction of health and the environment. Reporting on the situation in Africa, Olive Shisana, the director of the South African research program on HIV/AIDS and Health points out that because of the withdrawal of those ill or dying from the workforce, "the economic status of individuals, families, and communities is reduced, exacerbating what is most likely an already impoverished situation. This leads to the mushrooming of informal urban settlements, contributing to environmental degradation" in the form of lower food production, deforestation, and water contamination (quoted in Merriam et al., 2006, p. 206). Sachs (2008) concurs, noting that in some locations in our interconnected global economy, "societies have outstripped the carrying capacity of the land, resulting in chronic hunger, environmental degradation and large-scale exodus of desperate populations; [We are] crowded into an interconnected society of global trade, migration, ideas and, yes, risk of pandemic diseases, terrorism, refugee movements and conflict" (p. 38).

The consequences of globalization are not all bleak, however. Communication technology has enabled the flow of information, ideas, and values. Our television news might be reporting on an event in another part of the world as it happens; dictators cannot hide; the Internet cannot effectively be shut down; all cell phones cannot be confiscated. People everywhere come to see that no single culture, country, or people is at the center of the universe. We are, in fact, an incredibly diverse world. If the demographics of the world were represented by a community of 100 people, there would be 61 Asians, 14 North and South Americans, 13 Africans, 12 Europeans, and 1 Australian; 70 would be non-White, and 30 would be White; 67 would be non-Christians, and 33 would be Christian. About 59% of the entire wealth of the community would be in the hands of only six people, and all six would be citizens of the United States. Finally, of relevance to educators is the fact that 25.5 of those over 15 years of age would be illiterate, only 7 would have a secondary education, and only 1 would have a college education; 72 of the 100 would struggle to live on U.S.$2 per day or less (http://www.miniature-earth.com). Globalization has connected us with other parts of the planet on which we live and enlarged our horizons both to its problems and to its incredible diversity.

Learning in a Globalized World

Globalization has fostered two powerful trends of particular importance to the field of adult education—the infusion of non-Western perspectives into our thinking about learning and the emergence of lifelong learning as a unifying concept for our practice (for a discussion of the issues related to the use of the term "non-Western," see Merriam & Associates, 2007). Communication, travel, and immigration have had a positive impact on the field of adult education in that the historical hegemony of Western perspectives on what counts as knowledge, who "owns" knowledge, and how knowledge is constructed is being challenged. Non-Western perspectives on learning and knowing are entering our field's discourse through conferences, research in non-Western settings, journals (see, for example, the special issue of *Advances in Developing Human Resources,* devoted to different worldviews of adult learning in the workplace, 2006, Vol. 8, No. 3), and books such as *Non-Western Perspectives on Learning and Knowing,* which has chapters on Islam, American Indian, Hinduism, Maori, Buddhist, Latin American, and African indigenous knowledge, as well as Confucianism (Merriam & Associates, 2007). Most of these systems predate Western science by thousands of years and even today are held by the majority of the world's peoples. Globalization has led to our examining the heretofore privileged position of Western assumptions about learning and knowing, assumptions that value the *individual* learner over the collective and that promote *autonomy* and *independence* of thought and action over community and interdependence. In adult learning theory, for example, andragogy, self-directed learning, and much of the literature on transformational learning position self-direction, independence, rational discourse, and reflective thought as pinnacles of adult learning.

What we are beginning to learn from our exposure to non-Western perspectives is that learning in other cultures is a communal activity; learning is the responsibility of all members of the community because it is through this learning that the community itself can develop. Furthermore, one defines him- or herself in

terms of the community, and interdependency is valued over independency. Acquired knowledge is communal. For example, from an Islamic perspective, "if there is no medical doctor to serve a community, then it is obligatory upon the community to send one or more of its members for medical training, and failure to do so will result in each member sharing the community sin" (Kamis & Muhammad, 2007, p. 28).

Another shift in our understanding of learning and knowing influenced by exposure to non-Western perspectives is that learning is more than a cognitive activity; learning also involves the body, emotions, and the spirit. In 2005, a catastrophic tsunami killed hundreds of thousands of Southeast Asians. Off the coast of Thailand, a group of nomads known as the Moken village sea gypsies survived. Why? Because they "knew" it was coming; they "felt" it (Freiler, 2008). This is embodied learning. Learning that occurs in the community, in the experience, is holistic— it has not only a cognitive but physical, emotional, and sometimes spiritual dimensions. The Hindu tradition of yoga, for example, employs the mind, body, and spirit in concert to work toward enlightenment. In most traditions, balance is sought among these dimensions. Native Americans assume that if a person has a disease (dis-ease), it means that the person's spiritual, emotional, physical, and mental functions are out of balance (Hart, 1996).

Learning in non-Western societies is a lifelong journey. Western discourse around lifelong learning is relatively recent, having evolved from the more institutionalized and vocational ideology of lifelong education. Avoseh (2001) speaks to the interaction between the community and lifelong learning in traditional African society: Learning is "a lifelong process that could not be separated from the rest of the life's activities" (p. 482), and "anyone who fails to learn . . . is regarded as *oku eniyan* (the living dead)" (p. 483). Not only is learning lifelong, it is primarily nonformal (i.e., sponsored by community groups, not formal educational institutions) and informal, embedded in everyday life. Although certainly the majority of lifelong learning is informal even in Western settings, the difference is that most Westerners do not recognize nor value learning that occurs outside classroom walls.

This notion, firmly lodged in non-Western societies, that learning is a lifelong activity converges with the second outcome/fallout of globalization and the information economy, that of lifelong learning. According to Uggla (2008), lifelong learning is "the new life narrative," which "is constituted as a process of constant learning. And every person is expected to refigure his/her life in accordance with this narrative identity" (p. 215). Lifelong learning is not a new concept, having been articulated by early writers in adult education (such as Lindeman, 1926) and by UNESCO's 1972 report, *Learning to Be* (Faure et al.). However, this was a somewhat humanist version of lifelong education; the change in emphasis to *learning* is in direct response to globalization and the need for workers to constantly learn to keep pace with a changing global job market. Learning is something to be engaged in from preschool to postretirement, with a great emphasis on learning skills and practical knowledge that can transfer to the workplace. Learning is not only lifelong, but life-wide, encompassing all aspects of our life and all contexts (work, community, family). Learning is also very much the responsibility of the individual rather than the state (Jarvis, 2007). Lifelong learning acknowledges that learning can and does occur outside of formal educational institutions; indeed, much learning occurs informally or in community settings. Green (2006) captures how the "most globalized of educational discourses" is challenging traditional educational thinking:

> As technological change drives up the employer demand for skills, and as individuals increasingly compete for career-enhancing certificates, so governments have to find new ways to meet the demand. Lifelong learning is an ingenious solution, made possible in part by the new learning technologies. By declaring learning a lifelong and "lifewide" process— occurring everywhere from the school to the home, the workplace and the community— governments are able both to respond to individual demands for more diverse learning opportunities which mesh with their modern lifestyles, and to shift the costs, which they can no longer bear, onto employers, individuals and their families and communities. . . . We have been used to thinking about education in terms of schools and colleges and other institutions. In years to come these may well cease to be the main locus of learning activity. . . . We will have to start to think more about informal learning, workplace learning, and learning in the community and home. (p. 41)

But this notion of lifelong learning is more comprehensive than just preparing for work; it includes other facets of human development that are captured by the 1996 UNESCO report, *Learning: The Treasure Within* (Delors, 1996). This report lays out the implications for education in a globalized world, which must "simultaneously provide maps of a complex world in constant turmoil and the compass that will enable people to find their way in it" (p. 85). To do this, education needs to address four fundamental types of learning or pillars of knowledge:

> *Learning to know*, that is acquiring the instruments of understanding; *learning to do*, so as to be able to act creatively on one's environment; *learning to live together*, so as to participate and co-operate with other people in all human activities; and *learning to be*, an essential progression which proceeds from the previous three. (Delors, 1996, p. 86)

More recently UNESCO's Institute for Lifelong Learning has added a fifth pillar, *learning to change*. This fifth pillar can be found in the Literacy Decade (2003–2012) document in a section on "Learning Through Life in Different Cultural Contexts" (http://portal.unesco.org/education).

To summarize, we are all affected by globalization, by living in a world of instant communication, travel, and the movement of people, services, goods, and ideas across national borders. There are both positives and negatives associated with this phenomenon. Those nations or segments of society that are not part of the global economy are poorer and more marginalized than ever before. However, this interconnectedness on various levels is showing us the diversity of the world and hopefully turning our attention to some of the major issues on the planet today. Globalization has also informed educational theory and practice. Of particular relevance to adult education is the challenging of Western epistemological hegemony by other systems of knowing and learning and the emergence of lifelong learning as a response.

How Adult Education Can Respond

What can adult educators do to respond to the challenges of globalization? How can we maximize the benefits but at the same time ameliorate the problems associated with globalization? Historically, adult education in the West has had a social action agenda; that is, adult education has been seen as a means of improving people's lives and the society in which they live. This mission has been eclipsed in some areas of practice by the rise of workplace learning. Billions of dollars each year are spent on training workers for today's global market. As Friedman (2005), author of *The World Is Flat*, writes, "There is only one message: You have to constantly upgrade your skills" (p. 237). We also need to make ourselves "untouchable" by preparing for jobs that cannot be outsourced. Furthermore, some feel we are moving toward a standardized global curriculum characterized by "two inseparable meditational tools, technology and English; proficiencies in these tools have been referred to as global literacy skills" (Tsui & Tellefson, 2007, p. 1). That globalization is dominated by the West is underscored by the fact that only 7.6% of the world's population speaks English (Spring, 2008).

But what of the social aspects of our practice? In 2004, lecturers, resource specialists, and 38 adult education scholars from the United States, Latin America, and Southern Africa gathered in Salzburg, Austria, for a week-long seminar on "Global Issues: The Roles and Responsibilities of Adult Education." From this event, the following responses emerged: Adult educators can (1) create space and listen to people's voices; (2) adopt a critical stance; (3) attend to policy; and (4) engage in collective learning and action (Merriam et al., 2006).

Create Space and Listen

Adult education cannot respond to the needs of its learners if we do not know what those needs are. As trained practitioners, we may feel we can guess what those needs are, but at best, it is only a guess. Understaffed programs, budgetary restrictions, and institutional regulations often get in the way of practitioners finding out what learners' real needs and concerns are. For those who do make space and listen, the rewards are great. Folkman (2006), for example, reports on an adult education program with the Hmong refugee community in Milwaukee, Wisconsin. The three-stage program began with listening to the refugees' stories of coming to the United States, of trying to survive and adapt to our culture without losing

their own. In the second stage, a group dialogue was held with representatives from community-based agencies that served this population. In time, the group moved to the third stage, where solutions were sought to some of their issues; this led to organizing an action coalition across the community.

Creating space for learning to occur is also being promoted in the workplace. Research has shown that most of the learning in the workplace is informal and not through formal training programs, although billions of dollars a year are spent on training. Allowing employees to interact informally, rather than distracting from work getting done, actually increases problem-solving efficiency and work productivity (Rowden, 2007). So, no matter what our work setting as adult education practitioners, the challenge is to make space, physically and psychologically, for hearing the voices of our learners.

Adopt a Critical Stance

As mentioned above, the field of adult education has historically been concerned with improving the lives of individual learners, but also with bringing about a more equitable and democratic society. This goal cannot be met without becoming aware of inequities in one's society and the oppression and marginalization of groups as a result of unequal distribution of power and other resources. The status quo has to be scrutinized in order for a better society to be possible. Adult educators writing about globalization, for example, question whose interests it serves, who stands to gain by companies becoming transnational, and what the downside of global media is when ownership is in the hands of a few. Communications technology, a big part of what makes globalization possible, is also viewed with a critical eye—who has access to the Internet, how does information flow and through what media, and so on. Even the "bottom line" or profitability motive of corporate human resource development (HRD) is being critically scrutinized:

> The work to make HRD more socially responsible in a globalizing context demands that the performance-based assumptions of performativity, discourse, credibility, and power be questioned. This challenge calls for both adult educators and HRD professionals to critically assess how HRD

knowledge is created and identify constructive measures that can be taken to provide a more balanced perspective for HRD research, theory, and practice. (Bierema, 2000, p. 286)

Linked to a critical stance on adult education is a more inclusive view of who is included in practice, what needs and interests different groups of people may have, how institutions and social forces have marginalized many, and how what we do as adult educators can address these inequities. Indeed, a critical stance is permeating much of the writing and theorizing in adult education in the West with regard to program development and the goals of adult education and adult learning. Brookfield (2000) writes that "a critically reflective pose increases our chance of taking informed actions in pursuit" of "a world organized according to the ideals of fairness and social justice" (p. 47).

Attend to Policy

Adult educators are busy people; they manage programs, teach, raise money, and in general have too little time and too few resources to meet the needs of adults whom they serve. But there are numerous situations where our practice could be more effective with more attention to policies established and implemented by governmental agencies. Even in societies like the United States, where education is decentralized and under the purview of individual states, the voices of adult educators are needed perhaps even more in the present climate of recession and looming "scarcity of resources and social inequities" (Quigley, 2000, p. 216). Through "being heard at the state and national policy-level and becoming part of social policy formation," social movements bring about change (Quigley, 2000, p. 216). Public policy with regard to women's rights, environmental education, and low-income adult learners are all important issues for adult educators, whether in the first world or in developing countries.

In preparation for the Sixth UNESCO International Conference on Adult Education (called CONFINTEA VI) held in Belém, Brazil, in December 2009, UNESCO requested that each government establish a national committee with representatives of all stakeholders, hold preparatory regional conferences to explore policy, and hold national conferences to validate the work of national committees. Finally, each country submitted a national report on The Development and State of the Art of Adult Learning and Education. Also, from multiple data sources and these national reports, an overview of trends and challenges in adult learning and education was produced as input to CONFINTEA VI. This overview, called the Global Report on Adult Learning and Education (GRALE), played an important role at the conference. Furthermore, in an effort to include civil society representation at CONFINTEA VI, 500 people from 80 countries participated in the International Civil Society Forum held immediately before CONFINTEA VI. This preparation and the conference itself were incredible opportunities for adult educators, institutions, and organizations to come together and engage in national and international dialogue around policy formation.

Globalization has raised our awareness of these issues, and now we need to respond with policies that address these challenges. "Great social transformations," Sachs (2008) writes, "all began with public awareness and engagement. . . . Each of us has a role to play and a chance for leadership" (p. 40). He goes on to say that "there is no substitute for meeting and engaging with people across cultures, religions and regions to realize that we are all in this together." And most important of all, we need to "demand" that our politicians respond: "If the public leads, politicians will surely follow" (p. 40).

Engage in Collective Learning and Action

To effectively deal with the challenges of globalization and their impact on adult education, adult educators need to form partnerships and engage in collective learning and action. Developing partnerships was, in fact, one of the items in the Agenda for the Future forged at the UNESCO world conference on adult education in 1997 and recently reaffirmed at CONFINTEA VI. That agenda states,

> The development of adult learning requires partnership between government departments, intergovernmental and non-governmental organizations, employers and trade unions, universities and research centres, the media, civil and community-level associations, facilitators of adult learning and the adult learners themselves. (UNESCO, 1997, p. 9)

Partnerships have many advantages and few drawbacks. Sharing resources, whether they be physical or human and expertise can help carry out shared goals. The needs of low-income adult learners in higher education, for example, can be better addressed by partnering with business, both in terms of identifying the skills needed in today's workplace and in supporting students financially (Hansman, 2006).

Adult education's mission to bring about social change has always been fostered through collective learning and action. Whether tackling social justice issues, environmental issues, women's rights, poverty, health, or welfare, collective learning and action have long been recognized as more effective than individual approaches. At present, collective learning is being expressed through the formation of learning communities, both geographical and interest- or activity-based. Learning communities are being formed and studied throughout education: through online courses, in the workplace, and in the promotion of continuing professional education. Geographic learning communities are also on the rise. China, for example, encountering a growing gap between those benefiting from the market economy and the poor, has implemented a massive, country-wide learning cities program designed to bring about a harmonious society. Learning cities, districts, neighborhoods, streets, and families are designed to engage residents in collective learning. Japan, South Korea, Australia, and a number of European countries also have forms of the learning city, town, or village. These learning communities are part of several nations' lifelong learning or learning society policies.

Jarvis (2007) concludes that "this movement towards learning cities and learning regions might be described as a new social movement or, better, as part of the wider new social movement which is lifelong learning itself" (p. 117).

SUMMARY

"Adult education does not occur in a vacuum. What one needs or wants to learn, what opportunities are available, the manner in which one learns—all are to a large extent determined by the society in which one lives" (Merriam, Caffarella, & Baumgartner, 2007, p. 25). The society in which we now live is a globalized world where the movement of people, goods, culture, services, and ideas flows across national boundaries. Globalization, with its market-driven economy supported by information technologies, has solved some problems and created others. While we can instantly communicate with someone on the other side of the world and produce consumer goods ever more cheaply, there are people and nations excluded from the benefits of globalization. Such divisions only exacerbate the differences between rich and poor, creating ethnic hatred and global instability (Chua, 2003). Adult educators can respond to the challenges of globalization by creating space for the voices of our adult learners to be heard; by adopting a critical stance toward our values, goals, and practices; by attending to social policy that invariably affects our practice; and by fostering collective learning and action.

REFERENCES

Avoseh, M. B. M. (2001). Learning to be active citizens: Lessons of traditional Africa for lifelong learning. *International Journal of Lifelong Education, 20*(6), 479–486.

Barlyn, S. (2008, April 14). Call my lawyer . . . in India. *TIME* magazine, Global 1–2.

Bierema, L. L (2000). Moving beyond performance paradigms in human resource development. In A. L. Wilson & E. R. Hayes (Eds.), *Handbook of adult and continuing education* (pp. 278–293). San Francisco: Jossey-Bass.

Brookfield, S. (2000). The concept of critically reflective practice. In A. L. Wilson & E. R. Hayes (Eds.), *Handbook of adult and continuing education* (pp. 33–50). San Francisco: Jossey-Bass.

Chang, B. (2009). Patterns of knowledge construction. In R. Lawrence (Ed.), *Honoring our past embracing our future; Proceedings of the 50th Annual Adult Education Research Conference* (pp. 90–95). Chicago: National-Louis University.

Chua, A. (2003). Globalization and ethnic hatred. *Phi Kappa Phi Forum, 83*(4), 13–16.

Delors, J. (Chair). (1996). *Learning: The treasure within* (Report to UNESCO of the International Commission on Education for the Twenty-first Century). Paris: UNESCO.

Faure, E. (Chair) et al. (1972). *Learning to be.* Paris: UNESCO.

Folkman, D. V. (2006). Framing a critical discourse on globalization. In S. B. Merriam, B. C. Courtenay, & R. M. Cervero (Eds.), *Global issues and adult education* (pp. 78–90). San Francisco: Jossey-Bass.

Freiler, T. J. (2008). Learning through the body. In S. B. Merriam (Ed.), *The third update on adult learning theory* (pp. 37–47). New Directions in Adult and Continuing Education. San Francisco: Jossey-Bass.

Friedman, T. L. (2005). *The world is flat; A brief history of the twenty-first century.* New York: Farrar, Straus & Giroux.

Glastra, F. J., Hake, B. J., & Schedler, P. E. (2004). Lifelong learning as transitional learning. *Adult Education Quarterly, 54*(4), 291–307.

Green, A. (2006). National educational systems and comparative education: From state formation to globalization. In N. Pang (Ed.), *Globalization: Educational research, change and reform* (pp. 25–50). Hong Kong: The Chinese University Press.

Hansman, C. A. (2006). Low-income adult learners in higher education: Politics, policies, and praxis. In S. B. Merriam, B. C. Courtenay, & R. M. Cervero (Eds.), *Global issues and adult education* (pp. 399–411). San Francisco: Jossey-Bass.

Hart, M. A. (1996). Sharing circles: Utilizing traditional practice methods for teaching, helping, and supporting. In S. O'Meara & D. A. West (Eds.), *From our eyes: Learning from indigenous peoples* (pp. 59–72). Toronto, Ontario: Garamond Press.

Jarvis, P. (2004). *Adult education and lifelong learning: Theory and practice* (3rd ed.). London and New York: Routledge/Falmer Press.

Jarvis, P. (2007). *Globalisation, lifelong learning and the learning society.* London: Routledge.

Jarvis, P. (2008). The consumer society: Is there a place for traditional adult education? *Convergence, 51*(1), 11–27.

Kamis, M., & Muhammad, M. (2007). Islam's lifelong learning mandate. In S. B. Merriam & Associates (Eds.), *Non-Western perspectives on learning and knowing* (pp. 21–40). Malabar, FL: Krieger.

Lindeman, E. C. (1926). *The meaning of adult education,* New York: New Republic.

Medel-Anonuevo, C. (1997). Moving across borders, cultures, and mindsets: Prospects for migrant and refugee education in the 21st century. In CONFINTEA V Background Papers, Special Issue. *Adult Education and Development,* pp. 165–171.

Merriam, S. B., & Associates (2007). *Non-Western perspectives on learning and knowing.* Malabar, FL: Krieger.

Merriam, S. B., Caffarella, R. S., & Baumgartner, L. M. (2007). *Learning in adulthood.* San Francisco: Jossey-Bass.

Merriam, S. B., Courtenay, B. C., & Cervero, R. M. (Eds.), (2006). *Global issues and adult education.* San Francisco: Jossey-Bass.

Newsweek. (2006, January). *The knowledge revolution: Why victory will go to the smartest nations & companies* [Special edition].

Quigley B. A. (2000). Adult education and democracy: Reclaiming our voice through social policy. In A. L. Wilson & E. R. Hayes (Eds.), *Handbook of adult and continuing education* (pp. 208–223). San Francisco: Jossey-Bass.

Rowden, R. (2007). *Workplace learning: Principles and practice.* Malabar, FL: Krieger.

Sachs, J. D. (2008, March 14). Common Wealth. *TIME* magazine, pp. 36–40.

Spring, J. (2008). Research on globalization and education. *Review of Educational Research, 78*(2), 330–336.

Tsui, A., & Tellefson, J. (Eds.). (2007). *Language policy, culture, and identity in Asian contexts.* Mahwah, NJ: Lawrence Erlbaum.

Uggla, B. K. (2008). Who is the lifelong learner? Globalization, lifelong learning and hermeneutics. *Studies in the Philosophy of Education, 27,* 211–226.

UNESCO. (1997, July). *Adult education: The Hamburg Declaration, the agenda for the future* (CONFINTEA '97: Fifth International Conference on Adult Education). Hamburg: UNESCO-Institute for Education.

Youngman, F. (2000). *The political economy of adult education and development.* London & New York: Zed Books.

38

PARADOX AND PROMISE IN THE KNOWLEDGE SOCIETY

ELISABETH E. BENNETT AND ALEXANDRA A. BELL

The rapid pace of change and the quest for knowledge in modern society have created a new landscape in adult and continuing education. Some scholars believe we are transitioning to a new era, the effects of which cannot be fully comprehended until the transition is complete (Sentell, 1998). This transition is not limited to Western civilization but now is part of one world history and civilization (Drucker, 2003). Aspects of the new era are captured in the concept of the knowledge society with profound implications for the field. Certainly, technical advances have dramatically altered the social context of adult and continuing education practice and have made information more accessible to most areas of the world, thus paving the way for the knowledge society.

A central and largely implicit premise behind the knowledge society is that open access to information will improve society and quality of life. This premise incorporates both individual adult learning as well as collective learning for the betterment of civil institutions and social structures, and it is consistent with the long-held emphasis of social justice in adult and continuing education. Knowledge and action are intertwined in the knowledge society to create progress. Also consistent with the historical foundations of the field is the goal of learning for economic advantage. Shifts in labor markets and employment trends create corresponding learning needs and challenges. Jobs and careers are changing at unprecedented levels, particularly as technological leaps occur with a quickened pace. Technology is transferred to public life with staggering speed as devices become better, faster, smaller, and cheaper. As we show in this chapter, technology is a critical component of the growth of the knowledge society.

In this era of postmodernity, the nature of knowledge and how one comes "to know" is a complex question. Indeed, the very concept of the knowledge society is likely contested, as we may ask "whose knowledge and whose society?" In the field of adult and continuing education, an emphasis on life-long learning helps adults cope with growing demands for new knowledge and the rapidity of change. Danger exists, however, in having too much information that can obscure knowledge building over the life span. This is but one example of paradoxes inherent in a knowledge society that affect the field. To borrow an old adage, the more one knows, the more one realizes how little one knows. Adults come to this understanding through the search for new knowledge. Due to human limitations, what one person can know is minuscule in comparison to the volume of extant information; yet personal or highly specialized knowledge applied at the right moment can make all the difference for success.

HISTORICAL PERSPECTIVES

The thirst for openness of knowledge in democratic society began during the Enlightenment and is revolutionized through new public knowledge forums found on the Internet; but the very characteristics that define the knowledge society also bring concerns about inequality and exclusion (UNESCO, 2005). A fundamental concern for the field is the growing distinction between the "haves" and the "have nots." A part of this divide is the role of technology in providing open access to information and connecting knowledge communities. Yet, infrastructure is necessary to support access, for example: Sending computers to a developing country does not help much if there are insufficient electrical outlets to provide power. Although the differential between developed and developing nations is vast, there has been a significant global growth of knowledge through information exchange.

Peter Drucker (1969) is often credited with advancing the term *knowledge society* in the mid-1960s as he described his thoughts on new social structures in which knowledge is integral to the economy. The term, however, does not appear in prior *Handbooks of Adult Education*. A retrospective of the past four decades' *Handbooks* reveals changes in contributors' conceptions about the nature of society, knowledge, and technology that lay a path to this chapter.

In the 1970 *Handbook of Adult Education* (Smith, Aker, & Kidd, 1970), which documented the 1960s decade, the United States was described as an industrial society. Digital technologies were beginning to change the nature of work, yet Johnson (1970) observed, "Although the computer is widely used for administrative and research tasks, it has made little impact to date on the actual practice of education" (p. 95). The impact of technology on practice and society as a whole becomes dramatically apparent in the 1990 *Handbook*. The backdrop is a postindustrial information age, and Lewis (1989) cogently described how technological breakthroughs enabled access, storage, and dissemination of tremendous amounts of information across geographic and demographic boundaries, triggering challenges to educational and social conventions in terms of power, choice, access, and wealth. At the same time, new technologies enabled new realities, such as computer simulations and teleconferencing, challenging conventions about knowledge.

In 1970, De Crow portrayed knowledge as something acquired, separate from the knower. By 2000, Holford and Jarvis described "a fundamental shift in the conception of knowledge itself—from something certain and true to something changing and relative" (p. 646). To cope with constant changes in what is known, they explained, reflective learning becomes a "way of life" (p. 646) and society a learning society. As described in this chapter, exponential leaps in technology demand not only constant learning but also skills for managing what is known. Spear and Mocker's (1989) forecast in the 1990 *Handbook* that "ideas [will] become the principle and most prized product" (p. 645) has been realized in Western society. Knowledge has become part of the social infrastructure, and adult and continuing education plays a pivotal role in the knowledge society. In this chapter, we describe the growth of the knowledge society with implications for the field and illuminate the inherent paradoxes found in the concept.

DEFINING THE KNOWLEDGE SOCIETY

The nature of the knowledge society is abstract and defies exact definition. Over the past 20 years, several iterations of terms have led to use of the term *knowledge society* to describe the predominant social paradigm among developed and developing nations. *Information economy* gave rise to *information society,* followed by *knowledge economy* and now *knowledge society.* The earlier terms reflect a narrower technical and economic emphasis. A shift from describing economy to society reflects the social and cultural transformation that occurs as a community adjusts to new technologies, industries, and ways of living.

An information economy expresses the centrality of information technology needed for a sound economy, whereas information society reflects how the growing volume of information has altered daily life. A knowledge economy can be defined as "all jobs, companies, and industries in which the knowledge and capabilities of people, rather than the capabilities of machines or technologies, determine competitive advantage" (Lengnick-Hall & Lengnick-Hall, 2003, p. 17). Knowledge society is qualitatively different from the former terms because it is more holistic and views people as possessing rich and diverse forms of knowledge important for a progressive society. A marked change has been a greater recognition of what humans contribute to organizations, captured in such terms as *human capital* and *intellectual capital.* Codifiable information, primarily accessible to information technology specialists, is but one form of knowledge alongside intuition, judgment, and expertise.

Possessing the physical network infrastructure for information access is insufficient to create a knowledge society (UNESCO, 2005). Rather, the focus is creativity and innovation resulting from the process of using information to build new knowledge, products, services, and philosophies of living. As the world has seen from recent financial crises, the ability to derive value from intangible knowledge products can be troublesome. In the same way that new social structures occurred as a result of the industrial age, social changes can be expected when knowledge is the key ingredient in the economy.

Knowledge is more valuable than information. Lor and Britz (2007) wrote, "'knowledge' implies a resource that is richer, more structured, more organized, more complex and more qualitative than 'information'" (p. 389). Knowledge requires an exercise of judgment. At the time it became law, the G.I. Bill of Rights seemed incongruous to pre-war educational patterns among working-class men, but the enthusiastic response by American veterans signaled a shift to a society in which specialized knowledge was the main resource for economic growth, with land and capital necessary but secondary in the economic equation (Drucker, 2003). Drucker further noted that certain fields such as education, medicine, religion, and law have always been knowledge professions, but now specialized knowledge is necessary for many professions. Specialized or expert knowledge is productive only when it is integrated into a task, whereas general knowledge is applicable in more contexts. Schools often teach general knowledge, although many adult educators have become more facile with incorporating practice to jump-start expertise development and knowledge application.

Knowledge society has become an accepted term in the last decade. It is most often used as a singular term, that is, we are all moving to one larger knowledge society rather than parallel knowledge societies (Jakobi, 2007). Biesta (2007) described two interpretations of the knowledge society, that of the knowledge economy, discussed

previously, and knowledge democracy, which allows the freedom to pursue knowledge for both individual and political effects. He also suggested that expertise could make democracy superfluous because of the reliance on expert opinion to solve complex issues. Stehr (2006) alluded to this paradox inherent in the knowledge society where there is a growing dependence on expert knowledge in modern society and a gap between experts with an understanding of the complexity of modern problems and the public without full knowledge of a subject; this situation creates tension and contradiction for democratic representation. This cognitive distance disenfranchises the public from discussions that require scientific or topical literacy. For example, the debate on global warming is based on complex and at times inaccessible scientific data. When the debate influences legislation to curb emissions and amend international treaties, the economic viability for many countries and their constituents can be severely impacted. The public relies on scientists to be correct in forecasting climate change but has little ability to verify the prediction models or make sense of theoretical disagreements. The Internet can help bridge the divide if it is accessible; however, a person cannot be expert in all things. The knowledge society, then, must successfully balance knowledge democracy and expertise to avoid oppression.

Communications technology and the Internet have been steadily changing information access patterns for new knowledge creation. A knowledge society is a society that "operates within the paradigm of the economics of information" (Lor & Britz, 2007, p. 390). Participation in this new economic paradigm depends heavily on infrastructure and also on how cultures and communities regulate access. In some countries, such as China, leaders have severely restricted Internet access of the populace. Participation and knowledge growth can be curtailed by any ideology that views open access to information as a threat to sociopolitical stability. We believe that how the paradox of expertise and knowledge democracy is negotiated in the coming years will have profound implications for the ethical practice of adult and continuing education and for society as a whole. This is as true for governments and businesses as it is for academic institutions because organizational values can place restrictions on the flow of information and determine who participates in the knowledge society.

Education and the World Economy

Academic institutions have long relied on knowledge as a primary resource, presenting many potential areas for collaboration and knowledge exchange with businesses. Conversely, the potential for prohibiting access to new knowledge exists, which is in opposition to the premise of the knowledge society. Higher education has become, to an extent, commodified and marketable in the global arena. Universities can no longer claim a monopoly on research; but by credentialing professionals, higher education maintains a high degree of control over participation (Biesta, 2007). The rise of proprietary and corporate universities blurs the lines between education and business. In addition, corporate research and development activities now extend beyond the hard sciences and include social science and educational research. Knowledge creation and sharing are necessary in the global knowledge society (UNESCO, 2005), but there is much debate about intellectual property rights that erect knowledge-sharing boundaries. In all arenas, private or public, experts have the potential to become the new oppressors or to open doors to participation.

Globalization, powered by technology, has created a delimited and increasingly interdependent world. National boundaries can be easily crossed with technology, providing opportunities for greater knowledge of and, we hope, appreciation for the differences among cultures. Transnational organizations exist beyond the boundaries of any one country, and they are positioned to become the most muscular force in global politics. According to Lor and Britz (2007), the global race for information in the knowledge society is not unlike an arms race. Another paradox exists here when countries attempt to maintain exclusivity of information because information cannot be exhausted in the same way as physical resources. Information can be reused and reformed many times and for many purposes, limited only by human desire and imagination. A new formula for plastic, for example, can create a life-saving medical device or a weapon undetectable to airport scanners. Knowledge can be reformulated in innovative and agile ways, but not all formulations are desirable.

Pressures in the global economy are sparking change in education. Many countries are adopting common educational policies and best practices as a result of globalization (Jakobi, 2007). In addition, the phenomenon of the "brain drain" affects educational as well as political practices internationally, as academic institutions and businesses alike vie for knowledge talent. The gain and loss of knowledge workers will have global consequences for developing and industrial countries alike.

Knowledge Workers and Knowledge Management

Although knowledge professions have always existed, the growth of new knowledge fields, such as the technology sector, has created major labor forces in industrial countries that were once driven by manufacturing positions. This specialization has been achieved primarily through formal education (Drucker, 2003) and, we would add, experience. Knowledge as the primary resource in a knowledge society brings new challenges: With all the information available, how does one create something of value through knowledge processes, and how does one manage the knowledge?

Knowledge management theory addresses these questions and has applications for adult and continuing education in the knowledge society. Knowledge management relates to how knowledge is acquired, created, and distributed (Lengnick-Hall & Lengnick-Hall, 2003) with emphasis on the social activity of sharing knowledge through technology. The idea of managing knowledge through technology may seem like a paradox because knowledge exists in the human brain. One way to conceptualize knowledge management is by looking at the use of mnemonics. Creating a rhyme or an acronym to aid memorization is an example of managing knowledge with a tool that can be embedded in software and serve as a reminder. Technology offers cognitive tools for off-loading and manipulating information. Knowledge can be found in the dynamic interplay between brain and device. New knowledge is created, for example, when one plays with numbers in an electronic savings calculator and preserves different scenarios to revisit later. This allows an adult to build knowledge through experimentation.

Because knowledge is at the center of knowledge management, theorists have struggled with what to do with different forms of knowledge.

First, knowledge management distinguishes between tacit and explicit knowledge. Explicit knowledge can be communicated through text. Tacit knowledge is rooted in action and intuition and is difficult to articulate (Choo, 1995). According to Polanyi (1966), people know more than they can say, and attempting to say everything one knows, such as every discrete motion needed to ride a bike, can destroy meaning when isolated from the skill, once it is learned as a whole.

Another way that knowledge management defines forms of knowledge is through the distinction of bits of information, or data, to build more valuable knowledge and wisdom. Harris (1998) suggested that information is dynamic and evolutionary as value is added to transform observations into wisdom. He proposed a model that begins with data flowing from observation, which, when analyzed for classifications, produces information. Information explained leads to understanding, and the ability to predict produces knowledge. Wisdom is achieved when knowledge is used to create general laws. Very little data make it all the way through the process to the plane of wisdom, which is continually redefined in each era; what is wise in one historical moment is commonplace in another. This progression of refinement is greater than the sum of individual learning and affects the collective imagination of society.

Forms of knowledge and culture are the basis of society (UNESCO, 2005). How individuals perceive and apply data to build knowledge and how knowledge becomes part of culture are mysterious in many ways. The Internet, which has been a driving force for globalization, and other communication technologies have played important roles in these processes. Bennett (2006) described how the capabilities of Web technology to incorporate graphics, colors, sounds, and video clips can tap into diverse forms of knowledge to shape culture. Web sites provide a virtual space for adults to experience new things. For example, the very colors and font styles of a Web site can communicate a feeling of the macabre, whereas cartoons and crayon-drawn stick figures create a childlike and seemingly safe environment. Designers use literary techniques to manage public perception. But seeing is not necessarily believing, as many Web sites are hoaxes. Critical consumption of information is as important, if not more so, in the knowledge society. An important role of adult educators is fostering critical thinking about the trustworthiness of Web sources. Increasingly, adults are entering classrooms, workplaces, and community settings with greater diversity of technical skills and experiences. In many ways, adult learners are already engaging in knowledge management because they must choose what must be learned versus what can be looked up to find the most up-to-date information. We explore adult learning in the knowledge society further in the next section.

ADULT LEARNING IN THE KNOWLEDGE SOCIETY

Although the knowledge society will shape and be shaped by adult learning in many ways, two phenomena in particular influence the field of adult and continuing education. First is the preeminence of lifelong learning in determining the viability of the knowledge society. Second is the role of technology in creating new learning environments for adults.

Lifelong Learning and the Knowledge Society

Because what is known is changing continually, the viability of a knowledge society—its "performance capacity" (Drucker, 2001, p. 289)—is dependent on the ability of individuals to be lifelong learners. Jarvis (2007) explained: "Because society is fluid and always changing, learning itself is changing and needs to become lifelong rather than recurrent at times of status change; lifelong learning is an individual necessity for all people" (p. 39). For this chapter, we adopted Jarvis's (2007) broad definition of lifelong learning that includes preconscious as well as conscious learning resulting from the transformation of experience in all contexts and stages in life and integration into the individual's personal biography. This definition underscores the social context of learning and the continual changes in self-identity and life world that are both the outcome and genesis of new learning. In the knowledge society, individuals' ability to learn from experience in ways that enable them to cope with continual change becomes the curriculum for lifelong learning.

Whereas the curriculum for industrialized societies emphasized the skills of language literacy, rationality, analysis, and predictability, the knowledge society requires its own curriculum for lifelong learning. Most notable are cognitive skills that enable individuals to cope with and optimally thrive on the complexities, uncertainties, multiple choices, and multiple realities in the knowledge society. Perceptual skills (Drucker, 2001) and the ability to appreciate alternative perspectives (Quirk, 2006) take priority over analytical skills. These skills allow individuals to acquire meaningful knowledge and to make viable choices amid constantly changing options. They also enable individuals to appreciate and function in increasingly broader societies, resulting in expanded conceptions of *me* and *we*, dissolving boundaries between *them* and *us* (O'Hara, 2007). Additional cognitive skills needed in the knowledge society include multitasking, nonlinear and systems reasoning, information navigation, reflective practice, pattern recognition, and the ability to "distinguish between the significant and the banal" (O'Hara, p. 939) in ever-changing contexts.

Technology plays a pivotal role in the curriculum for the knowledge society. Advances in storing and retrieving information may reduce demand for the most essential of cognitive functions—recognition and recall, resulting in changes in the nature of cognition itself. An increasing number of technologies offer opportunities to assume alternative personae and experience new realities, expanding and intensifying what Jarvis (2007) described as continual changes in self-identity and life-world associated with lifelong learning. Educators in adult and continuing education are in a unique position to support learners through a spectrum of experiences, whether intrinsic, social, or virtual. Technology will be an integral part of that support as well.

Technology and New Learning Environments

The knowledge society cannot be separated from the technology that enables it. A paradox of technology is that it can both isolate people and overcome barriers of space and time to bring people closer together. This era is characterized by fragmentation but also opportunities for new alliances and interactions (Merriam, Caffarella,

& Baumgartner, 2007), for example, knowledge networks, which are groups that form around expertise or interest in a specialized topic. The growth of the Internet has altered the environment in which adults live and work. For example, alternative workplace strategies are becoming more popular as organizations develop sophisticated and culturally relevant technology that fosters human interaction and informal virtual learning (Bennett, 2009).

Virtual reality offers a distinctly different environment for interaction and learning. It allows for multiple representations of one's self and for gaining experiences that are largely impossible in the physical world. The overlay of an individual adult's knowledge with that of a knowledge network suggests a state in which both idiosyncratic and collective knowledge can exist simultaneously. Objectifying technology and seeing it as something outside the self is appealing; however, humans strive for community through interaction whether face to face or facilitated through technology. Interaction patterns shape communication technology and in turn are shaped by technology (Palloff & Pratt, 1999). The phenomenon of cell phone texting, for example, is changing the language and timetable of social communication. The dynamic between humans and technology creates new knowledge and extends human capability, but some knowledge may be lost as old ways are left behind.

Technology has revolutionized adult and continuing education in that there are more things to be learned by adults and more ways in which to learn them. Adults can join knowledge networks to find resources for hobbies and learning projects. Knowledge networks clustered around specialized interests can form overnight to solve a problem, only to disconnect after the problem is resolved. In this manner, knowledge networks afford powerful environments for learning, analysis, and action and with unprecedented flexibility and agility.

Social networking sites provide another learning environment. The success of sites such as Facebook.com and MySpace.com may be due to participants' conception that membership in various networks is fluid and temporal. In reality, however, information a person places out on the Internet should be considered released forever and part of the public domain. Internet content can be printed or cached to a backup copy of a Web site, which is available even if the original source is removed. The metacognitive and reflective skills needed to maximize learning through social networking sites are largely unknown and represent a new area of practice and research for adult educators. Another fascinating example is massive multiplayer online gaming, such as Xbox Live™, which necessitates quick formation and negotiation of virtual teams. These abilities are shaping the next generation of adult learners.

Virtual environments can also provide a space for experimentation with self-identity through avatars that become a virtual representation of self. In her studies of sociological issues of the Internet, Turkle (1995) found that individuals questioned and explored notions of gender and identity online. Internet role-playing and chat rooms allow participants to hide or enhance personal attributes or pretend to be something different altogether. Business, too, incorporates virtual spokespeople to interact with Web guests. The meaning virtual experiences hold for adults can be a matter of individual perspective but also negotiated in virtual community. Turkle described how an Internet community struggled with the meaning of a virtual rape when a male character violated a female character. Messages posted on virtual bulletin boards about the incident ranged from defending the rape because it was merely fantasy and not embodied, to viewing the act as a crime against the mind because the avatar was an extension of a real person. When individuals participate in new realities afforded by technology in the knowledge society their lifeworld is altered. Their values may be challenged, and questions arise that are not easily answered in the new paradigm.

Physical limitations are overcome in virtual environments although long-standing social problems still exist. Avatars in Second Life defy gravity and fly over mountains and seas to experience new destinations in the virtual world, but adults still need solid relational skills. Some universities hold class in Second Life where learners are represented by their avatars. Presentations can be uploaded to screens in a virtual classroom, and the instructor can see who is present and engaged in learning. Support groups are also widely available in virtual environments and can help adults find semi-anonymous help with difficult personal circumstances.

Technology also allows for the practice of skills in safe environments. Avatars that were once limited to the realm of fantasy games are now incorporated into architectural planning software, allowing clients to "walk through" a design before it is built. Simulation and gaming programs have become commonplace in many fields. For example, virtual trainers are used in medical education to teach physicians foundational surgical skills before they practice on live patients. Other types of trainers, such as patient mannequins, simulate medical emergencies so that a medical team reacts more quickly in real-life emergencies. Some mannequins mimic heart rhythms and possess gas exchangers to add to the realism of cardiovascular functions.

Not all learning technology has to be virtual or high fidelity. Low-cost mobile devices for task training have helped fuel the use of simulation in education (Ramalay & Zia, 2005) and help incorporate skill building and cognitive knowledge. Technology provides a means for educating adults, who now expect education "to go" in the form of online classes, blogs, and podcasts. These are but a few of the many new learning environments afforded by technology in the knowledge society. In the knowledge society, learning environments and the lifelong learning of adults will be mutually determined. These trends have interesting implications for research and practice in adult and continuing education.

FUTURE TRENDS

The social context of adult and continuing education is changing, as are global needs for education. The field will undergo dramatic changes as it accommodates the newest generation of adults and grapples with generational differences. The Net generation (Hartman, Moskal, & Dziuban 2005), born between 1981 and 1994, is entering adulthood, and members bring with them a set of traits that includes familiarity with technology, optimism, ability to multitask, diversity, and acceptance of authority. Other traits, however, may pose challenges for supporting their learning. According to Hartman et al. (2005), members of the Net generation are also characterized by shallowness in reading, lack of critical thinking, and naïveté about intellectual property and information authenticity of Internet resources. Other changes for adult and continuing education will stem from international demographic shifts and emerging industries.

The knowledge society will have diverse global effects due to demographic shifts and changing cultural expectations. Some nations may become increasingly open to global influence in the knowledge society whereas others may become more closed and isolationist. Drucker (2003) predicted that accommodating the aging population, with its increased life expectancy and need for new services, will require widespread immigration of knowledge workers and alterations in work patterns, including flexible options for retaining older workers in part-time roles. Due to low birthrates, European countries will need to increase immigration to stay economically viable. The United States will also need to address workforce shortages, but it is better positioned because of past experience with immigration. Developing countries have tremendous opportunities and challenges ahead. Major challenges in the short run include the recruitment of top knowledge workers; if successful, long-term opportunities abound. With increased mobility, there will be important avenues for adult and continuing education to bridge cultural and economic divides through education. There will also be many potential points of cultural conflict and misunderstanding.

In a knowledge society, ideally people should be able to move easily through the flow of information and distinguish between helpful and valueless information (UNESCO, 2005); however, the paradox is that one cannot always predict what information will be useful later. Existing data may suddenly become important when it is used in new ways. Information about a wild plant local to one region may be the next pharmaceutical miracle, with great benefit to society, when matched with specialized scientific knowledge in another region. The ongoing challenge for members of the knowledge society will be to live successfully in the tension between the public and the private, the individual and the collective, the open and the closed. Negotiating these tensions will be what balances the paradoxes of the knowledge society.

Implications for Research

The knowledge society has many implications for research in adult and continuing education. One prominent implication is that research is needed to test new knowledge and to understand adult learning in this era. Given how necessary lifelong learning is to the viability of the knowledge society, more resources should be applied to support adult education research, especially in developing countries where economic success is overshadowed by pandemics. Little is known of how the knowledge society will affect, for example, adult cognitive development or political empowerment. The role of technology in adult learning, especially Web-based and simulation approaches, should be part of the research agenda. Many effects of technology on adult learning are unknown, flying under the research radar in many universities. The very context in which we live and practice helps us to pose fascinating and relevant questions to advance the field. No doubt the knowledge society concept touches research in ways not conceived of when adult and continuing education was in its infancy.

As we have demonstrated, separating the concept of the knowledge society from the technology that enables it is difficult. How knowledge, technology, and research can interrelate is captured in the acronym TRASO or "technology as research aid, subject, and object" (Bennett, 2003). Technology can be seen through at least three lenses in relation to research. First, it can be viewed as an aid to managing research. Computing has aided statistical analysis and, more recently, qualitative data analysis. Word processors, online search engines, and e-mail are tremendous tools in producing dissertations and in speeding findings to electronic repositories. Second, technology can be seen as a research subject. Many questions exist about how instructional technology affects adult learning and where the boundaries of the classroom lie. In the third and possibly most interesting lens, technology can be viewed as a research object. As described earlier in this chapter, technology in the knowledge society can reflect more forms of knowledge than in previous decades.

We project that research products will increasingly use graphics, colors, and sounds to represent the experience of the researcher in ways that text alone cannot convey. When a researcher produces a thesis as a Web site, for example, the design choices, inflections, emotion, and expression in video clips, and so on blur the lines between the findings and the technology. The challenge for the field will be how to critique this work. Technology also allows members of the field to experience more of the researcher's perspective. This aspect opens up many new possibilities for understanding how research is conducted and how new knowledge is created by researchers. The knowledge society will demand greater understanding of knowledge creation through all avenues of research and practice.

IMPLICATIONS FOR PRACTICE

Practice of adult and continuing education will adjust to the knowledge society. The field will need to negotiate a global identity and generate ways to interface with the new and changing world. A major gap exists between research on learning and what instructors actually practice, especially regarding technology (Ramalay & Zia, 2005). Clearly, adult and continuing education needs to connect theory and practice for improved educational outcomes. Online learning will continue to be a flexible delivery mode that can make learners' thinking patterns and knowledge creation methods explicit. Ramalay and Zia (2005) offered that "in cyberspace, the whole thought process is laid open in the building of understanding through much richer conversation" (p. 8.16). This perspective complements the idea that conversation is a form of experiential learning whereby people achieve collaborative understanding through interplay of contradictions such as reflection and action (Baker, Jensen, & Kolb, 2005). Still, we believe that face-to-face interaction is also important to facilitate shared understandings and to convey embodied or tacit knowledge not found in technology. The need for personal connection and interaction is ever present.

With regard to classroom-based practice, the andragogical model of adult learning (Knowles, 1984) described the desire for control of one's learning and the rich set of prior experiences with which adults enter the classroom. The role of the instructor, according to Knowles (1984), is to promote mutual respect among learners and to facilitate each adult's purpose for learning. We believe that this perspective is highly relevant in the knowledge society. Instructors can help adults with technical literacy, including the critical consumption of information. The skills adults need go beyond logic and analysis; they include intuition, judgment, and depth of insight. Because so much of the Internet is vanity press or polemic, Dyson (1998) recommended adults build webs of trust, defined as trusted sources of knowledge and expertise. This could be a challenge for instructors if, as Hartman et al. (2005) contended, newer generations of adults are less critical in their consumption of information and must be encouraged to form independent opinions. Independence of mind is pivotal for the knowledge society and should be an aim of adult and continuing education.

CONCLUSION

In this chapter, we have described the growth of the knowledge society with implications for the field of adult and continuing education. Inherent in the concept are many paradoxes in social progress. We anticipate that, for some colleagues in the field, many ideas presented in this chapter may cause deep concern and, for others, exhilaration in the endless possibilities. We recognize and respect that some adult educators are leery of technology, perhaps out of concern for its potential to dehumanize and deskill. So much remains unknown about the complex interrelationships among technologies, knowledge, and adult learning in the knowledge society. The opportunities, however, have never been richer for adult educators to be at the planning table to negotiate democratically for adult and continuing education (Cervero & Wilson, 2006). We look forward with great anticipation to see how the knowledge society develops for the 2020 *Handbook.*

REFERENCES

Baker, A., Jensen, P., & Kolb, D. A. (2005). Conversation as experiential learning. *Management Learning, 36*(4), 411–427.

Bennett, E. E. (2003). *Technology: Cracking the research code.* Oral presentation in the Department of Adult Education, University of Georgia, Athens.

Bennett, E. E. (2006). Organizational intranets and the transition to managing knowledge. In M. Anandarajan, T. Teo, & C. Simmers (Eds.), *The Internet and transformation of the workplace* (pp. 83–103). Advances in Management

Information Systems. Armonk, NY: M. E. Sharpe.

Bennett, E. E. (2009). Virtual HRD: The intersection of knowledge management, culture, and Intranets. *Advances in Developing Human Resources, 11*(3), 362–374.

Biesta, G. (2007). Towards the knowledge democracy? Knowledge production and the civic role of the university. *Studies in Philosophy of Education, 26,* 467–479.

Cervero, R. M., & Wilson, A. L. (2006). *Working the planning table: Negotiating democratically for adult, continuing, and workplace education.* San Francisco: Jossey-Bass.

Choo, C. W. (1995). *Information management for the intelligent organization: The art of scanning the environment.* Medford, NJ: Information Today.

De Crow, R. (1970). Information resources and services. In R. M. Smith, G. F. Aker, & J. R. Kidd (Eds.), *Handbook of adult education* (pp. 75–90). New York: Macmillian.

Drucker, P. (1969). *The age of discontinuity: Guidelines to our changing society.* New York: Harper & Row.

Drucker, P. F. (2001). The educated person. In P. F. Drucker, *The essential Drucker* (pp. 287–295). New York: HarperCollins.

Drucker, P. (2003). *A functioning society: Selections from sixty-five years of writing on community, society, and polity.* Piscataway, NJ: Transaction.

Dyson, E. (1998). *Release 2.1: A design for living in the digital age.* New York: Broadway Books.

Harris, M. C. (1998). *Value leadership: Winning competitive advantage in the information age.* Milwaukee, WI: Quality Press.

Hartman, J., Moskal, P., & Dziuban, C. (2005). Preparing the academy of today for the learner of tomorrow. In D. C. Oblinger & J. L. Oblinger (Eds.), *Educating the Net generation* (pp. 6.1–6.15). Washington, DC: Educause.

Holford, P., & Jarvis, P. (2000). The learning society. In A. L. Wilson & E. R. Hayes (Eds.), *Handbook of adult and continuing education* (pp. 643–659). San Francisco: Jossey-Bass.

Jakobi, A. P. (2007). The knowledge society and global dynamics in education politics. *European Educational Research Journal, 6*(1), 39–51.

Jarvis, P. (2007). *Globalization, lifelong learning, and the learning society.* Lifelong Learning and the Learning Society. London: Routledge.

Johnson, E. I. (1970). Technology in adult education. In R. M. Smith, G. F. Aker, & J. R. Kidd (Eds.), *Handbook of adult education* (pp. 91–108). New York: Macmillan.

Knowles, M. S. (1984). *Andragogy in action.* San Francisco: Jossey-Bass.

Lengnick-Hall, M. L., & Lengnick-Hall, C. A. (2003). *Human resource management in the knowledge economy: New challenges, new roles, and new capabilities.* San Francisco: Barrett-Koehler.

Lewis, L. H. (1989). New educational technologies for the future. In S. B. Merriam & P. Cunningham (Eds.), *Handbook of adult and continuing education* (pp. 613–627). San Francisco: Jossey-Bass.

Lor, P. J., & Britz, J. J. (2007). Is a knowledge society possible without freedom of access to information? *Journal of Information Science, 33*(4), 387–397.

Merriam, S. B., Caffarella, R. S., & Baumgartner, L. M. (2007). *Learning in adulthood: A comprehensive guide* (3rd ed.). San Francisco: Jossey-Bass.

O'Hara, M. (2007). Strangers in a strange land: Knowing, learning, and education for the global knowledge society. *Futures, 39,* 930–941.

Palloff, R. M., & Pratt, K. (1999). *Building learning communities in cyberspace: Effective strategies for the online classroom.* San Francisco: Jossey-Bass.

Polanyi, M. (1966). *The tacit dimension.* Garden City, NY: Anchor Books.

Quirk, M. (2006). *Intuition and metacognition in medical education: Keys to developing expertise.* New York: Springer.

Ramalay, J., & Zia, L. (2005). The real versus the possible: Closing the gaps in engagement and learning. In D. G. Oblinger & J. L. Oblinger (Eds.), *Educating the Net generation* (pp. 8.1–8.21). Washington, DC: Educause.

Sentell, G. (1998). *Creating change-capable cultures.* Alcoa, TN: Pressmark International.

Smith, R. M., Aker, G. F., & Kidd, J. R. (Eds.). (1970). *Handbook of adult education.* New York: Macmillan.

Spear, G. E., & Mocker, D. W. (1989). The future of adult education. In S. B. Merriam & P. Cunningham (Eds.), *Handbook of adult and continuing education* (pp. 640–649). San Francisco: Jossey-Bass.

Stehr, N. (2006). Comment: Is democracy a daughter of knowledge? In G. Neave (Ed.), *Knowledge, power and dissent: Critical perspectives on higher education and research in knowledge society.* Paris: UNESCO.

Turkle, S. (1995). *Life on the screen: Identity in the age of the Internet.* New York: Touchstone.

UNESCO. (2005). *Towards knowledge societies.* Condé-sur-Noireau, France: Imprimerie Corlet.

39

INFORMAL LEARNING IN A VIRTUAL ERA

KATHLEEN P. KING

In the 21st century, knowledge is increasing at lightning speed, and people of every age and background face the continuing challenge of uncovering the information they need and mastering the ways of obtaining it, which are also evolving rapidly. In every area of life, from medical information to book reviews, refinancing homes to home remodeling, adults constantly need to find the latest data to make informed decisions. Formal learning is inadequate to meet these lifelong learning needs: people do not have time to enroll in formal classes at every new life stage and for every decision they must make.

Ubiquitous (but not always obvious) informal learning opportunities make it possible for adults to tap the exploding information and learning resources of our times. Informal learning today goes beyond book-based self-study to include a plethora of Web-based, digital, and community resources, along with opportunities for worldwide collaboration with people of similar interests and needs. The world is rich with new learning opportunities—for example, iPods, TV programs, digital radio and virtual simulations—that can fit anyone's schedule and learning style.

Informal learning is commonly viewed as embedded in a typology of learning that includes formal, nonformal, and informal learning (Coombs, 1989). What distinguishes informal learning is the independence of the learner and the context of daily life. A central issue is the conundrum that while educational systems often view formal learning as the pride of pedagogy, informal learning predates it and necessitates greater learner responsibility.

Marsick and Watkins (1990) discuss the nonlinear development of a theory of informal learning, beginning with Lindeman's view that "a central feature of informal and incidental learning is learning from experience" (p. 15). They note that no one theorist's views entirely capture the process, but some of the key works have been contributed by Dewey (1938), Polanyi (1967), Tough (1971, 1999), Argyris and Schön (1974), Kolb (1984), Marsick and Watkins (1990), Garrick (1998), Livingstone (1999), and Schugurensky (2000). While these scholars have begun researching and building awareness of this area, much remains to be revealed as we enhance our understanding of informal learning.

Informal learning is one way to achieve information literacy. As carefully demonstrated by the American Library Association (2006), adults need to determine what and how they need to find; to evaluate, analyze, interpret available information; and then apply the information in the context of various issues surrounding the use of information. Synthesizing several sources, King and Sanquist (2009) note that information literacy skills today include skills such as research and logic, visual literacy, technology literacy, copyright laws, and more.

OPPORTUNITIES AND CHALLENGES

In prior centuries, informal learning was characterized by direct observation, modeling, and mentorship (Tough, 1971). However, the virtual and digital ages have opened new possibilities as adults can engage in learning outside the constraints of time and place. Examples include the use of digital audio to provide tutoring and language learning; digital audio and video to develop new skills in relaxation, memory skills, and critical thinking; as well as computer-based simulations to explore career opportunities. Many authors point to the U.S. 2008 presidential election to illustrate how digital and online petitions, instructions, and notifications have clearly emerged as powerful ways to inform, educate, and mobilize voters (McGirt, 2009).

The digital age has put a profusion of information at our fingertips. Every institution, academic or otherwise, seems to have a Web site offering information, and the Internet also offers access to an expanding library of online books, online encyclopedias, and a host of more or less authoritative information sources.

At the same time, the virtual age offers personal access to different experiences and alternate lives/realities (Milanovic, 2006). Vast numbers of adults of all ages engage in computer-based and Web-based simulations, which enable them to interact in an environment much like real experience. In these simulations, they learn and practice how to navigate obstacles, make decisions, use controls, and strategize in a safe environment. This medium is already integrated into K–12 education, medical training, flight controller training, online and video games (Flight Simulator etc.), online environments (Second Life, for example), and movies.

There are also challenges to the use of new technologies for informal learning. The principal one is the lack of universal access, which leaves many unable to develop lifelong learning skills in this way. Because the need for successful lifelong learning skills has never been more urgent, this handicap may lead to disadvantages in economic, professional, political, social, health, and personal domains (Brown & Thomas, 2006).

PATTERNS OF PARTICIPATION

Examination of inequities in participation in informal learning is facilitated by some excellent recent data collected by several groups, notably the New Approaches to Lifelong Learning (NALL) group in Canada and the National Center for Education Statistics (NCES), in the United States. The development of new technologies has had a major impact in this area.

In one of the earliest studies of informal learning, Tough (1971) found that 70% of the adult population was involved in intentional learning that was informal in nature but still purposeful. In 1991, he said the figure was about 90% and that people spent on average 15 hours per week engaged in this learning. However, something pivotal happened in 1992 (Tapscott & Williams, 2006). With the development of the World Wide Web (www), graphical user interface browsers (i.e., Netscape, then Internet Explorer), and affordable desktop computers, adoption of Internet use soared. Soon, technology for everyday use in business, education, and general public use extended from free computer-based video conferencing (e.g., Skype), to full-body simulation games and sports (e.g., Wii), Web-connected cell phones, online learning environments (e.g., Blackboard.com, Moodle.org), and virtual environments (e.g., Second Life).

By 2001, NCES data revealed, more than 63% adults participated in work-related informal learning, while only 46% adults participated in formal learning endeavors. These findings confirm prior studies that adults with college educations and family income of $50,000 or more are more likely to pursue education in all its modalities (U.S. Department of Education, 2004). Most recent findings about the adoption of technology reveal trends that could greatly expand the participation rate and potentially shed light on differing ways that individuals use technology. For instance, a recent Pew study (Li, 2007) reveals how people of different ages use Web-based technologies and new media in different ways.

The research looks beyond patterns of participation to examine motivations. Early studies found many reasons for participation, building on Tough's (1971) initial focus. For example, Boshier's (1991) Educational Participation Scale (EPS) provided a psychometric instrument to measure the motivation for participation in learning across the dimensions of Escape/Stimulation, Social Welfare, Social Contact, and Cognitive Interest. It remains to be seen if these dimensions for motivation change as the means of participation change.

An increasingly diverse adult population and instantaneous global collaboration offer avenues for additional research perspectives and efforts. King and Sanquist (2009) provide one example of how varied contexts (podcasting) and multiple lenses (lesbian, gay, bisexual, transgender, and questioning [LGBTQ] adults) can assist our specific understanding with broader insights of adult learning.

Workplace Issues

Garrick (1998) suggests that we examine the context for the continuing and renewed interest in informal learning by questioning changing political and economic climates and their roles in our pursuits. He asks, "Why is it that informal learning is, at this particular moment, a focus of industry's gaze?" (p. 5). In recent years, the workplace has been the site for much research on informal learning (Livingstone, 1999; Schugurensky, 2000). Indeed, economic conditions, as well as the rapid adoption of technology, provide the major impetus for renewed attention to informal learning. The following scenario shows how adult learners may use technology for informal learning on the job.

> This week Sharlene, Carrie, Merlyn, and Brady volunteer to be the office's team for the "Managerial Face-Off." They are competing in an online simulation among sales managers of Magnolia Interior Make Overs sponsored by one of their vendors.
>
> Sharlene was this week's team leader. They were using the Web-based environment to explore Week Six's sales market, learn the conditions and rules of this episode, and successfully complete the quests, which were revealed successively. Their office's previous teams gathered with them to prepare for the competition and provided strategies about navigating the system to look for patterns in the simulated sales market, along with economic and production conditions, and to recognize cooperative and aggressive competitors.
>
> Everyone was hooked on this impromptu learning experience. It was a tangible, fun way to problem solve, collaborate, and strategize. After Week Three, many people in the office began to wonder, "Why don't we do this with our regular work?" And by Week Four, they had begun to hold the same sort of meetings about their clients, customers, and projects. Sharlene could see a different environment emerging.

This scenario illustrates the effectiveness of gaming as informal learning because it is entertaining and interactive; it reminds us that any analysis of informal leaning has to include several dimensions.

Modalities and Means: Variable Dimensions

In examining how a particular example of informal learning compares and differs from other efforts, several dimensions may be useful. This section addresses technology-no technology, mind-body, and face to face-virtual.

Technology—no technology. One way to differentiate informal learning is the extent of the use of technology in its delivery. The range begins with no technology use, progressing to occasional or optional technology use, integrated use, and finally means that are fully dependent on technology. At opposite poles, reading a book requires no technology whereas learning with podcasts would be entirely technology dependent. Searching for a book in an online bookstore, ordering it there, and then reading it in hard copy would be a midway point because technology was used extensively in gaining the learning resource.

Mind-body. Another approach is to consider a mind-body dimension to illustrate how adults experience informal learning. The mind-body dimension represents a scale of continuity between cognitive/intellectual activities and awareness of the body. While Western cultures have not usually been attuned to the full range of possibilities, Eastern philosophies and religions make frequent use of the mind-body connection, and it is beginning to appear in many more cultures through wider adoption of yoga, relaxation techniques, and some holistic training of educators and counselors (Schure, Christopher, & Christopher, 2008; Schwartz & Begley, 2002).

Toward the mind end of the range would be the realm of concepts, cognitive development, intellectual knowledge, and learning objectives. At the other end of the scale is body, where learning and understanding are evidenced in behavior, action, and experience. At the scale's midpoint is a perfect balance of the two emphases, where intellect and action are integrated. Examples of mind-focused informal learning would be reading and language learning whereas body-focused learning examples include apprenticeship, crafts, and fully mastered relaxation techniques.

Recent studies demonstrate the positive impact on learning experiences of meditative practices, which build greater connectivity between mind and body (e.g., Schure et al., 2008). These and other recent findings in neuroscience indicate how much there is to learn about how the brain works and how it interacts with body (Katz, Goldstein, & Beers, 2001). Using such information with a framework that recognizes the interface and synergistic mind-body relationship, we are better prepared to realize new learning opportunities for adults of all ages.

Face to face-virtual. Consider the mentor relationship, which may begin with face-to-face mentoring with an instructor and then continue more informally via letters to students at work placements. This situation illustrates an informal learning experience that can be placed along the face-to-face to virtual dimension. An example of completely virtual informal learning is remote language learning via radio, which has been popular for many decades and is particularly popular among Asian, African, and Spanish-speaking people and in countries where the government restricts access to information.

Virtual learning may also include using online technologies or cell phones to share information and learn from people you know. Conversely, it may involve interacting in an artificial world with simulated characters or computer-generated representations of real people (avatars) (online games and virtual spaces like Second Life often use this approach). Virtual informal learning experiences represent a host of new possibilities for exploring alternate perspectives, interactions, and risk taking in informal learning (Bischoff & Rohrig, 2004). Such risks are much less frequently approached in formal learning because of academic or accountability consequences; instead, learners must discover these new talents, skills, and potentials through such informal learning as virtual explorations.

Of course, all of these dimensions fall within the underlying range for *formal* versus *informal*

education. Literature and practice suggest a progression here, too, in which some learners may lean toward formal characterizations whereas others are more or less informal. A multidimensional foundation for examining informal learning increases options for planning, facilitation, and content development. It also supports mixed approaches, addresses contextual and learner needs, and affords greater opportunities to learn. Examining informal learning in this manner provides a richer variation of possibilities for learning, instruction, and research.

21st-Century Living and Information Literacy

Perhaps nothing today is pushing informal learning into the limelight more than the dynamics of 21st-century life. The rushing rate of technological change and its integration into daily life requires that people of all ages continue to learn constantly. From online shopping to ATMs and online banking, automatic bill pay to driver's license renewals, people have to use different forms of technology to meet their everyday needs. Everyone needs to work to prepare educators and learners alike to cope and succeed in this morphing context.

21st-Century Workplace Skills

In the 21st century, changing technology and constant problem-solving permeate adult lives. For instance, from filing taxes to requesting books at the local library, adults need to use technology to navigate their daily lives. The informal learning skills needed to be successful in the 21st century include the specific set of skills termed 21st-century learning skills: critical thinking, problem solving, creativity, flexibility, coping strategies, collaboration, self-direction, multiple literacies (language, information technology, information, visual, cultural, and more) and research strategies (Partnership for 21st-Century Skills, 2004). Such learning skills and strategies apply to both adults' professional work and their nonwork daily needs. In the modern workplace, individuals need to continuously adapt to changing procedures, processes, and technologies. In addition to the "how to" of the specific technology-related device, they also need the skills to apply the tools deftly

(American Library Association, 2006; King & Sanquist, 2009; Partnership for 21st-Century Skills, 2004).

Those adults who do not possess these skills are at great disadvantage in trying to deal with the technological problems that daily confront them. Yet, for the most part these skills are learned informally in the workplace. In a sense, these skills are "caught," not explicitly taught. This tacit knowledge is problematic. Within the diverse world and workplace, it is misguided and borders on discrimination (Schugurensky, 2000). Therefore, preparation in preschool through secondary schools and workplace training needs to assess the needs of learners and build the necessary repertoire of skills and learning strategies to enable them to learn informally for a lifetime in varied contexts.

Lifelong Learning Skills

The set of skills needed across the many contexts of the lifespan may be both similar to and different from those needed in the workplace. Certainly, collaboration balanced with self-directedness and initiative helps adults find successful solutions to many situations they confront (Argyris, & Schön, 1974). However, the approach to managing a workplace team through a change process may not be what's needed in other relationships (Partnership for 21st-Century Skills, 2004).

The list of lifelong learning skills frequently includes self-directed learning, problem solving, creativity, flexibility, critical thinking, coping strategies, research strategies, analysis, interpretation, independence, initiative, collaboration, multiple literacies (language, technical, information, visual, cultural, and more), and goal setting. It illustrates the extensive scope of skills needed to succeed as a lifelong learner. Adults need to be able to chase down information they need, determine its accuracy, and evaluate how to integrate it into their schema and practice. Unlike formal learning, this informal lifelong learning never ends: it permeates most areas of our lives.

Creating a *hunger* for independent, informal learning among all learners is an essential element of providing the skills to accomplish it. A useful enthusiasm can be fostered by pointing out the opportunities to explore new information, develop new skills, uncover hidden talents, and cultivate additional applications. Helping learners of all ages to see the possibilities for learning in the world around them—in their rooms, on their computers, with their MP3 player, on a hike, in the grocery store, on the job, or in the nursing home—can unleash new generative power that will add to personal fulfillment and success. Conversely, without these skills and an enthusiastic approach to learning, adults face constant barriers and dead ends. Stopped from advancement, they may eventually not be able to accomplish basic living tasks (like paying for groceries or transit) and become dependent on those who can. Informal learning is the means to successfully continue lifelong and professional learning, living independently in the 21st century.

NEW PERSPECTIVES AND OPPORTUNITIES

Considering informal learning in a virtual era raises provocative questions. The following sections highlight particular concerns that informal learning can both address and perhaps ameliorate.

Environmental Concerns

At a time of global warming, environmental concerns have become prominent in informal learning (Gore, 2006; HGTV.com, 2008; Regeneration.com, 2008). While virtual learning requires many of the same resources used in traditional formal learning settings, it reduces travel, helps preserve fossil fuels, and uses fewer resources for distribution across time, space, and users. These reductions can simultaneously enhance content geared toward environmental concerns. The two in fact complement each other.

A unique example of combining environmental resources with informal learning is the example of CALI Bamboo (www.calibamboo.com), a site that appeals to the desire to "go green" because it sells bamboo products, a rapidly renewable resource. Many homeowners needing to build a fence also must learn to construct it. CALI Bamboo (2008) developed a virtual learning space for informal, self-directed learning. The site has photos of different fence styles, completed products, and video tutorials, and it provides daily telephone support. This illustration shows how businesses can use informal learning to recognize customer sensitivities and agendas and address their learning needs in comprehensive, scalable, and accessible formats.

Access and Equity

Access and equity can also be addressed via informal learning in the virtual age (King & Griggs, 2006), as the Internet allows for collaboration across borders or across communities. Although some may say the digital divide has been bridged, visiting impoverished inner-city, small rural, and violence-torn areas around the globe reveals scores of people who do not have access to electricity, technology, and the outside world. Among those responding to these concerns is iEARN.org (2008), which provides collaborative space and support for worldwide learning projects to address such issues. Educators can identify a project in their community and post an iEARN.org-wide invitation for partnering groups to collaborate. Projects include solving sanitation and water supply problems for villages and sharing cultural stories between nations.

Democratization of the Media

The power of informal learning is illustrated by podcasting, which emerged in 2004 as a technology for freely creating and distributing digital audio worldwide. In 2009, podcasting has become a powerful medium, with its original tagline, "Democratization of the Media." King and Gura (2009) watched language learning podcasts consistently ranked most popular during the last 4 years, demonstrating the hunger for informal learning.

Studies reveal significant development of voice and empowerment among podcasters (King, 2008; King & Gura, 2009). Crafting a message, recording in private, and broadcasting across the globe have a powerful impact extending from the context of podcasting to face-to-face interactions (King, 2008). When educators, adult students, and others use podcasts to share their cultural histories, conduct original research, or interview people, for example, they are adding to the burgeoning body of information and resources that others can use for their formal and informal learning. (Recommendations for copyright issues may be found in Vogele, Garlick, & The Berkman Center, 2007.) Organizations and individuals alike need to pursue new policies and practices to preserve privacy and exercise virtual responsibility, but we need to use the rich resources for learning they offer.

INFORMAL LEARNING STRATEGIES

Introducing and using a problem-solving paradigm as a focus for informal learning strategies early in people's learning experiences will afford opportunities to practice, watch, and test multiple approaches. Such experiences enable people to find approaches that are most comfortable and successful for them, thereby cultivating habits of informal learning.

Technologies

New technologies and new software have expanded ideas about informal learning, both as learning strategies and as learning tools. For example, medicine uses virtual reality for continuing professional learning (Schoor, Mecke, & Rehfeld, 2006). In addition, standard counseling, neuropsychology, and neurobiology texts now include discussions of alternative methods for biofeedback, mind mapping, and EMDR (Eye Movement Desensitization and Reprocessing) for cognitive and medical rehabilitation of learning disability clients (Katz et al., 2001). A few years ago, computer-based relaxation biofeedback was used only with highly specialized and costly equipment. Now clients can independently continue their practice of biofeedback learning with inexpensive personal computer biofeedback programs.

The Teachers' Podcast (TTPOD) (www.teachers podcast.org) is a successful, long-standing series reaching more than 4 million educators who seek professional development on the topic of educational technology. Many people listen to the talk show-like audio series, hosted by King and Gura (2009), at their computers. Other educators transfer the files to mobile devices like MP3 players, iPods, or cell phones and engage in mobile learning while traveling or working out at the gym (Li, 2007).

Two further examples in technology-assisted informal learning are from the American Society for Training and Development community. The Cascadia chapter (http://www.astdcascadia.org/podcast/Default.html) provides interviews, multiple perspectives, and professional learning opportunities via audio interviews that are posted on their organization Web site and iTunes. Both TTPOD and ASTD Cascadia demonstrate instructional design, personalization, and learning community opportunities through virtual informal learning. Their listeners can not only listen and learn, but also respond via e-mail, blog posts, comments, and suggested topics. ASTD T&D Podcast (www.astd.org) provides another popular format. This podcast series allows the general public to listen to featured journal articles in audio format. More research is needed on the outcomes of such approaches. Certainly, the flexibility of this technology has the potential to change how individuals interact with the media.

In recent years, many studies have found a positive relationship between video and computer games and various cognitive and psychomotor skills such as critical thinking, rapid reaction times, small motor coordination, and strategic decision making (Thomas, & Fout, 2005). Future research needs to examine the ways that action in advanced games may involve continuous and anticipatory problem-solving, global collaboration, and rapid response time. Moreover, virtual gaming experiences including multiplayer role-playing games are actively being used in job placement, advancement, and some executive training (Brown & Thomas, 2006; Southwood, 2007).

Strategy for Practice

Both within the workplace and in other contexts, situated learning (Argyris & Schön, 1974; Lave & Wenger, 1991) is a powerful means of modeling strategies for continued informal learning endeavors (Kolb, 1984; Tough, 1971). Using virtual tools and strategies provides the possibility for extending this situated learning to a broader audience. For example, adult basic education learners can investigate community development and the building permit application process as part of a literacy lesson. Having learners conduct investigations, interview community members about related issues, and look up information on their community Web sites provides a rich platform for situated learning. Learners decide what information is true, how to gather information quickly, and what the information means. Structured settings may help students learn how to overcome perceived

barriers to new modes of learning, thus building new patterns of success and confidence that encourage them to continue on their own in informal settings. Cultivating a *hunger* and *vision* for learning opportunities provides sustained results. By drawing on our learners' interests in sports, health, recreation, family, and academics, we leverage those areas closest to their core intrinsic interests. These areas are prime sources to practice finding additional local, independent, and virtual informal learning venues.

A final strategy for informal learning practice is that of continuous improvement. Developing and sustaining a perspective of formative development, continual assessment, and building better approaches and strategies affords a timeless strategy to create contextual, situated, and successful learning. Action research or evaluation of data about informal learning can be powerful for informing direction, development, and delivery.

RECOMMENDATIONS

Understanding the current and future needs of formal and nonformal learners is an ideal place to start in preparing them for lifelong informal learning.

Creating informal learning opportunities. Publicly available resources, along with strategies to use and analyze their findings, are invaluable to adult learners. Creating space for sharing prior informal learning experiences also provides opportunities for peer-to-peer learning and validation of their efforts.

Researching informal learning. Of critical importance are studies that examine the impact and effect of informal learning. All research methods can be effective in this regard; however, mixed methods research may be especially valuable in providing the breadth and depth needed to fully understand the impact of these technologies and strategies (Tashakkori & Teddlie, 1998). The very rich contexts of informal learning provide fertile environment for innovative research. Possible directions include how informal learning helps people explore their lives, showing the connections between learning and different aspects of their lives, and demonstrating the vital, constant, lifelong learning footprint. We need to challenge and question informal learning's currently minimized role and lack of visibility (Garrick, 1998).

Advancing informal learning. The area of informal learning continues to need academic and practitioner leaders who have the vision and strategies to develop and advance its visibility and understanding. Building on advances in neuroscience, nanotechnology, and social adoption of technology, we can reach beyond the status quo, charting a new territory of possibilities that will continue to open opportunities for informal learners around the globe.

CONCLUSION

Understanding informal learning can lead to the establishment of a rich framework that expands understanding of the breadth of adult learning across the lifespan. Rather than regulating learning to formal or even nonformal settings, informal learning responds to the creative and inquiring mind. This chapter has laid out a framework of the history, the current conditions, and possibilities for informal learning. Educators and researchers need to equip adults everywhere with new ways for appropriating the learning at hand.

REFERENCES

American Library Association. (2006, September 1). *Information literacy competency standards for higher education.* Retrieved July 23, 2008, from http://www.ala.org/ala/acrl/acrlstandards/informationliteracycompetency.cfm

Argyris, C., & Schön, D. (1974). *Theory in practice.* San Francisco: Jossey-Bass.

Bischoff, A., & Rohrig, C. (2004). *Streaming audio/video and multi-user virtual reality.* Proceedings of the 21st ICDE Conference on Open Learning and Distance Education, Hong Kong. Retrieved July 27, 2008, from http://prt.fernuni-hagen.de/~bischoff/research/pdf/Bischoff04a_icde2004_fuh_bischoff_lab_final.pdf

Boshier, R. (1991). Psychometric properties of the alternative form of the Education Participation Scale. *Adult Education Quarterly 41*(3), 150–167.

Brown, J. S., & Thomas, D. (2006, April). You play world of warcraft? You're hired. *WIRED Magazine 14*(1), Retrieved July 20, 2008, from http://www.wired.com/wired/archive/14.04/learn.html

CALI Bamboo (2008). How to install. Retrieved June 25, 2008, from http://calibamboo.com/instructions.html

Coombs, P. H. (1989). Formal and nonformal education: Future strategies. In C. Titmus (Ed.), *Lifelong learning education for adults: An international handbook* (pp. 57–60). Oxford, UK: Pergamon.

Dewey, J. (1938). *Experience and education.* New York: Collier Books.

Garrick, J. (1998). *Unmasking informal learning in the workplace.* New York: Routledge.

Gore, A. (2006). *An inconvenient truth.* Retrieved July 15, 2008, from http://www.climatecrisis.net/

HGTV.com. (2008, July 25). *Special presentation: 20 ways your home can save the planet.* Retrieved July 26, 2008, from http://www.hgtv.com/hgtv/spcl_prsntn/episode/0,,HGTV_3909_54049,00.html

iEARN.org (2008). International Education and Research Network homepage. Retrieved July 1, 2008, from http://www.iearn.org

Katz, L. J., Goldstein, G., & Beers, S. R. (2001). *Learning disabilities in older adolescents and adults: Critical issues in neuropsychology.* New York: Springer.

King, K. P. (2008). Slamming the closet door and taking control: Analysis of personal transformation and social change as LGBTQ podcasting. In T. Bettinger & J. Gedro (Eds.), *Proceedings 2008 Adult Education Research Conference, LGBTQ&A Pre-Conference.* St Louis: University of Missouri.

King, K. P., & Griggs, J. (2006). *Harnessing innovative technologies in higher education: Access, equity, policy and instruction.* Madison, WI: Atwood Press.

King, K. P., & Gura, M. (2009). *Podcasting for teachers: Using a new technology to revolutionize teaching and learning* (2nd ed.). Emerging Technologies for Evolving Learning. Charlotte, NC: Information Age Publishing.

King, K. P., & Sanquist, S. (2009). 21st-century learning and human performance. In V. Wang, & K. P. King (Eds.), *Fundamentals of human performance and training issues* (pp. 61–88). Adult Education Special Topics. Charlotte, NC: Information Age Publishing.

Kolb, D. A. (1984). *Experiential learning.* Englewood Cliffs, NJ: Prentice Hall.

Lave, J., & Wenger, E. (1991). *Situated learning.* Cambridge, UK: University of Cambridge Press.

Li, C. (2007, April 22). *Forrester's new social technographics report.* Retrieved August 28, 2007, from http://blogs.forrester.com/charleneli/2007/04/index.html

Livingstone, D. (1999). Exploring the icebergs of adult learning. *Canadian Journal of Studies in Adult Education 13*(2), 49–72.

Marsick, V. J., & Watkins, K. (1990). *Informal and incidental learning in the workplace.* New York: Routledge.

McGirt, E. (2009, March 17). How Chris Hughes helped launch Facebook and the Barack Obama campaign. *Fast Company,* pp. 22–23.

Milanovic, Z. (2006). Lecturing with a virtual whiteboard. *Physics Teacher, 44*(6), 354–357.

Partnership for 21st-Century Skills. (2004). *Learning for the 21st century.* Retrieved July 23, 2008, from http://www.21stcenturyskills.org/images/stories/otherdocs/P21_Report.pdf

Polanyi, M. (1967). *The tacit dimension.* New York: Doubleday.

Regeneration.com. (2008). Home page. Retrieved July 23, 2008, from http://www.regeneration.org/

Schoor, W., Mecke, R., & Rehfeld, M. (2006). *VR based knowledge transfer in medical technology and techniques.* Proceedings of the Congress Computational Science and Its Applications, Glasgow. Retrieved July 19, 2008, from http://cat.inist.fr/?aModele=afficheN&cpsidt=19968236

Schugurensky, D. (2000). *The forms of informal learning* (NALL Working Paper No. 19–2000). Retrieved July 285, 2008, from http://www.oise.utoronto.ca/depts/sese/csew/nall/res/19formsofinformal.htm

Schure, M. B., Christopher, J., & Christopher, S. (2008). Mind-body medicine and the art of self-care. *Journal of Counseling & Development, 86*(1), 47–56.

Schwartz, J., & Begley, S. (2002). *The mind and the brain: Neuroplasticity and the power of mental force.* New York: HarperCollins.

Southwood, D. (2007, October 1). It's not just a game—it's skills for life. *TechLearning Magazine.* Retrieved July 20, 2008, from http://www.techlearning.com/showArticle.php?articleID=196604728

Tapscott, D., & Williams, A. D. (2006). *Wikinomics.* New York: Portfolio.

Tashakkori, A., & Teddlie, C. (1998). *Mixed methodology.* Thousand Oaks, CA: Sage.

Thomas, D., & Fout, J. (2005). *Public diplomacy and virtual worlds.* Paper presented at DiGRA 2005: Changing Views: International Conference, Simon Fraser University, Vancouver. Retrieved July 21, 2008, from http://ir.lib.sfu.ca/handle/1892/1616?mode=simple

Tough, A. (1971). *The adult's learning projects learning.* Toronto, Ontario: OISE.

Tough, A. (1999). *The iceberg of informal learning* (NALL Working Paper No. 42-2002). Retrieved July 20, 2008, from http://www.oise.utoronto.ca/depts/sese/csew/nall/res/49AllenTough.pdf

U.S. Department of Education. (2004). *National household education surveys of 2001: Participation in adult education and lifelong learning.* Washington, DC: National Center for Education Statistics.

Vogele, C., Garlick, M., & The Berkman Center. (2007). *Podcasting legal guide.* Retrieved on May 21, 2008, from http://wiki.creativecommons.org/Podcasting_Legal_Guide

40

CREATING AND RE-CREATING COMMUNITY

COLLEEN AALSBURG WIESSNER, VANESSA SHEARED, POONEH LARI, SUZANNE Z. KUCHARCZYK, AND DORIS FLOWERS

I f human learning is a social enterprise, then recognizing, developing, and drawing on strengths of community contributive to learning will enhance learning processes. Acceptance of the importance of community is common in the field of adult education. Creating community is a central role of adult educators, for often adult learning takes place in community with other learners. Yet, meanings of community vary, and realization of community can be elusive.

REFRAMING

In this chapter, we propose reframing how we think about community and roles adult educators play in fostering it. To reframe community, we employ multiple lenses of gender, race, culture, and ability. In addition, we suggest that community should be viewed from multiple perspectives. Individualism and independence characterize mainstream U.S. culture. However, emerging voices of indigenous cultures and immigrant groups value interdependence over independence and collective perspectives over the individual. As virtual communities proliferate, we must shift how we conceptualize and engage in community.

In the past, proximity, alikeness, structure, and hierarchy determined and characterized how we operated and acted within forms of community that we reframe in this chapter. In this section, we introduce the notion of reframing. In the second, we explore community by recognizing multiple theoretical perspectives. Then we suggest expanding the concept of community by connecting the importance of commonality *and* diversity, community's existence in boundless *and* shared spaces, with the intention for learning, and as a center for development and creativity. Finally, we suggest that the role of adult educators includes sustaining community by embracing its richness. Since becoming colleagues and friends who live in different parts of the country and who are interested in working with each other as colleagues, we have found ourselves having to redefine and rethink how we as scholars begin to work together in community, as shared in this chapter.

RECOGNIZING MULTIPLE INTERSECTING COMMUNITY REALITIES

Various theoretical, developmental, cultural, spiritual, and global viewpoints conceptualize various community realities. For instance, *theoretically,* Wenger (1998) joins concepts of practice and community in describing communities of practice (CoP), characterized by mutual engagement, joint enterprise, and shared repertoire. Wenger, McDermott, and Snyder (2002) define CoP as "groups of people who share a concern, a set of problems, or a passion about a topic, and who deepen their knowledge and expertise" (p. 4). Avis and Fisher (2006) state engagement in CoP is increasingly important to adult learning, and participation within such communities provides dialogic space for learning. According to Lave and Wenger (1991), CoP view learning as social activity that occurs as learners move through established communities' professional hierarchies toward expertise. Learning opportunities occur through informal interaction among colleagues in work contexts. New learners gain access to communities' professional knowledge in authentic contexts through encounters with people, tools, tasks, and social norms (Schlager, Fusco, & Schank, 2002). Over time, CoP adopt new policies and practices.

Developmentally, Merriam and Clark (2006) state connecting with others contributes to development in adult learning. "Learning is a social activity, one that involves others in dialogue and community. In fact, it is difficult to think about any learning that is linked to development that occurs in isolation from others" (p. 41). Achieving personal mastery involves sense of connection and vision beyond self-interest, evidenced in commitment to the whole (Senge, 1990). Daloz (2000) identifies constructive engagement with otherness—as a dimension of one's development—as the single, strongest contributor to growth of commitment to social responsibility, leading to empathic connection. In Kegan's (1982) schema, adults move from dependence to independence to interdependence. Belenky, Clinchy, Goldberger, and Tarule (1986) say that stages of women's cognitive development culminate in constructed knowing and facility for separate and connected knowing. Sinott and Berlanstein (2006) posit three categories of development related to feeling connected: connecting with sides of self, others, and the transcendent. Developmental stages can impact perspectives on and participation in community.

Reviewing community through theoretical and developmental lenses is important, yet both can be devoid of how culture and race lead to people's coming together to connect so that they can collectively resolve political, social, or historical falsehoods and concerns. So, *culturally,* we find ourselves moving from an individual standpoint to one centered on collective response. "Adult educators who work with marginalized groups of learners need not underestimate the power of community and its impact on the educational experience of the learner" (Guy, 1999, p. 95). For example, Confucianism impacts Asian cultural perspectives, characterized by integration and harmony; collective power; collaborative learning; sense of membership in family, class, community, and society; and connection to nature (Zhang, 2008). Guidance, kinship, diversity, special status of children as gifts, ethical models, clear roles, customs and practices, recognition of life stages and accomplishments that benefit the whole, unique ways of learning, community work, environment, and spirit characterize indigenous education's communal nature, based in a belief that we are all related (Cajete, 1994). A holistic metaphor that contrasts with dominant culture, this perspective emphasizes beneficial intertwine, harmony of natural and human community, and personhood or wholeness understood through community, connection, and responsibility.

Jeria (1999) advocates for popular education approaches, grounded in creating shared understandings and bases for action, as means for empowerment of learners in minority communities. Hidalgo (1998) identifies relevant cultural perspectives valued by Latinos/as: collective wisdom and experience, family-centered rather than individual-centered achievement, networks of familial and social relationships, retention of ethnic identity, language, geographical priority, and cultural citizenship across country groups.

Afrocentric adult education "speaks to a way of knowing grounded in making connections with one's history, race and ancestors . . . Learning is purposeful with a community goal as motivator" (Flowers, 2003). It emphasizes interdependence, interconnectedness, responsibility, and harmony.

Often, these cultural perspectives contrast with those of dominant U.S. culture. Concern exists about erosion of community. Putnam (2000) describes people as socially isolated, less participatory than in the past, and individualized. Bellah, Madson, Sullivan, Swidler, and Tipton (1996) describe the culture of individualism, and Taylor (1991) refers to fragmentation.

Spiritually, communities support people who experience oppression. hooks (2003) cites the radical nature of community and commitment to community, broadly defined, in Christian life:

> Caring together is the basis of community life. We don't come together simply to console each other or even to support each other. Important as those things may be, long term community life is directed in other ways. Together we reach out to others . . . The mystery of this caring together is that it not only asks for community, but also creates it. (p. 171)

Sharing her Buddhist perspective, hooks (2003) continues:

> To be guided by love is to live in community with all life. However, a culture of domination, like ours, does not strive to teach us how to live in community. As a consequence, learning to live in community must be a core practice for all of us who desire spirituality in education. (p. 163)

English, Fenwick, and Parsons (2003) explore weaving spirituality as a dimension of learning communities and propose that "educators can do much to suffuse the spaces and communities around them with invitation, compassion and care—and a sense of anchor beyond productivity and material gain" (p. 107).

Globally, awareness of connection to world community is growing, fueled by economic globalization, ecological challenges, and concern for social sustainability. Everything connects in the life web as systems bound together in communities of organisms (Capra, 1996). Capra defines system as "an integrated whole whose essential properties arise from the relationships between its parts" (p. 27). He compares human communities to ecological communities; both are living systems that exhibit similar principles of organization and openness to flow of energy and resources. He expresses usable principles of organization to guide human communities:

interdependence, recycling, partnership, flexibility, and diversity. *Interdependence* is interconnectedness and dependence in networks of relationships, where success of the whole community depends on success of its individual members; success of each member depends on success of the community as a whole. *Recycling* means waste from one community member may be useful for another. Capra defines *partnership* as democracy and empowerment resulting in co-evolution where each partner learns to change and develop and better understand others' needs. *Flexibility* results from feedback into the system and re-establishes balance, allowing it to find stability. *Diversity* involves different relationships and approaches to the same problem. Diverse communities are capable of adapting to changing situations but can survive only through relationships, partnerships, and interdependencies of individual members.

RECOGNIZING AND MOVING TOWARD A REDEFINITION OF COMMUNITY

What constitutes community? For some, creating community is not challenging; it exists as a way of knowing and being. Others, enveloped in cultures of individualism, may or may not seek community, which is not always occurring around them naturally. Adult educators, engaged in social justice, feminist and critical pedagogies, and community-based learning in particular, recognize community as essential to teaching and learning. Building community requires intentionality to foster conjoint experience, shared meanings, common interests and endeavors, interconnectedness and communion, and responsibility (Greene, 1995). Communities provide a sense of identity and security and places of shared values and beliefs (Wlodkowski, 1999). They sustain themselves through continuous growth (Dewey, 1916/1966). We believe that strength of community exists in both alikeness *and* difference.

COMMUNITY AS COMMONALITY AND DIVERSITY

Who identifies what is and isn't community? Is community always viewed positively? Identifying with and participating in community based on one's sexual orientation can provide a haven for people who feel excluded in the heterosexist dominant culture. Conversely, being labeled and placed there by others is marginalizing (Chapman & Gedro, 2009). We also want to acknowledge and include individuals with physical or other disabilities, often overlooked among those who are marginalized. Terms such as *people who have disabilities, the disabled, the handicapped* among others are used to establish boundaries of membership within or outside these communities (Linton, 1998).

Underscoring diversity of perspectives on community, some, such as those who self-identify as being part of deaf culture (Lane, Hoffmeister, & Bahan, 1996), establish clear purposes and boundaries of their community. Others are discouraged from including themselves in community with those who have disabilities, perhaps "for fear that they will be identified with the socially marginal group" (Linton, 1998, p. 103).

Community sometimes emerges through experiencing shared enterprises or commitments, such as social action, learning, or other life events. Alternately, community results from intentional fostering. "Adult educators and trainers have long recognized the advantages of building community among a group of learners" (Merriam & Clark, 2006, p. 43). Often, people participate in multiple communities, both short term and sustained, simultaneously. Daily, a worldwide community connects us ecologically.

The communities we refer to are contexts that stimulate change rather than maintain status quo and that embrace diverse perspectives rather than foster insular thinking. Sites of knowledge creation (Stein & Imel, 2002), communities include multiple perspectives and realities. They encompass shared histories and stories. A community "is always in the making. Marked by an emerging solidarity, a sharing of certain beliefs, and a dialogue about others, it must remain open to newcomers, those too long thrust aside" (Greene, 1995, p. 39).

Often, as women, the authors of this chapter find we must redefine community. Community is about having a group of sister friends, who may not always be in the same *place* but are in the same *space*. To engage about what is happening with and to us, we must create intentional acts to talk and work together. It does not matter if we are of the same race, language, or economic background in order for us to be able to share similar sets of experiences about how being a woman impacts how we are viewed and treated within higher education contexts and other arenas.

Community as Boundless and Shared Space

Community can supersede proximity, once thought essential. For example, the five of us began this endeavor because of our desire to establish a connection to a community of women who respect and tolerate difference and recognize similarities that exist between us. While proximity ensures people see each other, as in scheduled meetings, it does not always lead to finding or sharing community. Community can be viewed through the lens of family; not being near family does not affect membership. Rather, we seek ways to transcend time and space to remain connected. The same is true of community; especially for those of us who find ourselves moving through and within institutions where we were not necessarily intended to have a larger role. Literature about community would have us believe that community is shaped by space and proximity; as with family, women in higher education must seek alternative ways to pursue relationships with one another.

Whittaker, Isaacs, and O'Day (1997) provide descriptors of online communities: a shared goal, interest, need, or activity that provides members with a reason for belonging to the community; repeated active participation, including intense interactions and strong emotional ties between participants; shared access to resources and policies for determining access to those resources; member reciprocity for information, support, and services; and common context of social conventions, language, and protocols. Degrees of relationships differ, intensifying or weakening depending on participation (Preece & Maloney-Krichmar, 2003). Online, instructors bear responsibility for facilitating and creating spaces to experience social presence and create learning experiences (Palloff & Pratt, 2007). Kasworm, Polson, and Fishback (2002) note faculty member responsibility to create learning communities among participants.

Without meeting face to face, students become acquainted through initial introductions and demonstration of effective and appropriate interaction in online environments. "Promoting human relationships, affirming and recognizing students' input; providing opportunities for students to develop a sense of group cohesiveness, maintaining the group as a unit, and in other ways helping members to work together in a mutual cause" (Collins & Berge, 2001, p. 7) are tasks that build and maintain online communities (Palloff & Pratt, 2007).

Rheingold (1994), an early online pioneer, describes online communities as "cultural aggregations that emerge when enough people bump into each other often enough in cyberspace" (p. 57). Boundlessness allows us to find what is like us that may not exist in our place-based context *and* to experience diversity beyond that context.

COMMUNITY WITH INTENTION FOR LEARNING

For some, community offers means for preserving life and spirit. Intersecting dimensions of race, gender, language, and location contribute to identifying meanings of community in adult education. To illustrate, let us ask: How do women find community? Why is it important for women, regardless of race, economic background, or position, to remain in community? hooks (1994) notes that when she enters classrooms, she does so assuming that "we must build community in order to create a climate of openness and intellectual rigor," and that "rather than focusing on issues of safety . . . a feeling of community creates a sense that there is shared commitment and common good that binds us" (p. 4). If hooks's assessment is taken on its merits, community is about minds meeting about things that matter to those involved. We can, therefore, have community with our sister friends whether we are in the same location or thousands of miles apart.

Those of us in higher education find community out of necessity for survival as scholars, teachers, and administrators. Women, regardless of and sometimes in spite of our roles, find ways to come together because of similarities of struggles and our interpretations about how

and what we must do to resolve or overcome these struggles.

COMMUNITY AS A CENTER FOR DEVELOPMENT AND CREATIVITY

Whether virtual or place-based, communities can offer creative sites for developing individual capacity (Greene, 1995; Welton, 2005) and for self-expression (Lindeman, 1961; Welton, 2005); a space to "imagine alternative possibilities for their own becoming and their group's becoming . . . and an opportunity to be otherwise" (Greene, 1995, p. 39). English et al. (2003) refer to community as soul friends; Palmer (2004) as circles of trust; Belenky, Bond, and Weinstock (1997) as other mothers and public homeplaces; and Daloz (2000) as commons for which we share social responsibility. Although it is tempting to idealize communities, they offer places of negotiation to work out conflicts (St. Clair, 1998). They can reveal differences or mask and homogenize them. St. Clair defines communities as relationships: "Educators must recognize the complexities of the relationships of community linking the setting to wider social structures. The relationships of community bring us together in the commonplace, where we may explore what we mean to ourselves and to our communities" (p. 13).

Given these variants, community involves developing individual and collective voice (Hayes & Flannery, 2000) among those who may or may not have similar cultural, racial, sexual, age, physical, or mental connections or abilities. Educators are called to

> seek out and encourage engagement with those different from ourselves, to foster critical reflection on the meaning of our differences, to create mentoring communities where socially responsible commitments can be formed and sustained, and to make available opportunities to practice these emerging and vital commitments. (Daloz, 2000, p. 121)

Criticality, transcendence, continual search for intellectual freedom and freedom of articulation, envisaging what might be, and wide-awakeness—"awareness of what it is to be in the world" (Greene, 1995, p. 35)—are potential ways that occur in community.

Connecting and Embracing Community

Community takes many forms in adult education, including formal, informal, and nonformal contexts. They can be bounded or unbounded, local or global, virtual or place-based. Adult education literature most often cites community action, community development, and community education. What characterizes contexts of such activities that enable people to connect and embrace community? While varied, the following perspectives provide an understanding about how organizations can support spaces necessary to engage in learning through acts of community. For those engaged in organizational development, community may be defined by the purpose, function, and mission of tasks or activities; accountability; and recognition of and respect for the individual or group (Brown & Duguid, 2001; Cook & Brown, 1999; Fisher, Rooke, & Torbert, 2003; Henriksson, 2000; Senge, 1990; Vera & Crossan, 2005; Wenger et al., 2002). For those actively engaged in creating spaces for marginalized or oppressed groups, community engagement takes on a more radical approach, which often focuses on the intersection of culture, history, spirit, politics, and mental and physical attributes of the individual or group (English et al., 2003; Flowers, 2003; Greene, 1995; Lindeman 1961; Tisdell, 2003; Vella, 2000; Welton, 2005; Wiessner, 2005).

So how, and under what conditions, one embraces community is dependent on the purpose and function of the organizational setting and how one perceives or perceived oneself or group identity within a given setting. Factors such as diversity, class, racial, sexual orientation, gender, religion, age, size, or ability help to determine to what extent an individual or group is able to embrace others in any given community context.

Greene (1995) concluded, "In thinking of community, we need to emphasize and process words: making, creating, weaving, saying and the like. Community cannot be achieved through rational formulation nor through edict" (p. 39). Overall, embracing community requires, as hooks (2003) suggests, being engaged in both/and thinking. What Greene (1995) calls imagination and sense of possibility, Sheared (1994) describes as recognition of one's multiple ways of knowing and being, along with an understanding of one's polyrhythmic realities. In other words, to embrace community requires an understanding of ways in which race, class, gender, age—and equality, justice, freedom, and democracy—intersect and impact how one experiences his or her lifeworld.

In addition to focusing on the impact of community engagement on one's spiritual being, building trust is a "cornerstone of community orientation" (Collinson & Cook, 2007, p. 157). According to Lipshitz, Friedman, and Popper (2007), trust is crucial to psychological safety necessary for individuals to feel committed to learning productively on behalf of organizations. As adult educators, we need to engage in varied processes and practices for facilitating and sustaining community.

While there are multiple activities one might use to establish community, we believe that storytelling, teaching defiance, and fostering inclusion through action illustrate things one needs to consider in the development of community, activities that can help individuals or group members connect with and embrace each other within a community context.

Wiessner (2005) discovered that storytelling allows people to enter into others' experiences and lives, develop understanding across differences, connect people to each other and to society as a whole, create new spaces, engage imagination, and develop voice. In each case, "Community results not from *sameness* made clear through narrative, but rather through understanding and appreciation of *difference* that leads to discovery of deeper levels of acceptance and connection" (p. 104). Connections with others, which include an understanding and respect for their commonalities as well as differences, can also be made through the incorporation of poetry, music, drama, and other artistic expressions.

In addition to storytelling, Newman (2006) emphasized the value of teaching defiance through community and social action, and Hugo (2002) concluded that the "characteristics of community education include a focus on real-life problems identified by community residents, coordination of service delivery, community collaboration through shared resources, and links between home, school, and community" (p. 14). Shor (1992) states, "A learning community emerges from mutual communication, meaningful work, and empowering methods" (p. 258). Walker, Golde, Jones, Bueschel, and Hutchings (2008) write about formation of scholars and students' entry into intellectual communities that build knowledge, reduce isolation and attrition, and share collective wisdom. By offering individuals or group members an opportunity to engage in reflective discourse through journal writing, short stories, and letters to themselves or significant other(s), the individual or group can begin to gain a handle on their own talents, as well as insights into others' perceptions. In other words, people view themselves as individuals and as part of a collective or community. Participation in a community builds a sense of inclusion and dispels isolation and marginalization.

For example, a group of women over 30 years old, experiencing first pregnancies and living across the United States, engaged in learning together online. Homogeneity brought them together, but diversity sustains the evolution of their community. Diverse in race, socioeconomic class, professional identity, and experiences, they also represented multiple perspectives on preparation for stages of pregnancy, birth, and motherhood; ways of processing disorientation; and modes for modeling openness to difference. They evidence similarities and differences and exemplify perspectives and actions that foster community.

Fostering inclusion through action, reflection, and dialogue with others (or alone if journaling) can decrease or eliminate the sense of isolation and marginalization people feel when they are not in community. Reflective discourse, as means for developing social responsibility and commitment to the collective, is a first step in moving individuals toward becoming part of a community. The next step occurs after they begin to articulate and take control over their own voice, as well as recognize the validity of the *other's* voice. Consequently, an individual no longer sees the world through his or her own lens but begins to make space for other voices to be heard (Sheared & Sissel, 2001). While in community, people hear as well as listen to others; they find ways to ensure equal inclusion of diverse voices in discourse and take collective action.

By acting collectively, people begin to move toward organizational or social change, challenging hegemonic norms, beliefs, and actions that foster exclusion. This practice then allows individuals and the collective to gain greater access to powers and structures that delimit the existence of individuals or groups previously excluded or marginalized from resources or decision-making opportunities as a result of race, culture/ethnicity, language, religion, age,

size or ability. In other words, as Giroux (1992) concluded, community provides locations for border crossing as well as bridging assigned and desired locations along "a shifting sphere of multiple and heterogeneous borders where different histories, languages, experiences and voices intermingle amid diverse relations of power and privilege" (p. 32). And as Sheared (1994) intimated, while it is important to recognize one's individual uniqueness, it is also equally important to see oneself in context and connection to others within the community or society. By embracing both one's individual uniqueness and one's group membership, community can be achieved and sustained.

SUSTAINING AND CONTINUOUSLY (RE)CREATING COMMUNITY

Embracing static definitions of community or "believing that community is a thing of the past rather than an experience that undergoes transformation in relation to society" is problematic (Hugo, 2002, p. 8). Nostalgia for past forms prevents imagining and creating new ones. The strength of learning in community has ebbed and flowed in response to perceived or experienced urgency of social problems and change. Our current local and global contexts demand new conceptualizations of community and its creation.

Reading this chapter may stimulate thinking about community and catalyze questions about conceptions of creating community in the field of adult education. To some extent, the concept of community suffers from idealization. We often invoke it unquestioningly and view it in a positive haze. In this final section, we present issues to consider in critically reflecting on concepts and practices of creating community. This chapter would not be complete without viewing creation of community through lenses of ethics, social justice, and current societal contexts.

Only by *recognizing* and *embracing* community can it flourish. As previously stated, all life interconnects in webs: Whatever we do or allow, we do to ourselves. This biological reality is not new to those among us whose cultures recognize connection in community and emphasize respect for all life. A challenge for adult educators is creating *awareness* of community that already exists. From this perspective, acts such as overconsumption no longer represent individual choice but rather borrowing or stealing from the greater community. Responses to this community present dialectics: recognize/ignore, embrace/resist, foster/work against, participate/isolate.

Ecological and social sustainability should change our perspectives on connection within the worldwide web.

> The goal of education is ultimately to change individuals and the community. For this to occur, individuals need to see themselves as part of a larger community. Separatist or exclusionary perspectives, therefore, do not aid in the achievement of individual and social change. (Guy, 1999, p. 97)

Cajete (1994) suggests indigenous approaches to education as means to address challenges of the 21st century and encourages educators to move their focus from specialized to holistic knowledge, from structures to processes, from objective science to systemic science, and from building to networking.

What does this mean for our adult education practices?

> Organizations, professional educators, and formal and informal leaders meld learning and the experience of community in order to strengthen connections between people, facilitate ability to keep up with the rapid social change that comes with industrial and scientific change, and right social injustice. (Hugo, 2002, p. 21)

Within the global community, we come together in multiple local communities that reflect polyrhythmic realities of our lives. We connect and cluster within a wider community. Adult educators can create community with intentionality by embracing elements:

1. Embracing varied perspectives on community. For example,

- Resisting the urge to uncritically laud value in creating community; rather engaging in critical reflection on purposes, processes, ethical issues, and power
- Recognizing and attending to *de facto* communities, sustainability, and interdependence in a global context
- Developing shared cultures with space for everyone while respecting cultures of origin or choice
- Acknowledging that although we value community in our rhetoric, our theoretical and andragogical foundations often are individually oriented and at epistemological odds

2. Embracing diversity within community, for example,

- Learning from varied cultural perspectives and from those who share community as ways of knowing and being, without appropriating or co-opting them
- Valuing diverse perspectives
- Addressing barriers to creating community, such as privilege, marginalization, manipulation, safety, control, and oppression
- Participating in communities without engaging in marginalization or exclusion from the wider community or using them to escape diversity or segregate ourselves

3. Embracing community as daily practice, for example,

- Committing to shifting mind-sets, ways of viewing our lifeworlds
- Dwelling in dialectics of communities and using them as content in learning
- Balancing complex relationships between individuals and community
- Making community a pedagogy as well as a goal through action and creative approaches
- Embodying connection and relationship
- Acting *as if*, living into new ways of thinking and being
- Creating new forms of community so that *creating community* takes on new meanings

Community will become what we make it or what we choose to foster as we recognize and become more intentional about growing and developing together. Not long ago, virtual communities were as unimagined as new forms of communities that will emerge by the time the 2020 *Handbook* is written. "Future historians will write the stories of how adults discovered and challenged that community energy" (Hugo, 2002, p. 22). We can innovate what we want and need; creating community will be what we *continuously* envision, construct, and sustain. It will not be a benign, generic nicety; hard work will result in multiple configurations and processes and *radical* community as we engage in recognizing, connecting, and sustaining one another, our collective body, our world.

REFERENCES

Avis, J., & Fisher, R. (2006, July). Reflections on communities of practice, online learning and transformation: Teachers, lecturers and trainers. *Research in Post-Compulsory Education, 11*(2), 141–151.

Belenky, M. F., Bond, L. A., & Weinstock, J. S. (1997). *A tradition that has no name: Nurturing the development of people, families, and communities.* New York: Basic Books.

Belenky, M. F., Clinchy, B. M. V., Goldberger, N. R., & Tarule, J. M. (1986). *Women's ways of knowing: The development of self, voice, and mind.* New York: HarperCollins.

Bellah, R. N., Madson, R., Sullivan, W. M., Swidler, A., & Tipton, S. M. (1996). *Habits of the heart: Individualism and commitment in American life.* Berkeley: University of California Press.

Brown, J. S., & Duguid, P. (2001). Organizational learning and communities-of-practice: Toward a unified view of working, learning and innovation. *Organization Science, 2*(1), 40–57.

Cajete, G. (1994). *Look to the mountain: An ecology of indigenous education.* Durango, CO: Kavaki Press.

Capra, F. (1996). *The web of life: A new scientific understanding of living systems.* New York: Doubleday.

Chapman, D. D., & Gedro, J. (2009). Queering the HRD curriculum: Preparing students for success in the diverse workforce. *Advances in Developing Human Resources, 11*(1).

Collins, M., & Berge, Z. (2001). Facilitating interaction in computer mediated online courses. Retrieved on September 2, 2008, from http://www.emoderators.com/moderators/flcc.html

Collinson, V., & Cook, T. F. (2007). *Organizational learning: Improving learning, teaching, and leading in school systems.* Thousand Oaks, CA: Sage.

Cook, S. D. N., & Brown, J. S. (1999). Bridging epistemologies: The generative dance between organizational knowledge and organizational knowing. *Organization Science, 10*(4), 381–400.

Daloz, L. A. P. (2000). Transformative learning for the common good. In J. D. Mezirow (Ed.), *Learning as transformation: Critical perspectives on a theory in progress* (pp. 103–123). San Francisco: Jossey-Bass.

Dewey, J. (1966). *Democracy and education: An introduction to the philosophy of education.* New York: Free Press. (Original work published 1916)

English, L. M., Fenwick, T. J., & Parsons, J. (2003). *Spirituality of adult education and training.* Malabar, FL: Krieger.

Fisher, D., Rooke, D., & Torbert, B. (2003). *Personal and organisational transformations: Through action inquiry.* Great Britain: Edge\Work Press.

Flowers, D. (2003). An Afrocentric view of adult learning theory. In L. Baumgartner (Ed.), *Adult learning theory: An exploration of perspectives* (pp. 11–16). Columbus, OH: Educational Resources Information Center.

Giroux, H. A. (1992). *Border crossings: Cultural workers and the politics of education.* New York: Routledge.

Greene, M. (1995). *Releasing the imagination: Essays on education, the arts, and social change.* San Francisco: Jossey-Bass.

Guy, T. (1999). Culture as context for adult education: The need for culturally relevant adult education. In *Culture as context for adult education* (pp. 5–18). New Directions for Adult and Continuing Education, No. 82. San Francisco: Jossey-Bass.

Hayes, E., & Flannery, D. D. (Eds.). (2000). *Women as learners: The significance of gender in adult learning.* San Francisco: Jossey-Bass.

Henriksson, K. (2000). *When communities of practice come to town: On culture and contradiction in emerging theories of organizational learning.* Lund, Sweden: Lund University, Institute of Economic Research.

Hidalgo, N. M. (1998). Toward a definition of a Latino family research paradigm. *International Journal of Qualitative Studies in Education, 11*(1), 103–120.

hooks, b. (1994). *Teaching to transgress: Education as the practice of freedom.* New York: Routledge.

hooks, b. (2003). *Teaching community: A pedagogy of hope.* New York: Routledge.

Hugo, J. (2002). Learning community history . In D. A. Stein & S. Imel (Eds.), *Adult learning in community* (pp. 5–26). New Directions for Adult and Continuing Education, No. 95. San Francisco: Jossey-Bass.

Jeria, J. (1999). Popular education: Models that contribute to the empowerment of learners in minority communities. In *Culture as context for adult education* (pp. 49–65). New Directions for Adult and Continuing Education, No. 82. San Francisco: Jossey-Bass.

Kasworm, C. E., Polson, C. J., & Fishback, S. J. (2002). *Responding to adults in higher education.* Malabar, FL: Krieger.

Kegan, R. (1982). *The evolving self: Problem and process in human development.* Cambridge, MA: Harvard University Press.

Lane, H., Hoffmeister, R., & Bahan, B. (1996). *A journey into the deaf-world.* San Diego: Dawn Sign Press.

Lave, J., & Wenger, E. (1991). *Situated learning: Legitimate peripheral participation.* New York: Cambridge University Press.

Lindeman, E. (1961). *The meaning of adult education.* Montreal, Quebec: Harvest House.

Linton, S. (1998). *Claiming disability: Knowledge and identity.* New York: New York University Press.

Lipshitz, R., Friedman, V. J., & Popper, M. (2007). *Demystifying organizational learning*. Thousand Oaks, CA: Sage.

Merriam, S. B., & Clark, M. C. (2006). Learning and development: The connection in adulthood. In C. Hoare (Ed.), *Handbook of adult development and learning*. New York: Oxford University Press.

Newman, M. (2006). *Teaching defiance: Stories and strategies for activist educators*. San Francisco: Jossey-Bass.

Palloff, R. M., & Pratt, K. (2007). *Building online learning communities: Effective strategies for the virtual classroom*. San Francisco: Jossey-Bass.

Palmer, P. J. (2004). *A hidden wholeness: The journey toward an undivided life*. San Francisco: Jossey-Bass.

Preece, J., & Maloney-Krichmar, D. (2003). Online communities. In J. Jacko & A. Sears, A. (Eds.), *Handbook of human-computer interaction*. Mahwah, NJ: Lawrence Erlbaum.

Putnam, R. (2000). *Bowling alone: The collapse and revival of American community*. New York: Simon & Schuster.

Rheingold, H. (1994). A slice of life in my virtual community. In L. M. Harasim (Ed.), *Global networks: Computers and international communication* (pp. 57–80). Cambridge, MA: MIT Press.

Schlager, M. S., Fusco, J., & Schank, P. (2002). Evolution of an online education community of practice. In K. A Renninger & W. Shumar (Eds.), *Building virtual communities: Learning and change in cyberspace*. New York: Cambridge University Press.

Senge, P. (1990). *The fifth discipline: The art and practice of the learning organization*. New York: Doubleday.

Sheared, V. (1994). Giving voice: An inclusive model of instruction. In E. Hayes & S. A. J. Colin, III (Eds.), *Confronting racism and sexism*. New Directions for Adult and Continuing Education, No. 61. San Francisco: Jossey-Bass.

Sheared, V., & Sissel, P. A. (2001). *Making space: Merging theory and practice in adult education*. Westport, CT: Greenwood Press.

Shor, I. (1992). *Empowering education: Critical teaching for social change*. Chicago: University of Chicago Press.

Sinott, J. D., & Berlanstein, D. (2006). The importance of feeling whole: Learning to "feel connected," community and adult development. In C. Hoare (Ed.), *Handbook of adult development and learning*. New York: Oxford University Press.

St. Clair, R. (1998). On the commonplace: Reclaiming community in adult education. *Adult Education Quarterly, 49*(1), 5–14.

Stein, D., & Imel, S. (2002). Adult learning in community: Themes and threads. *Adult learning in community* (pp. 93–97). New Directions in Adult and Continuing Education, No. 95. San Francisco: Jossey-Bass.

Taylor, C. (1991). *The ethics of authenticity*. Cambridge, MA: Harvard University Press.

Tisdell, E. J. (2003). *Exploring spirituality and culture in adult and higher education*. San Francisco: Jossey-Bass.

Vella, J. (2000). A spirited epistemology: Honoring the adult learner as subject. In L. M. English & M. A. Gillen (Eds.), *Addressing the spiritual dimensions of adult learning* (pp. 7–16). New Directions for Adult and Continuing Education, No. 85. San Francisco: Jossey-Bass.

Vera, D., & Crossan, M. (2005). Organizational learning and knowledge management: Towards an integrative framework. In M. Easterby-Smith & M. A. Lyles (Eds.), *Handbook of organizational learning and knowledge management* (pp. 122–141). Malden, MA: Blackwell.

Walker, G. E., Golde, C. M., Jones, L., Bueschel, A. C., & Hutchings, P. (2008). *The formation of scholars: Rethinking doctoral education for the twenty-first century*. San Francisco: Jossey-Bass.

Welton, M. (2005). *Designing the just learning society: A critical inquiry*. Leichester, UK: NIACE.

Wenger, E. (1998). *Communities of practice: Learning, meaning, and identity*. New York: Cambridge University Press.

Wenger, E., McDermott, R., & Snyder, W. E. (2002). *Cultivating communities of practice*. Boston: Harvard Business School Press.

Whittaker, S., Isaacs, E., & O'Day, V. (1997). Widening the net. Workshop report on the theory and practice of physical and network communities. *SIGCHI Bulletin, 29*(3), 27–30.

Wiessner, C. A. (2005). Storytellers: Women crafting new knowing and better worlds. *Convergence, 38*(4), 101–119.

Wlodkowski, R. J. (1999). Motivation and diversity: A framework for teaching. In M. Theall (Ed.), *Motivation from within: Approaches for encouraging faculty and students to excel* (pp. 7–16). New Directions for Teaching and Learning, No. 78. San Francisco: Jossey-Bass.

Zhang, W. (2008). Conceptions of lifelong learning in Confucian culture: Their impact on adult learners. *International Journal of Lifelong Education, 27*(5), 551–557.

Looking Back, Looking Forward

CAROL E. KASWORM, AMY D. ROSE, AND JOVITA M. ROSS-GORDON

That this is an age of change is an expression frequently heard to-day. Never before in the history of mankind have so many and so frequent changes occurred

Ogburn, 1922, p. 199

Writing in 1922, William Ogburn expressed what for him was a commonplace notion, the ways that culture needed to adapt. He specifically was concerned about culture change in relation to changing technological innovations. As part of this 1920s discussion, he used the term *cultural lag* to focus on the differential between the state of culture and the state of technology. For Ogburn, cultural lag occurred when one part of a culture changed more quickly than another. Although he had many examples of this phenomenon, he was primarily concerned with the cultural shifts occurring behind technological change. For Ogburn, cultural lag meant that the social institutions and cultures of the times were not keeping up with an era of perpetual change. In simplest terms, cultural lag meant that, for example, cultural and social institutions as well as individual values had not kept pace with the ever-changing technological landscape. One example considered the variance between city designs and changing transportation needs, which had resulted in great disagreement about the planning and development of cities.

Ogburn's notion of cultural lag was profoundly influential. It seemed to explain many of the technological changes and social dislocations occurring during the post-World War I period. Of particular importance for adult education was his idea that this cultural lag led to what he called social maladjustment; that is, social and cultural institutions were lagging behind change, and this led to a disorienting dislocation and hence maladjustment. Much of Ogburn's theory rested on perceptions of cultural diffusion. For adult education, which was emerging as a field in the period after Ogburn's work, the idea of cultural and social maladjustment lay at the heart of much of the thinking of the time. Adult education could be used as a means of helping societies again achieve cultural equilibrium with societal change.

Of course, many of Ogburn's discussions were dated. He divided the world into the biological (unchanging) and the cultural (which included, from his perspective, social and cultural associations). In the early 21st century, we now know that the biological world is constantly changing and that a great part of cultural lag these days is in relation to the social environment. Yet, Ogburn is still an interesting starting point for a discussion of adult education and change. Surely, one of the chief unifying themes of these chapters is their constant iteration on the ways that society and culture are changing, particularly due to technology.

As we think broadly about the current state and the possible futures of adult education, we are struck by the essential themes that resonate through all of the parts of this *Handbook*. In essence, they revolve around the centrality of change (in its broadest possible definition) and the honoring of diversity in these changes. In Ogburn's terms, the changing technologies of the last century, combined with the social changes accompanying urbanization and immigration, have combined in substantial cultural dislocation. Many of the current cultural debates in the early 21st century revolve around these same dislocations; adult education, like other cultural and social arenas, continues to grapple with these changes. Thus, many of the issues that we see as new and pressing are in fact quite old and complex.

Adult and continuing education, as with education in general, blends a vision of social change with more pragmatic concerns of curriculum and program development. As a dynamic and evolving field, adult and continuing education has always been influenced and has attempted to influence the impact of social change on adult society. However, there continues to be little agreement about the central purposes of the field and the varied ways that the field has embraced and honored diversity in its many forms, contexts, and processes. Thus, in our continuing explorations, the 2010 *Handbook* presents a picture of the field as it is today, interpreted through many prisms, and simultaneously viewed from many angles.

In this final chapter, we structure our concluding discussion through the lenses of the intellectual commons, explicating a number of the key realities and challenges facing the field as we move forward in the early 21st century. As we look to the past and the future, we revisit the broad commitments of the intellectual commons for adult and continuing education and discuss how each has been represented within the *Handbook*. This intellectual commons is the public forum for honoring our dialogue about contemporary state-of-the-art adult and continuing education practices, new understandings of adult learning, innovative scholarship, and the many new challenges facing the field. Those core commitments of the intellectual commons of adult and continuing education include:

- Centrality of the adult learner and adult learning

- Creation of open exchanges of knowledge, theory, and practice

- Adult and continuing education as a field of practice

- Diversity of adult learning venues and collective endeavors

- Centrality of social justice

- Future of adult and continuing education within a global context

CENTRALITY OF THE ADULT LEARNER AND ADULT LEARNING

The adult learner and the adult learning process, whether occurring individually, in groups, in organizations, or in communities, remain at the heart of the study and practice of adult and continuing education. Yet, in the first decade of the 21st century, North American adult educators have increasingly turned their attention to a broader audience of adult learners and extended their interest in adult learning beyond a nearly exclusive focus on the psychological and rational dimensions of adult learning. Chapters in this *Handbook* point to several themes related to adult learning that have gained prominence in the first decade of the 21st century, with promise to suggest new directions for theory, research, and practice.

Handbook chapters on adult learning (Chapter 3), facilitating adult instruction (Chapter 13), and spirituality (Chapter 26) all point to recent trends toward more holistic and multifaceted conceptions of adult learning. Gone are the days when adult learning was conceived of as a psychological process engaged in by isolated learners. In recent decades, adult educators have increasingly become interested in previously unexplored aspects of adult learning, including somatic, emotional, and spiritual dimensions. As suggested by Chapter 3, Freiler (2008) describes recent work on learning through the body, which has been referred to as embodiment, embodied learning, and somatic learning. She defines embodiment as "a way to construct knowledge through direct engagement in bodily experiences and inhabiting one's body through a felt sense of being-in-the-world" (p. 40). Alternative conceptions of this construct of embodiment suggest a process of making meaning from direct bodily experiences, cognitive manifestations of bodily engagement, and a way to construct knowledge through unity of body and mind. Beyond the update on current considerations of emotions in learning in Chapter 3, Dirkx (2008) observes that the discussion of emotion in learning is partly situated within the conversation on embodied learning, through discussions of how our bodies react in certain teaching and learning situations. He also points to alternative conceptions of the connection between emotions and learning that emphasize either innate physiological response to stimuli, the cognitive mediation of those responses, or the socially constructed nature of human emotions. Spirituality also has become an important focal point. For example, Tisdell (2008) suggests that spirituality can be defined as a journey toward wholeness and points to several indicators of a more explicit focus on spirituality in adult learning and adult education. Other authors also suggest these connections, including the work of authors such as Dirkx (2001) and English and Gillen (2000), who have discussed the influence of spirituality and soul on individual learning. In addition, English, Fenwick, and Parsons (2003) suggest the role of spirituality in learning in the workplace, and Dillard (2006) has focused on spirituality as a part of social justice in adult education. Each of these strands of work remains vibrant at the time this *Handbook* goes to press, and each promises to reveal a more complex and holistic picture of adult learning in various settings and contexts, extending our knowledge and informing our practice in adult and continuing education.

Another related trend in the work on adult learning, as suggested in Chapter 3 and in several other chapters throughout the *Handbook,* is the increasing awareness of ways of knowing linked to cultural traditions that extend beyond European traditions. A key influence driving this trend has been attention to indigenous and non-Western perspectives on learning. Once rarely addressed in adult education literature beyond the work of Africentric scholars and of journals with an international scope like *Convergence* and the *International Journal of Lifelong Education,* this trend has moved into the mainstream of adult education literature in recent decades. As a key example, Merriam, Caffarella, and Baumgartner (2007) identified four themes apparent within indigenous and non-Western perspectives, including: (a) an emphasis on interdependence in learning; (b) a linked emphasis on the communal nature of learning; (c) a holistic approach to learning that includes spirit, mind, body, and emotions; and (d) an emphasis on learning that is informal and lifelong. Furthermore, as noted in several *Handbook* chapters and particularly Chapter 33 (on race and adult education) and Chapter 6 (on theoretical frameworks), non-Eurocentric understandings bring significant insights to our field. For example, Merriweather Hunn (2004) pays particular attention to the Africentric perspective, emphasizing that it questions the right of dominant cultures to legitimize knowledge, making way for an African-centered way of knowing that resonates with the cultural experiences of African Americans, while also supporting other cultural perspectives. She notes as well that Africentrism is holistic in orientation; embraces communal, affective, and spiritual dimensions of adult learning; and offers guidance for adult education practice that honors this perspective.

In the last decade, adult and continuing educators have shown an invigorated interest in the connections between emerging scientific understandings of the brain and adult learning. This interest has been spurred by a number of trends that are likely to continue and potentially grow stronger in coming years. As also noted in the chapter on adult learning, neuroscience has recognized the plasticity of the human brain throughout the life span and the role that social interaction and learning play in promoting neural plasticity (Cozolino & Sprokay, 2006). This current research has noted increasing awareness of the links between emotion and learning as well as the impact of stress on learning, both positive and negative. For example, Cozolino and Sprokay suggest that such links also help explain the impact of narratives, both personal and shared, on learning. Computer imaging technologies have enabled neuroscientists to see what is happening in living brains as information and experiences are processed, enhancing understanding of brain functioning in individuals with learning disabilities and traumatic brain injuries. Yet, it can be argued that the growing volume of neuroscientific research on the brain introduces new questions about adult learning even as it answers some older ones, promising that this area of work is likely to be a vibrant one for at least the decade to come. This first theme of the intellectual commons will continue to be at the center of our work and provide significant impact to our future research and practice.

Creation of Open Exchanges of Knowledge, Theory, and Practice

Adult and continuing education, like many professional fields, is grappling with a multiplicity of views about its purposes, methods, and strategies. Within this atmosphere, there is a constant tension between understanding the individual (the learner) and understanding the social context within which individuals operate. This is a complex issue; many of the chapters in this *Handbook* have attempted to address this tension; specifically, Chapter 38 examines globalization and the knowledge society. On one level, the research-to-practice paradigm of adult continuing education seems relatively straightforward. Identify a problem in practice, try to understand its dimensions, devise ways to ameliorate the situation, and then adapt these findings to real life situations. On another level however, this progression inadequately defines the actual ways that knowledge and theory interact in practice (Merriam, 1991).

Recent years have seen a shift in thinking about the nature of knowledge and its relation to practice. Early models of the relationship between knowledge, theory, and practice emphasized the search for general theory that could be applied to all situations. There was a continual lament that theoretical research and the building on prior research toward grand theory was often missing from adult continuing education literature. Instead, research was epitomized as an accumulation of knowledge, based almost solely on efforts to improve the practice of adult education (Rubenson, 2000). More recently, the search for generalizable knowledge has given way to a more context-based sense of reality.

The 2000 *Handbook* posited critically reflective practice as the key link between theory and practice. Diversity of perspective was an integral part of the philosophical thrust. Wilson and Hayes (2000) state:

> To capture the theme of practice as critically informed choice, we propose that the complex combinations of organized knowledge, assumptions, values, and experiences that define professional practice require an openness to critical inspection and a willingness to engage the new forms of knowledge construction that have proliferated in recent decades. (p. xvi)

If anything, the basic conceptualizations inherent in the Wilson and Hayes (2000) *Handbook* have become only more complex. Inherent within the debates are theories and understandings of human nature, disagreements about evolutionary psychology and epistemologies of knowledge, and the infinite contextual ramifications that affect translating theory into practice.

A particular issue, which underlies many of these *Handbook* chapters, is the problem of developing a coherent policy for adult and continuing education. As discussed in chapters on professionalization of the field (Chapter 11), professional identity (Chapter 12), and policy (Chapter 9), part of the reason for this conundrum lies in the weakness of the field's professional associations, but other reasons come from the increasingly narrow and context-based approaches to research. Whereas, on the one hand, these forms of research provide a richer understanding of particular programs and groups of learners, they fail to broaden the development of the field and hence to be helpful in developing policy. Finally, the diversity of the field and the related diversity of perspectives fail to unite us to affect policy. There is a continuing tension over this lack of consensus, while at the same time a deep belief in diversity and almost disdain for consensus. Consensus is usually defined sociologically, in terms of the values that a society has identified as guiding understandings in order to function. Critiques of consensus, in this sense, note that such a view about how society in general functions can be epitomized as a problem that leads to politics bereft of consideration of the power relationships that can affect both programming and political decision making (Rubenson, 1989). However, it is also clear that within the United States as well as potentially other nations, there is no agreement about general purposes or how to achieve a singular focus as a field.

These tensions among adult educators and their worldviews are evident in many of the chapters and specifically in those on theoretical frameworks (Chapter 6), histories of adult education (Chapter 7), international and comparative adult education (Chapter 8), and sociology of adult education (Chapter 10) and in the six chapters of *Part V: Centrality of Social Justice*. The authors of these chapters all attempt to bring new perspectives to the field, while simultaneously summarizing or synthesizing their perspectives on the present state of the field. In so doing, they illustrate the nature of the intellectual commons. These chapters aim to present divergent theories and approaches, to open up thinking about adult education and its impact on society, and to both integrate and disrupt thinking about the field.

A related issue in this commitment to an open exchange is the lack of consensus regarding the kinds of current research endeavors. Many of the chapters rely on tantalizing research about the forms and impact of adult education programming. Yet, often the kinds of close, qualitative studies that can add enormously to our understanding of a particular, unique organization or event do little to help us understand broader trends. This research tension surfaces explicitly in this *Handbook*. The task of identifying broad trends in the field is difficult when the research focuses on the particular. It is hard not to lapse into a form of relativism. However, broad outlines are beginning to emerge. The principal conundrum continues to be that there can be no field without common understandings, and yet we are not sure what these common understandings should be. Are we concerned with the practice (and the improvement) of adult and continuing education? Are we interested in understanding the dynamic relationships among varying stakeholders? What is at the heart of the field? Thus, we see in many chapters, but particularly in the six chapters of *Part III: Adult and Continuing Education as a Field of Practice*, an attempt to synthesize and simultaneously create new approaches and emphases to the practices within adult and continuing education. We hope that this *Handbook* stimulates dialogue and promotes reflection, while simultaneously working toward a more coherent field.

ADULT AND CONTINUING EDUCATION AS A FIELD OF PRACTICE

As a field of practice, adult and continuing education can be best understood as a set of educational activities, based in collective influences that impact individuals, groups, and organizations in relation to understanding and acting in the world. At its best, adult and continuing education can influence the transformation of individual lives and begin to address societal ills through collective action. We view this field of practice as a collaborative of change made up of adult learners, organizations, and the broader society. Throughout many chapters of the *Handbook*, we hear eloquent ideas and actions in the field of practice and scholarship for making a difference in society with a caring ethic.

As we face a new decade of many challenges, one of the central concerns for our field is a broader societal discussion focused on policies and funding for K–12 schooling and higher education based in educational accountability and outcomes. As suggested by Chapter 14 (Planning and Delivering of Programs), Chapter 15 (Assessment and Evaluation) and Chapter 9 (Policy and Adult Learning and Education), there are similar questions facing our field. Whether it is concerns about learner outcomes or meeting intended purposes, we also desire to identify causal or probable impacts of our work and our actions in both individual and collective enterprises. There is varied evidence of these forces in our work, such as suggested by employer-sponsored workforce learning (Chapter 22), adult basic education (Chapter 17), military adult education (Chapter 24), 2- and 4-year higher education (Chapters 20 and 21), and continuing professional education (Chapter 25).

This broader public debate is concerned with "knowable truths" and predictable impacts, a debate that has long been inherent in the field of education. Unlike earlier decades, the current period features a national discourse where dominant concerns are based in a culture of evidence and accountability. This evidence-based reform agenda is often characterized through the phrasing of "what works in education" (Slavin, 2008, p. 47). However, as suggested through the previous *Handbook* (Wilson & Hayes, 2000), we are now engaged in critically reflective efforts to understand how research can inform practice and how practice can inform research. We view our world of practice and our world of research from broader and more complex lenses. Thus, the field often seeks to illuminate meanings and webs of significance and to considering unique environments, groupings of adults of varied educational background and goals, and unique organizational environments presenting diverse expectations and cultures for learning (Eisenhart & DeHaan, 2005; Geertz, 1973). For the new decade, research and practice need to address both this new culture of evidence and accountability by seeking general principles and theories and of outcomes accountability, while others continue to value the situated descriptive understandings of the particular.

Compounding this disjuncture between the search for specific understandings and generalizable outcomes is the additional trauma of diminishing resources and competing needs, sometimes linked to justification for our work and our impact. We also have experienced the press toward a corporate mentality, sometimes defined as academic capitalism and commodification of knowledge (Slaughter & Leslie, 1997). As suggested by Jarvis (2007), "lifelong learning has become a process of consumption in the learning market . . . we have to recognize the power of the consumers" (p. 125). This culture of evidence and accountability, of a learning market orientation, and of the growing dominance of the power of the consumer is subtly interwoven throughout discussions in the *Handbook*.

Adult and continuing education, as a field of practice, is complex work based in expertise and skill. Thus, the second major concern for the field in this coming decade is the challenge of many practitioners who directly serve adults, yet lack professional knowledge of adult and continuing education theory and practice. As noted by Ball and Forzani (2007), engagement in education "is a common experience, familiarity masks its complexity." Powell (1980), for example, referred to education as a 'fundamentally uncertain profession' about which the perception exists that ingenuity and art matter more than professional knowledge" (p. 529). Thus, many individuals who serve adult learners require additional professional knowledge to best serve their constituencies. As noted in the Introduction and in the discussion of the professionalization of the field (Chapter 11) and *Part IV: Diversity of Adult Learning Venues and Collective Endeavors*, many individuals who lack formal coursework or formal preparation in adult education serve as instructors, program designers, administrators, mentors, and facilitators of adult learning experiences. These individuals bring to the intellectual commons a spectrum of new and existing frameworks and principles for viewing research and practice. However, these rich and complex ways of understanding and acting also create tension within

the field. The artistry of the individual practitioner may at times clash with the day-to-day tasks related to the production of programs.

The structure of the profession of adult and continuing education differs from other professions in that individuals working in the field range from those with no formal background or training to those who hold advanced degrees in adult education. This diversity of preparation, as discussed in Chapters 12 and 13, works to create a tension in the field as well as an awareness of the richness that nonprofessionals can add to practice.

This section of the *Handbook* adds to the intellectual commons through the chapters on the field and on professional identity. Although Jarvis (1999) and Wilson and Hayes (2000) both deal with this issue, we hope that the present discussions offer more insight into the integration and engagement of these varied practitioners. But the issue goes beyond just those who are not professionally trained. The vitality of the field rests in the combination of expertise and the tacit beliefs of practitioners.

DIVERSITY OF ADULT LEARNING VENUES AND COLLECTIVE ENDEAVORS

Adrienne Rich (1978) suggested, "Whatever we do together is pure invention. The maps they gave us were out of date by years" (p. 31). It is evident that the creativity and dynamism of adult and continuing educators, as well as the intentional acts of adults engaging in new ways of learning, are reforming our world maps of adult learners and of adult provider organizations. This changing diversity of adult learning landscape has been partially mapped in the *Handbook, Part IV: Diversity of Adult Learning Venues and Collective Endeavors*. These 14 chapters explicitly focus on a select set of current forms and understandings as well as tensions of adult learning engagement by particular providers, venues, or mission foci. However, these chapters provide only a glimpse of adult and continuing education providers and venues.

As noted by Rich's quote, we face the important paradox that we are both leaders and partners of historic forms of adult learning, while also being creators of new venues, delivery systems, and collaborations within our world of adult and continuing education. We attempt to be responsive to the changing needs and interests of adults and society; we also attempt to be proactive in creating greater adult access, participation, and learner-relevant programs. In addition, in this age of technological access to knowledge and social networks, many adult learners have independently reframed our understandings of the world of self-directed learning engagements (autodidacts) and are redefining our historic understandings of informal adult learning. Furthermore, across the many chapters of Part IV considering the global context, it is evident that we no longer collaborate only in local or regional spaces. Adult and continuing education is informed and has become transformed through international exchanges and professional dialogues and through the growing worldwide interest in lifelong learning.

We acknowledge the evolving tensions in the field, such as the suggested commodification of formal structures of education and a growing ethos of credential-seeking in adult learners (Chapter 20), limited societal supports for adult literacy and English as a Second Language programs (Chapter 17 and 18), as well as important impacts of inequitable funding and malnourished policy (Chapter 2, Chapter 9). Furthermore, adults are challenging traditional educational provider venues by crafting their own learning experiences and generating their own sense of learning community (Chapters 30, 39, 40) through social networking, technology-based worlds of communication, and self-stylized learning-focused efforts (e.g., book clubs and self-help groups). In addition, unique and exciting collectives of adult learners are constructing organized pursuits for common societal issues, such as adult education for empowerment of individuals and communities (Chapter 19) and environmental adult education (Chapter 28).

How can we make sense of these shifting worlds and understandings in adult and continuing education? About half a century ago, Knowles (1962/1977) suggested,

> the field is highly expansive and flexible . . . adult education is an open system which any institution may enter at a time and under conditions of its own choosing. As a result the institutional sponsorship of adult education in this country has expanded continuously and rapidly, although unevenly. (p. 249)

In particular, Knowles characterized institutions of adult education as

> typically emerg[ing] in response to specific needs, rather than as part of a general design for the continuing education of adults . . . adult educational institutions as a whole [are] more sensitive than most educational institutions to the changing pressures of society for service. . . [Furthermore] "the developmental process of adult education tends to be more episodic than consistent. In a sense, adult education has thrived on crises, since needs are greatest and clearest then. Similarly, it has tended to retrench in periods of placidity. (pp. 257–258).

With the growth of a knowledge-based culture in our society and of more individuals who have longer pedigrees of learning and educational engagement (whether through formal or informal structures), there has emerged a more complex, layered, complementary, and at times more competitive, organizational landscape. One of these "crises to stimulate growth," as suggested by Knowles, is this development of a knowledge society with multiple and evolving sets of providers and format venues. Through these changes, it is also evident that there is a blurring of formal, nonformal, and informal organization structures and learning formats, as well as the blurring of lifestyles of work, learning, and leisure. Clear life-role demarcations and provider territories have fallen away in this postmodern world. As noted in Chapter 37 on globalization and adult education and Chapter 38 on the knowledge society, our place in this contemporary arena is paradoxical; the construct of the knowledge society is contested. What are the important areas of knowledge that will be valued? What is the nature of society in this discussion? And we face the most important question: Who should be providing these adult learning experiences?

In this reconfiguration, one of the growing concerns is the burgeoning opportunities and options for institutions and individuals who have social and cultural capital. In the midst of this wealth of opportunities, there is a contrasting underclass of adult learners who are not being served or who cannot access these opportunities (Chapter 2, Access and Participation). Thus, it appears that innovation in creating diverse structures and learning formats may be unintentionally fostering additional barriers for adult learners demarcated by access and resource supports. In this time of change, we are facing the continuing challenge to serve and support adult learners across all life conditions in our society. Our commitment to social justice is clear. However, how do we nurture a viable and dynamic network of providers and supports for adult learner for this evolving knowledge society? How do we continue our commitment to the field of practice in adult and continuing education?

CENTRALITY OF SOCIAL JUSTICE

Recent data suggest increased participation in adult education of all types—formal, nonformal, and informal—with somewhat greater representation of historically underrepresented adult learner populations, including African Americans, Hispanics, and older adults (Kleiner, Carver, Hagedorn, & Chapman, 2005; O'Donnell, 2006; Snyder, Dillow, & Hoffman, 2008). At the same time, chapters in this *Handbook,* including those on adult learners, access and participation, and policy (Chapters 1, 2, and 9, respectively), point to continuing issues of equitable access and persistence in adult education programs. Of significant concern for our field, Part V of this *Handbook* has been devoted to specific perspectives of social justice in adult and continuing education, focusing on aging, class and place, disability, gender, sexuality, and race. Each of these five chapters discusses efforts within the field to use adult education as a vehicle to address social inequities; other chapters across the *Handbook* suggest integrating discussions of social justice. A scan of scholarly literature of the field during the decade since the last *Handbook* points to a proliferation of conferences proceedings, articles, and books focusing on social justice as it relates to diverse aspects of the field including the arts, globalization, health literacy, social movements, and welfare reform (Alfred, Butterwick, & Hansman, 2007; Clover & Stalker, 2007; Hill, 2004; Holst, 2006; McKinley Parrish, 2007). Yet, current *Handbook* chapter titles, including terms like *dream, hope,* and *utopia,* symbolize chapter authors' assessments that the field has yet to achieve its ideals with regard to social justice. Recent articles by Tennant (2005) and Armstrong and Miller (2006) suggest others also share these sentiments, as they reflect on the state of adult education from a global perspective.

Going forward into the next decade of the 21st century, one might ask what indicators portend continued progress toward achievement of these ideals and what challenges seem most critical at this historical juncture.

In the realm of theory and research, there is growing integration of epistemologies that foster greater understanding of those who have been at the margins, as well as the forces that have contributed to that marginalization. New perspectives as suggested in Parts II and V (on theoretical frameworks and social justice) have been offered by critical theory, feminist theories, Africentrism, critical race theory, queer theory, disability studies, and postmodernist theory. Understanding such perspectives can help adult educators examine their own personal assumptions about teaching, learning, and organizational change, as well as the degree to which existing classroom and organizational practices either challenge or support inequalities.

Discussions of pedagogies with these emergent frameworks (e.g., Africentric, feminist, and critical pedagogies) in this *Handbook,* as well as other literature, have provided concrete suggestions for modifying learning environments in ways that challenge the status quo of cultural hegemony and power relations. These trends suggest significant potential for adult and continuing education practitioners and scholars alike toward the attainment of goals for social justice through adult education as espoused by previous generations of *Handbook* authors.

Yet, looking into the future, it is evident that numerous challenges remain. These challenges are figural, whether from the perspective of realizing the ideals of social justice *within* the field or from the perspective of hoping for a day when adult and continuing education truly serves to diminish the gaps between the haves and have nots. One challenge is found in the persistent associations between race/ethnicity, income level, and prior educational attainment correlated to the likelihood of participation in various forms of adult and continuing education (O'Donnell, 2006). Another challenge is the current inadequate public resources for adult and continuing education and the concomitant problems of policy-mandated accountability of program outcomes for learners to "contribute" (economically) to society, without adequate educational supports. There are also challenges for adult educators in maintaining the commitment to social justice at both a personal and programmatic level.

FUTURE OF ADULT AND CONTINUING EDUCATION WITHIN A GLOBAL CONTEXT

One of the more notable changes in our field during the last decade is the growth of international connections and interglobal engagements in adult and continuing education across governments, organizations, and collectives of adult learners. As characterized in Chapter 37 on globalization and through many *Handbook* chapters, the field has developed more complex understandings and connections through an international frame of practice and research. In addition, the *Handbook* authors suggest unique societal forces of globalization across our world of adult and continuing education. No matter the setting or context, whether it be literacy, environmental issues, health, or workplace learning, the local environment of adult education and the global context of adult lifelong learning have become united in many of our understandings.

Past *Handbooks* have largely focused on adult and continuing education research and practice in North American context and have more often considered comparative international studies in select ways. Predominant international explorations and discussions have historically focused upon the European cultural context, with more limited efforts to document and consider adult and continuing education endeavors in Asia, Africa, and Central and South America. Furthermore, our limitations have occurred through the silos of language, with limited engagement in non-English dialogues.

It is evident in these last decades that our world of practice and research has broadened its boundaries and incorporated international connections to individual and collective professional gatherings. Through multicultural and international professional organizations, policy venues, and interglobal exchange of publications and research, we have enhanced our understandings of best practices and research to serve adult learners. Among major engagements to stimulate the global-local worldview of adult and continuing education are recent involvements with UNESCO, the International Council on Adult Education, the International Commission of the American Association for Adult and Continuing Education,

and University Continuing Education Association partnerships. In addition, many institutional, group, and individual collaborations across national boundaries have fostered important dialogues for exchange of ideas and best practices. There have also been a number of notable research and publication initiatives, including select *Handbooks of Adult and Continuing Education*—which have provided focused contributions to the field in relation to global understandings,] as well as a number of international handbooks and encyclopedias on adult education and lifelong learning.

As suggested by one recent project focused on the importance of adult education in responding to the challenges of global issues,

> Globalization's attempts to integrate the world have marginalized nations and groups of people. Environmental disasters and health problems, and their manifestation in marginalized communities, signal the circular nature of the interrelationships. Lifelong learning and community empowerment are two global issues that hold potential for adult educators to address the unfortunate outcomes of globalization. (Merriam, Courtenay, & Cervero, 2006, p. 489)

Merriam et al. (2006) suggested five roles and responsibilities for adult educators in this global society, to include: "create space and listen to voices; adopt a critical stance; attend to policy; develop partnerships; and foster collective learning and action" (p. 490). These roles and responsibilities have also been suggested in a number of the current chapters in the *Handbook* and in relation to our current challenges of globalization.

We face many future challenges in this turbulent internationalized society. However, many dynamic international adult and continuing education leaders and scholars bring new collective understandings and research to our field. In particular, many of the current chapters have integrated international perspectives and practices in the field of adult and continuing education. As we think of the future of adult and continuing education, the key challenge for us is to understand that our work, as part of the local and the particular, is strengthened through our collaborating and partnering with others at a national and international level.

Thus, this *Handbook* provides the field and specifically the readership with new understandings of how the local and the global unite. It also highlights the phenomenon of globalization, technological communications, and interrelated economics of the workplace and society as it influences our worldview of the field of adult and continuing education. Throughout this *Handbook*, there is a clearly stated need for adult and continuing education to provide leadership toward a strong and vital adult learning agenda.

Concluding Thoughts

For this decade, the intellectual commons provides us a metaphor to define our public stance and key markers in current and future engagement in the field of adult and continuing education. As we face a troubled world in need of peace and respect for all of humanity, environmental sustainability, economic vitality, and of world citizens who have knowledge and skills to protect and nurture this planet, our future has many challenges. It is clear our work is important, our impact significant, and our world, as envisioned through the intellectual commons of adult and continuing education, will embody these multifaceted opportunities and challenges.

References

Alfred, M., Butterwick, S., & Hansman, C. (2007). *Neoliberal welfare reform, poverty and adult education: Identifying the problem and engaging in resistance.* Adult Education Research Conference, Halifax, Nova Scotia. Retrieved on June 9, 2009, from http://www.adulterc.org/Proceedings/2007/Proceedings/Alfred.pdf

Armstrong, P., & Miller, N. (2006). Whatever happened to social purpose? Adult educators' stories of political commitment and change. *International Journal of Lifelong Education, 25*(3), 291–305.

Ball, D. L., & Forzani, F. M. (2007). What makes education research "educational"? *Educational Researcher, 36*(9), 529–540.

Clover, D., & Stalker, J. (Eds.). (2007). *The arts and social justice: Re-crafting adult education and community cultural leadership.* Leicester, UK: National Institute of Adult and Continuing Education.

Cozolino, L., & Sprokay, S. (2006). Neuroscience and adult learning. In S. Johnson & K. Taylor (Eds.), *The new update on adult learning theory* (pp. 11–19). New Directions for Adult and Continuing Education, No. 110. San Francisco: Jossey-Bass.

Dillard, C. (2006). When the music changes, so should the dance: Cultural and spiritual considerations in paradigm "proliferation." *International Journal of Qualitative Studies in Education (QSE), 19*(1), 59–76.

Dirkx, J. (2001). The power of feelings: Emotion, imagination, and the construction of meaning in adult learning. In S. Merriam (Ed.), *The new update on adult learning theory* (pp. 63–72). New Directions for Adult and Continuing Education, No. 89. San Francisco: Jossey-Bass.

Dirkx, J. M. (2008). The meaning and role of emotions in adult learning. In J. M. Dirkx (Ed.), *The new update on adult learning theory* (pp. 7–18). New Directions for Adult and Continuing Education, No. 120. San Francisco: Jossey-Bass.

Eisenhart, M., & DeHaan, R. (2005). Doctoral preparation of scientifically based educational researchers. *Educational Researcher, 34*(4), 3–14.

English, L. M., Fenwick, T. J., & Parsons J. (2003). *Spirituality of adult education and training.* Malabar, FL: Krieger.

English, L. M., & Gillen, M. A. (2000). Editor's notes. In L. M. English & M. A. Gillen (Eds.), *The new update on adult learning theory* (pp. 1–5). New Directions for Adult and Continuing Education, No. 85. San Francisco: Jossey-Bass.

Freiler, T. J. (2008). Learning through the body. In S. Merriam (Ed.), *The new update on adult learning theory* (pp. 37–47). New Directions for Adult and Continuing Education, No. 119. San Francisco: Jossey-Bass.

Geertz, C. (1973). *The interpretation of cultures.* New York: Basic Books.

Hill, L. (2004). Health literacy is a social justice issue that affects us all. *Adult Learning, 15*(1/2), 4–6.

Holst, J. (2006). *The politics and economics of globalization and social change in radical adult education: A critical review of recent literature.* Proceedings from the Adult Education Research Conference, Minneapolis, MN. Retrieved on June 9, 2009, from http://www.adulterc.org/Proceedings/2006/Proceedings/Holst.pdf

Jarvis, P. (1999). *The practitioner researcher.* San Francisco: Jossey-Bass.

Jarvis, P. (2007). *Globalisation, lifelong learning, and the learning society: Sociological perspectives.* Lifelong Learning and the Learning Society, No. 2. London: Routledge.

Kleiner, B., Carver, P., Hagedorn, M., & Chapman, C. (2005). *Participation in adult education for work-related reasons: 2002–2003* (NCES 2006-040). Washington, DC: National Center for Education

Statistics. Retrieved March 4, 2009, from http://nces.ed.gov/pubsearch/pubsinfo.asp?pubid=2006040

Knowles, M. (1977). *A history of the adult education movement in the United States: Includes adult education institutions through 1976* (Rev. ed.). Huntington, NY: Krieger. (Original work published 1962)

McKinley Parrish, M. (2007). *View from the stoop: Exploring the impact of place on learning in social movements.* Proceedings of the Adult Education Research Conference. Halifax, Nova Scotia. Retrieved on June 9, 2009, from http://www.adulterc.org/Proceedings/2007/Proceedings/Parrish.pdf

Merriam, S. B. (1991). How research contributes to the field of adult education. In J. M. Peters, P. Jarvis, & Associates. *Adult education: Evolution and achievement in a developing field of study.* San Francisco: Jossey-Bass.

Merriam, S. B., Caffarella, R. S., & Baumgartner, L.M. (2007). *Learning in adulthood: A comprehensive guide* (3rd ed.). San Francisco: Jossey-Bass.

Merriam, S., Courtenay, B., & Cervero, R. (2006). The role of adult education in addressing global issues. In S. Merriam, B. Courtenay, & R. Cervero (Eds.), *Global issues and adult education* (pp. 485–496). San Francisco: Jossey-Bass.

Merriweather Hunn, L. (2004). Africentric philosophy: A remedy for Eurocentric dominance. In J. Sandlin & R. St. Clair (Eds.), *The new update on adult learning theory* (pp. 65–74). New Directions for Adult and Continuing Education, No. 102. San Francisco: Jossey-Bass.

O'Donnell, K. (2006). *Adult education participation in 2005-05* (NCES 2006-077). Washington, DC: U. S. Department of Education, National Center for Education Statistics.

Ogburn, W. F. (1922). *Social change with respect to culture and original nature.* New York: Viking Press.

Powell, AG. (1980). *The uncertain profession: Harvard and the search for educational authority.* Cambridge, MA: Harvard University Press.

Rich, A. (1978). Twenty-One Love Poems –XIII. *The Dream of a Common Language, Poems 1974–1977.* New York: W. W. Norton.

Rubenson, K. (1989). Sociology of adult education. In S. Merriam & P. Cunningham (Eds.), *Handbook of adult and continuing education* (pp. 51–69). San Francisco: Jossey-Bass.

Rubenson, K. (2000). *Revisiting the map of the territory.* Proceedings of the 2000 Adult Education Research Conference. Retrieved June, 2009, from http://www.adulterc.org/Proceedings/2000/rubensonk1-final.PDF

Slaughter, S., & Leslie, L. (1997). *Academic capitalism.* Baltimore: Johns Hopkins University Press.

Slavin, R. E. (2008). Evidence-based reform in education: Which evidence counts? *Educational Researcher, 37*(1), 47–50.

Snyder, T. D., Dillow, S. A., & Hoffman, C. M. (2008). *Digest of education statistics: 2007* (NCES 2008-022). Table 182. Retrieved March 8, 2009, from http://nces.ed.gov/programs/digest/d07/tables/dt07_182asp?referrer=list

Tennant, M. (2005). Adult and continuing education: continuities and discontinuities. *International Journal of Lifelong Education, 24*(6), 525–533.

Tisdell, E. J. (2008). Spirituality and adult learning. In S. Merriam (Ed.), *The new update on adult learning theory* (pp. 27–36). New Directions for Adult and Continuing Education, No. 119. San Francisco: Jossey-Bass.

Wilson, A. L., & Hayes, E. R. (2000). *Handbook of adult and continuing education* (new ed.). San Francisco: Jossey-Bass.

Author Index

SUBJECT INDEX

Academic capitalism, 221, 446

Academy of Human Resource Development, 139

Accelerated learning programs, 25, 224

Access, 26

Access/participation issues, 25–26, 447–448

accelerated/intensive learning formats and, 31–32

adult basic education students and, 28

barriers to participation, 18, 20, 28–29

chain of response model and, 27

cost of participation, 18, 20, 25

diversity challenges and, 20

Education Participation Scale and, 28

enrollment policies, liberalization of, 29

equitable/inequitable participation, influences on, 29–32, 120–121

expanded educational opportunities, strategies for, 31–32

globalization pressures and, 29

higher education opportunities, 28, 29, 30, 31, 226–227

low-income students and, 28, 29–30

online learning and, 29, 30

participants, description of, 27

persistence and, 26, 27

Prior Learning Assessment and, 31

psychological perspective and, 27–28

race/ethnicity and, 365

readiness to learn and, 28

remedial/developmental education programs and, 30–31

sociological perspective and, 28

statistics on, 18–19, 25

status quo, reinforcement of, 31

stopping out phenomenon and, 28, 29, 32

supportive practices and, 32

technology, disparate access to, 29–30

terminology for adult education, 26–27

See also Adult basic education (ABE); Adult and Continuing Education practice; Adult learning; Community colleges

Accreditation of Continuing Medical Education (ACCME), 280

Achieving the Dream, 234

Action learning (AL), 64–65

Action research, 64, 214

Adult basic education (ABE), 18, 26, 189

compulsory educational settings and, 191, 193, 194

Equipped for the Future initiative and, 192

evidence-based practices, best practices model and, 195

flexibility in, 190

funding for, 189, 190, 191, 193

health-related learning and, 297

immigrant populations and, 195

instructor diversity in, 190, 195–196

intermittent students in, 28

international dimensions of, 193–195

liberatory approach to literacy and, 192

locations of, 190–191

nature of, 189–190

new influences/challenges in, 195–196

participants in, 27, 28, 29, 190

persistence and, 26, 27, 32

policy influences on, 193

REFLECT program, 192

relevant/real-life instruction and, 194

remedial education and, 190

responsive programs and, 191

rural-urban gap in literacy, 194

skills-based approach to, 192, 194–195, 195

social practices approach and, 190, 192, 194

standardization/accountability, demands for, 191, 193

stopping out phenomenon and, 28

supportive practices and, 32

theoretical foundations of, 191–193

traditional education programs and, 191

transition-to-postsecondary education programs and, 32

universal primary schooling and, 194

welfare reform policy and, 193

Workforce Investment Act and, 193

See also Adult and Continuing Education practice; Adult learners; Adult learning; English as a Second Language (ESL) programs

Supporting researchers
for more than 40 years

Research methods have always been at the core of SAGE's publishing program. Founder Sara Miller McCune published SAGE's first methods book, *Public Policy Evaluation*, in 1970. Soon after, she launched the *Quantitative Applications in the Social Sciences* series—affectionately known as the "little green books."

Always at the forefront of developing and supporting new approaches in methods, SAGE published early groundbreaking texts and journals in the fields of qualitative methods and evaluation.

Today, more than 40 years and two million little green books later, SAGE continues to push the boundaries with a growing list of more than 1,200 research methods books, journals, and reference works across the social, behavioral, and health sciences. Its imprints—Pine Forge Press, home of innovative textbooks in sociology, and Corwin, publisher of PreK–12 resources for teachers and administrators—broaden SAGE's range of offerings in methods. SAGE further extended its impact in 2008 when it acquired CQ Press and its best-selling and highly respected political science research methods list.

From qualitative, quantitative, and mixed methods to evaluation, SAGE is the essential resource for academics and practitioners looking for the latest methods by leading scholars.

For more information, visit **www.sagepub.com**.

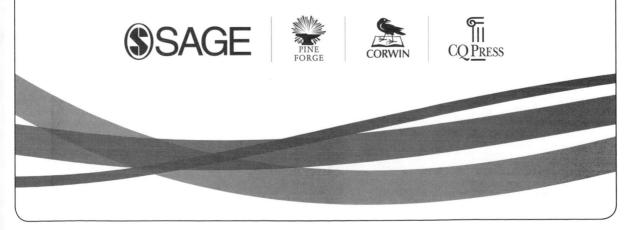